To Suzanne, Barbara, Marvin, Muis, and the memory of Sweetie π

CONTENTS

2   THE PHYSICAL LAYER   52

3 THE MEDIUM ACCESS SUBLAYER   116

PREFACE

Computer networking has changed enormously over the past decade, and this book has changed along with it. Ten years ago, computer networks were exotic research tools used only by few specialists. Today, computers ranging from personal computers to supercomputers are more likely to be part of a network than not. Most organizations that use computers either already have, or are soon planning to install, one or more local area networks. Worldwide electronic mail is a daily reality for millions of people. In short, networks have evolved from an academic curiosity to an essential tool for users in business, government, and universities.

Only a few short years ago, the design of a computer network was something of a black art. Every computer manufacturer had its own network architecture, no two of which were compatible. All that has changed now. Virtually the entire computer industry has now agreed to a series of International Standards for describing network architectures. These standards are known as the OSI Reference Model. In the near future, almost all other network architectures will disappear, and computers from one vendor will be able to communicate effortlessly with computers from another vendor, thus stimulating network usage even more.

This book uses the OSI Reference Model as a framework. The model is based on a principle first enunciated by Julius Caesar: Divide and Conquer. The idea is to design networks as a sequence of layers, one based upon the previous one. By reducing the study of the whole to the study of its parts, the entire process becomes more manageable.

Because networking has changed so much since the first edition, this second edition is almost a completely new book. Over half of the material is completely new, and much of the remainder has also been heavily updated and improved. Whole new areas are now discussed in detail, including ISDN, LANs, fiber optics, and bridges. The treatment of the upper OSI layers has been completely rewritten and expanded by over a hundred pages to include important topics such as the OSI transport protocols, ASN.1, FTAM, and VTP. New networks, including MAP, TOP, and USENET are now examined in some detail and network software is also given more coverage.

The idea of organizing the book around the seven OSI layers has proved very successful and has been retained in this second edition. Chapter 1 provides an introduction to the subject of computer networks in general and layered protocols in particular. The next five chapters deal with the lower layers, physical through transport, which collectively are the providers of the transport service. Chapter 2 covers physical media, analog and digital transmission, the telephone system and ISDN. Chapter 3 looks at the MAC sublayer and local area networks, including IEEE standard 802. Chapter 4 is about the data link layer and its protocols: algorithms for reliably transmitting data over unreliable lines. Chapter 5 treats the network layer, especially routing, congestion control, and internetworking. Finally, chapter 6 studies the transport layer, in particular, connection management and end-to-end protocols.

The last three chapters deal with the upper layers, the users of the transport service. Chapter 7 is about the session layer, which is concerned with providing reliable service, even in the face of unreliable hardware. Chapter 8 covers the presentation layer, including the OSI abstract syntax notation, data compression, and cryptography. Chapter 9 provides an introduction to some application layer issues, including file transfer, electronic mail, virtual terminals, remote job entry, and directory services. Chapter 10 contains a reading list and bibliography.

Queueing theory is a basic mathematical tool that is used to analyze computer networks, so an appendix is provided on it for the benefit of readers not familiar with this subject.

The book can be used as a text for undergraduates or beginning graduate students in computer science, electrical engineering, and related disciplines. The only prerequisites are a general familiarity with computer systems and programming, although a little knowledge of elementary calculus and probability theory is useful in a few places, but is not essential. Some of the examples are given in Pascal, so some knowledge of this, or a similar programming language is a plus. Since the amount of material in the book may be too much for a one semester course, depending on the level of the students, I have made a serious attempt to make each chapter relatively independent of the other ones. In this way an instructor could choose to emphasize, for example, data communication and the lower layers, or alternatively, software and the upper layers.

The book can also be used by computer professionals who are interested in networking. For this reason, I have attempted to limit the amount of mathematics used, and have included numerous practical examples instead of providing many pages of abstract derivations. Even programmers or technical managers who are not network specialists should be able to follow a considerable amount of the book.

Many people have helped me during the preparation of the second edition. I would especially like to thank Imrich Chlamtac Bdale Garbee, John Henshall, Brian Kernighan, John Limb, Chris Makemson, Daniel Pitt, Sandy Shaw, Jennifer Steiner and my editor, John Wait. I would also like to thank my students for helping to debug the text. Special thanks go to Jeroen Belien, Berend Jan Beugel, Remco Feenstra, Anneth de Gee, Cornelis Kroon, Roemer Lievaart, Maarten Litmaath, Paul Polderman, Rob van Swinderen, Luuk Uljee, and Felix Yap.

Last but not least, I would like to thank Suzanne, Barbara, Marvin, and Muis. Suzanne for still being so understanding after all these years; Barbara and Marvin for using their computer instead of mine, thus making this book possible; and and Muis for being as quiet as a mouse while I was writing.

ANDREW S. TANENBAUM

1

INTRODUCTION

Each of the past three centuries has been dominated by a single technology. The eighteenth century was the time of the great mechanical systems accompanying the Industrial Revolution. The nineteenth century was the age of the steam engine. During the twentieth century, the key technology has been information gathering, processing, and distribution. Among other developments, we have seen the installation of worldwide telephone networks, the invention of radio and television, the birth and unprecedented growth of the computer industry, and the launching of communication satellites.

As we move toward the final years of this century, these areas are rapidly converging, and the differences between collecting, transporting, storing, and processing information are quickly disappearing. Organizations with hundreds of offices spread over a wide geographical area routinely expect to be able to examine the current status of even their most remote outpost at the push of a button. As our ability to gather, process, and distribute information grows, the demand for even more sophisticated information processing grows even faster.

Although the computer industry is young compared to other industries (e.g., automobiles and air transportation), computers have made spectacular progress in a short time. During the first two decades of their existence, computer systems were highly centralized, usually within a single large room. Not infrequently, this room had glass walls, through which visitors could gawk at the great electronic wonder inside. A medium-size company or university might have had one or two

1

computers, while large institutions had at most a few dozen. The idea that within 20 years equally powerful computers smaller than postage stamps would be mass produced by the millions was pure science fiction.

The merging of computers and communications has had a profound influence on the way computer systems are organized. The concept of the "computer center" as a room with a large computer to which users bring their work for processing is rapidly becoming obsolete. This model has not one, but at least two flaws: the concept of a single large computer doing all the work, and the idea of users bringing work to the computer instead of bringing the computer to the users.

The old model of a single computer serving all of the organization's computational needs, is rapidly being replaced by one in which a large number of separate but interconnected computers do the job. These systems are called **computer networks**. The design and analysis of these networks are the subjects of this book.

Throughout the book we will use the term "computer network" to mean an *interconnected* collection of *autonomous* computers. Two computers are said to be interconnected if they are able to exchange information. The connection need not be via a copper wire; lasers, microwaves, and communication satellites can also be used. By requiring the computers to be autonomous, we wish to exclude from our definition systems in which there is a clear master/slave relation. If one computer can forcibly start, stop, or control another one, the computers are not autonomous. A system with one control unit and many slaves is not a network; nor is a large computer with remote card readers, printers, and terminals.

There is considerable confusion in the literature between a computer network and a **distributed system**. The key distinction is that in a distributed system, the existence of multiple autonomous computers is transparent (i.e., not visible) to the user. He† can type a command to run a program, and it runs. It is up to the operating system to select the best processor, find and transport all the input files to that processor, and put the results in the appropriate place.

In other words, the user of a distributed system is not aware that there are multiple processors; it looks like a virtual uniprocessor. Allocation of jobs to processors and files to disks, movement of files between where they are stored and where they are needed, and all other system functions must be automatic.

With a network, a user must *explicitly* log onto one machine, *explicitly* submit jobs remotely, *explicitly* move files around and generally handle all the network management personally. With a distributed system, nothing has to be done explicitly; it is all automatically done by the system without the user's knowledge.

In effect, a distributed system is a special case of a network, one whose software gives it a high degree of cohesiveness and transparency. Thus the distinction between a network and a distributed system lies with the software (especially the operating system), rather than with the hardware.

---

† "He" should be read as "he or she" throughout this book.

Nevertheless, there is a lot of overlap between the two subjects. For example, both distributed systems and computer networks need to move files around. The difference lies in who invokes the movement, the system or the user. Although this book primarily focuses on networks, many of the topics are also important in distributed systems. For more information about distributed systems, see Crichlow (1988), Sloman and Kramer (1987), and Tanenbaum and van Renesse (1985).

1.1. USES OF COMPUTER NETWORKS

Before we start to examine the technical issues in detail, it is worth devoting some time to pointing out why people are interested in computer networks and what they can be used for.

1.1.1. Network Goals

Many organizations already have a substantial number of computers in operation, often located far apart. For example, a company with many factories may have a computer at each location to keep track of inventories, monitor productivity, and do the local payroll. Initially, each of these computers may have worked in isolation from the others, but at some point, management may have decided to connect them to be able to extract and correlate information about the entire company.

Put in slightly more general form, the issue here is **resource sharing**, and the goal is to make all programs, data, and equipment available to anyone on the network without regard to the physical location of the resource and the user. In other words, the mere fact that a user happens to be 1000 km away from his data should not prevent him from using the data as though they were local. Load sharing is another aspect of resource sharing. This goal may be summarized by saying that it is an attempt to end the "tyranny of geography."

A second goal is to provide **high reliability** by having alternative sources of supply. For example, all files could be replicated on two or three machines, so if one of them is unavailable (due to a hardware failure), the other copies could be used. In addition, the presence of multiple CPUs means that if one goes down, the others may be able to take over its work, although at reduced performance. For military, banking, air traffic control, and many other applications, the ability to continue operating in the face of hardware problems is of great importance.

Another goal is **saving money**. Small computers have a much better price/performance ratio than large ones. Mainframes are roughly a factor of ten faster than the fastest single chip microprocessors, but they cost a thousand times more. This imbalance has caused many systems designers to build systems consisting of powerful personal computers, one per user, with data kept on one or more shared **file server** machines.

This goal leads to networks with many computers located in the same building.

Such a network is called a **LAN** (**local area network**) to contrast it with the far-flung **WAN** (**wide area network**), which is also called a **long haul network**.

A closely related point is the ability to increase system performance gradually as the workload grows just by adding more processors. With central mainframes, when the system is full, it must be replaced by a larger one, usually at great expense and with even greater disruption to the users.

Yet another goal of setting up a computer network has little to do with technology at all. A computer network can provide a powerful **communication medium** among widely separated people. Using a network, it is easy for two or more people who live far apart to write a report together. When one author makes a change to the document, which is kept online, the others can see the change immediately, instead of waiting several days for a letter. Such a speedup makes cooperation among far-flung groups of people easy where it previously had been impossible. In the long run, the use of networks to enhance human-to-human communication may prove more important than technical goals such as improved reliability.

In Fig. 1-1 we give a classification of multiple processor systems arranged by physical size. At the top are **data flow machines**, highly parallel computers with many functional units all working on the same program. Next come the **multiprocessors**, systems that communicate via shared memory. Beyond the multiprocessors are the true networks, computers that communicate by exchanging messages. Finally, the connection of two or more networks is called **internetworking**.

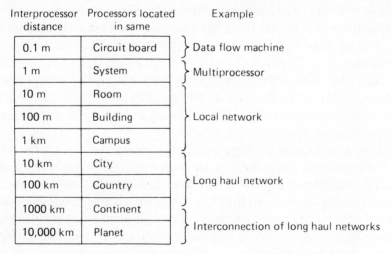

Interprocessor distance	Processors located in same	Example
0.1 m	Circuit board	Data flow machine
1 m	System	Multiprocessor
10 m	Room	
100 m	Building	Local network
1 km	Campus	
10 km	City	
100 km	Country	Long haul network
1000 km	Continent	
10,000 km	Planet	Interconnection of long haul networks

Fig. 1-1. Classification of interconnected processors by scale.

1.1.2. Applications of Networks

Replacing a single mainframe by workstations on a LAN does not make many new applications possible, although it may improve the reliability and performance. In contrast, the availability of a (public) WAN makes many new applications feasible. Some of these new applications may have important effects on society as a whole. To give an idea about some important uses of computer networks, we will now briefly look at just three examples: access to remote programs, access to remote databases, and value-added communication facilities.

A company that has produced a model simulating the world economy may allow its clients to log in over the network and run the program to see how various projected inflation rates, interest rates, and currency fluctuations might affect their businesses. This approach is often preferable to selling the program outright, especially if the model is constantly being adjusted or requires an extremely large mainframe computer to run.

Another major area of network use is access to remote databases. It may soon be easy for the average person sitting at home to make reservations for airplanes, trains, buses, boats, hotels, restaurants, theaters, and so on, anywhere in the world with instant confirmation. Home banking and the automated newspaper also fall in this category. Present newspapers offer a little bit of everything, but electronic ones can be easily tailored to each reader's personal taste, for example, everything about computers, the major stories about politics and epidemics, but no football, thank you.

The next step beyond automated newspapers (plus magazines and scientific journals) is the fully automated library. Depending on the cost, size, and weight of the terminal, the printed word may become obsolete. Skeptics should take note of the effect the printing press had on the medieval illuminated manuscript.

All these applications use networking for economic reasons: calling up a distant computer via a network is cheaper than calling it directly. The lower rate is possible because a normal telephone call ties up an expensive, dedicated circuit for the duration of the call, whereas access via a network ties up long-distance lines only while data are actually being transmitted.

A third category of potential widespread network use is as a communication medium. Computer scientists already take it for granted that they can send electronic mail from their terminals to their colleagues anywhere in the world. In the future, it will be possible for everyone, not just people in the computer business, to send and receive electronic mail. Furthermore, this mail will also be able to contain digitized voice, still pictures and possibly even moving television and video images. One can easily imagine children in different countries trying to learn each other's languages by drawing a picture of a child on a shared screen and labeling it girl, jeune fille, or meisje.

Electronic bulletin board systems already exist, but these tend to be used by computer experts, are oriented towards technical topics, and are often limited in geographic scope. Future systems will be national or international, be used by millions of nontechnical people, and cover a much broader range of subjects. Using a bulletin board may be as common as reading a magazine.

It is sometimes said that there is a race going on between transportation and communication, and whichever one wins will make the other unnecessary. Using a computer network as a sophisticated communication system may reduce the amount of traveling done, thus saving energy. Home work may become popular, especially for part-time workers with young children. The office and school as we now know them may disappear. Stores may be replaced by electronic mail order catalogs. Cities may disperse, since high-quality communication facilities tend to reduce the need for physical proximity. The information revolution may change society as much as the Industrial Revolution did.

1.2. NETWORK STRUCTURE

It is now time to turn our attention from the social implications of networking to the technical issues involved in network design. In any network there exists a collection of machines intended for running user (i.e., application) programs. We will follow the terminology of one of the first major networks, the ARPANET, and call these machines **hosts**. The term **end system** is sometimes also used in the literature. The hosts are connected by the **communication subnet**, or just **subnet** for short. The job of the subnet is to carry messages from host to host, just as the telephone system carries words from speaker to listener. By separating the pure communication aspects of the network (the subnet) from the application aspects (the hosts), the complete network design is greatly simplified.

In most wide area networks, the subnet consists of two distinct components: transmission lines and switching elements. Transmission lines (also called **circuits**, **channels**, or **trunks**) move bits between machines.

The switching elements are specialized computers used to connect two or more transmission lines. When data arrive on an incoming line, the switching element must choose an outgoing line to forward them on. Again following the original ARPANET terminology, we will call the switching elements **IMPs** (**Interface Message Processors**) throughout the book, although the terms **packet switch node**, **intermediate system**, and **data switching exchange** are also commonly used. Unfortunately, there is no consensus on terminology here; every writer on the subject seems to use a different name. The term "IMP" is probably as good as any. In this model, shown in Fig. 1-2, each host is connected to one (or occasionally several) IMPs. All traffic to or from the host goes via its IMP.

Broadly speaking, there are two types of designs for the communication subnet:

1. Point-to-point channels.

2. Broadcast channels.

In the first one, the network contains numerous cables or leased telephone lines, each one connecting a pair of IMPs. If two IMPs that do not share a cable nevertheless wish to communicate, they must do this indirectly, via other IMPs.

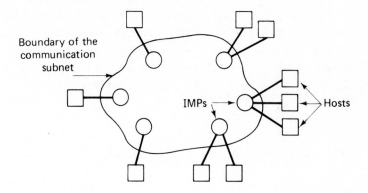

Fig. 1-2. Relation between hosts and the subnet.

When a message (in the context of the subnet often called a **packet**), is sent from one IMP to another via one or more intermediate IMPs, the packet is received at each intermediate IMP in its entirety, stored there until the required output line is free, and then forwarded. A subnet using this principle is called a **point-to-point**, **store-and-forward**, or **packet-switched** subnet. Nearly all wide area networks have store-and-forward subnets.

When a point-to-point subnet is used, an important design issue is what the IMP interconnection topology should look like. Figure 1-3 shows several possible topologies. Local networks that were designed as such usually have a symmetric topology. In contrast, wide area networks typically have irregular topologies.

The second kind of communication architecture uses broadcasting. Most local area networks and a small number of wide area networks are of this type. In a local area network, the IMP is reduced to a single chip embedded inside the host, so there is always one host per IMP, whereas in a wide area network there may be many hosts per IMP.

Broadcast systems have a single communication channel that is shared by all the machines on the network. Packets sent by any machine are received by all the others. An address field within the packet specifies for whom it is intended. Upon receiving a packet, a machine checks the address field. If the packet is intended for some other machine, it is just ignored.

As an analogy, consider someone standing at the end of a corridor with many rooms off it and shouting "Watson, come here. I want you." Although the packet may actually be received (heard) by many people, only Watson responds. The others just ignore it.

Broadcast systems generally also allow the possibility of addressing a packet to *all* destinations by using a special code in the address field. When a packet with this code is transmitted, it is received and processed by every machine on the network. Some broadcast systems also support transmission to a subset of the machines, something known as **multicasting**. A common scheme is to have all

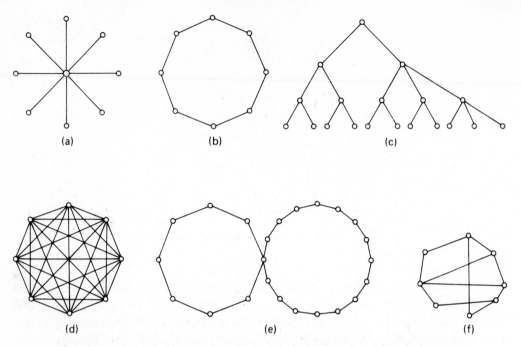

Fig. 1-3. Some possible topologies for a point-to-point subnet. (a) Star. (b) Ring. (c) Tree. (d) Complete. (e) Intersecting rings. (f) Irregular.

addresses with the high-order bit set to 1 be reserved for multicasting. The remaining $n-1$ addresses bits form a bit map corresponding to $n-1$ groups. Each machine can "subscribe" to any or all of the $n-1$ groups. If a packet with, say, bits x, y, and z set to 1 is transmitted, it is accepted by all machines subscribing to one or more of those three groups.

Figure 1-4 shows some of the possibilities for broadcast subnets. In a bus or cable network, at any instant one machine is the master and is allowed to transmit. All other machines are required to refrain from sending. An arbitration mechanism is needed to resolve conflicts when two or more machines want to transmit simultaneously. The arbitration mechanism may be centralized or distributed.

A second possibility is a satellite or ground radio system. Each IMP has an antenna through which it can send and receive. All IMPs can hear the output *from* the satellite, and in some cases they can also hear the upwards transmissions of their fellow IMPs *to* the satellite as well.

A third broadcast system is the ring. In a ring, each bit propagates around on its own, not waiting for the rest of the packet to which it belongs. Typically, each bit circumnavigates the entire ring in the time it takes to transmit a few bits, often before the complete packet has even been transmitted. Like all other broadcast systems, some rule is needed for arbitrating simultaneous accesses to the ring. Various methods are in use and will be discussed later in this book.

Broadcast subnets can be further divided into static and dynamic, depending on

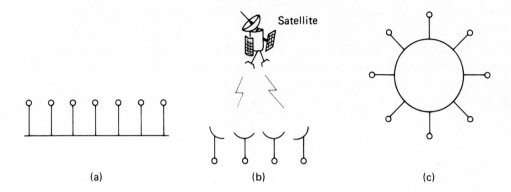

Fig. 1-4. Communication subnets using broadcasting. (a) Bus. (b) Satellite or radio. (c) Ring.

how the channel is allocated. A typical static allocation would be to divide up time into discrete intervals, and run a round robin, allowing each machine to broadcast only when its time slot comes up. Static allocation wastes channel capacity when a machine has nothing to say during its allocated slot, so some systems attempt to allocate the channel dynamically (i.e., on demand).

Dynamic allocation methods for a common channel are either centralized or decentralized. In the centralized channel allocation method, there is a single entity, for example a bus arbitration unit, which determines who goes next. It might do this by accepting requests and making a decision according to some internal algorithm. In the decentralized channel allocation method, there is no central entity; each machine must decide for itself whether or not to transmit. You might think that this always leads to chaos, but it does not. Later we will study many algorithms designed to bring order out of the potential chaos.

1.3. NETWORK ARCHITECTURES

Modern computer networks are designed in a highly structured way. In the following sections we examine the structuring technique in some detail.

1.3.1. Protocol Hierarchies

To reduce their design complexity, most networks are organized as a series of **layers** or **levels**, each one built upon its predecessor. The number of layers, the name of each layer, the contents of each layer, and the function of each layer differ from network to network. However, in all networks, the purpose of each layer is to offer certain services to the higher layers, shielding those layers from the details of how the offered services are actually implemented.

Layer n on one machine carries on a conversation with layer n on another machine. The rules and conventions used in this conversation are collectively known as the layer n **protocol**, as illustrated in Fig. 1-5 for a seven-layer network. The entities comprising the corresponding layers on different machines are called **peer processes**. In other words, it is the peer processes that communicate using the protocol.

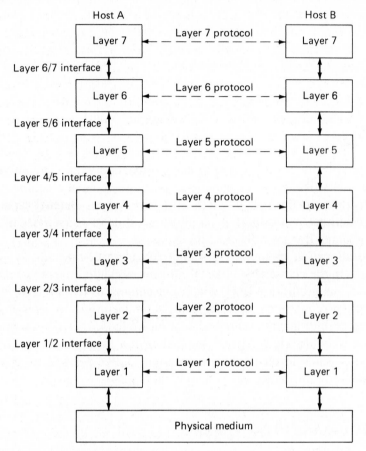

Fig. 1-5. Layers, protocols, and interfaces.

In reality, no data are directly transferred from layer n on one machine to layer n on another machine. Instead, each layer passes data and control information to the layer immediately below it, until the lowest layer is reached. Below layer 1 is the **physical medium** through which actual communication occurs. In Fig. 1-5, virtual communication is shown by dotted lines and physical communication by solid lines.

Between each pair of adjacent layers there is an **interface**. The interface defines which primitive operations and services the lower layer offers to the upper one. When network designers decide how many layers to include in a network and what each one should do, one of the most important considerations is defining clean interfaces between the layers. Doing so, in turn, requires that each layer perform a specific collection of well-understood functions. In addition to minimizing the amount of information that must be passed between layers, clean-cut interfaces also make it simpler to replace the implementation of one layer with a completely different implementation (e.g., all the telephone lines are replaced by satellite channels), because all that is required of the new implementation is that it offer exactly the same set of services to its upstairs neighbor as the old implementation did.

The set of layers and protocols is called the **network architecture**. The specification of the architecture must contain enough information to allow an implementer to write the program or build the hardware for each layer so that it will correctly obey the appropriate protocol. Neither the details of the implementation nor the specification of the interfaces are part of the architecture because these are hidden away inside the machines and not visible from the outside. It is not even necessary that the interfaces on all machines in a network be the same, provided that each machine can correctly use all the protocols. The subjects of network architectures and protocols are the principal topics of this book.

An analogy may help explain the idea of multilayer communication. Imagine two philosophers (peer processes in layer 3), one in Kenya and one in Indonesia, who want to communicate. Since they have no common language, they each engage a translator (peer processes at layer 2), each of whom in turn contacts an engineer (peer processes in layer 1). Philosopher 1 wishes to convey his affection for *oryctolagus cuniculus* to his peer. To do so, he passes a message (in Swahili) across the 2/3 interface, to his translator, who might render it as "I like rabbits" or "J'aime des lapins" or "Ik hou van konijnen," depending on the layer 2 protocol.

The translator then gives the message to his engineer for transmission, by telegram, telephone, computer network, or some other means, depending on what the two engineers have agreed on in advance (the layer 1 protocol). When the message arrives, it is translated into Indonesian and passed across the 2/3 interface to philosopher 2. Note that each protocol is completely independent of the other ones as long as the interfaces are not changed. The translators can switch from French to Dutch at will, provided that they both agree, and neither changes his interface with either layer 1 or layer 3.

Now consider a more technical example: how to provide communication to the top layer of the seven-layer network in Fig. 1-6. A message, m, is produced by a process running in layer 7. The message is passed from layer 7 to layer 6 according to the definition of the layer 6/7 interface. In this example, layer 6 transforms the message in certain ways (e.g., text compression), and then passes the new message, M, to layer 5 across the layer 5/6 interface. Layer 5, in the example, does not modify the message but simply regulates the direction of flow (i.e., prevents an incoming message from being handed to layer 6 while layer 6 is busy handing a series of outgoing messages to layer 5).

In many networks, there is no limit to the size of messages accepted by layer 4,

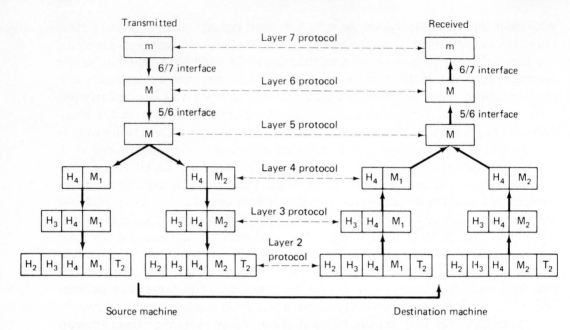

Fig. 1-6. Example information flow supporting virtual communication in layer 7.

but there is a limit imposed by layer 3. Consequently, layer 4 must break up the incoming messages into smaller units, prepending a **header** to each unit. The header includes control information, such as sequence numbers, to allow layer 4 on the destination machine to get the pieces back together in the right order if the lower layers do not maintain sequence. In many layers, headers also contain contain sizes, times and other control fields.

Layer 3 decides which of the outgoing lines to use, attaches its own headers, and passes the data to layer 2. Layer 2 adds not only a header to each piece, but also a trailer, and gives the resulting unit to layer 1 for physical transmission. At the receiving machine the message moves upward, from layer to layer, with headers being stripped off as it progresses. None of the headers for layers below n are passed up to layer n.

The important thing to understand about Fig. 1-6 is the relation between the virtual and actual communication and the difference between protocols and interfaces. The peer processes in layer 4, for example, conceptually think of their communication as being "horizontal," using the layer 4 protocol. Each one is likely to have a procedure called *SendToOtherSide* and a procedure *GetFromOtherSide*, even though these procedures actually communicate with lower layers across the 3/4 interface, not with the other side.

The peer process abstraction is crucial to all network design. Without this abstraction technique, it would be difficult, if not impossible, to partition the design of the complete network, an unmanageable problem, into several smaller, manageable, design problems, namely the design of the individual layers.

1.3.2. Design Issues for the Layers

Some of the key design issues that occur in computer networking are present in several layers. Below, we will briefly mention some of the more important ones.

Every layer must have a mechanism for connection establishment. Since a network normally has many computers, some of which have multiple processes, a means is needed for a process on one machine to specify with whom it wants to establish a connection. As a consequence of having multiple destinations, some form of addressing is needed in order to specify a specific destination.

Closely related to the mechanism for establishing connections across the network is the mechanism for terminating them once they are no longer needed. As we will see in Chapter 6, this seemingly trivial point can actually be quite subtle.

Another set of design decisions concerns the rules for data transfer. In some systems, data only travel in one direction (**simplex communication**). In others they can travel in either direction, but not simultaneously (**half-duplex communication**). In still others they travel in both directions at once (**full-duplex communication**). The protocol must also determine how many logical channels the connection corresponds to, and what their priorities are. Many networks provide at least two logical channels per connection, one for normal data and one for urgent data.

Error control is an important issue because physical communication circuits are not perfect. Many error-detecting and error-correcting codes are known, but both ends of the connection must agree on which one is being used. In addition, the receiver must have some way of telling the sender which messages have been correctly received and which have not.

Not all communication channels preserve the order of messages sent on them. To deal with a possible loss of sequencing, the protocol must make explicit provision for the receiver to allow the pieces to be put back together properly. An obvious solution is to number the pieces, but this solution still leaves open the question of what should be done with pieces that arrive out of order.

An issue that occurs at every level is how to keep a fast sender from swamping a slow receiver with data. Various solutions have been proposed and will be discussed later. All of them involve some kind of feedback from the receiver to the sender, either directly or indirectly, about the receiver's current situation.

Another problem that must be solved at several levels is the inability of all processes to accept arbitrarily long messages. This property leads to mechanisms for disassembling, transmitting, and then reassembling messages. A related issue is what to do when processes insist upon transmitting data in units that are so small that sending each one separately is inefficient. Here the solution is to gather together several small messages heading toward a common destination into a single large message, and dismember the large message at the other side.

When it is inconvenient or expensive to set up a separate connection for each pair of communicating processes, the underlying layer may decide to use the same connection for multiple, unrelated conversations. As long as this multiplexing and demultiplexing is done transparently, it can be used by any layer. Multiplexing is needed in the physical layer, for example, where all the traffic for all connections has to be sent over at most a few physical circuits.

When there are multiple paths between source and destination, a route must be chosen. Sometimes this decision must be split over two or more layers. For example, to send data from London to Rome, a high level decision might have to be made to go via France or Germany based on their respective privacy laws, and a low-level decision might have to be made to choose one of the many available circuits based on current traffic.

1.4. THE OSI REFERENCE MODEL

Now that we have discussed layered networks in the abstract, it is time to look at the set of layers that will be used throughout this book. The model is shown in Fig. 1-7. This model is based on a proposal developed by the International Standards Organization (ISO) as a first step toward international standardization of the various protocols (Day and Zimmermann, 1983). The model is called the **ISO OSI Open Systems Interconnection) Reference Model** because it deals with connecting open systems—that is, systems that are open for communication with other systems. We will usually just call it the OSI model for short.

The OSI model has seven layers. The principles that were applied to arrive at the seven layers are as follows:

1. A layer should be created where a different level of abstraction is needed.

2. Each layer should perform a well defined function.

3. The function of each layer should be chosen with an eye toward defining internationally standardized protocols.

4. The layer boundaries should be chosen to minimize the information flow across the interfaces.

5. The number of layers should be large enough that distinct functions need not be thrown together in the same layer out of necessity, and small enough that the architecture does not become unwieldy.

In Sections 1.5.1 through 1.5.7 we will discuss each layer of the model in turn, starting at the bottom layer. Note that the OSI model itself is not a network architecture because it does not specify the exact services and protocols to be used in each layer. It just tells what each layer should do. However, ISO has also produced standards for all the layers, although these are not strictly speaking part of the model. Each one has been published as a separate international standard.

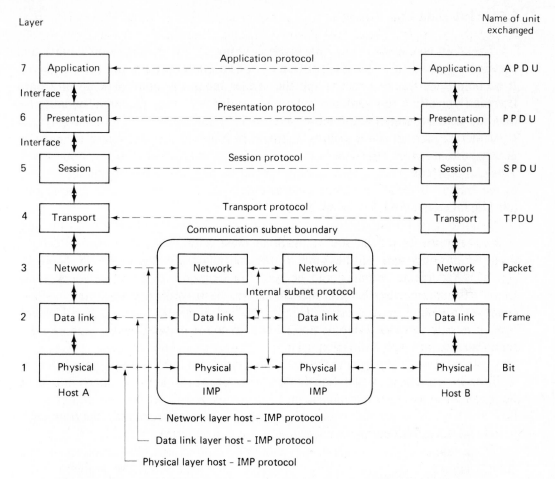

Fig. 1-7. The network architecture used in this book. It is based on the OSI model.

1.4.1. The Physical Layer

The **physical layer** is concerned with transmitting raw bits over a communication channel. The design issues have to do with making sure that when one side sends a 1 bit, it is received by the other side as a 1 bit, not as a 0 bit. Typical questions here are how many volts should be used to represent a 1 and how many for a 0, how many microseconds a bit lasts, whether transmission may proceed simultaneously in both directions, how the initial connection is established and how it is torn down when both sides are finished, and how many pins the network connector has and what each pin is used for. The design issues here largely deal with mechanical, electrical, and procedural interfaces, and the physical transmission medium, which lies below the physical layer. Physical layer design can be properly considered to be within the domain of the electrical engineer.

1.4.2. The Data Link Layer

The main task of the **data link layer** is to take a raw transmission facility and transform it into a line that appears free of transmission errors to the network layer. It accomplishes this task by having the sender break the input data up into **data frames** (typically a few hundred bytes), transmit the frames sequentially, and process the **acknowledgement frames** sent back by the receiver. Since the physical layer merely accepts and transmits a stream of bits without any regard to meaning or structure, it is up to the data link layer to create and recognize frame boundaries. This can be accomplished by attaching special bit patterns to the beginning and end of the frame. If these bit patterns can accidentally occur in the data, special care must be taken to avoid confusion.

A noise burst on the line can destroy a frame completely. In this case, the data link layer software on the source machine must retransmit the frame. However, multiple transmissions of the same frame introduce the possibility of duplicate frames. A duplicate frame could be sent, for example, if the acknowledgement frame from the receiver back to the sender was destroyed. It is up to this layer to solve the problems caused by damaged, lost, and duplicate frames. The data link layer may offer several different service classes to the network layer, each of a different quality and with a different price.

Another issue that arises in the data link layer (and most of the higher layers as well) is how to keep a fast transmitter from drowning a slow receiver in data. Some traffic regulation mechanism must be employed to let the transmitter know how much buffer space the receiver has at the moment. Frequently, this flow regulation and the error handling are integrated, for convenience.

If the line can be used to transmit data in both directions, this introduces a new complication that the data link layer software must deal with. The problem is that the acknowledgement frames for A to B traffic compete for the use of the line with data frames for the B to A traffic. A clever solution (piggybacking) has been devised; we will discuss it in detail later.

1.4.3. The Network Layer

The **network layer** is concerned with controlling the operation of the subnet. A key design issue is determining how packets are routed from source to destination. Routes could be based on static tables that are "wired into" the network and rarely changed. They could also be determined at the start of each conversation, for example a terminal session. Finally, they could be highly dynamic, being determined anew for each packet, to reflect the current network load.

If too many packets are present in the subnet at the same time, they will get in each other's way, forming bottlenecks. The control of such congestion also belongs to the network layer.

Since the operators of the subnet may well expect remuneration for their efforts, there is often some accounting function built into the network layer. At the very least, the software must count how many packets or characters or bits are sent by each customer, to produce billing information. When a packet crosses a national border, with different rates on each side, the accounting can become complicated.

When a packet has to travel from one network to another to get to its destination, many problems can arise. The addressing used by the second network may be different from the first one. The second one may not accept the packet at all because it is too large. The protocols may differ, and so on. It is up to the network layer to overcome all these problems to allow heterogenous networks to be interconnected.

In broadcast networks, the routing problem is simple, so the network layer is often thin or even nonexistent.

1.4.4. The Transport Layer

The basic function of the **transport layer**, is to accept data from the session layer, split it up into smaller units if need be, pass these to the network layer, and ensure that the pieces all arrive correctly at the other end. Furthermore, all this must be done efficiently, and in a way that isolates the session layer from the inevitable changes in the hardware technology.

Under normal conditions, the transport layer creates a distinct network connection for each transport connection required by the session layer. If the transport connection requires a high throughput, however, the transport layer might create multiple network connections, dividing the data among the network connections to improve throughput. On the other hand, if creating or maintaining a network connection is expensive, the transport layer might multiplex several transport connections onto the same network connection to reduce the cost. In all cases, the transport layer is required to make the multiplexing transparent to the session layer.

The transport layer also determines what type of service to provide the session layer, and ultimately, the users of the network. The most popular type of transport connection is an error-free point-to-point channel that delivers messages in the order in which they were sent. However, other possible kinds of transport service are transport of isolated messages with no guarantee about the order of delivery, and broadcasting of messages to multiple destinations. The type of service is determined when the connection is established.

The transport layer is a true source-to-destination or **end-to-end** layer. In other words, a program on the source machine carries on a conversation with a similar program on the destination machine, using the message headers and control messages. In the lower layers, the protocols are between each machine and its immediate neighbors, and not by the ultimate source and destination machines, which may be separated by many IMPs. The difference between layers 1 through 3, which are chained, and layers 4 through 7, which are end-to-end, is illustrated in Fig. 1-7.

Many hosts are multiprogrammed, which implies that multiple connections will be entering and leaving each host. There needs to be some way to tell which message belongs to which connection. The transport header (H_4 in Fig. 1-6) is one place this information could be put.

In addition to multiplexing several message streams onto one channel, the transport layer must take care of establishing and deleting connections across the network. This requires some kind of naming mechanism, so that a process on one machine has a way of describing with whom it wishes to converse. There must also be a mechanism to regulate the flow of information, so that a fast host cannot overrun a slow one. Flow control between hosts is distinct from flow control between IMPs, although we will later see that similar principles apply to both.

1.4.5. The Session Layer

The session layer allows users on different machines to establish **sessions** between them. A session allows ordinary data transport, as does the transport layer, but it also provides some enhanced services useful in a some applications. A session might be used to allow a user to log into a remote time-sharing system or to transfer a file between two machines.

One of the services of the session layer is to manage dialogue control. Sessions can allow traffic to go in both directions at the same time, or in only one direction at a time. If traffic can only go one way at a time (analogous to a single railroad track), the session layer can help keep track of whose turn it is.

A related session service is **token management**. For some protocols, it is essential that both sides do not attempt the same operation at the same time. To manage these activities, the session layer provides tokens that can be exchanged. Only the side holding the token may perform the critical operation.

Another session service is **synchronization**. Consider the problems that might occur when trying to do a two-hour file transfer between two machines on a network with a 1 hour mean time between crashes. After each transfer was aborted, the whole transfer would have to start over again, and would probably fail again when the network next crashed. To eliminate this problem, the session layer provides a way to insert checkpoints into the data stream, so that after a crash, only the data after the last checkpoint have to be repeated.

1.4.6. The Presentation Layer

The **presentation layer** performs certain functions that are requested sufficiently often to warrant finding a general solution for them, rather than letting each user solve the problems. In particular, unlike all the lower layers, which are just interested in moving bits reliably from here to there, the presentation layer is concerned with the syntax and semantics of the information transmitted.

A typical example of a presentation service is encoding data in a standard agreed upon way. Most user programs do not exchange random binary bit strings. They exchange things such as people's names, dates, amounts of money, and invoices. These items are represented as character strings, integers, floating point numbers, and data structures composed of several simpler items. Different computers have different codes for representing character strings (e.g., ASCII and EBCDIC), integers (e.g., one's complement and two's complement), and so on. In order to make it possible for computers with different representations to communicate, the data structures to be exchanged can be defined in an abstract way, along with a standard encoding to be used "on the wire." The job of managing these abstract data structures and converting from the representation used inside the computer to the network standard representation is handled by the presentation layer.

The presentation layer is also concerned with other aspects of information representation. For example, data compression can be used here to reduce the number of bits that have to be transmitted and cryptography is frequently required for privacy and authentication.

1.4.7. The Application Layer

The application layer contains a variety of protocols that are commonly needed. For example, there are hundreds of incompatible terminal types in the world. Consider the plight of a full screen editor that is supposed to work over a network with many different terminal types, each with different screen layouts, escape sequences for inserting and deleting text, moving the cursor, etc.

One way to solve this problem is to define an abstract **network virtual terminal** that editors and other programs can be written to deal with. To handle each terminal type, a piece of software must be written to map the functions of the network virtual terminal onto the real terminal. For example, when the editor moves the virtual terminal's cursor to the upper left-hand corner of the screen, this software must issue the proper command sequence to the real terminal to get its cursor there too. All the virtual terminal software is in the application layer.

Another application layer function is file transfer. Different file systems have different file naming conventions, different ways of representing text lines, and so on. Transferring a file between two different systems requires handling these and other incompatibilities. This work, too, belongs to the application layer, as do electronic mail, remote job entry, directory lookup, and various other general-purpose and special-purpose facilities.

1.4.8. Data Transmission in the OSI Model

Figure 1-8 shows an example of how data can be transmitted using the OSI model. The sending process has some data it wants to send to the receiving process. It gives the data to the application layer, which then attaches the application header, *AH* (which may be null), to the front of it and gives the resulting item to the presentation layer.

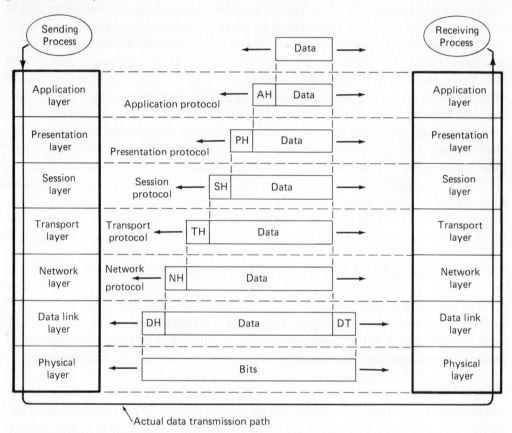

Fig. 1-8. An example of how the OSI model is used. Some of the headers may be null. (Source: H.C. Folts. Used with permission.)

The presentation layer may transform this item in various ways, and possibly add a header to the front, giving the result to the session layer. It is important to realize that the presentation layer is not aware of which portion of the data given to it by the application layer is *AH*, if any, and which is true user data. Nor should it be aware.

This process is repeated until the data reach the physical layer, where they are actually transmitted to the receiving machine. On that machine the various headers are stripped off one by one as the message propagates up the layers until it finally arrives at the receiving process.

The key idea throughout is that although actual data transmission is vertical in Fig. 1-8, each layer is programmed as though it were really horizontal. When the sending transport layer, for example, gets a message from the session layer, it attaches a transport header and sends it to the receiving transport layer. From its point of view, the fact that it must actually hand the message to the network layer on its own machine is an unimportant technicality. As an analogy, when an Uighur-speaking diplomat is addressing the United Nations, he thinks of himself as addressing the other assembled diplomats. That, in fact, he is really only speaking to his translator is seen as a technical detail.

1.5. SERVICES

The real function of each layer in the OSI model is to provide services to the layer above it. In this section we will look at precisely what a service is in more detail, but first we will give some of the OSI terminology.

1.5.1. OSI Terminology

The active elements in each layer are called **entities**. An entity can be a software entity (such as a process), or a hardware entity (such as an intelligent I/O chip). Entities in the same layer on different machines are called **peer entities**. The layer 7 entities are called **application entities**; the layer 6 entities are called **presentation entities,** and so on.

The entities in layer N implement a service used by layer $N + 1$. In this case layer N is called the **service provider** and layer $N + 1$ is called the **service user**. Layer N may use the services of layer $N - 1$ in order to provide its service. It may offer several classes of service, for example, fast, expensive communication and slow, cheap communication.

Services are available at **SAP**s. (**service access points**), The layer N SAPs are the places where layer $N + 1$ can access the services offered. Each SAP has an address that uniquely identifies it. To make this point clearer, the SAPs in the telephone system are the sockets into which modular telephones can be plugged, and the SAP addresses are the telephone numbers of these sockets. To call someone, you must know his SAP address. Similarly, in the postal system, the SAP addresses are street addresses and post office boxes. To send a letter, you must know the addressee's SAP address. In Berkeley UNIX†, the SAPs are the sockets and the SAP addresses are the socket numbers. The SAP concept is discussed in detail by Tomas et al. (1987).

In order for two layers to exchange information, there has to be an agreed upon set of rules about the **interface**. At a typical interface, the layer $N + 1$ entity passes an **IDU (Interface Data Unit)** to the layer N entity through the SAP as shown in Fig. 1-9. The IDU consists of an **SDU (Service Data Unit)** and some control information. The SDU is the information passed across the network to the peer entity

---

† UNIX is a registered trademark of AT&T Bell Laboratories.

and then up to layer $N + 1$. The control information is needed to help the lower layer do its job (e.g., the number of bytes in the SDU), but is not part of the data itself.

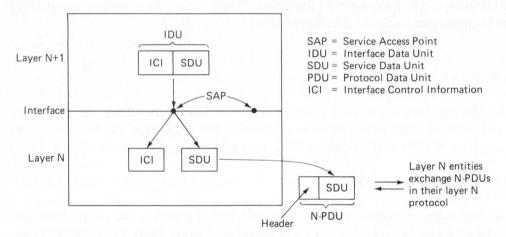

Fig. 1-9. Relation between layers at an interface.

In order to transfer the SDU, the layer N entity may have to fragment it into several pieces, each of which is given a header and sent as a separate **PDU (Protocol Data Unit)** such as a packet. The PDU headers are used by the peer entities to carry out their peer protocol. They identify which PDUs contain data and which contain control information, provide sequence numbers and counts, and so on. The transport, session and application PDUs are often referred to as TPDUs, SPDUs, and APDUs, respectively. No one talks much about the other PDUs.

This language is often known as **internationalbureaucratspeak**. We will avoid it where possible in favor of the more familiar nomenclature actually used by working computer scientists and engineers.

1.5.2. Connection-Oriented and Connectionless Services

Layers can offer two different types of service to the layers above them: connection-oriented and connectionless. In this section we will look at these two types, and examine the differences between them. Additional material can be found in (Bucciarelli and Caneschi, 1985; and Chapin, 1983).

Connection-oriented service is modeled after the telephone system. To talk to someone, you pick up the phone, dial the number, talk, and then hang up. Similarly, to use a connection-oriented network service, the service user first establishes a connection, uses the connection, and then terminates the connection. The essential aspect of a connection is that it acts like a tube: the sender pushes objects in at one end, and the receiver takes them out in the same order at the other end.

In contrast, **connectionless service** is modeled after the postal system. Each message (letter) carries the full destination address, and each one is routed through the system independent of all the others. Normally, when two messages are sent to the same destination the first one sent will be the first one to arrive. However, it is possible that the first one sent can be delayed so that the second one arrives first. With a connection-oriented service this is impossible.

Each service can be characterized by a quality of service. Some services are reliable in the sense that they never lose data. Usually a reliable service is implemented by having the receiver acknowledge the receipt of each message, so the sender is sure that it arrived. The acknowledgement process introduces overhead and delays, which are often worth it, but are sometimes undesirable.

A typical situation in which a reliable connection-oriented service is appropriate is file transfer. The owner of the file wants to be sure that all the bits arrive correctly and in the same order they were sent. Very few file transfer customers would prefer a service that occasionally scrambles or loses a few bits, even if it is much faster.

Reliable connection-oriented service has two minor variations: message sequences and byte streams. In the former, the message boundaries are preserved. When two 1K messages are sent, they arrive as two distinct 1K messages, never as one 2K message. In the latter, the connection is simply a stream of bytes, with no message boundaries. When 2K bytes arrive at the receiver, there is no way to tell if they were sent as one 2K message, two 1K messages, or 2048 one-byte messages. If the pages of a book are sent over a network to a phototypesetter as separate messages, it might be important to preserve the message boundaries. On the other hand, with a terminal logging into a remote time-sharing system, a byte stream from the terminal to the computer is all that is needed.

As mentioned above, for some applications, the delays introduced by acknowledgements are unacceptable. One such application is digitized voice traffic. It is preferable for telephone users to hear a bit of noise on the line or a garbled word from time to time than to introduce a delay to wait for acknowledgements.

Not all applications require connections. For example, as electronic mail becomes more common, can electronic junk mail be far behind? The electronic junk mail sender probably does not want to go to the trouble of setting up and later tearing down a connection just to send one item. Nor is 100 percent reliable delivery essential, especially if it costs more. All that is needed is a way to send a single message that has a high probability of arrival, but no guarantee. Unreliable (meaning not acknowledged) connectionless service is often called **datagram service**, in analogy with telegram service, which also does not provide an acknowledgement back to the sender.

In other situations, the convenience of not having to establish a connection to send one short message is desired, but reliability is essential. The **acknowledged datagram service** can be provided for these applications. It is like sending a registered letter and requesting a return receipt. When the receipt comes back, the sender is absolutely sure that the letter was delivered to the intended party.

Still another service is the **request-reply service**. In this service the sender transmits a single datagram containing a request; the reply contains the answer. For example, a query to the local library asking where Uighur is spoken falls into this category. Figure 1-10 summarizes the types of services discussed above.

	Service	Example
Connection-oriented	Reliable message stream	Sequence of pages
	Reliable byte stream	Remote login
	Unreliable connection	Digitized voice
Connection-less	Unreliable datagram	Electronic junk mail
	Acknowledged datagram	Registered mail
	Request-reply	Database query

Fig. 1-10. Six different types of service.

1.5.3. Service Primitives

A service is formally specified by a set of **primitives** (operations) available to a user or other entity to access the service. These primitives tell the service to perform some action or report on an action taken by a peer entity. In the OSI model, the service primitives can be divided into four classes as shown in Fig. 1-11.

Primitive	Meaning
Request	An entity wants the service to do some work
Indication	An entity is to be informed about an event
Response	An entity wants to respond to an event
Confirm	An entity is to be informed about its request

Fig. 1-11. Four classes of service primitives

The first class of primitive is the *request* primitive. It is used to get work done, for example, to establish a connection or to send data. When the work has been performed, the peer entity is signaled by an *indication* primitive. For example, after a *CONNECT.request* (in OSI notation), the entity being addressed gets a *CONNECT.indication* announcing that someone wants to set up a connection to it. The entity getting the *CONNECT.indication* then uses the *CONNECT.response* primitive to tell whether it wants to accept or reject the proposed connection. Either way, the entity issuing the initial *CONNECT.request* finds out what happened via a *CONNECT.confirm* primitive.

Primitives can have parameters, and most of them do. The parameters to a

CONNECT.request might specify the machine to connect to, the type of service desired, and the maximum message size to be used on the connection. The parameters to a *CONNECT.indication* might contain the caller's identity, the type of service desired, and the proposed maximum message size. If the called entity did not agree to the proposed maximum message size, it could make a counterproposal in its *response* primitive, which would be made available to the original caller in the *confirm*. The details of this **negotiation** are part of the protocol. For example, in the case of two conflicting proposals about maximum message size, the protocol might specify that the smaller value is always chosen.

As an aside on terminology, the OSI model carefully avoids the terms "open a connection" and "close a connection" because to electrical engineers, an "open circuit" is one with a gap or break in it. Electricity can only flow over "closed circuits." Computer scientists would never agree to having information flow over a closed circuit. To keep both camps pacified, the official terms are "establish a connection" and "release a connection."

Services can be either **confirmed** or **unconfirmed**. In a confirmed service, there is a *request*, an *indication*, a *response*, and a *confirm*. In an unconfirmed service, there is just a *request* and an *indication*. *CONNECT* is always a confirmed service because the remote peer must agree to establish a connection. Data transfer, on the other hand, can be either confirmed or unconfirmed, depending on whether or not the sender needs an acknowledgement. Both kinds of services are used in networks.

To make the concept of a service more concrete, let us consider as an example a simple connection-oriented service with eight service primitives as follows:

1. *CONNECT.request* — Request a connection to be established.

2. *CONNECT.indication* — Signal the called party.

3. *CONNECT.response* — Used by the callee to accept/reject calls.

4. *CONNECTION.confirm* — Tell the caller whether the call was accepted.

5. *DATA.request* — Request that data be sent.

6. *DATA.indication* — Signal the arrival of data.

7. *DISCONNECT.request* — Request that a connection be released.

8. *DISCONNECT.indication* — Signal the peer about the request.

In this example, *CONNECT* is a confirmed service (an explicit response is required), whereas *DISCONNECT* is unconfirmed (no response).

It may be helpful to make an analogy with the telephone system to see how these primitives are used. For this analogy, consider the steps required to call Aunt Millie on the telephone and invite her to to your house for tea.

1. *CONNECT.request* — Dial Aunt Millie's phone number.

2. *CONNECT.indication* — Her phone rings.

3. *CONNECT.response* — She picks up the phone.

4. *CONNECT.confirm* — You hear the ringing stop.

5. *DATA.request* — You invite her to tea.

6. *DATA.indication* — She hears your invitation.

7. *DATA.request* — She says she would be delighted to come.

8. *DATA.indication* — You hear her acceptance.

9. *DISCONNECT.request* — You hang up the phone.

10. *DISCONNECT.indication* — She hears it and hangs up too.

Figure 1-12 shows this same sequence of steps as a series of service primitives, including the final confirmation of disconnection. Each step involves an interaction between two layers on one of the computers. Each *request* or *response* causes an *indication* or *confirm* at the other side a little later. In this example, the service users (you and Aunt Millie) are in layer $N + 1$ and the service provider (the telephone system) is in layer N.

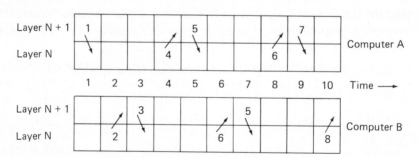

Fig. 1-12. How a computer would invite its Aunt Millie to tea. The numbers near the tail end of each arrow refer to the eight service primitives discussed in this section.

1.5.4. The Relationship of Services to Protocols

Services and protocols are distinct concepts, although they are frequently confused. This distinction is so important, however, that we emphasize it again here. A *service* is a set of primitives (operations) that a layer provides to the layer above it. The service defines what operations the layer is prepared to perform on behalf of its users, but it says nothing at all about how these operations are implemented. A service relates to an interface between two layers, with the lower layer being the service provider and the upper layer being the service user.

A *protocol*, in contrast, is a set of rules governing the format and meaning of the frames, packets, or messages that are exchanged by the peer entities within a layer. Entities use protocols in order to implement their service definitions. They are free to change their protocol at will, provided they do not change the service visible to their users. In this way, the service and the protocol are completely decoupled.

An analogy with programming languages is worth making. A service is like an abstract data type. It defines operations that can be performed on an object, but does not specify how these operations are implemented. A protocol relates to the *implementation* of the service, and as such is not visible to the user of the service.

Many of the pre-OSI protocols did not distinguish the service from the protocol. In effect, a typical layer might have had a service primitive *SEND PACKET* with the user providing a pointer to a fully assembled packet. This arrangement meant that all changes to the protocol were immediately visible to the users. It is now universally accepted that such a design is a blunder of major proportions.

1.6. NETWORK STANDARDIZATION

In the early days of networking, each computer manufacturer had its own network protocols. IBM had more than a dozen. The result was that users who had computers from several vendors could not connect them together into a single network. This chaos led many users to demand standardization.

Not only do standards allow different computers to communicate, but they also increase the market for products adhering to the standard, which leads to mass production, economies of scale in manufacturing, VLSI implementations, and other benefits that decrease price and further increase acceptance. In this section we will take a quick look at the important, but little-known, world of international standardization.

Standards fall into two categories: de facto and de jure. **De facto** (Latin for "from the fact") standards are those that have just happened, without any formal plan. The IBM PC and its successors are de facto standards for small office computers because dozens of manufacturers have chosen to copy IBM's machines very closely. UNIX is the de facto standard for operating systems in university computer science departments.

De jure (Latin for "by law") standards, in contrast, are formal, legal standards adopted by some authorized standardization body. International standardization authorities are generally divided into two classes: those established by treaty among national governments, and voluntary, nontreaty organizations. In the area of computer network standards, there are two principal organizations, one of each type. Both standards organizations are important and will be discussed below.

1.6.1. Who's Who in the Telecon

The legal status of the world's
country to country. At one extrem
privately owned telephone compani
that time the world's largest corpoi
vided telephone service to about
throughout half of its geographical a
vicing the remaining (mostly rural) c
to provide long distance service, witl
providing local service.

Companies in the United States
public are called **common carriers**.
document called a **tariff**, which must
Commission for the interstate and inte   ... ..ue Public Utili-
ties Commissions for intrastate traffic.

In recent years a new breed of telecommunication company has emerged to provide specialized data communication services, often in direct competition with the
telephone companies. Some of these companies offer high-performance long-
distance transmission facilities (e.g., using satellites), whereas others provide time-
sharing, networking, or other services using transmission facilities that they themselves rent from other common carriers.

At the other extreme are countries in which the national government has a complete monopoly on all communication, including the mail, telegraph, telephone, and
often radio and television as well. Most of the world falls in this category. In some
cases the telecommunication authority is a nationalized company, and in others it is
simply a branch of the government, usually known as the **PTT** (**Post, Telegraph &
Telephone** administration).

With all these different suppliers of services, there is clearly a need to provide
compatibility on a worldwide scale to ensure that people (and computers) in one
country can call their counterparts in another one. This coordination is provided by
an agency of the United Nations called **ITU** (**International Telecommunication
Union**). ITU has three main organs, two of which deal primarily with international
radio broadcasting and one of which is primarily concerned with telephone and data
communication systems.

The latter group is called **CCITT**, an acronym for its French name: Comité
Consultatif International de Télégraphique et Téléphonique. CCITT has five
classes of members: *A* members, which are the national PTTs; *B* members, which
are recognized private administrations (e.g., AT&T); *C* members, which are
scientific and industrial organizations; *D* members, which are other international
organizations; and *E* members, which are organizations whose primary mission is
in another field but which have an interest in CCITT's work. Only *A* members may
vote. Since the U.S. does not have a PTT, somebody else had to represent it in

CCITT. This task fell to the State Department, probably on the grounds that CCITT had to do with foreign countries, the State Department's specialty.

CCITT's task is to make technical recommendations about telephone, telegraph, and data communication interfaces. These often become internationally recognized standards. Two examples are V.24 (also known as EIA RS-232 in the United States), which specifies the placement and meaning of the various pins on the connector used by most asynchronous terminals, and X.25, which specifies an interface between a computer and a (packet-switched) computer network.

1.6.2. Who's Who in the Standards World

International standards are produced by **ISO (International Standards Organization†)**, a voluntary, nontreaty organization founded in 1946. Its members are the national standards organizations of the 89 member countries. These members include ANSI (U.S.), BSI (Great Britain), AFNOR (France), DIN (W. Germany), and 85 others.

ISO issues standards on a vast number of subjects, ranging from nuts and bolts (literally) to telephone pole coatings. ISO has almost 200 Technical Committees, numbered in the order of their creation, each dealing with a specific subject. TC1 deals with the nuts and bolts (standardizing screw thread pitches). TC97 deals with computers and information processing. Each TC has subcommittees (SCs) divided into working groups (WGs).

The real work is done largely in the WGs by over 100,000 volunteers world-wide. Many of these "volunteers" are assigned to work on ISO matters by their employers, whose products are being standardized. Others are government officials keen on having their country's way of doing things become the international standard. Academic experts also are active in many of the WGs.

On issues of telecommunication standards, ISO and CCITT *sometimes* cooperate (ISO is a *D* class member of CCITT) to avoid the irony of two official and mutually incompatible international standards.

The U.S. representative in ISO is **ANSI (American National Standards Institute)**, which despite its name, is a private, nongovernmental, nonprofit organization. Its members are manufacturers, common carriers, and other interested parties. ANSI standards are frequently adopted by ISO as international standards.

The procedure used by ISO for adopting standards is designed to achieve as broad a consensus as possible. The process begins when one of the national standards organizations feels the need for an international standard in some area. A working group is then formed to come up with a **DP (Draft Proposal)**. The DP is then circulated to all the member bodies, which get six months to criticize it. If a

---

† For the purist, despite the acronym, ISO's true name is the International Organization for Standardization.

substantial majority approves, a revised document, called a **DIS (Draft International Standard)** is produced and circulated for comments and voting. Based on the results of this round, the final text of the **IS (International Standard)** is prepared, approved, and published. In areas of great controversy, a DP or DIS may have to go through several versions before acquiring enough votes, and the whole process can take years.

NBS (National Bureau of Standards), is an agency of the U.S. Dept. of Commerce. It issues standards that are mandatory for purchases made by the U.S. Government, except for those of the Department of Defense, which has its own.

Another major player in the standards world is **IEEE (Institute of Electrical and Electronics Engineers)**, the largest professional organization in the world. In addition to publishing scores of journals and running numerous conferences each year, IEEE has a standardization group that develops standards in the area of electrical engineering and computing. IEEE's 802 standard for local area networks is the key standard for LANs. It has subsequently been taken over by ISO as the basis for ISO 8802.

1.6.3. Discussion of the Standardization of the OSI model

The time at which a standard is established is absolutely critical to its success. David Clark of M.I.T. has a theory of standards that he calls the *apocalypse of the two elephants*, and which is illustrated in Fig. 1-13.

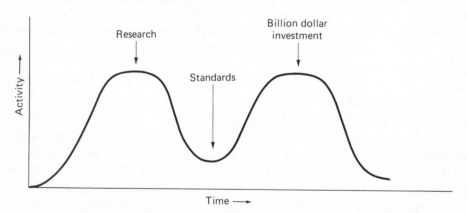

Fig. 1-13. The apocalypse of the two elephants.

This figure shows the amount of activity surrounding a new subject. When the subject is first discovered, there is a lot of research activity in the form of discussions, papers, and meetings. After a while this subsides, corporations discover the subject, and the billion-dollar wave of investment hits.

It is essential that the standards be written in the trough between the two "elephants." If they are written too early, before the research is finished, the subject may still be poorly understood, which leads to bad standards. If they are written too late, so many companies may have already made major investments in different ways of doing things that the standards are effectively ignored. If the interval between the two elephants is very short (because everyone is in a hurry to get started), the people developing the standards may get crushed.

It is the belief of some workers in the field that this is what happened with the OSI model. Most discussions of the seven-layer model give the impression that the number and contents of the layers eventually chosen were the only way, or at least the obvious way. In the paragraphs that follow, we present some dissenting arguments.

It would have been nice if all seven layers had roughly the same size and importance. This is far from true. The session layer has little use in most applications, and the presentation layer is nearly empty. In fact, the British proposal to ISO only had 5 layers, not 7. In contrast to the session and presentation layers, the data link and network layers are so full that subsequent work has split them into multiple sublayers, each with different functions.

The model, along with the associated service definitions and protocols, is extraordinarily complex. When piled up, the printed standards occupy a significant fraction of a meter of paper. They are also difficult to implement and inefficient in operation. One problem is that some functions, such as addressing, flow control, and error control reappear again and again in each layer. Saltzer et al. (1984), for example, have pointed out that to be effective, error control must be done in the highest layer, so that repeating it over and over in each of the lower layers is unnecessary and inefficient.

Another issue is that the placement of certain features in particular layers is not always obvious. The virtual terminal handling (now in the application layer) was in the presentation layer during part of the development of the standard. It was moved to the application layer because the committee had trouble deciding what the presentation layer was good for. Data security and encryption were so controversial that no one could agree which layer to put them in, so they were left out altogether. Network management was also omitted from the model for similar reasons.

Another criticism of the original standard is that it completely ignored connectionless services and connectionless protocols, even though that is the way most local area networks work. Subsequent addenda (known in the software world as bug fixes) have addressed this issue.

Perhaps the most serious criticism is that the model is completely dominated by a communications mentality. The relationship of computing to communications is barely mentioned anywhere, and some of the choices made are wholly inappropriate to the way computers and software work. As an example, consider the set of primitives discussed in Sec. 1.5.3 and listed in Fig. 1-11. In particular, think carefully about the primitives and how one might use them in a programming language.

The *CONNECT.request* primitive is simple. One can imagine a library procedure, *connect*, that programs can call to establish a connection. Now think about

CONNECT.indication. When a message arrives, the destination process has to be signaled. In effect, it has to get an interrupt, hardly an appropriate concept for programs written in any modern high-level language.

If the program was expecting the attempt to connect to it, it could call a library procedure *receive* to block itself, but if this were the case, why was *receive* not the primitive instead of *indication*? *Receive* is clearly oriented toward the way computers work, whereas *indication* is equally clearly oriented toward the way telephones work. Computers are different from telephones. Computers do not ring. In short, the semantic model of an interrupt-driven system is conceptually a very poor idea and totally at odds with all modern ideas of structured programming. This problem and similar ones are discussed by Langsford (1984).

1.7. EXAMPLE NETWORKS

Numerous networks are currently operating around the world. Some of these are public networks run by common carriers or PTTs, others are research networks, yet others are cooperative networks run by their users, and still others are commercial or corporate networks. In the following sections we will take a look at a few representative networks to get an idea of what they are like and how they differ from one another. Other networks are described by Quarterman and Hoskins (1986).

Networks differ in their history, administration, facilities offered, technical design, and user communities. The history and administration can vary from a network carefully planned by a single organization with a well-defined goal, to an ad-hoc collection of machines that have been connected to one another over the years without any master plan or central administration at all. The facilities available range from arbitrary process-to-process communication to electronic mail, file transfer, remote login, and remote execution. The technical designs can differ in the transmission media used, the naming and routing algorithms employed, the number and contents of the layers present, and the protocols used. Finally, the user community can vary from a single corporation to all the academic computer scientists in the industrialized world.

1.7.1. Public Networks

In many countries the government or private companies have begun to offer networking services to any organization that wishes to subscribe. The subnet is owned by the network operator, providing communication service for the customers' hosts and terminals. Such a system is called a **public network**. It is analogous to, and often a part of, the public telephone system.

Although public networks in different countries are frequently quite different internally, virtually all of them use the OSI model and the standard CCITT or OSI protocols for all the layers. In addition, many private networks also use the OSI protocols, or are planning to use them in the near future.

For the lowest three layers, CCITT has issued recommendations that have been universally adopted by public networks worldwide. These layers are always known collectively as **X.25** (the CCITT recommendation number), although ISO has also adopted and numbered them as standards.

The physical layer protocol, called **X.21**, specifies the physical, electrical, and procedural interface between the host and the network. Very few public networks actually support this standard, because it requires digital, rather than analog signaling on the telephone lines, but it may conceivably become more important in the future. As an interim measure, an analog interface similar to the familiar RS-232 standard has been defined.

The data link layer standard has a number of (slightly incompatible) variations. They all are designed to deal with transmission errors on the telephone line between the user's equipment (host or terminal) and the public network (IMP).

The network layer protocol deals with addressing, flow control, delivery confirmation, interrupts and related issues.

Because the world is still full of terminals that do not speak X.25, another set of standards has been defined that describes how an ordinary (nonintelligent) terminal communicates with an X.25 public network. In effect, the user or network operator installs a "black box" to which these terminals can connect. The black box is called a **PAD (Packet Assembler Disassembler)**, and its function is described in a CCITT recommendation known as **X.3**. A standard protocol has been defined between the terminal and the PAD, called **X.28**; another standard protocol exists between the PAD and the network, called **X.29**. Together, these three recommendations are often called **triple X**. We will discuss these standards in Chap. 9.

Above the network layer, the situation is less uniform. ISO has developed standards for a connection-oriented transport layer service definition (ISO 8072) and a connection-oriented transport layer protocol (ISO 8073). Most public networks will no doubt eventually adopt these. The transport service has five different variants. These will be discussed later in the book in the chapter on the transport layer.

ISO has also adopted standards for the connection-oriented session service and protocol (ISO 8326 and ISO 8327) and presentation service and protocol (ISO 8822 and ISO 8823). These will also be adopted eventually by most public networks, although the need is less critical than for a uniform transport service since many applications have no real need for session or presentation services at all.

The application layer contains not just one, but a whole collection of protocols for various applications. The **FTAM (File Transfer, Access, and Management)** protocol provides a way to transfer, access, and generally manipulate remote files in a uniform way. The **MOTIS (Message-Oriented Text Interchange Systems)** protocol is used for electronic mail. It is similar to the CCITT **X.400** series of recommendations. The **VTP (Virtual Terminal Protocol)** protocol provides a terminal-independent way for programs to access remote terminals (e.g., for full-screen editors). The **JTM** (**Job Transfer and Manipulation**) protocol is used for submitting jobs to remote mainframe computers for batch processing. It can be used to move both programs and data files. Numerous other industry-specific and application-specific protocols have also been defined, and new ones are being thought up and standardized all the time.

Figure 1-14 shows the numbers of a few of the key international standards. The style of the standards changes radically between layers 3 and 4, since the lower ones were done by CCITT and the upper ones were done by ISO. In particular, CCITT never bothered to distinguish between the service and the protocol, something ISO has meticulously done. Many other standards, including most of the connectionless ones, are not listed. Copies of all the standards are available from national standards organizations (e.g., ANSI).

Layer	Standard	Description
1-7	ISO 7498	ISO OSI Basic reference model
7	ISO 8571	File transfer, access and manipulation service
	ISO 8572	File transfer, access and manipulation protocol
	ISO 8831	Job transfer and manipulation service
	ISO 8832	Job transfer and manipulation protocol
	ISO 9040	Virtual terminal service
	ISO 9041	Virtual terminal protocol
	CCITT X.400	Message handling (electronic mail)
6	ISO 8822	Connection-oriented presentation service
	ISO 8823	Connection-oriented presentation protocol
5	ISO 8326	Connection-oriented session service
	ISO 8327	Connection-oriented session protocol
4	ISO 8072	Connection-oriented transport service
	ISO 8073	Connection-oriented transport protocol
3	CCITT X.25	X.25 layer 3 protocol
2	ISO 8802	Local area networks
	CCITT X.25	HDLC/LAPB data link layer
1	CCITT X.21	Physical layer digital interface

Fig. 1-14. A few of the key ISO and CCITT network standards. ISO refers to an ISO International Standard. ISO 8802 is derived from IEEE 802.

1.7.2. The ARPANET

The ARPANET is the creation of ARPA (now DARPA), the (Defense) Advanced Research Projects Agency of the U.S. Department of Defense. Starting in the late 1960s it began stimulating research on the subject of computer networks by providing grants to computer science departments at many U.S. universities, as well as to a few private corporations. This research led to an experimental four-node network that went on the air in December 1969. It has been operating ever since, and has subsequently grown to several hundred computers spanning half the globe, from Hawaii to Sweden. Much of our present knowledge about networking is a direct result of the ARPANET project. To honor this pioneering work, we have adopted some of the original ARPANET terminology (e.g., host, IMP, subnet).

After the ARPANET technology had proven itself by years of highly reliable service, a military network, MILNET, was set up using the same technology. An extension of MILNET in Europe, called MINET, was also created. MILNET and MINET are connected to the ARPANET, but the traffic between the parts is tightly controlled. Two satellite networks, SATNET and WIDEBAND, were also hooked up later. Since many of the universities and government contractors on the ARPANET had their own LANs, eventually these were also connected to the IMPs, leading to the **ARPA internet** with thousands of hosts and well over 100,000 users. The ARPANET will be frequently cited throughout this book, but most of what is said about the ARPANET (e.g., the protocols used) also holds for the entire internet.

The original ARPANET IMPs were Honeywell DDP-516 minicomputers with 12K 16-bit words of memory. As time has gone on, the IMPs have been replaced several times by more powerful machines. They are now called **PSNs** (**Packet Switch Nodes**), but their function is the same as it was.

Some of the IMPs have been configured to allow user terminals to call them directly, instead of logging into a host. These were called **TIPs** (**Terminal Interface Processors**) and are now called **TACs** (**Terminal Access Controllers**). The IMPs were originally connected by 56 kbps leased lines, although higher speed (e.g., 230.4 kbps), lines are now also used. The original IMPs could handle one to four hosts apiece. The current ones can handle tens of hosts and hundreds of terminals simultaneously.

The ARPANET does not follow the OSI model at all (it predates OSI by more than a decade). The IMP-IMP protocol really corresponds to a mixture of the layer 2 and layer 3 protocols. Layer 3 also contains an elaborate routing mechanism. In addition, there is a mechanism that explicitly verifies the correct reception at the destination IMP of each and every packet sent by the source IMP. Strictly speaking, this mechanism is another layer of protocol, the source IMP to destination IMP protocol. However, this protocol does not exist in the OSI model. We will treat it as part of layer 3, since it is closer to that layer than to any other.

The ARPANET does have protocols that roughly cover the same territory as the

OSI network and transport protocols. The network protocol, called **IP** (**Internet Protocol**), is connectionless and was designed to handle the interconnection of the vast number of WAN and LAN networks comprising the ARPA internet. The OSI model only grudgingly dealt with internetworking at all, as an afterthought, whereas the concept was central to the design of IP.

The ARPANET transport protocol is a connection-oriented protocol called **TCP** (**Transmission Control Protocol**). It resembles the OSI transport protocol in its general style, but it differs in all the formats and details. TCP is used in Berkeley UNIX, which makes it very widespread even though it is not part of the OSI suite. Just as an aside, it should be pointed out that TCP is the second generation transport protocol. The first one is no longer used.

There are no session or presentation layer protocols in the ARPANET as no one has had any use for them in the first 20 years of operation. Various application protocols exist, but they are not structured the same way as their OSI counterparts. The ARPANET services include file transfer, electronic mail, and remote login. These services are supported by the well-known protocols **FTP** (**File Transfer Protocol**), **SMTP** (**Simple Mail Transfer Protocol**), and **TELNET** (remote login). Various specialized protocols are available for other applications.

1.7.3. MAP and TOP

If two sites each use the OSI model, there is no guarantee that they will be able to communicate with each other. The model consists of a framework telling what the layers are, but does not itself specify the protocols to be used in each layer. While ISO has standardized certain protocols, other nonstandard protocols also exist. Furthermore, in some layers, multiple, incompatible standard protocols also exist. If two sites use different protocols in any layer, they will not be able to communicate.

Many readers may just throw up their hands in disgust and say: "Why can't the experts just agree on one standard protocol in each layer?" It is instructive to look at a concrete example to see how the problem arises. In 1973, Robert Metcalfe wrote a Ph.D. thesis at M.I.T. in which he described his research on LANs. Metcalfe then moved to the Xerox Corporation where he teamed up with David Boggs and others to implement the **Ethernet**† LAN based on the ideas in Metcalfe's thesis. Ethernet was quickly adopted by many companies and Intel later built a single-chip controller for it. It did not take long before Ethernet became the de facto standard for LANs.

Shortly thereafter, some people felt that there should be an *official* standard for LANs. A group of people working under the auspices of IEEE was set up to write

---

† Ethernet is a trademark of the Xerox Corporation.

one. Many people were invited to join the committee and contribute to the work. Some of these people came from General Motors, which was also carefully looking at LANs.

In order to compete with the Japanese automobile companies, GM wanted to set up a network covering all its offices, factories, dealers and suppliers. The idea was that when a customer ordered a car anywhere in the world, the dealer's computer would instantly send the order to GM, which would then send orders to its suppliers ordering the necessary steel, glass, and other raw materials.

An important part of the GM network was factory automation, in which all the robots working on the assembly lines would all be connected by LANs. Since the cars on the assembly lines move by at a fixed rate, whether the robots are ready or not, GM felt it essential to have a LAN in which the worst case transmission time had an upper bound that was known in advance. Ethernet does not have this property.

Essentially, Ethernet works by having all the machines listen to the cable. If the cable is idle, any machine may transmit. If two machines transmit at the same time, there is a collision, in which case they all stop, wait a random period of time, and try again later. In theory, there is no upper bound on the time a machine might have to wait to send a message. GM wanted a LAN called the **token bus** in which the machines took turns, round-robin, thus giving a deterministic worst-case performance rather than a statistical one.

While all this was going on, IBM announced that it had adopted yet a third LAN, the **token ring**, as its standard. The token ring was based on a prototype built at IBM's Zurich lab. IBM chose this design due to its high reliability and serviceability as well as some other technical advantages.

In short order, the IEEE committee had three proposals, one backed by DEC, Xerox, Intel, and the office automation people, one backed by GM, its suppliers, and other people concerned about factory automation, and one backed by IBM and many others. The necessary majority to approve a standard was simply lacking. Finally, the committee threw in the towel and approved all three LAN standards, known now as IEEE 802.3 (based on Ethernet), 802.4 (token bus), and 802.5 (token ring) on the theory that three standards were better than no standards.

Anyway, GM and other companies concerned with factory automation clearly saw the need to adopt specific protocols in each OSI layer to avoid further incompatibilities. This work led to the **MAP** (**Manufacturing Automation Protocol**) using the token bus, which was quickly adopted by many companies in the manufacturing world.

At about the same time, Boeing was interested in standards for office automation. Boeing preferred the Ethernet to the token bus because it had no real time requirements (747s do not roll down assembly lines) and Ethernet already had a huge installed base. Boeing eventually developed a set of protocols for office automation called **TOP** (**Technical and Office Protocols**) that many other companies also adopted for office automation. Although MAP and TOP differ at the lowest layers, GM and Boeing worked closely to ensure that they would be fully compatible in the middle and upper layers.

A collection of protocols, one per layer, such as MAP or TOP, is called a **protocol suite** or **protocol stack**. In addition to MAP and TOP, the protocol suites used by the public networks and the ARPANET are also widely used. Others can be expected in the future, so compatibility between different ones may become a crucial issue.

Now let us turn from the history of MAP and TOP to a closer examination of their technical contents. Both suites follow the OSI model very closely, as shown in Fig. 1-15. MAP uses the token bus for the physical medium and TOP uses the Ethernet (or token ring, which was added in 1987). Both use the IEEE 802.2 data link protocol **LLC** (**Logical Link Control**) in the data link layer in connectionless mode as the service available to the network layer.

Layer

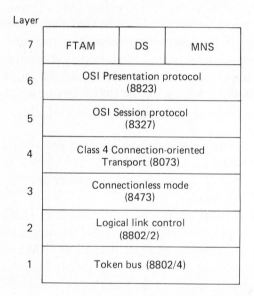
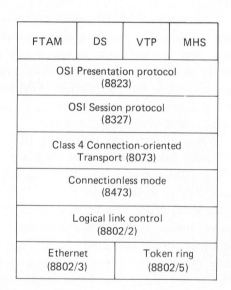

Fig. 1-15. TOP and MAP protocol suites.

Both suites also use a connectionless network layer protocol, ISO 8473. This protocol is very close to the ARPA internet's IP protocol, but completely different in style and details from the CCITT X.25 protocol used on public networks. The reason for this choice is that years of experience with the ARPA internet have shown that the datagram approach is much more flexible and robust when connecting multiple heterogenous networks together, an important aspect of MAP and TOP.

The MAP and TOP transport layer is ISO 8072/8073, using class 4 service. This class assumes the network layer is not completely reliable, and handles all the error control and flow control itself. By making this choice, MAP and TOP have made it possible to connect to almost any kind of network, no matter how bad. The price paid, of course, is a complex transport layer that must deal with an unreliable network service. The ARPANET, which works the same way, made this decision years ago after observing that network service *was* unreliable, so the transport protocol had to deal with it, whether or not it wanted to. In contrast, X.25 service is supposed to be highly reliable, allowing for a simpler class of transport service to be used with it.

The OSI connection-oriented standards ISO 8326/8327 and ISO 8822/8823 are used in MAP and TOP in the session and presentation layers. The OSI standards are also used in the application layer. In particular, the file transfer protocol, virtual terminal protocol, and others are used.

TOP recognizes five types of systems that may be present in a TOP network: an end system, a repeater, a bridge, a router, and a gateway. The **end system** (host) is a user machine, containing all seven OSI layers. The other four types are used to connect together different networks. They differ in the layer at which the connection is made, as shown in Fig. 1-16.

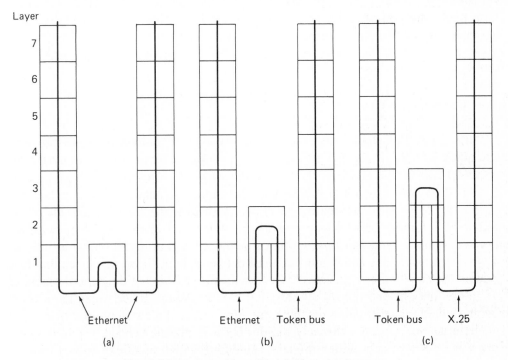

Fig. 1-16. (a) A repeater. (b) A bridge. (c) A router.

A **repeater**, as shown in Fig. 1-16(a), just forwards bits from one network to another, making the two networks look logically like one network. Networks are often split into two (or more) pieces due to maximum cable length restrictions on the individual pieces. Repeaters are dumb (no software); they just copy bits blindly without understanding what they are doing.

A **bridge**, as shown in Fig. 1-16(b), can be used to connect two networks at the data link layer. This approach is useful, for example, when the networks have different data link layers but the same network layer. A connection between an Ethernet and a token bus would normally be a bridge. The frames from the Ethernet arrive at the bridge in Ethernet form and are copied to the token bus in token bus form, or vice versa. Bridges are smart (full of software); they can be programmed to copy frames selectively and make necessary changes while doing so.

A **router**, as shown in Fig. 1-16(c), is needed when the two networks use the same transport layer, but have different network layers. A connection between a token bus and an X.25 public network would need a router to convert the token bus frames to the form required by the X.25 network.

The final type of TOP node, the **gateway**, is used to connect to a network that does not use the OSI model at all. In many cases the connection will have to be done in the application layer.

has six types of nodes, including the MAP end system, bridge, router, and gateway. It does not have the repeater (using bridges for that purpose), but it does has two additional node types, the **MINIMAP** node and the MAP/EPA gateway. These nodes are compatible with the PROWAY LAN standard, which was common in factory environments prior to MAP. They only have layers 1 and 2, and are important for critical real time work. It is expected that over a million MAP and TOP nodes will be in service by the early 1990s.

1.7.4. USENET

When UNIX first came into widespread use at Bell Laboratories, researchers there quickly realized that they needed a way to copy files from one UNIX system to another. To solve this problem, they wrote the *uucp* (UNIX to UNIX CoPy) program.

As UNIX systems acquired modems and automatic telephone dialers, it became possible to copy files automatically between distant machines using *uucp*. A number of informal networks sprung up in which one central machine with an automatic dialer would call up a group of machines late at night, one at a time, to log in and transfer files and electronic mail between them. Two machines that had modems but no automatic dialer could communicate by having the central machine call up the first one and upload all outgoing files and mail. Later, when the central machine called the destination machine, the files and mail were downloaded to it.

These networks grew extremely rapidly because all one needed to join the network was a UNIX system with a modem, something which practically every university computer science department in the Western world had. These networks have since joined up to form a single network, sometimes referred to as **UUCP** with about 10,000 machines and a million users. It is probably the largest network in the world.

Unlike the various public networks or the ARPANET, which are centrally administered, this network can best be described as near total anarchy. Each site can run any version of the software it wants to, and many of them use this freedom to the fullest. On the other hand, the user community has hundreds of competent and dedicated *wizards* (experts) who keep the network running extremely well, despite the total lack of central control.

The European segment even has an official name: EUnet, and also has a more organized structure. Each European country has a single gateway machine run by a single administrator. The administrators keep in close touch to coordinate the network. All international traffic goes between the gateways. The gateways then feed the traffic out into the national networks. Europe and the U.S. are connected by a leased line between Amsterdam and a site in Virginia called **uunet** that is also on the ARPANET. Segments also exist in Japan, Korea, Australia, and other countries.

The only service offered is electronic mail, but a companion network called **USENET**, started at Duke University and the University of North Carolina, also offers an unusual service called **network news**. While some UNIX machines in the U.S. are only on one or the other, most of them are on both. In Europe, EUnet carries both mail and news, so there is only one network. Since both networks are administered the same way and run the same protocols, throughout this book we will often treat them as a single network under the name of USENET, even though this is not strictly true.

Network news is divided into hundreds of newsgroups on a variety of topics, some technical and some not. There are groups for each popular programming language, for each common microcomputer, and for several operating systems, as well as groups for people offering or seeking jobs, people wanting to buy or sell things, and groups for many recreational activities and sports. USENET users can subscribe to whatever groups they are interested in.

Users can also post messages, which are then copied (usually by *uucp*) to all the machines in the entire world that carry that news group. A user with a question or opinion on some subject can post a message and perhaps start a discussion that may eventually involve hundreds or thousands of people all over the world. Many "bulletin board systems" run by computer hobbyists have similar features, but none of these have anywhere near the number of subscribers or the worldwide reach that USENET does.

1.7.5. CSNET

By 1980, the enormous value of the ARPANET for communication among researchers had become obvious. The main problem with the ARPANET was that it was owned by the Department of Defense, and those universities not having federal contracts were not permitted to use it. To provide networking facilities to the computer science community as a whole, NSF (National Science Foundation) set up **CSNET**, which was to be accessible to all computer science departments in the U.S. (Comer, 1983; Landweber et al., 1986; Partridge et al., 1987).

Actually, CSNET is not a real network like the ARPANET, but a metanetwork. It uses transmission facilities provided by other networks and adds a uniform protocol layer on top to make the whole thing look like a single logical network to the users. Physically, CSNET initially consisted of three components; later a fourth one was added. All the pieces are tied together by a machine called CSNET-RELAY located at a company called BBN in Cambridge, Mass. BBN was chosen to run CSNET due to its considerable experience running the ARPANET. Altogether, about 150 campuses are on CSNET.

The first component is the ARPANET. Many CS departments are already on it, and these hosts are already connected by a subnet using 56-kbps leased lines, much higher bandwidth than CSNET could possibly afford.

The second component is the public X.25 network. Those departments that are on one of the X.25 networks, such as Telenet or Uninet, can use that network to reach CSNET-RELAY.

For those departments not on the ARPANET or an X.25 network, **PHONENET** was set up. This network consists of having the PHONENET hosts simply calling up CSNET-RELAY whenever they want to. Most use automatic dialers to call every hour or two. This is similar to USENET, except here, all traffic is to or from CSNET-RELAY, whereas with USENET, there is no centralized control. Each USENET machine can directly communicate with any other machine it wants to.

The fourth component, called **CYPRESS**, is an attempt to duplicate the ARPANET technology on a lower budget (Comer and Narten, 1988). It has packet-switching nodes, called **IMPLET**s, and hosts. The IMPLETs are DEC Microvaxes connected by leased lines. To join CYPRESS, an organization has to acquire a Microvax and lease a line to some other IMPLET.

The basic service provided to all CSNET sites is electronic mail, using the ARPANET protocols and formats. Except for the PHONENET hosts, file transfer and remote login are also possible.

Having seen how well CSNET worked, NSF set up another network to provide access to supercomputers spread around the U.S. Since supercomputer programs often need large amounts of data, this network uses 1.5 Mbps microwave links for long-haul transmission. At this rate, a full 1600 bpi magnetic tape can be sent in under 5 minutes. This network, called **NSFNET** (Mills and Braun, 1987), uses the same TCP/IP protocols as the ARPA internet, CSNET, and Berkeley UNIX. By now it should be clear that the large number of networks and machines running the internet protocols means that it will be a considerable time before the whole world is converted to the OSI protocols, if ever.

1.7.6. BITNET

Another interesting network is **BITNET (Because It's Time NETwork)**, started in 1981 by City University of New York and Yale University (Landweber et al., 1986). The idea behind it was to create a university network, like CSNET, but for all departments, not just computer science. It has now spread to about 175 sites in the U.S. and about 260 sites in Europe via its counterpart there, called **EARN** (**European Academic Research Network**).

Technically, BITNET is somewhat similar to CYPRESS, with each BITNET site leasing a line to some other site. Unlike CYPRESS, the BITNET hosts themselves do the communication; there is no subnet of IMPLETs. Also unlike CYPRESS, BITNET uses a protocol and software donated to it by IBM that is not compatible with either OSI or TCP/IP (or anything else). It is based on the idea of transmitting 80-column punched card images, a frequent source of problems.

The financing of BITNET is unusual, and accounts for part of its popularity. To join, a university must lease a line to some other BITNET site and pay the rental cost of the line. It must also permit some other university to lease a line to it in the future (at the other university's expense). Finally, it must agree to forward traffic passing through it for free. Other than the loss of some computing power for forwarding third-party traffic, the only real cost is one leased line. Unlike just about every other network, there are no charges based on the volume of traffic sent.

The basic BITNET service is file transfer, which also includes electronic mail and remote job entry. Each file entered into the system contains its final destination, and may be stored and forwarded many times before it gets there. A limited amount of remote login is possible, but since the interactive traffic is stored and forwarded just like the file transfer traffic, response time is very slow and reliability is low.

Work is in progress to add a CYPRESS-like subnet to BITNET, and to try to integrate it better into the ARPA internet, USENET, and CSNET worlds.

1.7.7. SNA

No discussion of networking would be complete without at least a few words about IBM's network architecture, **SNA** (**Systems Network Architecture**). The OSI model was patterned after SNA to a considerable extent, including the concept of layering, the number of layers chosen, and their approximate functions.

SNA is a network architecture intended to allow IBM customers to construct their own private networks, both the hosts and the subnet. A bank, for example, might have one or more CPUs in its data-processing department and numerous terminals in each of its branch offices. Using SNA, all these isolated components could be transformed into a coherent system.

Prior to SNA, IBM had several hundred communication products, using three dozen teleprocessing access methods, with more than a dozen data link protocols alone. The idea behind SNA was to eliminate this chaos and to provide a coherent framework for loosely coupled distributed processing. Given the desire of many of IBM's customers to maintain compatibility with all these (mutually incompatible) programs and protocols, the SNA architecture is more complicated in places than it might have been had these constraints not been present. SNA also performs a large number of functions not found in other networks, which, although valuable for certain applications, tend to add to the overall complexity of the architecture.

SNA has evolved considerably over the years and is still evolving. The original release in 1974 permitted only centralized networks, that is, tree-shaped networks with only a single host and its terminals. From our point of view, that is no network at all. The 1976 release allowed multiple hosts with their respective trees, with intertree communication possible only between the roots of the trees. The 1979 release removed this restriction, allowing somewhat more general communication. Finally, in 1985, arbitrary topologies of hosts and LANs were supported.

An SNA network consists of a collection of machines called **nodes**, of which there are four types, approximately characterized as follows. Type 1 nodes are terminals. Type 2 nodes are controllers, machines that supervise the behavior of terminals and other peripherals. Type 4 nodes are front end processors, devices whose function is to relieve the main CPU of the work and interrupt handling associated with data communication. Type 5 nodes are the main hosts themselves, although with the advent of low-cost microprocessors, some controllers have acquired some host-like properties. Strangely enough, there are no type 3 nodes.

Each node contains one or more **NAU**s (**Network Addressable Units**). A NAU is a piece of software that allows a process to use the network. It can be regarded as a SAP plus the entities that provide the upper layer services. To use the network, a process must connect itself to a NAU, at which time it can be addressed and can address other NAUs. The NAUs are thus the entry points into the network for user processes.

There are three kinds of NAUs. An **LU** (**logical unit**) is the usual variety to which user processes can be attached. A **PU** (**physical unit** is a special administrative NAU associated with each node. The PU is used by the network to bring the node online, take it offline, test it, and perform similar network management functions. A PU provides a way for the network to address a physical device, without reference to which processes are using it. The third kind of NAU is the **SSCP** (**System Services Control Point**) of which there is normally one per type 5 node and none in the other nodes. The SSCP has complete knowledge of, and control over, all the front ends, controllers, and terminals attached to the host. The collection of hardware and software managed by an SSCP is called a **domain**. Figure 1-17 depicts a simple two-domain SNA network.

While it is possible to make a rough mapping of the SNA layers to the OSI layers, when you look at them in detail, the two models do not correspond especially well, especially in layers 3, 4, and 5. A summary of the SNA layers follows.

The lowest SNA layer, shown in Fig. 1-18 takes care of physically transporting bits from one machine to another. The protocols used in this layer generally conform to the appropriate industry standards.

The next layer, the **data link control** layer, constructs frames from the raw bit stream, detecting and recovering from transmission errors in a way transparent to higher layers. Many networks have directly or indirectly copied their layer 2

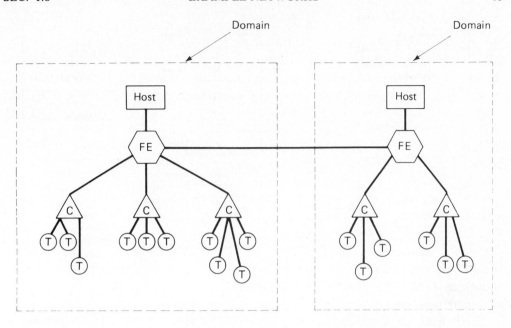

Fig. 1-17. A two domain SNA network. FE = Front End, C = Controller, T = Terminal.

protocol from SNA's layer 2 data communication protocol, **SDLC (Synchronous Data Link Control)**. In particular, ISO's **HDLC (High Level-Data Link Control)** is closely patterned on SDLC. SNA also supports a token ring LAN in this layer.

Layer 3 in SNA, called **path control** by IBM, is concerned with establishing a logical path from the source NAU to the destination NAU. Many SNA networks are split up into subnetworks, called **subareas**, each of which has a special subarea node that acts as a gateway. A subarea often corresponds to a domain. This design leads to a hierarchical structure, with the subarea nodes connected together to form a backbone, and each node connected to some subarea node.

Path control consists of three sublayers. The highest sublayer does the global routing, deciding which sequence of subareas should be used to get from the source subarea to the destination subarea. This sequence is called a **virtual route**. Two subareas may be connected by several different kinds of communication lines (e.g., leased line and satellite), so the next sublayer chooses the specific lines to use, giving an **explicit route**. The lowest sublayer splits traffic among several parallel communication links of the same type to achieve greater bandwidth and reliability.

Information concerned with finding virtual and explicit routes, and managing network congestion is passed in the **transmission header**, shown in Fig. 1-18. Path control can also block unrelated packets together into large units for greater efficiency.

Above the path control layer is the **transmission control** layer whose job it is

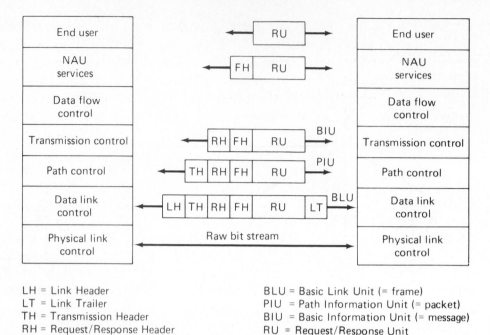

LH = Link Header
LT = Link Trailer
TH = Transmission Header
RH = Request/Response Header
FH = Function Header

BLU = Basic Link Unit (= frame)
PIU = Path Information Unit (= packet)
BIU = Basic Information Unit (= message)
RU = Request/Response Unit

Fig. 1-18. Protocol hierarchy and units exchanged in SNA.

to create, manage, and delete transport connections (sessions). All communication in SNA uses sessions; connectionless communication is not supported. The purpose of a session in SNA, as in the OSI model, is to provide the upper layers with an error-free channel that is independent of the underlying hardware technology.

SNA distinguishes five different kinds of sessions:

1. SSCP—SSCP: for interdomain control and management messages.

2. SSCP—PU: to allow the SSCP to initialize, control, and stop PUs.

3. SSCP—LU: to enable LUs to manage sessions.

4. LU—LU: for transmitting user data.

5. PU: for network management.

In the OSI model, any process can send a message to any other process requesting that a session be established. If the called party agrees, it sends back a response that establishes the session. In SNA, the situation is much more complicated and differs for each of the session types. We will just consider user to user (i.e., LU—LU) sessions below.

To establish a session, a process must talk to the session control manager in its domain. If the destination is local (same domain), it can be established directly.

However, if the destination is in a remote domain, the SSCP must first contact the SSCP controlling the remote domain. Virtual and explicit routes must also be chosen. This mechanism is quite cumbersome, requiring the exchange of over a dozen control messages. Once a session has been established, the transmission control layer regulates the rate of flow between the processes, controls buffer allocation, manages the different message priorities, handles multiplexing and demultiplexing of data and control messages for the benefit of higher layers, and performs encryption and decryption when requested to do so.

Above transmission control comes **data flow control**, which has nothing at all to do with controlling the flow of data in the usual sense. Instead, it has to do with keeping track of which end of a session is supposed to talk next, assuming that the processes want such a service.

This layer is also heavily involved in error recovery. A somewhat unusual feature of the data flow control layer is the absence of a header used to communicate with the corresponding software on the other end. Instead, the information that would normally be communicated in a header is passed to transmission control as parameters and included in the transmission header.

The sixth layer within SNA, **NAU services**, provides two classes of services to user processes. First, there are **presentation services**, such as text compression. Second, there are **session services**, for setting up connections. In addition, there are **network services**, which have to do with the operation of the network as a whole.

SNA is a vast and complex subject. An excellent book on the subject is (Meijer, 1987).

1.8. OUTLINE OF THE REST OF THE BOOK

This book is structured according to the OSI model. While this model may or may not be a good way to organize real, live computer networks, it makes an excellent framework for organizing books about them.

Starting with Chapter 2, we begin working our way up the protocol hierarchy beginning at the bottom. The second chapter provides some background in the field of data communication. It covers analog and digital transmission, multiplexing, and switching. This material is concerned with the physical layer, although we cover only the architectural rather than the hardware aspects. Several examples of the physical layer are also discussed.

Chapter 3 concerns the Medium Access Sublayer. When the IEEE 802 committee invented this sublayer, they thought it belonged at the bottom of layer 2. ISO disagreed initially, thinking that it belonged at the top of layer 1. Either way, it goes between the physical transmission and the data link protocols, and is important enough to warrant an entire chapter. The basic question it deals with is how to determine who may use the network next when the network consists of a single shared channel, as in most LANs and some satellite networks.

Chapter 4 discusses the data link layer and its protocols by means of a number of increasingly complex examples. The analysis of these protocols is also covered.

Chapter 5 deals with the network layer, especially routing, congestion control, and internetworking. It discusses both static and dynamic routing algorithms. Broadcast routing is also covered. The effect of poor routing, congestion, is also discussed in some detail. Connecting heterogenous networks together to form internetworks leads to numerous problems that are discussed here.

Chapter 6 deals with the transport layer. Much of the emphasis is on connection-oriented protocols, since both the OSI transport protocol and TCP are of this type. An example transport service and its implementation are discussed in detail.

Chapter 7 is about the session layer. First some of the design issues concerning the OSI session layer are discussed. Like the transport layer, this is a connection-oriented service and protocol. Then comes a discussion of a connectionless session protocol, the remote procedure call. This protocol is very popular among researchers building distributed operating systems.

Chapter 8 is about the presentation layer. A large part of the chapter deals with an internationally standardized language for describing data types, such as packet formats, and how these data types are represented "on the wires." This chapter also deals with network security and privacy since the presentation layer is a reasonable place to put these functions (but not the only one).

Chapter 9 goes into some of the issues that occur in the application layer. Among these are file servers, electronic mail, virtual terminal protocols, directory services, and remote job entry.

Chapter 10 contains an annotated list of suggested readings arranged by chapter. It is intended to help those readers who would like to pursue their study of networking further. The chapter also has an alphabetical bibliography of all references cited in this book.

Throughout the book we will use four networks as running examples to illustrate the principles discussed. These are the public networks (such as X.25 networks), the ARPANET (and ARPA internet), MAP/TOP, and USENET.

1.9. SUMMARY

Networks are being developed both to connect existing machines and to take advantage of the low-cost, high-performance microprocessors the semiconductor industry is turning out. Most wide area networks have a collection of hosts communicating via a subnet. The subnet may utilize multiple point-to-point lines between its IMPs, or a single common broadcast channel, as in a satellite network. Local-area networks connect the hosts directly onto a cable using an interface chip that is somewhat analogous to the IMP in a wide area network.

Networks are always designed as a series of protocol layers, with each layer responsible for some aspect of the network's operation. The seven-layer OSI model, consisting of the physical link layer, data link layer, network layer, transport layer, session layer, presentation layer, and application layer, forms the conceptual backbone of this book.

The physical layer is concerned with standardizing network connectors and their electrical properties. The data link layer breaks the raw bit stream up into discrete units and exchanges these units using a protocol. The network layer takes care of routing. The transport layer provides reliable, end-to-end connections to the higher layers. The session layer enhances the transport layer by adding facilities to help recover from crashes and other problems. The presentation layer deals with standardizing the way data structures are described and represented. Finally, the application layer contains file transfer, electronic mail, virtual terminal, and a number of application specific protocols.

Quite a few networks are now in operation. Some of the ones we have touched upon are the public networks, the ARPANET, MAP and TOP, USENET, CSNET, BITNET, and SNA.

PROBLEMS

1. Imagine that you have trained your St. Bernard, Bernie, to carry a box of three floppy disks instead of a flask of brandy. (When your disk fills up, you consider that an emergency.) These floppy disks each contain 250,000 bytes. The dog can travel to your side, wherever you may be, at 18 km/hour. For what range of distances does Bernie have a higher data rate than a 300 bps telephone line?

2. In the future, when everyone has a home terminal connected to a computer network, instant public referendums on important pending legislation will become possible. Ultimately, existing legislatures could be eliminated, to let the will of the people to be expressed directly. The positive aspects of such a direct democracy are fairly obvious; discuss some of the negative aspects.

3. Consider $2^n - 1$ IMPs connected by the following topologies:
   (a) Star (central node is just a switch, not an IMP).
   (b) Ring.
   (c) Complete interconnection.
   For each, give the number of hops needed for the average IMP-IMP packet (no self traffic).

4. A collection of five IMPs are to be connected in a point-to-point subnet. Between each pair of IMPs, the designers may put a high-speed line, a medium-speed line, a low-speed line, or no line. If it takes 100 ms of computer time to generate and inspect each topology, how long will it take to inspect all of them?

5. A group of $2^n - 1$ IMPs are interconnected in a centralized binary tree, with an IMP at each tree node. IMP i communicates with IMP j by sending a message to the root of the tree. The root then sends the message back down to j. Derive an approximate expression for the mean number of hops per message for large n, assuming that all IMP pairs are equally likely.

6. A disadvantage of a broadcast subnet is the capacity wasted due to multiple hosts attempting to access the channel at the same time. As a simplistic example, suppose that time is divided into discrete slots, with each of the n hosts attempting to use the channel with probability p during each slot. What fraction of the slots are wasted due to collisions?

7. The president of the Specialty Paint Corp. gets the idea to work together with a local beer brewer for the purpose of producing an invisible beer can (as an anti-litter measure). The president tells his legal department to look into it, and they in turn ask engineering for help. As a result, the chief engineer calls his counterpart at the other company to discuss the technical aspects of the project. The engineers then report back to their respective legal departments, which then confer by telephone to arrange the legal aspects. Finally the two corporate presidents discuss the financial side of the deal. Is this an example of a multilayer protocol in the sense of the OSI model?

8. Redraw Fig. 1-6 for a system in which layer 3, not layer 4, splits up the messages.

9. In most networks, the data link layer handles transmission errors by requesting damaged frames to be retransmitted. If the probability of a frame being damaged is p, what is the mean number of transmissions required to send a frame if acknowledgements are never lost?

10. Which of the OSI layers handles each of the following:
    (a) Breaking the transmitted bit stream into frames.
    (b) Determining which route through the subnet to use.
    (c) Providing synchronization.

11. In the OSI model, do TPDUs encapsulate packets or the other way around? Discuss.

12. What are the SAP addresses in FM radio broadcasting?

13. What is the principal difference between connectionless communication and connection-oriented communication?

14. Two networks both provide reliable connection-oriented service. One of them offers a reliable byte stream and the other offers a reliable message stream. Are these identical? If so, why is the distinction made? If not, give an example of how they differ.

15. What is the difference between a confirmed service and an unconfirmed service? For each of the following, tell whether it might be a confirmed service, and unconfirmed service, both or neither.
    (a) Connection establishment.
    (b) Data transmission.
    (c) Connection release.

16. What does "negotiation" mean when discussing network protocols? Give an example of it.

17. List two advantages and two disadvantages of having international standards for network protocols.

18. When transferring a file between two computers, (at least) two acknowledgement strategies are possible. In the first one, the file is chopped up into packets, which are individually acknowledged by the receiver, but the file transfer as a whole is not acknowledged. In the second one, the packets are not acknowledged individually, but the entire file is acknowledged when it arrives. Discuss these two approaches.

19. Why is a virtual terminal protocol needed? What kinds of applications are likely to use it?

20. Ethernet is sometimes said to be inappropriate for real time computing because the worst case retransmission interval is not bounded. Under what circumstances can the same argument be leveled at the token ring? Under what circumstances does the token ring have a known worst case? Assume the number of stations on the token ring is fixed and known.

2

THE PHYSICAL LAYER

In this chapter we will look at the lowest layer depicted in the hierarchy of Fig. 1-7. We will begin with a theoretical analysis of data transmission, only to discover that Mother Nature puts some limits on what can be sent over a given channel. Then we will look at how data is transmitted, both in analog and digital form. After that we will examine the design of the new digital telephone system that will replace the old analog one in years to come. Finally, we will look briefly at terminal handling in computer networks.

2.1. THE THEORETICAL BASIS FOR DATA COMMUNICATION

Information can be transmitted on wires by varying some physical property such as voltage or current. By representing the value of this voltage or current as a single valued function of time, $f(t)$, we can model the behavior of the signal and analyze it mathematically. This analysis is the subject of the following sections.

2.1.1. Fourier Analysis

In the early 19th century, the great French mathematician Jean Fourier proved that any reasonably behaved periodic function, $g(t)$, with period T can be constructed by summing a (possibly infinite) number of sines and cosines:

$$g(t) = \frac{1}{2}c + \sum_{n=1}^{\infty} a_n \sin(2\pi n f t) + \sum_{n=1}^{\infty} b_n \cos(2\pi n f t) \qquad (2\text{-}1)$$

where $f = 1/T$ is the fundamental frequency and a_n and b_n are the sine and cosine amplitudes of the nth **harmonics** (terms). Such a decomposition is called a **Fourier series**. From the Fourier series, the function can be reconstructed; i.e., if the period, T, is known and the amplitudes are given, the original function of time can be found by performing the sums of Eq. (2-1).

A data signal that has a finite duration (which all of them do) can be handled by just imagining that it repeats the entire pattern over and over forever (i.e., the interval from T to $2T$ is the same as from 0 to T, etc).

The a_n amplitudes can be computed for any given $g(t)$ by multiplying both sides of Eq. (2-1) by $\sin(2\pi k f t)$ and then integrating from 0 to T. Since

$$\int_0^T \sin(2\pi k f t) \sin(2\pi n f t)\, dt \;=\; \begin{cases} 0 \text{ for } k \neq n \\ T/2 \text{ for } k = n \end{cases}$$

only one term of the summation survives: a_n. The b_n summation vanishes completely. Similarly, by multiplying Eq. (2-1) by $\cos(2\pi k f t)$ and integrating between 0 and T, we can derive b_n. By just integrating both sides of the equation as it stands, c can be found. The results of performing these operations are as follows:

$$a_n = \frac{2}{T}\int_0^T g(t)\sin(2\pi n f t)\, dt \qquad b_n = \frac{2}{T}\int_0^T g(t)\cos(2\pi n f t)\, dt \qquad c = \frac{2}{T}\int_0^T g(t)\, dt$$

2.1.2. Bandwidth-Limited Signals

To see what all this has to do with data communication, let us consider a specific example, the transmission of the ASCII character "b" encoded in an 8-bit byte. The bit pattern to be transmitted is 01100010. The left-hand part of Fig. 2-1(a) shows the voltage output by the transmitting computer. The Fourier analysis of this signal yields the coefficients:

$$a_n = \frac{1}{\pi n}[\cos(\pi n/4) - \cos(3\pi n/4) + \cos(6\pi n/4) - \cos(7\pi n/4)]$$

$$b_n = \frac{1}{\pi n}[\sin(3\pi n/4) - \sin(\pi n/4) + \sin(7\pi n/4) - \sin(6\pi n/4)]$$

$$c = 3/8$$

The root-mean-square amplitudes, $\sqrt{a_n^2 + b_n^2}$, for the first few terms are shown on the right-hand side of Fig. 2-1(a). These values are of interest because their squares are proportional to the energy transmitted at the corresponding frequency.

No transmission facility can transmit signals without losing some power in the process. If all the Fourier components were equally diminished, the resulting signal would be reduced in amplitude but not distorted [i.e., it would have the same nice squared-off shape as Fig. 2-1(a)]. Unfortunately, all transmission facilities diminish different Fourier components by different amounts, thus introducing distortion. Usually, the amplitudes are transmitted undiminished from 0 up to some frequency f_c [measured in cycles/sec or Hertz (Hz)] with all frequencies above this cutoff frequency strongly attenuated. In some cases this is a physical property of the transmission medium, and in other cases a filter is intentionally introduced into the circuit to limit the amount of (scarce) bandwidth available to each customer.

Now let us consider how the signal of Fig. 2-1(a) would look if the bandwidth were so low that only the lowest frequencies were transmitted [i.e., the function were being approximated by the first few terms of Eq. (2-1)]. Figure 2-1(b) shows the signal that results from a channel that allows only the first harmonic (the fundamental, f) to pass through. Similarly, Fig. 2-1(c)-(e) show the spectra and reconstructed functions for higher bandwidth channels.

The time T required to transmit the character depends on both the encoding method and the signaling speed [the number of times per second that the signal changes its value (e.g., its voltage)]. The number of changes per second is measured in **baud**. A b baud line does not necessarily transmit b bits/sec, since each signal might convey several bits. If the voltages 0, 1, 2, 3, 4, 5, 6, and 7 were used, each signal value could be used to convey 3 bits, so the bit rate would be three times the baud rate. In our example, only 0s and 1s are being used as signal levels, so the bit rate is equal to the baud rate.

Given a bit rate of b bits/sec, the time required to send 8 bits (for example) is $8/b$ sec, so the frequency of the first harmonic is $b/8$ Hz. An ordinary telephone line, often called a **voice grade line**, has an artificially introduced cutoff frequency near 3000 Hz. This restriction means that the number of the highest harmonic passed through is $3000/(b/8)$ or $24000/b$, roughly (the cutoff is not sharp). For some commonly used data rates, the numbers work out as follows:

Bps	T (msec)	First harmonic (Hz)	# harmonics sent
300	26.67	37.5	80
600	13.33	75	40
1200	6.67	150	20
2400	3.33	300	10
4800	1.67	600	5
9600	0.83	1200	2
19200	0.42	2400	1
38400	0.21	4800	0

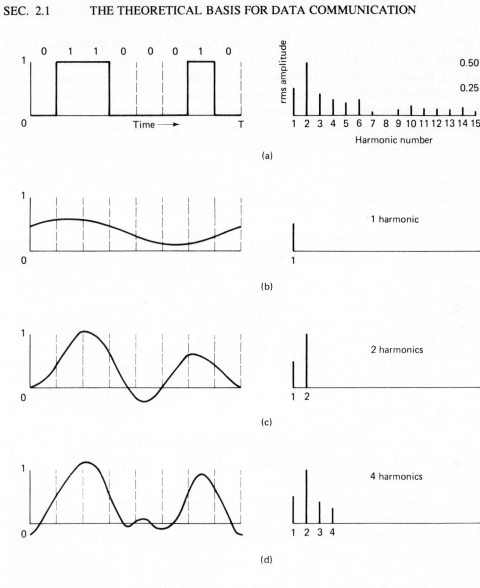

(a)

(b)

(c)

(d)

(e)

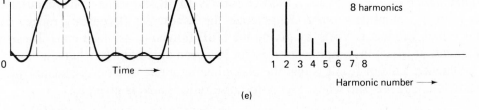

Fig. 2-1. (a) A binary signal and its rms Fourier amplitudes. (b)-(e) Successive approximations to the original signal.

From the numbers above, it is clear that trying to send at 9600 bps over a voice-grade telephone line will transform Fig. 2-1(a) into something looking like Fig. 2-1(c), making accurate reception of the original binary bit stream unlikely. It should be obvious that at data rates much higher than 38.4 kbps there is no hope at all for binary signals, even if the transmission facility is completely noiseless. In other words, limiting the bandwidth limits the data rate, even for perfect channels. However, sophisticated coding schemes that use several voltage levels do exist and can achieve higher data rates.

2.1.3. The Maximum Data Rate of a Channel

As early as 1924, H. Nyquist realized the existence of this fundamental limit and derived an equation expressing the maximum data rate for a finite bandwidth noiseless channel. In 1948, Claude Shannon carried Nyquist's work further and extended it to the case of a channel subject to random (thermal) noise. We will just briefly summarize their now classical results here.

Nyquist proved that if an arbitrary signal has been run through a low-pass filter of bandwidth H, the filtered signal can be completely reconstructed by making only $2H$ (exact) samples per second. Sampling the line faster than $2H$ times per second is pointless because the higher frequency components that such sampling could recover have already been filtered out. If the signal consists of V discrete levels, Nyquist's theorem states:

$$\text{maximum data rate} = 2H \log_2 V \text{ bits/sec}$$

For example, a noiseless 3-kHz channel cannot transmit binary (i.e., two-level) signals at a rate exceeding 6000 bps.

So far we have considered only noiseless channels. If random noise is present, the situation deteriorates rapidly. The amount of thermal noise present is measured by the ratio of the signal power to the noise power, called the **signal-to-noise ratio**. If we denote the signal power by S and the noise power by N, the signal-to-noise ratio is S/N. Usually, the ratio itself is not quoted; instead, the quantity $10 \log_{10} S/N$ is given. These units are called **decibels** (dB). An S/N ratio of 10 is 10 dB, a ratio of 100 is 20 dB, a ratio of 1000 is 30 dB and so on. The manufacturers of stereo amplifiers often characterize the bandwidth (frequency range) over which their product is linear by giving the 3-dB frequency on each end. These are the points at which the amplification factor has been approximately halved.

Shannon's major result is that the maximum data rate of a noisy channel whose bandwidth is H Hz, and whose signal-to-noise ratio is S/N, is given by

$$\text{maximum number of bits/sec} = H \log_2 (1 + S/N)$$

For example, a channel of 3000-Hz bandwidth, and a signal to thermal noise ratio of 30 dB (typical parameters of the telephone system) can never transmit more than

30,000 bps, no matter how many or few signal levels are used and no matter how often or how infrequent samples are taken. Shannon's result was derived using information-theory arguments and has very general validity. Counterexamples should be treated in the same category as perpetual motion machines. It should be noted, however, that this is only an upper bound. In practice, it is difficult to even *approach* the Shannon limit. A bit rate of 9600 bps on a voice-grade line is considered excellent, and is achieved by sending 4-bit groups at 2400 baud. We will look at such coding systems later.

2.2. TRANSMISSION MEDIA

The purpose of the physical layer is to transport a raw bit stream from one machine to another. Various physical media can be used for the actual transmission. In the following sections we will look briefly at the characteristics of some common media.

2.2.1. Magnetic Media

One of the most common ways to transport data from one computer to another is to write them onto magnetic tape or floppy disks, physically transport the tape or disks to the destination machine, and read them back in again. While this method is not as sophisticated as using a geosynchronous communication satellite, it is often much more cost effective, especially for applications in which high bandwidth or cost per bit transported is the key factor.

A simple calculation makes this point clear. An industry standard 6250 bpi magnetic tape can hold 180 megabytes. A station wagon or light truck can easily transport 200 tapes at one time. Suppose the source and destination machines are an hour's drive apart. The effective data rate between these two machines is then 288,000 megabits in 3600 sec or 80 Mbps. No wide-area network comes within an order of magnitude of this bandwidth. Few local networks can even match it. For a bank with gigabytes of data to be backed up daily on a second machine (so the bank can continue to function even if the primary machine fails), it is likely that no other transmission technology can even begin to approach magnetic tape for performance or cost effectiveness.

The moral of the story is: *Never underestimate the bandwidth of a station wagon full of tapes hurtling down the highway.*

2.2.2. Twisted Pair

Although the bandwidth characteristics of magnetic tape are excellent, the delay characteristics are poor. Transmission time is measured in minutes or hours, not milliseconds. For many applications an on-line connection is needed. The oldest and still most common transmission medium is **twisted pair**. A twisted pair consists of two insulated copper wires, typically about 1 mm thick. The wires are twisted together in a helical form, just as a DNA molecule. The twisted form is used to reduce electrical interference to similar pairs close by. (Two parallel wires constitute a simple antenna; a twisted pair does not.)

The most common application of the twisted pair is the telephone system. Nearly all telephones are connected to the telephone company office by a twisted pair. Twisted pairs can run several km without amplification, but for longer distances, repeaters are needed. When many twisted pairs run in parallel for a substantial distance, such as all the wires coming from an apartment building to the telephone company office, they are bundled together and encased in a protective sheath. The pairs in these bundles would interfere with one another if it were not for the twisting. In parts of the world where telephone lines run on poles above ground, it is common to see bundles several centimeters in diameter.

Twisted pairs can be used for either analog or digital transmission. The bandwidth depends on the thickness of the wire and the distance traveled, but several megabits/sec can be achieved for a few km in many cases. Due to their adequate performance and low cost, twisted pairs are widely used and are likely to remain so for years to come.

2.2.3. Baseband Coaxial Cable

Another common transmission medium is the **coaxial cable** (known to its many friends as just "coax"). Two kinds of coaxial cable are widely used. One kind, 50-ohm cable, is used for digital transmission and is the subject of this section. The other kind, 75-ohm cable, is used for analog transmission and will be described in the next section.

A coaxial cable consists of a stiff copper wire as the core, surrounded by an insulating material. The insulator is encased by a cylindrical conductor, often as a closely woven braided mesh. The outer conductor is covered in a protective plastic sheath. A cutaway view of a coaxial cable is shown in Fig. 2-2.

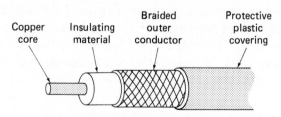

Fig. 2-2. A coaxial cable.

The construction of the coaxial cable gives it a good combination of high bandwidth and excellent noise immunity. The bandwidth possible depends on the cable length. For 1 km cables, a data rate of 10 Mbps is feasible. Higher data rates are possible on shorter cables. Longer cables can also be used, but only at lower data rates. Coaxial cables are widely used for local area networks and for long-distance transmission within the telephone system.

There are two ways to connect computers to a coaxial cable. The first way is to cut the cable cleanly in two and insert a **T junction**, a connector that reconnects the cable but also provides a third wire leading off to the computer. The second way is to use a **vampire tap**, which is a hole of exceedingly precise depth and width drilled into the cable, terminating in the core. Into this hole is screwed a special connector that achieves the same goal as a T junction, but without the need to cut the cable in two.

There is much folklore about the advantages and disadvantages of the two techniques. Inserting a T junction requires cutting the cable, which means bringing down the network for a few minutes. For a large production network onto which new users are being attached all the time, stopping the network even for a few minutes may be objectionable. Furthermore, the more connectors a cable has, the more likely that one of them will have a poor connection and cause intermittent problems. Vampire taps do not have either of these problems, but must be installed very carefully. If the hole is drilled too deep, it may break the core into two unconnected pieces. If it is not deep enough, the connection may give intermittent errors. The cables used for vampire taps are thicker and more expensive than the cables used with T junctions.

Although straight binary signaling is sometimes used on coaxial cable (e.g., 1 volt for a 1 bit and 0 volts for a 0 bit), this method gives the receiver no way of determining when each bit starts and ends. Instead a technique called **Manchester encoding** or a related technique called **differential Manchester encoding** is preferred. With Manchester encoding, each bit period is divided into two equal intervals. A binary 1 bit is sent by having the voltage be high during the first interval and low in the second one. A binary 0 is just the reverse: first low and then high. This scheme ensures that every bit period has a transition in the middle, making it easy for the receiver to synchronize with the sender. A disadvantage of Manchester encoding is that it requires twice as much bandwidth as straight binary encoding, because the pulses are half the width. Manchester encoding is shown in Fig. 2-3.

Differential Manchester encoding is a variation of basic Manchester encoding. In it, a 1 bit is indicated by the absence of a transition at the start of the interval. A 0 bit is indicated by the presence of a transition at the start of the interval. In both cases, there is a transition in the middle as well. The differential scheme requires more complex equipment, but offers better noise immunity.

2.2.4. Broadband Coaxial Cable

The other kind of coaxial cable system uses analog transmission on standard cable television cabling. It is called **broadband**. Although the term "broadband" comes from the telephone world, where it refers to anything wider than 4 kHz, in

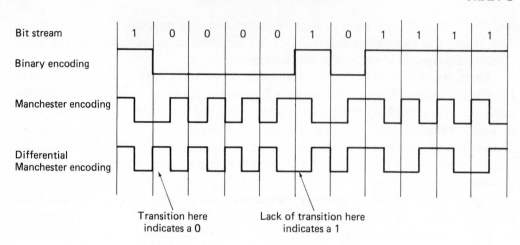

Fig. 2-3. Three different encoding techniques.

the computer networking world "broadband" means any cable network using analog transmission (see Cooper, 1986).

Since broadband networks use standard cable television technology, the cables can be used up to 300 MHz (and sometimes up to 450 MHz) and can run for nearly 100 km due to the analog signaling, which is much less critical than digital signaling. To transmit digital signals on an analog network, each interface must contain electronics to convert the outgoing bit stream to an analog signal, and the incoming analog signal to a bit stream. Depending on the type (and price) of these electronics, 1 bps may occupy anywhere from 1 to 4 Hz of bandwidth. Typically, a 300-MHz cable will support a total data rate of 150 Mbps.

Broadband systems are normally divided up into multiple channels, frequently the 6-Mhz channels used for television broadcasting. Each channel can be used for analog television, high-quality audio, or a digital bit stream at, say, 3 Mbps, independent of the other channels. Television and data can be mixed on the same cable.

One key difference between baseband and broadband is that broadband systems need analog amplifiers to strengthen the signal periodically. These amplifiers can only transmit signals in one direction, so a computer outputting a packet will not be able to reach computers "upstream" from it if an amplifier lies between them. To get around this problem, two types of broadband systems have been developed: dual cable and single cable systems.

Dual cable systems have two identical cables running next to each other. To transmit data, a computer outputs the data onto cable 1, which runs to a device called the **headend** at the root of the cable tree. The headend then transfers the signal to cable 2 for transmission back down the tree. All computers transmit on cable 1 and receive on cable 2. A dual cable system is shown in Fig. 2-4(a).

The other scheme allocates different frequency bands for inbound and outbound

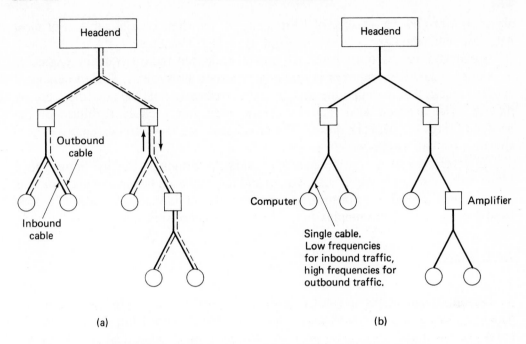

Fig. 2-4. Broadband networks. (a) Dual cable. (b) Single cable.

communication on a single cable [see Fig. 2-4(b)]. The low frequency band is used for communication from the computers to the headend, which then shifts the signal to the high frequency band and rebroadcasts it. In the **subsplit** system, frequencies from 5 to 30 MHz are used for inbound traffic, and frequencies from 40 to 300 MHz are used for outbound traffic.

In the **midsplit** system, the inbound band is 5 to 116 MHz and the outbound band is 168 MHz to 300 MHz. The choice of these frequency bands is historical, having to do with how the U.S. Federal Communications Commission has assigned frequencies for television broadcasting, for which broadband was designed. Both split systems require an active headend that accepts inbound signals on one band and rebroadcasts them on another. These techniques and frequencies were developed for cable television and have been taken over for networking without modification due to the availability of reliable and relatively inexpensive hardware.

Broadband can be used in various ways. Some computer pairs may be given a permanent channel for their exclusive use. Other computers may be able to request a channel for a temporary connection on a control channel, and then switch their frequencies to that channel for the duration of the connection. Still another arrangement is to have all the computers compete for access to a single channel or a group of channels, using techniques to be covered in Chapter 3.

Much has been said and written about the choice of baseband versus broadband (Hopkins and Meisner, 1987). Baseband is simple and inexpensive to install, and requires inexpensive interfaces. It offers a single digital channel with a data rate of about 10 Mbps over a distance of 1 km using off-the-shelf coaxial cable. For most data communication applications baseband is perfectly adequate.

Broadband, on the other hand, requires experienced radio frequency engineers to plan the cable and amplifier layout and to install the system. Skilled personnel are also required to maintain the system and periodically tune the amplifiers during its use. The headend also requires careful servicing because a failure of the headend brings the network down. The broadband interfaces are also more expensive than the baseband ones.

However, broadband offers multiple channels (although usually limited to 3 Mbps each) and can transmit data, voice, and television on the same cable for tens of kilometers if need be. For most applications, the additional bandwidth of broadband does not justify its complexity and expense, so baseband is more widely used.

2.2.5. Fiber Optics

Recent developments in optical technology have made it possible to transmit data by pulses of light. A light pulse can be used to signal a 1 bit; the absence of a pulse signals a 0 bit. Visible light has a frequency of about 10^8 MHz, so the bandwidth of an optical transmission system is potentially enormous.

An optical transmission system has three components: the transmission medium, the light source, and the detector. The transmission medium is an ultrathin fiber of glass or fused silica. The light source is either an **LED (Light Emitting Diode)**, or a **laser diode**, both of which emit light pulses when an electrical current is applied. The detector is a **photodiode**, which generates an electrical pulse when light falls on it. By attaching an LED or laser diode to one end of an optical fiber and a photodiode to the other, we have a unidirectional data transmission system that accepts an electrical signal, converts and transmits it by light pulses, and then reconverts the output to an electrical signal at the receiving end.

This transmission system would leak light and be useless in practice except for an interesting principle of physics. When a light ray passes from one medium to another, for example, from fused silica to air, the ray is refracted (bent) at the silica/air boundary as shown in Fig. 2-5. Here we see a light ray incident on the boundary at an angle α_1 emerging at an angle β_1. The amount of refraction depends on the properties of the two media (in particular, their indices of refraction). For angles of incidence above a certain critical value, the light is refracted back into the silica; none of it escapes into the air. Thus a light ray incident at or above the critical angle is trapped inside the fiber, as shown in Fig. 2-5(b), and can propagate for many kilometers with virtually no loss.

The sketch of Fig. 2-5(b) shows only one trapped ray, but since any light ray incident on the boundary above the critical angle will be reflected internally, many different rays will be bouncing around at different angles. This situation is called a **multimode fiber**.

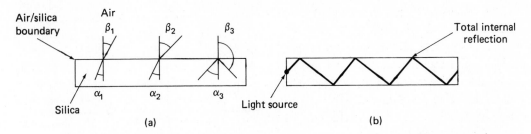

Fig. 2-5. (a) Three examples of a light ray from inside a silica fiber impinging on the air/silica boundary at different angles. (b) Light trapped by total internal reflection.

However, if the fiber's diameter is reduced to one wavelength of light, the fiber acts like a wave guide, and the light will propagate in a straight line, without bouncing, yielding a **single mode fiber**. Single mode fibers require (expensive) laser diodes to drive them, rather than (inexpensive) LEDs, but they are more efficient and can be run for longer distances. Currently available fiber optics systems can transmit data at about 1000 Mbps for 1 km. Higher data rates have been achieved in the laboratory for shorter distances. Experiments have shown that powerful lasers can drive a fiber 100-km long without repeaters, although at much lower speeds.

Fiber optic links are being installed for long-distance telephone lines in many countries. This trend will continue during the next few decades, with coaxial cable being replaced by fiber on more and more routes.

Fibers can also form the basis for LANs, although the technology is more complex. The basic problem is that while vampire taps can be made on fiber LANs by fusing the incoming fiber from the computer with the LAN fiber, the process of making a tap is very tricky and substantial light is lost.

One way around the problem is to realize that a ring network is really just a collection of point-to-point links, as shown in Fig. 2-6. The interface at each computer passes the light pulse stream through to the next link and also serves as a T junction to allow the computer to send and accept messages.

Two types of interfaces are used. A passive interface consists of two taps fused onto the main fiber. One tap has an LED or laser diode at the end of it (for transmitting), and the other has a photodiode (for receiving). The tap itself is completely passive and is thus extremely reliable because a broken LED or photodiode does not break the ring. It just takes one computer off-line.

The other interface type, shown in Fig. 2-6, is the **active repeater**. The incoming light is converted to an electrical signal, regenerated to full strength if it has been weakened, and retransmitted as light. The interface with the computer is an ordinary copper wire that comes into the signal regenerator. If an active repeater fails, the ring is broken and the network goes down. On the other hand, since the signal is regenerated at each interface, the individual computer-to-computer links can be kilometers long, with virtually no limit on the total size of the ring. The

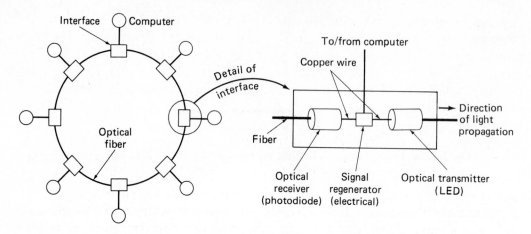

Fig. 2-6. A fiber optic ring with active repeaters.

passive interfaces lose light at each junction, so the number of computers and total ring length are greatly restricted.

A ring topology is not the only way to build a LAN using fiber optics. It is also possible to have hardware broadcasting using the **passive star** construction of Fig. 2-7. In this design, each interface has a fiber running from its transmitter to a silica cylinder, with the incoming fibers fused to one end of the cylinder. Similarly, fibers fused to the other end of the cylinder are run to each of the receivers. Whenever an interface emits a light pulse, it is diffused inside the passive star to illuminate all the receivers, thus achieving broadcast. In effect, the passive star performs a Boolean OR of all the incoming signals and transmits the result out on all lines. Since the incoming energy is divided among all the outgoing lines, the number of nodes in the network is limited by the sensitivity of the photodiodes.

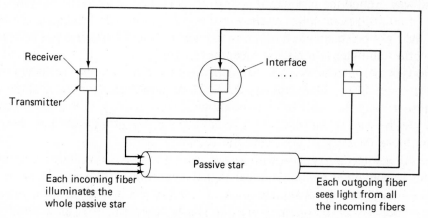

Fig. 2-7. A passive star connection in a fiber optics network.

It is instructive to compare coaxial cable to fiber optics. Fiber provides extremely high bandwidth with little power loss, so it can run for long distances between repeaters. The fibers themselves are not affected by power line surges, electromagnetic interference, or corrosive chemicals in the air, so they can be used in harsh factory environments unsuitable for coaxial cable. Fibers are also very thin, a big plus for companies with thousands of cables and bulging cable ducts. (One of the main motivations for using fibers in the telephone system is simply the lack of room for any more coaxial cables on many routes.)

On the minus side, fiber optics is an unfamiliar technology requiring skills most network engineers do not have. Fibers are difficult to splice and even more difficult to tap. (The latter point can also be seen as an advantage: security is excellent because fiber does not radiate and wiretappers will have as much trouble as the network owners in tapping it.) Fiber networks are also inherently unidirectional, and the interfaces are considerably more expensive than electrical interfaces. However, the advantages of fiber optics are so great that much work is being directed to improving the technology and reducing the cost.

2.2.6. Line-of-Sight Transmission

Although many data communication systems use copper wire or fiber, some just send the data out into the air. In particular, transmission by infrared, lasers, microwave, and radio does not require any physical medium. Each of these techniques is well suited for certain applications.

A common application for which running a cable or fiber is frequently undesirable is a LAN that runs between several buildings on a college campus or industrial office park or factory complex. Within each building, the LAN may use copper or fiber, but connecting the buildings may require digging up the streets to lay a cable trench, an expensive proposition at best. If the trench has to cross a public road, in many areas it is also illegal.

On the other hand, putting a laser or infrared transmitter and receiver on the roof of each building (or maybe just pointing them out a window) is inexpensive, easy to do, and nearly always legal. This design yields a hierarchical network, with the backbone being the laser or infrared network between the buildings. Each building's LAN is attached to the backbone by a gateway. Laser or infrared communication is fully digital, and is highly directional, making it almost immune to tapping or jamming. On the other hand, rain and fog may interfere with the communication, depending on the wavelength chosen.

For long distance communication, microwave radio transmission is widely used as an alternative to coaxial cable. Parabolic antennas can be mounted on towers to send a beam to another antenna tens of kilometers away. This system is widely used for both telephone and television transmission. The higher the tower, the greater the range. With a 100-meter high tower, distances of 100 km between towers are feasible.

The advantage of microwave is that building two towers is frequently much cheaper than digging a 100-km trench, laying cable or fiber in it, and closing it up again. The difficulties of digging long trenches should not be underestimated, especially if they happen to go through people's houses. Laying the cable is not the only problem. Repeaters along the way need to be maintained periodically, and cables can be broken by a variety of causes ranging from rodents to overzealous gardeners digging in their backyards. None of these problems exists with microwave.

On the other hand, signals from a single antenna may split up and propagate by slightly different paths to the receiving antenna. When these out-of-phase signals recombine, they interfere, reducing signal strength. Microwave propagation is also affected by thunderstorms and other atmospheric phenomena.

Most microwave transmission occurs at frequencies between 2 and 40 GHz, corresponding to wavelengths of 15 and 0.75 cm. These frequencies have been divided into bands for common carrier, government, military, and other uses. Most long distance telephone traffic takes place in the 4-6 GHz range although it is increasingly overcrowded. Higher frequencies are available, but they are less useful for long-distance traffic since the attenuation is greater at higher frequencies.

2.2.7. Communication Satellites

Communication satellites have some interesting properties that make them attractive for certain applications. A communication satellite can be thought of as a big microwave repeater in the sky. It contains one or more **transponders**, each of which listens to some portion of the spectrum, amplifies the incoming signal, and then rebroadcasts it at another frequency, to avoid interference with the incoming signal. The downward beams can be broad, covering a substantial fraction of the earth's surface, or narrow, covering an area hundreds of kilometers in diameter.

According to Kepler's law, the orbital period of a satellite varies as the orbital radius to the 3/2 power. Near the surface of the earth, the period is about 90 min. Communication satellites at such low altitudes are not useful because they are within sight of the ground stations for too short a time interval.

However, at an altitude of approximately 36,000 km above the equator, the satellite period is 24 hours, so it revolves at the same rate as the earth under it. An observer looking at a satellite in a circular equatorial orbit sees the satellite hang in a fixed spot in the sky, apparently motionless. Having the satellite be fixed in the sky is extremely desirable, because otherwise an expensive steerable antenna would be needed to track it.

With current technology, it is unwise to have satellites spaced much closer than 4 degrees in the 360-degree equatorial plane. At smaller separations, the upward beam from a ground station illuminates not only the desired satellite, but also its neighbors. With a spacing of 4 degrees, there can only be 360/4 = 90 geosynchronous communication satellites in the sky at once. In addition to these technological limitations, there is also competition for orbit slots with other classes of users (e.g., television broadcasting, government and military use, etc.). Television satellites need to be spaced 8 degrees apart on account of their high power.

Fortunately, satellites using different parts of the spectrum do not compete, so each of the 90 possible satellites could have several data streams going up and down simultaneously. Alternatively, two or more satellites could occupy one orbit slot if they operate at different frequencies.

To prevent total chaos in the sky, there have been international agreements about who may use which orbit slots and frequencies. The 3.7 to 4.2 GHz and 5.925 to 6.425 GHz bands have been designated as telecommunication satellite frequencies for downward and upward beams, respectively. These bands, usually referred to as 4/6 GHz, are already overcrowded because they are also used by the common carriers for terrestrial microwave links.

The next highest bands available to telecommunication are at 12/14 GHz. These bands are not (yet) congested, and at these frequencies satellites can be spaced as close as 1 degree. However, another problem exists: rain. Water is an excellent absorber of these short microwaves. Fortunately, heavy storms are usually localized, so by using several widely separated ground stations instead of just one, the problem can be gotten around at the price of extra antennas, extra cables, and extra electronics to switch rapidly between stations. Frequency bands at 20/30 GHz have also been set aside for telecommunication but the equipment needed to use them is still expensive.

A typical satellite splits its 500 MHz bandwidth over a dozen transponders, each with a 36 MHz bandwidth. Each transponder can be used to encode a single 50-Mbps data stream, 800 64-kbps digital voice channels, or various other combinations. Furthermore, two transponders can use different polarizations of the signal, so they can use the same frequency range without interfering. In the earliest satellites, the division of the transponders into channels was static, by splitting the bandwidth up into fixed frequency bands. Nowadays, the channel is split up by time, first one station, then another, and so on. This scheme is much more flexible. It is called time division multiplexing, and we will study it later in this chapter in detail.

The first satellites had a single spatial beam that covered all the ground stations. With the enormous decline in the price, size, and power requirements of microelectronics, a much more sophisticated broadcasting strategy has become possible. Each satellite is equipped with multiple antennas and multiple transponders. Each downward beam can be focused on a small geographical area, so multiple upward and downward transmissions can take place simultaneously. These so called **spot beams** are typically elliptically shaped, and can be as small as a few hundred km in diameter.

Figure 2-8(a) illustrates a satellite with two antennas, corresponding to two geographically spaced areas. In this example, each area has two ground stations. The two stations within each area take turns broadcasting to the satellite. The numbers within the upward beams indicate the intended receiver of the message. As the messages come in, they are switched to the appropriate antenna and beamed downward. Figure 2-8(b) shows the retransmission of the messages sent upward in Fig. 2-8(a) By providing a satellite with many spot beams, one satellite can do the work of many.

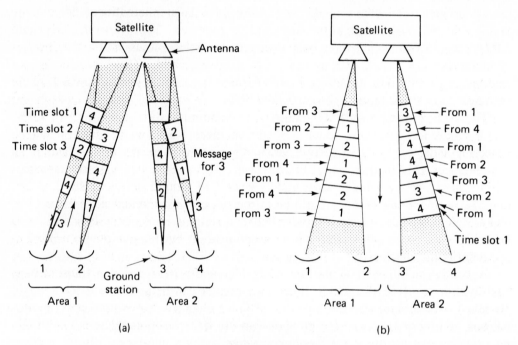

Fig. 2-8. A two-antenna satellite.

Communication satellites have several properties that are radically different from terrestrial point-to-point links. To begin with, even though signals to and from a satellite travel at the speed of light (300,000 km/sec), the large round-trip distance introduces a substantial delay. Depending on the distance between the user and the ground station, and the elevation of the satellite above the horizon, the end-to-end transit time is between 250 and 300 msec. For comparison purposes, terrestrial microwave links have a propagation delay of roughly 3 μsec/km and coaxial cable links have a delay of approximately 5 μsec/km (electromagnetic signals travel slower in copper wire than in air).

It is often said that satellite links have a longer delay than terrestrial links (especially by people operating terrestrial links). Although it is incontrovertibly true that the propagation delay is longer, the total delay depends on the bandwidth and error rate as well. For example, the total delay to send x kilobits over a 9600 bps terrestrial line is $x/9.6$ sec. To send the same message over a 5-Mbps satellite link requires $x/5000 + 0.270$ sec, including the 270 msec typical propagation delay. For messages longer than 2.6 kilobits, the satellite is faster. If we include the effect of the delay introduced by retransmissions, the lower error rate of the satellite channel will drive the crossover point even lower.

In addition to a propagation delay that is independent of the distance between sender and receiver, satellites also have the property that the cost of transmitting a message is independent of the distance traversed. A call across the ocean costs no more to service than a call across the street. Present-day common carrier price structures were developed under very different conditions, and it will be many years before the two are reconciled.

Another potentially revolutionary difference between satellites and terrestrial links is the bandwidth available. The highest speed leased telephone lines in normal use run at 56 kbps, although 1.544 Mbps lines are used in a few places where the high cost is acceptable. Rooftop-to-rooftop satellite transmission bypasses the entire telephone system and potentially offers data rates 1000 times higher. Alternatively, a cheap rooftop antenna can be used to communicate directly with a powerful satellite ground station nearby. Either way, the ability to acquire an immense bandwidth for a short time is attractive owing to the burstiness of computer traffic. Sending a magnetic tape over a 56 kbps phone line takes 7 hours; sending the same tape using a single 50-Mbps satellite transponder takes 30 sec.

Another interesting property of satellite broadcasting is precisely that: it is broadcasting. All stations under the downward beam can receive the transmission, including "pirate stations" the common carrier may know nothing about. The implications for privacy are obvious. Some form of encryption is required to keep the data secret. We will study cryptography in detail in Chapter 8.

Satellites are not only used for telephone and data transmission. They can also be used for direct broadcasting of television signals to homes. This subject, however interesting, is beyond the scope of this book, so we will not mention it further.

A comparison of satellite communication with fiber optics is instructive. While a single fiber has, in principle, more potential bandwidth than all the satellites ever launched, this bandwidth is not available to most users. The fibers that are now being installed are used within the telephone system to handle many long distance calls at once, not to provide individual users with high bandwidth. Furthermore, few users even have access to a fiber channel. Calling up the local telephone company office at 9600 bps will never give more bandwidth than 9600 bps, no matter how wide the intermediate link is. With satellites, it is practical for a user to erect an antenna on the roof of his building and completely bypass the telephone system. For Third World countries with hostile terrain and little existing infrastructure, satellites are an attractive idea. Indonesia, for example, has its own satellite for domestic telephone traffic.

For this reason, it is likely that satellite communication will increase in popularity until all the copper in the telephone system has been replaced by fiber (sometime in the middle of the twenty-first century), at which time fiber will be the ultimate winner, except perhaps for those applications requiring broadcasting, such as television transmission.

2.3. ANALOG TRANSMISSION

For the past 100 years, analog transmission has dominated all communications. In particular, the telephone system is based entirely on analog signaling. While digital transmission is becoming more and more popular, it will be decades before analog transmission has disappeared. Thus it is still important to learn about analog systems and their limitations. In the following sections we will study the telephone system, modems, and two common analog interfaces, RS-232-C and RS-449.

2.3.1. The Telephone System

When two computers owned by the same company or organization and located close to each other need to communicate, it is often easiest just to run a cable between them. However, when the distances are large, or there are many computers, or the cables would have to pass through a public road or other public right of way, the costs of running private cables are usually prohibitive. Furthermore, in just about every country in the world, stringing private transmission lines across (or underneath) public property is also illegal. Consequently, the network designers must rely upon the existing telecommunication facilities.

These facilities, especially the public switched telephone network, were usually designed many years ago, with a completely different goal in mind: transmitting the human voice in a more or less recognizable form. Their suitability for use in computer-computer communication is often marginal at best, but since there is rarely an alternative, it is worth devoting some attention to them and the obstacles they present.

To see the order of magnitude of the problem, let us make a rough but illustrative comparison of the properties of a typical computer-computer connection via a local cable and via a dial-up telephone line. A cable running between two computers can transfer data at memory speeds, typically 10^7 to 10^8 bps. The error rate is usually so low that it is hard to measure, but one error per day would be considered poor at most installations. One error per day at these speeds is equivalent to one error per 10^{12} or 10^{13} bits sent.

In contrast, a dial up line has a maximum data rate on the order of 10^4 bps and an error rate of roughly 1 per 10^5 bits sent, varying somewhat with the age of the telephone switching equipment involved. The combined bit rate times error rate performance of a local cable is thus 11 orders of magnitude better than a voice-grade telephone line. To make an analogy in the field of transportation, the ratio of the cost of the entire Apollo project, which landed men on the moon to the cost of a bus ride downtown is about 11 orders of magnitude.

The trouble, of course, is that computer systems designers are used to working with computer systems, and when suddenly confronted with another system whose performance (from their point of view) is 11 orders of magnitude worse, it is not surprising that much time and effort have been devoted to trying to figure out how to use it efficiently.

There are 300 million telephones in the world. From each one of them it is possible to call any of the other ones. The number of different potential connections is therefore 4.5×10^{16}. The most straightforward way of implementing the telephone network would simply be to run 300 million copper wires into everyone's house, each one leading to a different telephone. This method, although conceptually simple, has some drawbacks, to put it mildly. Consider, for example, the implications of installing a new telephone somewhere. Figure 2-9(a) illustrates the idea of a complete interconnection on a somewhat modest scale.

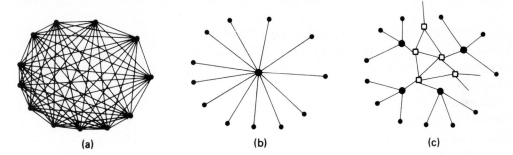

(a)   (b)   (c)

Fig. 2-9. (a) Fully interconnected network. (b) Centralized switch. (c) Two-level hierarchy.

The next simplest approach might be to have one gigantic switch somewhere, with one line running to each of the world's telephones, as illustrated in Fig. 2-9(b). This, too, is absurd due to the gargantuan problems of building, operating, and maintaining the switch.

In reality, the telephone system is organized as a highly redundant, multilevel hierarchy. The following description is highly simplified but gives the essential flavor nevertheless. Each telephone has two copper wires coming out of it that go directly to the telephone company's nearest **end office** (also called a **local central office**). The distance is typically 1 to 10 km, being smaller in cities than in rural areas. In the United States alone there are about 20,000 end offices. The concatenation of the area code and the first three digits of the telephone number uniquely specify an end office, which is why the rate structure uses this information. The two-wire connections between each subscriber's telephone and the end office are known in the trade as the **local loop**. If the world's local loops were stretched out end to end, they would extend to the moon and back 1000 times.

If a subscriber attached to a given end office calls another subscriber attached to the same end office, the switching mechanism within the office sets up a direct electrical connection between the two local loops. This connection remains intact for the duration of the call.

If the called telephone is attached to another end office, a different procedure is used. Each end office has a number of outgoing lines to one or more nearby switching centers, called **toll offices** (or **tandem offices**). These lines are called **toll connecting trunks**. If both the caller's and callee's end offices happen to have a toll connecting trunk to the same toll office (a likely occurrence if they are relatively close by), the connection may be established within the toll office. A telephone network consisting only of end offices (the large dots) and toll offices (the squares) is shown in Fig. 2-9(c).

If the caller and callee do not have a toll office in common, the path will have to be established somewhere higher up in the hierarchy. There are sectional and regional offices that form a network by which the toll offices are connected. The toll, sectional, and regional exchanges communicate with each other via high bandwidth **intertoll trunks**. The number of different kinds of switching centers and their topology (e.g., may two sectional offices have a direct connection or must they go through a regional office?) varies from country to country depending on its telephone density. Figure 2-10 shows how a medium-distance connection might be routed.

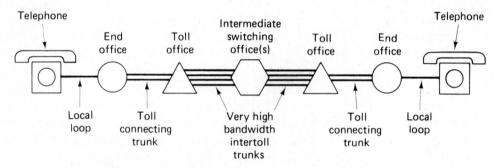

Fig. 2-10. Typical circuit route for a medium-distance call.

A variety of transmission media are used for telecommunications. Local loops consist of pairs of insulated copper wires nowadays, although at the beginning of the century, uninsulated wires spaced 25 cm apart on telephone poles were common. Between switching offices, coaxial cables, microwaves, and waveguides are used. Fiber-optics systems using lasers are also becoming more widespread, primarily because their enormous bandwidth allows a single bundle to replace many copper cables, alleviating the critical overcrowding within existing cable ducts.

2.3.2. Modems

The local loop consists of a pair of copper wires running between the subscriber's telephone and an end office. If it were not for the difficulties mentioned below, such a conductor could carry traffic at 1 or 2 Mbps without any trouble. The signals used on the local loop are dc, limited by filters to the frequency range 300 Hz to 3kHz. If a digital signal were to be applied to one end of the line, the received signal at the other end would not show a square wave form, owing to capacitance and inductance effects. Rather it would rise slowly and decay slowly. This effect makes baseband (dc) signaling unsuitable except at slow speeds and over short distances. The variation of signal propagation speed with frequency also contributes to the distortion.

To get around the problems associated with dc signaling, ac signaling is used. A continuous tone in the 1000 to 2000 Hz range is introduced, called a **sine wave carrier**. Its amplitude, frequency, or phase can be modulated to transmit information. In **amplitude modulation**, two different voltage levels are used to represent 0 and 1, respectively. In **frequency modulation**, also known as **frequency shift keying**, two (or more) different tones are used. In the most common form of **phase modulation**, the carrier wave is systematically shifted 45, 135, 225, or 315 degrees at uniformly spaced intervals. Each phase shift transmits 2 bits of information. Figure 2-11 illustrates the three forms of modulation. A device that accepts a serial stream of bits as input and produces a modulated carrier as output (or vice versa) is called a **modem** (for modulator-demodulator). The modem is inserted between the (digital) computer and the (analog) telephone system.

Some advanced modems use a combination of modulation techniques. In Fig. 2-12(a), we see dots at 0, 90, 180, and 270 degrees, with two amplitude levels per phase shift. Amplitude is indicated by the distance from the origin. In Fig. 2-12(b) we see a different modulation scheme, in which 30-degree phase shifts are used. Eight of the phase shifts can have only one legal amplitude, but the other four have two possible values, allowing for 16 combinations in all. Thus Fig. 2-12(a) can be used to transmit 3 bits per baud and Fig. 2-12(b) can be used to transmit 4 bits per baud. The scheme of Fig. 2-12(b) when used to transmit 9600 bps over a 2400-baud line is called **QAM (Quadrature Amplitude Modulation)**.

At the junction between the local loop, which is (usually) a two-wire circuit, and the trunk, which is a four-wire circuit, echoes can occur. As an illustration of electromagnetic echoes, try shining a flashlight from a darkened room through a closed window at night. You will see a reflection of the flashlight in the window (i.e., some of the energy has been reflected at the air-glass junction and sent back toward you). The same thing happens in the end office.

The effect of the echo is that a person speaking on the telephone hears his own words after a short delay. Psychological studies have shown that this is annoying to many people, often making them stutter or become confused. To eliminate the problem of echoes, echo suppressors are installed on lines longer than 2000 km. (On short lines the echoes come back so fast that people cannot detect them.) An **echo suppressor** is a device that detects human speech coming from one end of the connection and suppresses all signals going the other way.

When the first person stops talking and the second begins, the echo suppressor switches directions. While it is functioning, however, information can only travel in one direction. Figure 2-13(a) shows the state of the echo suppressors while *A* is talking to *B*. Figure 2-13(b) shows the state after *B* has started talking. When echo suppressors are used, full-duplex communication is impossible.

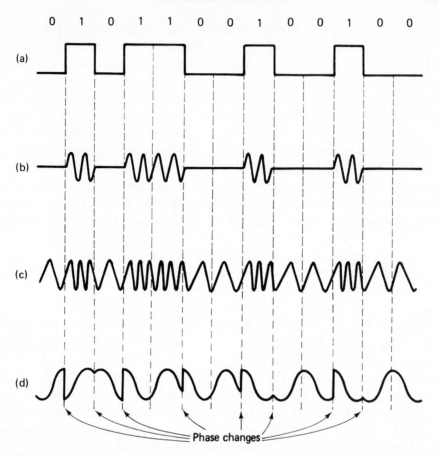

Fig. 2-11. (a) A binary signal. (b) Amplitude modulation. (c) Frequency modulation. (d) Phase modulation.

The echo suppressors have several properties that are undesirable for data communication. First, they prevent full-duplex data transmission, which would otherwise be possible, even over the two-wire local loop (by allocating part of the bandwidth to the forward channel and part to the reverse channel). Even if half-duplex transmission is adequate, they are a nuisance because the time required to switch directions can be substantial. Furthermore, they are designed to reverse upon detecting human speech, not digital data.

To alleviate these problems, an escape hatch has been provided. When the echo suppressors hear a pure tone at 2100 Hz, they shut down, and remain shut down as long as a carrier is present. This arrangement is one of the many examples of **in-band signaling**, so called because the control signals that activate and deactivate internal control functions lie within the band accessible to the user.

In recent years a new form of local distribution has appeared on the horizon: cable tv. Since a television channel requires 6 MHz of bandwidth and most cable systems offer many channels, typically cables with a bandwidth of 300 MHz are

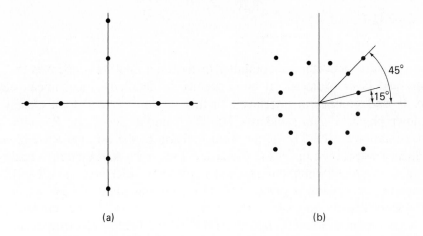

Fig. 2-12. (a) 3 bits/baud modulation. (b) 4 bits/baud modulation.

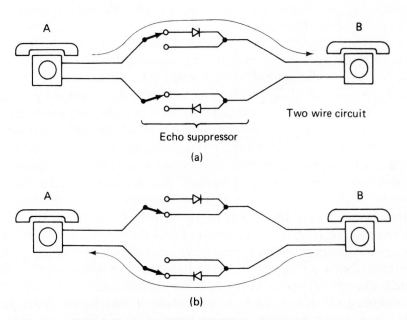

Fig. 2-13. (a) *A* talking to *B*. (b) *B* talking to *A*.

used. It bears watching in the future as a possible data transmission facility. Unlike the local loops, cable TV does not use a star pattern radiating out from an end office. Instead, everyone in the same neighborhood shares the same cable, which is like having hundreds of extension telephones on a single outgoing line. Nevertheless, high-performance data transmission systems can be built using a shared cable. In Chapter 3 we will see how multiple users can share a single channel in a fair and efficient way.

2.3.3. RS-232-C and RS-449

The interface between the computer or terminal and the modem is an example of a physical layer protocol. It must specify in detail the mechanical, electrical, functional, and procedural interface. In this section we will look closely at two well-known physical layer standards: RS-232-C and its successor, RS-449.

Let us start with **RS-232-C**, the third revision of the original RS-232 standard. The standard was drawn up by the Electronic Industries Association, a trade organization of electronics manufacturers, and is properly referred to as EIA RS-232-C. The international version is given in CCITT recommendation **V.24**, which is similar, but differs slightly on some of the rarely used circuits. In the standards, the terminal or computer is officially called a **DTE (Data Terminal Equipment)** and the modem is officially called a **DCE (Data Circuit-Terminating Equipment)**.

The mechanical specification is for a 25 pin connector 47.04 ± .13 mm wide (screw center to screw center), with all the other dimensions equally well specified. The top row has pins numbered 1 to 13 (left to right); the bottom row has pins numbered 14 to 25 (also left to right).

The electrical specification for RS-232-C is that a voltage more negative than −3 volts is a binary 1 and a voltage more positive than +4 volts is a binary 0. Data rates up to 20 kbps are permitted, as are cables up to 15 meters.

The functional specification tells which circuits are connected to each of the 25 pins, and what they mean. Figure 2-14 shows 9 pins that are nearly always implemented. The remaining ones are frequently omitted. When the terminal or computer is powered up, it asserts (i.e., sets to a logical 1) Data Terminal Ready (pin 20). When the modem is powered up it asserts Data Set Ready (pin 6). When the modem detects a carrier on the telephone line, it asserts Carrier Detect (pin 8). Request to Send (pin 4) indicates that the terminal wants to send data. Clear to Send (pin 5) means that the modem is prepared to accept data. Data is transmitted on the Transmit circuit (pin 2) and received on the Receive circuit (pin 3).

Other circuits are provided for selecting the data rate, testing the modem, clocking the data, detecting ringing signals, and sending data in the reverse direction on a secondary channel. They are hardly ever used in practice.

The procedural specification is the protocol, that is, the legal sequence of events. The protocol is based on action-reaction pairs. When the terminal asserts Request to Send, for example, the modem replies with Clear to Send, if it is able to accept data. Similar action-reaction pairs exist for other circuits as well.

It commonly occurs that two computers must be connected using RS-232-C. Since neither one is a modem, there is an interface problem. This problem is solved by connecting them with a device called a **null modem**, which connects the transmit line of one machine to the receive line of the other. It also crosses some of the other lines in a similar way.

RS-232-C has been around for years. Gradually, the limitation of the data rate

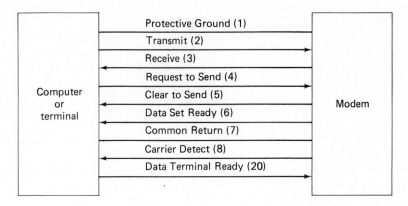

Fig. 2-14. Some of the principal RS-232-C circuits. The pin numbers are given in parentheses.

to not more than 20 kbps and the 15 meter maximum cable length have become increasingly annoying. EIA had a long debate about whether to try to have a new standard that was compatible with the old one (but technically not very advanced) or a new and incompatible one that would meet all needs for years to come. They eventually compromised by choosing both.

The new standard, called **RS-449**, is actually three standards in one. The mechanical, functional, and procedural interfaces are given in RS-449, but the electrical interface is given by two different standards. The first of these, **RS-423-A**, is similar to RS-232-C in that all its circuits share a common ground. This technique is called **unbalanced transmission**. The second electrical standard, **RS-422-A**, in contrast, uses **balanced transmission**, in which each of the main circuits requires two wires, with no common ground. As a result, RS-422-A can be used at speeds up to 2 Mbps over 60 meter cables, and at even higher speeds over shorter cables.

The circuits used in RS-449 are shown in Fig. 2-15. Several new circuits not present in RS-232-C have been added. In particular, circuits for testing the modem both locally and remotely were included. Due to the inclusion of a number of 2 wire circuits (when RS-422-A is used), more pins are needed in the new standard, so the familiar 25 pin connector was dropped. In its place is a 37 pin connector and a 9 pin connector. The 9 pin connector is only required if the second (reverse) channel is being used. If it is not being used, the 37 pin connector is sufficient.

2.4. DIGITAL TRANSMISSION

Historically, analog transmission has dominated the telecommunication industry since its inception. Signals have been sent by having some physical quantity (e.g., voltage) continuously vary as a function of time. With the advent of digital

RS-232-C			CCITT V.24			RS-449		
Code	Pin	Circuit	Code	Pin	Circuit	Code	Pin	Circuit
AA	1	Protective ground	101	1	Protective ground	—	1	
AB	7	Signal ground	102	7	Signal ground	SG	19	Signal ground
						SC	37	Send common
						RC	20	Receive common
BA	2	Transmitted data	103	2	Transmitted data	SD	4, 22	Send data
BB	3	Received data	104	3	Received data	RD	6, 24	Receive data
CA	4	Request to send	105	4	Request to send	RS	7, 25	Request to send
CB	5	Clear to send	106	5	Ready for sending	CS	9, 27	Clear to send
CC	6	Data set ready	107	6	Data set ready	DM	11, 29	Data mode
CD	20	Data terminal ready	108	20	Data terminal ready	TR	12, 30	Terminal ready
CE	22	Ring indicator	125	22	Calling indicator	IC	15	Incoming call
CF	8	Line detector	109	8	Line detector	RR	13, 31	Receiver ready
CG	21	Signal quality	110	21	Signal quality	SQ	33	Signal quality
CH	23	DTE rate	111	23	DTE rate	SR	16	Signaling rate
CI	18	DCE rate	112	18	DCE rate	SI	2	Signaling indicators
						IS	28	Terminal in service
			136		New signal	NS	34	New signal
			126	11	Select frequency	SF	16	Select frequency
DA	24	DTE timing	113	24	DTE timing	TT	17, 35	Terminal timing
DB	15	DCE timing	114	15	DCE timing	ST	5, 23	Send timing
DD	17	Receiver timing	115	17	Receiver timing	RT	8, 26	Receive timing
SBA	14	Transmitted data	118	14	Transmitted data	SSD	3	Send data
SBB	16	Received data	119	16	Received data	SRD	4	Receive data
SCA	19	Request to send	120	19	Line signal	SRS	7	Request to send
SCB	13	Clear to send	121	13	Channel ready	SCS	8	Clear to send
SCF	12	Line detector	122	12	Line detector	SRR	2	Receiver ready
						LL	10	Local loopback
						RL	14	Remote loopback
						TM	18	Test mode
						SS	32	Select standby
						SB	36	Standby indicator

Secondary Channel — brackets SBA through SCF rows.

Fig. 2-15. Comparison of RS-232-C, V.24, and RS-449.

electronics and computers, the high speed intertoll trunks in industrialized countries are being converted to digital transmission (i.e., strings of 0s and 1s are transmitted instead of continuous signals). Due to the immense investment in existing facilities, it will be decades before the complete system, including all the local loops, have been converted. This process, however, is well underway, and will be discussed in Sec. 2.6.

Digital transmission is superior to analog transmission in several important ways. First, it potentially has a very low error rate. Analog circuits have amplifiers that attempt to compensate for the attenuation in the line, but they can never compensate exactly for it, especially if the attenuation is different for different frequencies. Since the error is cumulative, long-distance calls that go through many amplifiers are likely to suffer considerable distortion. Digital regenerators, in contrast can restore the weakened incoming signal to its original value exactly, because the only possible values are 0 and 1. Digital regenerators do not suffer from cumulative error.

A second advantage of digital transmission is that voice, data, music, or even images, such as television, facsimile, or video telephone, can all be multiplexed (mixed) together to make more efficient use of the equipment. Another advantage is that much higher data rates are possible using existing lines. As the cost of digital computers and integrated circuit chips continues to drop, digital transmission and its associated switching are likely to become much cheaper than analog transmission as well.

2.4.1. Pulse Code Modulation

When a telephone subscriber attached to a digital end office makes a call, the signal emerging from his local loop is an ordinary analog signal. This analog signal is then digitized at the end office by a **codec** (coder-decoder), producing a 7- or 8-bit number. A codec, in a sense, is the inverse of a modem: the latter converts a digital bit stream into a modulated analog signal; the former converts a continuous analog signal into a digital bit stream. The codec makes 8000 samples per second (125 μsec/sample) because the Nyquist theorem says that this is sufficient to capture all the information from a 4-kHz bandwidth. This technique is called **PCM** (**Pulse Code Modulation**).

When digital transmission began emerging as a feasible technology, CCITT was unable to reach agreement on an international standard. Consequently, there are now a variety of incompatible schemes in use in different countries around the world. International hookups between incompatible countries require (often expensive) "black boxes" to convert the originating country's system to that of the receiving country.

One method that is in widespread use is the Bell System's T1 carrier, depicted in Fig. 2-16. The T1 carrier can handle 24 voice channels multiplexed together. Usually, the analog signals are periodically sampled on a round-robin basis with the resulting analog stream being fed to the codec rather than having 24 separate codecs and then merging the digital output. Each of the 24 channels, in turn, gets to insert 8 bits into the output stream. Seven of these are data, and one is for control, yielding $7 \times 8000 = 56,000$ bps of data, and $1 \times 8000 = 8000$ bps of signaling information per channel.

A frame consists of $24 \times 8 = 192$ bits, plus one extra bit for framing, yielding 193 bits every 125 μsec. This gives a gross data rate of 1.544 Mbps. The 193rd bit is used for frame synchronization. It contains the pattern 0101010101 .... Normally, the receiver keeps checking this bit to make sure that it has not lost synchronization. If it does get out of sync, the receiver can scan for this pattern to get resynchronized. Analog customers cannot generate the bit pattern at all, because it corresponds to a sine wave at 4000 Hz, which would be filtered out. Digital customers can, of course, generate this pattern, but the odds are against it being present when the frame slips.

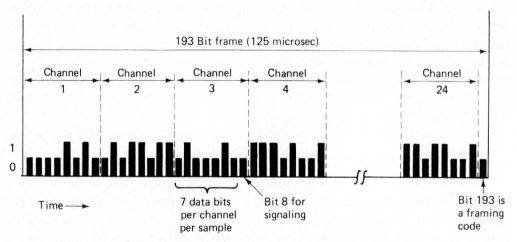

Fig. 2-16. The Bell System T1 carrier (1.544 Mbps).

When CCITT finally did reach agreement, they felt that 8000 bps of signaling information was far too much, so their 1.544-Mbps standard is based upon an 8- rather than a 7-bit data item; that is, the analog signal is quantized into 256 rather than 128 discrete levels. Two (incompatible) variations are provided. In **common-channel signaling**, the extra bit (which is attached onto the front rather than the rear of the 193 bit frame) takes on the values 10101010 . . . in the odd frames and contains signaling information for all the channels in the even frames.

In the other variation, **channel associated signaling**, each channel has its own private signaling subchannel. A private subchannel is arranged by allocating one of the eight user bits in every sixth frame for signaling purposes, so five out of six samples are 8 bits wide, and the other one is only 7 bits wide. CCITT also has a recommendation for a PCM carrier at 2.048 Mbps. This carrier has 32 8-bit data samples packed into the basic 125-μsec frame. Thirty of the channels are used for information and two are used for signaling. Each group of four frames provides 64 signaling bits, half of which are used for channel associated signaling and half of which are used for frame synchronization or are reserved for each country to use as it wishes. Outside North America and Japan, the 2.048 Mbps carrier is in widespread use.

Just as there is little agreement on the basic carrier, there is equally little agreement on how it is to be multiplexed into higher bandwidth carriers. The Bell system has standards called T2, T3, and T4 at 6.312, 44.736, and 274.176 Mbps, whereas CCITT's recommendations are for 8.848, 34.304, 139.264, and 565.148 Mbps.

2.4.2. Encoding Systems

Once the voice signal has been digitized, it is tempting to try to use statistical techniques to reduce the number of bits needed per channel. These techniques are appropriate not only to encoding speech, but to the digitization of any analog signal. All of the compaction methods are based upon the principle that the signal changes relatively slowly compared to the sampling frequency, so that much of the information in the 7- or 8-bit digital level is redundant.

One method, called **differential pulse code modulation**, consists of outputting not the digitized amplitude, but the difference between the current value and the previous one. Since jumps of ±16 or more on a scale of 128 are unlikely, 5 bits should suffice instead of seven. If the signal does occasionally jump wildly, the encoding logic may require several sampling periods to "catch up." For speech, the error introduced can be ignored.

A variation of this compaction method requires each sampled value to differ from its predecessor by either +1 or −1. A single bit is transmitted, telling whether the new sample is above or below the previous one. This technique, called **delta modulation**, is illustrated in Fig. 2-17. Like all compaction techniques that assume small level changes between consecutive samples, delta encoding can get into trouble if the signal changes too fast, as shown in the figure.

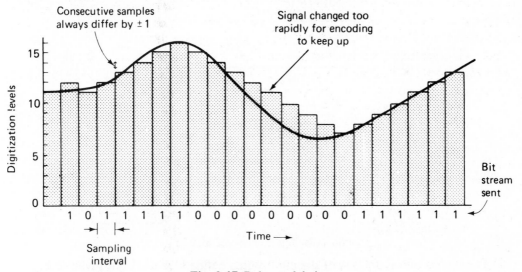

Fig. 2-17. Delta modulation.

An improvement to differential PCM is to extrapolate the previous few values to predict the next value and then to encode the difference between the actual signal and the predicted one. The transmitter and receiver must use the same prediction algorithm, of course. Such schemes are called **predictive encoding**. They are useful because they reduce the size of the numbers to be encoded, hence the number of bits to be sent.

Although PCM is widely used on interoffice trunks, the computer user gets relatively little benefit from it if he must send his data to his end office in the form of a modulated analog sine wave at 2400 bps. It would be nice if the carrier would attach the local loop directly to the PCM trunk system, so that the computer could output digital data directly onto the local loop at 1.544 or 2.048 Mbps. The twisted pairs used for local loop distribution can handle this data rate if the loading coils used to reduce the frequency dependence of the attenuation factor at low frequencies are removed and digital regenerators are inserted every 2 km. These steps are gradually being taken, so the day of end-to-end digital communication is coming closer.

2.4.3. The X.21 Digital Interface

As early as 1969, CCITT realized that carriers would eventually bring true digital lines (although not necessarily at T1 speeds) onto customer premises. To encourage compatibility in their use, in 1976, CCITT recommended a digital signaling interface called **X.21**. The recommendation specifies how the customer's computer, the DTE, sets up and clears calls by exchanging signals with the carrier's equipment, the DCE.

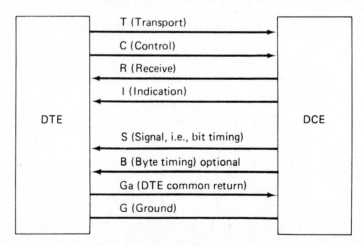

Fig. 2-18. Signal lines used in X.21.

The names and functions of the eight wires defined by X.21 are given in Fig. 2-18. The physical connector has 15 pins, but not all of them are used. The DTE uses the T and C lines to transmit data and control information, respectively. (The C line is analogous to the on-hook/off-hook signal in a telephone.) The DCE uses the R and I lines for data and control. The S line contains a signal stream emitted by the DCE to provide timing information, so the DTE knows when each bit interval starts and stops. At the carrier's option, a B line may also be provided to group the bits into 8-bit frames. If this option is provided, the DTE must begin each character on a frame boundary. If the option is not provided, both DTE and DCE must begin every control sequence with at least two SYN characters, to enable the other one to deduce the implied frame boundaries. In fact, even if the byte timing is provided, the DTE must send the two SYNs before control sequences, to maintain compatibility with networks that do not provide byte timing. The SYNs and all other control characters are in the International Alphabet number 5 (similar to ASCII), with odd parity.

Although X.21 is a long and complicated document, which references other long and complicated documents, the simple example of Fig. 2-19 illustrates the main features. In this example we will show how the DTE places a call to a remote DTE, and how the originating DTE clears the call when it is finished. To make the explanation clearer, we will describe the calling and clearing procedures in terms of an analogy with the telephone system.

Step	C	I	Event in telephone analogy	DTE sends on T	DCE sends on R
0	Off	Off	No connection-line idle	T = 1	R = 1
1	On	Off	DTE picks up phone	T = 0	
2	On	Off	DCE gives dial tone		R = "+ + + . . . +"
3	On	Off	DTE dials phone number	T = address	
4	On	Off	Remote phone rings		R = call progress
5	On	On	Remote phone picked up		R = 1
6	On	On	Conversation	T = data	R = data
7	Off	On	DTE says goodbye	T = 0	
8	Off	Off	DCE says goodbye		R = 0
9	Off	Off	DCE hangs up		R = 1
10	Off	Off	DTE hangs up	T = 1	

Fig. 2-19. An example of X.21 usage.

When the line is idle (i.e., no call on it), the four signaling lines are all one. When referring to C and I, we will follow CCITT practice and call one OFF and zero ON. When the DTE wishes to place a call, it sets T to 0 and C to ON, which is analogous to a person picking up the telephone receiver to place a call. When the DCE is ready to accept a call, it begins transmitting the ASCII "+" character on the R line, in effect, a digital dial tone, telling the DTE that it may commence dialing. The DTE "dials" the number by sending the remote DTE's address as a series of ASCII characters using the T line, 1 bit at a time. At this point the DCE sends what are called **call progress signals** to inform the DTE of the result of the call. The call progress signals, defined in CCITT recommendation X.96, consist of two-digit numbers, the first of which gives the general class of the result, and the second the details. The general classes include: call put through, try again (e.g., number busy), call failed and will probably fail again next time (e.g., access barred, remote DTE out of order, DTEs incompatible), short term network congestion, and long term network congestion. If the call can be put through, the DCE sets I to ON to indicate that the data transfer may begin.

At this point a full-duplex digital connection has been established, and either side can send information at will. Either DTE can say "goodbye" by setting its C line to OFF. Having done so, it may not send more data, although it must be prepared to continue receiving data until the other DTE has finished. In step 7 of Fig. 2-19, the originating DTE says goodbye first. Its local DCE acknowledges this signal by turning its I line to OFF. When the remote DTE also has turned off its C line, the DCE at the originating side sets R to 1. Finally, the DTE sets T to 1 as an acknowledgement, and the interface is back in the idle state, waiting for another call.

The procedure for incoming calls is analogous to that for outgoing calls. If an incoming call and an outgoing call take place simultaneously, known as a **call collision**, the incoming call is canceled and the outgoing call is put through. CCITT made this decision because it may be too late at this point for some DTEs to reallocate resources already committed to the outgoing call.

Carriers are likely to offer a variety of special features on X.21 networks such as fast-connect, in which setting the C line ON is interpreted by the DCE as a request to reconnect to the number previously dialed. This feature eliminates the dialing stage, and might be useful, for example, to place a separate call to a time-sharing computer every time the person at the terminal hit return. Another possible X.21 option is the closed user group, by which a group of customers (e.g., company offices) could be prevented from making calls to, or receiving calls from, anyone outside the group. Call redirection, collect calls, incoming or outgoing calls barred, and caller identification are other possibilities.

2.5. TRANSMISSION AND SWITCHING

In the following sections we will look at some of the issues involved in transmitting information, especially in digital form.

2.5.1. Frequency Division and Time Division Multiplexing

Economies of scale play an important role in the telephone system. It costs essentially the same amount of money to install and maintain a high-bandwidth cable as a low-bandwidth wire between two switching offices (i.e., the costs come from having to dig the trench and not from the copper conductor). Consequently, telephone companies have developed elaborate schemes for multiplexing many conversations over a single physical channel.

These multiplexing schemes can be divided into two basic categories: **FDM (Frequency Division Multiplexing)** and **TDM (Time Division Multiplexing)**. In FDM the frequency spectrum is divided among the logical channels, with each user having exclusive possession of his frequency band. In TDM the users take turns (in a round robin), each one periodically getting the entire bandwidth for a little burst of time.

AM radio broadcasting provides illustrations of both kinds of multiplexing. The allocated spectrum is about 1 MHz, roughly 500 to 1500 kHz. Different frequencies are allocated to different logical channels (stations), each operating in a portion of the spectrum, with the interchannel separation great enough to prevent interference. This system is an example of frequency-division multiplexing. In addition (in some countries), the individual stations have two logical subchannels: music and advertising. These two alternate in time on the same frequency, first a burst of music, then a burst of advertising, then more music, and so on. This situation is time-division multiplexing.

Figure 2-20 shows how three voice-grade telephone channels are multiplexed using FDM. Filters limit the usable bandwidth to about 3000 Hz per voice-grade channel. When many channels are multiplexed together, 4000 Hz is allocated to each channel to keep them well separated. First the voice channels are raised in frequency, each by a different amount. Then they can be combined, because no two channels occupy the same portion of the spectrum now. Notice that even though there are gaps (guard bands) between the channels, there is some overlap between adjacent channels, because the filters do not have sharp edges. This overlap means that a strong spike at the edge of one channel will be felt in the adjacent one as nonthermal noise.

The FDM schemes used around the world are to some degree standardized. A widespread standard is twelve 4000-Hz voice channels (3000 Hz for the user, plus two guard bands of 500 Hz each) multiplexed into the 60 to 108 kHz band. This unit is called a **group**. The 12- to 60-kHz band is sometimes used for another group. Many carriers offer a 48- to 56-kbps leased line service to customers, based on the group. Five groups (60 voice channels) can be multiplexed to form a **supergroup**. The next unit is the **mastergroup**, which is five supergroups (CCITT standard) or ten supergroups (Bell system). Other standards up to 230,000 voice channels also exist.

Computer to computer traffic has some properties that are fundamentally different from you talking to your grandmother on the telephone. When people are talking, it is unusual for gaps in the conversation to last for many minutes. When interactive computers are communicating, such gaps are the rule, not the exception. A burst of data will need to be sent quickly, and then there may be silence for the next 30 min. In other words, human-to-human traffic needs continuous use of a low-bandwidth channel, whereas (some) computer-to-computer traffic needs

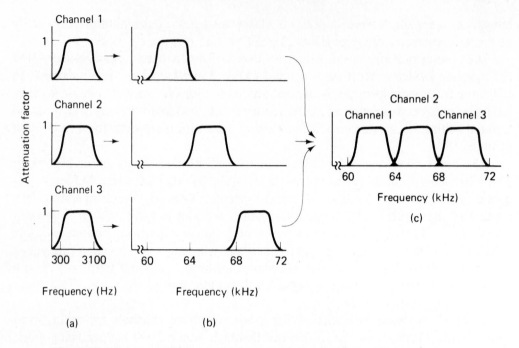

Fig. 2-20. Frequency-division multiplexing. (a) The original bandwidths. (b) The bandwidths raised in frequency. (c) The multiplexed channel.

intermittent use of a high bandwidth channel. There is a difference in kind between eating an ice cream cone every day, and eating 365 ice cream cones on your birthday, even though the mean consumption rate is the same.

The existing telephone plant was set up for human-to-human communication, not computer-to-computer communication. It uses TDM and FDM, neither of which is appropriate for data traffic. A fundamentally different kind of switching is needed. In the following sections we will discuss the two principal switching techniques, circuit switching and packet switching.

2.5.2. Circuit Switching

When you or your computer places a telephone call, the switching equipment within the telephone system seeks out a physical "copper" path all the way from your telephone to the receiver's telephone. This technique is called **circuit switching** and is shown schematically in Fig. 2-21(a). Each of the six rectangles represents a carrier switching office (end office, toll office, etc.). In this example, each office has three incoming lines and three outgoing lines. When a call passes through a switching office, a physical connection is (conceptually) established between the line on which the call came in and one of the output lines, as shown by the dotted lines. In the early days of the telephone, the connection was made by having the operator plug a jumper cable into the input and output sockets.

The model shown in Fig. 2-21(a) is highly simplified of course, because parts of the "copper" path between the two telephones may, in fact, be microwave links onto which thousands of calls are multiplexed. Nevertheless, the basic idea is valid: once a call has been set up, a dedicated path between both ends exists, and will continue to exist until the call is finished.

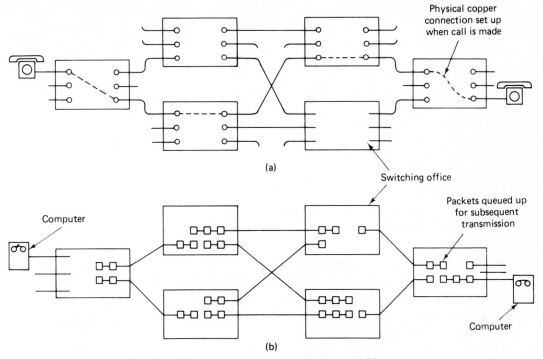

Fig. 2-21. (a) Circuit switching. (b) Packet switching.

An important property of circuit switching is the need to set up an end-to-end path *before* any data can be sent. The elapsed time between the end of dialing and the start of ringing can easily be 10 sec, more on long-distance or international calls. During this time interval, the telephone system is hunting for a copper path, as shown in Fig. 2-22(a). Note that before data transmission can begin, the call request signal must propagate all the way to the destination, and be acknowledged. For many computer applications (e.g., point-of-sale credit verification), long setup times are undesirable.

As a consequence of the copper path between the calling parties, once the setup has been completed, the only delay for data is the propagation time for the electromagnetic signal, about 6 msec per 1000 km. Also as a consequence of the established path, there is no danger of congestion—that is, once the call has been put through, you never get busy signals, although you might get one before the connection has been established due to lack of internal switching or trunk capacity.

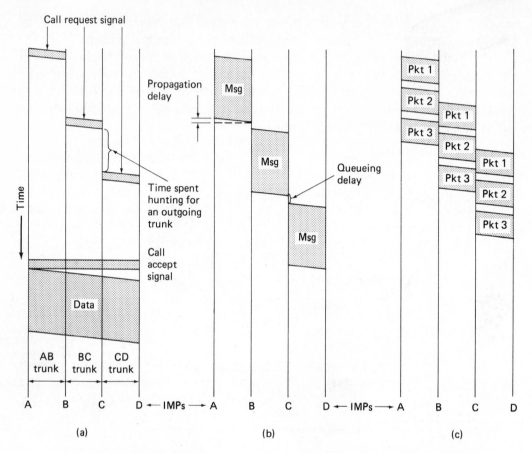

Fig. 2-22. Timing of events in (a) circuit switching, (b) message switching, (c) packet switching.

2.5.3. Packet Switching

An alternative switching strategy is **message switching**, shown in Fig. 2-22(b). When this form of switching is used, no physical copper path is established in advance between sender and receiver. Instead, when the sender has a block of data to be sent, it is stored in the first switching office (i.e., IMP) and then forwarded later, one hop at a time. Each block is received in its entirety, inspected for errors, and then retransmitted. A network using this technique is called a **store-and-forward** network, as mentioned earlier.

Yet another possibility is **packet switching**. With message switching, there is no limit on block size, which means that IMPs must have disks to buffer long blocks. It also means that a single block may tie up an IMP-IMP line for many minutes, rendering message switching useless for interactive traffic. In contrast, packet switching networks place a tight upper limit on block size, allowing packets to be buffered in IMP main memory instead of on disk. By making sure that no user can monopolize any transmission line for more than a few tens of milliseconds, packet switching networks are well suited to handling interactive traffic. A further advantage of packet switching over message switching is shown in Fig. 2-22(b) and (c): the first packet of a multipacket message can be forwarded before the second one has fully arrived, reducing delay and improving throughput. For these reasons, computer networks are usually packet switched, occasionally circuit switched, but never message switched.

Circuit switching and packet switching differ in many respects. The key difference is that circuit switching statically reserves the required bandwidth in advance, whereas packet switching acquires and releases it as it is needed. With circuit switching, any unused bandwidth on an allocated circuit is just wasted. With packet switching it may be utilized by other packets from unrelated sources going to unrelated destinations, because circuits are never dedicated. However, just because no circuits are dedicated, a sudden surge of input traffic may overwhelm an IMP, exceeding its storage capacity and causing it to lose packets.

In contrast with circuit switching, when packet switching is used, it is straightforward for the IMPs to provide speed and code conversion. Also, they can provide error correction to some extent. In some packet-switched networks, however, packets may be delivered in the wrong order to the destination. Reordering of packets can never happen with circuit switching.

A final difference between the two methods is the charging algorithm. Packet carriers usually base their charge on both the number of bytes (or packets) carried and the connect time. Furthermore, transmission distance usually does not matter, except perhaps internationally. With circuit switching, the charge is based on the distance and time only, not the traffic.

2.5.4. Hybrid Switching

As computer and communication technology move closer together, variants and hybrid forms of circuit switching and packet switching become possible. We will now briefly touch upon four of these.

The main reason packet switching was invented is to get around the long call connection time present in the existing telephone system. A much more direct, although expensive, approach is to build a new telephone system, one in which calls are put through in milliseconds instead of seconds. With such a system, called **fast connect circuit switching** for obvious reasons, each line typed at a terminal causes the microprocessor inside the terminal to "dial" the computer, send the line, and then hang up.

Just as fast-connect networks are a variation on circuit switching, there are variations on packet switching. An especially interesting one is **time-division switching**, in which each IMP scans its input lines in strict rotation. Each packet is immediately retransmitted on the correct output line, often starting as soon as the header has been read. By using fixed-size packets and a rigid time synchronization, no buffer space is needed, and the whole IMP can be reduced to a few chips. The chief virtue of time-division switching is that it offers high performance (>100 Mbps throughput) at low cost using a technology that has already proven itself in the context of the telephone system.

If nothing else, all these possibilities should make clear the importance of designing networks hierarchically, as in Fig. 1-7, to insulate the higher layers from possible drastic changes in the lower ones.

2.6. ISDN—INTEGRATED SERVICES DIGITAL NETWORK

For more than a century, the primary international communication infrastructure has been the telephone system. This system was designed for analog voice transmission and is proving inadequate for modern communication needs such as data transmission, facsimile, and video. User demands for these and other services have led to an international undertaking to replace a major portion of the worldwide telephone system with an advanced digital system by the early part of the twenty-first century. This new system, called **ISDN (Integrated Services Digital Network)**, has as its primary goal the integration of voice and nonvoice services.

Since ISDN is basically a redesign of the telephone system, the international coordination is taking place within CCITT and its many study groups, rather than within ISO. CCITT works on a four year cycle, with study groups preparing recommendations for submission to the Plenary Session held every four years. The key ISDN recommendations were approved in 1984, with refinements in 1988. Figure 2-23 lists some of the key recommendations (Decina, 1986). In the following sections we will look at the objectives, evolution, architecture, and design of ISDN.

Number	Title
I.120	Integrated Services Digital Networks
I.210	Principles of telecommunication services supported by an ISDN
I.211	Bearer services supported by an ISDN
I.310	ISDN network functional principles
I.320	ISDN protocol reference manual
I.411	ISDN user/network interfaces–reference configurations
I.412	ISDN user/network interfaces–interface structure and access
I.420	Basic network/user interface
I.421	Primary rate network/user access
I.430	Basic user/network interface–Layer 1 specification
I.431	Primary rate user/network interface–Layer 1 specification
I.440	ISDN user/network interface Data Link Layer protocol–general aspects
I.441	ISDN user/network interface Data Link Layer specification
I.450	ISDN user/network interface Layer 3–general aspects
I.451	ISDN user/network interface Layer 3–specification

Fig. 2-23. Some of the principal CCITT ISDN Recommendations

2.6.1. ISDN Services

Since the driving force behind ISDN has been the demand for new services and the desire to integrate these services with voice telephony, it is appropriate to begin our study of ISDN with a short review of some of the home and business services CCITT is planning.

The key service will continue to be voice, although many enhanced features will be added. For example, many corporate managers have an intercom button on their telephone that rings their secretaries instantly (no call setup time). One ISDN feature is telephones with multiple buttons for instant call setup to arbitrary telephones anywhere in the world. Another feature is telephones that display the caller's telephone number, name, and address on a display while ringing. A more sophisticated version of this feature allows the telephone to be connected to a computer, so that the caller's database record is displayed on the screen as the call comes in. For example, a stock broker could arrange that when he answered the telephone, the caller's portfolio was already on the screen along with the current prices of all the caller's stocks.

Other advanced voice services are call transfer and forwarding to any number worldwide and conference calls (more than two parties) worldwide. Furthermore, speech digitization techniques make it possible for callers who get a busy signal or discover no one at home to leave a message. Although answering machines already exist, most homes do not have one and never will, but they might use the service if it were part of the telephone system itself and only cost a few cents per message. Finally, an automatic wakeup call service would be of great interest to hotels to save their operators the trouble of making hundreds of daily wakeup calls manually.

ISDN data transmission services will allow users to connect their ISDN terminal or computer to any other one in the world. At present such connections are frequently impossible internationally due to incompatible national telephone systems. Connections may also involve three or more parties, along with the possibility of a broadcast mode, in which, say, the president of a multinational corporation sends an electronic message about changes in the retirement policy to all employees over the age of 60.

Another important data transmission feature is the closed user group, in which the members of the group can only call other members of the group, and no calls from outside the group can come in (except in carefully controlled ways). This feature makes it possible for a company to use the telephone system as a private network. Private networks are of great importance for privacy and security reasons to many corporate, government, diplomatic, and military agencies.

A new communication service that is expected to become widespread with ISDN is **videotex**, which is interactive access to a remote database by a person at a terminal. In France, for example, the PTT has already started to abolish all the telephone books and information operators (at enormous savings) by providing each subscriber with a small terminal for accessing the on-line telephone book.

Directory assistance is only one small application of videotex. One could also imagine having the Yellow Pages on-line, at which time people will be able to type in a product name to get a list of companies that sell it. Then they can select a company and get its price list on the terminal. Finally, they can buy the product by just typing in its order number and have it charged to their credit card or telephone bill. Airline, hotel, theater, and restaurant reservations, bank-by-terminal, and numerous other applications are also possible once the basic videotex system is in place.

Another ISDN service that is expected to become popular is **teletex** which is essentially a form of electronic mail for home and business. In virtually every country, the telephone system makes a large profit and the postal system makes an even larger loss. (It is cheaper to send bits electronically from New York to California than to transport them physically by planes, trucks, and ultimately, on foot.) Consequently, it makes good economic sense to turn every telephone into a telephone/terminal workstation not only for videotex, but also for composing, editing, sending, receiving, archiving, and printing electronic mail, to reduce the load on the postal system.

Teletex service must be cheap to give it wide acceptance, so it is designed for simple terminals suitable only for text and some basic graphics. Many businesses need to send contracts with handwritten signatures, charts, diagrams, blueprints, illustrations and other graphic materials to distant destinations. These can use another ISDN terminal and service, **facsimile** (often called **fax**), in which an image is scanned and digitized electronically. The resulting bit stream is then transmitted to the destination and then redrawn on a piece of paper—in effect, a distributed photocopy machine, with the input window and output tray in different cities. As with teletex, there is a need to archive, edit, forward, and broadcast facsimile images.

Facsimile need not be restricted to the copying of paper documents, but is generally useful for transmitting any image. For example, automated bank teller machines could photograph their customers for identification to help prevent fraud and robbery. Business conference calls could be augmented by having charts and drawings on blackboards transmitted along with the voices. Slow-scan video (one image every few seconds) can also be used. In the distant future, when enough bandwidth is available, full-motion video will also be possible.

Facsimile is an example of a service requiring high bandwidth, but there are also potential services requiring low bandwidth. These go by the name of **telemetry** or **alarm** services. For example, it is obviously wasteful to set up a large organization of people and automobiles just to go around collecting a 32-bit number from everyone's house (electricity meter readers). It would be much more efficient to have the meter on-line, so that the electricity company could read it by just calling it on the telephone.

Alarm services include smoke and fire detectors in homes and businesses that automatically call the fire department when they detect smoke or fire. If the fire department's telephone automatically displays the telephone number, name, and address of the calling party, the detectors can be made cheaply because then the detectors do not have to identify themselves when making the call.

Another important application is the medical alarm, in which a patient who has a high risk of, for example, heart attack, could have a button in each room of his house. If a button is pressed, it makes an instant connection with the ambulance department of a local hospital, displaying on their terminal the patient's name, address, medical history, and best route to the patient's house, taking into account the normal traffic patterns at the time of the call.

Some of these proposed ISDN services are already available in primitive form, but they all require different networks and are poorly integrated. While all offices have telephones and many have computers or facsimile machines, few executives have the ability to call someone up on the telephone and during the conversation display a contract they are negotiating, with both parties being able to change the contract by editing it (data transmission) or writing on it (facsimile). The goal of ISDN is to integrate all the services described above and make them as commonplace as the telephone is now.

2.6.2. Evolution of ISDN

ISDN will not happen overnight. The investment in the current telephone system is so great that ISDN will have to be phased in over a period of decades, and it will have to coexist with the present analog system for many years. These requirements have had a major influence on the final form ISDN will take and the way the current system will gradually evolve toward ISDN. In this section we will provide some background information that will make it clearer why the ISDN architecture described in the next section was designed that way.

The analog voice telephone system (the **public switched network** in telephone jargon) originally sent all its control information in the same 4 kHz channel used for voice. Pure tones at various frequencies were used for signaling by the system itself. This scheme, known as **in-band signaling**, meant that in theory users could interfere with the internal signaling system.

Some years ago, a popular children's breakfast cereal included a free whistle in each box. Unfortunately, the frequency emitted by this whistle was also used by the telephone system, so whenever a child called up his grandmother to demonstrate the whistle, the call was cut off. The child naturally called the grandmother again with predictable results. Eventually the child's parent called the telephone company to report a broken telephone, and a truck with crew was dispatched to fix it.

Another property of in-band signaling was that sophisticated users could manipulate the system to avoid paying. For a long time, the only way coin telephone operators could tell which coins had been deposited was to listen for the sounds they made as they struck bells inside the pay phone. Slugs, pieces of ice the shape of a quarter, and tape recorders wielded by mischievious undergraduates were a nuisance, but serious commercial billing fraud was also a problem.

To eliminate these and other problems caused by in-band signaling, in 1976 AT&T built and installed a packet switching network separate from the main public switched network. This network, called **Common Channel Interoffice Signaling (CCIS)**, ran at 2.4 kbps and was designed to move the signaling traffic out-of-band. With CCIS, when an end office needed to set up a call, it chose a channel on an outgoing trunk of the public switched network. Then it sent a packet on the CCIS network to the next switching office along the chosen route telling which channel had been allocated. This CCIS node then chose the next outgoing trunk channel, and reported it on the CCIS network. Thus, the management of the analog connections was done on a separate packet switched network to which the users had no access.

CCIS came to be regarded as a great success, and was soon used by more and more applications. The four major uses now are:

1. Call setup, routing, and termination.

2. Internal database access.

3. Network operations and support.

4. Accounting and billing.

Call setup, as we have just said, relates to choosing trunks and channels at each step of the way for calls that must pass through multiple exchanges. The internal databases are used for verifying telephone credit card numbers, routing and charging collect calls (including calls to 800 numbers) among other applications. Network operations and support has to do with monitoring the performance of the whole system, keeping track of trunk utilization, installing and removing exchanges and lines, distributing new software to exchanges, and so on. Finally, accounting and billing also use the CCIS network, to reduce customer fraud. The success of CCIS has greatly influenced the design of ISDN, which also handles signaling out-of-band.

Another development that has been taking place since the mid 1970s is the growth of commercially available packet switching networks. The public switched network is a circuit switching network, which means that a physical connection is reserved all the way from end to end throughout the duration of the call. For intermittent traffic, such as terminal access to a remote database or time-sharing system, simply calling up the remote machine and staying on the phone all day is too expensive. Thus many users prefer to call the local office of a packet switching network, so the long telephone call is a local one, with additional charges from the packet network based primarily on traffic volume, not connect time.

Thus the current telephone system really has three distinct components inside of it: the analog public switched network for voice, CCIS for controlling the voice network, and packet switching networks for data. Furthermore, the installed base of twisted pair local loops from the 20,000 end offices in the U.S. alone (over 1 billion kilometers) exceeds 130 billion dollars. Replacing the local loops with say, fiber optics, to satisfy the needs of ISDN is unthinkable. On the other hand, replacing interexchange trunks with fiber optic links is feasible because there are fewer of them and they can be easily upgraded one at a time.

These facts mean that ISDN was designed from the beginning to live with the limitations of the existing local loops and the voice, CCIS, and packet networks. In particular, the bandwidth available on the local loops is about 2 Mbps for the 80 percent of the loops shorter than 7 or 8 km, and somewhat less on the longer ones.

The first step towards ISDN was to define and standardize the user-to-ISDN interface. The next step was to slowly start replacing existing end offices with ISDN exchanges that support the ISDN interface. At this point, those users connected to an ISDN exchange can use ISDN services on calls to other ISDN users even though these calls use the facilities of the existing networks, as shown in Fig. 2-24(a). Eventually the existing transmission and switching networks will be replaced by an integrated one, as shown in Fig. 2-24(b), but this will not occur until well into the twenty-first century.

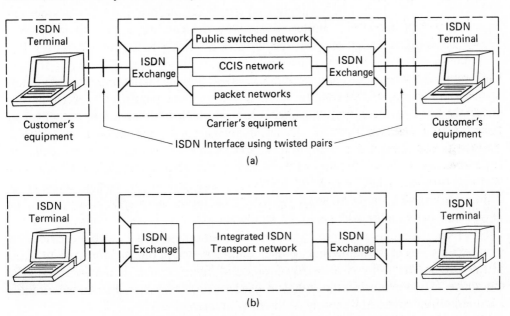

Fig. 2-24. (a) Initial stage of ISDN evolution. (b) Later stage.

2.6.3. ISDN System Architecture

It is now time to look at the ISDN architecture in detail, particularly the customer's equipment and the interface between the customer and the telephone company or PTT (Gifford, 1986). The key idea behind ISDN is that of the **digital**

bit pipe, a conceptual pipe between the customer and the carrier through which bits flow. Whether the bits originated from a digital telephone, a digital terminal, a digital facsimile machine, or some other device is irrelevant. All that matters is that bits can flow through the pipe in both directions.

The digital bit pipe can, and normally does, support multiple independent channels by time division multiplexing of the bit stream. The exact format of the bit stream and its multiplexing is a carefully defined part of the interface specification for the digital bit pipe. Two principal standards for the bit pipe have been developed, a low bandwidth standard for home use and a higher bandwidth standard for business use that supports multiple channels that are identical to the home use channel. Furthermore, businesses may have multiple bit pipes if they need additional capacity beyond what the standard business pipe can provide.

In Fig. 2-25(a) we see the normal configuration for home or small business use. The carrier places a network terminating device, **NT1,** on the customer's premises and then connects it to the ISDN exchange in the carrier's office, several kilometers away, using the twisted pair that was previously used to connect to the customer's telephone. The NT1 box has a connector on it into which a passive bus cable can be inserted. Up to eight ISDN telephones, terminals, alarms, and other devices can be connected to the cable, similar to the way devices are connected to a LAN. From the customer's point of view, the network boundary is the connector on NT1.

Actually, NT1 is more than just a patch panel. It contains electronics for network administration, local and remote loopback testing, maintenance, and performance monitoring. For example, each device on the passive bus must have a unique address so it can be addressed. One approach is to have a thumbwheel on each ISDN device, and instruct the users to make sure that when a new burglar alarm it is installed, it has a different address than the telephone, smoke detector, and thermostat. The probability of the average user getting this right is pretty close to zero. Instead, when a new device is powered up on the bus, it requests an address from NT1, which checks its list of addresses currently in use, and then downloads an available address to the new device.

NT1 also contains logic for contention resolution, so that if several devices try to access the bus at the same time, it can determine which one should win. In terms of the OSI model, NT1 is primarily a physical layer device. It is concerned with the shape of the plug and the voltages used to represent bits, but knows nothing about how frames are built on top of the raw bit stream.

For large businesses, the model of Fig. 2-25(a) is inadequate because it is common to have more telephone conversations going on simultaneously than the bus can handle. Therefore, the model of Fig. 2-25(b) is used. In this model we find a device, **NT2,** called a **PBX (Private Branch eXchange),** connected to NT1 and providing the real interface for telephones, terminals and other equipment. An ISDN PBX is not very different conceptually from an ISDN exchange, although it is usually smaller and cannot handle as many conversations at the same time. Calls between two telephones or terminals within the company, usually dialed using 4-

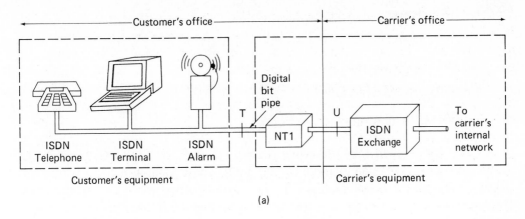

(a)

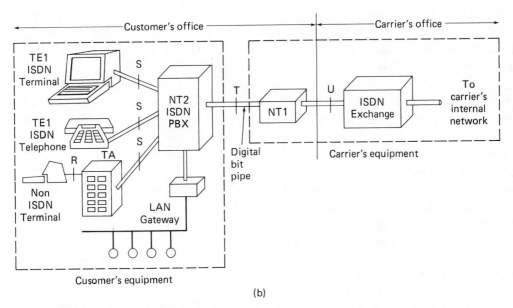

(b)

Fig. 2-25. (a) Example ISDN system for home use. (b) Example ISDN system with a PBX for use in large businesses.

digit extension numbers, are connected inside the PBX, without the carrier's ISDN exchange being aware. When an employee dials "9" (or some other code) to get an outside line, the PBX allocates a channel on the outgoing digital bit pipe and connects the caller to it. If no channel is available, the caller gets a busy signal. PBXes cover at least layers 1 through 3 in the OSI model.

An ISDN PBX can directly interface to ISDN terminals and telephones. However, the world is still full of non-ISDN devices, such as RS-232-C terminals. To accommodate these, the customer can install one or more terminal adapters that speak RS-232-C to the terminal and ISDN to the PBX. In summary, Fig. 2-25(b) depicts five kinds of devices on the customer premises as follows:

1. NT1: network boundary.

2. NT2: customer PBX.

3. TE1: ISDN terminal.

4. TE2: non-ISDN terminal.

5. TA: terminal adapter.

CCITT has defined four **reference points**, called **R, S, T**, and **U**, between the various devices. These are marked in Fig. 2-25. The U reference point is the connection between the ISDN exchange in the carrier's office and NT1. At present it is a two-wire copper twisted pair, but at some time in the future it may be replaced by fiber optics. The T reference point is what the connector on NT1 provides to the customer. The S reference point is the interface between the ISDN PBX and the ISDN terminals. The R reference point is the connection between the terminal adapter and non-ISDN terminals. Many different kinds of interfaces will be used at R.

The ISDN situation is greatly complicated by the national politics in various countries. In the U.S. the government is actively trying to encourage competition in the telecommunications industry in an effort to inject some fresh blood. In most European countries, the PTT still has a complete monopoly on telecommunications, although it is weakening here and there. These different policies give rise to a number of controversies.

First, who should own NT1 and NT2? Three possibilities suggest themselves:

1. The customer buys and owns both NT1 and NT2.

2. The carrier leases NT1 to the customer, but the customer buys NT2.

3. The carrier leases both NT1 and NT2 to the customer.

In cases 1 and 3 it may make economic sense to integrate both NT1 and NT2 into a single unit. In effect, these are modified PBXes that connect directly to the carrier's ISDN exchange at the U reference point over the local loop. These modified PBXes are called **NT12** devices.

In the U.S. many companies will want to buy this kind of equipment to avoid having to lease NT1 from the carrier. In those European countries in which the PTT monopoly extends to PBXes, the PTT may provide NT12 PBXes in order to lower its own costs. The advantage of NT1, however, is that it isolates the customer from changes in the local loop technology. When fiber optics finally arrives, retrofitting NT1 is much simpler than retrofitting or replacing the whole PBX. On the other hand, some customers argue that since the local loop has not changed in the past 100 years, they will take their chances about it changing in the next 100 years, preferring the immediate cash benefits of NT12 as opposed to NT1 and NT2.

Another controversy is at the S reference point. The PTTs want a single standard interface for all telephones and terminals, since in the long run the world will be simpler with only one interface. Many PBX manufacturers want to offer PBXes that speak not only ISDN, but also RS-232-C, RS-449, X.21, analog telephone, fiber optics, IBM PC bus, Ethernet, and anything else for which their customers are willing to pay. As a result of these and similar issues, we may see different and incompatible ISDN systems in different countries.

2.6.4. The Digital PBX

In the previous section, we looked at the ISDN system architecture and saw the key role played by the PBX. In this section we will take a closer look at this device to get an idea of how it works internally. PBX design is a large and complex area, and much of the technology is proprietary, so this will of necessity be a brief summary.

The modern PBX, also known as a **PABX (Private Automatic Branch eXchange)** or **CBX (Computerized Branch eXchange)**, is a third-generation system. First-generation PBXes were patch panels run by a human operator. To make a call, an employee picked up the telephone, which signaled the operator who then asked: "Number, please?" The operator then connected the caller to the desired extension or an outside line by inserting both ends of a short jumper cable into the PBX to make a physical circuit between the caller and the destination. Second-generation PBXes worked the same way, except with electromechanical relays making the connection instead of a human operator.

Third-generation PBXes have the general structure of Fig. 2-26. The heart of the PBX is a circuit switch into which modules can be inserted. Each module card interfaces with some class of device and produces an ISDN bit stream as output. An ISDN module does not have much work to do, but a module for analog telephones must digitize the signal in ISDN format. Trunk modules connect to the ISDN exchange.

The control unit is a general-purpose computer that runs the PBX. When a telephone is picked up or a terminal powered on, the control module gets an interrupt from the appropriate line module. The control unit then collects the digits of the number called, and sets up the switch to create a circuit between the calling and called devices. The services unit provides dial tones, busy signals, and other services for the control unit.

Two kinds of switches are in common use. One type, the **crosspoint switch**, is shown in Fig. 2-27. In a PBX with n input lines and n output lines (i.e., n full duplex lines), the crosspoint switch has n^2 intersections where an input and an output line may be connected by a semiconductor switch, as shown in Fig. 2-27(a). In Fig. 2-27(b) we see an example in which line 0 is connected to line 4, line 1 is connected to line 7, and line 2 is connected to line 6. Lines 3 and 5 are not connected. All the bits that arrive at the PBX from line 4, for example, are immediately sent

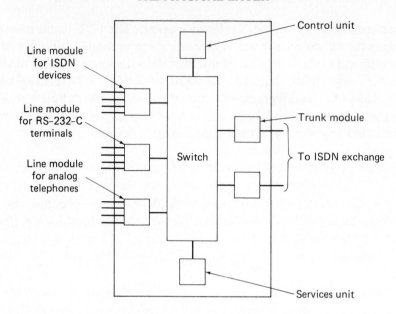

Fig. 2-26. Block structure of a digital PBX.

out of the PBX on line 0. Thus the crosspoint switch implements circuit switching by making a direct electrical connection, just like the jumper cables in the first-generation PBXes, only automatically and within microseconds.

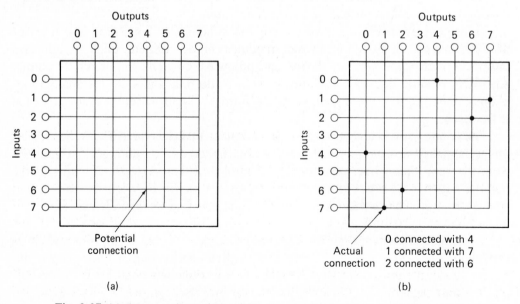

Fig. 2-27. (a) A crosspoint switch with no connections. (b) A crosspoint switch with three connections set up.

The problem with a crosspoint switch is that the number of crosspoints grows as the square of the number of lines into the PBX. If we assume that all lines are full duplex and that there are no self-connections, only the crosspoints above the diagonal are needed. Still, $n(n-1)/2$ cross points are needed. For $n = 1000$, we need 499,500 crosspoints. While building a VLSI chip with this number of transistor switches is at least conceivable, having 1000 pins on the chip is not. Nevertheless, by splitting the crosspoint switch into small chunks and interconnecting them, it is possible to build feasible multistage switches.

A completely different kind of switch is the **time division switch**, shown in Fig. 2-28. With time division switching, the n input lines are scanned in sequence to build up an input frame with n slots. Each slot has k bits. For ISDN PBXes, the slots would normally have 8 bits, with 8000 frames built and processed per second (ISDN uses the PCM standard).

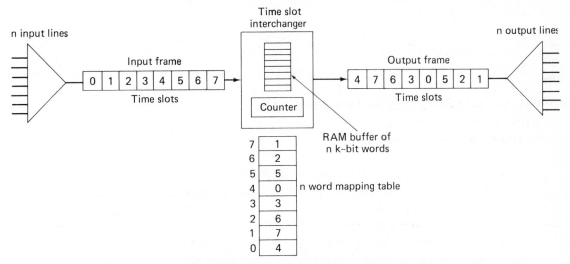

Fig. 2-28. A time division switch.

The heart of the time division switch is the **time slot interchanger**, which accepts input frames and produces output frames in which the time slots have been reordered. In Fig. 2-28, input slot 4 is output first, then slot 7, and so on. Finally, the output frame is demultiplexed, with output slot 0 (input slot 4) going to line 0, and so on. In essence, the switch has moved a byte from input line 4 to output line 0, another byte from input line 7 to output line 1, and so on. Viewed from the outside, the whole arrangement is a circuit switch, even though there are no physical connections.

The time slot interchanger works as follows: When an input frame is ready to be processed, each slot (i.e., byte) is written into a RAM buffer inside the interchanger. The slots are written in order, so buffer word i contains slot i.

After all the slots of the input frame have been stored in the buffer, the output frame is constructed by reading out the words again, but in a different order. A counter goes from 0 to $n-1$. At step j, the contents of word j of a mapping table is read out and used to address the RAM table. Thus if word 0 of the mapping table contains a 4, word 4 of the RAM buffer will be read out first, and the first slot of the output frame will be slot 4 of the input frame. Thus the contents of the mapping table determine which permutation of the input frame will be generated as the output frame, and thus which input line is connected to which output line.

The role of the control unit in a time division switch is now clear. Its function is to set up connections by adjusting the contents of the slot mapping table. If a full duplex connection is set up between slots i and j, slot i in the mapping table gets value j, and slot j gets value i.

Time division switches use tables that are linear in the number of lines, rather than quadratic, but they have another limitation. It is necessary to store n slots in the buffer RAM and then read them out again within one frame period of 125 μsec. If each of these memory accesses takes T microsec, the time needed to process a frame is $2nT$ microsec, so we have $2nT = 125$ or $n = 125/2T$. For a memory with 100 nsec cycle time, we can support at most 625 lines. We can also turn this relation around and use it to determine the required memory cycle to support a given number of lines. As with a crosspoint switch, it is possible to devise multistage switches that split the work up into several parts and then combine the results in order to handle larger numbers of lines.

2.6.5. The ISDN Interface

Let us now turn from PBX design to the ISDN interface. Remember that the goal of ISDN is to present the user with a digital bit pipe at either the T or S reference point. Before we look closely at this interface, it is worth noting that the term "interface" has a different meaning in the ISDN world than it has in the OSI world. In Fig. 2-29(a) we see the by now familiar OSI picture, in which the term "interface" refers to the boundary between two layers on the same machine. The horizontal lines are the peer protocols.

The CCITT view of the world is different. CCITT is primarily concerned with the interface between the carrier's equipment and the customer's equipment, so they have defined "interface" to mean the peer protocols in the lower layers, as shown in Fig. 2-29(b). When discussing ISDN, we will use "interface" in the CCITT sense.

ISDN is layered in a way similar to the OSI model, although the correspondence is far from exact and many of the ISDN protocols are unrelated to the OSI protocols found in the same layer. Like its OSI counterpart, the ISDN physical layer deals with the mechanical, electrical, functional, and procedural aspects of the interface. To start with, ISDN uses a new kind of connector, completely unrelated to the 25-, 37-, and 9-pin D connectors used for RS-232-C and RS-449. The ISDN connector has eight contacts. Two are used for transmit and transmit ground. Two more are used for receive and receive ground. The remaining four are used to

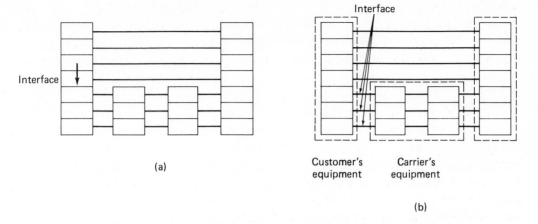

(a)

Customer's   Carrier's
equipment   equipment

(b)

Fig. 2-29. (a) Interfaces in the OSI model. (b) Interfaces in the ISDN model.

allow NT1 or NT2 to power the terminal or vice versa. By using this balanced transmission scheme, like RS-422-A, the ISDN cable can be 1 km long with good noise immunity.

As mentioned earlier, the ISDN bit pipe supports multiple channels interleaved by time division multiplexing. Several channel types have been standardized:

A - 4 kHz analog telephone channel
B - 64 kbps digital PCM channel for voice or data
C - 8 or 16 kbps digital channel
D - 16 or 64 kbps digital channel for out-of-band signaling
E - 64 kbps digital channel for internal ISDN signaling
H - 384, 1536, or 1920 kbps digital channel

It is not CCITT's intention to allow an arbitrary combination of channels on the digital bit pipe. Three combinations have been standardized so far:

1. **Basic rate**: 2B + 1D

2. **Primary rate**: 23B + 1D (U.S. and Japan) or 30B + 1D (Europe)

3. **Hybrid**: 1A + 1C

The basic rate and primary rate channels are illustrated in Fig. 2-30.

The basic rate should be viewed as a replacement for **POTS (Plain Old Telephone Service)** for home or small business use, and for individual employees in a large company. Each of the 64-kbps B channels can handle a single PCM voice channel with 8-bit samples made 8000 times a second (note that 64 kbps means 64,000 here, not 65,536). Signaling is on a separate D channel, so the full 64 kbps are available to the user (as in the CCITT 2.048 Mbps system and unlike the U.S. and Japanese T1 system).

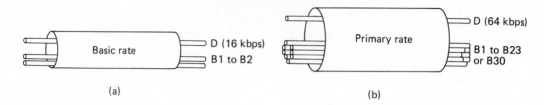

Fig. 2-30. (a) Basic rate digital pipe. (b) Primary rate digital pipe.

The idea of giving the user two channels instead of one is primarily for marketing reasons. Customers are encouraged to perceive the two ISDN channels as an improvement over the one channel POTS system. Without some visible improvement, the carrier might have a hard time convincing customers that ISDN is a good idea, since it is more expensive and many customers are not really all that interested in whether the signaling is analog or digital. A typical use for two channels might be for two people to talk on the telephone while looking at a document on the second channel. For data transmission, the B channels may be submultiplexed into 32 kbps, 16 kbps, or lower rates, but of course all the subchannels must begin and end at the same terminals.

The basic rate D channel is 16 kbps. Calls are requested by sending messages on it. A typical call-setup message would specify which of the B channels to use, the ISDN telephone number to call, and various other options (e.g., collect calls).

The D channel is divided into three logical subchannels: the *s* subchannel for signaling (e.g., call setup), the *t* subchannel for telemetry (e.g., smoke detectors), and the *p* subchannel for low bandwidth packet data.

The primary rate interface is intended for use at the T reference point for businesses with a PBX. It has 23 B channels and 1 D channel (at 64 kbps) in the U.S. and Japan and 30 B channels and 1 D channel (at 64 kbps) in Europe. The 23B + 1D choice was made to allow an ISDN frame fit nicely on AT&T's T1 system. The 30B + 1D choice was made to allow an ISDN frame fit nicely in CCITT's 2.048 Mbps system. The thirty-second time slot in the CCITT system is used for framing and general network maintenance. Note that the amount of D channel per B channel in the primary rate is much less than in the basic rate, so it is not expected that there will be much telemetry or low bandwidth packet data there.

The hybrid configuration is intended to allow ordinary analog telephones to be combined with a C channel to produce something vaguely reminiscent of the basic rate. It is not very close and everyone knows it, but it is better than nothing.

The physical layer frame format for basic rate traffic from NT1 or NT2 to TE1 is shown in Fig. 2-31. (TE to NT1 or NT2 traffic uses L instead of the E and S bits.) The frame is 48 bits, of which 36 are data. It is sent in 250 μsec, giving a data rate of 144 kbps, but occupying 192 kbps of bandwidth including the overhead. The F bits contain a well defined pattern to help keep both sides in synchronization. The L bits are there to adjust the average bit value (T1 systems do not like frames containing only 0s). The E bits are used for contention resolution when several terminals on a passive bus are contending for a channel. The A bit is used for activating devices. The S bits have not yet been assigned. Finally, the B1, B2, and D bits are for user data.

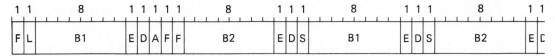

48 bits in 250 microsec = gross data rate of 192 kbps
36 data bits (16 B1, 16 B2, 4 D) in 250 microsec = net data rate of 144 kbps

F = Framing bit
L = DC load balancing
E = Echo of previous D bit (for contention resolution)
D = D channel (4 bits X 4000 frames/sec = 16 kbps)
A = Activation bit
S = Spare bit

Fig. 2-31. Physical layer frame format for basic rate NT to TE traffic at the S or T reference points.

It is important to realize that Fig. 2-31 is the physical layer frame format. The user data is just a raw bit stream. There is no error checking, no checksum, no redundancy, no acknowledgement, and no retransmission. If errors occur, they must be handled by higher layers in the OSI model. All ISDN does is provide the user with raw physical bit streams using the B channels (and to a lesser extent, the D channel).

The ISDN bit streams can be used to support either circuit switching or packet switching, depending on how bursty the traffic is. In the circuit switching scenario, the ISDN customer calls up the destination and uses a 64-kbps channel as a physical layer connection for transmitting digitized voice, data, or anything else. The entire 64-kbps is dedicated to the call throughout its duration. The charge will typically be proportional to both the duration of the call and the distance, but not to the volume of data sent.

In the packet-switching scenario, the ISDN customer calls up a nearby IMP. This connection is used to transmit packets from the customer's equipment to the IMP, which transmits them to the final destination via a traditional packet-switching network. The advantage of this scheme is that the call to the IMP will generally be a local call, so the charge for the service will be the cost of a local call plus a certain amount per packet. If the volume of traffic is low, for example, an interactive terminal, this method of usage may be cheaper.

When used to access a packet-switching network, the ISDN line is analogous a host-IMP link in the ARPANET. In effect, ISDN gives home users high-bandwidth access to a packet-switching network as well as the possibility of dialing direct calls where that is more appropriate. More information about the ISDN interface can be found in (Julio and Pellegrini, 1986; and Kano, 1986).

2.6.6. ISDN Signaling—SS #7

ISDN uses the out-of-band signaling concept pioneered by CCIS. Notice that this idea is quite different from how LANs are used, with data and control packets interleaved on the same cable (not to mention that data packets also have control information in their headers). The sequence of D bits, four per frame in Fig. 2-31, is viewed by ISDN as an independent digital channel with its own frame formats, messages, and so on. All the signaling (i.e., sending of control packets) is done on the D channel.

The full 64 kbps on each B channel can be regarded as pure user data, with no required headers or other overhead. ISDN does not specify the contents of the B channels. Put in other terms, for the B channels, ISDN only specifies the physical layer. If an ISDN customer calls up another ISDN customer they can format their channel into frames in any way. If an ISDN customer calls up a packet switching network or a database system, he will, of course, have to use the formats and protocols in layers 2 through 7 that are compatible with what the packet network or database system requires, but ISDN itself does not care.

The situation with the D channel is fundamentally different. The D channel is used by customers to communicate with the ISDN system itself. To place a call, for example, an ISDN device sends a packet in a certain format to NT1. The exact packet format, position of the callee's ISDN telephone number within the packet, and so on are specified in detail by CCITT recommendations. The format and content of packets exchanged by the customer and the carrier on the D channel are specified by CCITT **SS #7 (Signaling System Number 7)**, which was developed during the late 1970s.

SS #7 is a strange system. It was originally based on SS #6, the international version of CCIS, but has been (and is still being) modified to make it fit the OSI model better. Initially, SS #7 had four layers, the lowest three of which were functionally somewhat similar to X.25. The top layer, called the **user part**, was a gigantic unstructured mess, containing everything not directly connected with controlling the network. Recently, some protocol suites have been defined within the user part to perform specific applications. Nevertheless, SS #7 basically remains a scheme for controlling telephone switching equipment, not a general purpose computer-to-computer communication scheme.

The SS #7 protocol hierarchy is shown in Fig. 2-32. We have already seen the format of the physical layer bit stream in Fig. 2-31. The principal layer 2 protocol is LAPD, which is similar to the X.25 layer 2 protocol LAPB (see Chapter 4). LAPB and LAPD are concerned with delimiting frames, assigning sequence numbers to each one, computing and verifying checksums, and in general converting the potentially error prone bit stream provided by layer 1 into a reliable, sequenced frame stream for use by layer 3.

SS #7 layer 3 is divided into two sublayers. The bottom one is concerned with routing calls and messages through the network of telephone exchanges. In

it puts a polling message addressed to its neighbor on the line. If this terminal is also idle, it sends a poll to its neighbor (on the controller side). The poll propagates from terminal to terminal until one can be found that has something to say or until the poll gets back to the controller. The advantage here is that it is not necessary to keep turning the line around just to discover that a terminal has nothing to say. Sometimes hub polling uses a separate side channel for the polls.

For the case of a star controller, as in Fig. 2-33(b), polling is not required to avoid chaos on the lines. Nevertheless, roll-call polling is often used anyway, to allow the master to acquire input in an orderly fashion. These poll messages differ from those of the multidrop case because there are no site addresses needed; a terminal only receives those polls directed to it.

The **BISYNC** (**BI**nary **SYN**chronous **Communication**) protocol, developed by IBM, is widely used in the computer industry for polling remote terminals, as well as for other applications. It is intended for lines operating in half-duplex mode, either multidrop or point-to-point. BISYNC supports three character sets: ASCII, EBCDIC, and IBM's 6-bit Transcode.

The BISYNC message format is shown in Fig. 2-34. The contents of the header field are up to the network; they are not defined by the protocol. ETB is used to terminate a block when there are more blocks to follow. ETX is used to terminate the last block. Addressing of terminals on a multidrop line is not done in the header, but by a separate control message.

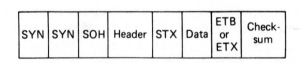

SYN = SYNchronize
SOH = Start Of Header
STX = Start of TeXt
ETB = End of Transmission Block
ETX = End of TeXt

Fig. 2-34. BISYNC message format.

When ASCII code is used, the parity bit is set and the checksum is simply a vertical parity check. With EBCDIC or 6-bit Transcode, the individual characters are not parity-checked. Instead cyclic redundancy checksums are used. These checksums will be described in Chapter 4.

2.7.2. Multiplexing versus Concentration

Terminal controllers can be divided into two general classes, multiplexers and concentrators. A **multiplexer** is a device that accepts input from a collection of lines in some static, predetermined sequence, and outputs the data onto a single output line in the same sequence. Since each output time slot is dedicated to a specific input line, there is no need to transmit the input line numbers. The output line must have the same capacity as the sum of the input line capacities. Figure 2-35(a) depicts a multiplexer with four terminals. With four-terminal TDM, each terminal is allocated one-fourth of the output time slots, regardless of how busy it is. If each of the terminals operates at 1200 bps, the output line must be $4 \times 1200 = 4800$ bps, since four characters *must* be sent during each polling cycle.

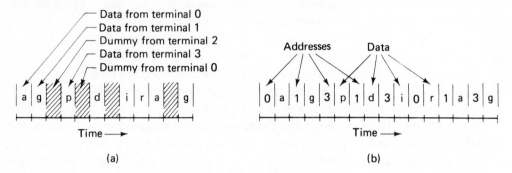

Fig. 2-35. (a) Four terminal multiplexing. (b) Four terminal concentration.

The big disadvantage of TDM is that when a terminal has no traffic, an output time slot is wasted. The output slots are filled in strict rotation, as in Fig. 2-35(a). If there are no data, dummy characters are used. It is not possible to skip a time slot, because the receiving end keeps track of which character came from which terminal by its position in the output stream. Initially, the multiplexer and the computer synchronize themselves. Both know that the order to be used, for example, is 012301230123 .... The data themselves carry no identification of their origin. If the multiplexer skipped a time slot when there were no data from a terminal, the receiver would get out of phase and interpret the origin of succeeding characters incorrectly.

If each terminal has traffic only a small fraction of the time, TDM makes inefficient use of the output line capacity. When the actual traffic is far below the potential traffic, most of the time slots on the output line are wasted. Consequently, it is often possible to use an output line with less capacity than the sum of the input lines. This arrangement is called **concentration**. The usual approach is to only transmit actual data and not dummy characters. However, this strategy introduces the problem of telling the receiver which character came from which input line. One solution to this problem is to send two output characters for each input character: the terminal number and the data. Figure 2-35(b) shows what the output might look like if each data character were preceded by its terminal number. Concentrators using this principle are often referred to as **statistical multiplexers** or **ATDMs (Asynchronous Time Division Multiplexers)**, in contrast with the true (synchronous) multiplexers, or **STDMs**, although strictly speaking, a statistical multiplexer that had as much output capacity as input capacity would not be a concentrator.

Unfortunately, concentration has an inherent difficulty. If each terminal suddenly starts outputting data at its maximum rate, there will be insufficient capacity on the output line to handle it all. Some data may be lost. For this reason, concentrators are always provided with extra buffers in order to survive short data surges. The more memory a concentrator has, the more it costs but the less likely it is to lose data. Choosing the appropriate parameters for the output line bandwidth and concentrator memory size involves trade-offs. If either is too small, data may be lost. If either is too large, the whole arrangement may be unnecessarily expensive. Furthermore, the optimum choices depend on the traffic statistics, which are not always known at system design time.

2.8. SUMMARY

In this chapter we have studied the physical layer and some of the more common physical layer protocols. We began with a look at the theory behind data communications and saw two fundamental limits that Mother Nature puts on the bandwidth of a channel, the Shannon limit and the Nyquist limit. Then we enumerated some of the principal transmission media, including twisted pair, coaxial cable, fiber optics, microwave, and satellite.

The next two sections dealt with analog and digital transmission over these media. Analog transmission uses modems to convert binary data to analog form for transmission over a telephone line. The most important standards here are RS-232-C and RS-449. Digital transmission typically uses PCM, with or without encoding schemes such as delta modulation and predictive coding to reduce the bandwidth needed. Both circuit switching and packet switching were discussed.

In the future, the telephone system will be digital from end to end, and will carry both voice and nonvoice traffic over the same lines. This new system is known as ISDN, and was discussed at some length. Finally, the issue of terminal handling was covered, along with multiplexing and concentration.

PROBLEMS

1. Compute the Fourier coefficients for the function $f(t) = t$ $(0 \leq t \leq 1)$.

2. A noiseless 4-kHz channel is sampled every millisecond. What is the maximum data rate?

3. Television channels are 6 MHz wide. How many bits/sec can be sent if four-level digital signals are used?

4. If a binary signal is sent over a 3-kHz channel whose signal-to-noise ratio is 20 dB, what is the maximum achievable data rate?

5. What signal-to-noise ratio is needed to put a T1 carrier on a 50-kHz line?

6. A simple telephone system consists of two end offices and a single toll office to which each end office is connected by a 1-MHz full-duplex trunk. The average telephone is used to make four calls per 8-hour workday. The mean call duration is 6 min. Ten percent of the calls are long-distance (i.e., pass through the toll office). What is the maximum number of telephones an end office can support? (Assume 4 kHz per circuit.)

7. Why has the PCM sampling time been set at 125 μsec?

8. What is the percent overhead on a T1 carrier, that is, what percent of the 1.544 Mbps are not delivered to the end user?

9. Compare the maximum data rate of a noiseless 4-kHz channel using:
   (a) Analog encoding with 2 bits per sample.
   (b) The T1 PCM system.

10. What is the difference, if any, between the demodulator part of a modem and the coder part of a codec? (After all, both convert analog signals to digital ones.)

11. A signal is transmitted digitally over a 4-kHz noiseless channel with one sample every 125 μsec. How many bits per second are actually sent for each of these encoding methods?
    (a) CCITT 2.048 Mbps standard.
    (b) DPCM with a 4-bit relative signal value.
    (c) Delta modulation.

12. A pure sine wave of amplitude A is encoded using delta modulation, with x samples/sec. An output of $+1$ corresponds to a signal change of $+A/8$, and an output signal of -1 corresponds to a signal change of $-A/8$. What is the highest frequency that can be tracked without cumulative error?

13. Figure 2-19 depicts the events happening at the calling DTE during call setup but does not show what the sequence is at the receiving DTE. Make a proposal for a scheme that would allow the receiving DTE to answer calls, accepting or rejecting reverse charging if requested.

14. Sketch the Manchester encoding for the bit stream: 0001110101.

15. Sketch the differential Manchester encoding for the bit stream of the previous problem. Assume the line is initially in the low state.

16. What is the difference between a passive star and an active repeater in a fiber optic network?

17. The cost of a powerful microprocessor has dropped to the point where it is now possible to include one in each modem. How does that affect the handling of telephone line errors?

18. A modem constellation diagram similar to Fig. 2-13 has data points at the following coordinates: $(1, 1)$, $(1, -1)$, $(-1, 1)$, and $(-1, -1)$. How many bps can a modem with these parameters achieve at 1200 baud?

19. A modem constellation diagram similar to Fig. 2-13 has data points at (0, 1) and (0, 2). Does the modem use phase modulation or amplitude modulation?

20. Three packet switching networks each contain n nodes. The first network has a star topology with a central switch, the second is a (bidirectional) ring, and the third is fully interconnected, with a wire from every node to every other node. What are the best, average, and worst case transmission paths in hops?

21. Compare the delay in sending an x-bit message over a k-hop path in a circuit-switched network and in a (lightly loaded) packet-switched network. The circuit set up time is s sec, the propagation delay is d sec per hop, the packet size is p bits, and the data rate is b bps. Under what conditions does the packet network have a lower delay?

22. Suppose that x bits of user data are to be transmitted over a k-hop path in a packet-switched network as a series of packets, each containing p data bits and h header bits, with $x \gg p + h$. The bit rate of the lines is b bps and the propagation delay is negligible. What value of p minimizes the total delay?

23. How long does it take to transmit an 8 inch by 10 inch image by facsimile over an ISDN B channel? The facsimile digitizes the image into 300 pixels per inch and assigns 4 bits per pixel.

24. Give an advantage and a disadvantage of NT12 (as opposed to NT1 and NT2) in an ISDN network.

25. How many lines can a PBX handle using time division switching if the RAM access time is 50 nsec?

26. How many bits of RAM buffer does a time switch interchanger need if the input line samples are 10 bits and there are 80 input lines?

27. A terminal multiplexer has six 1200-bps terminals and n 300-bps terminals connected to it. The outgoing line is 9600 bps. What is the maximum value of n?

28. Write a procedure that computes the value of a periodic function after it has been passed through a low-pass filter. The function itself, its period, and the cutoff frequency are parameters to your procedure.

29. Write a procedure that encodes an input function using delta modulation. The number of digitization levels and the interval between layers should be given as procedure inputs. Use half the levels for positive and half for negative values. The sampling interval should also be a parameter.

30. Write a program to simulate the behavior of a concentrator with n input lines. Assume a Poisson arrival pattern (see the Appendix) but fixed-length messages. Simulate the concentrator for various loads, and compare the measured mean queue length with that predicted by queueing theory.

3

THE MEDIUM ACCESS SUBLAYER

Networks can be divided into two categories: those using point-to-point connections and those using broadcast channels. This chapter deals with broadcast networks and their protocols.

In any broadcast network, the key issue is how to determine who gets to use the channel when there is competition for it. To make this point clearer, consider a conference call in which six people, on six different telephones, are all connected together so that each one can hear and talk to all the others. It is very likely that when one of them stops speaking, two or more will start talking at once, leading to chaos. In a face-to-face meeting, chaos is avoided by external means, for example people raise their hands to request permission to speak. When only a single channel is available, determining who should go next is much harder. Many protocols for solving the problem are known, and form the contents of this chapter. In the literature, broadcast channels are sometimes referred to as **multiaccess channels** or **random access channels**. Some general references are (Abramson, 1985; Gallager, 1985; Mehravari, 1984; Tobagi et al., 1984; and Tsybakov, 1985).

3.1. LOCAL AND METROPOLITAN AREA NETWORKS

This book is organized according to the layers of the OSI model. This chapter deals with what is called the **MAC (Medium Access Control)** sublayer. The MAC sublayer is especially important in LANs, nearly all of which use a multiaccess channel as the basis of their communication. WANs, in contrast, use point-to-point links, except for satellite networks. Because multiaccess channels and LANs are so closely related, we will use this chapter for discussing LANs in general, as well as satellite and some other broadcast networks.

To start off, let us say what we mean by a local area network. LANs generally have three characteristic features:

1. A diameter of not more than a few kilometers.

2. A total data rate of at least several Mbps.

3. Complete ownership by a single organization.

WANs in contrast, typically span entire countries, have data rates below 1 Mbps, and are owned by multiple organizations (the carrier owns the communications subnet and numerous clients own the hosts).

In between the LAN and the WAN is the **MAN** (**Metropolitan Area Network**). A MAN is a network that covers an entire city, but uses LAN technology. Cable television (CATV) networks are examples of analog MANs for television distribution. The MANs we are interested in are digital and are intended to connect computers together, not televisions sets, although some of them may use broadband coaxial cable as the transmission medium. Most of the discussion on LAN protocols in this chapter also holds for MANs, so we will not mention the latter explicitly much more.

Why is anyone interested in building a LAN? Basically the reasons are the same as for building networks in general. In some cases, the purpose of the LAN is to connect existing machines together, for example, departmental computers on a campus, to allow all of them to communicate. In other cases, incremental growth is the goal. In still others, the superior price/performance ratio of a network of workstations is the attractions. In any event, there is a great deal of interest in LANs nowadays.

Local area networks differ from their wide area cousins in several ways. The key difference is that WAN designers are nearly always forced by legal, economic, or political reasons to use the existing public telephone network, regardless of its technical suitability. In contrast, nothing prevents LAN designers from laying their own high-bandwidth cable, which they nearly always do.

From this one difference spring numerous advantages. To start with, bandwidth is no longer the precious resource that it is in the long-haul case, so the protocol designers do not have to stand on their heads to squeeze out the last drop of performance. Quite different, and usually much simpler, protocols can be used, making the implementation easier.

Another difference is that LAN cable is highly reliable; error rates 1000 times lower than in WANs are normal. This difference also impacts the protocols. With WANs, the low reliability means that error handling must be done in each layer.

With LANs, it may be sufficient to skip the error checking in the lower layers and just do it higher up, leading to simpler and more efficient protocols in the lower layers.

3.1.1. Static Channel Allocation in LANs and MANs

Let us now get back to the central theme of this chapter: how to allocate a single broadcast channel among competing users. The traditional way of allocating a single channel, such as a telephone trunk, among multiple competing users is **FDM** (**Frequency-Division Multiplexing**). If there are N users, the bandwidth is divided into N equal sized portions (see Fig. 2-21) each user being assigned one portion. Since each user has his own private frequency band, there is no interference between users. When there is only a small and fixed number of users, and each of which has a heavy (buffered) load of traffic (e.g., carriers' switching offices), FDM is a simple and efficient allocation mechanism.

However, when the number of stations is large and continuously varying, or the traffic is bursty, FDM presents some problems. If the spectrum is cut up into N regions, and fewer than N users are currently interested in communicating, a large piece of valuable spectrum will be wasted. If more than N users want to communicate, some of them will be denied permission, for lack of bandwidth, even if some of the users who have been assigned a frequency band hardly ever transmit or receive anything.

However, even assuming that the number of users could somehow be held constant at N, dividing the single available channel into static subchannels is inherently inefficient. The basic problem is that when some users are quiescent, their bandwidth is simply lost. They are not using it, and no one else is allowed to use it either. Furthermore, in most computer systems, data traffic is extremely bursty (peak traffic to mean traffic ratios of 1000:1 are common). Consequently, most of the channels will be idle most of the time.

The poor performance of static FDM can easily be seen from a simple queueing theory calculation. (If you are not familiar with queueing theory, please read the Appendix.) Let us start with the mean time delay, T, for a channel of capacity C bps, with an arrival rate of λ frames/sec, each frame† having a length drawn from an exponential probability density function with mean $1/\mu$ bits/frame:

$$T = \frac{1}{\mu C - \lambda}$$

Now let us divide the single channel up into N independent subchannels, each with

---

† Since this chapter deals with the MAC sublayer, we will use the term "frame" when referring to the transmission units, except for "packet radio" which is a well established term.

capacity C/N bps. The mean input rate on each of the subchannels will now be λ/N. Recomputing T we get

$$T_{\text{FDM}} = \frac{1}{\mu(C/N) - (\lambda/N)} = \frac{N}{\mu C - \lambda} = NT \tag{3-1}$$

The mean delay using FDM is N times worse than if all the frames were somehow magically orderly arranged in a big central queue.

Precisely the same arguments that apply to FDM also apply to synchronous time-division multiplexing. Each user is statically allocated every Nth time slot. If a user does not use his allocation, it just lies fallow.

At first it might appear that asynchronous time-division multiplexing (concentration) could be used, but there is a problem here, too. In the traditional ATDM scheme, each terminal has a private (dedicated) port into the concentrator (see Fig. 2-34). If two terminals decide to send characters simultaneously, each one is loaded into a different memory location in the concentrator for queueing and subsequent transmission. Even if all terminals transmit at once, there will be no collisions at the concentrator. If there is sufficient memory, all terminals may send continuously indefinitely with no data loss. With uncoordinated, geographically dispersed users who have only a single shared channel to communicate on, there is no private port, and two simultaneous transmissions will collide.

To avoid conflicts, we could give each user a private portion of the spectrum, but this is just FDM, which we have already shown to be inefficient with many bursty users. None of the traditional data communication methods works here. We need a genuinely new channel allocation method.

3.1.2. Dynamic Channel Allocation in LANs and MANs

Before we get into the first of the many channel allocation methods to be discussed in this chapter, it is worthwhile carefully formulating the allocation problem. Underlying all the work done in this area are five key assumptions, described below.

1. **Station model**. The model consists of N independent **stations** (computers or terminals), each with a program or user that generates frames for transmission. The probability of a frame being generated in an interval of length Δt is $\lambda \Delta t$, where λ is a constant (the arrival rate of new frames). Once a frame has been generated, the station is blocked and does nothing until the frame has been successfully transmitted.

2. **Single Channel Assumption**. A single channel is available for all communication. All stations can transmit on it and all can receive from it. As far as the hardware is concerned, all stations are equivalent, although protocol software may assign priorities to them.

3.   **Collision Assumption**. If two frames are transmitted simultaneously, they overlap in time and the resulting signal is garbled. This event is called a **collision**. All stations can detect collisions. A collided frame must be transmitted again later. There are no errors other than those generated by collisions.

4a. **Continuous Time**. Frame transmission can begin at any instant. There is no master clock dividing time into discrete intervals.

4b. **Slotted Time**. Time is divided into discrete intervals (slots). Frame transmissions always begin at the start of a slot. A slot may contain 0, 1, or more frames, corresponding to an idle slot a successful transmission, or a collision, respectively.

5a. **Carrier Sense**. Stations can tell if the channel is in use before trying to use it. If the channel is sensed as busy, no station will attempt to use it until it goes idle.

5b. **No Carrier Sense**. Stations cannot sense the channel before trying to use it. They just go ahead and transmit. Only later can they determine whether or not the transmission was successful.

Some discussion of these assumptions is in order. The first one says that stations are independent, and that work is generated at a constant rate. It also implicitly assumes that each station only has one program or user, so while the station is blocked, no new work is generated. More sophisticated models allow multiprogrammed stations that can generate work while a station is blocked, but the analysis of these stations is much more complex.

The single channel assumption is the heart of the matter. There are no external ways to communicate. Stations cannot raise their hands to request that the teacher call on them.

The collision assumption is also basic, although in some systems (notably packet radio), when a collision occurs, stronger signals can still be detected. This is known as the **capture effect**, but we will ignore it until we come to packet radio late in the chapter.

There are two alternative assumptions about time. Either it is continuous or it is slotted. Some systems use one and some systems use the other, so we will discuss and analyze both. Obviously, for a given system, only one of them holds.

Similarly, a network can either have carrier sensing or not, but not both. LANs generally have carrier sense, but satellite networks do not (due to the long propagation delay). Stations on carrier sense networks can terminate their transmission prematurely if they discover that it is colliding with another transmission. Note that the word "carrier" in this sense refers to an electrical signal on the cable, and has nothing to do with the common carriers (e.g., telephone companies) that date back to the Pony Express days.

3.2. ALOHA PROTOCOLS

In the 1970s, Norman Abramson and his colleagues at the University of Hawaii devised a new and elegant method to solve the channel allocation problem. Their work has been extended by many researchers since then (Abramson, 1985). Although Abramson's work, called the ALOHA system, used ground-based radio broadcasting, the basic idea is applicable to any system in which uncoordinated users are competing for the use of a single shared channel. We will examine ground radio in general and the University of Hawaii ALOHA system in particular, later in this chapter.

3.2.1. Pure ALOHA and Slotted ALOHA

The basic idea of an ALOHA system is simple: let users transmit whenever they have data to be sent. There will be collisions, of course, and the colliding frames will be destroyed. However, due to the feedback property of broadcasting, a sender can always find out whether or not its frame was destroyed by listening to the channel output. With a LAN, the feedback is immediate; with a satellite, there is a delay of 270 msec before the sender knows if the transmission was successful. If the frame was destroyed, the sender just waits a random amount of time and sends it again. The waiting time must be random or the same frames will collide over and over, in lockstep. Systems in which multiple users share a common channel in a way that can lead to conflicts are widely known as **contention** systems.

A sketch of frame generation in an ALOHA system is given in Fig. 3-1. We have made the frames all the same length because the throughput of ALOHA systems is maximized by having a uniform frame size rather than allowing variable length frames.

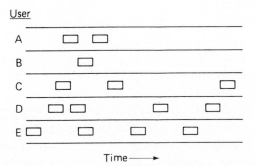

Fig. 3-1. In pure ALOHA, frames are transmitted at completely arbitrary times.

Whenever two frames try to occupy the channel at the same time there will be a collision and both will be garbled. You should realize that if the first bit of a new frame overlaps with just the last bit of a frame almost finished, both frames will be totally destroyed, and both will have to be retransmitted later. The checksum cannot (and should not) distinguish between a total loss and a near miss. Bad is bad.

A most interesting question is: What is the efficiency of an ALOHA channel? That is, what fraction of all transmitted frames escape collisions under these chaotic circumstances? Let us first consider an infinite collection of interactive users sitting at their terminals (stations). A user is always in one of two states: thinking or blocked. Initially, all users are in the thinking state. Whenever someone decides what to do next, he types a line of text followed by a carriage return. At this point he is blocked and stops thinking. The microcomputer inside the terminal immediately locks the keyboard to prevent any more input. It then transmits a frame containing the line and checks the channel to see if it was successful. If so, the user's keyboard is unlocked. If not, the keyboard remains locked and the frame is retransmitted over and over until it has been successfully sent.

Let the "frame time" denote the amount of time needed to transmit the standard, fixed-length frame (i.e., the frame length divided by the bit rate). At this point we assume that the infinite population of users generates new frames according to a Poisson distribution with mean S frames per frame time. (The infinite-population assumption is needed to ensure that S does not decrease as users become blocked.) If $S > 1$, the user community is generating frames at a higher rate than the channel can handle, and nearly every frame will suffer a collision. For reasonable throughput we would expect $0 < S < 1$.

In addition to the new frames, the stations also generate retransmissions of frames that previously suffered collisions. Let us further assume that the probability of k transmission attempts per frame time, old and new combined, is also Poisson, with mean G per frame time. Clearly, $G \geq S$. At low load (i.e., $S \approx 0$), there will be few collisions, hence few retransmissions, so $G \approx S$. At high load there will be many collisions, so $G > S$. Under all loads, the throughput is just the offered load, G, times the probability of a transmission being successful—that is, $S = GP_0$, where P_0 is the probability that a frame does not suffer a collision.

A frame will not suffer a collision if no other frames are sent within one frame time of its start, as shown in Fig. 3-2. Under what conditions will the shaded frame arrive undamaged? Let t be the time required to send a frame. If any other user has generated a frame between time t_0 and $t_0 + t$, the end of that frame will collide with the beginning of the shaded one. In fact, the shaded frame's fate was already sealed even before the first bit was sent, but since in pure ALOHA a station does not listen to the channel before transmitting, it has no way of knowing that another frame was already underway. Similarly, any other frame started between $t_0 + t$ and $t_0 + 2t$ will bump into the end of the shaded frame.

The probability that k frames are generated during a given frame time is given by the Poisson distribution:

$$\Pr[k] = \frac{G^k e^{-G}}{k!} \qquad (3\text{-}2)$$

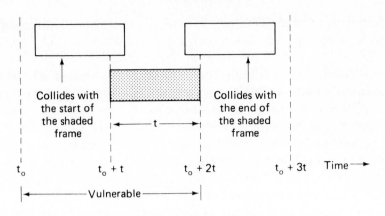

Fig. 3-2. Vulnerable period for the shaded frame.

so the probability of zero frames is just e^{-G}. In an interval two frame times long, the mean number of frames generated is $2G$. The probability of no other traffic being initiated during the entire vulnerable period is thus given by $P_0 = e^{-2G}$. Using $S = GP_0$, we get

$$S = Ge^{-2G}$$

The relation between the offered traffic and the throughput is shown in Fig. 3-3. The maximum throughput occurs at $G = 0.5$, with $S = 1/(2e)$, which is about 0.184. In other words, the best we can hope for is a channel utilization of 18%. This result is not very encouraging, but with everyone transmitting whenever he wants to, we could hardly have expected a 100% success rate.

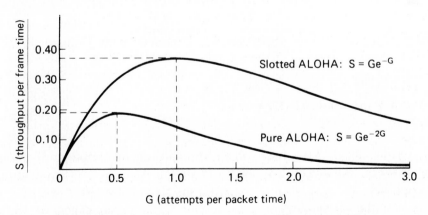

Fig. 3-3. Throughput versus offered traffic for ALOHA systems.

In 1972, Roberts published a method for doubling the capacity of an ALOHA system. His proposal was to divide time up into discrete intervals, each interval corresponding to one frame. One way to achieve synchronization among the users would be to have one special station emit a pip at the start of each interval, like a clock.

In Roberts' method, which has come to be known as **slotted ALOHA**, in contrast to Abramson's **pure ALOHA**, a terminal is not permitted to send whenever a carriage return is typed. Instead, it is required to wait for the beginning of the next slot. Thus the continuous pure ALOHA is turned into a discrete one. Since the vulnerable period is now reduced in half, the probability of no other traffic during the same slot as our test frame is e^{-G} which leads to

$$S = Ge^{-G} \qquad (3\text{-}3)$$

As you can see from Fig. 3-3, slotted ALOHA peaks at $G = 1$, with a throughput of $S = 1/e$ or about 0.368, twice that of pure ALOHA. If the system is operating at $G = 1$, the probability of an empty slot is 0.368 (from Eq. 3-2). The best we can hope for using slotted ALOHA is 37% of the slots empty, 37% successes, and 26% collisions. Operating at higher values of G reduces the number of empties but increases the number of collisions exponentially. To see how this rapid growth of collisions with G comes about, consider the transmission of a test frame. The probability that it will avoid a collision is e^{-G}, the probability that all the other users are silent in that slot. The probability of a collision is then just $1 - e^{-G}$. The probability of a transmission requiring exactly k attempts, (i.e., $k - 1$ collisions followed by one success) is

$$P_k = e^{-G}(1 - e^{-G})^{k-1}$$

The expected number of transmissions, E, per carriage return typed is then

$$E = \sum_{k=1}^{\infty} kP_k = \sum_{k=1}^{\infty} ke^{-G}(1 - e^{-G})^{k-1} = e^G$$

As a result of the exponential dependence of E upon G, small increases in the channel load can drastically reduce its performance.

3.2.2. Finite Population ALOHA

The results above have been obtained using the assumption of an infinite number of users. Abramson also analyzed slotted ALOHA systems with a finite number of users. We now briefly summarize his results (see also Abramson, 1985).

Let S_i be the probability of a successful transmission generated by user i. Remember that at equilibrium the throughput rate must equal the rate at which new frames are generated. Let G_i be the total transmission probability (per slot) of user i, including both new frames and retransmissions. Clearly, $S_i \leq G_i$. The probability that a given slot will contain a successful frame sent by user i is the probability that user i sends a frame, times the probability that none of the $N-1$ other users sends a frame:

$$S_i = G_i \prod_{j \neq i}(1 - G_j) \tag{3-4}$$

Let us now specialize Eq. (3-4) to the case of N identical users, each having a throughput of $S_i = S/N$ frames/slot and a total transmission rate of $G_i = G/N$ frames/slot, where $G = \Sigma G_i$. Substituting into Eq. (3-4), we get

$$S = G\left[1 - \frac{G}{N}\right]^{N-1}$$

As $N \to \infty$, we can use the fact that

$$\lim_{k \to \infty}\left[1 + \frac{x}{k}\right]^k = e^x$$

to arrive at Eq. (3-3).

From Fig. 3-3 we see that the maximum throughput for an infinite-population slotted ALOHA system occurs at $G = 1$. This intuitively reasonable result also holds for systems with a finite number of users. The condition for maximum throughput is

$$\sum_{i=1}^{N} G_i = 1 \tag{3-5}$$

Now let us consider two classes of users, for example file transfer users and interactive users. Let there be N_1 of the first kind and N_2 of the second, with throughput S_1 and S_2 respectively (per user). Then Eq. (3-4) reduces to

$$S_1 = G_1(1 - G_1)^{N_1 - 1}(1 - G_2)^{N_2} \tag{3-6}$$

and

$$S_2 = G_2(1 - G_2)^{N_2 - 1}(1 - G_1)^{N_1} \tag{3-7}$$

For maximum throughput, we must obey Eq. (3-5), which becomes

$$N_1 G_1 + N_2 G_2 = 1 \tag{3-8}$$

We now have three equations in four unknowns (S_1, S_2, G_1, G_2). By using Eq. (3-8), we can eliminate G_2 from the two-class throughput equations [Eqs. (3-6) and (3-7)] to yield parametric equations for the throughput, parametrized by G_1.

As a first example, consider $N_1 = 1$ and $N_2 = 1$. This leads to $S_1 = G_1^2$ and $S_2 = (1 - G_1)^2$. S_1, S_2 and $S = S_1 + S_2$ are plotted in Fig. 3-4(a). Notice that when G_1 is close to 0, user 1 hardly ever attempts to send, and user 2 is free to use nearly every slot, so the total throughput is close to one frame per slot. The worst case is when both users attempt to send on every slot with a probability of 0.5. If that happens, there is a 25% chance that user 1 will try and user 2 will refrain. Similarly, there is a 25% chance that user 2 will try and user 1 will refrain. The total throughput is therefore 0.5 frame per slot. The conclusion to be drawn from this example is that an asymmetric situation yields a higher throughput than does a symmetric one. Later we will see algorithms that exploit this fact.

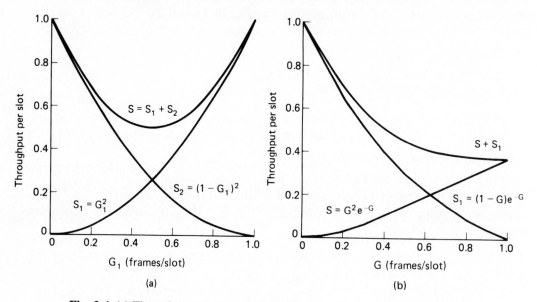

Fig. 3-4. (a) Throughput of a two-user ALOHA system. (b) Throughput of an ALOHA system with one large and many small users.

Next let us specialize Eqs. (3-6) and (3-7) to the case of $N_1 = 1$ and $N_2 = \infty$. User 1 might be trying to transfer a large file, whereas the remaining users are doing interactive work. To keep the total traffic finite, we must let $G_2 \rightarrow 0$ in such a way that $G = N_2 G_2$ remains finite. Letting $S = N_2 S_2$ we get

$$S_1 = G_1 e^{-G}$$

and

$$S = Ge^{-G}(1 - G_1)$$

The condition for maximum total throughput is now $G_1 + G = 1$, which allows us to plot S_1, S, and the total throughput, $S_1 + S$, as a function of G. This plot is given in Fig. 3-4(b). When G is small, the interactive users are not doing much, and the single "large" user can continuously send frames without collisions, thus achieving a very high total channel utilization. As G increases, the interactive traffic claims a larger portion of the available bandwidth and the large user is forced to send less to maintain the total offered traffic at one frame per slot.

3.3. LOCAL AREA NETWORK PROTOCOLS

With slotted ALOHA the best channel utilization that can be achieved is $1/e$. This is hardly surprising, since with stations transmitting at will, without paying attention to what the other stations are doing, there are bound to be many collisions. In local area networks, however it is possible for stations to detect what other stations are doing, and adapt their behavior accordingly. These networks can achieve a much better utilization than $1/e$. In Sec. 3-3, we will study LAN protocols in general. In Sec. 3-4, we will look at some standards in this area.

3.3.1. Persistent and Nonpersistent CSMA

Protocols in which stations listen for a carrier (i.e., a transmission) and act accordingly are called **carrier sense protocols**. Kleinrock and Tobagi (1975) have analyzed several such protocols in detail.

The first carrier sense protocol is **1-persistent CSMA** (Carrier Sense Multiple Access). When a station has data to send, it first listens to the channel to see if anyone else is transmitting. If the channel is busy, the station waits until it becomes idle. When the station detects an idle channel, it transmits a frame. If a collision occurs, the station waits a random amount of time and starts all over again. The protocol is called 1-persistent because the station transmits with a probability of 1 whenever it finds the channel idle.

The propagation delay has an important effect on the performance of the protocol. There is a small chance that just after a station begins sending, another station will become ready to send and sense the channel. If the first station's signal has not yet reached the second one, the latter will sense an idle channel and will also begin sending, resulting in a collision. The longer the propagation delay is, the more important this effect becomes, and the worse the performance of the protocol.

Even if the propagation delay is zero, there will still be collisions. If two stations become ready in the middle of a third station's transmission, both will wait politely until the transmission ends and then both will begin transmitting exactly simultaneously, resulting in a collision. If they were not so impatient, there would be fewer collisions. Even so, this protocol is far better than pure ALOHA, because both stations have the decency to desist from interfering with the third station's frame. Intuitively, this will lead to a higher performance than pure ALOHA. Exactly the same holds for slotted ALOHA.

A second carrier sense protocol is **nonpersistent CSMA**. In this protocol, a conscious attempt is made to be less greedy than in the previous one. Before sending, a station senses the channel. If no one else is sending, the station begins doing so itself. However, if the channel is already in use, the station does not continually sense it for the purpose of seizing it immediately upon detecting the end of the previous transmission. Instead, it waits a random period of time and then repeats the algorithm. Intuitively this algorithm should lead to better channel utilization and longer delays than 1-persistent CSMA.

The last protocol is **p-persistent CSMA**. It applies to slotted channels and works as follows. When a station becomes ready to send, it senses the channel. If it is idle, it transmits with a probability p. With a probability $q = 1 - p$ it defers until the next slot. If that slot is also idle, it either transmits or defers again, with probabilities p and q. This process is repeated until either the frame has been transmitted or another station has begun transmitting. In the latter case, it acts as if there had been a collision (i.e., it waits a random time and starts again). If the station initially senses the channel busy, it waits until the next slot and applies the above algorithm. Figure 3-5 shows the throughput versus offered traffic for all three protocols, as well as pure and slotted ALOHA.

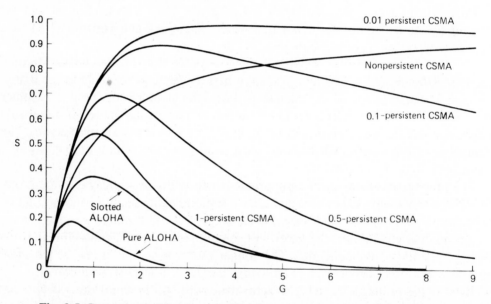

Fig. 3-5. Comparison of the channel utilization versus load for various random access protocols.

3.3.2. CSMA with Collision Detection

Persistent and nonpersistent CSMA protocols are clearly an improvement over ALOHA because they ensure that no station begins to transmit when it senses the channel busy. Another improvement is for stations to abort their transmissions as soon as they detect a collision. In other words, if two stations sense the channel to be idle and begin transmitting simultaneously they will both detect the collision almost immediately. Rather than finish transmitting their frames, which are irretrievably garbled anyway, they should abruptly stop transmitting as soon as the collision is detected. Quickly terminating damaged frames saves time and bandwidth. This protocol, known as **CSMA/CD (Carrier Sense Multiple Access with Collision Detection)**, is widely used on LANs in the MAC sublayer.

CSMA/CD, as well as many other LAN protocols, uses the conceptual model of Fig. 3-6. At the point marked t_0, a station has finished transmitting its frame. Any other station having a frame to send may now attempt to do so. If two or more stations decide to transmit simultaneously, there will be a collision. Each will detect the collision, abort its transmission, wait a random period of time, and then try again, assuming that no other station has started transmitting in the meantime. Therefore, our model for CSMA/CD will consist of alternating contention and transmission periods, with idle periods occurring when all stations are quiet (e.g., for lack of work).

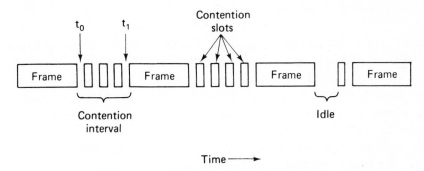

Fig. 3-6. CSMA/CD can be in one of three states: contention, transmission, or idle.

Now let us look closely at the details of the contention algorithm. Suppose that two stations both begin transmitting at exactly time t_0. How long will it take them to realize that there has been a collision? The answer to this question is vital to determining the length of the contention period, and hence what the delay and throughput will be. The minimum time to detect the collision is then just the time it takes the signal to propagate from one station to the other.

Based on this reasoning, you might think that a station not hearing a collision for a time equal to the full cable propagation time after starting its transmission could be sure it had seized the cable. By "seized," we mean that all other stations knew it was transmitting and would not interfere. This conclusion is wrong. Consider the following worst-case scenario. Let the time for a signal to propagate between the two farthest stations be τ. At t_0, one station begins transmitting. At $\tau - \varepsilon$, an instant before the signal arrives at the most distant station, that station also begins transmitting. Of course, it detects the collision almost instantly and stops, but the little noise burst caused by the collision does not get back to the original station until time $2\tau - \varepsilon$. In other words, in the worst case a station cannot be sure that it has seized the channel until it has transmitted for 2τ without hearing a collision.

For this reason we will model the contention interval as a slotted ALOHA system with slot width 2τ. On a 1-km long coaxial cable, $\tau \approx 5$ μsec. For simplicity we will assume that each slot contains just 1 bit. Once the channel has been seized, a station can transmit at any rate it wants to, of course, not just at 1 bit per 2τ sec.

It is important to realize that collision detection is an *analog* process. The station's hardware must listen to the cable while it is transmitting. If what it reads back is different from what it is putting out, it knows a collision is occurring. The implication is that the signal encoding must allow collisions to be detected (e.g., a collision of two 0-volt signals may well be impossible to detect). For this reason, Manchester encoding is commonly used.

CSMA/CD is an important protocol. Later in this chapter we will study one version of it, IEEE 802.3, which is an international standard.

3.3.3. Collision-Free Protocols

Although collisions do not occur with CSMA/CD once a station has unambiguously seized the channel, they can still occur during the contention period. These collisions adversely affect the system performance, especially when the cable is long (i.e., large τ) and the frames short. As very long, high-bandwidth fiber optic networks come into use, the combination of large τ and short frames will become an increasingly serious problem. In this and the following sections, we will examine some protocols that resolve the contention for the channel without any collisions at all, not even during the contention period.

In all the protocols to be described, we make the assumption that there are N stations, each with a unique address from 0 to $N - 1$ "wired" into it. That some stations may be inactive part of the time does not matter. The basic question remains: Which station gets the channel after a successful transmission? We continue using the model of Fig. 3-6 with its discrete contention slots.

In our first collision-free protocol, the **basic bit-map method**, each contention period consists of exactly N slots. If station 0 has a frame to send, it transmits a 1 bit during the first slot. No other station is allowed to transmit during this slot. Regardless of what station 0 does, station 1 gets the opportunity to transmit a 1 during slot 1, again only if it has a frame queued. In general, station j may announce the fact that it has a frame to send by inserting a 1 bit into slot j. After all N slots have passed by, each station has complete knowledge of which stations wish to transmit. At that point, they begin transmitting in numerical order (see Fig. 3-7). Since everyone agrees on who goes next, there will never be any collisions. After the last ready station has transmitted its frame, an event all stations can easily monitor, another N bit contention period is begun. If a station becomes ready just after its bit slot has passed by, it is out of luck and must remain silent until everyone has had his say and the bit map comes around again.

Let us briefly analyze the performance of this protocol. A simulation model is discussed in (Knott, 1985). For convenience, we will measure time in units of the

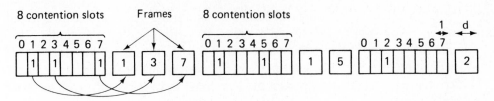

Fig. 3-7. The basic bit-map protocol.

contention bit slot, with data frames consisting of d time units. Under conditions of low load, the bit map will simply be repeated over and over, for lack of data frames.

Consider the situation from the point of view of a low-numbered station, such as 0 or 1. Typically, when it becomes ready to send, the "current" slot will be somewhere in the middle of the bit map. On the average, the station will have to wait $N/2$ slots for the current scan to finish and another full N slots for the following scan to run to completion before it may begin transmitting.

The prospects for high-numbered stations are brighter. Generally these will only have to wait half a scan ($N/2$ bit slots) before starting to transmit. High numbered stations rarely have to wait for the next scan. Since low-numbered stations must wait on the average $1.5N$ slots and high-numbered stations must wait on the average $0.5N$ slots, the mean for all stations is N slots. The channel efficiency at low load is easy to compute. The overhead per frame is N bits, and the amount of data is d bits, for an efficiency of $d/(N + d)$.

At high load, when all the stations have something to send all the time, the N bit contention period is prorated over N frames, yielding an overhead of only 1 bit per frame, or an efficiency of $d/(d + 1)$. The mean delay for a frame is equal to the sum of the time it queues inside its station, plus an additional $N(d + 1)/2$ once it gets to the head of its internal queue.

3.3.4. BRAP—Broadcast Recognition with Alternating Priorities

The basic bit-map protocol has several drawbacks, the most blatant of which is the asymmetry with respect to station number: higher numbered stations get better service than lower numbered ones. Another drawback is that under conditions of light load a station must always wait for the current scan to be finished (at the very least) before it may transmit. Our next protocol eliminates both these problems. It was discovered independently by Chlamtac (1976) and Scholl (1976). Chlamtac's version is called **BRAM (Broadcast Recognition Access Method)**; Scholl's version is called **MSAP (Mini Slotted Alternating Priorities)**. As a compromise, we will adopt the name **BRAP**.

In BRAP, as soon as a station inserts a 1 bit into its slot, it begins transmission of its frame immediately thereafter. In addition, instead of starting the bit scan with station 0 each time, it is started with the station following the one that just transmitted. In effect, permission to send rotates among the stations in a round-robin fashion. Any station wishing to exercise its permission to send simply does so without further ado. Any station not wishing to send lets its bit slot go idle. BRAP is illustrated in Fig. 3-8, with the same pattern of ready stations as in Fig. 3-7. Notice that each contention period always consists of a run of (zero or more) empty slots, terminated by a single 1 bit. As soon as someone announces that he wants the channel, he gets it immediately.

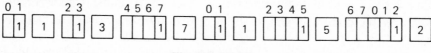

Fig. 3-8. BRAP.

BRAP can also be described in a slightly different form. Going back to 1-persistent CSMA, we could say that BRAP consists of having each station delay its attempt to seize the channel, with the delay time being proportional to the difference between the station's number and the number of the last successful transmission, modulo N. Since the delays are staggered, there are no collisions.

Although the channel efficiency of BRAP is identical to the basic bit-map method, its delay characteristics are better. In particular, at low load a station only has to wait an average of $N/2$ bit slots before starting (for large N), versus N for the earlier protocol. At high load, BRAP and the basic method are similar, since the major delay comes from the frames, not the contention slots.

3.3.5. MLMA—The Multi-Level Multi-Access Protocol

The problem with BRAP is not with the channel utilization, which is excellent in the case of high load, but with the delay when the system is lightly loaded. When no stations are ready, there are no data frames, and the N-bit headers just go on and on until some station inserts a 1 bit in its bit slot. On the average, a station will have to wait $N/2$ bit slots before it may begin sending.

Rothauser and Wild (1977) have devised a method that is nearly as efficient under conditions of high channel load but has a shorter delay under conditions of low channel load. In their method, a station announces that it wants to send by broadcasting its address in a particular format. We will illustrate the idea by means of an example using radix 10 arithmetic and $N = 1000$. An address in this system consists of three decimal digits, each decimal digit represented by a group of 10 bits called a "decade." For example, 472 is represented by setting bit 4 in the first decade, bit 7 in the middle decade, and bit 2 in the last decade.

If only one station attempts to transmit during a frame slot, it uses the 30-bit header to announce itself and then it sends its frame. The trouble arises when two or more stations try to insert their addresses into the same header. To disambiguate all of the addresses, the stations behave as follows. The first decade in every frame slot corresponds to the hundreds place in the station number. After the first decade is finished, stations that have not transmitted a bit must remain silent until all the stations that did set a bit have transmitted their data. Call the highest occupied bit position in the first decade x. In the second decade, all stations with x as their leading digit announce their ten's place. Call the highest occupied bit here y. In the third decade, all the stations whose addresses begin with xy may set the bit corresponding to their last digits. There are at most 10 of them.

This example is illustrated in Fig. 3-9 for five stations, with addresses 122, 125, 705, 722, and 725. Here $x = 7$ and $y = 2$. After decade 2, all stations now know that 722 and 725 want to send, and that furthermore one or more stations with addresses between 700 and 709, and one or more stations with addresses between 100 and 199 also want to send. Decade three identifies 705. Decade four is used for the ten's place of all stations in the highest "century" not yet fully identified. In this case the 100 series stations get to broadcast their tens places next. If station 342 had also set its bit in decade 0, decade 4 would have been devoted to the 300 series stations instead of the 100 series. After the 100 series stations have broadcast their tens places, everyone knows that the highest (and only) remaining group of stations is 120-129, so the following decade is used to separate them out. Finally, the data are sent in numerical order of the station addresses.

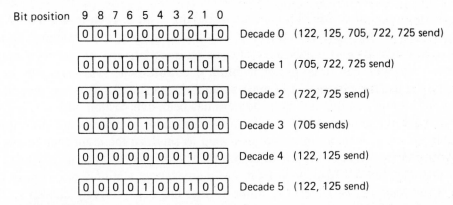

Fig. 3-9. MLMA. The recognition of stations 122, 125, 705, 722, and 725 requires 60 bits.

The number of decades needed to resolve conflicts depends on the addresses themselves. To separate 122 and 129 requires only three decades, but to separate 122 and 229 requires five decades. If all 1000 stations want to send, decade 0 is 0-999, decade 1 is for the 900 series, decade 2 is for 990-999, decade 3 is for 980-989, and so on. Decade 10 is for 900-909, decade 11 is for the ten's place of the 800 series stations, and so forth. In all, 111 decades are needed for the header (the initial one, the 10 "centuries," and the 100 decades that differentiate on the ones place).

The channel efficiency is difficult to calculate exactly, but for a minimum channel load, 30 bits of header are needed, giving an efficiency of $d/(d + 30)$. In the limit of a very heavy load, a frame consists of 111 decades of header and 1000 data frames, for an efficiency of $d/(d + 1.11)$, which is close to the efficiency of the bit-map method. The mean delay under conditions of light load is just 25 bits (if station 485 becomes ready just after the first 5 bits of the first decade have gone idle, it is not too late to capture the slot).

By now it should be clear that the choice of radix 10 was an arbitrary choice. Any other radix would do, also. For example, with radix 2 and 1000 stations, 10 levels are needed, each containing 2 bits. The first "decade" (bicade?) is used to separate stations 0-511 from stations 512-999. To minimize the number of bits in the header for the case of only one request per frame, consider some radix, r, with l levels ("decades"). The number of levels for a given r is the smallest value of l such that $r^l \geq N$. We seek to minimize the number of bits in the header, lr, subject to the constraint $r^l \geq N$. The minimum occurs at $r = e$. For 1000 stations, $r = 2$ and $l = 10$ is best, but for 2000 stations the optimum radix is 3, with seven levels.

3.3.6. Binary Countdown

The limiting case of MLMA consists of having 1 bit at each level. For N stations, the number of levels needed is $\log_2 N$ rounded upward to an integer. To signal that it wants to send, a station writes its address into the header as a binary number. We will call this protocol **binary countdown**. However, to avoid conflicts, the usual arbitration rule must be applied: as soon as a station sees that a high-order bit position that is 0 in its address has been overwritten with a 1, it gives up. After the winning station has transmitted its address, there is no information available telling how many other stations want to send, so the algorithm begins all over with the next frame. The channel efficiency of this method, $d/(d + \ln N)$, is better than decimal MLMA when there are many bursty stations, but slightly less under a full load. If, however, the frame format has been cleverly chosen so that the sender's address is the first field in the frame, even these $\ln N$ bits are not wasted.

Mok and Ward (1979) have described a variation of binary countdown using a parallel rather than a serial interface. They also suggest using virtual station numbers, with the virtual station numbers from 0 up to and including the successful station being circularly permuted after each transmission, in order to give higher priority to stations that have been silent unusually long. For example, if stations C, H, D, A, G, B, E, F have priorities 7, 6, 5, 4, 3, 2, 1, and 0, respectively, then a successful transmission by D puts it at the end of the list, giving a priority order of C, H, A, G, B, E, F, D. Thus C remains virtual station 7, but A moves up from 4 to 5 and D drops from 5 to 0. Station D will now only be able to acquire the channel if no other station wants it.

3.3.7. Limited-Contention Protocols

We have now considered two basic strategies for channel acquisition in a cable network: contention, as in CSMA, and collision-free methods. Each strategy can be rated as to how well it does with respect to the two important performance measures, delay at low load and channel efficiency at high load. Under conditions of light load, contention (i.e., pure or slotted ALOHA) is preferable due to its low delay. As the load increases, contention becomes increasingly less attractive, because the overhead associated with channel arbitration becomes greater. Just the reverse is true for the collision-free protocols. At low load, they have high delay, but as the load increases, the channel efficiency improves rather than getting worse as it does for contention protocols.

Obviously, it would be nice if we could combine the best properties of the contention and collision-free protocols, arriving at a new protocol that used contention at low loads to provide low delay, but used a collision-free technique at high load to provide good channel efficiency. Such protocols, which we will call **limited contention protocols**, do, in fact, exist, and will conclude our study of carrier sense networks.

Up until now the only contention protocols we have studied have been symmetric, that is, each station attempts to acquire the channel with some probability, p, with all stations using the same p. As we mentioned earlier, the overall system performance can sometimes be improved by using a protocol that assigns different probabilities to different stations.

Before looking at the asymmetric protocols, let us quickly review the performance of the symmetric case. The probability that some station successfully acquires the channel during a given slot if there are k stations contending for it, each transmitting with probability p is $kp(1-p)^{k-1}$. To find the optimal value of p, we differentiate with respect to p, set the result to zero, and solve for p. Doing so, we find that the best value of p is $1/k$. Substituting $p = 1/k$ we get

$$\Pr[\text{success with optimal } p] = \left(\frac{k-1}{k}\right)^{k-1} \tag{3-9}$$

This probability is plotted in Fig. 3-10. For small numbers of stations, the chances of success are good, but as soon as the number of stations reaches even five, the probability has dropped close to its asymptotic value of $1/e$.

From Fig. 3-10, it is fairly obvious that the probability of some station acquiring the channel can be increased only by decreasing the amount of competition. The limited-contention protocols do precisely that. They first divide the stations up into (not necessarily disjoint) groups. Only the members of group 0 are permitted to compete for slot 0. If one of them succeeds, it acquires the channel and transmits its frame. If the slot lies fallow or if there is a collision, the members of group 1 contend for slot 1, etc. By making an appropriate division of stations into groups,

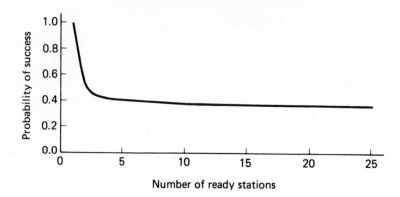

Fig. 3-10. Acquisition probability for a symmetric contention channel.

the amount of contention for each slot can be reduced, thus operating each slot near the left end of Fig. 3-10.

The trick is how to assign stations to slots. Before looking at the general case, let us consider some special cases. At one extreme, each group has but one member. Such an assignment guarantees that there will never be collisions, because at most one station is contending per slot. We have seen this protocol before; it is just BRAP. The next special case is to assign two stations per group. The probability that both will try to transmit during a slot is p^2, which for small p is negligible. Assigning two stations per slot reduces the number of slots in the BRAP bit map from $N/2$ to $N/4$, halving the delay. As more and more stations are assigned to the same slot, the probability of a collision grows, but the length of the bit map scan needed to give everyone a chance shrinks. The limiting case is a single group containing all stations (i.e., slotted ALOHA). What we need is a way to assign stations to slots dynamically, with many stations per slot when the load is low and few (or even just one) station per slot when the load is high.

3.3.8. The Adaptive Tree Walk Protocol

One particularly simple way of performing the necessary assignment is to use the algorithm devised by the U.S. Army for testing soldiers for syphilis during World War II (Dorfman, 1943). In short, the Army took a blood sample from N soldiers. A portion of each sample was poured into a single test tube. This mixed sample was then tested for antibodies. If none were found, all the soldiers in the group were declared healthy. If antibodies were present, two new mixed samples were prepared, one from soldiers 1 through $N/2$ and one from the rest. The process was repeated recursively until the infected soldiers were determined.

For the computer version of this algorithm (Capetanakis, 1979) it is convenient to think of the stations as being organized in a binary tree as illustrated in Fig. 3-11. In the first contention slot following a successful frame transmission, slot 0, all stations are permitted to try to acquire the channel. If one of them does so, fine. If there is a collision, then during slot 1 only those stations falling under node B may compete. If one of them acquires the channel, the slot following the frame is reserved for those stations under node C. If, on the other hand, two or more stations under node B want to transmit, there will be a collision during slot 1, in which case it is node D's turn during slot 2.

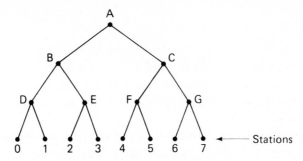

Fig. 3-11. The tree for eight stations.

In essence, if a collision occurs during slot 0, the entire tree is searched, depth first, to locate all ready stations. Each bit slot is associated with some particular node in the tree. If a collision occurs, the search continues recursively with the left and right children of that node. If a bit slot goes idle or if there is exactly one station that transmits into it, the searching of its node can stop, because all ready stations have been located. (If there were more than one, there would have been a collision.)

When the load on the system is heavy, it is hardly worth the effort to dedicate slot 0 to node A, because that makes sense only in the unlikely event that precisely one station has a frame to send. Similarly, one could argue that nodes B and C should be skipped as well for the same reason. Put in more general terms, at what level in the tree should the search begin? Clearly, the heavier the load, the farther down the tree the search should begin. For the time being, let us assume that each station has a good estimate of the number of ready stations, q. We will come back to the question of how to obtain such estimates later.

To proceed, let us number the levels of the tree from the top, with node A in Fig. 3-11 at level 0, nodes B and C at level 1, etc. Notice that each node at level i has a fraction 2^{-i} of the total tree below it. If the q ready stations are uniformly distributed, the expected number of them below a specific node at level i is just $2^{-i}q$. Intuitively, we would expect the optimal level to begin searching the tree as the one at which the mean number of contending stations per slot is 1, that is, the level at which $2^{-i}q = 1$. Solving this equation we find that $i = \log_2 q$.

Numerous improvements to the basic algorithm have been discovered and are discussed by Bertsekas and Gallager (1987). For example, consider the case of stations 6 and 7 being the only ones wanting to transmit. At node A a collision will occur, so B will be tried and discovered idle. It is pointless to probe C since it is guaranteed to have a collision (we know that two or more stations under A are ready and none of them are under B, so they must all be under C. The probe of C can be skipped and F tried next. When this probe also turns up nothing, G can be skipped and node 6 tried next.

3.3.9. Urn Protocol

Kleinrock and Yemini (1978) have described another protocol that is similar to the tree walk protocol, but uses an urn rather than a tree as its basis. Like the tree walk protocol, it limits the number of stations entitled to transmit during each slot in such a way as to maximize the probability of getting exactly one ready station per contention slot.

In this protocol, an analogy is made between the stations and the balls in an urn. Green balls correspond to stations that are ready (have a frame to send). Red balls correspond to stations that do not have a frame to send. The probability of selecting exactly x green balls if we withdraw n balls without replacement is

$$\frac{\binom{k}{x} \binom{N-k}{n-x}}{\binom{N}{n}}$$

The first factor in the numerator is the number of ways of selecting x green balls from among the k green balls in the urn. The second factor in the numerator is the number of ways of selecting $n - x$ red balls from among the $N - k$ red balls in the urn. The denominator is the number of ways of selecting n balls from the N balls in the urn.

What we are really interested in is the probability of drawing exactly one green ball, since that is the only way a successful transmission can occur. When $x = 1$, the probability of success is maximized by choosing $n = N/k$ (truncated to an integer). The mean number of green balls in the sample is equal to the sample size, n, times the probability that a given ball is green, k/N. This value is always close to 1 (it is not exactly 1 due to the truncation). Figure 3-12 shows the probability of getting exactly one green ball for the case $N = 100$. For $k > N/2$, only one ball will be sampled, and the throughput will be equal to the fraction of stations wanting to transmit.

After having determined what n should be, the next question is which stations are to be chosen. This decision must be made in a distributed way, and all stations must agree on the decision for the method to work. Several methods have been proposed (Kleinrock and Yemini, 1978). A particularly attractive one is as follows. The stations are imagined to be arranged in numerical order along the circumference of a hypothetical circle. A window of size n rotates around the circle. During

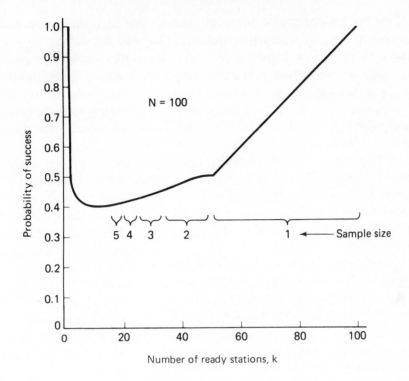

Fig. 3-12. Success probability with the urn method.

each slot, those stations inside the window are given permission to send. (Being in the window is analogous to being under the node in Fig. 3-12 that owns the current slot.) If there was a successful transmission or no transmission at all, the window is advanced n positions. If there was a collision, the window is shrunk back to half its size, and the process is repeated until the collision ceases. (Shrinking the window is analogous to recursively walking one of the subtrees of a Fig. 3-11 node.)

Let us consider how the entire algorithm works under two conditions, light load and heavy load. If the estimate of the number of ready stations is 1 or fewer, the window size will be N. In other words, the window will go all the way around, and all stations will be allowed to send at will. Under these conditions, the protocol degenerates to slotted ALOHA. If the estimate of k remains stable at 2 for a while, n will be N/2 and the stations will be partitioned into two groups, with half the stations operating under slotted ALOHA in the odd slots, and the other half operating the same way in the even slots. Finally, if k > N/2, the sample size (i.e., the window size) will be 1. During each slot, exactly one station will be given permission to send, so there will be no collisions. The position of the lucky station will rotate around the circle. In this limit, the system becomes identical to synchronous time-division multiplexing. Thus the urn method acts like slotted ALOHA at low load and automatically goes over to STDM at high load. Chlamtac and Ganz (1986a) give a more rigorous analysis.

All of the limited-contention protocols assume that each station has an estimate of the number of stations wanting to transmit. One way for stations to estimate the system state is to have a logically separate subchannel used for signaling state changes. Such a subchannel can be obtained by traditional multiplexing. For example, by allocating a narrow frequency band on the cable for signaling only (FDM), or by setting aside the first contention slot following each successful frame transmission for signaling only (TDM). Either way, we assume that the signaling subchannel is slotted.

Each station must maintain a running estimate of the number of ready stations. This estimate must be updated when either one of two events happens: a successful transmission occurs (state is decremented), or a new station becomes ready (state is incremented). The former is easy to detect because all stations can easily keep track of successful transmissions. The latter is trickier and is the reason the separate subchannel is needed. When a station becomes ready, it announces itself on the signaling subchannel. If only one station becomes ready during a signaling slot, this can be unambiguously detected by everyone else. However, if two or more become ready during one signaling slot, there will be a collision.

At this point, we explicitly assume that these collisions can be detected. When a collision occurs on the subchannel, all the stations know that two or more stations have become ready, but they do not know exactly how many. To make an estimate of the mean number of newly ready stations represented by each collision, let us assume that the number of stations that become ready in each slot is a Poisson process with mean m. The probability of zero stations becoming ready in a given slot is e^{-m}, by Eq. (3-2). Similarly, the probability of one station becoming ready in a signaling slot is me^{-m}. Both of these quantities can be accurately estimated by recording the fraction of subchannel slots containing zero or one "I am ready" messages. From this information, two estimates of m can be made and then the average used.

With m known, we can now deduce the probability that exactly r stations become ready using the Poisson law and the formula for conditional probabilities,

$$\Pr[A \text{ given } B] = \frac{\Pr[A \text{ and } B]}{\Pr[B]}$$

we find that

$$\Pr[\text{exactly } r \text{ stations in a collision}] = \frac{m^r e^{-m}/r!}{1 - e^{-m} - me^{-m}}$$

Given the probabilities, we can find the mean. In general the mean number of stations in a collision will not be an integer, so the running estimate of the system state will also take on continuous rather than integer values. This is not a problem as long as we force n to be an integer.

3.4. IEEE STANDARD 802 FOR LOCAL AREA NETWORKS

As discussed in Sec. 1.7.4, IEEE has produced several standards for LANs. These standards, collectively known as **IEEE 802**, include CSMA/CD, token bus, and token ring. The various standards differ at the physical layer and MAC sublayer, but are compatible at the data link layer. The IEEE 802 standards have been adopted by ANSI as American National Standards, by NBS as government standards, and by ISO as international standards (known as ISO 8802). They are surprisingly readable (as standards go).

The standards are divided in parts, each published as a separate book. The 802.1 standard gives an introduction to the set of standards and defines the interface primitives. The 802.2 standard describes the upper part of the data link layer, which uses the **LLC** (**Logical Link Control**) protocol. Parts 802.3 through 802.5 describe the three LAN standards, the CSMA/CD, token bus, and token ring standards, respectively. Each standard covers the physical layer and MAC sublayer protocol. The next three sections cover these three systems.

3.4.1. IEEE Standard 802.3 and Ethernet

The IEEE 802.3 standard is for a 1-persistent CSMA/CD LAN. To review the idea, when a station wants to transmit, it listens to the cable. If the cable is busy, the station waits until it goes idle, otherwise it transmits immediately. If two or more stations simultaneously begin transmitting on an idle cable, they will collide. All colliding stations then terminate their transmission, wait a random time, and repeat the whole process all over again.

The 802.3 standard has an interesting history. The real beginning was Abramson's ALOHA system in Hawaii, to be discussed later in this chapter. Later, carrier sensing was added, and Xerox built a 2.94-Mbps CSMA/CD system to connect over 100 personal workstations on a 1-km cable (Metcalfe and Boggs, 1976; Shoch, 1987). This system was called **Ethernet** after the *luminiferous ether*, through which electromagnetic radiation was once thought to propagate. (When the Nineteenth Century British physicist James Clerk Maxwell discovered that electromagnetic radiation could be described by a wave equation, scientists assumed that space must be filled with some ethereal medium in which the radiation was propagating. Only after the famous Michelson-Morley experiment in 1887, did physicists discover that electromagnetic radiation could propagate in a vacuum.)

The Xerox Ethernet was so successful that Xerox, DEC, and Intel drew up a standard for a 10-Mbps Ethernet. This standard formed the basis for 802.3. The published 802.3 standard differs from the Ethernet specification in that it describes a whole family of 1-persistent CSMA/CD systems, running at speeds from 1 to 10 Mbps on various media. The initial standard also gives the parameters for a 10 Mbps baseband system using 50-ohm coaxial cable. Other parameter sets for other media and speeds are under consideration. The discussion below will focus on the 10 Mbps baseband version.

Many people (incorrectly) use the name "Ethernet" in a generic sense to refer to all CSMA/CD protocols, even though it really refers to a specific product that implements 802.3. We will use the terms "802.3" and "CSMA/CD" except when specifically referring to the Ethernet product in the next few paragraphs.

Since the name "Ethernet" refers to the cable (the ether), let us start our discussion there. Two types of coaxial cable are commonly used. These are popularly called "thick Ethernet" and "thin Ethernet." Thick Ethernet resembles a yellow garden hose, with markings every 2.5 meters to show where the taps go. (The 802.3 standard does not actually *require* the cable to be yellow, but it does *suggest* it.) Thin Ethernet is smaller and more flexible, and it uses industry standard BNC connectors to form T junctions, rather than using taps. Thin Ethernet is much cheaper, but it can only run for short distances. The two types are compatible and can be connected in certain ways. Under certain restricted conditions, a twisted pair can also be used instead of coax.

Detecting cable breaks, bad taps, or loose connectors can be a major problem with all kinds of media. For this reason, techniques have been developed to track them down. Basically, a pulse of known shape is injected into the cable. If the pulse hits an obstacle or the end of the cable, an echo will be generated and sent back. By carefully timing the interval between sending the pulse and receiving the echo, it is possible to locate the origin of the echo quite accurately. This technique is called **time domain reflectometry**.

All 802.3 implementations, including Ethernet, use straight Manchester encoding, as shown in Fig. 2-3. The presence of a transition in the middle of each bit makes it possible for the receiver to synchronize with the sender. At any instant, the cable can be in one of three states: transmitting a 0 bit (low followed by high), transmitting a 1 bit (high followed by low), or idle (0 volts). The high signal is +0.85 volts and the low signal is −0.85 volts, giving a dc value of 0 volts.

The usual configuration for Ethernet is shown in Fig. 3-13(a). Here we see a **transceiver** clamped securely onto the cable so that its tap makes contact with the inner core. The transceiver contains the electronics that handle carrier detection and collision detection. When a collision is detected, the transceiver also puts a special invalid signal on the cable to insure that all other transceivers also realize that a collision has occurred.

A **transceiver cable** connects the transceiver to an interface board in the computer. The transceiver cable may be up to 50 meters long, and contains five individually shielded twisted pairs. Two of the pairs are for data in and data out, respectively. Two more are for control signals in and out. The fifth pair, which is not always used, allows the computer to power the transceiver electronics. Some transceivers allow up to eight nearby computers to be attached to them, to reduce the number of transceivers needed.

The transceiver cable terminates on an interface board inside the computer.

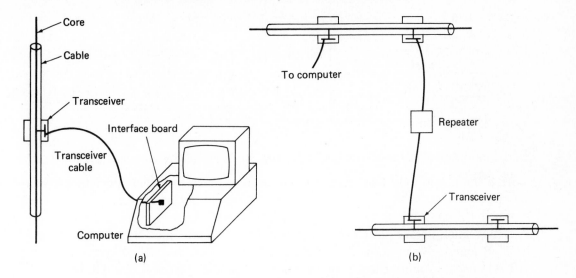

Fig. 3-13. (a) Position of the transceiver and interface. (b) Connecting two cable segments with a repeater.

The interface board contains a controller chip that transmits frames to, and receives frames from, the transceiver. The controller is responsible for assembling the data into the proper frame format, as well as computing checksums on outgoing frames and verifying them on incoming frames. Some controller chips also manage a pool of buffers for incoming frames, a queue of buffers to be transmitted, DMA transfers with the host computers, and other aspects of network management.

The maximum cable length permitted by 802.3 is 500 meters. To allow the network to extend to a larger distance, multiple cables can be connected by **repeaters**, as shown in Fig. 3-13(b). A repeater is a physical layer device. It receives, amplifies, and retransmits signals in both directions. As far as the software is concerned, a series of cable segments connected by repeaters is no different than a single cable (except for some delay introduced by the repeaters). A system may contain multiple cable segments and multiple repeaters, but no two transceivers may be more than 2.5 km apart and no path between any two transceivers may traverse more than four repeaters.

Figure 3-14 shows different ways of wiring up a building. In Fig. 3-14(a), a single cable is snaked from room to room, with each station tapping onto it at the nearest point. In Fig. 3-14(b), a vertical spine runs from the basement to the roof, with horizontal cables on each floor connected to it by repeaters. In some buildings the horizontal cables are thin, and the backbone is thick. The most general topology is the tree, as in Fig. 3-14(c), because a network with two paths between some pairs of stations would suffer from interference between the two signals.

An alternative way to organize a cable network is as a collection of separate segments connected by **bridges** (also called **selective repeaters**). Unlike ordinary repeaters, which just pass through bits without examining them, bridges examine

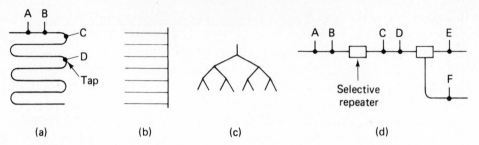

Fig. 3-14. Cable topologies. (a) Linear. (b) Spine. (c) Tree. (d) Segmented.

each frame and only forward those that need to reach the other segment. A frame sent by *A* to *B* in Fig. 3-14(d), for example, would not be forwarded, but a frame sent by *A* to either *C* or *F* would be forwarded. Bridges make it possible for a conversation to take place between *A* and *B* at the same time *C* is talking to *D* or *E*.

Bridges have to know the locations of all stations in order to know whether or not to copy a frame onto a given segment. How they discover this will be revealed when we study them in Chapter 5.

The 802.3 MAC Sublayer Protocol

The 802.3 (IEEE, 1985) frame structure is shown in Fig. 3-15. Each frame starts with a *Preamble* of 7 bytes, each containing the bit pattern 10101010. The Manchester encoding of this pattern produces a 10-MHz square wave for 5.6 μsec to allow the receiver's clock to synchronize with the sender's. Next comes a *Start of frame* byte containing 10101011 to denote the start of the frame itself. (As an aside, we will indicate field names *Like this* and frame types *LIKE THIS.*)

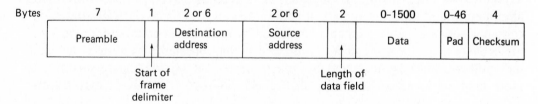

Fig. 3-15. The 802.3 frame format.

The frame contains two addresses, one for the destination and one for the source. The standard allows 2-byte and 6-byte addresses, but the parameters defined for the 10-Mbps baseband standard use only the 6-byte addresses. The high-order bit of the destination address is a 0 for ordinary addresses and 1 for group addresses. Group addresses allow multiple stations to listen to a single address. When a frame is sent to a group address, all the stations in the group receive it. Sending to a group of stations is called **multicast**. The address consisting of all 1 bits is reserved for **broadcast**. A frame containing all 1s in the destination field is delivered to all stations on the network and is propagated by all bridges.

Another interesting feature of the addressing is the use of bit 46 (adjacent to the high-order bit) to distinguish local from global addresses. Local addresses are assigned by each network administrator and have no significance outside the local network. Global addresses, in contrast, are assigned by IEEE to ensure that no two stations anywhere in the world have the same global address. With $48 - 2 = 46$ bits available, there are about 7×10^{13} global addresses. The idea is that any station can uniquely address any other station by just giving the right 48-bit number. It is up to the network layer to figure out how to find the destination.

The *Length* field tells how many bytes are present in the data field, from a minimum of 0 to a maximum of 1500. While a data field of 0 bytes is legal, it causes a problem. When a transceiver detects a collision, it truncates the current frame, which means that stray bits and pieces of frames appear on the cable all the time. To make it easier to distinguish valid frames from garbage, 802.3 states that valid frames must be at least 64 bytes long, from destination address to checksum. If the data portion of a frame is less than 46 bytes, the pad field is used to fill out the frame to the minimum size. Another reason for having a minimum length frame is to prevent a station from completing the transmission of a short frame before the first bit has even reached the far end of the cable, where it may collide with another frame.

The final field is the *Checksum*. It is effectively a 32-bit hash code of the data. If some data bits are erroneously received (due to noise on the cable), the checksum will almost certainly be wrong, and the error will be detected. The checksum algorithm is a cyclic redundancy check (to be described in Chapter 4).

As mentioned before, if two stations both detect an idle ether and begin transmitting at the same time, a collision will occur. Any station detecting a collision aborts its transmission, generates a noise burst to warn all other stations, and then waits a random time before repeating the entire cycle. Let us now see how the randomization is done. The model is that of Fig. 3-6. After a collision, time is divided up into discrete slots whose length is equal to the worst case round trip propagation time on the ether (2τ). To accommodate the longest path allowed by 802.3 (2.5 km and four repeaters), the slot time has been set to 512 bit times, or 51.2 μsec.

After the first collision, each station waits either 0 or 1 slot times before trying again. If two stations collide and each one picks the same random number, they will collide again. After the second collision, each one picks either 0, 1, 2, or 3 at random and waits that number of slot times. If a third collision occurs (the probability of this happening is 0.25), then the next time the number of slots to wait is chosen at random from the interval 0 to $2^3 - 1$.

In general, after i collisions, a random number between 0 and $2^i - 1$ is chosen, and that number of slots is skipped. However, after 10 collisions have been reached, the randomization interval is frozen at a maximum of 1023 slots. After 16 collisions, the controller throws in the towel and reports failure back to the computer. Further recovery is up to higher layers.

This algorithm, called **binary exponential backoff**, was chosen to dynamically adapt to the number of stations trying to send. If the randomization interval for all collisions was 1023, the chance of two stations colliding for a second time would be negligible, but the average wait after a collision would be hundreds of slot times, introducing significant delay. On the other hand, if each station always delayed for either 0 or 1 slot, then if 100 stations ever tried to send at once, they would collide over and over until 99 of them picked 0 and the remaining station picked 1, or vice versa. This might take years. By having the randomization interval grow exponentially as more and more consecutive collisions occur, the algorithm ensures a low delay when only a few stations collide, but also ensures that the collision is resolved in a reasonable interval when many stations collide.

As described so far, CSMA/CD provides no acknowledgements. Since the mere absence of collisions does not guarantee that bits were not garbled by noise spikes on the cable, for reliable communication the destination must verify the checksum, and if correct, send back an acknowledgement frame to the source. Normally, this acknowledgement would be just another frame as far as the protocol is concerned, and would have to fight for channel time just like a data frame. However, a simple modification to the contention algorithm allows speedy confirmation of frame receipt and lets the sender know that its frame has been received correctly (Tokoro and Tamaru, 1977). All that is needed is to reserve the first contention slot following successful transmission for the destination station.

802.3 Performance

Now let us briefly examine the performance of 802.3 under conditions of heavy and constant load, that is, k stations always ready to transmit. A complete analysis of the binary exponential backoff algorithm is very complex, so instead we will follow Metcalfe and Boggs (1976) and assume a constant retransmission probability in each slot. If each station transmits during a contention slot with probability p, the probability A, that some station acquires the ether during that slot is

$$A = kp(1 - p)^{k-1} \tag{3-10}$$

A is maximized when $p = 1/k$, with $A \to 1/e$ as $k \to \infty$. The probability that the contention interval has exactly j slots in it is $A(1 - A)^{j-1}$, so the mean number of slots per contention is given by

$$\sum_{j=0}^{\infty} jA(1 - A)^{j-1} = \frac{1}{A}$$

Since each slot has a duration 2τ, the mean contention interval, w, is $2\tau/A$.

Assuming optimal p, the mean number of contention slots is never more than e, so w is at most $2\tau e \approx 5.4\tau$.

If the mean frame takes P sec to transmit, when many stations have frames to send,

$$\text{Channel efficiency} = \frac{P}{P + 2\tau/A} \qquad (3\text{-}11)$$

Here we see where the maximum cable distance between any two stations enters into the performance figures, giving rise to topologies other than that of Fig. 3-14(a). The longer the cable, the longer the contention interval. By allowing no more than 2.5 km of cable and four repeaters between any two transceivers, the round trip time can be bounded to 51.2 μsec, which at 10 Mbps corresponds to 512 bits or 64 bytes, the minimum frame size.

It is instructive to formulate Eq. (3-11) in terms of the frame length, F, the network bandwidth, B, the cable length, L, and the speed of signal propagation, c, for the optimal case of e contention slots per frame. With $P = F/B$, Eq. (3-11) becomes

$$\text{Channel efficiency} = \frac{1}{1 + 2BLe/cF} \qquad (3\text{-}12)$$

When the second term in the denominator is large, network efficiency will be low. More specifically, increasing network bandwidth or distance (the BL product) reduces efficiency for a given frame size. Unfortunately, much research on network hardware is aimed precisely at increasing this product. People want high bandwidth over long distances (fiber optic MANs, for example), which suggests that 802.3 may not be the best system for these applications.

In Fig. 3-16, the channel efficiency is plotted versus number of ready stations for $2\tau = 51.2$ μsec and a data rate of 10 Mbps using Eq. (3-12). With a 64-byte slot time, it is not surprising that 64-byte frames are not efficient. On the other hand, with 1024-byte frames and an asymptotic value of e 64-byte slots per contention interval, the contention period is 174 bytes long and the efficiency is 0.85.

To determine the mean number of stations ready to transmit under conditions of high load, we can use the following (crude) observation. Each frame ties up the channel for one contention period and one frame transmission time, for a total of $P + w$ sec. The number of frames per second is therefore $1/(P + w)$. If each station generates frames at a mean rate of λ frames/sec, when the system is in state k the total input rate of all unblocked stations combined is $(N - k)\lambda$ frames/sec. Since in equilibrium the input and output rates must be identical, we can equate these two expressions and solve for k. (Notice that w is a function of k.)

More sophisticated analyses are given by Bertsekas and Gallager (1987), Hammond and O'Reilly (1987), and Hayes (1984).

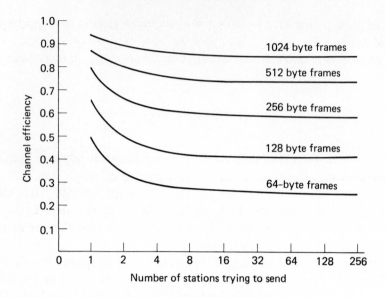

Fig. 3-16. Efficiency of 802.3 at 10 Mbps with 512-bit slot times.

3.4.2. IEEE Standard 802.4: Token Bus

Although 802.3 is widely used in offices, during the development of the 802 standard people from General Motors and other companies interested in factory automation had serious reservations about it. For one thing, due to the probabalistic MAC protocol, with a little bad luck a station might have to wait arbitrarily long to send a frame (i.e., the worst case is unbounded). For another, 802.3 frames do not have priorities, making them unsuited for real time systems in which important frames should not be held up waiting for unimportant frames.

A simple system with a known worst case is a ring in which the stations take turns sending frames. If there are n stations and it takes T sec to send a frame, no frame will ever have to wait more than nT sec to get a chance. The factory automation people in the 802 committee liked the conceptual idea of a ring, but did not like the physical implementation because a break in the ring cable would bring the whole network down. Furthermore, they noted that a ring is a poor fit to the linear topology of most assembly lines. As a result, a new standard was developed, having the robustness of the 802.3 broadcast cable, but the known worst-case behavior of a ring.

This standard, 802.4 (Dirvin and Miller, 1986; IEEE, 1985; Phinney and Jelatis, 1983), is called a **token bus**. Physically, the token bus is a linear or tree-shaped cable onto which the stations are attached. Logically, the stations are organized into a ring (see Fig. 3-17), with each station knowing the address of the station to its "left" and "right." When the logical ring is initialized, the highest numbered station may send the first frame. After it is done, it passes permission to its immediate neighbor by sending the neighbor a special control frame called a **token**. The token propagates around the logical ring, with only the token holder being permitted to transmit frames. Since only one station at a time holds the token, collisions do not occur.

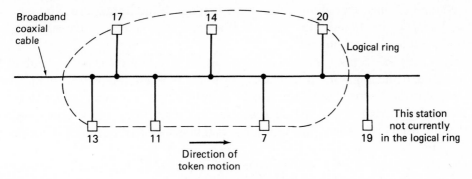

Fig. 3-17. A token bus.

An important point to realize is that the physical order in which the stations are connected to the cable is not important. Since the cable is inherently a broadcast medium, each station receives each frame, discarding those not addressed to it. When a station passes the token, it sends a token frame specifically addressed to its logical neighbor in the ring, irrespective of where that station is physically located on the cable. It is also worth noting that when stations are first powered on, they will not be in the ring (e.g., stations 14 and 19 in Fig. 3-17), so the MAC protocol has provisions for adding to, and deleting stations from, the ring.

The 802.4 MAC protocol is very complex, with each station having to maintain 10 different timers and more than two dozen internal state variables. The 802.4 standard is much longer than 802.3, filling more than 200 pages. The two standards are also quite different in style, with 802.3 giving the protocols as Pascal procedures, whereas 802.4 gives them as finite state machines, with the actions written in Ada†.

For the physical layer, the token bus uses the 75-ohm broadband coaxial cable used for cable television. Both single and dual cable systems are allowed, with or without headends. Three different analog modulation schemes are permitted: phase continuous frequency shift keying, phase coherent frequency shift keying, and multilevel duobinary amplitude modulated phase shift keying. Speeds of 1, 5, and 10 Mbps are possible. Furthermore, the modulation schemes not only provide ways to represent 0, 1, and idle on the cable, but also three other symbols used for network control. All in all, the physical layer is totally incompatible with 802.3, and a lot more complicated.

---

† Ada is a registered trademark of the U.S. Department of Defense Joint Ada program.

The Token Bus MAC Sublayer Protocol

When the ring is initialized, stations are inserted into it in order of station address, from highest to lowest. Token passing is also done from high to low addresses. Each time a station acquires the token, it can transmit frames for a certain amount of time, then it must pass the token on. If the frames are short enough, several consecutive frames may be sent. If a station has no data, it passes the token immediately upon receiving it.

The token bus defines four priority classes, 0, 2, 4, and 6 for traffic, with 0 the lowest and 6 the highest. It is easiest to think of each station internally being divided into four substations, one at each priority level. As input comes in to the MAC sublayer from above, the data are checked for priority and routed to one of the four substations. Thus each substation maintains its own queue of frames to be transmitted.

When the token comes into the station over the cable, it is passed internally to the priority 6 substation, which may begin transmitting frames, if it has any. When it is done (or when its timer expires), the token is passed internally to the priority 4 substation, which may then transmit frames until its timer expires, at which point the token is passed internally to the priority 2 substation. This process is repeated until either the priority 0 substation has sent all its frames or its timer has expired. Either way, at this point the token is sent to the next station in the ring.

Without getting into all the details of how the various timers are managed, it should be clear that by setting the timers properly, we can ensure that a guaranteed fraction of the total token holding time can be allocated to priority 6 traffic. The lower priorities will have to live with what is left over. If the higher priority substations do not need all of their allocated time, the lower priority substations can have the unused portion, so it is not wasted.

This priority scheme, which guarantees priority 6 traffic a known fraction of the network bandwidth, can be used to implement voice and other real time traffic. For example, suppose the parameters of a 50-station network running at 10 Mbps have been adjusted to give priority 6 traffic 1/3 of the bandwidth. Then each station has a guaranteed 67 kbps for priority 6 traffic. This bandwidth could be used to carry one ISDN voice channel per station, with a little left over for control information.

The token bus frame format is shown in Fig. 3-18. It is unfortunately different from the 802.3 frame format. The preamble is used to synchronize the receiver's clock, as in 802.3, except that here it may be as short as 1 byte. The *Starting delimiter* and *Ending delimiter* fields are used to mark the frame boundaries. Both of these fields contain analog encoding of symbols other than 0s and 1s, so that they cannot occur accidentally in the user data. As a result, no length field is needed.

The *Frame control* field is used to distinguish data frames from control frames. For data frames, it carries the frame's priority. It can also carry an indicator requiring the destination station to acknowledge correct or incorrect receipt of the frame. Without this indicator, the destination would not be allowed to send anything

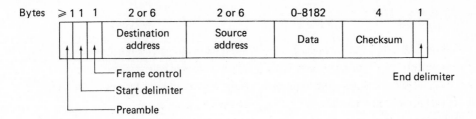

Fig. 3-18. The 802.4 frame format.

because it does not have the token. This indicator turns the token bus into something resembling the acknowledgement scheme of Tokoro and Tamaru.

For control frames, the *Frame control* field is used to specify the frame type. The allowed types include token passing and various ring maintenance frames, including the mechanism for letting new stations enter the ring, the mechanism for allowing stations to leave the ring, and so on. Note that the 802.3 protocol does not have any control frames. All the MAC layer does there is provide a way to get frames onto the cable; it does not care what is in them.

The *Destination address* and *Source address* fields are the same as in 802.3 (yes, the two groups did talk to each other; no, they did not agree on very much). As in 802.3, a given network must use all 2-byte addresses or all 6-byte addresses, not a mixture on the same cable. The initial 802.4 standard allows either size. The individual and group addressing and the local and global address assignments are identical to 802.3.

The *Data* field may be up to 8182 bytes long when 2-byte addresses are used, and up to 8174 bytes long when 6-byte addresses are used. This is more than five times as long as the maximum 802.3 frame, which was made short to prevent one station from hogging the channel too long. With the token bus, the timers can be used as an antihogging measure when need be, but it is nice to be able to send long frames when real-time traffic is not an issue. The *Checksum* is used to detect transmission errors. It uses the same algorithm and polynomial as 802.3.

The token bus control frames are shown in Fig. 3-19. They will be discussed below. The only one we have seen so far is the *token* frame, used to pass the token from station to station. Most of the rest relate to adding and deleting stations from the logical ring.

Logical Ring Maintenance

From time to time, stations are powered on and want to join the ring. Other stations are turned off and want to leave the ring. The MAC sublayer protocol provides a detailed specification of exactly how this is done while maintaining the known worst case bound on token rotation. Below we will just briefly sketch the mechanisms used.

Once the ring has been established, each station's interface maintains the

Frame control field	Name	Meaning
00000000	Claim—token	Claim token during ring initialization
00000001	Solicit—successor—1	Allow stations to enter the ring
00000010	Solicit—successor—2	Allow stations to enter the ring
00000011	Who—follows	Recover from lost token
00000100	Resolve—contention	Used when multiple stations want to enter the ring
00001000	Token	Pass the token
00001100	Set—successor	Allow station to leave the ring

Fig. 3-19. The token bus control frames.

addresses of the predecessor and successor stations internally. Periodically, the token holder solicits bids from stations not currently in the ring that wish to join by sending one of the *SOLICIT_SUCCESSOR* frames shown in Fig. 3-19. The frame gives the sender's address and the successor's address. Stations inside that range may bid to enter (to keep the ring sorted in descending order of station address).

If no station bids to enter within a slot time (2τ, as in 802.3), the **response window** is closed and the token holder continues with its normal business. If exactly one station bids to enter, it is inserted into the ring, and becomes the token holder's successor.

If two or more stations bid to enter, their frames will collide and be garbled, as in 802.3. The token holder then runs an arbitration algorithm, starting with the broadcast of a *RESOLVE_CONTENTION* frame. The algorithm is a variation of binary countdown, using two bits at a time.

Furthermore, all station interfaces maintain two random bits inside. These bits are used to delay all bids by 0, 1, 2, or 3 slot times, to further reduce contention. In other words, two stations only collide on a bid if the current two address bits being used are the same and they happen to have the same two random bits. To prevent stations that must wait 3 slot times from being at a permanent disadvantage, the random bits are regenerated every time they are used or periodically every 50 msec.

The solicitation of new stations may not interfere with the guaranteed worst case for token rotation. Each station has a timer that is reset whenever it acquires the token. When the token comes in, the old value of this timer (i.e., the previous token rotation time) is inspected just before the timer is reset. If it exceeds a certain threshold value, there has been too much traffic recently, so no bids may be solicited this time around. In any event, only one station may enter at each solicitation, to put a bound on how much time can be consumed in ring maintenance. No guarantee is provided for how long a station may have to wait to join the ring when traffic is heavy, but in practice it should not be more than a few seconds.

Leaving the ring is easy. A station, *X*, with successor *S*, and predecessor *P*, leaves the ring, by sending *P* a *SET_SUCCESSOR* frame telling it that henceforth its successor is *S* instead of *X*. Then *X* just stops transmitting.

Ring initialization is a special case of adding new stations. Consider an idle system with all stations powered off. When the first station comes on line, it notices that there is no traffic for a certain period. Then it sends a *CLAIM_TOKEN* frame. Not hearing any competitors contending for the token, it creates a token and sets up a ring containing only itself. Periodically, it solicits bids for new stations to join. As new stations are powered on, they will respond to these bids and join the ring using the contention algorithm described above. Eventually every station that wants to join the ring will be able to do so. If the first two stations are powered on simultaneously, the protocol deals with this by letting them bid for the token using the standard modified binary countdown algorithm and the two random bits.

Due to transmission errors or hardware failures, problems can arise with the logical ring or the token. For example, if a station tries to pass the token to a station that has gone down, what happens? The solution is straightforward. After passing the token, a station listens to see if its successor either transmits a frame or passes the token. If it does neither, the token is passed a second time.

If that also fails, the station transmits a *WHO_FOLLOWS* frame specifying the address of its successor. When the failed station's successor sees a *WHO_FOLLOWS* frame naming its predecessor, it responds by sending a *SET_SUCCESSOR* frame to the station whose successor failed, naming itself as the new successor. In this way, the failed station is removed from the ring.

Now suppose that a station fails to pass the token to its successor and also fails to locate the successor's successor, which may also be down. It adopts a new strategy by sending a *SOLICIT_SUCCESSOR_2* frame to see if *anyone* else is still alive. Once again the standard contention protocol is run, with all stations that want to be in the ring now bidding for a place. Eventually the ring is re-established.

Another kind of problem occurs if the token holder goes down and takes the token with it. This problem is solved using the ring initialization algorithm. Each station has a timer that is reset whenever a frame appears on the network. When this timer hits a threshold value, the station issues a *CLAIM_TOKEN* frame, and the modified binary countdown algorithm with random bits determines who gets the token.

Still another problem is multiple tokens. If a station holding the token notices a transmission from another station, it discards its token. If there were two, there will now be one. If there were more than two, this process will be repeated sooner or later until all but one are discarded. If, by accident, all the tokens are discarded, then the lack of activity will cause one or more stations to try to claim the token.

3.4.3. IEEE Standard 802.5: Token Ring

Ring networks have been around for many years (Pierce, 1972) and have long been used for both local and wide area networks. Among their many attractive features is the fact that a ring is not really a broadcast medium, but a collection of individual point-to-point links that happen to form a circle. Point-to-point links involve a well-understood and field-proven technology, and can run on twisted pair, coaxial cable, or fiber optics. Ring engineering is also almost entirely digital, whereas 802.3, for example, has a substantial analog component for collision detection. A ring is also fair and has a known upper bound on channel access. For these reasons, IBM has chosen the ring as its LAN and IEEE has included a ring standard in 802 (compatible with IBM's). The 802.5 and IBM rings are described in (Dixon, 1987; IEEE, 1985; Pitt, 1987; Strole, 1987; and Willett, 1987).

Several kinds of rings exist. The one standardized in 802.5 is called a **token ring**. In this section we will first describe token rings in general and then IEEE 802.5 in particular. At the end of the section we will briefly describe some other kinds of rings.

A major issue in the design and analysis of any ring network is the "physical length" of a bit. If the data rate of the ring is R Mbps, a bit is emitted every $1/R$ μsec. With a typical signal propagation speed of about 200 m/μsec, each bit occupies $200/R$ meters on the ring. This means, for example, that a 1-Mbps ring whose circumference is 1000 meters can contain only 5 bits on it at once. The implications of the number of bits on the ring will become clearer later.

As mentioned above, a ring really consists of a collection of ring interfaces connected by point-to-point lines. Each bit arriving at an interface is copied into a 1-bit buffer and then copied out onto the ring again. While in the buffer, the bit can be inspected and possibly modified before being written out. This copying step introduces a 1-bit delay at each interface. A ring and its interfaces are shown in Fig. 3-20.

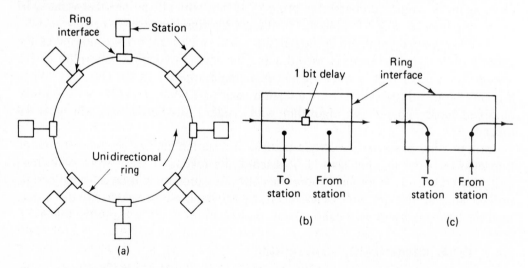

Fig. 3-20. (a) A ring network. (b) Listen mode. (c) Transmit mode.

In a token ring a special bit pattern, called the **token**, circulates around the ring whenever all stations are idle. When a station wants to transmit a frame, it is required to seize the token and remove it from the ring before transmitting.

Because there is only one token, only one station can transmit at a given instant, thus solving the channel access problem the same way the token bus solves it.

An implication of the token ring design is that the ring itself must have a sufficient delay to contain a complete token to circulate when all stations are idle. The delay has two components: the 1-bit delay introduced by each station, and the signal propagation delay. In almost all rings, the designers must assume that stations may be powered down at various times, especially at night. If the interfaces are powered from the ring, shutting down the station has no effect on the interface, but if the interfaces are powered externally, they must be designed to connect the input to the output when power goes down, thus removing the 1-bit delay. The point here is that on a short ring an artificial delay may have to be inserted into the ring at night to ensure that a token can be contained on it.

Ring interfaces have two operating modes, listen and transmit. In listen mode, the input bits are simply copied to output, with a delay of 1 bit time, as shown in Fig. 3-20(b). In transmit mode, which is entered only after the token has been seized, the interface breaks the connection between input and output, entering its own data onto the ring. To be able to switch from listen to transmit mode in 1 bit time, the interface usually needs to buffer one or more frames itself rather than having to fetch them from the station on such short notice.

As bits that have propagated around the ring come back, they are removed from the ring by the sender. The sending station can either save them, to compare with the original data to monitor ring reliability, or discard them. This ring architecture puts no limit on the size of the frames, because the entire frame never appears on the ring at one instant. After a station has finished transmitting the last bit of its last frame, it must regenerate the token. When the last bit of the frame has gone around and come back, it must be removed, and the interface must switch back into listen mode immediately, to avoid removing the token that might follow if no other station has removed it.

It is straightforward to handle acknowledgements on a token ring. The frame format need only include a 1-bit field for acknowledgements, initially zero. When the destination station has received a frame, it inverts the bit. Of course, if the acknowledgement means that the checksum has been verified, the bit must follow the checksum, and the ring interface must be able to verify the checksum as soon as its last bit has arrived. When a frame is broadcast to multiple stations, a more complicated acknowledgement mechanism must be used (if any is used at all).

When traffic is light, the token will spend most of its time idly circulating around the ring. Occasionally a station will seize it, transmit a frame, and then output a new token. However, when the traffic is heavy, so that there is a queue at each station, as soon as a station finishes its transmission and regenerates the token, the next station downstream will see and remove the token. In this manner the permission to send rotates smoothly around the ring, in round-robin fashion. The network efficiency can approach 100 percent under conditions of heavy load.

Now let us turn from token rings in general to the 802.5 standard in particular.

At the physical layer, 802.5 calls for shielded twisted pairs running at 1 or 4 Mbps. The IBM version runs at 4 Mbps and most others do too. Signals are encoded using differential Manchester encoding (see Fig. 2-3) with high and low being positive and negative signals of absolute magnitude 3.0 to 4.5 volts. Normally, differential Manchester encoding uses high-low or low-high for each bit, but 802.5 also uses high-high and low-low in certain control bytes (e.g., to mark the start and end of a frame). These nondata signals always occur in consecutive pairs so as not to introduce a dc component into the ring voltage.

One of the criticisms of ring networks is that if the cable breaks somewhere, the ring dies. This problem can be solved very elegantly by the use of a **wire center**, as shown in Fig. 3-21. While logically still a ring, physically each station is connected to the wire center by a cable containing (at least) two twisted pairs, one for data to the station and one for data from the station.

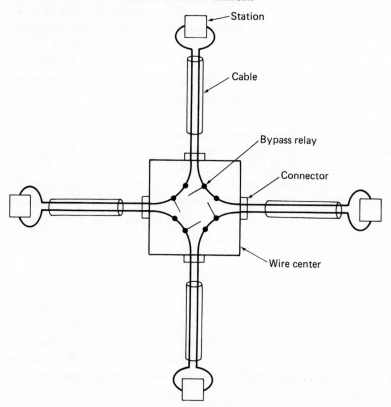

Fig. 3-21. Four stations connected via a wire center.

Inside the wire center are bypass relays that are energized by current from the stations. If the ring breaks or a station goes down, loss of the drive current will release the relay and bypass the station. The relays can also be operated by software to permit diagnostic programs to remove stations one at a time to find faulty stations and ring segments. The ring can then continue operation with the bad segment bypassed. Although the 802.5 standard does not formally require this kind of ring, often called a **star-shaped ring** (Saltzer et al., 1983), it is expected that most 802.5 LANs will, in fact, use wire centers to improve their reliability and maintainability.

When a network consists of many clusters of stations far apart, a topology with multiple wire centers can be used. Just imagine that the cable to one of the stations in Fig. 3-21 was replaced by a cable to a distant wire center. Although logically all the stations are on the same ring, the wiring requirements are greatly reduced.

The Token Ring MAC Sublayer Protocol

The basic operation of the MAC protocol is straightforward. When there is no traffic on the ring, a 3-byte token circulates endlessly, waiting for a station to seize it by setting a specific 0 bit in the second byte to 1. This action converts the first two bytes into the start-of-frame sequence. The station then outputs the rest of a normal data frame, as shown in Fig. 3-22.

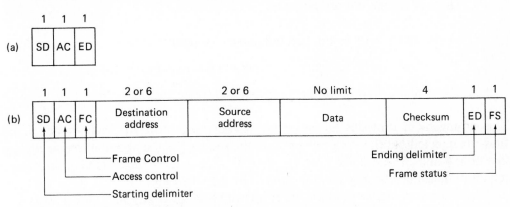

Fig. 3-22. (a) Token format. (b) Data frame format.

Under normal conditions, the first bit of the frame will go around the ring and return to the sender before the full frame has been transmitted. Only a very long ring will be able to hold even a short frame. Consequently, the transmitting station must drain the ring while it continues to transmit. As shown in Fig. 3-20(c), this means that the bits that have completed the trip around the ring come back to the sender and are removed.

A station may hold the token for the **token-holding time**, which is 10 msec unless an installation sets a different value. If there is enough time left after the first frame has been transmitted to send more frames, these may be sent as well. After all pending frames have been transmitted or the transmission of another frame would exceed the token-holding time, the station regenerates the 3-byte token frame and puts it out onto the ring.

The *Starting delimiter* and *Ending delimiter* fields of Fig. 3-22(b) mark the beginning and ending of the frame. Each contains invalid differential Manchester patterns (HH and LL) to distinguish them from data bytes. The *Access control* byte contains the token bit, and also the *Monitor bit*, *Priority bits*, and *Reservation bits* (described below). The *Frame control* byte distinguishes data frames from various control frames.

Next come the *Destination address* and *Source address* fields, which are the same as in 802.3 and 802.4. These are followed by the data, which may be as long as necessary, provided that the frame can still be transmitted within the token-holding time. The *Checksum* field, like the destination and source addresses, is also the same as 802.3 and 802.4.

An interesting byte not present in the other two protocols is the *Frame status* byte. It contains the *A* and *C* bits. When a frame arrives at the interface of a station with the destination address, the interface turns on the *A* bit as it passes through. If the interface also copies the frame to the station, it also turns on the *C* bit. A station might fail to copy a frame due to lack of buffer space or other reasons.

When the sending station drains the frame from the ring, it examines the *A* and *C* bits. Three combinations are possible:

1. $A = 0$ and $C = 0$: destination not present or not powered up.

2. $A = 1$ and $C = 0$: destination present but frame not accepted.

3. $A = 1$ and $C = 1$: destination present and frame copied.

This arrangement provides an automatic acknowledgement for each frame. If a frame is rejected but the station is present, the sender has the option of trying again in a little while. The *A* and *C* bits are present twice in the *Frame status* to increase reliability inasmuch as they are not covered by the checksum.

The *Ending delimiter* contains an *E* bit which is set if any interface detects an error (e.g., a non-Manchester pattern where that is not permitted). It also contains a bit that can be used to mark the last frame in a logical sequence, sort of like an end-of-file bit.

The 802.5 protocol has an elaborate scheme for handling multiple priority frames. The 3-byte token frame contains a field in the middle byte giving the priority of the token. When a station wants to transmit a priority *n* frame, it must wait until it can capture a token whose priority is less than or equal to *n*. Furthermore, when a data frame goes by, a station can try to reserve the next token by writing the priority of the frame it wants to send into the frame's *Reservation bits*. However, if a higher priority has already been reserved there, the station may not make a reservation. When the current frame is finished, the next token is generated at the priority that has been reserved.

A little thought will show that this mechanism acts like a ratchet, always jacking the reservation priority higher and higher. To eliminate this problem, the protocol contains some complex rules. The essence of the idea is that a station raising the reservation priority is also responsible for lowering the priority again when it is done.

Notice that this priority scheme is substantially different from the token bus scheme, in which each station always gets its fair share of the bandwidth, no matter what other stations are doing. In the token ring, a station with only low priority frames may starve to death waiting for a low priority token to appear. Clearly the two committees had different taste when trading off good service for high priority traffic vs. fairness to all stations.

Ring Maintenance

The token bus protocol goes to considerable lengths to do ring maintenance in a fully decentralized way. The token ring protocol handles maintenance quite differently. Each token ring has a **monitor station** that oversees the ring. If the monitor goes down, a contention protocol insures that another station is elected monitor quickly. (Every station has the capability of becoming the monitor.) While the monitor is functioning properly, it alone is responsible for seeing that the ring operates correctly.

When the ring comes up or any station notices that there is no monitor, it can transmit a *CLAIM TOKEN* control frame. If this frame circumnavigates the ring before any other *CLAIM TOKEN* frames are sent, the sender becomes the new monitor (each station has monitor capability built in). The token ring control frames are shown in Fig. 3-23.

Frame control field	Name	Meaning
00000000	Duplicate address test	Test if two stations have same address
00000010	Beacon	Used to locate breaks in the ring
00000011	Claim token	Attempt to become monitor
00000100	Purge	Reinitialize the ring
00000101	Active monitor present	Issued periodically by the monitor
00000110	Stand by monitor present	Announces the presence of potential monitors

Fig. 3-23. Token ring control frames.

Among the monitor's responsibilities are seeing that the token is not lost, taking action when the ring breaks, cleaning the ring up when garbled frames appear, and watching out for orphan frames. An orphan frame occurs when a station transmits a short frame in its entirety onto a long ring and then crashes or is powered down before the frame can be drained. If nothing is done, the frame will circulate forever.

To check for lost tokens, the monitor has a timer that is set to the longest possible tokenless interval, namely, each station transmitting for the full token-holding time. If this timer goes off, the monitor drains the ring and issues a new token.

When a garbled frame appears, the monitor can detect it by its invalid format or checksum, and then open the ring to drain it, issuing a new token when the ring has been cleaned up. Finally, the monitor detects orphan frames by setting the *monitor* bit in the *Access control* byte whenever it passes through. If an incoming frame has this bit set, something is wrong since the same frame has passed the monitor twice without having been drained, so the monitor drains it.

One last monitor function concerns the length of the ring. The token is 24 bits long, which means that the ring must be big enough to hold 24 bits. If the 1-bit delays in the stations plus the cable length add up to less than 24 bits, the monitor inserts extra delay bits so that a token can circulate.

One maintenance function that cannot be handled by the monitor is locating breaks in the ring. When a station notices that either of its neighbors appears to be dead, it transmits *BEACON* frame giving the address of the presumably dead station. When the beacon has propagated around as far as it can, it is then possible to see how many stations are down, and delete them from the ring using the bypass relays in the wire center, all without human intervention.

It is instructive to compare the approaches taken to controlling the token bus and the token ring. The 802.4 committee was scared to death of having any centralized component that could fail in some unexpected way and take the system down with it. Therefore they designed a system in which the current token holder had special powers (e.g., soliciting bids to join the ring), but no station was otherwise different from the others (e.g., currently assigned administrative responsibility for maintenance).

The 802.5 committee, on the other hand, felt that having a centralized monitor made handling lost tokens, orphan frames and so on much easier. Furthermore, in a normal system, stations hardly ever crash, so occasionally having to put up with contention for a new monitor is not a great hardship. The price paid is that if the monitor ever really goes berserk, but continues to issue *ACTIVE MONITOR PRESENT* control frames periodically, no station will ever challenge it. Monitors cannot be impeached.

This difference in approach comes from the different application areas the two committees had in mind. The 802.4 committee was thinking in terms of factories with large masses of metal moving around under computer control. Network failures could result in severe damage, and had to be prevented at all costs. The 802.5 committee was interested in office automation, where a failure once in a rare while could be tolerated as the price for a simpler system. Whether 802.4 is, in fact, more reliable than 802.5 is a matter of some controversy.

Slotted Rings

The token ring is not the only kind of ring in widespread use. We will now briefly examine two other popular LAN rings, even though they are not part of 802. The first of these is the **slotted ring** so-called because it is slotted into a number of fixed-size frames. Unless the physical distance around the ring is very large or there are many stations, it is unlikely that there will be enough delay to hold several frames, so artificial delays are needed. These can be obtained easily by putting shift registers in the ring interfaces. Instead of the 1-bit delay of Fig. 3-20(b), there are multiple-bit delays. Figure 3-24 shows a conceptual model of a slotted ring.

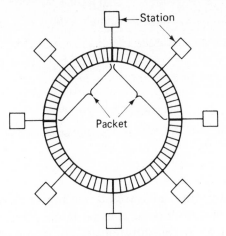

Fig. 3-24. A slotted ring.

Each frame contains a bit that tells whether it is full or empty. When a station wishes to transmit, it simply waits for an empty frame to come around, marks it as full, and puts its data in the frame. Of course, frames must be small enough to fit in a frame, in contrast to the token ring, which support frames of arbitrarily large size. The performance of slotted rings is analyzed in (Wu and Spratt, 1987).

Register Insertion Rings

The other kind of ring, the **register insertion ring**, is a more sophisticated version of the slotted ring. It was developed by Liu (1978). To understand how the register insertion ring works, we must examine the ring interface, shown in Fig. 3-25. The interface contains two registers, a shift register and an output buffer. When a station has a frame to transmit, it loads the frame into the output buffer. Frames may be of variable length, up to the size of the output buffer.

When the ring is started up, the input pointer shown in Fig. 3-25 points to the rightmost bit position in the shift register, meaning that all the bit slots at and to the left of where it is pointing are empty. When a bit arrives from the ring, it is placed at the position pointed to by the input pointer, and the pointer is moved 1 bit to the left. As soon as the address field of the frame has arrived, the interface can determine whether or not the frame is addressed to it. If so, the rest of the frame is diverted to the station, removing the frame from the ring. The input pointer is then reset to the extreme right.

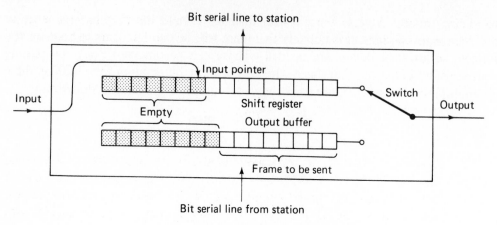

Fig. 3-25. Interface of a register insertion ring.

If, however, the frame is not addressed to the local station, the interface begins forwarding it. As each new bit arrives, it is put in the place pointed to by the input pointer. The entire contents of the shift register are then shifted right one position, pushing the rightmost bit out onto the ring. The input pointer is not advanced. If no new input arrives, for example due to an interframe gap, the contents of the shift register can be reduced by 1 bit and the input pointer moved right one position.

Now let us see how output from the station happens. Whenever the shift register has pushed out the last bit of a frame, it checks to see if (1) there is an output frame waiting, and (2) the number of empty slots in the shift register is at least as large as the output frame. Only if both conditions are met can output proceed, in which case the output switch is flipped and the output buffer is now shifted out onto the ring, 1 bit at a time, in synchronization with the input. New input is accumulated in the shift register, which is why there must be enough empty slots there to accommodate all the input while the output buffer is being emptied. Not all the slots may be needed, since an interframe gap may arrive during output, but the interface must be prepared for the worst case. As soon as the output buffer has been emptied, the switch is flipped again, and the shift register is emptied (if it has anything in it).

An interesting property of this ring architecture is the way it prevents a station from monopolizing the ring. If the ring is idle, the shift register will be empty when an output frame has been finished, so the next output frame can be sent as soon as it can be loaded into the output buffer by the station. In effect, if the ring is idle, any station can have the entire bandwidth if it so desires. If the ring is busy, however, after sending a frame the station will not be allowed to send another one because there will usually be insufficient empty slots in the shift register. Only when enough interframe gaps have been saved up can output occur again. In essence, to send a b-bit frame, the interface must accumulate b bits of empty space on the ring in which to insert the frame. The *b* bits need not be consecutive, however, because the interframe gaps are accumulated in the left-hand portion of the shift register.

3.4.4. Comparison of Local Area Networks

With three different LAN standards available, many organizations are faced with the question: "Which one should we install?" In this section we will look at all three of the 802 LAN standards, pointing out their strengths and weaknesses, comparing and contrasting them. The following section compares LANs with PBXes.

To start with, it is worth noting that the three LAN standards use roughly similar technology and get roughly similar performance. While computer scientists and engineers can discuss the merits of coax versus twisted pair for hours on end if given half a chance, the people in the marketing, personnel, or accounting departments probably do not really care that much one way or the other.

Let us start with the advantages of 802.3. It is far and away the most widely used type at present, with a huge installed base and considerable operational experience. The algorithm is simple. Stations can be installed on the fly, without taking the network down. A passive cable is used and modems are not required. Furthermore, the delay at low load is practically zero (stations do not have to wait for a token; they just transmit immediately).

On the other hand, 802.3 has a substantial analog component. Each station has to be able to detect the signal of the weakest other station even when it itself is transmitting, and all of the collision detect circuitry in the transceiver is analog. Due to the possibility of having frames aborted by collisions, the minimum valid frame is 64 bytes, which represents substantial overhead when the data is just a single character from a terminal.

Furthermore, 802.3 is nondeterministic, which is often inappropriate for real time work. It has no priorities. The cable length is limited to 2.5 km (when repeaters are used) because the round trip cable length determines the slot time, hence the performance. Getting CSMA/CD networks such as 802.3 to run at high speeds is difficult, and as the speed increases, the efficiency drops because the frame transmission times drop but the contention interval does not (the slot width is 2τ no matter what the data rate is). As technology improves and networks get faster, this efficiency issue will become very significant (Chlamtac and Ganz, 1988).

At high load, the presence of collisions becomes a major problem, and can seriously affect the throughput. Moreover, 802.3 is not well suited to fiber optics due to the difficulty of installing taps.

Now let us consider the 802.4, the token bus. It uses highly reliable cable television equipment, which is available off-the-shelf from numerous vendors. It is more deterministic than 802.3, although repeated losses of the token at critical moments can introduce more uncertainty than its supporters like to admit. It can handle short minimum frames.

Token bus also supports priorities and can be configured to provide a guaranteed fraction of the bandwidth to high-priority traffic, such as digitized voice. It also has excellent throughput and efficiency at high load, effectively becoming TDM. Finally, broadband cable can support multiple channels, not only for data, but also for voice and television.

On the down side, broadband systems use a lot of analog engineering, include modems and wideband amplifiers. The protocol is extremely complex and has substantial delay at low load (stations must always wait for the token, even in an otherwise idle system). Finally, it is poorly suited for fiber optic implementations.

Now consider the token ring. It uses point-to-point connections, meaning that the engineering is easy and fully digital. Rings can be built using virtually any transmission medium from carrier pigeon to fiber optics. The standard twisted pair is cheap and simple to install. The use of wire centers make the token ring the only LAN that can detect and eliminate cable failures automatically.

Like the token bus, priorities are possible, although the scheme is not as fair. Also like the token bus, short frames are possible, but unlike the token bus, so are arbitrarily large ones, limited only by the token-holding time. Finally, the throughput and efficiency at high load are excellent, like the token bus and unlike 802.3.

The major minus is the presence of centralized monitor function, which introduces a critical component. Even though a dead monitor can be replaced, a sick one can cause headaches. Furthermore, like all token passing schemes, there is some delay at low load because the sender must wait for the token.

It is also worth pointing out that there have been numerous studies of all three LANs (Bux, 1987; Ferguson, 1986; Hammond and O'Reilly, 1986; Sachs et al., 1985; Schwartz, 1987; and Stuck, 1983). The principle conclusion we can draw from these studies is that we can draw no conclusions from them. One can always find a set of parameters that makes one of the LANs look better than the others.

The only general statement that is inarguable is that an overloaded 802.3 LAN will collapse totally, but an overloaded token-based system will have an efficiency approaching 100 percent. For people planning to run their LAN in overloaded mode, 802.3 is definitely not the way to go. For people planning to run with light to moderate load, all three perform well, so that factors other than the performance are probably more important.

Since all three LAN types are likely to coexist for years to come, the issue of interconnecting different LANs is an important one. We will defer our discussion of LAN bridges (layer 2) and gateways (layer 3) to Chapter 5, partly because bridges and gateways are very similar and can best be examined together, and partly because routing among LAN bridges in complex networks is definitely a layer 3 subject.

ISDN PBXes versus LANs

Now let us briefly compare ISDN PBXes to LANs. A PBX can be used to connect all the stations in a building, so it is clearly a competitor to the LAN. The PBX can use existing telephone wiring, eliminating the need to rewire the building, a huge plus. It can also carry voice and data over the same network, another big plus. Furthermore, the PBX can connect stations not only to other local stations, but also to those far away in a totally transparent way, yet another major advantage over the LANs, which need gateways and all kinds of other complicated mechanisms. Finally, the total throughput of a PBX can easily exceed 500 Mbps, something no LAN can even begin to approach.

The problem with PBXes is that they do everything in a big way. The advantages over LANs are enormous, but so are the disadvantages. The worst is the minuscule 64-kbps bandwidth on each ISDN channel. Trying to page virtual memory to a remote disk over a 64-kbps channel would be agonizingly slow. Even trying to read a file from a remote file server at 8000 bytes/sec would be unbearable.

Another very serious problem is that PBXes are circuit switched, which is fine for continuous traffic but terrible for the kind of bursty traffic that computers generate. Thus a PBX with a rated capacity of 500 Mbps may, in practice, offer a lower total throughput than a 10-Mbps LAN because most of the 500 Mbps is dedicated to channels that do not need it, but those channels that do need high bandwidth cannot have it.

Finally, a PBX is a highly complex, centralized component. It is conceivable that a problem in the PBX could bring the entire network down. On the other hand, some PBXes contain enough redundancy to make this event unlikely, although this redundancy always costs extra.

The PBX-LAN controversy will no doubt go on for years, with neither side achieving a definitive victory. In fact, many organizations will probably install both a PBX and a LAN, with the PBX used primarily for traffic with distant machines and the LAN used primarily for in-house traffic. Gateways between the two will make life easier for users needing access to both. The design of LAN-PBX gateways is discussed in (Gray et al., 1987; and Maebara and Takeuchi, 1987).

3.5. FIBER OPTIC NETWORKS

The three 802 LANs we have just studied are all based on copper media. However, fiber optics is becoming increasingly important, not only for wide-area point-to-point links, but also for metropolitan and local area networks. Fiber has high bandwidth, is thin and lightweight, is not affected by electromagnetic interference from heavy machinery (important when cabling runs through elevator shafts), power surges, or lightning, and has excellent security because it is nearly impossible to wiretap without detection. In the following sections we will look at some networks that use fiber optics, either exclusively or in combination with copper. Several additional systems are described in (Kummerle et al., 1987).

3.5.1. FDDI

FDDI (Fiber Distributed Data Interface) is a high performance fiber optic token ring LAN running at 100 Mbps over distances up to 200 km with up to 1000 stations connected (Burr, 1986; Joshi, 1986; and Ross, 1986, 1987). It can be used in the same way as any of the 802 LANs, but with its high bandwidth, another common use is as a backbone to connect copper LANs, as shown in Fig. 3-26. FDDI-II is the successor to FDDI, modified to handle synchronous circuit switched PCM data for voice or ISDN traffic, in addition to ordinary data. We will refer to both of them as just FDDI. This section deals with both the physical layer and the MAC sublayer of FDDI.

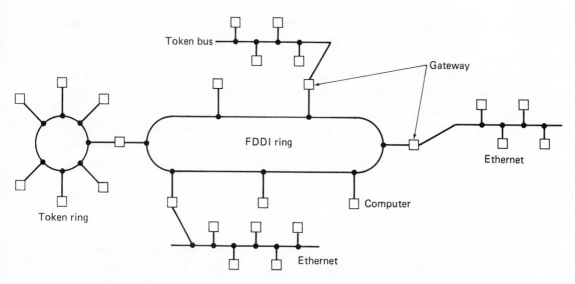

Fig. 3-26. An FDDI ring being used as a backbone to connect LANs and computers.

FDDI uses multimode fibers [see Fig. 2-5(b)] because the additional expense of single mode fibers is not needed for networks running at only 100 Mbps. It also uses LEDs rather than lasers, not only due to their lower cost, but also because FDDI may sometimes be used to connect directly to user workstations. There is a danger that curious users may occasionally unplug the fiber connector and look directly into it to watch the bits go by at 100 Mbps. With a laser the curious user might end up with a hole in his retina. LEDs are too weak to do any eye damage but are strong enough to transfer data accurately at 100 Mbps. The FDDI design specification calls for no more than 1 error in 2.5×10^{10} bits. Many implementations will do much better.

The FDDI cabling consists of two fiber rings, one transmitting clockwise and the other transmitting counterclockwise, as illustrated in Fig. 3-27(a). If either one breaks, the other can be used as a backup. If both break at the same point, for example, due to a fire or other accident in the cable duct, the two rings can be joined into a single ring approximately twice as long, as shown in Fig. 3-27(b). Each station contains relays that can be used to join the two rings or bypass the station in the event of station problems. Wire centers can also be used, as in 802.5.

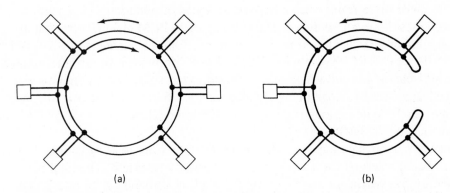

(a)   (b)

Fig. 3-27. (a) FDDI consists of two counterrotating rings. (b) In the event of failure of both rings at one point, the two rings can be joined together to form a single long ring.

FDDI defines two classes of stations, *A* and *B*. Class *A* stations connect to both rings. The cheaper class *B* stations only connect to one of the rings. Depending on how important fault tolerance is, an installation can choose class *A* or class *B* stations, or some of each.

The physical layer does not use Manchester encoding because 100 Mbps Manchester encoding requires 200 megabaud, which was deemed too expensive. Instead a scheme called **4 out of 5** encoding is used. Each group of 4 MAC symbols (0s, 1s, and certain nondata symbols such as start-of-frame) are encoded as a group of 5 bits on the medium. Sixteen of the 32 combinations are for data, 3 are for delimiters, 2 are for control, 3 are for hardware signaling, and 8 are unused.

The advantage of this scheme is that it saves bandwidth, but the disadvantage is the loss of the self-clocking property of Manchester encoding. To compensate for this loss, a long preamble is used to synchronize the receiver to the sender's clock. Furthermore, all clocks are required to be stable to at least 0.005 percent. With this stability, frames up to 4500 bytes can be sent without danger of the receiver's clock drifting too far out of sync with the data stream.

The basic FDDI protocols are closely modeled on the 802.5 protocols. To transmit data, a station must first capture the token. Then it transmits a frame and removes it when it comes around again. One difference between FDDI and 802.5 is that in 802.5, a station may not generate a new token until its frame has gone all the way around and come back. In FDDI, with potentially 1000 stations and 200 km of fiber, the amount of time wasted waiting for the frame to circumnavigate the ring could be substantial. For this reason, it was decided to allow a station to put a new token back onto the ring as soon as it is done transmitting its frames. In a large ring, several frames might be on the ring at the same time.

FDDI permits data frames similar to 802.5, including the acknowledgement bits in the *frame status* byte. However, it also permits special synchronous frames for circuit switched PCM or ISDN data. The synchronous frames are generated every 125 μsec by a master station to provide the 8000 samples/sec needed by PCM systems. Each of these frames has a header, 16 bytes of noncircuit switched data, and up to 96 bytes of circuit-switched data (i.e., up to 96 PCM channels per frame).

The number 96 was chosen because it allows four T1 channels (4×24) at 1.544 Mbps or three CCITT channels (3×32) at 2.048 Mbps to fit in a frame, thus making it suitable for use anywhere in the world. One synchronous frame every 125 μsec consumes 6.144 Mbps of bandwidth for the 96 circuit-switched channels. A maximum of 16 synchronous frames every 125 μsec allows up to 1536 PCM channels and eats up 98.3 Mbps.

Once a station has acquired one or more time slots in a synchronous frame, those slots are reserved for it until they are explicitly released. The total bandwidth not used by the synchronous frames is allocated on demand. A bit mask is present in each of these frames to indicate which slots are available for demand assignment. The nonsynchronous traffic is divided into priority classes, with the higher priorities getting first shot at the leftover bandwidth.

The MAC protocol requires each station to have a token rotation timer to keep track of how long it was since the last token was seen. A priority algorithm similar to 802.4 is used to determine which priority classes may transmit on a given token pass. If the token is ahead of schedule, all priorities may transmit, but if it is behind schedule, only the highest ones may send.

3.5.2. Fibernet II

A group of researchers (Schmidt et al., 1983) at Xerox have built a fiber LAN compatible with Ethernet at the transceiver interface so that stations could be plugged into it using their existing station to transceiver cable (see Fig. 3-14). The hard part about building any CSMA/CD network out of fiber optics is getting the collision detection to work. Several methods are possible using the passive star configuration of Fig. 2-7 (Reedy and Jones, 1985):

1. **Power sensing.** If a station senses more power than it is putting out, its transmission must be colliding with another station's.

2. **Pulse width.** If two stations collide, the incoming pulse will be wider than the outgoing pulse. This difference can be detected.

3. **Time delay.** When two stations collide, the one transmitting last will receive power from the first one earlier than its own signal should be coming back. It can detect this difference.

4. **Directional coupling.** It is possible to design the transmit and receive equipment so that a receiver does not pick up transmissions from its own station. Any transmissions it does receive while transmitting must therefore be collisions.

All of these are quite tricky to implement. Furthermore, passive stars greatly weaken the signal because the incoming energy has to be divided over all the outgoing lines. Consequently, Schmidt et al. used an active star instead of a passive one. In their system, each transceiver has two point-to-point fibers running to the central star, one of them for input and the other for output. The active star is sketched in Fig. 3-28.

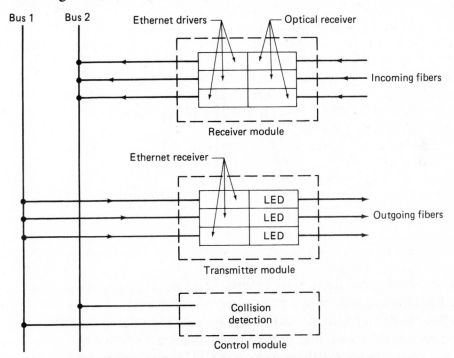

Fig. 3-28. The Fibernet II active star for collision detection.

At the star, each incoming optical signal is converted to an electrical signal, processed electronically, and then reconverted to an optical signal for output on the other fiber. Connected to each incoming fiber is an opto-electrical coupler that converts the pulse stream coming off the fiber into an electrical signal. This signal is fed into a tiny CSMA/CD driver inside the active star. All the signals from the drivers go onto a common electrical bus.

If two signals collide, this event will be detected electrically the same way as in an ordinary CSMA/CD. If there is no collision, the one incoming signal is transferred to a second internal bus that drives the transmitter module. The incoming signal is broadcast to all the transceivers by modulating each one's individual LED. This scheme does not require dividing the incoming power among N ways to spread it among the N transceivers. Each transceiver gets full power.

3.5.3. S/NET

S/NET (Ahuja, 1983) is another fiber optic network with an active star for switching. It was designed and implemented at Bell Laboratories. Unlike Fibernet II, whose goal was compatibility with Ethernet, the goal of S/NET was very fast switching. The structure of the active star is illustrated in Fig. 3-29.

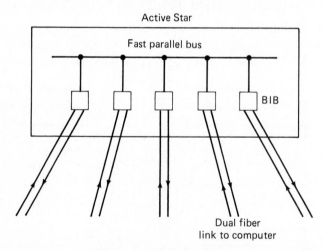

Fig. 3-29. The S/NET switch.

Each computer in the network has two 20-Mbps fibers running to the switch, one for input and one for output. The fibers terminate in a **BIB** (**Bus Interface Board**). The CPUs each have an I/O device register that acts like a one-word window into BIB memory. When a word is written to that device register, the interface board in the CPU transmits the bits serially over the fiber to the BIB, where they are reassembled as a word in BIB memory. When the whole frame to be transmitted has been copied to BIB memory, the CPU writes a command to another I/O device register to cause the switch to copy the frame to the memory of the destination BIB and interrupt the destination CPU.

Access to the bus is done by a priority algorithm. Each BIB has a unique priority. When a BIB wants access to the bus it asserts a signal on the bus line corresponding to its priority. The requests are recorded and granted in priority order, with one word transferred (16 bits in parallel) at a time. When all requests have been granted, another round of bidding is started and BIBs can again request the bus. No bus cycles are lost to contention, so switching speed is 16 bits every 200 nsec, or 80 Mbps.

3.5.4. FASNET AND EXPRESSNET

FASNET is a high performance network suitable for use as a LAN or MAN. It was designed at Bell Laboratories and is described in (Limb, 1984; and Limb and Flores, 1987). Related work is discussed in (Fratta and Gerla, 1985; Tobagi and Fine, 1983; and Ulug, 1985).

FASNET uses two linear unidirectional buses, as shown in Fig. 3-30. Each station taps onto both buses and can send and receive on either one. When a station wants to send a frame to a higher numbered station it transmits on bus A; when it wants to send to a lower numbered station, it transmits on bus B. Stations 1 and N play special roles in this network, as we shall see.

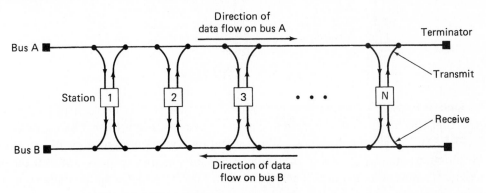

Fig. 3-30. FASNET.

A transmission cycle is started when station 1 begins transmitting a sequence of fixed-size slots on bus A and station N begins transmitting an identical sequence in the opposite direction on bus B. These slots provide the clocking for the bus. Other stations synchronize their transmissions to them as they propagate by. The slots can be thought of as a train of empty flatcars onto which data can be loaded.

When a station wanting to transmit to a higher numbered station detects the start of the train of bus A, it waits until the first empty slot passes by. The station then sets a bit in the first byte of the slot marking it as busy, and places the source and destination addresses and the data in the empty slot. If the data do not fit in a single slot, several consecutive slots may be allocated. When the downstream station to whom the frame is addressed sees the frame, it just copies it to its memory, leaving the slot on the bus, still marked as busy. An analogous mechanism is used on bus B.

When the last station on either bus detects the end of the train, it sends an announcement frame on the other bus. When it arrives, a new train is started. The interval between train departures on either bus is equal to the round trip propagation time plus the time required to transmit all the frames on that cycle.

EXPRESSNET (Tobagi et al., 1987) is similar to FASNET in a number of ways. However, rather than using two buses, EXPRESSNET uses a single bus folded as illustrated in Fig. 3-31. Each station attaches to the bus in two places, once on the outbound portion, for transmission, and once on the inbound portion, for reception.

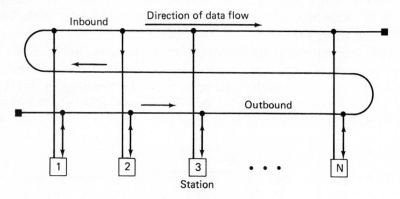

Fig. 3-31. EXPRESSNET

Unlike FASNET, which is synchronous (the first station on each bus generates the complete train and the other stations have to align their clocks with it), EXPRESSNET is asynchronous. When a station has a frame to transmit, it senses the inbound channel to see if the cable is already in use. If it is, the station just waits until the cable is quiet. Then the station hooks its frame on the end, to form a train. When the train reaches the inbound portion it is accepted by the station to whom it is addressed.

Due to the nonzero propagation time, a problem can occur if two stations, say 2 and 3, try to transmit simultaneously. A few microseconds after station 3 has started sending, the front of station 2's frame will arrive on the outbound channel and collide with station 3's frame. To deal with this problem, all stations monitor the outbound channel and terminate transmission instantly if they detect a frame from a lower-numbered station coming in from the left. Implicitly, this algorithm resolves collisions in favor of the lower-numbered station, but it also garbles a few bits at the front of its frame.

The obvious solution is for each station to transmit a few bytes of preamble before its frame. The preamble is not part of the data. It is designed to absorb collisions. If we stick to the train model, the preamble is the cowcatcher.

EXPRESSNET differs from FASNET in a few ways. For one thing, there is the issue of synchronous versus asynchronous transmission (analogous to the difference between a slotted ring and a token ring). For another, FASNET requires N

taps on each of two cables, whereas EXPRESSNET requires 2*N* taps on one cable, potentially a significant difference with fiber optics since the taps are lossy. Finally, the propagation time for a frame from station 1 to station *N* is three times as long in EXPRESSNET as FASNET. Tobagi and Fine (1983) model the performance of both systems.

3.5.5. DATAKIT

DATAKIT (Fraser, 1987) is a network that was designed at Bell Labs and is currently sold by AT&T. It differs from most other networks in that it is a single integrated network to be used as a LAN, MAN, and WAN. Furthermore, it allows copper and fiber to be intermixed in arbitrary ways.

Architecturally, DATAKIT consists of switches, each with various kinds of lines coming out of it. These lines may go to terminals, computers, or other DATAKIT switches. The lines going to terminals are typically twisted pairs, but the lines connecting two DATAKIT switches may be fiber optic trunks running at T1 speed (1.544 Mbps) or higher. Thus a DATAKIT network consists of multiple interconnected stars, rather than a bus or ring.

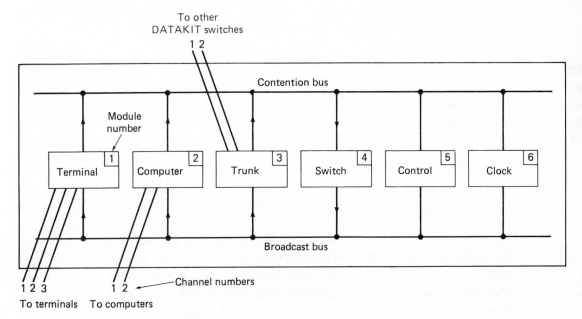

Fig. 3-32. A DATAKIT switch.

The structure of a DATAKIT switch is given in Fig. 3-32. The switch backplane has two buses, a contention bus and a broadcast bus. Various cards can be inserted into the switch, each card connected to both buses. Some cards contain RS-232-C interfaces for terminals, others contain computer interfaces, and still others contain interfaces for copper or fiber optic trunks to other switches. When a terminal, computer or other DATAKIT switch has a byte to transmit to a device attached to a different card, it competes for the contention bus, and when it acquires the bus, puts the byte on the bus. The switch card removes the byte from the contention bus and puts it on the broadcast bus, where the destination card takes it off.

Unlike all the other networks we have studied so far, DATAKIT uses virtual circuits. When a terminal or computer wants to communicate with another terminal or computer, it sends a request to the control computer in its local switch to find a path to the destination. The control computer records the path in its tables, and uses that path when the data arrive later.

Consider, for example, what happens when terminal 3 connected to module 1 in Fig. 3-32 wants to communicate with the computer connected to the same switch via line 1 on module 2. First a virtual circuit must be established by the control computer. Establishment of the virtual circuit results in a table entry being made in the switch. For example $(1,3) \rightarrow (2,1)$ might map module 1, channel (i.e., line) 3 onto module 2, channel 1.

Later, when a character arrives from the terminal, the terminal card builds a DATAKIT frame (see Fig. 3-33), and tries to acquire the contention bus. The contention bus protocol is the binary countdown algorithm described earlier. When the bus has been acquired, it outputs the frame with its own module number (1) in the module field and the terminal's channel number (3) in the channel field.

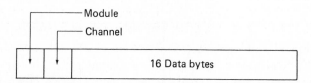

Fig. 3-33. A DATAKIT frame. The module and channel fields contain the source module and channel when on the contention bus, and the destination module and channel when on the broadcast bus. All the "bytes" are 9 bits wide. The ninth bit is used to distinguish control bytes from data bytes.

When the switch module sees the frame, it looks up the combination (1,3) in the switching table and performs the mapping onto (2,1). The switch then copies the frame from the contention bus to the broadcast bus, replacing the source module and channel by the destination module and channel. All the cards receive the frame from the broadcast bus, but only card 2 accepts it, sending it off on its line 1.

This switching scheme not only works locally, but also over metropolitan or wide area networks. A frame destined for a different DATAKIT switch will be mapped onto one of the channels of the appropriate outgoing trunk. When a data frame arrives, it will be switched to the trunk card, which then outputs it over one of the trunks. At the other end, it comes into another trunk card, where it is buffered until it can acquire the contention bus in that system and be switched again.

In a way, a DATAKIT switch resembles a PBX. It has incoming and outgoing lines, and uses circuit switching. On the other hand, the DATAKIT switched data streams are just byte streams, in any format (not just PCM), and at any speed (not just 64 kbps). Furthermore, DATAKIT is not synchronous like a time division switch, so an idle module consumes no bandwidth. In that respect, internally DATAKIT is more like a packet switch than a circuit switch, even though externally it appears to do circuit switching.

3.6. SATELLITE NETWORKS

Having finished with channel allocation in broadcast LANs, let us now turn our attention to channel allocation in broadcast WANs. In this section, we will deal with satellite networks; in the following one we will study packet radio networks. Both of these subjects are becoming increasingly important.

Communication satellites generally have a dozen or so transponders. Each transponder has a beam that covers some portion of the earth below it. Stations within the beam area can send frames to the satellite on the uplink frequency. The satellite shifts these frames to the downlink frequency and rebroadcasts them. Different frequencies are used for uplink and downlink so that upward and downward frames do not interfere with each other.

Just as with LANs, one of the key design issues is how to allocate the transponder channels. However, unlike LANs, carrier sensing is impossible due to the 270-msec propagation delay. When a station senses the state of a transponder channel, it hears what was going on 270 msec ago. It has no way of hearing whether any other stations are trying to transmit right now. As a result, the CSMA/CD protocols (which assume that a transmitting station can detect collisions within the first few bit times, and then pull back if one is occurring) cannot be used with satellites. Thus unlike LAN protocols, in which collisions only occupy a small number of bit times, each satellite collision wastes an entire frame. Hence the need for new protocols.

In theory, a protocol such as the token bus protocol could be used. However, with a propagation time of 270 msec, it would take 27 sec to pass the token around a 100 station ring, even if no frames were queued for transmission. Hardly an attractive proposition.

In the following sections we will discuss various allocation algorithms for satellite channels. We will start out with classical FDM and TDM schemes, then look at some variations on ALOHA. Next we will consider algorithms that reserve channel slots in advance. Finally, we will conclude with a method that combines the best properties of the foregoing techniques into a single protocol that has been used in several satellites.

3.6.1. SPADE

Traditionally, satellites have been used to connect a limited number of telephone switching offices, each of which has a continuous flow of data to transmit. Under these conditions, it makes sense to use FDM or TDM. FDM is the simplest. Each transponder channel is divided into disjoint subchannels at different frequencies, with (unused) guard bands between the subchannels to keep two adjacent channels from interfering. When a telephone call requiring a satellite channel is placed, for example, an intercontinental call, a subchannel is allocated to that call and not deallocated until the call is terminated. The entire subchannel bandwidth is dedicated to that one call throughout its duration. As long as there are enough calls to keep the satellite reasonably busy, this scheme works moderately well.

An alternative to FDM is TDM, in which the satellite channel is not divided into subchannels by frequency, but by time. The channel is divided into slots, which are grouped into frames. For digital telephony, a frame would be 125 μsec to accommodate the PCM sampling rate. When a call is placed, a free slot is allocated and dedicated to the call in every frame until the call is finished. If no slot is available, the caller gets a busy signal and has to try again later.

Although FDM and TDM are similar, they do have some differences. For one, FDM requires guard bands to keep the signals well separated. The guard bands occupy a nonnegligible amount of the spectrum. For another, TDM can be used to broadcast control and status messages to all stations by just setting a header bit. After all, every station receives every slot. FDM does not have this broadcast property. On the other hand, TDM needs careful time slot synchronization, something FDM does not need.

As an example of how FDM works, let us consider the **SPADE** system used on some early Intelsat satellites. Each SPADE transponder is divided into 794 simplex (64 kbps) PCM channels, along with a 128 kbps common signaling channel. The PCM channels are used in pairs to provide full duplex service. The total transponder bandwidth used is 50 Mbps for the uplink portion and another 50 Mbps for the downlink. The channels are allocated by FDM, although TDM could also have been chosen.

The common signaling channel is divided into units of 50 msec. A unit contains 50 slots of 1 msec (128 bits). Each slot is "owned" by one of (not more than) 50 ground stations. When a ground station has data to send, it picks a currently unused channel at random and writes the number of that channel in its next 128-bit slot. If the selected channel is still unused when the request is seen on the downlink, the channel is considered allocated and all other stations refrain from trying to acquire it. If two or more stations try to allocate the same channel in the same frame, the first one wins and the others must try again later. When a station is finished using its channel, it sends a deallocation message in its slot on the common channel.

3.6.2. ALOHA Revisited

Systems using TDM, FDM, or SPADE are only feasible when the number of stations is small and relatively static, and all of them have continuous traffic. When there are hundreds or thousands of stations, or stations with bursty traffic, none of these algorithms are attractive. Instead, ALOHA becomes a serious candidate again.

The problem with ALOHA, of course, is the low channel efficiency. With pure ALOHA it is $1/2e$ or 0.184. Even with slotted ALOHA it is only $1/e$ or 0.368. Various proposals have been made to improve this efficiency. In this section we will examine some of these proposals.

The obvious way to run a slotted ALOHA system on a satellite is to have an uplink channel and a downlink channel, each of bandwidth B bps for a total of $2B$ allocated bandwidth. The throughput will be B/e bps. The channel efficiency is then $(B/e)/2B$ or $1/2e$, which is 0.184. Thus the requirement that frames must be explicitly rebroadcast by the satellite costs a factor of two in efficiency compared to an ALOHA system in which each station can hear the original transmissions.

Now consider what happens if we go from a system with one uplink and one downlink channel, as shown in Fig. 3-34(a), to one with two uplink channels and one downlink channel, as shown in Fig. 3-34(b).

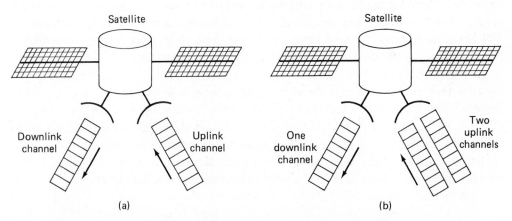

Fig. 3-34. (a) An ALOHA system with one uplink and one downlink channel. (b) An ALOHA system with two uplink and one downlink channels.

A station with a frame to transmit chooses one of the two uplink channels at random and sends the frame in the next slot. Each uplink is an independent slotted ALOHA channel. If we assume each channel is operated optimally ($G = 1$), then according to Eq. (3-2) the probability of an empty slot is 0.368, the probability of a successful transmission is 0.368, and the probability of a collision is 0.264. With two independent channels, nine events are possible in each slot. The probability of each event is listed in Fig. 3-35.

	Channel 1		
	Empty	Success	Collision
Empty	.135	.135	.097
Channel 2 Success	.135	.135	.097
Collision	.097	.097	.070

Fig. 3-35. Joint probabilities for a two channel slotted ALOHA system.

From the table of Fig. 3-35, we can see that the probability of exactly one success is 0.464. The one successful frame can be shifted to the downlink and rebroadcast. Furthermore, in 0.135 of the slots both channels will have exactly one frame, so the satellite chooses one of them and rebroadcasts it, discarding the other one. The station whose frame is discarded treats the event the same way it treats collisions—wait a random number of slots and try again. Adding up these numbers we see that the utilization of the downlink is 0.599. The total bandwidth occupied by this scheme is $3B$ and the throughput is $0.599B$, so the efficiency of the scheme is about 0.200, or about 9 percent better than the system with one uplink and one downlink.

To make this example more concrete, suppose 1 Mbps of bandwidth is available for data transmission. If this bandwidth is allocated as 500 kbps uplink and 500 kbps downlink, the throughput will be at most 184 kbps. However, if two uplink channels of 333 kbps each are allocated along with a single downlink channel at 333 kbps, the throughput will be at most 200 kbps. The gain comes from the fact that the system with two uplinks makes better use of the downlink channel.

It should be clear that other schemes are also possible. Instead of two uplink channels, we could have n of them. A little thought will reveal that as n increases, the throughput on the downlink increases. The calculation is straightforward. A slot can be wasted by being idle or by a collision. The probability that a slot is wasted is $p = 1 - 1/e$. If there are n channels, the probability that the downlink is wasted is just the probability that *all* the uplink slots are wasted, namely p^n. Thus the downlink utilization is $1 - p^n$. The efficiency is then the downlink utilization divided by the allocated bandwidth:

$$\text{efficiency} = \frac{1 - (1 - 1/e)^n}{n + 1}$$

The maximum occurs for $n = 2$.

In the previous model, if two frames successfully arrive together, one of them must be discarded because there is only one downlink. Two improvements are possible here. One is to add storage capacity to the satellite, so the frame not immediately rebroadcast can be saved for a later slot. The other is to add multiple downlinks. Onboard memory requires additional power, which means more solar cells and a greater weight to carry into space. For this reason, early satellites did not have any way to store frames for future rebroadcasting. As technology has improved, onboard storage is becoming more common. Several authors have developed models of satellites with onboard memory and multiple beams. For example, see (Chang, 1982, 1983; Chlamtac and Ganz, 1986b; and Lee and Mark, 1983) for more details.

If multiple uplinks are available, it is possible to modify the ALOHA protocol to reduce the average delay for high-priority frames. The way to achieve this reduction is to have these frames sent on several channels at once, increasing the chance that one of them is successful. Alternatively, if only one uplink is present, the frame could be sent normally, and then a little later (but well before the 270 msec propagation delay) it could be sent again. This repetition also improves the chance that at least one copy survives. Choudhury and Rappaport (1983) have analyzed the delay-throughput trade-offs of this scheme, which they call **diversity ALOHA**.

3.6.3. Reservation ALOHA

Even the most clever ALOHA-based protocol will never get the uplink channel efficiency above $1/e$. However, at high channel loads, there are other methods for making good use of a single shared channel, in particular, time-division multiplexing. Several researchers have proposed control schemes that act like normal or nearly normal slotted ALOHA at low channel utilization, and move gradually over to some kind of TDM as the channel load grows.

All these methods have one feature in common: some slots are reserved for specific stations. Stations are required to refrain from attempting to use a slot reserved for somebody else. The methods differ in the way reservations are made and released. For comparison, remember that in TDM the slots are organized into groups of N slots, with each slot permanently reserved for a specific station.

Binder (1975) proposed a method that starts out with the basic TDM model and adapts to slotted ALOHA for low channel utilization. As in TDM, N consecutive slots are grouped together into a group, with each station "owning" one position. If there are more slots than stations, the extra slots are not assigned to anyone. If the owner of a slot does not want it during the current group, he does nothing. An empty slot is a signal to everyone else that the owner has no traffic. During the next group, the slot becomes available to anyone who wants it, on a contention basis. If the owner wants to retrieve "his" slot, he transmits a frame, thus forcing a collision (if there was other traffic). After a collision, everyone except the owner must desist from using the slot. Thus the owner can always begin transmitting within two group times in the worst case. At low channel utilization the system does not perform as well as normal slotted ALOHA, since after each collision, the collidees must abstain for one group to see if the owner wants the slot back. Fig. 3-36(a) shows a group with eight slots, seven of which are owned.

One slight inefficiency with this method is that whenever the owner of a slot is

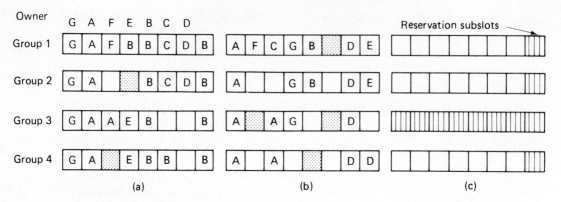

Fig. 3-36. Reservation schemes. (a) Binder. (b) Crowther. (c) Roberts. The shaded boxes indicate collisions.

through with it, the position must go idle during the next group to announce that its owner is done. To eliminate this wasted slot, an extra bit could be added to the header of all frames to announce that the owner did or did not have any more data for the next group.

A much more serious problem, however, is that the number of users must be known in advance. If this is not the case, several users could be assigned to the same slot, in the hope that it will not occur too often that both of them claim the slot simultaneously. To arbitrate when this does happen, each user could be given a static priority, with lower-priority users deferring to higher ones in the case of conflict.

Crowther et al. (1973) have proposed a different reservation method that is applicable even when the number of stations is unknown and varying dynamically. In their method, slots do not have permanent owners, as in Binder's, but instead, whenever a transmission is successful, the station making the successful transmission is entitled to that slot in the next group as well. Thus as long as a station has data to send, it can continue doing so indefinitely (subject to some "Please-do-not-be-a-pig" rules). Since it is unlikely that all stations will have long runs of data to send simultaneously, this method works well even when the number of slots per group is far less than the number of stations. In essence the proposal allows a dynamic mix of slotted ALOHA and TDM, with the number of slots devoted to each varying with demand. Fig. 3-36(b) shows a group with eight slots. Initially, E is using the last slot, but after two groups, it no longer needs it. It lies idle for one group, and then D picks it up and keeps it until he is done.

A third scheme, due to Roberts (1973), requires stations to make advance requests before transmitting. Each group contains, say, one special slot [the last one in Fig. 3-36(c)] which is divided into V smaller subslots used to make reservations. When a station wants to send data, it broadcasts a short request frame during one of the reservation subslots. If the reservation is successful (i.e., no collision), then the next regular slot (or slots) is reserved. At all times everyone must keep track of the queue length (number of slots reserved), so that when any station makes a successful reservation it will know how many data slots to skip before transmitting. Stations need not keep track of *who* is queued up; they merely need to know how long the queue is. When the queue length drops to zero, all slots revert to reservation subslots, to speed up the reservation process.

Jacobs et al. (1979) have proposed combining TDM and Roberts' protocol to handle both stream and bursty data. Their protocol, **PODA (Priority Oriented Demand Assignment)**, collects slots into groups as the other protocols do. It reserves some of these slots for data and others for reservation subslots. The boundary between the two varies with demand. Two strategies are possible for allocating reservation slots: fixed assignment of reservation subslots to users, called **FPODA (Fixed PODA)**, or contention assignment of the reservation subslots, called **CPODA (Contention PODA)**.

An interesting feature of PODA is the ability of a station to make a reservation by setting some bits in a data frame, so that heavy users rarely need to wait for the next reservation subslot (FPODA) or contend for a reservation subslot (CPODA). The reservation information includes the frame size and priority. Reservations can be made for a single frame, or a stream of frames. The protocol is intended to allow both data and voice, so channel scheduling takes all this information into account, rather than just scheduling frames first-come, first served as in Roberts' protocol.

Greene and Ephremides (1981) have also extended Roberts' original reservation scheme by pointing out that the reservation process is actually a surrogate for the real contention process, only using much smaller slots. Suppose that the number of reservation slots is equal to the number of slots available for data frames in a group, N. At the end of a group, the best one can hope for, on the average, is that N/e reservations have been successfully made, so that N/e frames can be sent in the next group. This result is no better than ordinary slotted ALOHA.

However, if the number of small slots for reservations is Ne, the expected number of reservations is N, so the next group will be fully utilized. If the ratio of a data slot to a reservation slot is L, the fractional overhead devoted to the reservations is $e/(L + e)$. For L in the range 100 to 1000, the reservation slots occupy at most a few percent of the bandwidth. Their paper describes and analyzes this **distributed reservation control** protocol in detail.

One last variation on the reservation idea is to use the reservation slots not for reserving channel time for the frames themselves, but for their retransmissions in the event of a collision (Raychaudhuri, 1985). If a frame collides, but its retransmission reservation (randomly chosen among the reservation slots of its frame) survives, then each station knows when the retransmission will be scheduled, and avoids using that slot in the next group. This protocol, called **ARRA (Announced Retransmission Random Access)** has the advantage over Roberts' scheme and its variants that when a frame is ready to be transmitted, it can be sent immediately. No delay is required to first try to reserve a slot. If the channel is lightly loaded, this scheme will have an appreciably lower average delay than those requiring a reservation before transmission.

3.7. PACKET RADIO NETWORKS

Ground radio packet (really frame) broadcasting differs from satellite packet broadcasting in several ways. In particular, stations have limited range, introducing the need for radio repeaters. Among other properties, if two stations are too far apart, they will not be able to hear each other's transmissions at all, making CSMA impossible and complicating the MAC sublayer protocol considerably. The propagation delay is also much less than for satellite broadcasting. Finally, there is no common clock as there is with a satellite, so protocols like Binder's or Crowther's that collect slots into groups are not feasible. In the following sections we will look at some of the ways in which ground radio differs from satellite broadcasting. More details about packet radio are provided in (Chlamtac and Kutten, 1985; Hahn and Stolle, 1984; Jubin, 1985; and Tobagi et al., 1984).

3.7.1. The University of Hawaii ALOHA System

The first computer system to employ radio instead of point-to-point wires for its communication facility was the ALOHA system at the University of Hawaii. The system first went on the air in 1971. Since this system is the ancestor of all packet broadcasting systems, we describe it below briefly. For a more complete description, see (Abramson, 1985).

The ALOHA system was begun to allow people at the University of Hawaii, who were spread out over seven campuses on four islands, to access the main computer center on Oahu without using telephone lines, which were expensive and unreliable. Communication is provided by equipping each station with a small FM radio transmitter/receiver with sufficient range (30 km) to talk to the computer center's transmitter/receiver. Later, a powerful repeater was introduced, increasing the theoretical range to 500 km.

All communication is either from a station to the computer center or from the computer center to a station. There is no station-to-station communication. When a packet is received at the computer center, it is processed there. It is not retransmitted for all other stations to hear. This arrangement is fundamentally different from the satellite broadcasting model, in which the satellite is merely a big repeater in the sky. Since incoming packets are not rebroadcast, a station has no way of knowing whether or not its transmission was received correctly by the central site. As a result, explicit acknowledgements are needed, just as in point-to-point connections.

After overcoming some initial skepticism about the unusual communication mechanism, the project was assigned two bands in the UHF part of the spectrum.

One frequency band, at 407.350 MHz, is used for inbound traffic, from stations to the central site. The other frequency band, at 413.475 MHz, is used for outbound traffic, from the central site to the stations. Transmission is at 9600 bps. The use of distinct channels for inbound and outbound traffic has important implications for the whole system organization. After several years of experience, the research group concluded that a single channel probably would have been a better idea.

The original rationale for having two distinct channels was the fundamental difference in the inbound and outbound traffic. Inbound, many uncoordinated users are competing for access to a shared resource. Outbound, a single site is in complete control of the channel, so there is no contention and there are no collisions. The basic idea is to use the inbound channel on a random access (what is now called pure ALOHA) basis, and the outbound channel on a straight broadcasting basis, with each station extracting those packets directed to it from the output stream.

Figure 3-37 shows the essential elements of the ALOHA system. At the central site is a minicomputer, called the Menehune (the Hawaiian word for "imp") that is connected to the antenna. All data in or out of the central site pass through it. The Menehune, in turn, is connected to two large computers, as well as to two other networks, ARPANET and PACNET. Each station has a control unit that buffers some text and handles retransmissions. The original control units were hardwired, but later microprocessors were used to provide more flexibility. Some stations are connected to concentrators to reduce transmitter/receiver costs.

Frames consist of four parts. First comes a 32-bit header, containing, among other things, the user identification and the packet length. To provide high reliability, the header is followed by a 16-bit checksum. Next come the data, up to 80 bytes followed by another checksum. The maximum packet is $32 + 16 + 640 + 16 = 704$ bits. At 9600 bps, the transmission time for the longest packet is 73 msec.

When a station has data to send, it just goes ahead and sends. This way of operating is ALOHA at its purest. When the Menehune correctly receives a packet, it inserts an acknowledgement packet into the output stream. If a station does not receive an acknowledgement within a preset time, it assumes that the packet suffered a collision, and retransmits it. The retransmission intervals are distributed between 200 and 1500 msec, with various distributions having been tried (e.g., uniform, three shorts and then a long, etc.).

3.7.2. Design Issues for Packet Radio Networks

In the preceding section we looked at the original ALOHA system as an example of a ground radio packet broadcasting system. In this section we will examine some additional design problems often present in these systems. The introduction of a large number of repeaters, in particular (to increase the geographic coverage of the system), brings with it a number of complications because repeaters store

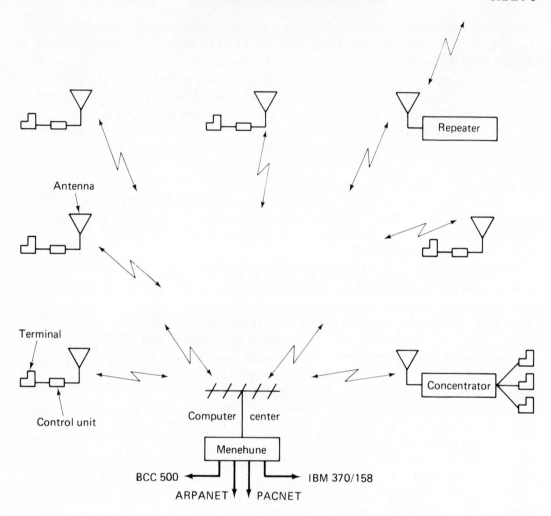

Fig. 3-37. The University of Hawaii ALOHA system.

incoming packets and then rebroadcast them on the same frequency. Simultaneous reception and transmission is therefore impossible.

Let us first look at the conceptual model of a packet radio system. There are (at least) three situations in which packet radio is attractive as a method of local distribution from a central site to remote stations.

1. The stations are located in areas where the telephone system is poorly developed or nonexistent: many rural areas, and most of the Third World falls into this category. Automated weather and seismic data collection stations are often parachuted into jungles, deserts, and hostile mountain terrain, which frequently lack the amenities of civilization, such as telephone poles.

2. The stations are mobile. A fleet of ships is a good example of a group of users that is inherently mobile. Police cars, ambulances, fire engines, and taxis are other examples.

3. The stations have a high peak-to-average traffic ratio, or a low data rate. In both cases, the cost of a dedicated line may make the application uneconomic. Packet radio offers the possibility of sharing a single channel instead of having a large number of channels with fixed (and mostly wasted) capacity. Equation (3-1) tells the whole story.

Although portable FM radio transmitters are usually equipped with a simple whip antenna, which makes them omnidirectional, repeaters may be equipped with omnidirectional or directional antennas, as needed. Repeaters may also be able to adjust their broadcasting power, to increase or decrease their range. If a substantial number of repeaters are battery powered, the system design must be sufficiently redundant to cope with repeaters whose batteries have gone dead, since this will be a regular occurrence.

When a packet radio system contains multiple repeaters, routing becomes an issue. Since routing in packet radio is closely tied to channel access, we will treat the issue (briefly) in this chapter. The most naive routing strategy, just having each repeater act as a transponder, storing and forwarding all incoming packets (flooding), does not work at all. Every packet would just bounce back and forth between adjacent repeaters forever, clogging up the channel.

When a repeater receives a packet, it must make a decision. To forward, or not to forward, that is the question. The choice of forwarding or discarding is analogous to an IMP's choice of output line in a point-to-point network. The goals of the routing procedure are the same as in all networks, of course: to achieve a high probability of delivering packets to the ultimate destination and to consume the minimum resources in the process.

Gitman et al. (1976) have suggested three possible routing strategies. In the first algorithm, each repeater just forwards all incoming packets, subject to one of two constraints. The first constraint is a hop counter, included in the header of each packet, which is decremented whenever the packet is forwarded. When it gets to zero, the packet is discarded. This rule guarantees that no packet lives forever. The second constraint is for repeaters to keep a list of the n most recently forwarded packets and refrain from retransmitting them if they come in again.

With these two extra rules, this is a reasonable algorithm to use in the case of highly mobile stations and/or repeaters. Its attractiveness lies in the fact that it does not depend on any repeater knowing the location of any other one. Nor does it assume any fixed assignment of stations to repeaters. The obvious disadvantage is the large amount of bandwidth it consumes.

The second of the routing algorithms proposed by Gitman et al. uses hierarchical routing. The repeaters are organized into a tree, with the central site at the root.

This algorithm requires that the central site be aware of the complete topology. Each data packet sent by the central site contains the sequence of repeaters by which the packet must be forwarded. In effect, the central site determines the complete path and includes it in each packet. This method is called **source routing**, and we will see it again when we study bridges in Chap. 5. At each hop, the receiver sends back an acknowledgement.

If a repeater along the required path has failed, all is not lost. The repeater, failing to get an acknowledgement, could set a bit in the header telling all repeaters to forward the packet. It could also announce the failure to the central site (assuming that it was still connected), requesting the central site to conduct another probe and relabel the tree.

The broadcast nature of packet radio makes a completely different strategy also possible: the repeater could simply turn up its power, blast away, and hope to skip over the failed repeater. This strategy obviously implies a conservative design, in which repeaters normally operate at less than full power. One problem, however, is that although the correct repeater may receive the packet, it may be too weak to get the acknowledgement all the way back.

In the third routing algorithm, a repeater only forwards a packet if it is closer to the destination than the last repeater that forwarded the packet. Each repeater is assumed to know its distance in hops from every other repeater. This information can be acquired by having each repeater broadcast its distance table periodically. Each data packet contains the identification of the destination and the current sender's distance from that destination.

Throughout this chapter, we have assumed that when two packets collide, both will be lost. For radio networks, this assumption is overly pessimistic, since FM receivers can be designed to extract the stronger of two overlapping packets without error. This phenomenon is known as the **capture effect** (Cidon et al., 1988). To see how this influences the system performance, imagine that there are two classes of stations, one broadcasting at high power, and one at low power, (or one group close by and one group far away, both at the same power). If two overlapping packets both originate from the same group, the receiver cannot disentangle them, and both are lost. If, however, they originate from different groups, the stronger one will be accepted. In half the cases, what was previously counted as a collision is now a success!

An interesting property of the capture effect is that under conditions of heavy load, stations close to the central site may generate so much traffic that stations farther out are locked out completely. This occurs because when a close in and a far out station collide, the close in station has a stronger signal and always wins.

Radio amateurs (ham operators) in the U.S., Canada, and Japan have developed an packet radio network that is worth mentioning here. The system has been standardized by the American Radio Relay League. The protocol is called **AX.25** (Karn et al., 1985) and is based on the CCITT X.25 protocol to be described in Chapter 5.

The standard describes the packet format, which contains an address field, a control field, and a data field, among others. It does not specify a channel access algorithm, so pure ALOHA or CSMA are both possible (amateur radio is too chaotic for slotted ALOHA, since that requires agreement on time slot boundaries). Most amateur radios are half duplex devices, so they cannot sense the channel while transmitting, thus making CSMA/CD impossible.

The most interesting feature of this network is the addressing and routing algorithm. Each radio amateur has a unique **call sign**, which is a string of 4 to 6 letters and digits that is assigned to him by the government when he passes his license examination. Like all other radio and television stations, amateur call signs begin with W or K (or N) in the U.S., C in Canada, and JA in Japan.

The address field of each AX.25 packet contains a list of call signs specifying the stations that are to store and forward packets, and their order. Thus the originator must choose the exact path. When any station forwards a packet, it sets the higher-order bit of its call sign to 1, so that if it hears a subsequent retransmission, it will know that it has already processed the packet and ignore it the second time.

In addition to this amateur packet network, radio amateurs also have a satellite network. How they got their satellites launched is an interesting story. When NASA or another space agency was testing a new experimental rocket for the first time, commercial satellite operators were often hesitant to use their 100 million dollar satellites as guinea pigs. Rather than using sandbags as the payload, the space agencies were sometimes willing to launch satellites built by radio amateurs in their spare time. Since many of these people were professional engineers who worked in the communications industry, the satellites were always low budget, but often ingenious devices. More than a dozen are currently in orbit and new ones (running at T1 speed) are in preparation.

The recent demand for telephones in cars has given rise to another interesting development in the area of packet radio, known **cellular radio**. In this system, each mobile telephone is attached to a radio antenna that broadcasts in the 800 to 900 MHz range (in the U.S.). The area covered by the cellular radio system is divided into cells. In theory the cells are hexagons (see Fig. 3-38); in practice they are less regular in shape.

The cell size corresponds to the range of the mobile transmitters, so that the signal from a transmitter can be heard in its own cell, and possibly in the neighboring ones, but usually not in cells beyond that. Within each cell, some set of frequencies is available for communication. All the cells adjoining it must be assigned a different set of frequencies, so there is no interference. Assigning frequencies is a form of graph coloring problem: how can one color the cells so that no two adjacent cells have the same color (set of frequencies). The problem is made more complex by irregular cell sizes, buildings, hills, and the fact that transmitters may be heard two cells away in some cases.

In each cell is a base station on top of a building or hill, positioned so that it can communicate with all the radios in its cell. When a mobile telephone is switched on, it hunts among the base-station frequencies to find the strongest signal

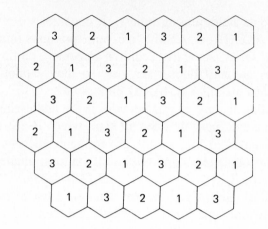

Fig. 3-38. Cell pattern for cellular radio. The numbers give an example of which frequencies could be assigned to which cell without interference assuming each base-station is in the center of its cell and the range of each transmitter is equal to the cell size.

(presumably the closest one), and sends a message announcing its telephone number. The base station then tells it which cell it is in and what frequencies to use.

When a mobile telephone wants to make a call, it sends a message to its base station, which then allocates an available frequency to it (if one is available). When the call is finished, the frequency is deallocated and made available for another caller in the same cell. The same frequency can be in use in many cells at the same time, provided they are out of range of each others transmitters (the graph coloring problem).

While switched on, each mobile telephone keeps monitoring the signals on all the base station frequencies to see which is strongest. Whenever it discovers that a different base station has become stronger (presumably because the car has now driven into a new cell), the telephone tells its base station, which then hands it over to the new base. The new base instructs the telephone to switch to its frequency. It is important that each base station knows the whereabouts of each mobile telephone at all times, so that incoming calls can be routed via the proper base station. The location of each car is kept track of continuously by a computer to which all the base stations have access.

3.8. EXAMPLES OF THE MAC SUBLAYER

In the following sections we will look at the medium access control sublayer in our four running examples.

3.8.1. The MAC Sublayer in Public Networks

The public networks all use the X.25 protocol for the lowest three layers. This protocol was designed for point-to-point networks, and does not have a MAC sublayer.

The only place where broadcast channels might be used in a public data network is on long-haul point-to-point satellite links. Invariably these channels are operated as TDM trunks to connect carrier switching offices. The small number of switching offices, the high traffic from each office, and the point-to-point nature of the connections all lead to TDM as the appropriate protocol.

3.8.2. The MAC Sublayer in the ARPANET

Almost all the IMP-IMP connections in the ARPANET proper are point-to-point leased telephone lines. Since none of these use multiple access in any form, no MAC sublayer is present.

However, if we widen our scope to encompass the ARPA Internet, we see various places where the MAC sublayer appears. Many universities with an ARPANET IMP have a campus network that is connected to the Internet via a gateway. These campus networks predominantly use Ethernet. Thus our discussion of CSMA/CD and 802.3 in this chapter applies to them.

A second place where the MAC sublayer appears in the Internet is on an experimental satellite network called **SATNET** This network was set up to connect nodes in Europe to the Internet and to experiment with satellite technology and protocols. It has ground stations in West Virginia, England, W. Germany, Italy, and Sweden. This network uses the CPODA protocol described earlier.

A third place where the MAC sublayer exists in the ARPA Internet is in the experimental packet radio network, **PRNET**, in the San Francisco Bay area. This network was set up to provide a testbed for packet radio technology and protocols. It has base stations on a hill in Berkeley overlooking the Bay Area, Mission Ridge in the East Bay, Menlo Park on the San Francisco peninsula, and elsewhere. Vans with packet radio transmitters roam around the Bay area communicating with the base stations and with the rest of the ARPA Internet via the IMP at SRI in Menlo Park.

3.8.3. The MAC Sublayer in MAP and TOP

Both MAP and TOP are based on the use of local area networks, so both have an extensive MAC sublayer. MAP specifies the use of the broadband token bus (802.4). TOP originally specified the use of CSMA/CD (802.3), but was later modified to allow the token ring (802.5) as well.

3.8.4. The MAC Sublayer in USENET

The physical links for USENET are mostly dialup telephone lines, which are all point-to-point and have no MAC sublayer. However, some experiments have tried a satellite for broadcasting news. This communication is largely one-way, so the problems of having a large number of independent stations vying for the same channel do not occur.

3.9. SUMMARY

Some networks have a single channel that is used for all communication. In these networks, the key design issue is the allocation of this channel among the competing stations wishing to use it. More than three dozen channel allocation algorithms have been discussed in this chapter. A large number of networks built to test or use these algorithms have also been discussed. A summary of the channel allocation methods described is given in Fig. 3-39.

The simplest allocation schemes are FDM and TDM. These are efficient when the number of stations is small and the traffic is continuous. Both are widely used under these circumstances, for example, for dividing up the bandwidth in satellite links used as telephone trunks.

When the number of stations is large and variable or the traffic bursty, FDM and TDM are poor choices. The ALOHA protocol, with and without slotting and control, has been proposed as an alternative. ALOHA and its many variants and derivatives have been widely discussed, analyzed, and used in real systems.

When the state of the channel can be sensed, stations can avoid starting a transmission while another station is transmitting. This technique, carrier sensing, has led to a variety of protocols that can be used on LANs and MANs.

A class of protocols that eliminate contention altogether, or at least reduce it considerably, is known. These include BRAP, MLMA, and binary countdown, which completely eliminate contention; and the tree walk and urn protocols, which reduce it. The latter two protocols work by dynamically dividing the stations into two disjoint groups, one of which is permitted to transmit and one of which is not. The protocols aim at making the division in such a way that only one station that is ready to send is permitted to do so.

We next looked at the IEEE 802 LANs: CSMA/CD, token bus and token ring. Each of these has its own unique advantages and disadvantages, and each has found its own user community and will probably continue to serve that community for years to come. Convergence to a single LAN standard is an unlikely event.

After examining the IEEE work, we went on to look at fiber optic networks. These included FDDI, Fibernet II, S/NET, EXPRESSNET, and to some extent, DATAKIT, which handles both copper and fiber. A wide variety of topologies and switching technologies are used in these examples.

FDM	Frequency division multiplexing
TDM	Time division multiplexing
Pure ALOHA	Unsynchronized transmission at any instant
Slotted ALOHA	Random transmission within well-defined time slots
Controlled ALOHA	Use of feedback to reduce channel load
1-Persistent CSMA	Standard carrier sense multiple access
Nonpersistent CSMA	Random delay when channel is sensed busy
p-Persistent CSMA	CSMA but with probability p of persisting
CSMA/collision detect	CSMA but abort transmission upon collision
Bit map	Round robin scheduling using a bit map
BRAP	BRAM/MSAP modification of bit map protocol
MLMA	Determine decimal addresses of ready stations
Binary countdown	Station with highest binary address goes next
Tree walk	Reduced contention by selective enabling
Urn	Reduced contention by variable rotating window
Ethernet	1-persistent CSMA/CD with exponential backoff
Token bus	Logical ring on a physical bus
Token ring	Stations must capture token before sending
Slotted ring	Full and empty slots circulate on the ring
Insertion ring	Frames transmitted by inserting buffer into ring
FDDI	Fiber optic ring based on token ring
Fibernet II	Fiber optic version of Ethernet with active star
S/NET	Fiber optic network with parallel active star
FASNET	Dual cable linear fiber optic token passing
EXPRESSNET	Folded cable fiber optic token passing
DATAKIT	Asynchronous switching in a multiple star network
SPADE	FDM with dynamic channel allocation
Multilink ALOHA	ALOHA with multiple uplinks and downlinks
Diversity ALOHA	ALOHA with multiple transmissions of each frame
Binder's protocol	TDM with ALOHA when slot owner not interested
Crowther's protocol	ALOHA with slot owner keeping it after use
Roberts' protocol	Channel time reserved in advanced by contention
PODA	Mixture of reservation and contention
Distributed reservation	Surrogate contention process with minislots
ARRA	ALOHA with announced retransmission slots
Packet radio	Menehune, repeaters, and flooding

Fig. 3-39. Channel allocation methods discussed in this chapter.

Then we went on to see how satellite networks differed from their terrestrial cousins. The major difference is the long propagation delay, which makes carrier sensing infeasible. Lack of carrier sensing means that other protocols are required. Several variants of ALOHA were discussed, as were a variety of protocols that reserved slots in advance.

The final subject of this chapter was packet radio. The problems here center around the mobility of the stations and the problems caused by some stations not being within broadcast range of other ones. A number of packet radio design issues were examined.

PROBLEMS

1. A group of N stations share a 56 kbps pure ALOHA channel. Each station outputs a 1000-bit frame on an average of once every 100 sec, even if the previous one has not yet been sent (e.g., the stations are buffered). What is the maximum value of N?

2. An infinite-population slotted ALOHA system has a frame time equal to k slot times. A frame can begin in any slot. The channel load is G frames per frame time. What is the throughput in frames per frame time? Find the throughput in the limiting cases of $k = 1$ and $k \to \infty$, and interpret these results.

3. Ten thousand airline reservation stations are competing for the use of a single slotted ALOHA channel. The average station makes 18 requests/hour. A slot is 125 μsec. What is the approximate total channel load?

4. A large population of ALOHA users manages to generate 50 requests/sec, including both originals and retransmissions. Time is slotted in units of 40 msec.
   (a) What is the chance of success on the first attempt?
   (b) What is the probability of exactly k collisions and then a success?
   (c) What is the expected number of transmission attempts needed?

5. Measurements of an infinite user slotted ALOHA channel show that 10% of the slots are idle.
   (a) What is the channel load, G?
   (b) What is the throughput?
   (c) Is the channel underloaded or overloaded?

6. In an infinite-population slotted ALOHA system, the mean number of slots a station waits between a collision and its retransmission is 4. Plot the delay versus throughput curve for this system.

7. A small slotted ALOHA system has only k customers, each of whom has a probability $1/k$ of transmitting during any slot (originals + retransmissions combined). What is the channel throughput as a function of k? Evaluate this expression numerically for $k = 2, 3, 4, 5, 10$ and lim $k \to \infty$.

8. Show that the maximum throughput of a finite population system with identical stations occurs at $G = 1$.

9. To reduce contention on its dispatcher's radio, a taxicab company has decided to slot time into 1-sec intervals. The company then begins hiring unemployed computer science Ph.D's as drivers, since the new system requires its users to speak digitally, in 1 sec bursts. Late one night, only two digital speaking drivers are out, both talking to the dispatcher. The probability that a driver has something to say during a slot is 0.3. In the event of a collision, each one repeats during the succeeding slots with a probability 0.2. Calculate the mean number of slots required per successful transmission. (The night dispatcher speaks only analog, and says nothing.)

10. How many "octades" does MLMA need to resolve all the conflicts if the stations whose octal addresses are 4052, 3052, 2162, 7722, 2712, 3662, and 3663 all decide to send at once?

11. Prove that at low channel load, the MLMA header is minimized when the radix of the system, r, is equal to e.

12. A CSMA/CD network uses Mok and Ward's version of binary countdown. At a certain instant, the ten stations have the virtual station numbers 8, 2, 4, 5, 1, 7, 3, 6, 9, and 0. The next three stations to send are 4, 3, and 9, in that order. What are the new virtual station numbers after all three have finished their transmissions?

13. Sixteen stations are contending for the use of a shared channel using the adaptive tree walk protocol. If all the stations whose addresses are prime numbers suddenly become ready at once, how many bit slots are needed to resolve the contention?

14. A collection of 2^n stations uses the adaptive tree walk protocol to arbitrate access to a shared cable. At a certain instant two of them become ready. What are the minimum, maximum, and mean number of slots to walk the tree if $2^n \gg 1$?

15. A biology student minoring in computer science has built a microprocessor-based, all-digital mousetrap in order to recapture one or more of the eight microprocessor-based, all-digital mice that have escaped from their cages. Unfortunately, there are also 11 ordinary, plain old analog mice in the lab. When the trap has reached its capacity of three mice, of either genre, the microprocessor emits an ASCII "Control G" character to alert the student. What is the probability of his having captured exactly one digital mouse?

16. If the urn protocol is used with 200 users, of whom 40 are ready to send, what is the probability of a collision? Of success?

17. A seven story office building has 15 adjacent offices per floor. Each office contains a wall socket for a terminal in the front wall, so the sockets form a rectangular grid in the vertical plane, with a separation of 4 m between sockets, both horizontally and vertically. Assuming that it is feasible to run a straight cable between any pair of sockets, horizontally, vertically, or diagonally, how many meters of cable are needed to connect all sockets using

(a) a star configuration with a single IMP in middle?

(b) an CSMA/CD?

(c) a ring net (without a wire center)?

18. What is the baud rate of the standard 10 Mbps 802.3 LAN (think carefully)?

19. A 1 km long, 10 Mbps CSMA/CD LAN has a propagation speed of 200 m/μsec. Data frames are 256 bits long, including 32 bits of header, checksum, and other overhead. The first bit slot after a successful transmission is reserved for the receiver to capture the channel to send a 32-bit acknowledgement frame. What is the effective data rate, excluding overhead, assuming that there are no collisions (e.g., urn protocol at heavy load)?

20. Two CSMA/CD stations are each trying to transmit long (multiframe) files. After each frame is sent, they contend for the channel using the binary exponential backoff algorithm. What is the probability that the contention ends on round k, and what is the mean number of rounds per contention period?

21. A token bus system works like this. When the token arrives at a station, a timer is reset to 0. The station then begins transmitting priority 6 frames until the timer reaches $T6$. Then it switches over to priority 4 frames until the timer reaches $T4$. This algorithm is then repeated with priority 2 and priority 0. If all stations have timer values of 40, 80, 90, and 100 msec for $T6$ through $T0$, respectively, what fraction of the total bandwidth is reserved for each priority class?

22. What happens in a token bus if a station accepts the token and then crashes immediately? How does the protocol described in the text handle this case?

23. At a transmission rate of 5 Mbps and a propagation speed of 200 m/μsec, how many meters of cable is the 1-bit delay in a token ring interface equivalent to?

24. A very heavily loaded 1 km long, 10-Mbps token ring has a propagation speed of 200 m/μsec. Fifty stations are uniformly spaced around the ring. Data frames are 256 bits, including 32 bits of overhead. Acknowledgements are piggybacked onto the data frames and are thus effectively free. The token is 8 bits. Is the effective data rate of this ring higher or lower than the effective data rate of a 10-Mbps CSMA/CD network?

25. In a token ring the sender removes the frame. What modifications to the system would be needed to have the receiver remove the frame instead, and what would the consequences be?

26. A large slotted ring contains 1024 bits, grouped in 32 frame slots. If 60% of the frame slots are empty on the average, what is the chance that a newly generated frame will have to wait more than two slots to get onto the ring?

27. A 4-Mbps token ring has a token holding timer value of 10 msec. What is the longest frame that can be sent on this ring?

28. Does the use of a wire center have any influence on the performance of a token ring?

29. A fiber optic token ring used as a MAN is 200 km long and runs at 100 Mbps. After sending a frame, a station breaks the ring and drains the frame from it before regenerating the token. The signal propagation speed in the fiber is 200,000 km/sec and the maximum frame size is 1K bytes. What is the maximum efficiency of the ring (ignoring all other sources of overhead)?

30. Repeat the previous question for a 200-km FASNET system with 100 stations.

31. A satellite uses slotted ALOHA with three uplinks and two downlinks. The satellite has no storage capacity. What is the maximum achievable utilization of the downlink channels?

32. Repeat the previous question, but now assume that the satellite has an infinite amount of onboard storage to store frames until they can be rebroadcast. What is the percent gain in efficiency over the system without storage?

33. A group of $2N$ stations communicate using a slotted ALOHA satellite. The satellite uses the capture effect to resolve collisions. The $2N$ stations are divided into N signal strength classes, each with two members. If each station has a probability p of transmitting during a slot, what is the throughput in the limit $N \to \infty$? Plot the throughput as a function of p and explain in words why the curve has the shape it does.

34. A packet radio system uses slotted ALOHA with perfect capture, that is, in the event of a collision, the destination is always able to correctly decode *some* packet. Every station can hear every other station, and propagation delay is negligible. Is the binary exponential backoff a good algorithm here? If not, suggest a better one.

35. Write a program to simulate slotted controlled ALOHA. Each station should monitor the channel load and increment its value of α by X percent whenever $G < 1$ and decrement it by the same amount if $G > 1$. Assume negligible propagation delay. Examine how X and the length of the shift register affect system performance.

36. Write a program to simulate the operation of a token ring with no priorities. Take into account the walk time between stations and the time required to drain the ring before regenerating the token. Now change the simulator to allow stations to regenerate the token as soon as they are done transmitting, without waiting to drain the ring.

4

THE DATA LINK LAYER

In this chapter we will study the design of layer 2, the data link layer. This study deals with the algorithms for achieving reliable, efficient communication between two adjacent machines at the data link layer. By adjacent, we mean that the two machines are physically connected by a communication channel that acts conceptually like a wire (e.g., a coaxial cable or a telephone line). The essential property of a channel that makes it "wire-like" is that the bits are delivered in exactly the same order in which they are sent.

At first you might think this problem is so trivial that there is no software to study—machine A just puts the data on the wire, and machine B just takes them off. Unfortunately, communication circuits make errors occasionally. Furthermore, they have only a finite data rate, and there is a nonzero propagation delay between the time a bit is sent and the time it is received. These limitations, coupled with the finite processing speed of the machines, have important implications for the efficiency of the data transfer. The protocols used for communications must take all these factors into consideration. These protocols are the subject of this chapter.

After an introduction to the key design issue present in the data link layer, we will start our study of its protocols by looking at the nature of errors, their causes and how they can be detected and corrected. Then we will study a series of increasingly complex protocols, each one solving more and more of the problems present in this layer. Finally, we will conclude with an examination of protocol performance and correctness, and give some examples of data link protocols.

4.1. DATA LINK LAYER DESIGN ISSUES

The data link layer has a number of specific functions to carry out. These functions include providing a well defined service interface to the network layer, determining how the bits of the physical layer are grouped into frames, dealing with transmission errors, regulating the flow of frames so that slow receivers are not swamped by fast senders, and general link management. In the following sections we will examine each of these issues in turn.

4.1.1. Services Provided to the Network Layer

The function of the data link layer is to provide services to the network layer. The principal service is transferring data from the network layer on the source machine to the network layer on the destination machine. On the source machine there is an entity, call it a process, in the network layer that hands some bits to the data link layer for transmission to the destination. The job of the data link layer is to transmit the bits to the destination machine, so they can be handed over to the network layer there, as shown in Fig. 4-1(a). The actual transmission follows the path of Fig. 4-1(b), but it is easier to think in terms of two data link layer processes communicating using a data link protocol. For this reason, we will implicitly use the model of Fig. 4-1(a) throughout this chapter.

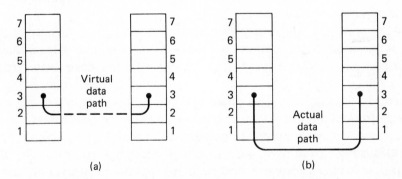

Fig. 4-1. (a) Virtual communication. (b) Actual communication.

The data link layer can be designed to offer various services. The actual services offered can vary from system to system. Three reasonable possibilities are:

1. Unacknowledged connectionless service.

2. Acknowledged connectionless service.

3. Connection-oriented service.

Let us consider each of these in turn.

Unacknowledged connectionless service consists of having the source machine send independent frames to the destination machine without having the destination machine acknowledge them. No connection is established beforehand or released afterwards. If a frame is lost due to noise on the line, no attempt is made to recover in the data link layer. This class of service is appropriate when the error rate is very low and recovery is left to higher layers. It is also appropriate for real time traffic, such as speech, in which late data are worse than bad data. Many LANs have unacknowledged connectionless service in the data link layer.

The next step up in terms of reliability is acknowledged connectionless service. When this service is offered, there are still no connections used, but each frame sent is individually acknowledged. In this way, the sender knows whether or not a frame has arrived safely. If it has not arrived within a specified time interval, it can be sent again.

The most sophisticated service the data link layer can provide to the network layer is connection-oriented service. With this service, the source and destination machines establish a connection before any data are transferred. Each frame sent over the connection is numbered, and the data link layer guarantees that each frame sent is indeed received. Furthermore, it guarantees that each frame is received exactly once and that all frames are received in the right order. With connectionless service, in contrast, it is conceivable that a lost acknowledgement causes a frame to be sent several times and thus received several times. Connection-oriented service, in contrast, provides the network layer processes with the equivalent of a reliable bit stream.

When connection-oriented service is used, transfers have three distinct phases. In the first phase the connection is established by having both sides initialize variables and counters needed to keep track of which frames have been received and which ones have not. In the second phase, one or more frames are actually transmitted. In the third and final phase, the connection is released, freeing up the variables, buffers, and other resources used to maintain the connection.

The communication between the network layer and the data link layer uses the standard OSI service primitives, which we will briefly review here. The primitives are: *request*, *indication*, *response*, and *confirm*. *Request* primitives are used by the network layer to ask the data link layer to do something, for example, establish or release a connection or send a frame. *Indication* primitives are used to indicate to the network layer that an event has happened, for example, another machine wishes to establish or release a connection, or a frame has arrived. *Response* primitives are used on the receiving side by the network layer to reply to a previous *indication*. *Confirm* primitives provide a way for the data link layer on the requesting side to learn whether the request was successfully carried out, and if not, why not.

Figure 4-2 illustrates these four primitives in two different ways. In Fig. 4-2(a), the layer structure is shown explicitly, as is the flow of data. In Fig. 4-2(b), To the left of the two vertical lines we have the data link service user on the sending side. Between the two vertical lines is the data link service provider. Finally, to the right of the lines is the data link service user on the receiving side. Time runs downward, so that events higher up occur before events lower down. We will use this type of diagram showing service users and providers (in different layers) repeatedly throughout the book.

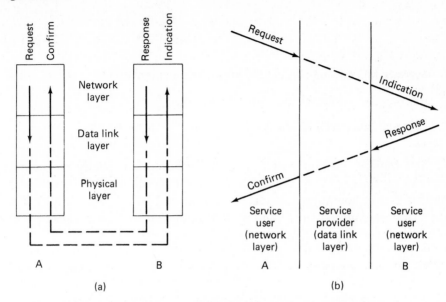

Fig. 4-2. Two different representations of the service primitives.

4.1.2. Framing

In order to provide service to the network layer, the data link layer must use the service provided to it by the physical layer. What the physical layer does is accept a raw bit stream and attempt to deliver it to the destination. This bit stream is not guaranteed to be error free. The number of bits received may be less than, equal to, or more than the number of bits transmitted, and they have different values. It is up to the data link layer to detect, and if necessary, correct errors.

The usual approach is for the data link layer to break the bit stream up into discrete frames and compute the checksum for each frame. (Checksum algorithms will be discussed later in this chapter.) When a frame arrives at the destination, the checksum is recomputed. If the newly computed checksum is different from the one contained in the frame, the data link layer knows that an error has occurred and takes steps to deal with it (e.g., discarding the bad frame and sending back an error report).

Breaking the bit stream up into frames is more difficult than it at first appears. One way to achieve this framing is to insert time gaps between frames, much like the spaces between words in ordinary text. However, networks rarely make any guarantees about timing, so it is possible these gaps might be squeezed out, or other gaps might be inserted during transmission.

Since it is too risky to count on timing to mark the start and end of each frame, other methods have been devised. In this section we will look at four commonly used methods:

1. Character count.

2. Starting and ending characters, with character stuffing.

3. Starting and ending flags, with bit stuffing.

4. Physical layer coding violations.

The first framing method uses a field in the header to specify the number of characters in the frame. When the data link layer at the destination sees the character count, it knows how many characters follow, and hence where the end of the frame is. This technique is shown in Fig. 4-3(a) for four frames of sizes 5, 5, 8, and 9 characters respectively.

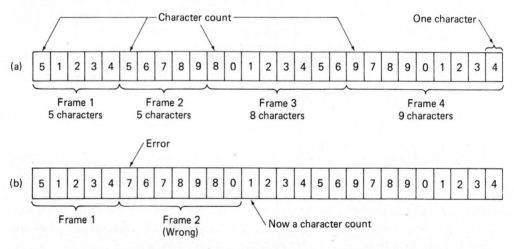

Fig. 4-3. A character stream. (a) Without errors. (b) With one error.

The trouble with this algorithm is that the count can be garbled by a transmission error. For example, if the character count of 5 in the second frame of Fig. 4-3(b) becomes a 7, the destination will get out of synchronization, and will be unable to locate the start of the next frame. Even if the checksum is incorrect so the destination knows that the frame is bad, it still has no way of telling where the next frame starts. Sending a frame back to the source asking for a retransmission does not help either, since the destination does not know how many characters to skip over to get to the start of the retransmission. For this reason, the character count method is rarely used anymore.

The second framing method gets around the problem of resynchronization after an error by having each frame start with the ASCII character sequence DLE STX and end with the sequence DLE ETX. (DLE is Data Link Escape, STX is Start of TeXt, and ETX is End of TeXt.) In this way, if the destination ever loses track of the frame boundaries, all it has to do is look for DLE STX or DLE ETX characters to figure out where it is.

A serious problem occurs with this method when binary data, such as object programs or floating point numbers, are being transmitted. It may easily happen that the characters for DLE STX or DLE ETX occur in the data, which would interfere with the framing. One way to solve this problem is to have the sender's data link layer insert an ASCII DLE character just before each "accidental" DLE character in the data. The data link layer on the receiving end removes the DLE before the data are given to the network layer. This technique is called **character stuffing**. Thus a framing DLE STX or DLE ETX can be distinguished from one in the data by the absence or presence of a single DLE. DLEs in the data are always doubled. Figure 4-4 gives an example data stream before stuffing, after stuffing, and after destuffing.

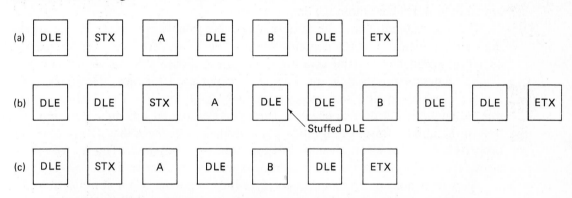

Fig. 4-4. (a) Data sent by the network layer. (b) Data after being character stuffed by the data link layer. (c) Data passed to the network layer on the receiving side.

A major disadvantage of using this framing method is that it is closely tied to 8-bit characters in general and the ASCII character code in particular. As networks developed, the disadvantages of embedding the character code in the framing mechanism became more and more obvious so a new technique was developed.

The new technique allows data frames to contain an arbitrary number of bits, and allows character codes with an arbitrary number of bits per character. It works like this. Each frame begins and ends with a special bit pattern, namely 01111110. Whenever the sender's data link layer encounters five consecutive ones in the data, it automatically stuffs a 0 bit into the outgoing bit stream. This **bit stuffing** is analogous to character stuffing, in which a DLE is stuffed into the outgoing character stream before DLE in the data.

When the receiver sees five consecutive incoming 1 bits, followed by a 0 bit, it automatically destuffs (i.e., deletes) the 0 bit. Just as character stuffing is completely transparent to the network layer in both computers, so is bit stuffing. If the user data contains the flag pattern 01111110, it is transmitted as 011111010 but stored in the receiver's memory as 01111110. Figure 4-5 gives an example of bit stuffing.

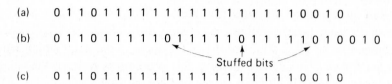

Fig. 4-5. Bit stuffing. (a) The original data. (b) The data as they appear on the line. (c) The data as they are stored in the receiver's memory after destuffing.

With bit stuffing, the boundary between two frames can be unambiguously recognized by the flag pattern. Thus if the receiver loses track of where it is, all it has to do is scan the input for flag sequences, since they can only occur at frame boundaries and never within the data.

The last method of framing is only applicable to networks in which the encoding on the physical medium contains some redundancy. For example, Manchester encoding encodes each 1 bit as a high-low pair and each 0 bit as a low-high pair. The combinations high-high and low-low are not used for data. However, some protocols use an invalid sequence such as high-high-low-low for framing. While this technique is a little like cheating (first you say that all bits must have a transition in the middle for clocking, then you introduce sequences that do not have this property), it has the clear advantage that no stuffing is required. This use of invalid physical codes is part of the 802 standard, as we saw in Chapter 3.

As a final note on framing, many data link protocols use a combination of a character count with one of the other methods for extra safety. When a frame arrives, the count field is used to locate the end of the frame. Only if the appropriate delimiter is present at that position and the checksum is correct, is the frame accepted as valid. Otherwise, the input stream is scanned for the next delimiter.

4.1.3. Error Control

Having solved the problem of marking the start and end of each frame, we come to the next problem: how to make sure all frames are eventually delivered to the network layer at the destination, and in the proper order. Suppose the sender just kept outputting frames without regard to whether they were arriving properly. This might be fine for unacknowledged connectionless service, but would most certainly not be fine for reliable, connection-oriented service.

The usual way to ensure reliable delivery is to provide the sender with some feedback about what is happening at the other end of the line. Typically the protocol calls for the receiver to send back special control frames bearing positive or negative acknowledgements about the incoming frames. If the sender receives a positive acknowledgement about a frame, it knows the frame has arrived safely. On the other hand, a negative acknowledgement means that something has gone wrong, and the frame must be transmitted again.

An additional complication comes from the possibility that hardware troubles may cause a frame to vanish completely (e.g., in a noise burst). In this case, the receiver will not react at all, since it has no reason to react. It should be clear that a protocol in which the sender transmitted a frame and then waited for an acknowledgement, positive or negative, would hang forever if a frame ever was completely lost due to malfunctioning hardware.

This possibility is dealt with by introducing timers into the data link layer. When the sender transmits a frame, it generally also starts a timer. The timer is set to go off after an interval long enough for the frame to reach the destination, be processed there, and have the acknowledgement propagate back to the sender. Normally the frame will be correctly received and the acknowledgement will get back before the timer runs out, in which case it will be canceled.

However, if either the frame or the acknowledgement is lost, the timer will go off, alerting the sender to a potential problem. The obvious solution is to just transmit the frame again. However, when frames may be transmitted multiple times, there is a danger that the receiver will accept the same frame two or more times, and pass it to the network layer more than once. To prevent this from happening, it is generally necessary to assign sequence numbers to outgoing frames, so that the receiver can distinguish retransmissions from originals.

The whole issue of managing the timers and sequence numbers so as to ensure that each frame is ultimately passed to the network layer at the destination exactly once, no more and no less, is an important part of the data link layer's duties. Later in this chapter, we will study in detail how this management is done by looking at a series of increasingly sophisticated examples.

4.1.4. Flow Control

Another important design issue that occurs in the data link layer (and higher layers as well) is what to do with a sender that systematically wants to transmit frames faster than the receiver can accept them? This situation can easily occur when the sender is running on a fast (or lightly loaded) computer and the receiver is running on a slow (or heavily loaded) machine. The sender keeps pumping the frames out at a high rate until the receiver is completely swamped. Even if the transmission is error-free, at a certain point the receiver will simply not be able to handle the frames as they arrive, and will start to lose some. Clearly something has to be done to prevent this situation.

The usual solution is to introduce **flow control** to throttle the sender into sending no faster than the receiver can handle the traffic. This throttling generally requires some kind of a feedback mechanism, so the sender can be made aware of whether or not the receiver is able to keep up.

Various flow control schemes are known, but most of them use the same basic principle. The protocol contains well-defined rules about when a sender may transmit the next frame. These rules generally prohibit frames from being sent until the receiver has granted permission, either implicitly or explicitly. For example, when a connection is set up, the receiver might say: "You may send me *n* frames now, but after they have been sent, do not send any more until I have told you to continue." We will study various flow control mechanisms in this chapter.

4.1.5. Link management

Another function of the data link layer is to manage the administration of the link. With connectionless service, the administration is minimal, but with connection-oriented service it is more complex. Connections must be established and released, sequence numbers must be initialized and possibly reinitialized in the face of errors, and so on.

Furthermore, the configuration of the link must be managed. In the simplest case, a physical wire just runs between two machines. However, it is commonplace that several machines share the same channel. Traditionally, one of these is the **primary** (e.g., a computer) and the others are **secondaries** (e.g., dumb terminals).

Traffic management is done by having the primary send a short frame, called a **poll** to the first secondary, asking if it has any data to send. If so, the terminal sends the data; otherwise the primary polls the next secondary. In other systems, the terminals are allowed to send data to the computer even in the absence of a poll. Finally, in still other systems, such as LANs, there are no primaries and secondaries. All stations are equal and have the same access rights to the channel. In any event, the whole issue of primaries and secondaries vs. peers is an issue that occurs in the data link layer.

4.2. ERROR DETECTION AND CORRECTION

As we have mentioned repeatedly above, transmission errors are a fact of life. Given the 40 year depreciation time on the existing telephone plant, transmission errors are going to continue being a fact of life for decades to come. In the following sections we will look at some of the problems more closely and see how the data link layer handles them.

Transmission errors on telephone lines are caused by a variety of different physical phenomena. One phenomenon that is always present is thermal noise. The electrons in the copper wires are buzzing around at high speed and in all directions, producing a broad-spectrum background noise level. It is the ratio of the signal to this noise that Shannon's result deals with.

A major source of noise for data transmission is impulse noise. These pulses or spikes on the line typically have a duration of 10 msec. To the human ear, such pulses sound like little clicks. To a 9600 bps line, they sound like the death knell for 96 bits. Most of them are caused by the arcing of relays and other electromechanical wheezes at older switching offices, although lightning, clumsy telephone repairpersons, backfiring cars, surges on the power line, and telephone system signaling tones also make contributions.

Another major source of errors is the fact that the amplitude, propagation speed, and phase of signals all are frequency dependent. The telephone system in effect Fourier-analyzes all signals, distorts each frequency component separately, and then recombines them at the end. It is usually possible to lease specially conditioned lines on which the carrier has tried to minimize these effects, but such lines are more expensive than regular lines and the equalization is never perfect, anyway.

Many other sources of error also exist. Crosstalk can occur between two wires that are physically adjacent. When the echo suppressors are turned off, there will be echoes. Microwave links are subject to fading, off-course birds, and the like. For voice transmission, it is desirable to compress the signal amplitude into a narrow range, because the amplifiers are not linear over wide ranges. This compression, called **companding**, can introduce errors. And finally, it is not possible to produce a perfect carrier wave. Its amplitude, frequency, and phase will always exhibit some jitter.

On PCM trunks, errors are introduced whenever the receiver gets out of sync with the transmitter. Typically, it takes a few tens of milliseconds to get back into sync, with all the data transmitted in the meanwhile delivered to the wrong destination (because the bits appearing in time slot n get delivered to user n, no matter whose they really are).

As a result of the physical processes causing the noise, errors tend to come in bursts rather than singly. Having the errors come in bursts has both advantages and disadvantages over isolated single-bit errors. On the advantage side, computer data are always sent in blocks of bits. Suppose that the block size is 1000 bits, and the error rate is 0.001 per bit. If errors were independent, most blocks would contain an error. If the errors came in bursts of 100 however, only one or two blocks in 100 would be affected, on the average. The disadvantage of burst errors is that they are much harder to detect and correct than are isolated errors, and they are also harder to model analytically.

If the mean error rate is e per character and a block contains n characters, then if we ignore burst errors (to make the analysis manageable), the probability that the block is transmitted perfectly is $(1 - e)^n$. The probability that the block is in error is $1 - (1 - e)^n$. If $e \ll 1$, this can be expanded using a binomial expansion to give an approximate probability of block error equal to en. The empirical data, however, gives a block error probability roughly equal to $10^{-4}n^{0.8}$ for blocks containing n 8-bit bytes and no start or stop bits. The results vary with line length, transmission speed, and other factors, so this is just an order of magnitude estimate.

4.2.1. Error-Correcting Codes

Network designers have developed two basic strategies for dealing with errors. One way is to include enough redundant information along with each block of data sent to enable the receiver to deduce what the transmitted character must have been. The other way is only to include enough redundancy to allow the receiver to deduce that an error occurred, but not which error, and have it request a retransmission. The former strategy uses **error-correcting codes** and the latter uses **error-detecting codes**.

To understand how errors can be handled, it is necessary to look closely at what an error really is. Normally, a frame consists of m data (i.e., message) bits and r redundant, or check bits. Let the total length be n (i.e., $n = m + r$). An n-bit unit containing data and checkbits is often referred to as an n-bit **codeword**.

Given any two codewords, say, 10001001 and 10110001, it is possible to determine how many corresponding bits differ. In this case, 3 bits differ. To determine how many bits differ, just EXCLUSIVE OR the two codewords, and count the number of 1 bits in the result. The number of bit positions in which two codewords differ is called the **Hamming distance** (Hamming, 1950). Its significance is that if two codewords are a Hamming distance d apart, it will require d single-bit errors to convert one into the other.

In most data transmission applications, all 2^m possible data messages are legal, but due to the way the check bits are computed, not all of the 2^n possible codewords are used. Given the algorithm for computing the check bits, it is possible to construct a complete list of the legal codewords, and from this list find the two codewords whose Hamming distance is minimum. This distance is the Hamming distance of the complete code.

The error-detecting and error-correcting properties of a code depend on its Hamming distance. To detect d errors, you need a distance $d + 1$ code because with such a code there is no way that d single-bit errors can change a valid codeword into another valid codeword. When the receiver sees an invalid codeword, it can tell that a transmission error has occurred. Similarly, to correct d errors, you need a distance $2d + 1$ code because that way the legal codewords are so far apart that even with d changes, the original codeword is still closer than any other codeword, so it can be uniquely determined.

As a simple example of an error-detecting code, consider a code in which a single **parity bit** is appended to the data. The parity bit is chosen so that the number of 1 bits in the codeword is even (or odd). Such a code has a distance 2, since any single-bit error produces a codeword with the wrong parity. It can be used to detect single errors.

As a simple example of an error-correcting code, consider a code with only four valid codewords:

0000000000, 0000011111, 1111100000, and 1111111111

This code has a distance 5, which means that it can correct double errors. If the codeword 0000000111 arrives, the receiver knows that the original must have been 0000011111. If, however, a triple error changes 0000000000 into 0000000111, the error will not be corrected properly.

Imagine that we want to design a code with m message bits and r check bits that will allow all single errors to be corrected. Each of the 2^m legal messages has n illegal codewords at a distance 1 from it. These are formed by systematically inverting each of the n bits in the n-bit codeword formed from it. Thus each of the 2^m legal messages requires $n + 1$ bit patterns dedicated to it. Since the total number of bit patterns is 2^n we must have $(n + 1)2^m \le 2^n$. Using $n = m + r$ this requirement becomes $(m + r + 1) \le 2^r$. Given m, this puts a lower limit on the number of check bits needed to correct single errors.

This theoretical lower limit can, in fact, be achieved using a method due to Hamming (1950). The bits of the codeword are numbered consecutively, starting with bit 1 at the left end. The bits that are powers of 2 (1, 2, 4, 8, 16, etc.) are check bits. The rest (3, 5, 6, 7, 9, etc.) are filled up with the m data bits. Each check bit forces the parity of some collection of bits, including itself, to be even (or odd). A bit may be included in several parity computations. To see which check bits the data bit in position k contributes to, rewrite k as a sum of powers of 2. For example, $11 = 1 + 2 + 8$ and $29 = 1 + 4 + 8 + 16$. A bit is checked by just those check bits occurring in its expansion (e.g., bit 11 is checked by bits 1, 2, and 8).

Char.	ASCII	Check bits
H	1001000	00110010000
a	1100001	10111001001
m	1101101	11101010101
m	1101101	11101010101
i	1101001	01101011001
n	1101110	01101010110
g	1100111	11111001111
	0100000	10011000000
c	1100011	11111000011
o	1101111	00101011111
d	1100100	11111001100
e	1100101	00111000101

Order of bit transmission

Fig. 4-6. Use of a Hamming code to correct burst errors.

When a codeword arrives, the receiver initializes a counter to zero. It then examines each check bit, k ($k = 1, 2, 4, 8, \ldots$) to see if it has the correct parity. If not, it adds k to the counter. If the counter is zero after all the check bits have been examined (i.e., if they were all correct), the codeword is accepted as valid. If the counter is nonzero, it contains the number of the incorrect bit. For example, if check bits 1, 2, and 8 are in error the inverted bit is 11, because it is the only one checked by bits 1, 2, and 8. Figure 4-6 shows some 7-bit ASCII characters encoded as 11-bit codewords using a Hamming code. Remember that the data are found in bit positions 3, 5, 6, 7, 9, 10, and 11.

Hamming codes can only correct single errors. However, there is a trick that can be used to permit Hamming codes to correct burst errors. A sequence of k consecutive codewords are arranged as a matrix, one codeword per row. Normally, the data would be transmitted one codeword at a time, from left to right. To correct burst errors, the data should be transmitted one column at a time, starting with the leftmost column. When all k bits have been sent, the second column is sent, and so on. When the frame arrives at the receiver, the matrix is reconstructed, one column at a time. If a burst error of length k occurs, at most 1 bit in each of the k codewords will have been affected, but the Hamming code can correct one error per codeword, so the entire block can be restored. This method uses kr check bits to make blocks of km data bits immune to a single burst error of length k or less.

4.2.2. Error-Detecting Codes

Error-correcting codes are sometimes used for data transmission, for example, when the channel is simplex, so retransmissions cannot be requested, but most often error detection followed by retransmission is preferred because it is more efficient. As a simple example, consider a channel on which errors are isolated and the error rate is 10^{-6} per bit. Let the block size be 1000 bits. To provide error correction for 1000-bit blocks, 10 check bits are needed; a megabit of data would require 10,000 check bits. To merely detect a bad block, a single parity bit per block will suffice. Once every 1000 blocks an extra block (1001 bits) will have to be transmitted. The total overhead for the error detection + retransmission method is only 2001 bits per megabit of data, versus 10,000 bits for a Hamming code.

If a single parity bit is added to a block and the block is badly garbled by a long burst error, the probability that the error will be detected is only 0.5, which is hardly acceptable. The odds can be improved considerably by regarding each block to be sent as a rectangular matrix n bits wide and k bits high. A parity bit is computed separately for each column and affixed to the matrix as the last row. The matrix is then transmitted one row at a time. When the block arrives, the receiver checks all the parity bits. If any one of them is wrong, it requests a retransmission of the block.

This method can detect a single burst of length n, since only 1 bit per column will be changed. A burst of length $n + 1$ will pass undetected, however, if the first bit is inverted, the last bit is inverted, and all the other bits are correct. (A burst error does not imply that all the bits are wrong, it just implies that at least the first and last are wrong.) If the block is badly garbled by a long burst or by multiple shorter bursts, the probability that any of the n columns will have the correct parity, by accident, is 0.5, so the probability of a bad block being accepted when it should not be is 2^{-n}.

Although the above scheme may be adequate sometimes, in practice, another method is in widespread use: the **polynomial code** (also known as a **cyclic redundancy code** or CRC code). Polynomial codes are based upon treating bit strings as representations of polynomials with coefficients of 0 and 1 only. A k-bit frame is regarded as the coefficient list for a polynomial with k terms, ranging from x^{k-1} to x^0. Such a polynomial is said to be of degree $k-1$. The high-order (leftmost) bit is the coefficient of x^{k-1}; the next bit is the coefficient of x^{k-2}, and so on. For example, 110001 has 6 bits and thus represents a six term polynomial with coefficients 1, 1, 0, 0, 0, and 1: $x^5 + x^4 + x^0$.

Polynomial arithmetic is done modulo 2, according to the rules of algebraic field theory. There are no carries for addition or borrows for subtraction. Both addition and subtraction are identical to EXCLUSIVE OR. For example:

$$
\begin{array}{cccc}
10011011 & 00110011 & 11110000 & 01010101 \\
+\,11001010 & +\,11001101 & -\,10100110 & -\,10101111 \\
\hline
01010001 & 11111110 & 01010110 & 11111010 \\
\end{array}
$$

Long division is carried out the same way as it is in binary except that the subtraction is done modulo 2, as above. A divisor is said "to go into" a dividend if the dividend has as many bits as the divisor.

When the polynomial code method is employed, the sender and receiver must agree upon a **generator polynomial**, $G(x)$, in advance. Both the high- and low-order bits of the generator must be 1. To compute the **checksum** for some frame with m bits, corresponding to the polynomial $M(x)$, the frame must be longer than the generator polynomial. The basic idea is to append a checksum to the end of the frame in such a way that the polynomial represented by the checksummed frame is divisible by $G(x)$. When the receiver gets the checksummed frame, it tries dividing it by $G(x)$. If there is a remainder, there has been a transmission error.

The algorithm for computing the checksum is as follows:

1. Let r be the degree of $G(x)$. Append r zero bits to the low-order end of the frame, so it now contains $m + r$ bits, and corresponds to the polynomial $x^r M(x)$.

2. Divide the bit string corresponding to $G(x)$ into the bit string corresponding to $x^r M(x)$ using modulo 2 division.

3. Subtract the remainder (which is always r or fewer bits) from the bit string corresponding to $x^r M(x)$ using modulo 2 subtraction. The result is the checksummed frame to be transmitted. Call its polynomial $T(x)$.

Figure 4-7 illustrates the calculation for a frame 1101011011 and $G(x) = x^4 + x + 1$.

It should be clear that $T(x)$ is divisible (modulo 2) by $G(x)$. In any division

Frame   :   1 1 0 1 0 1 1 0 1 1

Generator: 1 0 0 1 1

Message after appending 4 zero bits : 1 1 0 1 0 1 1 0 1 1 0 0 0 0

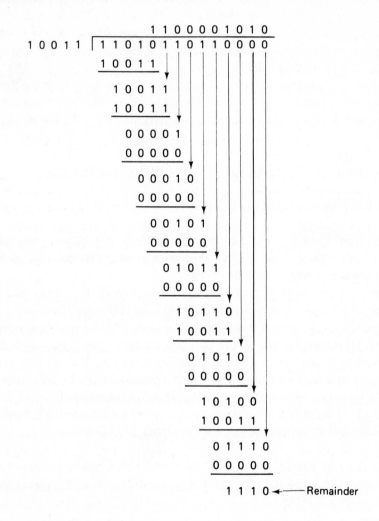

Transmitted frame: 1 1 0 1 0 1 1 0 1 1 1 1 1 0

Fig. 4-7. Calculation of the polynomial code checksum.

problem, if you diminish the dividend by the remainder, what is left over is divisible by the divisor. For example, in base 10, if you divide 210278 by 10941, the remainder is 2399. By subtracting off 2399 from 210278, what is left over (207879) is divisible by 10941.

Now let us analyze the power of this method. What kinds of errors will be detected? Imagine that a transmission error occurs, so that instead of the polynomial for $T(x)$ arriving, $T(x) + E(x)$ arrives. Each 1 bit in $E(x)$ corresponds to a bit that has been inverted. If there are k 1 bits in $E(x)$, k single-bit errors have occurred. A single burst error is characterized by an initial 1, a mixture of 0s and 1s, and a final 1, with all other bits being 0.

Upon receiving the checksummed frame, the receiver divides it by $G(x)$; that is, it computes $[T(x) + E(x)]/G(x)$. $T(x)/G(x)$ is always 0, so the result of the computation is simply $E(x)/G(x)$. Those errors that happen to correspond to polynomials containing $G(x)$ as a factor will slip by unnoticed, but all other errors will be caught.

If there has been a single-bit error, $E(x) = x^i$, where i determines which bit is in error. If $G(x)$ contains two or more terms, it will never divide $E(x)$, so all single-bit errors will be detected.

If there have been two isolated single-bit errors, $E(x) = x^i + x^j$, where $i > j$. Alternatively, this can be written as $E(x) = x^j(x^{i-j} + 1)$. If we assume that $G(x)$ is not divisible by x, a sufficient condition for all double errors to be detected is that $G(x)$ does not divide $x^k + 1$ for any k up to the maximum value of $i - j$ (i.e., up to the maximum frame length). Simple, low-degree polynomials that give protection to long frames are known. For example, $x^{15} + x^{14} + 1$ will not divide $x^k + 1$ for any k below 32768.

If there are an odd number of bits in error, $E(X)$ contains an odd number of terms (e.g., $x^5 + x^2 + 1$, but not $x^2 + 1$). Interestingly enough, there is no polynomial with an odd number of terms that has $x + 1$ as a factor in the modulo 2 system. By making $x + 1$ a factor of $G(x)$, we can catch all errors consisting of an odd number of inverted bits.

To see that no polynomial with an odd number of terms is divisible by $x + 1$, assume that $E(x)$ has an odd number of terms and is divisible by $x + 1$. Factor $E(x)$ into $(x + 1) Q(x)$. Now evaluate $E(1) = (1 + 1)Q(1)$. Since $1 + 1 = 0$ (modulo 2), $E(1)$ must be zero. If $E(x)$ has an odd number of terms, substituting 1 for x everywhere will always yield 1 as result. Thus no polynomial with an odd number of terms is divisible by $x + 1$.

Finally, and most important, a polynomial code with r check bits will detect all burst errors of length $\leq r$. A burst error of length k can be represented by $x^i(x^{k-1} + \ldots + 1)$, where i determines how far from the right hand end of the received frame the burst is located. If $G(x)$ contains an x^0 term, it will not have x^i as a factor, so if the degree of the parenthesized expression is less than the degree of $G(x)$, the remainder can never be zero.

If the burst length is $r + 1$, the remainder of the division by $G(x)$ will be zero if and only if the burst is identical to $G(x)$. By definition of a burst, the first and last bits must be 1, so whether it matches depends on the $r - 1$ intermediate bits. If all combinations are regarded as equally likely, the probability of such an incorrect frame being accepted as valid is $1/2^{r-1}$.

It can also be shown that when an error burst longer than $r + 1$ bits occurs, or several shorter bursts occur, the probability of a bad frame getting through unnoticed is $^1/_2{}^r$ assuming that all bit patterns are equally likely.

Three polynomials have become international standards:

$$\text{CRC–12} \quad = x^{12} + x^{11} + x^3 + x^2 + x^1 + 1$$
$$\text{CRC–16} \quad = x^{16} + x^{15} + x^2 + 1$$
$$\text{CRC–CCITT} = x^{16} + x^{12} + x^5 + 1$$

All three contain $x + 1$ as a prime factor. CRC-12 is used when the character length is 6 bits. The other two are used for 8-bit characters. A 16-bit checksum, such as CRC-16 or CRC-CCITT, catches all single and double errors, all errors with an odd number of bits, all burst errors of length 16 or less, 99.997% of 17-bit error bursts, and 99.998% of 18-bit and longer bursts.

Although the calculation required to compute the checksum may seem complicated, Peterson and Brown (1961) have shown that a simple shift register circuit can be constructed to compute and verify the checksums in hardware. In practice, this hardware is nearly always used.

4.3. ELEMENTARY DATA LINK PROTOCOLS

To introduce the subject of protocols, we will begin by looking at three protocols of increasing complexity. Before we look at the protocols, however, it is useful to make explicit some of the assumptions underlying the model of communication. To start with, we are assuming that the physical layer, data link layer, and network layer are independent processes that communicate by passing messages back and forth. In some cases, the physical and data link layer processes will be running on a microprocessor inside a special I/O chip and the network layer on the main CPU, but other implementations are also possible (e.g., three processes inside a single I/O chip; the physical and data link layers as procedures called by the network layer process, and so on). In any event, treating the three layers as separate processes makes the discussion conceptually cleaner and also serves to emphasize the independence of the layers.

Another key assumption is that machine A wants to send a long stream of data to machine B using a reliable, connection-oriented service. Later, we will consider the case where B also wants to send data to A simultaneously. A is assumed to have an infinite supply of data ready to send and never has to wait for data to be produced. When A's data link layer asks for data, the network layer is always able to comply immediately. (This restriction, too, will be dropped later.)

As far as the data link layer is concerned, the packet passed across the interface to it from the network layer is pure data, every bit of which is to be delivered to the destination's network layer. The fact that the destination's network layer may interpret part of the packet as a header is of no concern to the data link layer.

When the data link layer accepts a packet, it encapsulates the packet in a frame by adding a data link header and trailer to it (see Fig. 1-8). Thus a frame consists of an embedded packet and some control (header) information. The frame is then transmitted to the other data link layer. We will assume that there exist suitable library procedures *ToPhysicalLayer* to send a frame and *FromPhysicalLayer* to receive a frame. The transmitting hardware computes and appends the checksum, so that the data link layer software need not worry about it. The polynomial algorithm discussed earlier in this chapter might be used, for example.

Initially, the receiver has nothing to do. It just sits around waiting for something to happen. In the example protocols of this chapter we indicate that the data link layer is waiting for something to happen by the procedure call *wait*(*event*). This procedure only returns when something has happened (e.g., a frame has arrived). Upon return, the variable *event* tells what happened. The set of possible events differs for the various protocols to be described and will be defined separately for each protocol. Note that in a more realistic situation, the data link layer will not sit in a tight loop waiting for an event, as we have suggested, but will receive an interrupt, which will cause it to stop whatever it was doing and go handle the incoming frame. Nevertheless, for simplicity we will ignore all the details of parallel activity within the data link layer and assume that it is dedicated full time to handling just our one channel.

When a frame arrives at the receiver, the hardware computes the checksum. If the checksum is incorrect (i.e., there was a transmission error), the data link layer is so informed (*event* = *CksumErr*). If the inbound frame arrived undamaged, the data link layer is also informed (*event* = *FrameArrival*), so it can acquire the frame for inspection using *FromPhysicalLayer*. As soon as the receiving data link layer has acquired an undamaged frame, it checks the control information in the header, and if everything is all right, the packet portion is passed to the network layer. Under no circumstances is a frame header ever given to a network layer.

There is a good reason why the network layer must never be given any part of the frame header: to keep the network and data link protocols completely separate. As long as the network layer knows nothing at all about the data link protocol or the frame format, these things can be changed without requiring changes to the network layer's software. Providing a rigid interface between network layer and data link layer greatly simplifies the software design, because communication protocols in different layers can evolve independently. Figure 4-8 shows some declarations common to many of the protocols to be discussed later. Five data structures are defined there: *bit*, *SequenceNr*, *packet*, *FrameKind*, and *frame*. A *bit* is a 0 or a 1. A *SequenceNr* is a small integer used to number the frames in order to tell them apart. The constant *MaxSeq* is defined in each protocol. A *packet* is the unit of information exchanged between the network layer and the data link layer on the same machine, or between network layer peers. In our model it always contains exactly *LastBit* + 1 bits, but more realistically would be of variable length, from 0 up to a maximum of *LastBit* + 1 bits.

{Some data types and procedures common to a number of the protocols.}

const *LastBit* = ... ;   {determines packet size}
     doomsday = *false* ;   {used to repeat forever}
     MaxSeq = ... ;   {*MaxSeq* = highest seq = $2\uparrow n - 1$}

type *bit* = 0 .. 1;
     SequenceNr = 0 .. *MaxSeq* ;   {used to number the frames}
     packet = **packed array** [0 .. *LastBit*] **of** *bit* ;   {a packet from the upper layers}
     FrameKind = (*data* , *ack* , *nak*);
     frame = **packed record**
        kind : *FrameKind* ;
        seq : *SequenceNr* ;
        ack : *SequenceNr* ;
        info : *packet*
     end;

procedure *wait* (**var** *event* : *EvType*);
begin {Wait for an event to happen; return its type in *event*.} **end**;

procedure *FromNetworkLayer* (**var** *p* : *packet*);
begin {Fetch information from the network layer for transmission on the channel.} **end**;

procedure *ToNetworkLayer* (*p* : *packet*);
begin {Deliver information from an inbound frame to the network layer.} **end**;

procedure *FromPhysicalLayer* (**var** *r* : *frame*);
begin {Go get an inbound frame from the physical layer and copy it to *r*.} **end**;

procedure *ToPhysicalLayer* (*s* : *frame*);
begin {Pass the frame *s* to the physical layer for transmission.} **end**;

procedure *StartTimer* (*k* : *SequenceNr*);
begin {Start the clock running and enable *TimeOut* event.} **end**;

procedure *StopTimer* (*k* : *SequenceNr*);
begin {Stop the clock and disable *TimeOut* event.} **end**;

procedure *StartAckTimer* ;
begin {Start an auxiliary timer for sending separate acks.} **end**;

procedure *StopAckTimer* ;
begin {Stop the auxiliary timer and disable *NetworkLayerIdle* event.} **end**;

procedure *EnableNetworkLayer* ;
begin {Allow the network layer to cause a *NetworkLayerReady* event.} **end**;

procedure *DisableNetworkLayer* ;
begin {Forbid the network layer from causing a *NetworkLayerReady* event.} **end**;

procedure *inc* (**var** *k* : *SequenceNr*);
begin {Increment *k* circularly.} **if** *k* < *MaxSeq* **then** *k* := *k* + 1 **else** *k* := 0 **end**;

Fig. 4-8. Some definitions needed in the examples to follow.

A *frame* is composed of four fields: *kind*, *seq*, *ack*, and *info*, the first three of which contain control information, and the last of which may contain actual data to be transferred. These control fields are collectively called the **frame header**. The *kind* field tells whether or not there are any data in the frame, because some of the protocols distinguish frames containing exclusively control information from those containing data as well. The *seq* and *ack* fields are used for sequence numbers and acknowledgements, respectively; their use will be described in more detail later. The *info* field of a data frame contains a single packet; the *info* field of a control frame is not used. A more realistic implementation would use a variable-length *info* field, omitting it altogether for control frames.

It is important to realize the relationship between a packet and a frame. The network layer builds a packet by taking a message from the transport layer and adding the network layer header to it. This packet is passed to the data link layer for inclusion in the *info* field of an outgoing frame. When the frame arrives at the destination, the data link layer extracts the packet from the frame, and passes the packet to the network layer. In this manner, the network layer can act as though machines can exchange packets directly. Fig. 1-8 shows this relationship schematically.

A number of procedures are also listed in Fig. 4-8. These are library routines whose details are implementation-dependent and whose inner workings will not concern us further here. The procedure *wait* sits in a tight loop waiting for something to happen, as mentioned earlier. The procedures *ToNetworkLayer* and *FromNetworkLayer* are used by the data link layer to pass packets to the network layer and accept packets from the network layer, respectively. Note that *FromPhysicalLayer* and *ToPhysicalLayer* are used for passing frames between the data link and physical layers, whereas *ToNetworkLayer* and *FromNetworkLayer* are used for passing packets between the data link layer and network layer. In other words, *ToNetworkLayer* and *FromNetworkLayer* deal with the interface between layers 2 and 3, whereas *FromPhysicalLayer* and *ToPhysicalLayer* deal with the interface between layers 1 and 2.

In most of the protocols we assume an unreliable channel that loses entire frames upon occasion. To be able to recover from such calamities, the sending data link layer must start an internal timer or clock whenever it sends a frame. If no reply has been received within a certain predetermined time interval, the clock times out and the data link layer receives an interrupt signal.

In our protocols this is handled by allowing the procedure *wait* to return *event* = *TimeOut*. The procedures *StartTimer* and *StopTimer* are used to turn the timer on and off, respectively. Timeouts are possible only when the timer is running. It is explicitly permitted to call *StartTimer* while the timer is running; such a call simply resets the clock to cause the next timeout after a full timer interval has elapsed (unless it is reset or turned off in the meanwhile).

The procedures *StartAckTimer* and *StopAckTimer* are used to control an auxiliary timer used to generate acknowledgements under certain conditions.

The procedures *EnableNetworkLayer* and *DisableNetworkLayer* are used in the more sophisticated protocols, where we no longer assume that the network layer always has packets to send. When the data link layer enables the network layer, the network layer is then permitted to interrupt when it has a packet to be sent. We indicate this with *event = NetworkLayerReady*. When a network layer is disabled, it may not cause such events. By being careful about when it enables and disables its network layer, the data link layer can prevent the network layer from swamping it with packets for which it has no buffer space.

Frame sequence numbers are always in the range 0 to *MaxSeq* (inclusive), where *MaxSeq* is different for the different protocols. It is frequently necessary to advance a sequence number by 1 circularly (i.e., *MaxSeq* is followed by 0). The procedure *inc* performs this incrementing.

The declarations of Fig. 4-8 are part of each of the protocols to follow. To save space and to provide a convenient reference, they have been extracted and listed together, but conceptually they should be merged with the protocols themselves.

4.3.1. An Unrestricted Simplex Protocol

As an initial example we will consider a protocol that is as simple as can be. Data are transmitted in one direction only. Both the transmitting and receiving network layers are always ready. Processing time can be ignored. Infinite buffer space is available. And best of all, the communication channel between the data link layers never damages or loses frames. This thoroughly unrealistic protocol, which we will nickname "utopia," is shown in Fig. 4-9.

The protocol consists of two distinct procedures, a sender and a receiver. The sender runs in the data link layer of the source machine, and the receiver runs in the data link layer of the destination machine. No sequence numbers or acknowledgements are used here, so *MaxSeq* is not needed. The only event type possible is *FrameArrival* (i.e., the arrival of an undamaged frame).

The sender is in an infinite loop bracketed by **repeat until** *doomsday*, just pumping data out onto the line as fast as it can. The body of the loop consists of three actions: go fetch a packet from the (always obliging) network layer, construct an outbound frame using the variable *s*, and send the frame on its way. Only the *info* field of the frame is used by this protocol, because the other fields have to do with error and flow control, and there are no errors or flow control restrictions here.

The receiver is equally simple. Initially, it waits for something to happen, the only possibility being the arrival of an undamaged frame. Eventually, the frame arrives and the procedure *wait* returns, with *event* set to *FrameArrival* (which is ignored anyway). The call to *FromPhysicalLayer* removes the newly arrived frame from the hardware buffer and puts it in the variable *r*. Finally the data portion is passed on to the network layer and the data link layer settles back to wait for the next frame, effectively suspending itself until the frame arrives.

{Protocol 1 (utopia) provides for data transmission in one direction only, from sender to receiver. The communication channel is assumed to be error free, and the receiver is assumed to be able to process all the input infinitely fast. Consequently, the sender just sits in a loop pumping data out onto the line as fast as it can.}

type *EvType* = (*FrameArrival*);

procedure *sender1*;
var *s*: *frame*;   {buffer for an outbound frame}
   buffer: *packet*;   {buffer for an outbound packet}
begin
  repeat
    FromNetworkLayer(*buffer*);   {go get something to send}
    s.*info* := *buffer*;   {copy it into *s* for transmission}
    ToPhysicalLayer(*s*)   {send it on its way}
  until *doomsday*   {tomorrow, and tomorrow, and tomorrow,
                            creeps in this petty pace from day to day,
                            to the last syllable of recorded time;
                                              − Macbeth, V, v}

end; {*sender1*}

procedure *receiver1*;
var *r*: *frame*;
   event: *EvType*;   {filled in by *wait*, but not used here}
begin
  repeat
    wait(*event*);   {only possibility is *FrameArrival*}
    FromPhysicalLayer(*r*);   {go get the inbound frame}
    ToNetworkLayer(*r*.*info*)   {pass the data to the network layer}
  until *doomsday*
end; {*receiver1*}

Fig. 4-9. An unrestricted simplex protocol.

4.3.2. A Simplex Stop-and-Wait Protocol

Now we will drop the most unrealistic restriction used in protocol 1: the ability of the receiving network layer to process incoming data infinitely fast (or equivalently, the presence in the receiving data link layer of an infinite amount of buffer space in which to store all incoming frames while they are waiting their respective turns). The communication channel is still assumed to be error free however, and the data traffic is still simplex.

The main problem we have to deal with here is how to prevent the sender from flooding the receiver with data faster than the latter is able to process it. In essence, if the receiver requires a time *t* to execute *FromPhysicalLayer* + *ToNetworkLayer*, the sender must transmit at an average rate less than one frame per time t. More-over, if we assume that there is no automatic buffering and queueing done within the receiver's hardware, the sender must never transmit a new frame until the old one has been fetched by *FromPhysicalLayer*, lest the new one overwrite the old one.

In certain restricted circumstances (e.g., synchronous transmission and a receiv-ing data link layer fully dedicated to processing the one input line), it might be pos-sible for the sender to simply insert a delay into protocol 1 to slow it down sufficiently to keep from swamping the receiver. However, more usually, each data link layer will have several lines to attend to, and the time interval between a frame arriving and its being processed may vary considerably. If the network designers can calculate the worst-case behavior of the receiver, they can program the sender to transmit so slowly that even if every frame suffers the maximum delay, there will be no overruns. The trouble with this approach is that it is too conservative. It leads to a bandwidth utilization that is far below the optimum, unless the best and worst cases are almost the same (i.e., the variation in the data link layer's reaction time is small).

A more general solution to this dilemma is to have the receiver provide feed-back to the sender. After having passed a packet to its network layer, the receiver sends a little dummy frame back to the sender which, in effect, gives the sender permission to transmit the next frame. After having sent a frame, the sender is required by the protocol to bide its time until the little dummy (i.e., acknowledge-ment) frame arrives.

Protocols in which the sender sends one frame and then waits for an acknow-ledgement before proceeding are called **stop-and-wait**. Figure 4-10 gives an example of a simplex stop-and-wait protocol. As in protocol 1, the sender starts out by fetching a packet from the network layer, using it to construct a frame, and send-ing it on its way. Only now, unlike in protocol 1, the sender must wait until an acknowledgement frame arrives before looping back and fetching the next packet from the network layer. The sending data link layer need not even inspect the incoming frame: there is only one possibility.

The only difference between *receiver1* and *receiver2* is that after delivering a packet to the network layer, *receiver2* sends an acknowledgement frame back to the sender before entering the wait loop again. Because only the arrival of the frame back at the sender is important, not its contents, the receiver need not put any par-ticular information in it.

Although data traffic in this example is simplex, going only from the sender to the receiver, frames do travel in both directions. Consequently, the communication channel between the two data link layers needs to be capable of bidirectional infor-mation transfer. However, this protocol entails a strict alternation of flow: first the sender sends a frame, then the receiver sends a frame, then the sender sends another frame, then the receiver sends another one, and so on. A half-duplex physical chan-nel would suffice here.

{Protocol 2 (stop-and-wait) also provides for a one directional flow of data from sender to receiver. The communications channel is once again assumed to be error free, as in protocol 1. However, this time, the receiver has only a finite buffer capacity and a finite processing speed, so the protocol must explicity prevent the sender from flooding the receiver with data faster than it can be handled.}

type *EvType* = (*FrameArrival*);

procedure *sender2*;
var *s* : *frame* ;
    buffer : *packet* ;
    event : *EvType* ;
begin
  repeat
    FromNetworkLayer (*buffer*);   {fetch information from the network layer}
    s .*info* := *buffer* ; {copy it into *s* for subsequent transmission}
    ToPhysicalLayer (*s*);   {bye bye little frame}
    wait (*event*)   {do not proceed until given go ahead}
  until *doomsday*
end; {*sender2*}

procedure *receiver2*;
var *r* ,*s* : *frame* ;
    event : *EvType* ;
begin
  repeat
    wait (*event*);   {only possibility is *FrameArrival*}
    FromPhysicalLayer (*r*);   {go get the frame}
    ToNetworkLayer (*r* .*info*); {give the packet to the network layer}
    ToPhysicalLayer (*s*)   {send a dummy frame as a go ahead signal}
  until *doomsday*
end; {*receiver2*}

Fig. 4-10. A simplex stop-and-wait protocol.

4.3.3. A Simplex Protocol for a Noisy Channel

Now let us consider the unfortunately all-too-realistic situation of a communication channel that makes errors. Frames may be either damaged or lost completely. However, we assume that if a frame is damaged in transit, the receiver hardware will detect this when it computes the checksum. If the frame is damaged in such a way that the checksum is nevertheless correct, an exceedingly unlikely occurrence, this protocol (and all other protocols) can fail (i.e., deliver an incorrect packet to the network layer).

At first glance it might seem that a minor variation of protocol 2 would work.

The sender would send a frame, but the receiver would only send an acknowledgement frame if the data were correctly received. If a damaged frame arrived at the receiver, it would be discarded. After a while the sender would time out and send the frame again. This process would be repeated until the frame finally arrived intact.

The above scheme has a fatal flaw in it. Think about the problem and try to discover what might go wrong before reading further.

To see what might go wrong, remember that it is the task of the communication subnet to provide error free, transparent communication between network layers. The network layer on machine A gives a series of packets to its data link layer, which must ensure that an identical series of packets are delivered to the network layer on machine B by its data link layer. In particular, network layer on B has no way of knowing that a packet has been lost or duplicated, so the data link layer must guarantee that no combination of transmission errors, no matter how unlikely, can cause a duplicate packet to be delivered to a network layer.

Consider the following scenario:

1. The network layer on A gives packet 1 to its data link layer. The packet is correctly received at B and passed to the network layer on B. B sends an acknowledgement frame back to A.

2. The acknowledgement frame gets lost completely. It just never arrives at all. Life would be a great deal simpler if the channel only mangled and lost data frames and not control frames, but sad to say, the channel is not very discriminating.

3. The data link layer on A eventually times out. Not having received an acknowledgement, it (incorrectly) assumes that its data frame was lost or damaged and sends the frame containing packet 1 again.

4. The duplicate frame also arrives at data link layer on B perfectly and is unwittingly passed to the network layer there. If A is sending a file to B, part of the file will be duplicated (i.e., the copy of the file made by B will be incorrect and the error will not have been detected). In other words, the protocol will fail.

Clearly, what is needed is some way for the receiver to be able to distinguish a frame that it is seeing for the first time from a retransmission. The obvious way to achieve this is to have the sender put a sequence number in the header of each frame it sends. Then the receiver can check the sequence number of each arriving frame to see if it is a new frame or a duplicate to be discarded.

Since a small frame header is desirable, the question arises: What is the minimum number of bits needed for the sequence number? The only ambiguity in this protocol is between a frame, m, and its direct successor, $m + 1$. If frame m is lost or damaged, the receiver will not acknowledge it, so the sender will keep trying to send it. Once it has been correctly received, the receiver will send an acknowledgement back to the sender. It is here that the potential trouble crops up. Depending upon whether the acknowledgement frame gets back to the sender correctly or not, the sender may try to send m or $m + 1$.

The event that triggers the sender to start sending $m + 2$ is the arrival of an acknowledgement for $m + 1$. But this implies that m has been correctly received, and furthermore that its acknowledgement has also been correctly received by the sender (otherwise, the sender would not have begun with $m + 1$, let alone $m + 2$). As a consequence, the only ambiguity is between a frame and its immediate predecessor or successor, not between the predecessor and successor themselves.

A 1-bit sequence number (0 or 1) is therefore sufficient. At each instant of time, the receiver expects a particular sequence number next. Any arriving frame containing the wrong sequence number is rejected as a duplicate. When a frame containing the correct sequence number arrives, it is accepted, passed to the network layer, and the expected sequence number is incremented modulo 2 (i.e., 0 becomes 1 and 1 becomes 0).

An example of this kind of protocol is shown in Fig. 4-11. Protocols in which the sender waits for a positive acknowledgement before advancing to the next data item are often called **PAR (Positive Acknowledgement with Retransmission)**. Like protocol 2, this one also transmits data only in one direction. Although it can handle lost frames (by timing out), it requires the timeout interval to be long enough to prevent premature timeouts. If the sender times out too early, while the acknowledgement is still on the way, it will send a duplicate.

When the previous acknowledgement finally does arrive, the sender will mistakenly think that the just sent frame is the one being acknowledged and will not realize that there is potentially another acknowledgement frame somewhere "in the pipe." If the next frame sent is lost completely but the extra acknowledgement arrives correctly, the sender will not attempt to retransmit the lost frame, and the protocol will fail. In later protocols the acknowledgement frames will contain information to prevent just this sort of trouble. For the time being, the acknowledgement frames will just be dummies, and we will assume a strict alternation of sender and receiver.

Protocol 3 differs from its predecessors in that both sender and receiver have a variable whose value is remembered while the data link layer is in wait state. The sender remembers the sequence number of the next frame to send in *NextFrameToSend*; the receiver remembers the sequence number of the next frame expected in *FrameExpected*. Each protocol has a short initialization phase before entering the infinite loop.

After transmitting a frame, the sender starts the timer running. If it was already running, it will be reset to allow another full timer interval. The time interval must be chosen to allow enough time for the frame to get to the receiver, for the receiver to process it in the worst case, and for the acknowledgement frame to propagate

{Protocol 3 (par) allows data to be transmitted in one direction over a
noisy communication channel that garbles and even loses frames.}

const *MaxSeq* = 1;

type *EvType* = (*FrameArrival*, *CksumErr*, *TimeOut*);

procedure *sender3*;
var *NextFrameToSend*: *SequenceNr*;   {sequence number of next outgoing frame}
    s: *frame*;   {scratch variable}
    buffer: *packet*;   {buffer for outbound packet}
    event: *EvType*;
begin
  NextFrameToSend := 0;   {initialize outbound sequence numbers}
  FromNetworkLayer(*buffer*);   {fetch first packet}
  repeat
    s.*info* := *buffer*;   {construct frame for transmission}
    s.*seq* := *NextFrameToSend*;   {insert sequence number in frame}
    ToPhysicalLayer(*s*);   {send it on its way}
    StartTimer(*s*.*seq*);   {if answer takes too long, time out}
    wait(*event*);   {possibilities: *FrameArrival*, *CksumErr*, *TimeOut* }
    if *event* = *FrameArrival* **then**
      begin   {an acknowledgement has arrived intact}
        FromNetworkLayer(*buffer*);   {fetch the next one to send}
        inc(*NextFrameToSend*)   {invert *NextFrameToSend*}
      end
  until *doomsday*
end; {*sender3*}

procedure *receiver3*;
var *FrameExpected*: *SequenceNr*;   {*FrameExpected* = 0 or 1}
    r,*s*: *frame*;   {scratch variables}
    event: *EvType*;
begin
  FrameExpected := 0;
  repeat
    wait(*event*);   {possibilities: *FrameArrival*, *CksumErr*}
    if *event* = *FrameArrival* **then**
      begin   {a valid frame has arrived}
      FromPhysicalLayer(*r*);   {accept inbound frame}
      if *r*.*seq* = *FrameExpected* **then**
        begin   {this is what we have been waiting for}
          ToNetworkLayer(*r*.*info*);   {pass the data to the network layer}
          inc(*FrameExpected*)   {next time expect the other sequence nr}
        end;
      ToPhysicalLayer(*s*)   {none of the fields are used!}
      end
  until *doomsday*
end; {*receiver3*}

Fig. 4-11. A Positive Acknowledgement/Retransmission protocol.

back to the sender. Only when that time interval has elapsed is it safe to assume that either the transmitted frame or its acknowledgement has been lost, and to send a duplicate.

After transmitting a frame and starting the timer, the sender waits for something exciting to happen. There are three possibilities: an acknowledgement frame arrives undamaged, a damaged acknowledgement frame staggers in, or the timer goes off. If a valid acknowledgement comes in, the sender fetches the next packet from its network layer and puts it in the buffer, overwriting the previous packet. It also advances the sequence number. If a damaged frame arrives or no frame at all arrives, neither the buffer nor the sequence number are changed, so that a duplicate can be sent.

When a valid frame arrives at the receiver, its sequence number is checked to see if it is a duplicate. If not, it is accepted, passed to the network layer, and an acknowledgement generated. Duplicates and damaged frames are not passed to the network layer.

4.4. SLIDING WINDOW PROTOCOLS

In the previous protocols, data frames were transmitted in one direction only. In most practical situations, there is a need for transmitting data in both directions. One way of achieving full-duplex data transmission would be to have two separate communication channels, and use each one for simplex data traffic (in different directions). If this were done, we would have two separate physical circuits, each with a "forward" channel (for data) and a "reverse" channel (for acknowledgements). In both cases the bandwidth of the reverse channel would be almost entirely wasted. In effect, the user would be paying the cost of two circuits but only using the capacity of one.

A better idea is to use the same circuit for data in both directions. After all, in protocols 2 and 3 it was already being used to transmit frames both ways, and the reverse channel has the same capacity as the forward channel. In this model the data frames from A to B are intermixed with the acknowledgement frames from A to B. By looking at the *kind* field in the header of an incoming frame, the receiver can tell whether the frame is data or acknowledgement.

Although interleaving data and control frames on the same circuit is an improvement over having two separate physical circuits, yet another improvement is possible. When a data frame arrives, instead of immediately sending a separate control frame, the receiver restrains itself and waits until the network layer passes it the next packet. The acknowledgement is attached to the outgoing data frame (using the *ack* field in the frame header). In effect, the acknowledgement gets a free ride on the next outgoing data frame. The technique of temporarily delaying outgoing acknowledgements so that they can be hooked onto the next outgoing data frame is widely known as **piggybacking**.

The principal advantage of piggybacking over having distinct acknowledgement frames is a better use of the available channel bandwidth. The *ack* field in the frame header only costs a few bits, whereas a separate frame would need a header, the acknowledgement, and a checksum. In addition, fewer frames sent means fewer "frame arrived" interrupts, and perhaps fewer buffers in the receiver, depending on how the receiver's software is organized. In the next protocol to be examined, the piggyback field costs only 1 bit in the frame header. It rarely costs more than a few bits.

Piggybacking also introduces a complication not present with separate acknowledgements. How long should the data link layer wait for a packet onto which to piggyback the acknowledgement? If the data link layer waits longer than the sender's timeout period, the frame will be retransmitted, defeating the whole purpose of having acknowledgements. If the data link layer were an oracle and could foretell the future, it would know when the next network layer packet was going to come in, and could decide either to wait for it or send a separate acknowledgement immediately, depending on how long the projected wait was going to be. Of course, the data link layer cannot foretell the future, so it must resort to some ad hoc scheme, such as waiting a fixed number of milliseconds. If a new packet arrives quickly, the acknowledgement is piggybacked onto it; otherwise, if no new packet has arrived by the end of this time period, the data link layer just sends a separate acknowledgement frame.

In addition to it being only simplex, protocol 3 can deadlock if the sender times out too early. It would be nicer to have a protocol that remained synchronized in the face of any combination of garbled frames, lost frames, and premature timeouts. The next three protocols are all highly robust and continue to function properly even under pathological conditions. All three belong to a class of protocols called **sliding window** protocols. The three differ among themselves in terms of efficiency, complexity, and buffer requirements, as discussed later.

In all sliding window protocols, each outbound frame contains a sequence number, ranging from 0 up to some maximum. The maximum is usually $2^n - 1$ so the sequence number fits nicely in an n-bit field. The stop-and-wait sliding window protocol uses $n = 1$, restricting the sequence numbers to 0 and 1, but more sophisticated versions can use arbitrary n.

The essence of all sliding window protocols is that at any instant of time, the sender maintains a list of consecutive sequence numbers corresponding to frames it is permitted to send. These frames are said to fall within the **sending window**. Similarly, the receiver also maintains a **receiving window** corresponding to frames it is permitted to accept. The sender's window and the receiver's window need not have the same lower and upper limits, or even have the same size.

Although these protocols give the data link layer more freedom about the order in which it may send and receive frames, we have most emphatically not dropped the requirement that the protocol must deliver packets to the destination network layer in the same order that they were passed to the data link layer on the sending machine. Nor have we changed the requirement that the physical communication channel is "wire-like" (i.e., it must deliver frames in the order sent).

The sequence numbers within the sender's window represent frames sent but as yet not acknowledged. Whenever a new packet arrives from the network layer, it is given the next highest sequence number, and the upper edge of the window is advanced by one. When an acknowledgement comes in, the lower edge is advanced by one. In this way the window continuously maintains a list of unacknowledged frames.

Since frames currently within the sender's window may ultimately be lost or damaged in transit, the sender must keep all these frames in its memory for possible retransmission. Thus if the maximum window size is n, the sender needs n buffers to hold the unacknowledged frames. If the window ever grows to its maximum size, the sending data link layer must forcibly shut off the network layer until another buffer becomes free.

The receiving data link layer's window corresponds to the frames it may accept. Any frame falling outside the window is discarded without comment. When a frame whose sequence number is equal to the lower edge of the window is received, it is passed to the network layer, an acknowledgement is generated, and the window is rotated by one. Unlike the sender's window, the receiver's window always remains at its initial size. Note that a window size of 1 means that the data link layer only accepts frames in order, but for larger windows this is not so. The network layer, in contrast, is always fed data in the proper order, regardless of the data link layer's window size.

Figure 4-12 shows an example with a maximum window size of 1. Initially, no frames are outstanding, so the lower and upper edges of the sender's window are equal, but as time goes on, the situation progresses as shown.

4.4.1. A One Bit Sliding Window Protocol

Before tackling the general case, let us first examine a sliding window protocol with a maximum window size of 1. Such a protocol uses stop-and-wait, since the sender transmits a frame and waits for its acknowledgement before sending the next one.

Figure 4-13 depicts such a protocol. *NextFrameToSend* tells which frame the sender is trying to send. Similarly, *FrameExpected* tells which frame the receiver is expecting. In both cases, 0 and 1 are the only possibilities.

Normally, one of the two data link layers goes first. In other words, only one of the data link layer programs should contain the *ToPhysicalLayer* and *StartTimer* procedure calls outside the main loop. In the event both data link layers start off simultaneously, a peculiar situation arises, which is discussed later. The starting machine fetches the first packet from its network layer, builds a frame from it, and sends it. When this (or any) frame arrives, the receiving data link layer checks to

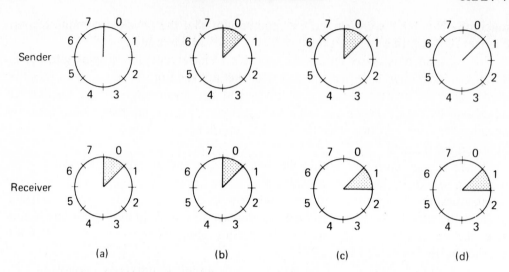

Fig. 4-12. A sliding window of size 1, with a 3-bit sequence number. (a) Initially. (b) After the first frame has been sent. (c) After the first frame has been received. (d) After the first acknowledgement has been received.

see if it is a duplicate, just as in protocol 3. If the frame is the one expected, it is passed to the network layer and the receiver's window is slid up.

The acknowledgement field contains the number of the last frame received without error. If this number agrees with the sequence number of the frame the sender is trying to send, the sender knows it is done with the frame stored in *buffer* and can fetch the next packet from its network layer. If the sequence number disagrees, it must continue trying to send the same frame. Whenever a frame is received, a frame is also sent back.

Now let us examine protocol 4 to see how resilient it is to pathological scenarios. Assume that *A* is trying to send its frame 0 to *B* and that *B* is trying to send its frame 0 to *A*. Suppose that *A* sends a frame to *B*, but *A*'s timeout interval is a little too short. Consequently, *A* may time out repeatedly, sending a series of identical frames, all with *seq* = 0 and *ack* = 1.

When the first valid frame arrives at *B*, it will be accepted, and *FrameExpected* set to 1. All the subsequent frames will be rejected, because their sequence numbers will be wrong. Furthermore, since all the duplicates have *ack* = 1 and *B* is still waiting for an acknowledgement of 0, *B* will not fetch a new packet from its network layer.

After every rejected duplicate comes in, *B* sends *A* a frame containing *seq* = 0 and *ack* = 0. Eventually, one of these arrives correctly at *A*, causing *A* to begin sending the next packet. No combination of lost frames or premature timeouts can cause the protocol to deliver duplicate packets to either network layer, or to skip a packet, or to get into a deadlock.

However, a peculiar situation arises if both sides simultaneously send an initial packet. This synchronization difficulty is illustrated by Fig. 4-14. In part (a), the

```
{Protocol 4 (sliding window) is bidirectional, and is more robust than
 protocol 3. It can withstand any combination of errors and timeouts without
 losing or duplicating network layer packets.}

const MaxSeq = 1;

type EvType = (FrameArrival, CksumErr, TimeOut);

procedure protocol4;
var NextFrameToSend : SequenceNr;        {0 or 1 only}
    FrameExpected : SequenceNr;          {0 or 1 only}
    r,s: frame;                          {scratch variables}
    buffer: packet;                      {current packet being sent}
    event: EvType;

begin
  NextFrameToSend := 0;                  {initialize outbound stream}
  FrameExpected := 0;                    {initialize inbound stream}
  FromNetworkLayer(buffer);              {fetch packet from network layer}
  s.info := buffer;                      {prepare to send initial frame}
  s.seq := NextFrameToSend;              {frame sequence number}
  s.ack := 1 - FrameExpected;            {piggybacked ack}
  ToPhysicalLayer(s);                    {transmit the frame}
  StartTimer(s.seq);                     {start the timer running}

  repeat
    wait(event);                         {FrameArrival, CksumErr, TimeOut}
    if event = FrameArrival then
      begin                              {an inbound frame made it without error}
        FromPhysicalLayer(r);            {go get it}

        if r.seq = FrameExpected then
          begin                          {handle inbound frame stream}
            ToNetworkLayer(r.info);      {pass the packet to the network layer}
            inc(FrameExpected)           {invert the receiver seq number}
          end;

        if r.ack = NextFrameToSend then
          begin                          {handle outbound frame stream}
            FromNetworkLayer(buffer);    {fetch a new packet from network layer}
            inc(NextFrameToSend)         {invert sender sequence number}
          end

      end;

    s.info := buffer;                    {construct outbound frame}
    s.seq := NextFrameToSend;            {insert sequence number into it}
    s.ack := 1 - FrameExpected;          {this is seq number of last received frame}
    ToPhysicalLayer(s);                  {transmit a frame}
    StartTimer(s.seq)                    {start the timer running}
  until doomsday

end; {protocol4}
```

Fig. 4-13. A 1-bit sliding window protocol.

normal operation of the protocol is shown. In (b) the peculiarity is illustrated. If *B* waits for *A*'s first frame before sending one of its own, the sequence is as shown in (a), and every frame is accepted. However, if *A* and *B* simultaneously initiate communication, their first frames cross, and the data link layers then get into situation (b). In (a) each frame arrival brings a new packet for the network layer; there are no duplicates. In (b) half of the frames contain duplicates, even though there are no transmission errors.

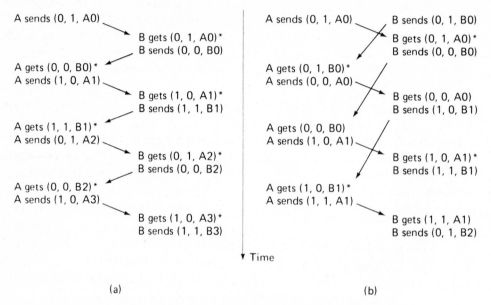

Fig. 4-14. Two scenarios for protocol 4. The notation is (seq, ack, packet number). An asterisk indicates where a network layer accepts a packet.

4.4.2. A Protocol Using Go Back n

Until now we have made the tacit assumption that the transmission time required for a frame to arrive at the receiver plus the transmission time for the acknowledgement to come back is negligible. Sometimes this assumption is patently false. In these situations the long round-trip time can have important implications for the efficiency of the bandwidth utilization. As an example, consider a 50-kbps satellite channel with a 500-msec round-trip propagation delay. Let us imagine trying to use protocol 4 to send 1000-bit frames via the satellite. At $t = 0$ the sender starts sending the first frame. At $t = 20$ msec the frame has been completely sent. Not until $t = 270$ msec has the frame fully arrived at the receiver, and not until $t = 520$ msec has the acknowledgement arrived back at the sender, under the best of circumstances (no waiting in the receiver and a short acknowledgement frame). This means that the sender was blocked during 500/520 or 96 percent of the time (i.e., only 4 percent of the available bandwidth was used). Clearly, the combination of a long transit time, high bandwidth and short frame length is disastrous in terms of efficiency.

The problem described above can be viewed as a consequence of the rule requiring a sender to wait for an acknowledgement before sending another frame. If we relax that restriction, much better efficiency can be achieved. Basically the solution lies in allowing the sender to transmit up to w frames before blocking, instead of just 1. With an appropriate choice of w the sender will be able to continuously transmit frames for a time equal to the round-trip transit time without filling up the window. In the example above, w should be at least 26. The sender begins sending frame 0 as before. By the time it has finished sending 26 frames, at $t = 520$, the acknowledgement for frame 0 will have just arrived. Thereafter, acknowledgements will arrive every 20 msec, so the sender always gets permission to continue just when it needs it. At all times, 25 or 26 unacknowledged frames are outstanding. Put in other terms, the sender's maximum window size is 26.

This technique is known as **pipelining**. If the channel capacity is b bits/sec, the frame size l bits, and the round-trip propagation time R sec, the time required to transmit a single frame is l/b sec. After the last bit of a data frame has been sent, there is a delay of $R/2$ before that bit arrives at the receiver, and another delay of at least $R/2$ for the acknowledgement to come back, for a total delay of R. In stop-and-wait the line is busy for l/b and idle for R, giving a line utilization of $l/(l + bR)$. If $l < bR$ the efficiency will be less than 50 percent. Since there is always a nonzero delay for the acknowledgement to propagate back, in principle pipelining can be used to keep the line busy during this interval, but if the interval is small, the additional complexity is not worth the trouble.

Pipelining frames over an unreliable communication channel raises some serious issues. First, what happens if a frame in the middle of a long stream is damaged or lost? Large numbers of succeeding frames will arrive at the receiver before the sender even finds out that anything is wrong. When a damaged frame arrives at the receiver, it obviously should be discarded, but what should the receiver do with all the correct frames following it? Remember that the receiving data link layer is obligated to hand packets to the network layer in sequence.

There are two basic approaches to dealing with errors in the presence of pipelining. One way, called **go back n**, is for the receiver simply to discard all subsequent frames, sending no acknowledgements. This strategy corresponds to a receive window of size 1. In other words, the data link layer refuses to accept any frame except the next one it must give to the network layer. If the sender's window fills up before the timer runs out, the pipeline will begin to empty. Eventually, the sender will time out and retransmit all unacknowledged frames in order, starting with the damaged or lost one. This approach, shown in Fig. 4-15(a), can waste a lot of bandwidth if the error rate is high.

The other general strategy for handling errors when frames are pipelined, called **selective repeat**, is to have the receiving data link layer store all the correct frames

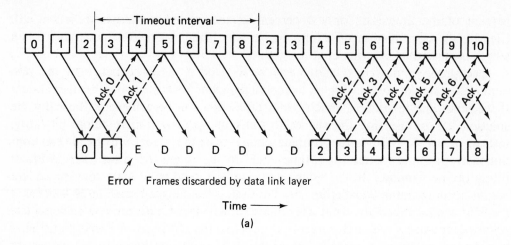

(a)

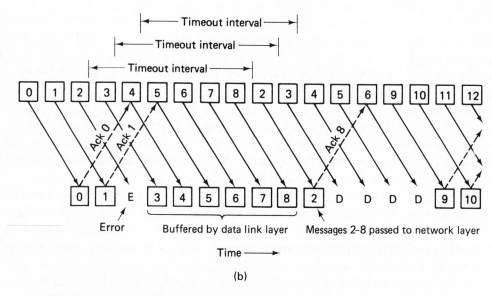

(b)

Fig. 4-15. (a) Effect of an error when the receiver window size is 1. (b) Effect of an error when the receiver window size is large.

following the bad one. When the sender finally notices that something is wrong, it just retransmits the one bad frame, not all its successors, as shown in Fig. 4-15(b). If the second try succeeds, the receiving data link layer will now have many correct frames in sequence, so they can all be handed off to the network layer quickly and the highest number acknowledged.

This strategy corresponds to a receiver window larger than 1. Any frame within the window may be accepted and buffered until all the preceding ones have been passed to the network layer. This approach can require large amounts of data link layer memory if the window is large.

These two alternative approaches are trade-offs between bandwidth and data link layer buffer space. Depending on which resource is more valuable, one or the other can be used. Figure 4-16 shows a pipelining protocol in which the receiving data link layer only accepts frames in order; frames following an error are discarded. In this protocol, for the first time, we have now dropped the assumption that the network layer always has an infinite supply of packets to send. When the network layer has a packet it wants to send, it can cause a *NetworkLayerReady* event to happen. However, in order to enforce the flow control rule of no more than *MaxSeq* unacknowledged frames outstanding at any time, the data link layer must be able to prohibit the network layer from bothering it with more work. The procedures *EnableNetworkLayer* and *DisableNetworkLayer* perform this function.

Note that a maximum of *MaxSeq* frames and not *MaxSeq* + 1 frames may be outstanding at any instant, even though there are *MaxSeq* + 1 distinct sequence numbers: 0, 1, 2, . . . , *MaxSeq*. To see why this restriction is needed, consider the following scenario with *MaxSeq* = 7.

1. The sender sends frames 0 through 7.

2. A piggybacked acknowledgement for frame 7 eventually comes back to the sender.

3. The sender sends another eight frames, again with sequence numbers 0 through 7.

4. Now another piggybacked acknowledgement for frame 7 comes in.

The question is: did all eight frames belonging to the second batch arrive successfully, or did all eight get lost (counting discards following an error as lost)? In both cases the receiver would be sending frame 7 as the acknowledgement. The sender has no way of telling. For this reason the maximum number of outstanding frames must be restricted to *MaxSeq*.

Although protocol 5 does not buffer the frames arriving after an error, it does not escape the problem of buffering altogether. Since a sender may have to retransmit all the unacknowledged frames at a future time, it must hang on to them until it knows for sure that they have been accepted by the receiver. When an acknowledgement comes in for frame *n*, frames *n* − 1, *n* − 2, and so on, are also automatically acknowledged. This property is especially important when some of the previous acknowledgement bearing frames were lost. Whenever any acknowledgement comes in, the data link layer checks to see if any buffers can now be released. If buffers can be released (i.e., there is some room available in the window), a previously blocked network layer can now be allowed to cause more *NetworkLayerReady* events.

Because this protocol has multiple outstanding frames, it logically needs multiple timers, one per outstanding frame. Each frame times out independently of all

{Protocol 5 (pipelining) allows multiple outstanding frames. The sender may transmit up to *MaxSeq* frames without waiting for an acknowledgement. In addition, unlike the previous protocols, the network layer is not assumed to have a new packet all the time. Instead, the network layer causes *NetworkLayerReady* events when there is a packet to be sent.}

type *EvType* = (*FrameArrival*, *CksumErr*, *TimeOut*, *NetworkLayerReady*);

procedure *protocol5*;
var *NextFrameToSend*: *SequenceNr*;   {*MaxSeq* > 1; used for outbound frame stream}
    AckExpected: *SequenceNr*;   {oldest frame as yet unacknowledged}
    FrameExpected: *SequenceNr*;   {next frame expected on inbound stream}
    r,*s*: *frame*;   {scratch variables}
    buffer: **array**[*SequenceNr*] **of** *packet*;   {buffers for the outbound stream}
    nbuffered: *SequenceNr*;   {how many buffer slots are currently in use}
    i: *SequenceNr*;   {used to index into buffer}
    event: *EvType*;

function *between*(*a*, *b*, *c*: *SequenceNr*): *boolean*;
{Return true if $a <= b < c$ circularly, false otherwise.}
begin
    if ((*a* <= *b*) **and** (*b* < *c*)) **or** ((*c* < *a*) **and** (*a* <= *b*)) **or** ((*b* < *c*) **and** (*c* < *a*))
        then *between* := *true*
        else *between* := *false*
end;   {*between*}

procedure *SendData*(*FrameNr*: *SequenceNr*);
{Construct and send a data frame.}
begin
    s.*info* := *buffer*[*FrameNr*];   {insert packet into frame}
    s.*seq* := *FrameNr*;   {insert seq into frame}
    s.*ack* := (*FrameExpected* + *MaxSeq*) **mod** (*MaxSeq* + 1);   {piggyback ack}
    ToPhysicalLayer(*s*);   {transmit the frame}
    StartTimer(*FrameNr*)   {start the timer running}
end;   {*SendData*}

begin
    EnableNetworkLayer;   {allow *NetworkLayerReady* events}
    NextFrameToSend := 0;   {initialize}
    AckExpected := 0;   {next ack expected on inbound stream}
    FrameExpected := 0;   {next data frame expected inbound}
    nbuffered := 0;   {initially no packets are buffered}

    repeat
        wait(*event*);   {*FrameArrival*, *CksumErr*, *TimeOut*,
                                  NetworkLayerReady}

        case *event* **of**

Fig. 4-16. A sliding window protocol using go back n.

```
NetworkLayerReady:                    {the network layer has a packet to send}
   begin                              {accept, save and transmit a new frame}
      FromNetworkLayer(buffer[NextFrameToSend]); {accept packet from network layer}
      nbuffered := nbuffered + 1;     {one more frame buffered now}
      SendData(NextFrameToSend);      {transmit the frame}
      inc(NextFrameToSend)            {expand sender's window}
   end;

FrameArrival:                         {a data or control frame has just arrived}
   begin
      FromPhysicalLayer(r);           {fetch the frame from the physical layer}

      if r.seq = FrameExpected then
         begin                        {frames are only accepted in proper order}
            ToNetworkLayer(r.info);   {pass packet to network layer}
            inc(FrameExpected)        {advance receiver's window}
         end;

      {ack n implies n − 1, n − 2, etc.; check for this}
      while between(AckExpected, r.ack, NextFrameToSend) do
         begin                        {handle the piggybacked ack}
            nbuffered := nbuffered − 1; {one frame fewer buffered}
            StopTimer(AckExpected);   {frame not lost, stop timer}
            inc(AckExpected)          {contract sender's window}
         end

   end;


CksumErr: ;                           {just ignore bad frames}


TimeOut:                              {trouble; retransmit all outstanding frames}
   begin
      NextFrameToSend := AckExpected;      {start retransmitting here}
      for i := 1 to nbuffered do
         begin
            SendData(NextFrameToSend);
            inc(NextFrameToSend)
         end
   end
end;

if nbuffered < MaxSeq then EnableNetworkLayer else DisableNetworkLayer
until doomsday
end; {protocol5}
```

the other ones. All of these timers can easily be simulated in software, using a single hardware clock that causes interrupts periodically. The pending timeouts form a linked list, with each node of the list telling how many clock ticks until the timer goes off, the frame being timed, and a pointer to the next node.

As an illustration of how the timers could be implemented, consider the example of Fig. 4-17. Assume that the clock ticks once every 100 msec. Initially the real time is 10:00:00.0 and there are three timeouts pending, at 10:00:00.5, 10:00:01.3, and 10:00:01.9. Every time the hardware clock ticks, the real time is updated and the tick counter at the head of the list is decremented. When the tick counter becomes zero, a timeout is caused and the node removed from the list, as shown in Fig. 4-17(b). Although this organization requires the list to be scanned when *StartTimer* or *StopTimer* is called, it does not require much work per tick. In protocol 5, both of these routines have been given a parameter, indicating which frame is to be timed.

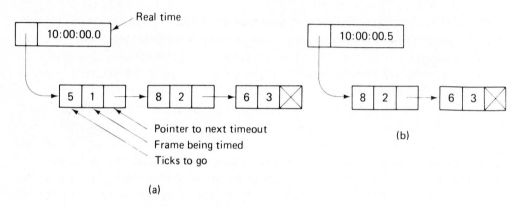

(a)

(b)

Fig. 4-17. Simulation of multiple timers in software.

4.4.3. A Protocol Using Selective Repeat

Protocol 5 works well if errors are rare, but if the line is poor it wastes a lot of bandwidth on retransmitted frames. An alternative strategy to handling errors is to allow the receiver to accept and buffer the frames following a damaged or lost one. Figure 4-18 illustrates our last, and most general, protocol. This protocol does not discard frames merely because an earlier frame was damaged or lost.

In this protocol, both sender and receiver maintain a window of acceptable sequence numbers. The sender's window size starts out at 0 and grows to some predefined maximum, *MaxSeq*. The receiver's window, in contrast, is always fixed in size and equal to *MaxSeq*. The receiver has a buffer reserved for each sequence number within its window. Associated with each buffer is a bit (*arrived*) telling whether the buffer is full or empty. Whenever a frame arrives, its sequence number is checked by the function *between* to see if it falls within the window. If so, and if it has not already been received, it is accepted and stored. This action is taken without regard to whether or not it contains the next packet expected by the network layer. Of course, it must be kept within the data link layer and not passed to the network layer until all the lower numbered frames have already been delivered to the network layer in the correct order.

Nonsequential receive introduces certain problems not present in protocols in which frames are only accepted in order. We can illustrate the trouble most easily with an example. Suppose that we have a 3-bit sequence number, so that the sender is permitted to transmit up to seven frames before being required to wait for an acknowledgement. It sends frames 0 through 6. Meanwhile, the receiver's window allows it to accept any frame with sequence number between 0 and 6 inclusive. If all seven transmitted frames arrive correctly, the receiver will acknowledge them, and advance its window to allow receipt of 7, 0, 1, 2, 3, 4, or 5. All seven buffers are marked empty.

It is at this point that disaster strikes in the form of a lightning bolt hitting the telephone pole, and wiping out all the acknowledgements. The sender eventually times out and retransmits frame 0. When this frame arrives at the receiver, a check is made to see if it is within the receiver's window. Unfortunately, it is within the new window, so it will be accepted. The receiver sends a piggybacked acknowledgement for frame 6, since 0 through 6 have been received.

The sender is happy to learn that all its transmitted frames did actually arrive correctly, so it advances its window and immediately sends frames 7, 0, 1, 2, 3, 4, and 5. Frame 7 will be accepted by the receiver and its packet will be passed directly to the network layer. Immediately thereafter, the receiving data link layer checks to see if it has a valid frame 0 already, discovers that it does, and passes the embedded packet to the network layer. Consequently, the network layer gets an incorrect packet, and the protocol fails.

The essence of the problem is that after the receiver advanced its window, the new range of valid sequence numbers overlapped the old one. The following batch of frames might be either duplicates (if all the acknowledgements were lost) or new ones (if all the acknowledgements were received). The poor receiver has no way of distinguishing these two cases.

The way out of this dilemma lies in making sure that after the receiver has advanced its window, there is no overlap with the original window. To ensure that there is no overlap, the maximum window size should be at most half the range of the sequence numbers. For example, if 4 bits are used for sequence numbers, these will range from 0 to 15. Only eight unacknowledged frames should be outstanding at any instant. That way, if the receiver has just accepted frames 0 through 7 and advanced its window to permit acceptance of frames 8 through 15, it can unambiguously tell if subsequent frames are retransmissions (0 through 7) or new ones (8 through 15). In general, the window size for protocol 6 will be $(MaxSeq + 1)/2$.

An interesting question is: How many buffers must the receiver have? Under no conditions will it ever accept frames whose sequence numbers are below the

{*Protocol 6 (nonsequential receive) accepts frames out of order, but passes*
packets to the network layer in order. Associated with each outstanding frame
is a timer. When the timer goes off, only that one frame is retransmitted, not
all the outstanding frames, as in protocol 5.}

const *NrBufs* = ... ;   {*NrBufs* = (*MaxSeq* + 1) **div** 2}
    MaxBuf = ... ;   {*MaxBuf* = *NrBufs* − 1}

type *bufnr* = 0 .. *MaxBuf*;
    EvType = (*FrameArrival*, *CksumErr*, *TimeOut*, *NetworkLayerReady*, *NetworkLayerIdle*);

procedure *protocol6*;
var *AckExpected* : *SequenceNr*;   {lower edge of sender's window}
    NextFrameToSend : *SequenceNr*;   {upper edge of sender's window + 1}
    FrameExpected : *SequenceNr*;   {lower edge of receiver window}
    TooFar : *SequenceNr*;   {upper edge of receiver window + 1}
    OldestFrame : *SequenceNr*;   {which frame timed out?}
    i : *bufnr*;   {index into buffer pool}
    r,*s* : *frame*;   {scratch variables}
    OutBuf : **array**[*bufnr*] **of** *packet*;   {buffers for outbound stream}
    InBuf : **array**[*bufnr*] **of** *packet*;   {buffers for inbound stream}
    arrived : **array**[*bufnr*] **of** *boolean*; {inbound bit map}
    nbuffered : *SequenceNr*;   {how many output buffers currently used}
    NoNak : *boolean*;   {set to false when a nak is sent}
    event : *EvType*;

function *between* (*a*,*b*,*c* : *SequenceNr*) : *boolean* ;
begin
  if ((*a* <= *b*) **and** (*b* < *c*)) **or** ((*c* < *a*) **and** (*a* <= *b*)) **or** ((*b* < *c*) **and** (*c* < *a*))
    then *between* := *true*
    else *between* := *false*
end; {*between*}

procedure *SendFrame* (*fk* : *FrameKind*; *FrameNr* : *SequenceNr*);
{Construct and send a data, ack, or nak frame.}
begin *s*.*kind* := *fk*;   {*kind* = *data*, *ack*, or *nak*}
  if *fk* = *data* **then** *s*.*info* := *OutBuf*[*FrameNr* **mod** *NrBufs*];
  s.*seq* := *FrameNr*;   {only meaningful for data frames}
  s.*ack* := (*FrameExpected* + *MaxSeq*) **mod** (*MaxSeq* + 1);
  if *fk* = *nak* **then** *NoNak* := *false*;   {one nak per frame, please}
  ToPhysicalLayer(*s*);   {transmit the frame}
  if *fk* = *data* **then** *StartTimer*(*FrameNr* **mod** *NrBufs*);
  StopAckTimer   {no need for separate ack frame}
end; {*SendFrame*}

begin
  EnableNetworkLayer;   {initialization begins here}
  NextFrameToSend := 0;   *AckExpected* := 0;   *FrameExpected* := 0;
  TooFar := *NrBufs*;   *nbuffered* := 0;   *NoNak* := *true*;
  for *i* := 0 **to** *MaxBuf* **do** *arrived*[*i*] := *false*;

  repeat
    wait (*event*);   {five possibilities; see *EvType* above}
    case *event* **of**

Fig. 4-18. A sliding window protocol using selective repeat.

```
  NetworkLayerReady:                {accept, save, and transmit a new frame}
    begin
      nbuffered := nbuffered + 1;   {expand window}
      FromNetworkLayer(OutBuf[NextFrameToSend mod NrBufs]); {fetch new packet}
      SendFrame(data, NextFrameToSend);      {transmit frame}
      inc(NextFrameToSend)          {advance upper window edge}
    end;

  FrameArrival:                     {a data or control frame has arrived}
    begin FromPhysicalLayer(r);     {fetch the frame from the physical layer}
      if r.kind = data then
      begin                         {an undamaged data frame has arrived}
        if (r.seq <> FrameExpected) and NoNak then SendFrame(nak,0);
        if between(FrameExpected, r.seq, TooFar) and
           (arrived[r.seq mod NrBufs] = false) then
        begin                       {frames may be accepted in any order}
          arrived[r.seq mod NrBufs] := true;  {mark buffer as full}
          InBuf[r.seq mod NrBufs] := r.info;  {insert data in buffer}
          while arrived[FrameExpected mod NrBufs] do
          begin                     {pass frames and advance window}
            ToNetworkLayer(InBuf[FrameExpected mod NrBufs]);
            NoNak := true;
            arrived[FrameExpected mod NrBufs] := false;
            inc(FrameExpected);     {advance lower edge of receiver window}
            inc(TooFar);            {advance upper edge + 1 of receiver window}
            StartAckTimer           {to see if separate ack needed}
          end
        end
      end; {end of code for data frame}

      if (r.kind = nak) and
        between(AckExpected, (r.ack + 1) mod (MaxSeq + 1), NextFrameToSend) then
        SendFrame(ack, (r.ack + 1) mod (MaxSeq + 1));

      while between(AckExpected, r.ack, NextFrameToSend) do
        begin nbuffered := nbuffered - 1;     {handle piggybacked ack}
          StopTimer(AckExpected mod NrBufs);          {frame arrived intact}
          inc(AckExpected)          {advance lower window edge}
        end

    end; {end of FrameArrival code}

  CksumErr: if NoNak then SendFrame(nak,0); {damaged frame received}

  TimeOut:  SendFrame(data, OldestFrame);   {we timed out}

  NetworkLayerIdle: SendFrame(ack, 0)       {network layer idle too long, send ack}

  end; {end of case}

  if nbuffered < NrBufs then EnableNetworkLayer else DisableNetworkLayer
 until doomsday
end; {protocol6}
```

lower edge of the window or frames whose sequence numbers are above the upper edge of the window. Consequently, the number of buffers needed is equal to the window size, not the range of sequence numbers. In the above example of a 4-bit sequence number, eight buffers, numbered 0 through 7, are needed. When frame i arrives, it is put in buffer i mod 8. Notice that although i and $(i + 8)$ mod 8 are "competing" for the same buffer, they are never within the window at the same time, because that would imply a window size of at least 9.

For the same reason, the number of timers needed is equal to the number of buffers, not the size of the sequence space. Effectively, there is a timer associated with each buffer. When the timer runs out, the contents of the buffer are retransmitted.

In protocol 5, there is an implicit assumption that the channel is heavily loaded. When a frame arrives, no acknowledgement is sent immediately. Instead, the acknowledgement is piggybacked onto the next outgoing data frame. If the reverse traffic is light, the acknowledgement will be held up for a long period of time. If there is a lot of traffic in one direction and no traffic in the other direction, only *MaxSeq* packets are sent, and then the protocol blocks. In protocol 6 this problem is fixed. After an in-sequence data frame arrives, an auxiliary timer is started by *StartAckTimer*. If no reverse traffic has presented itself before this timer goes off, a separate acknowledgement frame is sent. An interrupt due to the auxiliary timer is called a *NetworkLayerIdle* event. With this arrangement, one-directional traffic flow is now possible, because the lack of reverse data frames onto which acknowledgements can be piggybacked is no longer an obstacle.

Protocol 6 uses a more efficient strategy than protocol 5 for dealing with errors. Whenever the receiver has reason to suspect that an error has occurred, it sends a negative acknowledgement (*NAK*) frame back to the sender. Such a frame is a request for retransmission of the frame specified in the *NAK*. There are two cases when the receiver should be suspicious: a damaged frame has arrived or a frame other than the expected one arrived (potential lost frame). To avoid making multiple requests for retransmission of the same lost frame, the receiver should keep track of whether a *NAK* has already been sent for a given frame. The variable *NoNak* in protocol 6 is true if no *NAK* has been sent yet for *FrameExpected*. If the *NAK* gets mangled or lost, no real harm is done, since the sender will eventually time out and retransmit the missing frame anyway.

In some situations, the time required for a frame to propagate to the destination, be processed there, and have the acknowledgement come back is (nearly) constant. In these situations, the sender can adjust its timer to be just slightly larger than the normal time interval expected between sending a frame and receiving its acknowledgement. However, if this time is highly variable, the sender is faced with the choice of either setting the interval to a small value, and risking unnecessary retransmissions, thus wasting bandwidth, or setting it to a large value, going idle for a long period after an error, thus also wasting bandwidth. If the reverse traffic is sporadic, the time before acknowledgement will be irregular, being shorter when there is reverse traffic and longer when there is not. Variable processing time within the receiver can also be a problem here. In general, whenever the standard deviation of the acknowledgement interval is small compared to the interval itself, the timer can be set "tight" and *NAKs* are not useful. Otherwise, the timer must be set "loose," and *NAKs* can appreciably speed up retransmission of lost or damaged frames.

Closely related to the matter of timeouts and *NAKs* is the question of determining which frame caused a timeout. In protocol 5 it is always *AckExpected*, because it is always the oldest. In protocol 6, there is no trivial way to determine who timed out. Suppose that frames 0 through 4 have been transmitted, meaning that the list of outstanding frames is 01234, in order from oldest to youngest. Now imagine that 0 times out, 5 (a new frame) is transmitted, 1 times out, 2 times out, and 6 (another new frame) is transmitted. At this point the list of outstanding frames is 3405126, from oldest to youngest. If all inbound traffic is lost for a while, the seven outstanding frames will time out in that order. To keep the example from getting even more complicated than it already is, we have not shown the timer administration. Instead, we just assume that the variable *OldestFrame* is set upon timeout to indicate which frame timed out.

4.5. PROTOCOL PERFORMANCE

In principle, protocols 4, 5, and 6 are all equally good. They all serve to convert a line that makes errors into a virtual error free channel. In practice they can differ substantially in terms of performance. In the following sections, we will examine some aspects of protocol performance.

4.5.1. Performance of the Stop-and-Wait Protocol

Many factors influence the efficiency of a protocol. Among them are whether frames are of fixed or variable length, whether piggybacking is used or not, whether the protocol is pipelined or stop-and-wait, whether the line is half- or full-duplex, and the statistical characteristics of the transmission errors. For our protocol 1, for example, the channel efficiency is 100 percent, because the sender just keeps sending full blast. However, the other protocols are less efficient because they must occasionally wait for acknowledgements, or transmit frames a second time.

As an example, let us analyze a one directional stop-and-wait protocol with fixed-length frames and no piggybacking, such as our protocol 3. The basic approach we will use to determine the channel efficiency of any protocol, is to determine how much bandwidth is actually tied up to send the statistically average frame, taking account of all its retransmissions and timeouts. For the derivation we will need the following notation:

A = number of bits in an *ACK* frame

C = channel capacity in bps

D = number of data bits per frame

E = probability of a bit being in error

F = $D + H$ (total frame length)

H = number of bits in the frame header

I = interrupt and service time + propagation delay

L = probability that a frame or its *ACK* is lost or damaged

P_1 = probability that a data frame is lost or damaged

P_2 = probability that an *ACK* frame is lost or damaged

R = mean number of retransmissions per data frame

T = timeout interval

U = channel utilization (efficiency)

W = window size

Before considering the effects of errors, let us see what the channel utilization would be for a perfect line. Surprisingly enough, it can be far below 100 percent. Denote the time that the sender begins to send a frame as time 0. At time F/C the last bit has been sent. At time $(F/C) + I$ the last bit has arrived at the receiver, the interrupt has been serviced, and the receiver is ready to start sending the acknowledgement frame. At time $(F/C) + I + (A/C)$ the last bit of the acknowledgement frame has been sent. At time $(F/C) + I + (A/C) + I$, the sender has processed the acknowledgement and is ready to send the next data frame. The bandwidth occupied by this frame is C multiplied by the time taken, or $F + A + 2CI$. The number of data bits actually transferred is D, so the channel efficiency is $D/(H + D + A + 2CI)$. If the header and acknowledgements are negligible, the bandwidth low, and the propagation and service times are short, the channel utilization will be high; otherwise, not.

Now let us consider the effects of transmission errors. If a frame is damaged or lost, the sender will time out T sec after the last bit has been sent. Thus an unsuccessful transmission uses $F + CT$ bits worth of transmission capacity. If the mean number of retransmissions per frame is R, the total channel capacity used for the R bad frames and one good one is $R(F + CT) + (F + A + 2CI)$.

Now it remains to compute the mean number of retransmissions per frame. A frame is successful if both the data and acknowledgement are correctly received. The probability of success is $(1 - P_2)(1 - P_1)$. Therefore, the probability of failure is $L = 1 - (1 - P_2)(1 - P_1)$. The probability that exactly k attempts are needed (i.e., $k - 1$ retransmissions) is $(1 - L)L^{k-1}$. This result yields an expected number of transmissions per frame of $1/(1 - L)$ and an expected number of retransmissions one less, or $R = L/(1 - L)$.

Using this value of R, we arrive at a channel utilization

$$U = \frac{D}{(L/(1 - L))\,(F + CT) + (F + A + 2CI)}$$

If the receiver's service time has a low variance, the sender can set its timeout interval just above the time required for the acknowledgement to arrive: $T = A/C + 2I$ (approximately). The channel efficiency then becomes

$$U = \frac{D}{H + D} \times (1 - P_1)(1 - P_2) \times \frac{1}{1 + CT/(H + D)}$$

The first factor represents the loss due to header overhead. The second factor represents the loss due to errors. The third factor represents the loss due to stop-and-wait.

To proceed further, we need a model relating the probability of a frame's being in error to its length. To start with, let us make the (not terribly realistic) assumption that each bit has a probability E of being in error, independent of the preceding and succeeding bits. With this assumption and $A = H$ we find that the channel utilization is given by the formula

$$U = \frac{D}{H + D} \times (1 - E)^{H+D}(1 - E)^H \times \frac{1}{1 + CT/(H + D)} \qquad (4\text{-}1)$$

An interesting and important question now arises: What is the optimum frame size? If the frames are too short, the efficiency will be low due to the header overhead. If the frames are too long, the probability of a frame being received without error will be low, so the efficiency will drop due to the many retransmissions. This reasoning suggests that there must be an optimum frame size, with the optimum depending on the header size, error rate, raw bandwidth, and timeout interval. To find the optimum, take the partial derivative of U with respect to D and set it equal to zero. As Field (1976) has shown, this leads to the equation

$$D^2 + D(H + CT) + \frac{H + CT}{\ln(1 - E)} = 0$$

with solution

$$D_{\text{opt}} = \frac{H + CT}{2}\left[\sqrt{1 - 4/[(H + CT)\ln(1 - E)]} - 1\right]$$

If E is very small, which is commonly the case, $\ln(1 - E)$ can be accurately approximated by $-E$. Furthermore, a small E means that both the 1 under the radical and the 1 following the radical can be ignored, yielding the approximation

$$D_{opt} \approx \sqrt{(H + CT)/E} \tag{4-2}$$

Notice that $H + CT$ is the overhead due to headers and timeouts. As the line quality improves (i.e., $E \to 0$), the optimum frame size increases, as it should. If there are no errors, the only overhead comes from headers and the stop-and-wait protocol, both of which argue for as long a frame as possible. On the other hand, a high error rate drives the frame size down, to avoid retransmission of long frames.

To analyze the channel efficiency for frame sizes close to the optimum, let $D = xD_{opt}$, so values of x close to 1.0 represent frames close to the optimum size. Now substitute Eq. (4-2) into Eq. (4-1) and make the approximation $(1 - E)^D \approx 1 - ED$ to get

$$U \approx (1 - 2HE) \, \frac{1 - x\sqrt{(H + CT)E}}{1 + \dfrac{1}{x}\sqrt{(H + CT)E}}$$

As long as the radical remains relatively small, the channel utilization is not terribly sensitive to small deviations from the optimum frame size.

Actual measurements of the error characteristics of the telephone system show that errors do not befall individual bits at random. Instead, errors tend to come in bursts. Thus the model $P_1 = 1 - (1 - E)^{H+D}$ is not an accurate one. Experimentally, it appears that $P_1 = k(H + D)^{\alpha}$ provides a better fit. Finding the optimum frame size and channel efficiency for this model can be done using the method shown above.

Other protocols can also be analyzed using this procedure. As an example, consider protocol 5 under conditions of heavy traffic (i.e., there is always work to be done). Also assume that the window size is large enough that the sender never has to block because the window is full (unless there are errors, of course). For simplicity, assume that the piggybacked acknowledgements are free, and can be ignored in the analysis.

When an error occurs, the sender runs to the end of its window and then begins timing out. The bandwidth wasted during the timeout will be CT. After the timeout, the full window of W frames must be retransmitted. If the mean number of retransmissions is R, the total bandwidth occupied per successfully received frame is $H + D + R[W(H + D) + CT]$. The channel efficiency is then D divided by this amount of bandwidth.

For a more comprehensive analysis of protocol efficiency, see Field (1976) and Fraser (1977).

4.5.2. Performance of the Sliding Window Protocol

In this section we will give a simple analysis of sliding window protocols. To start with, let us assume that acknowledgements are piggybacked onto reverse traffic, so they can be ignored. Furthermore, let us assume that interrupt processing time is negligible, so I is equal to the one-way propagation time, τ. These assumptions simplify the analysis considerably.

We will first analyze an error-free channel; afterwards we will see how errors affect the performance. There are two cases to consider. If the window is large enough, the sender can just keep going at full speed because the acknowledgements get back before the sender's window fills up. The condition for continuous transmission can be derived as follows. The frame transmission time is F/C, so the sender may continue for a time WF/C at which point it must stop if the first frame has not yet been acknowledged. The first acknowledgement can come back $2I$ after the first frame has been transmitted so the acknowledgement arrives at $F/C + 2I$. The transmitter will be able to run continuously if $WF/C \geq F/C + 2I$. This inequality may also be solved for W giving:

Case 1: $W \geq 1 + 2CI/F$ (large window, no errors)

$$U = \frac{D}{H + D}$$

In other words, the channel runs at full speed, with the header bits being the only overhead.

If the window is small, the sender will have to stop at some point and wait for the first acknowledgement. Then it may send one more frame, at which time the next acknowledgement arrives, and so on. Each cycle takes $F/C + 2I$ and is good for W frames or WD data bits. Thus we have $U = WD/(F + 2CI)$ where the denominator represents the amount of bandwidth used up by each cycle. Algebraic simplification leads to:

Case 2: $W < 1 + 2CI/F$ (small window, no errors)

$$U = \frac{D}{H + D} \times \frac{W}{1 + 2CI/(H + D)}$$

Now let us consider the effect of errors. When errors are present, the performance of selective repeat and go back n protocols are different due to the different number of frames retransmitted upon an error. We will only treat selective repeat (protocol 6) here, but the analysis of go back n follows the same general line of reasoning.

In the large window case, transmission is still continuous, except that now extra frames must be sent to correct damaged frames. As we saw in the previous section, the expected number of transmissions per frame is $1/(1 - L)$, so to receive W frames without error, $W/(1 - L)$ of them must be transmitted. Thus we have:

Case 3: $W \geq 1 + 2CI/F$ (large window, with errors)

$$U = \frac{D}{H + D} \times (1 - L)$$

Similarly, with a small window, the efficiency also drops by the same factor due to retransmissions, so we get:

Case 4: $W < 1 + 2CI/F$ (small window, with errors)

$$U = \frac{D}{H + D} \times (1 - L) \times \frac{W}{1 + 2CI/(H + D)}$$

In the above models, the boundary between the large window and small window cases comes when $W = 1 + 2IC/F$. The time I is the one-way propagation time of the cable, so the product CI is the number of bits that can be sent in this time. In other words, it is the number of bits the cable can hold, or the cable length expressed in bits. Therefore, CI/F is the cable length in frames. W is thus one more than the number of frames it takes to fill up the cable in both directions.

If the window is at least one larger than the number of frames that fit on the cable, transmission can go on continuously. This statement is simply another way of expressing the idea that if the window is not full by the time the first frame has reached the receiver, been fully absorbed, and the acknowledgement propagated back, the sender never has to block due to a full window. The last factor in cases 2 and 4 above is just the ratio of the window size to the minimum window size required for continuous transmission.

The factor CI/F also occurs in the formulas for channel utilization in the guise of $CI/(H + D)$. Figure 4-19(a) shows the channel utilization for an error free channel with 20-byte headers and 80-byte data fields for $W = 1$ (stop-and-wait) and $W = 7$. As can be seen, as the cable gets longer, the performance of stop-and-wait drops quickly because most of the time is spent waiting for acknowledgements. A satellite channel is an extreme example. Figure 4-19(b) shows the channel utilization as a function of window size for three different cable lengths. Here we see that performance improves as the window size increases. For any given window size, it is worse for long cables than for short ones.

Before leaving the subject of protocol performance, we should take a quick look at the cable length in frames for various common situations. For a 10 Mbps 1 km LAN, CI is about 50 bits, so $CI/F \ll 1$. However, for a 64 kbps transcontinental line 3000 km long, CI is about 960 bits. For short frames, the cable will be several frames long. Finally, for a satellite channel at 64 kbps with a propagation time of 270 msec, the "cable" length is about 17,280 bits, so for many frames $CI/F \gg 1$.

4.6. PROTOCOL SPECIFICATION AND VERIFICATION

Realistic protocols, and the programs that implement them, are often quite complicated. Consequently, much research has been done trying to find formal, mathematical techniques for specifying and verifying protocols. In the following sections we will look at some popular models and techniques.

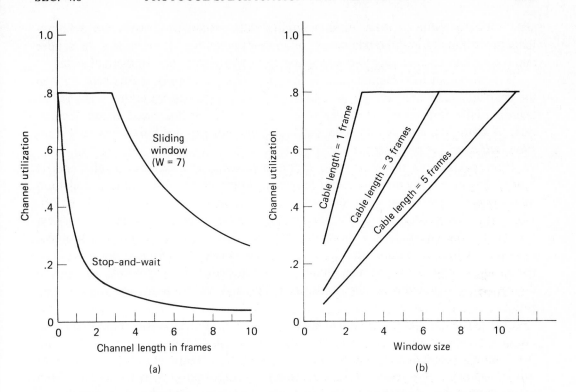

Fig. 4-19. (a) Channel utilization as a function of cable length. (b) Channel utilization as a function of window size. In both cases the header overhead is assumed to be 20 percent.

4.6.1. Finite State Machine Models

A key concept used in many protocol models is the **finite state machine**. With this technique, each **protocol machine** (i.e., sender or receiver) is always in a specific state at every instant of time. Its state consists of all the values of its variables, including the program counter.

In most cases, a large number of states can be grouped together for purposes of analysis. For example, considering the receiver in protocol 3, we could abstract out from all the possible states two important ones: waiting for frame 0 or waiting for frame 1. All other states can be thought of as transient, just steps on the way to one of the main states. Typically, the states are chosen to be those instants that the protocol machine is waiting for the next event to happen [i.e., executing the procedure call *wait*(*event*) in our examples]. At this point the state of the protocol machine is completely determined by the states of its variables. The number of states is then 2^n, where n is the number of bits needed to represent all the variables combined.

The state of the complete system is the combination of all the states of the two protocol machines and the channel. The state of the channel is determined by its contents. Using protocol 3 again as an example, the channel has four possible states: a zero frame or a one frame moving from sender to receiver, an acknowledgement frame going the other way, or an empty channel. If we model the sender and receiver as each having two states, the complete system has 16 distinct states.

A word about the channel state is in order. The concept of a frame being "on the channel" is an abstraction, of course. What we really mean is that a frame has been partially transmitted, partially received, but not yet processed at the destination. A frame remains "on the channel" until the protocol machine executes *FromPhysicalLayer* and processes it.

From each state, there are zero or more possible **transitions** to other states. Transitions occur when some event happens. For a protocol machine a transition might occur when a frame is sent, when a frame arrives, when a timer goes off, when an interrupt occurs, etc. For the channel, typical events are insertion of a new frame onto the channel by a protocol machine, delivery of a frame to a protocol machine, or loss of a frame due to a noise burst. Given a complete description of the protocol machines and the channel characteristics, it is possible to draw a directed graph showing all the states as nodes and all the transitions as directed arcs.

One particular state is designated as the **initial state**. This state corresponds to the description of the system when it starts running, or some convenient starting place shortly thereafter. From the initial state, some, perhaps all, of the other states can be reached by a sequence of transitions. Using well-known techniques from graph theory (e.g., computing the transitive closure of a graph), it is possible to determine which states are reachable and which are not. This technique is called **reachability analysis** (Lin et al., 1987). This analysis can be helpful in determining if a protocol is correct or not.

Formally, a finite state machine model of a protocol can be regarded as a quadruple: (S, M, I, T), where:

S is the set of states the processes and channel can be in.

M is the set of frames that can be exchanged over the channel.

I is the set of initial states of the processes.

T is the set of transitions between states.

At the beginning of time, all processes are in their initial states. Then events begin to happen, such as frames becoming available for transmission or timers going off. Each event may cause one of the processes or the channel to take an action and switch to a new state. By carefully enumerating each possible successor to each state, one can build the reachability graph and analyze the protocol.

Reachability analysis can be used to detect a variety of errors in the protocol specification. For example, if it is possible for a certain frame to occur in a certain state and the finite state machine does not say what action should be taken, the specification is in error (incompleteness). If there exists a set of states from which there is no exit and from which no progress can be made (correct frames received), we have another error (deadlock). A less serious error is protocol specification that tells how to handle an event in a state in which the event cannot occur (extraneous transition). Other errors can also be detected.

As an example of a finite state machine model, consider Fig. 4-20(a). This graph corresponds to protocol 3 as described above: each protocol machine has two states and the channel has four states. Each state is labeled by three characters, XYZ, where X is 0 or 1, corresponding to the frame the sender is trying to send; Y is also 0 or 1, corresponding to the frame the receiver expects, and Z is 0, 1, A, or empty (—), corresponding to the state of the channel. In this example the initial state has been chosen as (000). In other words, the sender has just sent frame 0, the receiver expects frame 0, and frame 0 is currently on the channel.

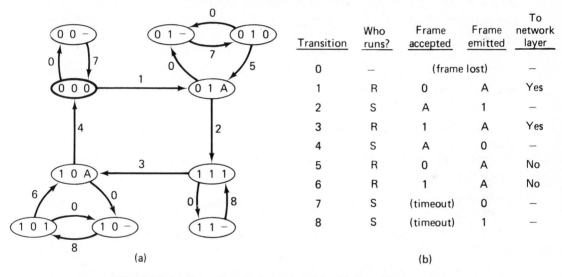

Transition	Who runs?	Frame accepted	Frame emitted	To network layer
0	—		(frame lost)	—
1	R	0	A	Yes
2	S	A	1	—
3	R	1	A	Yes
4	S	A	0	—
5	R	0	A	No
6	R	1	A	No
7	S	(timeout)	0	—
8	S	(timeout)	1	—

(a)   (b)

Fig. 4-20. (a) State diagram for protocol 3. (b) Transitions.

Nine kinds of transitions are shown in Fig. 4-20. Transition 0 consists of the channel losing its contents. Transition 1 consists of the channel correctly delivering packet 0 to the receiver, with the receiver then changing its state to expect frame 1 and emitting an acknowledgement. Transition 1 also corresponds to the receiver delivering packet 0 to the network layer. The other transitions are listed in Fig. 4-20(b). The arrival of a frame with a checksum error has not been shown because it does not change the state (in protocol 3).

During normal operation, transitions 1, 2, 3, and 4 are repeated in order over and over. In each cycle, two packets are delivered, bringing the sender back to the initial state of trying to send a new frame with sequence number 0. If the channel loses frame 0, it makes a transition from state (000) to state (00—). Eventually, the sender times out (transition 7) and the system moves back to (000). The loss of an acknowledgement is more complicated, requiring two transitions, 7 and 5, or 8 and 6, to repair the damage.

One of the properties that a protocol with a 1-bit sequence number must have is that no matter what sequence of events happens, the receiver never delivers two odd packets without an intervening even packet, and vice versa. From the graph of Figure 4-20 we see that this requirement can be stated more formally as "there must not exist any paths from the initial state on which two occurrences of transition 1 occur without an occurrence of transition 3 between them, or vice versa." From the figure it can be seen that the protocol is correct in this respect.

Another, similar requirement is that there not be any paths on which the sender changes state twice (e.g., from 0 to 1 and back to 0) while the receiver state remains constant. Were such a path to exist, then in the corresponding sequence of events two frames would be irretrievably lost, without the receiver noticing. The packet sequence delivered would have an undetected gap of two packets in it.

Yet another important property of a protocol is the absence of deadlocks. A **deadlock** is a situation in which the protocol can make no more forward progress (i.e., deliver packets to the network layer) no matter what sequence of events happen. In terms of the graph model, a deadlock is characterized by the existence of a subset of states that is reachable from the initial state and which has two properties:

1. There is no transition out of the subset.

2. There are no transitions in the subset that cause forward progress.

Once in the deadlock situation, the protocol remains there forever. Again, it is easy to see from the graph that protocol 3 does not suffer from deadlocks.

Now let us consider a variation of protocol 3, one in which the half-duplex channel is replaced by a full-duplex channel. In Fig. 4-21 we show the states as the product of the states of the two protocol machines and the states of the two channels. Note that the forward channel now has three states: frame 0, frame 1, or empty, and the reverse channel has two states, A or empty. The transitions are the same as in Fig. 4-20(b), except that when a data frame and an acknowledgement are on the channel simultaneously, there is a slight peculiarity. The receiver cannot remove the data frame by itself, because that would entail having two acknowledgements on the channel at the same time, something not permitted in our model (although it is easy to devise a model that does allow it). Similarly, the sender cannot remove the acknowledgement, because that would entail emitting a second data frame before the first had been accepted. Consequently, both events must occur together, for example, the transition between state (000A) and state (111A), labeled as 1 + 2 in the figure.

In Fig. 4-21(a) there exist paths that cause the protocol to fail. In particular, there are paths in which the sender repeatedly fetches new packets, even though the

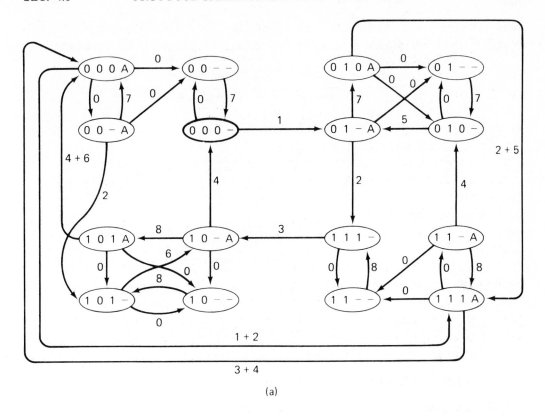

(a)

$(0\ 0\ 0\ -), (0\ 1\ -\ A), (0\ 1\ 0\ A), (1\ 1\ 1\ A), (1\ 1\ -\ A), (0\ 1\ 0\ -), (0\ 1\ -\ A), (1\ 1\ 1\ -)$

(b)

Fig. 4-21. (a) State graph for protocol 3 and a full-duplex channel. (b) Sequence of states causing the protocol to fail.

previous ones have not been delivered correctly. The problem arises because it is now possible for the sender to timeout and send a new frame without disturbing the acknowledgement on the reverse channel. When this acknowledgement arrives, it will be mistakenly regarded as referring to the current transmission and not the previous one.

One state sequence causing the protocol to fail is shown in Fig. 4-21(b). In the fourth and sixth states of this sequence, the sender changes state, indicating that it fetches a new packet from the network layer, while the receiver does not change state, that is, does not deliver any packets to the network layer.

The finite state machine examples given so far deal only with the details of frame transmission and acknowledgement. The model, however, can also be used for other aspects of protocol specification. Figure 4-22 gives a simplified version of the 802.5 token ring protocol, which is fully specified in the standard as a finite state machine. The specification of Fig. 4-22 differs from the actual standard because it does not include the priority and reservation aspects of the protocol.

Current State	Event number	Event/Action	New State
1	1	Frame available and token captured/	2
1	2	Frame error/Set E = 1	1
1	3	Destination = MA/Set A = 1	1
1	4	Frame copied/Set C = 1	1
2	5	Error (e.g. control frame seen)/Put token	1
2	6	End of frame transmission/	3
3	7	Frame header comes around/	4
3	8	Timer expires/Put token on ring	1
4	9	Frame drained/Put token on ring	1
4	10	Timer expires/Put token on ring	1

Fig. 4-22. A simplified finite state machine for IEEE 802.5.

In the model of Fig. 4-22 the station can be in one of four states:

1. In repeat mode, copying bits (i.e., not transmitting).

2. Transmitting a frame.

3. Waiting for the newly transmitted frame to come around.

4. Draining the frame from the ring.

In each state, one or more events are possible. Some of the events trigger actions (e.g., setting bits in the frame passing through the station) in addition to possible state changes. A brief description of the ten possible events follows:

1. The station has a frame to send and has captured the token.

2. An error has been detected on a frame being copied.

3. The frame is directed to the station (My Address, station busy).

4. The frame can be copied to the station (My Address, station idle).

5. Error detected after token captured (e.g., claim token frame seen).

6. The frame has been fully transmitted.

7. The header of the transmitted frame has circumnavigated the ring.

8. The frame just transmitted has apparently been lost.

9. The entire frame just transmitted has been removed from the ring.

10. The end-of-frame sequence has apparently been damaged.

4.6.2. The Estelle Protocol Specification Language

The main problem with finite state machines is that with any realistic protocol the number of states required is immense. Many of these states are similar in terms of what events the state machine is expecting and what it will do when they happen. For example, a state machine for a sliding window protocol is technically in a different state when it is expecting the arrival of frame 2 than when it is expecting the arrival of frame 7, even though the actions it will perform in both cases are almost identical.

This observation has led to the idea of extended state machines, in which states can have variables. Thus, for example, a state machine could have a state EXPECTING_DATA_FRAME, with a variable telling which one. The result of introducing states with variables is to collapse many of the states of the original finite state machine into a single parametrized state, thus reducing the size of the state graph substantially.

A considerable amount of research has been done on extended state machine modeling. This research has led to a protocol specification language, **Estelle (Extended State Transition Language)**, which we will briefly discuss in this section. Although we are looking at Estelle (and the other formal techniques) in the context of the data link layer, they are equally applicable to the higher layers as well.

An Estelle (Courtiat et al., 1985; Linn, 1985) specification is a collection of **modules** (typically one for each process being modeled) and **channels** over which the modules exchange frames. Each module contains a collection of transition rules, analogous to that of Fig. 4-22, but more detailed. Each transition rule belongs to a specific state and tells what events trigger the transition, what actions are performed when the transition is triggered, and what state the process moves to after the event. The events and actions are written in Pascal.

Figure 4-23 shows the form of a transition specification in Estelle. The Estelle programmer can define protocol states and give them symbolic names. These names appear in the **from** and **to** clauses of the transition and are analogous to the *Current state* and *New state* fields in Fig. 4-22. When the process of Fig. 4-23 is in state *state_1*, the transition described can occur. Otherwise it cannot occur. The **when** clause tells what event triggers the transition. Often this will be the arrival of a certain frame.

The **provided** clause allows the programmer to specify a Boolean condition of the process' state variables that must hold in order for the transition to happen. For example, the **when** clause might trigger the transition on the arrival of an acknowledgement frame, but the **provided** clause might further check to see if the sequence number fell inside the window of expected acknowledgements, and if not, ignore the frame.

The **priority** clause makes it possible to assign priorities to transitions. For example, suppose a sender transmits a frame and sets a timer. What happens if the

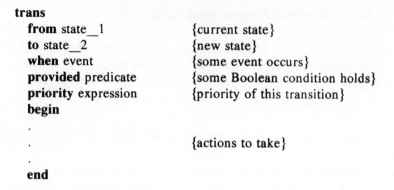

Fig. 4-23. A transition specification in Estelle.

timer goes off at the exact same instant as a frame arrives (possibly bearing an acknowledgement of the frame sent)? Using the **priority** clause it is possible to specify whether the timer event or the frame event should be processed first.

When the transition is triggered, the body of the transition is carried out. The body contains Pascal code that can examine and set internal state variables, output frames (using a special **out** statement), set timers, perform interactions with the layer above it, and so on.

A module consists of a set of definitions for data types, variables, auxiliary procedures, and a list of transitions. An Estelle specification is composed of one or more modules and channel definitions. Channel definitions provide a way to specify the external behavior of modules at interaction points. Mechanisms are provided to attach modules to channels.

4.6.3. Petri Net Models

The finite state machine is not the only technique for formally specifying protocols. Other work is described in (Choi, 1985; Rudin, 1985a, 1985b; Vissers et al., 1983). Other specification languages, such as LOTOS (Brinksma and Karjoth, 1984; Brinksma et al., 1986; Van Eijk, 1988), can also be used. In this section we will describe another technique, the **Petri Net** (Danthine, 1980). A Petri net has four basic elements: places, transitions, arcs, and tokens. A **place** represents a state which (part of) the system may be in. Figure 4-24 shows a Petri net with two places, A and B, both shown as circles. The system is currently in state A, indicated by the **token** (heavy dot) in place A. A **transition** is indicated by a horizontal or vertical bar. Each transition has zero or more **input arcs**, coming from its input places, and zero or more **output arcs**, going to its output places.

A transition is **enabled** if there is at least one input token in each of its input places. Any enabled transition may **fire** at will, removing one token from each input place and depositing a token in each output place. If the number of input arcs and output arcs differ, tokens will not be conserved. If two or more transitions are

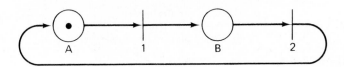

Fig. 4-24. A Petri net with two places and two transitions.

enabled, any one of them may fire. The choice of a transition to fire is indeterminate, which is why Petri nets are useful for modeling protocols. The Petri net of Fig. 4-24 is deterministic, and can be used to model any two-phase process (e.g., the behavior of a baby: eat, sleep, eat, sleep, and so on). As with all modeling tools, unnecessary detail is suppressed.

Figure 4-25 gives the Petri net model of Fig. 4-21. Unlike the finite state machine model, there are no composite states here; the sender's state, channel state, and receiver's state are represented separately. Transitions 1 and 2 correspond to transmission of frame 0 by the sender, normally, and on a timeout respectively. Transitions 3 and 4 are analogous for frame 1. Transitions 5, 6, and 7 correspond to the loss of frame 0, an acknowledgement, and frame 1, respectively. Transitions 8 and 9 occur when a data frame with the wrong sequence number arrives at the receiver. Transitions 10 and 11 represent the arrival at the receiver of the next frame in sequence and its delivery to the network layer.

Petri nets can be used to detect protocol failures in a way similar to the use of finite-state machines. For example, if some firing sequence included transition 10 twice without transition 11 intervening, the protocol would be incorrect. The concept of a deadlock in a Petri net is also similar to its finite state machine counterpart.

Petri nets can be represented in convenient algebraic form resembling a grammar. Each transition contributes one rule to the grammar. Each rule specifies the input and output places of the transition, for example, transition 1 in Fig. 4-25 is $BD \rightarrow AC$. The current state of the Petri net is represented as an unordered collection of places, each place represented in the collection as many times as it has tokens. Any rule all whose left-hand side places are present can be fired, removing those places from the current state, and adding its output places to the current state. The marking of Fig. 4-25 is ACG, so rule 10 ($CG \rightarrow DF$) can be applied but rule 3 ($AD \rightarrow BE$) cannot.

4.7. EXAMPLES OF THE DATA LINK LAYER

Having treated the general principles of data link protocols, it is now time to see what these protocols look like in practice. We will examine our usual running examples: public networks, ARPANET, MAP/TOP, and USENET.

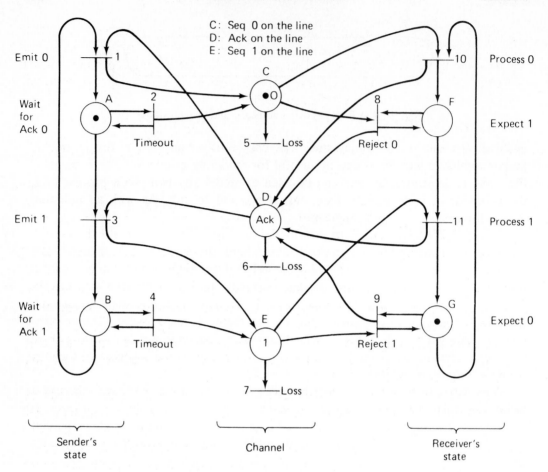

Fig. 4-25. A Petri net model for protocol 3.

4.7.1. The Data Link Layer in Public Networks.

In this section we will examine a group of closely related protocols that are widely used throughout the world. They are all derived from the data link protocol used in SNA, called **SDLC** (**Synchronous Data Link Control** protocol). After developing SDLC, IBM submitted it to ANSI and ISO for acceptance as U.S. and international standards, respectively. ANSI modified it to become **ADCCP** (**Advanced Data Communication Control Procedure**), and ISO modified it to become **HDLC** (**High-level Data Link Control**). CCITT then adopted and modified HDLC for its **LAP** (**Link Access Procedure**) as part of the X.25 network interface standard, but later modified it again to **LAPB**, to make it more compatible with a later version of HDLC. The nice thing about standards is that you have so many to choose from. Furthermore, if you do not like any of them, you can just wait for next year's model.

All of these protocols are based on the same principles. All are bit-oriented, and all use bit stuffing for data transparency. They differ only in minor, but nevertheless irritating, ways. The discussion of bit-oriented protocols that follows is intended as a general introduction. For the specific details of any one protocol, please consult the appropriate definition.

All the bit-oriented protocols use the frame structure shown in Fig. 4-26. The *Address* field is primarily of importance on multidrop lines, where it is used to identify one of the terminals. For point-to-point lines, it is sometimes used to distinguish commands from responses.

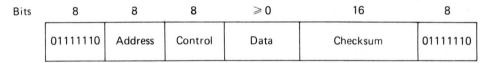

Bits	8	8	8	$\geqslant 0$	16	8
	01111110	Address	Control	Data	Checksum	01111110

Fig. 4-26. Frame format for bit-oriented protocols.

The *Control* field is used for sequence numbers, acknowledgements, and other purposes, as discussed below.

The *Data* field may contain arbitrary information. It may be arbitrarily long, although the efficiency of the checksum falls off with increasing frame length due to the greater probability of multiple burst errors.

The *Checksum* field is a minor variation on the well-known cyclic redundancy code, using CRC-CCITT as the generator polynomial. The variation is to allow lost flag bytes to be detected.

The frame is delimited with another flag sequence (01111110). On idle point-to-point lines, flag sequences are transmitted continuously, just as SYN characters are usually transmitted during idle periods when BISYNC is used. The minimum frame contains three fields and totals 32 bits, excluding the flags on either end.

There are three kinds of frames: **Information**, **Supervisory**, and **Unnumbered**. The contents of the *Control* field for these three kinds are shown in Fig. 4-27. The protocol uses a sliding window, with a 3-bit sequence number. Up to seven unacknowledged frames may be outstanding at any instant. The *Seq* field in Fig. 4-27(a) is the frame sequence number. The *Next* field is a piggybacked acknowledgement. However, all the protocols adhere to the convention that instead of piggybacking the number of the last frame received correctly, they use the number of the first frame not received (i.e., the next frame expected). The choice of using the last frame received or the next frame expected is arbitrary; it does not matter which convention is used, provided that it is used consistently of course.

The *P/F* bit stands for *Poll/Final*. It is used when a computer (or concentrator) is polling a group of terminals. When used as *P*, the computer is inviting the terminal to send data. All the frames sent by the terminal, except the final one, have the *P/F* bit set to *P*. The final one is set to *F*.

In some of the protocols, the *P/F* bit is used to force the other machine to send a

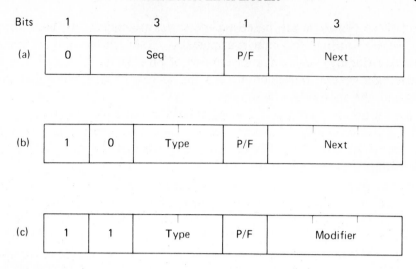

Fig. 4-27. Control field of (a) an information frame, (b) a supervisory frame, (c) an unnumbered frame.

Supervisory frame immediately rather than waiting for reverse traffic onto which to piggyback the window information. The bit also has some minor uses in connection with the Unnumbered frames.

The various kinds of Supervisory frames are distinguished by the *Type* field. Type 0 is an acknowledgement frame (officially called *RECEIVE READY)* used to indicate the next frame expected. This frame is used when there is no reverse traffic to use for piggybacking.

Type 1 is a negative acknowledgement frame (officially called *REJECT).* It is used to indicate that a transmission error has been detected. The *Next* field indicates the first frame in sequence not received correctly (i.e., the frame to be retransmitted). The sender is required to retransmit all outstanding frames starting at *Next.* This strategy is similar to our protocol 5 rather than our protocol 6.

Type 2 is *RECEIVE NOT READY.* It acknowledges all frames up to but not including *Next,* just as *RECEIVE READY,* but it tells the sender to stop sending. *RECEIVE NOT READY* is intended to signal certain temporary problems with the receiver, such as a shortage of buffers, and not as an alternative to the sliding window flow control. When the condition has been repaired, the receiver sends a *RECEIVE READY, REJECT,* or certain control frames.

Type 3 is the *SELECTIVE REJECT.* It calls for retransmission of only the frame specified. In this sense it is like our protocol 6 rather than 5 and is therefore most useful when the sender's window size is half the sequence space size, or less. Thus if a receiver wishes to buffer out of sequence frames for potential future use, it can force the retransmission of any specific frame using Selective Reject. HDLC and ADCCP allow this frame type, but SDLC and LAPB do not allow it (i.e., there is no Selective Reject), and type 3 frames are undefined.

The third class of frame is the Unnumbered frame. It is used for control purposes. The various bit-oriented protocols differ considerably here, in contrast with the other two kinds, where they are nearly identical. Five bits are available to indicate the frame type, but not all 32 possibilities are used.

All the protocols provide a command, *DISC* (DISConnect), that allows a machine to announce that it is going down (e.g., for preventive maintenance). They also have a command that allows a machine that has just come back on line to announce its presence and force all the sequence numbers back to zero. This command is called *SNRM* (Set Normal Response Mode). Unfortunately, "Normal Response Mode" is anything but normal. It is an unbalanced (i.e., asymmetric) mode in which one end of the line is the master and the other the slave. *SNRM* dates from a time when data communication meant a dumb terminal talking to a computer, which clearly is asymmetric. To make the protocol more suitable when the two partners are equals, HDLC and LAPB have an additional command, *SABM* (Set Asynchronous Balanced Mode), which resets the line and declares both parties to be equals. They also have commands *SABME* and *SNRME,* which are the same as *SABM* and *SNRM,* respectively, except that they enable an extended frame format that uses 7-bit sequence numbers instead of 3-bit sequence numbers.

A third command provided by all the protocols is *FRMR* (FRaMe Reject), used to indicated that a frame with a correct checksum but impossible semantics arrived. Examples of impossible semantics are a type 3 Supervisory frame in LAPB, a frame shorter than 32 bits, an illegal control frame, and an acknowledgement of a frame that was outside the window, etc. *FRMR* frames contain a 24-bit data field telling what was wrong with the frame. The data include the control field of the bad frame, the window parameters, and a collection of bits used to signal specific errors.

Control frames may be lost or damaged, just like data frames, so they must be acknowledged too. A special control frame is provided for this purpose, called *UA* (Unnumbered Acknowledgement). Since only one control frame may be outstanding, there is never any ambiguity about which control frame is being acknowledged.

The remaining control frames deal with initialization, polling, and status reporting. There is also a control frame that may contain arbitrary information, *UI* (Unnumbered Information). These data are not passed to the network layer, but are for the receiving data link layer itself.

4.7.2. The Data Link Layer in the ARPANET

The ARPANET does not have a pure data link protocol, but the subnet protocol is relatively close, so we will study it in this chapter. Actually, the subnet protocol consists of two distinct layers, as shown in Fig. 4-28. The lower layer is the IMP-IMP protocol between adjacent IMPs. The upper layer is the end-to-end subnet protocol.

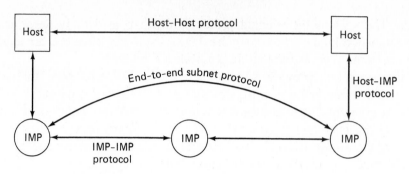

Fig. 4-28. The lower layer ARPANET protocols.

The IMP-IMP protocol is functionally similar to the protocols we have studied in this chapter. Its goal is to provide a reliable channel for transmitting frames from one IMP to its neighbor. At first you might think that if each individual hop along a path is reliable, there is no need for an additional end-to-end protocol, but there is. Consider the following scenario. An IMP passes a frame to a neighboring IMP, which acknowledges it. Then the neighboring IMP crashes before forwarding the frame.

The purpose of the end-to-end protocol is to make sure that each frame that starts along a multihop path reaches its final destination, at which time a special acknowledgement, called an *RFNM* (Request For Next Message), is sent back to the originating IMP. Only when this acknowledgement gets back to the sender is the frame discarded. If the end-to-end acknowledgement does not arrive within 30 sec, the source IMP sends a query to the destination IMP. Depending on the answer, if any—the destination IMP might have crashed—the source IMP may retransmit the message. The protocol has been designed to withstand losing *RFNMs,* as well as the queries and their responses.

Transmission of a data stream from the source host to the destination host works as follows. The source host's operating system is responsible for breaking the user's data stream into "messages" prefixed by 40-bit headers. These messages (up to 8063 bits) are transmitted transparently by the subnet, and delivered bit for bit to the receiving host. If two hosts agree to exchange ancient Babylonian parking tickets in EBCDIC, that is their business; the subnet will not complain.

How the host actually gets its message into the IMP is a somewhat involved story. Suffice it to say here that the host attaches a 96-bit host-IMP **leader** to the front of each message. The leader tells which host to send the message to, provides an identifier so the destination host knows which connection the message belongs to, and gives few other items the IMP needs to know. Data are sent from host to IMP one bit at a time with an explicit (hardware) go ahead signal after each bit. This signal is needed because the host and IMP may have different word lengths, and hence may have to pause to reference memory at different times. For most host-IMP pairs, the maximum data rate is about 10^5 bits/sec. The leader is stripped off by the IMP and is not transmitted, although the destination IMP constructs a new leader when passing the message to the destination host.

As the message pours into the IMP, it is split up into a maximum of eight frames (called "packets" in the ARPANET publications) each of which is a maximum of 1008 bits. When the complete message has arrived in the IMP's memory, the IMP begins sending the first frame along the path to the destination using the IMP-IMP protocol. The IMP-IMP protocol is character-oriented and uses character stuffing to allow DLE characters to be sent as data.

The IMP-IMP protocol is a living fossil. It was designed before the concept of the sliding window was invented, so it attempts to achieve the same effect as the sliding window protocol, but in a somewhat peculiar way. The IMP-IMP protocol multiplexes eight logically independent, full-duplex channels onto each physical line (16 in the case of the satellite links, owing to the long delay). Each of these logical channels operates using stop-and-wait.

Each IMP maintains a table containing 3 bits per logical channel [i.e., 24 bits per physical line (48 bits for satellite links)]. The 3 bits tell whether or not there is an outstanding frame on that logical channel, the sequence number of the next frame to send, and the sequence number of the next frame expected. When a frame needs to be sent, the lowest idle logical channel is marked busy and used. When the acknowledgement comes in, it is marked idle again.

When the sender wants to send a frame, it chooses the lowest idle logical channel and includes the current sequence number in the frame header. If this sequence number is one higher (modulo 2) than the last frame accepted, the receiver accepts this one, increments the sequence number (modulo 2), and sends an acknowledgement. If the incoming frame's sequence number matches the receiver's variable, the frame is a duplicate and is discarded. When the acknowledgement gets back to the transmitter, it is checked against the last sequence number sent. If the numbers agree, the transmit sequence number is complemented and the logical channel is marked idle.

Each frame sent contains in its header the last frame received on each of the logical channels rather than just an acknowledgement bit for the logical channel to which this frame belongs. Doing it this way ensures that even if a frame is lost, the next one will convey the complete acknowledgement status. When no reverse traffic exists, a special acknowledgement frame is sent.

The IMP-IMP protocol does not use *NAKs*. If a frame comes in damaged, it is just ignored. The sender will time out in 125 msec, and send it again. However, the use of eight distinct stop-and-wait logical channels rather than a 3-bit sliding window achieves the same effect as having *NAKs:* a damaged frame will be repeated quickly, without regard to the other seven frames.

We will discuss the details of the IMP-IMP frame header below (see Fig. 4-29). For the moment, suffice it to say that the header contains three fields used directly for exchanging frames between adjacent IMPs:

1. A 1-bit sequence number for the stop-and-wait protocol.

2. A 3-bit logical channel number.

3. An 8-bit acknowledgement field, one bit per logical channel.

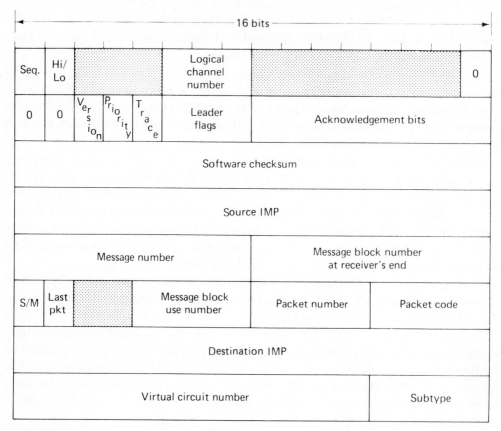

Fig. 4-29. The ARPANET IMP-IMP frame header. Shaded fields are reserved for future use.

The *Seq* field is the 1-bit sequence number used by the stop-and-wait protocol between adjacent IMPs.

The *Hi/Lo* field is used to tell which end of the line the frame came from. Nearly all the time, when an IMP sends a frame, it is delivered to the IMP at the other end. However, once in a rare while the carrier needs to take a line out of service for maintenance. The maintenance includes looping the line back onto itself, so data sent arrive back at the sender. If the IMP should decide to transmit a frame while the line was looped back, it would receive its own frame, inspect the acknowledgement bits, and behave incorrectly. The *Hi/Lo* bit enables each IMP to tell when a line is looped back. This may sound like an unimportant point, but you can just imagine how much time was wasted looking for software bugs until it was finally realized that leased lines can sometimes magically turn into mirrors without warning.

The *Logical channel number* tells which of the eight stop-and-wait channels available on the IMP-IMP line this frame belongs to.

The *Version* bit is needed because new versions of the IMP program are distributed and installed while the subnet is running. Since successive versions may differ in details, the IMPs must know whether a just arrived frame was generated by the current or previous version of the IMP program. You can see here the tremendous efforts the designers have made to make sure the subnet never goes down, not even for changing the IMP program. As a point of reference, how many computer manufacturers are able to switch over to a new version of the operating system without stopping the machine, and without affecting the jobs running during the changeover? Answer: not very many.

The *Priority* bit is used by the host to indicate which messages it considers important. The IMP just takes the bit at face value, so there has to be a gentlemen's agreement not to abuse it. Usually, hosts use it for transport protocol control messages or interactive traffic.

The *Trace* bit tells the subnet to trace the packet so that the network management can learn how it was routed. This feature is typically used while debugging new routing algorithms and tracking down sources of network congestion.

The *Leader flags* are passed by the source host to the source IMP, propagated through the subnet, and eventually transmitted to the destination host. These have to do with the host-IMP protocol.

The *Acknowledgement bits* give the sequence number of the last packet received on each of the eight logical channels. These are the piggybacked bits going home.

The *Software checksum* is computed by the source IMP and verified by each IMP along the way in order to detect IMP memory failures as well as transmission errors. Problems have arisen in the past with frames that were correctly transmitted between two adjacent IMPs and then damaged while sitting peacefully in memory waiting to be forwarded.

The *Source IMP* field speaks for itself. This format allows for up to 64K IMPs in the subnet.

The *Message number* is assigned by the source IMP. Consecutive messages between host *A* and host *B* are numbered consecutively. The *RFNMs* and source IMP to destination IMP protocol packets refer to this field.

The *Message block number* is used by the destination IMP as an index into its tables to find the variables pertaining to the traffic for this host-host pair.

The *S/M* field indicates single- or multiple-frame message. This bit is needed because the subnet attempts to provide good service to both interactive traffic and file transfer traffic. When the bit is set, the destination IMP knows that more frames are on the way for this message, and tries to allocate buffer space for them before they arrive. For single frame messages no extra buffers need be allocated.

The *Last packet* bit tells the destination IMP that this is the last piece of a multipacket message. Without it, the IMP would not know how long the message was.

The *Message block use number* is needed because message blocks are scarce resources. If a host-host pair has no traffic for a substantial period of time, the message blocks being used for that pair may be reclaimed and used for another host-host pair. If the former owner now suddenly starts sending traffic, this will be inserted into the data stream to which the message block now belongs. To prevent this, there is a 4-bit counter associated with each message block. This counter is incremented upon each use of the message block, so it is possible to detect sudden activity from long dormant transport pairs, by seeing that the message use number does not agree with the current one.

The *Packet number* numbers the packets of a message. Four bits have been provided to allow longer messages in the future.

The *Packet code* indicates the type of message. The code 0 is used for normal data; the remaining control codes are as follows:

1. Request for buffer allocation at destination IMP.

2. Source IMP returning multipacket allocation it does not need.

3. Incomplete message? Query from source IMP to destination IMP when no *RFNM*, Dead Destination, or other response has arrived within a prescribed timeout period.

4. *RFNM* (acknowledgement from destination IMP to source IMP).

5. *RFNM + ALLOCATE* (allows source to immediately send another message of the same kind—single or multiframe).

6. Dead destination (from destination IMP if host was down).

7. Incomplete reply (response to the packet code 3 query).

The *Destination IMP* field tells where to send the packet.

The *Virtual circuit number* is taken from the host-IMP leader at the source and reinserted into the IMP-host leader at the destination. The destination host needs this information in order to tell which connection the message belongs to.

The *Subtype* field is used to distinguish various special cases. For example, it is possible to disable the complete end-to-end subnet protocol for real-time voice traffic.

4.7.3. The Data Link Layer in MAP and TOP

The data link layer in the IEEE 802 LAN standard is split into two sublayers. The lower sublayer is the Medium Access Control sublayer, which has three variants: CSMA/CD, token bus, and token ring, as discussed in Chap. 3. The upper sublayer is the same for all three variants, to provide a uniform interface to the network layer independent of the MAC sublayer used. Above the data link layer, the particular type of LAN used is no longer relevant, since the protocol used at the top of the data link layer and the interface between the data link layer and the network layer are the same for all three LAN types.

Since both MAP and TOP are based on the 802 LANs, both of them use the 802 data link protocol, called **LLC** (**Logical Link Control**). This protocol is based closely on HDLC, and thus is similar in structure to the LAPB protocol described in detail above.

The LLC sublayer can provide either connectionless (called type 1) or connection-oriented (called type 2) services to the network layer. It also provides acknowledged connectionless (called type 3) service. When connectionless service is used, the LLC sublayer accepts a packet from the network layer and uses a best-efforts attempt to send it to the destination. There is no acknowledgement and no guarantee of delivery. With the connection-oriented service, a connection must first be set up between the source and destination. Using this connection, network layer packets can be transmitted in order with guaranteed delivery. When the connection is no longer needed, it must be released.

The LLC services are made available to the network layer by means of usual four types of service primitives: *request*, *indication*, *response*, and *confirm*. The network layer uses the *request* primitive to set up and release connections and to send data packets. These primitives cause the data link layer to transmit frames from the source to the destination and cause actions to happen there. These actions are signaled to the network layer on the destination machine by the *indication* primitives. The *response* and *confirm* primitives have their usual functions.

The LLC primitives and their parameters are given in Fig. 4-30. The connectionless service, shown in Fig. 4-30(a), only has two primitives, one for sending a frame and one for indicating that a frame has arrived. Both primitives have parameters *local_address* and *remote_address* to identify the sender and receiver. The actual data is in the *l_sdu* (Link Service Data Unit—see Fig. 1-9) parameter. The *service_class* parameter specifies the priority.

The connection-oriented primitives can be divided into five groups, as shown in Fig. 4-30(b). The first group is used to establish connections. The second one is for releasing them. The third group is for transferring data. These are straightforward and need little comment. The primitives specify the sender's and receiver's addresses, the priority, and the data. The *status* and *reason* parameters tell what happened and why, respectively. The reason for disconnection can be that the other party requested it or that it was internally generated due to hardware or software malfunction.

The fourth group is for resetting the connection after a serious error has been detected. It gets the connection back into its initial state and sets all protocol sequence numbers to 0. Data that was in transit at the time of the reset may be lost.

The fifth group is used to regulate the flow of information between the network

Unacknowledged connectionless service

L‑DATA.request (local_address, remote_address, I_sdu, service_class)
L‑DATA.indication (local_address, remote_address, I_sdu, service_class)

(a)

Connection-oriented service

L‑CONNECT.request (local_address, remote_address, service_class)
L‑CONNECT.indication (local_address, remote_address, status, service_class)
L‑CONNECT.response (local_address, remote_address, service_class)
L‑CONNECT.confirm (local_address, remote_address, status, service_class)
L‑DISCONNECT.request (local_address, remote_address)
L‑DISCONNECT.indication (local_address, remote_address, reason)
L‑DISCONNECT.response (local_address, remote_address)
L‑DISCONNECT.confirm (local_address, remote_address, status)
L‑DATA_CONNECT.request (local_address, remote_address, I_sdu)
L‑DATA_CONNECT.indication (local_address, remote_address, I_sdu)
L‑DATA_CONNECT.response (local_address, remote_address)
L‑DATA_CONNECT.confirm (local_address, remote_address, status)
L‑RESET.request (local_address, remote_address)
L‑RESET.indication (local_address, remote_address, reason)
L‑RESET.response (local_address, remote_address)
L‑RESET.confirm (local_address, remote_address, status)
L‑CONNECTION_FLOWCONTROL.request (local_address, remote_address, amount)
L‑CONNECTION_FLOWCONTROL.indication (local_address, remote_address, amount)

(b)

Fig. 4-30. IEEE 802 LLC primitives. (a) Connectionless. (b) Connection-oriented.

layer and the data link layer. Whenever it needs to, the network layer can issue a *L_CONNECTION_FLOWCONTROL* primitive to tell the data link layer how much data it is prepared to accept. Similarly, the data link layer can issue an *indication* to tell the network layer how much data may be passed without losing any.

The primitives of Fig. 4-30 define the interface between the network layer and the LLC sublayer. Furthermore, the 802 standard also defines the interface between the LLC sublayer and the three MAC sublayers below it. This interface contains: *MA_DATA.request*, *MA_DATA.indication*, and *MA_DATA.confirm*, to provide a way for the LLC sublayer to pass frames to the MAC sublayer and receive frames from the MAC sublayer. The LLC-MAC interface is completely connectionless.

The LLC frame structure has been designed to be similar to that of HDLC. It is illustrated in Fig. 4-31. The *DSAP address* and *SSAP address* fields identify the service access points on the interface between the network layer and the data link layer. Conceptually, that interface has some number of "holes" in it. When a connection is set up, the network layer chooses a hole (SSAP) and pushes the service request through it. At the other end, the information emerges through another hole

(DSAP). An SSAP-DSAP pair identifies a connection (or connectionless transfer). Without the SSAP and DSAP information, the data link layer would not know who sent a given frame and what to do with it.

Bytes	1	1	1 or 2	$\geqslant 0$
	DSAP address	SSAP address	Control	Information

Fig. 4-31. The IEEE 802 LLC frame format. This unit is carried in the data field of the MAC sublayer frame.

The *control* field in the LLC protocol is conceptually similar to the same field in the LAPB, HDLC, and ADCCP protocols. Information transfer, supervisory, and unnumbered control frames are permitted, as in the other protocols. There are four major differences between LLC and the others. First, the connection-oriented LLC frames have a 2-byte control field to permit the use of 7-bit sequence numbers. Second, LLC only supports the asynchronous balanced mode (i.e., peer-to-peer communication, and not computers polling terminals), so that those HDLC and LAPB frames relating to the other modes are absent from LLC.

The third and fourth differences relate to new frame types introduced in LLC. The XID frame is used for communicating information between the LLC peers about service types and window sizes. The TEST frame is used to request the other side to generate a response, just to test the transmission path.

The complete list of LLC control frames is given in Fig. 4-32. The *Format* column indicates the information, supervisory, or unnumbered frame type. The *Command* and *Response* columns show which frames can be commands and which responses to commands. The *Type1* and *Type2* columns show which frames may be used with connectionless and connection-oriented transmission, respectively.

4.7.4. The Data Link Layer in USENET

In all the other networks we have studied, the physical connection between the network nodes is always present. Nobody removes the wires and puts them back in the box when the work day is over at 5 P.M. With USENET, the situation is quite different because most of the traffic goes over dialup telephone lines, and these connections are not present all the time. Since one of the functions of the data link layer is management of the physical link, we will briefly describe how USENET manages connections in this section.

For our purposes, USENET offers three primary services, file transfer, electronic mail, and news. Mail and news are actually just front ends to the file transfer system. When a user wants to send mail to a user on a remote machine, the mail program constructs a file transfer command that ships the message to the remote user's mail box as a mail-file. Similarly, news is sent by moving news-files around

Name	Code	Format	Command	Response	Type 1	Type 2
INFORMATION	I	I	X	X		X
RECEIVE READY	RR	S	X	X		X
RECEIVE NOT READY	RNR	S	X	X		X
REJECT	REJ	S	X	X		X
UNNUMBERED INFORMATION	UI	U	X		X	
DISCONNECT	DISC	U	X			X
SET ASYNCH. BAL. MODE EXTENDED	SABMF	U	X			X
EXCHANGE INFORMATION	XID	U	X	X	X	
TEST	TEST	U	X	X	X	
UNNUMBERED ACKNOWLEDGEMENT	UA	U		X		X
DISCONNECTED MODE	DM	U		X		X
FRAME REJECT	FRMR	U		X		X

Fig. 4-32. The IEEE 802 LLC frame types.

using the file transfer protocol. Thus in this chapter we will concentrate on how the link is managed to enable higher layers to carry out file transfer.

When a file is scheduled for transfer, either directly by a person at a terminal explicitly typing a command (for example) of the form

uucp file_A machine_2!file_B

or by the mail or news programs, a work file is created in a system spooling directory. This work file specifies the source machine (the initiating machine in the example above), the destination machine (*machine_2*), the file names (*file_A*, *file_B*), the identity of the person or program requesting the transfer, and similar information.

Periodically, a **daemon process** can be started up to initiate file transfers. The daemon may be started up once an hour, once a day, or at any other interval the system administrator wishes. It is cheaper to call a remote system once a day and transfer many files than to call it once an hour for one or two files, but the service to the users is worse in the former case, so the administrator must make a choice about how to set the system parameters. There exist some large machines that are dedicated to USENET 24 hours a day and do nothing but wait to be called. In this respect they are like CSNET-RELAY.

Once a daemon is started up, it inspects the spooling directory to see if there is any work to be done. If there is, it chooses a remote system to contact and looks it up in a certain system file. This file tells how to contact that machine: which device to use (X.25 network, dialup line, etc.), what telephone number to call, what line speed is expected (1200 bps, 2400 bps, etc.), how to login there, which line protocol to use, and everything else required to call up and log in. Armed with this information, the daemon places the call, typically using a special modem able to dial phone numbers electronically.

After the remote machine answers the call, the daemon logs in under a special user name and starts up a slave process (called *uucico*) on remote machine. The calling process acts as the master and directs the slave process to accept whatever files the master has to send and send whatever files the master wants. After these have been transferred and properly stored (in mail boxes, news directories, or elsewhere), the roles reverse and the called machine becomes the master. It then sends files from its spooling directory and requests files it needs. When all the work has been completed, a log file is updated, the original work files are deleted, the caller logs out, and the connection is broken. The caller then goes back to its spooling directory to see if there are any more machines to call, to repeat the cycle all over.

A wide variety of data link protocols are used on the dialup lines, although many of them are variations of the **g protocol** developed at Bell Labs. In fact, there are so many variations in use that a detailed description of the protocol would only apply to a small fraction of the links. We will therefore just give the barest outline.

Data is transmitted as a sequence of packets containing 8-bit bytes using the sliding window protocol. Framing and transparency are handled with character stuffing. Two kinds of packets are permitted, data and control. Both types start out with a control byte containing three fields. The first field distinguishes data packets from control packets. In data packets, the other two fields are for the sequence number of the current packet and a piggybacked acknowledgement. In control packets, the second field is used for the command type, which might be *INIT, ACK, REJECT,* or *CLOSE.* The control byte, and in fact the entire protocol, bears a certain resemblance to LAPB.

4.8. SUMMARY

The task of the data link layer is to convert noisy lines into communication channels free of transmission errors for use by the network layer. To accomplish this goal, the data are broken up into frames, each of which is transmitted as many times as necessary to ensure that it has been received correctly. To prevent a fast sender from overrunning a slow receiver, the data link protocol always provides for flow control. The sliding window mechanism is widely used to integrate error control and flow control in a convenient way.

Sliding window protocols can be categorized by the size of the sender's window and the size of the receiver's window. When both are equal to 1, the protocol is stop-and-wait. When the sender's window is greater than 1, for example to prevent the sender from blocking on a circuit with a long propagation delay, the receiver can be programmed either to discard all frames other than the next one in sequence (protocol 5) or buffer out-of-order frames until they are needed (protocol 6).

Protocols can be analyzed for a variety of properties, for example, performance and correctness. Examples of each are presented in this chapter.

Many networks use one of the bit-oriented protocols—SDLC, HDLC, ADCCP, or LAPB—at the data link level. All of these protocols use flag bytes to delimit frames, and bit stuffing to prevent flag bytes from occurring in the data. All of them also use a sliding window for flow control. The ARPANET uses an older character-oriented protocol with multiple independent channels for the IMP-IMP protocol. MAP and TOP use IEEE 802 LLC, which is a variation on HDLC.

PROBLEMS

1. The following data fragment occurs in the middle of a data stream for which the character-stuffing algorithm described in the text is used: DLE, STX, A, DLE, B, DLE, ETX. What is the output after stuffing?

2. If the bit string 0111101111101111110 is subjected to bit stuffing, what is the output string?

3. Four methods of framing were discussed in this chapter. One of these used code violations to mark the frame boundaries. Is this technique applicable when Manchester encoding is used? What about when differential Manchester encoding is used?

4. Can you think of any circumstances under which an open-loop protocol, (e.g., a Hamming code) might be preferable to the feedback type protocols discussed throughout this chapter?

5. To provide more reliability than a single parity bit can give, an error detecting coding scheme uses one parity bit for checking all the odd numbered bits and a second parity bit for all the even numbered bits. What is the Hamming distance of this code?

6. One way of detecting errors is to transmit data as a block of n rows of k bits per row and adding parity bits to each row and each column. Will this scheme detect all single errors? Double errors? Triple errors?

7. What is the remainder obtained by dividing $x^7 + x^5 + 1$ by the generator polynomial $x^3 + 1$?

8. A channel has a bit rate of 4 kbps and a propagation delay of 20 msec. For what range of frame sizes does stop-and-wait give an efficiency of at least 50%?

9. A 3000-km long T1 trunk is used to transmit 64-byte frames using protocol 5. If the propagation speed is 6 μsec/km, how many bits should the sequence numbers be?

10. Imagine a sliding window protocol using so many bits for sequence numbers that wraparound never occurs. What relations must hold among the four window edges and the window size?

11. Frames of 1000 bits are sent over a 1-Mbps satellite channel. Acknowledgements are

always piggybacked onto data frames. The headers are very short. Three bit sequence numbers are used. What is the maximum achievable channel utilization for
(a) Stop-and-wait.
(b) Protocol 5.
(c) Protocol 6.

12. If the procedure *between* in protocol 5 checked for the condition $a \leq b \leq c$ instead of the condition $a \leq b < c$, would that have any effect on the protocol's correctness or efficiency? Explain.

13. Imagine that you are writing the data link layer software for a line used to send data to you, but not from you. The other end uses HDLC, with a 3-bit sequence number and a window size of seven frames. You would like to buffer as many out of sequence frames as possible to enhance efficiency, but you are not allowed to modify the software on the sending side. Is it possible to have a receiver window greater than one, and still guarantee that the protocol will never fail? If so, what is the largest window that can be safely used?

14. Consider the operation of protocol 6 over a 1-Mbps error-free line. The maximum frame size is 1000 bits. New packets are generated about one second apart. The timeout interval is 10 msec. If the special acknowledgement timer were eliminated, unnecessary timeouts would occur. How many times would the average message be transmitted?

15. In protocol 6 the code for *FrameArrival* has a section used for *NAKs*. This section is invoked if the incoming frame is a *NAK* and another condition is met. Give a scenario where the presence of this other condition is essential.

16. In protocol 6 $MaxSeq = 2^n - 1$. While this condition is obviously desirable to make efficient use of header bits, we have not demonstrated that it is essential. Does the protocol work correctly for $MaxSeq = 4$, for example?

17. Compute the fraction of the bandwidth that is wasted on overhead (headers and retransmissions) for protocol 6 on a heavily loaded 50 kbps satellite channel with data frames consisting of 40 header and 3960 data bits. *ACK* frames never occur. *NAK* frames are 40 bits. The error rate for data frames is 1%, and the error rate for *NAK* frames is negligible. The sequence numbers are 8 bits.

18. What is the optimum size of the data portion of the frame for stop-and-wait over a 1-Mbps channel with an error rate of 10^{-2} per bit, a 1-msec timeout, and 32-byte frame headers?

19. Consider an error-free 64-kbps satellite channel used to send 512-byte data frames in one direction, with very short acknowledgements coming back the other way. What is the maximum throughput for window sizes of 1, 7, 15, and 127?

20. Each of the N hosts attached to an IMP generates messages with a Poisson arrival pattern having a mean of λ messages/sec. The probability that a message has length m bits $(1 \leq m < \infty)$ is P_m. Each message acquires h bits of frame header while on the IMP's one-and-only IMP-IMP line. The line has a data rate of b bps. The probability

that a bit will be received in error is e. Acknowledgements come back instantly, and occupy negligible bandwidth. If all traffic is to distant hosts, what is the maximum value of N?

21. A 100 km long cable runs at the T1 data rate. The propagation speed in the cable is 2/3 the speed of light. How many bits fit in the cable?

22. Redraw Fig. 4-21 for a full-duplex channel that never loses frames. Is the protocol failure still possible?

23. Give the firing sequence for the Petri net of Fig. 4-25 corresponding to the state sequence (000), (01A), (01—), (010), (01A) in Fig. 4-20. Explain in words what the sequence represents.

24. Given the transition rules $AC \rightarrow B$, $B \rightarrow AC$, $CD \rightarrow E$, and $E \rightarrow CD$, draw the Petri net described. From the Petri net, draw the finite state graph reachable from the initial state ACD. What well-known computer science concept do these transition rules model?

25. In Fig. 4-25, transition 9 is $EG \rightarrow DG$. Under what conditions, if any, can the rule be simplified to $E \rightarrow D$?

26. Discuss the potential advantages and disadvantages of the ARPANET eight logical channel IMP-IMP protocol versus a 3-bit HDLC sliding window protocol.

27. The IEEE 802 LLC connectionless service sends data in U frames rather than I frames. Why do you think this choice was made?

28. The RR and REJ (NAK) frames used by HDLC, LAPB, and LLC both acknowledge correct receipt of frames up to $N - 1$, where N is the sequence number specified in the frame. What is the point of having two different control frames?

29. Write a program to simulate the communication of protocol 6. The program should read in the following parameters: transmission rate of the channel, length of a data frame, length of an ACK or NAK frame, probability of a frame being lost, propagation time of the channel, and mean rate at which a host produces new messages (assume an exponential interarrival distribution). For each set of parameters, the program should print out the effective data rate achieved.

30. Write a program to stochastically simulate the behavior of a Petri net. The program should read in the transition rules as well as a list of states corresponding to the network link layer issuing a new packet or the accepting a new packet. From the initial state, also read in, the program should pick enabled transitions at random and fire them, checking to see if a host ever accepts two messages without the other host emitting a new one in between.

5

THE NETWORK LAYER

The network layer is concerned with getting packets from the source all the way to the destination. Getting to the destination may require making many hops at intermediate nodes along the way. This function clearly contrasts with that of the data link layer, which has the more modest goal of just moving frames from one end of a wire to the other. Thus the network layer is the lowest layer that deals with end-to-end transmission.

In order to achieve its goals, the network layer must know about the topology of the communication subnet and choose appropriate paths through it. It must also take care to choose routes to avoid overloading some of the communication lines while leaving others idle. Finally, when the source and destination are in different networks, it is up to the network layer to deal with these differences and solve the problems that result from them.

5.1. NETWORK LAYER DESIGN ISSUES

In this section we will provide an introduction to some of the issues that the designers of the network layer must grapple with. These issues include the service provided to the transport layer, routing of packets through the subnet, congestion control, and connection of multiple networks together (internetworking). We will examine the latter three subjects in greater detail later in this chapter.

271

5.1.1. Services Provided to the Transport Layer

The network layer provides services to the transport layer. Since in some networks (e.g., the ARPANET and X.25 networks), the network layer runs in the IMPs and the transport layer runs in the hosts, the boundary between the network and transport layers in these networks is also the boundary between the subnet and the hosts. This means that the services provided by the network layer define the services provided by the subnet.

When the subnet is run by a common carrier or PTT and the hosts are run by the users, the network layer service becomes the interface between the carrier and the users. As such, it defines the carrier's duties and responsibilities, and is thus of great importance to both the carrier and the users. As you might expect under these circumstances, there has been a fair amount of discussion and controversy over the services that should be offered. We will look at this controversy shortly.

The network layer services have been designed with the following goals in mind.

1. The services should be independent of the subnet technology.

2. The transport layer should be shielded from the number, type, and topology of the subnets present.

3. The network addresses made available to the transport layer should use a uniform numbering plan even across LANs and WANs.

Given these goals, the designers of the network layer had a lot of freedom in writing detailed specifications of the services to be offered to the transport layer. This freedom quickly degenerated into a raging battle between two warring factions. The discussion centered on the question of whether the network layer should provide connection-oriented service or connectionless service.

This same issue occurs in the data link layer, as we saw in the previous chapter, but it is not as serious there. The LLC definition provides both, and since LANs are always owned and operated by the users, they can use whichever they prefer. With the network layer, the situation is different. If the carrier only offers one type of service and the users want the other, there is often no alternative.

One camp (represented by the ARPA Internet community) argues that the subnet's job is moving bits around and nothing else. In their view (based on nearly 20 years of actual experience with a real, working network), the subnet is inherently unreliable, no matter how it is designed. Therefore, the hosts should accept the fact that it is unreliable and do error control (i.e., error detection and correction) and flow control themselves.

This viewpoint leads quickly to the conclusion that the network service should be connectionless, with primitives *SEND PACKET* and *RECEIVE PACKET,* and little else. In particular, no error checking and flow control should be done, because the hosts are going to do that any way, and there is probably little to be gained by doing it twice. Furthermore, each packet must carry the full destination address, because each packet sent is carried independently of its predecessors, if any.

The other camp (represented by the carriers) argues that the network layer (and subnet) should provide a reliable, connection-oriented service with connections having the following properties:

1. Before sending data, the source transport entity must set up a connection to the destination transport entity. This connection, which is given a special identifier, is then used until there are no more data to send, at which time the connection is explicitly released.

2. When a connection is set up, the two transport entities and the network layer providing the service can enter into a negotiation about the parameters of the service and the quality and cost of the service to be provided.

3. Communication is in both directions, and packets are delivered in sequence without errors. The conceptual model behind this is a well-behaved queue with the first-in, first-out property.

4. Flow control is provided automatically to prevent a fast sender from dumping packets into the queue at a higher rate than the receiver can take them out, thus leading to overflow.

Other properties, such as explicit confirmation of delivery and high priority packets are optional.

An analogy between connection-oriented service and connectionless service may clarify the situation. The public telephone network offers a connection-oriented service. The customer first dials a number to set up a connection. Then the parties talk (exchange data). Finally the connection is broken. Although what happens inside the telephone system is undoubtedly very complicated, the two users are presented with the illusion of a dedicated, point-to-point channel that always delivers information in the order it was sent.

In contrast, the postal system (or telegraph system) is connectionless. Each letter carries the full destination address, and is carried independently of every other letter. Letters do not necessarily arrive in the order mailed. If a letter carrier accidentally drops a letter, the post office does not time out and send a duplicate. In short, error and flow control are handled by the users themselves, outside the postal system (subnet). Figure 5-1 summarizes the differences between connection-oriented and connectionless service.

The argument between connection-oriented and connectionless service really has to do with where to put the complexity. In the connection-oriented service, it is in the network layer (subnet); in the connectionless service, it is in the transport

Issue	Connection-oriented	Connectionless
Initial setup	Required	Not possible
Destination address	Only needed during setup	Needed on every packet
Packet sequencing	Guaranteed	Not guaranteed
Error control	Done by network layer (e.g., subnet)	Done by transport layer (e.g., hosts)
Flow control	Provided by network layer	Not provided by network layer
Is option negotiation possible?	Yes	No
Are connection identifiers used?	Yes	No

Fig. 5-1. Summary of the major differences between connection-oriented and connectionless service.

layer (hosts). Supporters of connectionless service say that user computing power has become cheap, so that there is no reason not to put the complexity in the hosts (frequently in a special network coprocessor chip). Furthermore, they argue that the subnet is a major national investment that will last for decades, so it should not be cluttered up with features that may become obsolete quickly, but will have to be calculated into the price structure for many years. Furthermore, some applications, such as digitized voice and real-time data collection may regard *speedy* delivery as much more important than *accurate* delivery.

On the other hand, supporters of connection-oriented service say that most users are not interested in running complex transport layer protocols in their machines. What they want is reliable, trouble-free service, and this service can be best provided with connections.

Finally, there is the very real issue of credibility. If the users are not willing to trust the carrier's claims that the subnet only loses a packet once in a blue moon, they will implement all the error checking anyway in the transport layer to protect themselves. However, if enough people do this, then it is wasteful to go to a lot of trouble and expense in the network layer to achieve high reliability. The subnet might just as well provide a cheap, bare-bones connectionless service and tell the users to do all the work, since many of them will do it anyway, no matter what the carrier tells them.

To make a long story short, the connection-oriented supporters outnumbered the connectionless supporters in the committee that wrote the network layer service definition, so the OSI network service was originally a connection-oriented service. (It has been said that the PTTs preferred connection-oriented service because they could not charge for connect time if there were no connections.) However, the people in favor of connectionless service kept lobbying for their cause, and ISO eventually modified the service definition to include both classes of service. Both types are now permitted and protocols for supporting both types have been incorporated into the OSI framework.

The network layer is not the only battleground between the two camps. The same issues arise in all the layers. The fight was finally resolved for all time by a revision to the OSI model to allow both kinds of service to be offered all the way up to the top. In Fig. 5-2 we see how the two service types relate to each other. At the top of each layer (except the application layer) are SAPs (Service Access Points) through which the layer above accesses the services. Each SAP has a unique address that identifies it. Starting with the data link layer, these services can be connection-oriented or connectionless (the issue is moot in the physical layer, since error control and flow control are not relevant there).

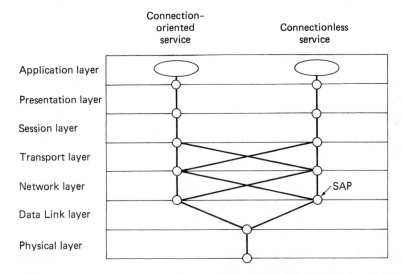

Fig. 5-2. Mixtures of connection-oriented and connectionless service in the OSI model.

Two obvious paths are fully connection-oriented service from top to bottom and fully connectionless service. However, it is also possible to have connection-oriented service be provided by the network or transport layers even though the lower layers are connectionless. In this case, the network or transport layers must handle the conversion. For example, a connection-oriented transport service could be built on a LAN with a connectionless data link service by putting the error control, flow control, and related functionality in either the network or transport layer.

The reverse mechanism, implementing a connectionless service for the upper layers on top of a connection-oriented service is also possible. Although this seems wasteful, it might be useful when connecting two fully connectionless LANs over a WAN that only offered connection-oriented network service. In any event, the conversion between the two service types can be done in either the network or transport layer, but not in higher layers.

The OSI Network Service Primitives

International Standard 8348 defines the network service by specifying the primitives that apply at the boundary between the network layer and transport layer. Both connection-oriented and connectionless primitives are provided.

The connection-oriented primitives use the model of Fig. 5-3. In this model, a connection is a pair of conceptual queues between two **NSAP**s (network addresses), one queue for traffic in each direction. Prior to establishing a connection, we have the situation of Fig. 5-3(a). After a successful establishment, we have the situation of Fig. 5-3(b). Finally, after three packets have been sent, the state of the connections might look like Fig. 5-3(c).

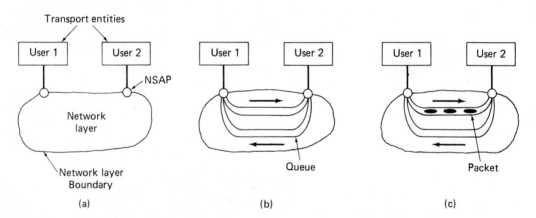

Fig. 5-3. (a) Prior to establishing a connection. (b) After establishing a connection. (c) After three packets have been sent but not yet received.

The OSI connection-oriented network service primitives are listed in Fig. 5-4(a). They can be grouped into four categories, for establishing, releasing, using, and resetting connections, respectively. Most of the primitives have parameters. The exact way the parameters are passed to the primitives is implementation dependent. The effect of each primitive can be described by the way it changes the state of the queues in Fig. 5-3.

The *N-CONNECT.request* primitive is used to set up a connection. It specifies the network address to connect to and the caller's network address. It also contains two Boolean variables used to request optional services. *Acks_wanted* is used to permit the caller to request acknowledgement of each packet sent. If the network

```
N-CONNECT. request (callee, caller, acks_wanted, exp_wanted, qos, user_data)
N-CONNECT. indication (callee, caller, acks_wanted, exp_wanted, qos, user_data)
N-CONNECT. response (responder, acks_wanted, exp_wanted, qos, user_data)
N-CONNECT. confirm (responder, acks_wanted, exp_wanted, qos, user_data)
```
```
N-DISCONNECT. request (originator, reason, user_data, responding_address)
N-DISCONNECT. indication (originator, reason, user_data, responding_address)
```
```
N-DATA. request (user_data)
N-DATA. indication (user_data)
N-DATA-ACKNOWLEDGE. request ( )
N-DATA-ACKNOWLEDGE. indication ( )
N-EXPEDITED-DATA. request (user_data)
N-EXPEDITED-DATA. indication (user_data)
```
```
N-RESET. request (originator, reason)
N-RESET. indication (originator, reason)
N-RESET. response ( )
N-RESET. confirm ( )
```

(a)

```
N-UNITDATA. request (source_address, destination_address, qos, user_data)
N-UNITDATA. indication (source_address, destination_address, qos, user_data)
```
```
N-FACILITY. request (qos)
N-FACILITY. indication (destination_address, qos, reason)
N-REPORT. indication (destination_address, qos, reason)
```

(b)

Notes on terminology:

Callee: Network address (NSAP) to be called
Caller: Network address (NSAP) used by calling transport entity
Acks_wanted: Boolean flag specifying whether acknowledgements are desired
Exp_wanted: Boolean flag specifying whether expedited data will be sent
Qos: Quality of service desired
User_data: 0 or more bytes of data transmitted but not examined
Responder: Network address (NSAP) connected to at the destination
Originator: Sepcification of who initiated the N-RESET
Reason: Specification of why the event happened

Fig. 5-4. (a) OSI connection-oriented network service primitives. (b) OSI connectionless network service primitives.

layer does not provide acknowledgements, the variable is set to *false* when delivered to the destination in the *N-CONNECT.indication* primitive. If the network layer does provide acknowledgements, but the destination does not want to use them, then it sets the flag to *false* in its *N-CONNECT.response*. Only if both transport entities and the network service provider want to use them are they used. This feature is an example of **option negotiation**.

The *exp_wanted* flag is a second example of option negotiation. If accepted by all three parties, it permits the use of **expedited data**, essentially packets may violate the normal queue ordering and skip to the head of the queue. Whether or not they actually do this, is implementation dependent. A typical example of expedited data is a user at a terminal hitting the DEL key to interrupt a running program. The DEL packet will go as expedited data.

The *qos* parameter is actually two lists of values that determine the **quality of service** provided by the connection. The first list gives the goal—what the caller really wants. The second list gives the minimum values considered acceptable. If the network service is unable to provide at least the minimum value for any parameter specified by either the caller (calling party) or the callee (called party), the connection establishment fails. The values that may be specified include throughput, delay, error rate, secrecy, and cost, among others.

The caller may include some user data in the connection request. The callee may inspect these data before deciding whether to accept or reject the request. Connection requests are accepted with the *N-CONNECT.response* primitive and rejected with the *N-DISCONNECT.request* primitive. When a request is rejected, the *reason* field allows the callee to tell why it was not willing to accept the connection and whether the condition is permanent or transient. The network layer itself may also reject attempts to establish connections, for example, if the quality of service desired is not available (permanent condition) or the subnet is currently overloaded (transient condition).

The remaining *N-CONNECT* primitives and the *N-DISCONNECT* primitives are straightforward, and need little further comment. After a connection has been established, either party can transmit data using *N-DATA.request*. When these packets arrive, an *N-DATA.indication* primitive is invoked on the receiving end. Expedited data uses primitives analogous to those for regular data.

If acknowledgements have been agreed upon, when a packet has been received, the recipient is expected to issue an *N-DATA-ACKNOWLEDGE.request*. This primitive contains no sequence number, so the party sending the original data must simply count acknowledgements. If the quality of service is low, and data and acknowledgements can be lost, this scheme is not very satisfactory. On the other hand, it is not the task of the network layer to provide an error-free service; that job is done by the transport layer. Network layer acknowledgements are merely an attempt to improve the quality of service, not make it perfect.

The *N-RESET* primitives are used to report catastrophes, such as crashes of either transport entity or the network service provider itself. After an *N-RESET* has been requested, indicated, responded to, and confirmed, the queues will be reset to their original empty state. Data present in the queues at the time of the *N-RESET* are lost. Again here, it is the job of the transport layer to recover from *N-RESET*s.

The OSI connectionless primitives are given in Fig. 5-4(b). The *N-UNITDATA* primitives are used to send up to 64,512 bytes of data (1K less than 2^{16}, to provide plenty of room for various headers and still keep the final unit less than 2^{16} bytes). The *N-UNITDATA* primitives provide no error control, no flow control, and no other control. The sender just dumps the packet into the subnet and hopes for the best.

The *N-FACILITY.request* primitive is designed to allow a network service user inquire about average delivery characteristics to the specified destination, such as percent of packets being delivered. The *N-FACILITY.indication* primitive comes from the network layer itself, not from a remote transport entity.

The *N-REPORT.indication* primitive allows the network layer to report problems back to the network service user. If, for example, a particular destination is unavailable, that fact could be reported using this primitive. The details of how the primitive is used are network dependent and not defined in the standard.

One of the functions of the network layer is to provide a uniform naming for the transport layer to use. Ideally, all the network operators in the world should get together and agree on a single name space, so that each wire running from a subnet into an office or home would have a world-wide unique address. Unfortunately, this is not going to happen.

To make the best of the existing situation, the OSI network layer addressing has been designed to incorporate today's diversity of network addressing schemes. All the network service primitives use NSAP addresses for identifying the source and destination. The format of these NSAP addresses is shown in Fig. 5-5. Each NSAP address has three fields. The first one, the **AFI** (**Authority and Format Identifier**), identifies the type of address present in the third field, the **DSP** (**Domain Specific Part**). Codes have been allocated to allow the DSP field to contain packet network addresses, telephone numbers, ISDN numbers, telex numbers, and similar existing numbering schemes, both in binary and in packed decimal. The AFI field can take on values from 10 to 99, leaving plenty of room for future numbering plans.

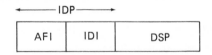

IDP: Initial Domain Part
AFI: Authority and Format Indicator
IDI: Initial Domain Identifier
DSP: Domain Specific Part

Fig. 5-5. The format of OSI network addresses (NSAPs).

The second, or **IDI** (**Initial Domain Identifier**) field, specifies the domain to which the number in the DSP part belongs. If, for example, the DSP is a telephone number, the IDI might be the country code for that number. The full NSAP address is variable length, up to 40 decimal digits or 20 bytes long.

To understand what NSAP addresses are for, it may be helpful to make an analogy with the telephone system. Most modern offices and homes nowadays are equipped with one or more sockets into which telephones can be plugged. Each socket has a wire running from it to a telephone switching office (or PBX). This socket is assigned a worldwide unique number consisting of a country code, area code, and subscriber number.

Whenever a telephone is plugged into a socket, the telephone can be reached by dialing the socket's number. Notice that the number really applies to the *socket,* not to the specific *telephone* currently plugged into it. When a telephone is moved from one office to another, it acquires the number of the new office. It does not take the old number with it. Thus the sockets give the telephone system a uniform name space, independent of which particular telephone that happens to be plugged in today, or which person will be answering it when it rings.

In this analogy, the telephone sockets are the NSAPs and the telephone numbers are the NSAP addresses. When a transport entity asks the network to make a call to a remote machine, it specifies the NSAP address (i.e., telephone number) to be called. The network layer does not care which transport entity (i.e., telephone) is currently attached (plugged in) to that NSAP, and certainly does not care which user owns the transport entity (i.e., which person will answer the telephone). How transport entities connect to NSAPs is an issue for the transport layer, not the network layer.

5.1.2. Internal Organization of the Network Layer

Having looked at the two classes of service the network layer can provide to its users, it is time to see how it works inside. Unfortunately, the OSI model does not provide a specification of the key algorithms, such as routing and congestion control. These are implementation dependent. Nevertheless, they are important and definitely worth studying in detail.

As a consequence, this chapter will cover many subnet design issues that are not strictly part of the network layer, although they are related to it. We will also discuss the OSI network layer where it is appropriate. To make it clear where we are discussing subnet design (as opposed to OSI), we will use the subnet terms "IMP" and "host" instead of "network layer" and "transport layer," although the latter are equivalent in some networks.

There are basically two different philosophies for organizing the subnet, one using connections and the other working connectionless. In the context of the *internal* operation of the subnet, a connection is usually called a **virtual circuit**, in analogy with the physical circuits set up by the telephone system. The independent packets of the connectionless organization are called **datagrams**, in analogy with telegrams.

Virtual circuits are generally used in subnets whose primary service is connection-oriented, so we will describe them in that context. The idea behind virtual circuits is to avoid having to make routing decisions for every packet sent. Instead, when a connection is established, a route from the source machine to the destination machine is chosen as part of the connection setup. That route is used for all traffic flowing over the connection, exactly the same way that the telephone system works. When the connection is released, the virtual circuit is discarded.

In contrast, with a datagram subnet no routes are worked out in advance, even if the service is connection-oriented. Each packet sent is routed independently of its predecessors. Successive packets may follow different routes. While datagram subnets have to do more work, they are also more robust and adapt to failures and congestion more easily than virtual circuit subnets. We will discuss the pros and cons of the two approaches later.

If packets flowing over a given virtual circuit always take the same route through the subnet, each IMP must remember where to forward packets for each of the currently open virtual circuits passing through it. Every IMP must maintain a table with one entry per open virtual circuit. Virtual circuits not passing through IMP X are not entered in X's table, of course. Each packet traveling through the subnet must contain a virtual circuit number field in its header, in addition to sequence numbers, checksums, and the like. When a packet arrives at an IMP, the IMP knows on which line it arrived and what the virtual circuit number is. Based only on this information, the packet must be forwarded to the correct IMP.

When a network connection is set up, a virtual circuit number not already in use on that machine is chosen as the connection identifier. Since each machine chooses virtual circuit numbers independently, the same virtual circuit number is likely to be in use on two different paths through some intermediate IMP, leading to ambiguities.

Consider the subnet of Fig. 5-6(a). Suppose that a process in A's host wants to talk to a process in D's host. A chooses virtual circuit 0. Let us assume that route $ABCD$ is chosen. Simultaneously, a process in B decides it wants to talk to a process in D (not the same one as A). If there are no open virtual circuits starting in B at this point, host B will also choose virtual circuit 0. Further assume that route BCD is selected as the best one. After both virtual circuits have been set up, the process at A sends its first message to D, on virtual circuit 0. When the packet arrives at D, the poor host does not know which user process to give it to.

To solve this problem, whenever a host wants to create a new outbound virtual circuit, it chooses the lowest circuit number not currently in use. The IMP (say X) does not forward this setup packet to the next IMP (say Y) along the route as is. Instead, X looks in its table to find all the circuit numbers currently being used for traffic to Y. It then chooses the lowest free number and substitutes that number for the one in the packet, overwriting the number chosen by the host. Similarly, IMP Y chooses the lowest circuit number free between it and the next IMP.

When this setup packet finally arrives at the destination, the IMP there chooses the lowest available inbound circuit number, overwrites the circuit number found in the packet with this, and passes it to the host. As long as the destination host always sees the same circuit number on all traffic arriving on a given virtual circuit, it does not matter that the source host is consistently using a different number.

Figure 5-6(b) gives eight examples of virtual circuits pertaining to the subnet of part (a). Part (c) of the figure shows the IMPs' tables, assuming the circuits were created in the order: $ABCD$, BCD, $AEFD$, BAE, $ABFD$, BF, AEC, and $AECDFB$. The last one ($AECDFB$) may seem somewhat roundabout, but if lines AB, BC, and EF were badly overloaded when the routing algorithm ran, this might well have been the best choice.

Each entry consists of an incoming and an outgoing part. Each of the two parts

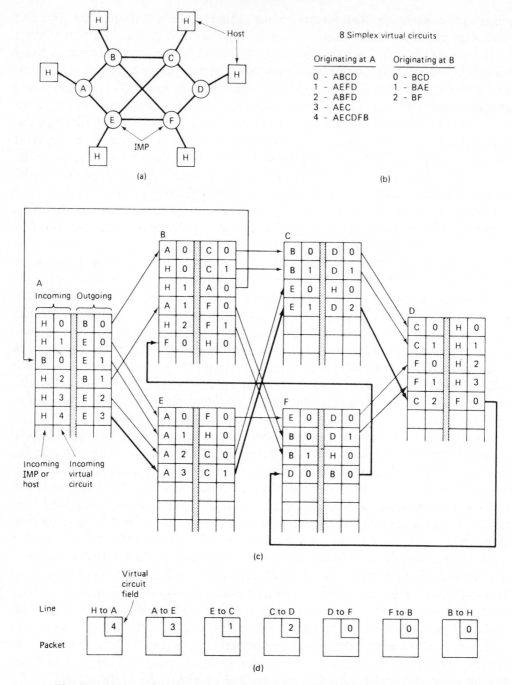

Fig. 5-6. (a) Example subnet. (b) Eight virtual circuits through the subnet. (c) IMP tables for the virtual circuits in (b). (d) The virtual circuit changes as a packet progresses.

has an IMP name (used to indicate a line) and a virtual circuit number. When a packet arrives, the table is searched on the left (incoming) part, using the arrival line and virtual circuit number found in the packet as the key. When a match is found, the outgoing part of the entry tells which virtual circuit number to insert into the packet and which IMP to send it to. *H* stands for the host, both on the incoming and outgoing sides.

As an example, consider a packet traveling from host *A* to host *B* on virtual circuit 4 (i.e., route *AECDFB*). When IMP *A* gets a packet from its own host, with circuit 4, it searches its table, finding a match for *H*4 at entry 5 (the top entry is 0). The outgoing part of this entry is *E*3, which means replace the circuit 4 with circuit 3 and send it to IMP *E*. IMP *E* then gets a packet from *A* with circuit 3, so it searches for *A*3 and finds a match at the third entry. The packet now goes to *C* as circuit 1. The sequence of entries used is marked by the heavy line. Figure 5-6(d) shows this sequence of packet numbers.

Because virtual circuits can be initiated from either end, a problem occurs when call setups are propagating in both directions at once along a chain of IMPs. At some point they have arrived at adjacent IMPs. Each IMP must now pick a virtual circuit number to use for the (full-duplex) circuit it is trying to establish. If they have been programmed to choose the lowest number not already in use on the link, they will pick the same number, causing two unrelated virtual circuits over the same physical line to have the same number. When a data packet arrives later, the receiving IMP has no way of telling whether it is a forward packet on one circuit or a reverse packet on the other. If circuits are simplex, there is no ambiguity.

Note that every process must be required to indicate when it is through using a virtual circuit, so that the virtual circuit can be purged from the IMP tables to recover the space. In public networks the motivation is the stick rather than the carrot: users are invariably charged for connect time as well as for data transported.

So much for the use of virtual circuits internal to the subnet. The other possibility is to use datagrams internally, in which case the IMPs do not have a table with one entry for each open virtual circuit. Instead, they have a table telling which outgoing line to use for each possible destination IMP. These tables are also needed when virtual circuits are used internally, to determine the route for a setup packet.

Each datagram must contain the full destination address (the machine and the NSAP address to which the destination process is attached). When a packet comes in, the IMP looks up the outgoing line to use and sends it on its way. Nothing in the packet is modified. Also, the establishment and release of network or transport layer connections do not require any special work on the part of the IMPs.

Comparison of Virtual Circuits and Datagrams within the Subnet

Both virtual circuits and datagrams have their supporters and their detractors. We will now attempt to summarize the arguments both ways. Inside the subnet the main trade-off between virtual circuits and datagrams is between IMP memory space and bandwidth. Virtual circuits allow packets to contain circuit numbers instead of full destination addresses. If the packets tend to be fairly short, a full destination address in every packet may represent a significant amount of overhead, and hence wasted bandwidth. The use of virtual circuits internal to the subnet becomes especially attractive when many of the "hosts" are actually interactive terminals with only a few characters per packet. The price paid for using virtual circuits internally is the table space within the IMPs. Depending upon the relative cost of communication circuits versus IMP memory, one or the other may be cheaper.

For transaction processing systems (e.g., stores calling up to verify credit card purchases), the overhead required to set up and clear a virtual circuit may easily dwarf the use of the circuit. If the majority of the traffic is expected to be of this kind, the use of virtual circuits inside the subnet makes little sense.

Virtual circuits also have a vulnerability problem. If an IMP crashes and loses its memory, even if it comes back up a second later, all the virtual circuits passing through it will have to be aborted. In contrast, if a datagram IMP goes down, only those users whose packets were queued up in the IMP at the time will suffer, and maybe not even all those, depending upon whether they have already been acknowledged or not. The loss of a communication line is fatal to virtual circuits using it, but can be easily compensated for if datagrams are used. Datagrams also allow the IMPs to balance the traffic throughout the subnet, since routes can be changed halfway through a connection.

It is worth explicitly pointing out that the service offered (connection-oriented or connectionless) is a separate issue from the subnet structure (virtual circuit or datagram). In theory, all four combinations are possible. Obviously, a virtual circuit implementation of a connection-oriented service and a datagram implementation of a connectionless service are reasonable. Implementing connections using datagrams also makes sense when the subnet is trying to provide a highly robust service.

The fourth possibility, a connectionless service on top of a virtual circuit subnet seems strange, but might happen in a subnet originally designed for connection-oriented service, with connectionless service thrown in as an afterthought. In such an arrangement, the subnet might have to set up, use, and release a virtual circuit for each packet sent, not a pleasant thought.

Figure 5-7 summarizes some of the differences between subnets using datagrams internally and subnets using virtual circuits internally.

5.1.3. Routing

The real function of the network layer is routing packets from the source machine to the destination machine. In most subnets, packets will require multiple hops to make the journey. The only notable exception is for broadcast networks,

Issue	Datagram subnet	VC subnet
Circuit setup	Not possible	Required
Addressing	Each packet contains the full source and destination address	Each packet contains a short vc number
State information	Subnet does not hold state information	Each established vc requires subnet table space
Routing	Each packet is routed independently	Route chosen when vc is set up; all packets follow this route
Effect of node failures	None, except for packets lost during the crash	All vcs that passed through the failed equipment are terminated
Congestion control	Difficult	Easy if enough buffers can be allocated in advance for each vc set up
Complexity	In the transport layer	In the network layer
Suited for	Connection–oriented and connectionless service	Connection–oriented service

Fig. 5-7. Comparison of datagram and virtual circuit subnets.
Notice the similarity with the connection-oriented and connectionless services of Fig. 5-1.

but even here routing is an issue if the source and destination are not on the same network. The algorithms that choose the routes and the data structures that they use are a major area of network layer design. In this section we will just outline the problem. Later in this chapter we will examine in detail many of the algorithms that have been proposed.

The **routing algorithm** is that part of the network layer software responsible for deciding which output line an incoming packet should be transmitted on. If the subnet uses datagrams internally, this decision must be made anew for every arriving data packet. However, if the subnet uses virtual circuits internally, routing decisions are made only when a new virtual circuit is being set up. Thereafter, data packets just follow the previously established route. The latter case is sometimes called **session routing**, because a route remains in force for an entire user session (e.g., a login session at a terminal or a file transfer).

Regardless of whether routes are chosen independently for each packet or only when new connections are established, there are certain properties that are desirable in a routing algorithm: correctness, simplicity, robustness, stability, fairness, and optimality. Correctness and simplicity hardly require comment, but the need for robustness may be less obvious at first. Once a major network comes on the air, it may be expected to run continuously for years without system-wide failures. During that period there will be hardware and software failures of all kinds. Hosts, IMPs, and lines will go up and down repeatedly, and the topology will change many times. The routing algorithm must be able to cope with changes in the topology and traffic without requiring all jobs in all hosts to be aborted and the network to be rebooted every time some IMP crashes.

Stability is also an important goal for the routing algorithm. There exist routing algorithms that never converge to equilibrium, no matter how long they run. Fairness and optimality may sound like Motherhood and Apple Pie—surely no one would oppose them—but as it turns out, they are often contradictory goals. As a simple example of this conflict, look at Fig. 5-8. Suppose that there is enough traffic between A and A', between B and B', and between C and C' to saturate the horizontal links. To maximize the total flow, the X to X' traffic should be shut off altogether. Unfortunately, X and X' may not see it that way. Evidently, some compromise between global efficiency and fairness to individual connections is needed.

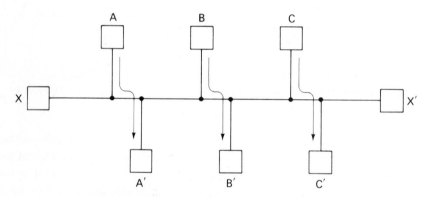

Fig. 5-8. Conflict between fairness and optimality.

Before we can even attempt to find trade-offs between fairness and optimality, we must decide what it is we seek to optimize. Minimizing mean packet delay is an obvious candidate, but so is maximizing total network throughput. Furthermore, these two goals are also in conflict, since operating any queueing system near capacity ($\rho \to 1$) implies a long queueing delay. As a compromise, many networks attempt to minimize the number of hops a packet must make, because reducing the number of hops tends to improve the delay and also reduce the amount of bandwidth consumed, which tends to improve the throughput as well.

Routing algorithms can be grouped into two major classes: nonadaptive and adaptive. Nonadaptive algorithms do not base their routing decisions on measurements or estimates of the current traffic and topology, whereas adaptive ones do. If an adaptive algorithm manages to adapt well to the traffic, it will naturally outperform an algorithm that is oblivious to what is going on in the network, but adapting well to the traffic is easier said than done. Adaptive algorithms can be further subdivided into centralized, isolated, and distributed (McQuillan, 1974), all of which are discussed in detail below.

5.1.4. Congestion

When too many packets are present in (a part of) the subnet, performance degrades. This situation is called **congestion**. Figure 5-9 depicts the symptom. When the number of packets dumped into the subnet by the hosts is within its carrying capacity, they are all delivered (except for a few that are afflicted with transmission errors), and the number delivered is proportional to the number sent. However, as traffic increases too far, the IMPs are no longer able to cope, and they begin losing packets. This tends to make matters worse. At very high traffic, performance collapses completely, and almost no packets are delivered.

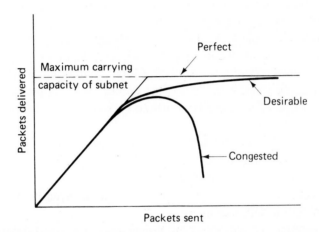

Fig. 5-9. When too much traffic is offered, congestion sets in, and performance degrades sharply.

Congestion can be brought about by several factors. If the IMPs are too slow to perform the various bookkeeping tasks required of them (queueing buffers, updating tables, etc.), queues can build up, even though there is excess line capacity. On the other hand, even if the IMP CPU is infinitely fast, queues will build up whenever the input traffic rate exceeds the capacity of the output lines. This can happen, for example, if three input lines are delivering packets at top speed, all of which need to be forwarded along the same output line. Either way, the problem boils down to not enough IMP buffers. Given an infinite supply of buffers, the IMP can always smooth over any temporary bottlenecks by just hanging onto all packets for as long as necessary. Of course, for stable operation, the hosts cannot indefinitely pump packets into the subnet at a rate higher than the subnet can absorb.

Congestion tends to feed upon itself and become worse. If an IMP has no free buffers, it must ignore newly arriving packets. When a packet is discarded, the IMP that sent the packet will time out and retransmit it, perhaps ultimately many times. Since the sending IMP cannot discard the packet until it has been acknowledged, congestion at the receiver's end forces the sender to refrain from releasing a buffer it would have normally freed. In this manner, congestion backs up, like cars approaching a toll booth.

It is definitely worth explicitly pointing out the difference between congestion control and flow control, as the authors of many books and papers on the subject do not seem to understand. Congestion control has to do with making sure the subnet is able to carry the offered traffic. It is a global issue, involving the behavior of all the hosts, all the IMPs, the store-and-forwarding processing within the IMPs, and all the other factors that tend to diminish the carrying capacity of the subnet.

Flow control, in contrast, relates to the point-to-point traffic between a given sender and a given receiver. Its job is to make sure that a fast sender cannot continually transmit data faster than the receiver can absorb it. Flow control nearly always involves some direct feedback from the receiver to the sender to tell the sender how things are doing at the other end.

To see the difference between these two concepts, consider a fiber optic network with a capacity of 1000 gigabits/sec on which a supercomputer was trying to transfer a file to a microcomputer at 100 Mbps. Although there would be no congestion at all (the network itself is not in trouble), flow control would be needed to force the supercomputer to stop frequently to give the microcomputer a chance to catch up.

At the other extreme, consider a store-and-forward network with 1-Mbps lines and 1000 large minicomputers, half of which were trying to transfer files at 100 kbps to the other half. Here the problem would not be that of fast senders overpowering slow receivers, but simply that the total offered traffic could easily exceed what the network could handle.

Later in this chapter we will examine congestion control in detail, and discuss various algorithms for dealing with it. It should be clear that congestion control and routing are closely related, with poor routing decisions being a major cause of congestion.

5.1.5. Internetworking

Just as congestion control is closely related to the primary function of the network layer, routing, so is internetworking. When the source and destination machines are in different networks, all the usual routing problems are present, only worse. For example, if the networks containing the source and destination machines are not directly connected, the routing algorithm will have to find a path through one or more intermediate networks. There may be many possible choices, all with different characteristics, advantages, and disadvantages.

Routing aside, another problem with internetworking is that not all networks use the same protocols. Different protocols imply different packet formats, headers, flow control procedures, acknowledgement rules, and more. As a consequence, when packets move from network to network, conversions are necessary. Sometimes they are straightforward, but often they are not. Just think about what happens when a packet must traverse both virtual circuit and datagram subnets on the way to the destination. Later in this chapter we will study internetworking, its problems and its solutions in detail.

5.2. ROUTING ALGORITHMS

Routing algorithms can be grouped into two major classes: nonadaptive and adaptive. **Nonadaptive algorithms** do not base their routing decisions on measurements or estimates of the current traffic and topology. Instead, the choice of the route to use to get from i to j (for all i and j) is computed in advance, off-line, and downloaded to the IMPs when the network is booted. This procedure is sometimes called **static routing**.

Adaptive algorithms, on the other hand, attempt to change their routing decisions to reflect changes in topology and the current traffic. Three different families of adaptive algorithms exist, differing in the information they use. The global algorithms use information collected from the entire subnet in an attempt to make optimal decisions. This approach is called centralized routing. The local algorithms run separately on each IMP and only use information available there, such as queue lengths. These are known as isolated algorithms. Finally, the third class of algorithms uses a mixture of global and local information. They are called distributed algorithms. All three classes are discussed in detail below. Additional information about routing can be found in Bell and Jabbour (1986).

5.2.1. Shortest Path Routing

Let us begin our study of routing algorithms with a technique that is widely used in many forms because it is simple and easy to understand. The idea is to build a graph of the subnet, with each node of the graph representing an IMP and each arc of the graph representing a communication line. To choose a route between a given pair of IMPs, the algorithm just finds the shortest path between them.

The concept **shortest path** deserves some explanation. One way of measuring path length is the number of hops. Using this metric, the paths *ABC* and *ABE* in Fig. 5-10 are equally long. Another metric is the geographic distance in kilometers, in which case *ABC* is clearly much longer than *ABE* (assuming the figure is drawn to scale).

However, many other metrics are also possible. For example, each arc could be labeled with the mean queueing and transmission delay for a standard test packet as determined by hourly or daily test runs. With this graph labeling, the shortest path is the fastest path, rather than the path with the fewest arcs or kilometers.

In the most general case, the labels on the arcs could be computed as a function of the distance, bandwidth, average traffic, communication cost, mean queue

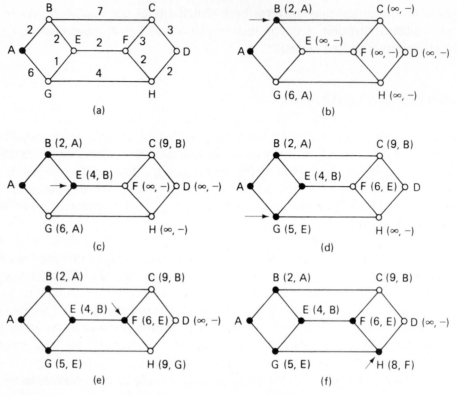

Fig. 5-10. The first five steps used in computing the shortest path from *A* to *D*. The arrows indicate the working node.

length, measured delay, and other factors. By changing the weighting function, the algorithm would then compute the "shortest" path according to any one of a number of criteria.

Several algorithms for computing the shortest path between two nodes of a graph are known. This one is due to Dijkstra (1959). Each node is labeled (in parentheses) with its distance from the source node along the best known path. Initially, no paths are known, so all nodes are labeled with infinity. As the algorithm proceeds and paths are found, the labels may change, reflecting better paths. A label may be either tentative or permanent. Initially, all labels are tentative. When it is discovered that a label represents the shortest possible path from the source to that node, it is made permanent and never changed thereafter.

To illustrate how the labeling algorithm works, look at the weighted, undirected graph of Fig. 5-10(a), where the weights represent, for example, distance. We want to find the shortest path from *A* to *D*. We start out by marking node *A* as permanent, indicated by a filled in circle. Then we examine, in turn, each of the nodes adjacent to *A* (the working node), relabeling each one with the distance to *A*. Whenever a node is relabeled, we also label it with the node from which the probe was made, so we can reconstruct the final path later. Having examined each of the nodes adjacent to *A*, we examine all the tentatively labeled nodes in the whole graph, and make the one with the smallest label permanent, as shown in Fig. 5-10(b). This one becomes the new working node.

We now start at *B*, and examine all nodes adjacent to it. If the sum of the label on *B* and the distance from *B* to the node being considered is less than the label on that node, we have a shorter path, so the node is relabeled.

After all the nodes adjacent to the working node have been inspected, and the tentative labels changed if possible, the entire graph is searched for the tentatively labeled node with the smallest value. This node is made permanent, and becomes the working node for the next round. Figure 5-10 shows the first five steps of the algorithm.

To see why the algorithm works, look at Fig. 5-10(c). At that point we have just made *E* permanent. Suppose that there were a shorter path than *ABE*, say *AXYZE*. There are two possibilities: either node *Z* has already been made permanent, or it has not been. If it has, then *E* has already been probed (on the round following the one when *Z* was made permanent), so the *AXYZE* path has not escaped our attention.

Now consider the case where *Z* is still tentatively labeled. Either the label at *Z* is greater than or equal to that at *E*, in which case *AXYZE* cannot be a shorter path than *ABE*, or it is less than that of *E*, in which case *Z* and not *E* will become permanent first, allowing *E* to be probed from *Z*.

This algorithm is given in Pascal in Fig. 5-11. The only difference between the program and the algorithm described above is that in Fig. 5-11, we compute the shortest path starting at the terminal node, *t*, rather than at the source node, *s*. Since the shortest path from *t* to *s* in an undirected graph is the same as the shortest path from *s* to *t*, it does not matter at which end we begin (unless there are several shortest paths, in which case reversing the search might discover a different one). The reason for searching backwards is that each node is labeled with its predecessor rather than its successor. When copying the final path into the output variable, *path*, the path is thus reversed. By reversing the search, the two effects cancel, and the answer is produced in the correct order.

5.2.2. Multipath Routing

So far we have tacitly assumed that there is a single "best" path between any pair of nodes and that all traffic between them should use it. In many networks, there are several paths between pairs of nodes that are almost equally good. Better performance can frequently be obtained by splitting the traffic over several paths, to reduce the load on each of the communication lines. The technique of using multiple routes between a single pair of nodes is called **multipath routing** or sometimes **bifurcated routing**.

Multipath routing is applicable both to datagram subnets and virtual circuit subnets. For datagram subnets, when a packet arrives at an IMP for forwarding, a

```
{Find the shortest path from the source to the sink of a given graph.}
const n = ... ;                         {number of nodes}
      infinity = ... ;                  {a number larger than any possible path length}

type node = 0 .. n;
     nodelist = array [1 .. n] of node;
     matrix = array [1 .. n, 1 .. n] of integer;

procedure ShortestPath (a: matrix; s,t: node;   var path: nodelist);
{Find the shortest path from s to t in the matrix a, and return it in path.}

type lab = (perm, tent);               {is label tentative or permanent?}
     NodeLabel = record predecessor: node; length: integer; labl: lab end;
     GraphState = array[1 .. n] of NodeLabel;

var state: GraphState;   i,k: node;   min: integer;
begin                                  {initialize}
  for i := 1 to n do
    with state [i] do
      begin predecessor := 0; length := infinity; labl := tent end;
  state [t].length := 0;   state [t].labl := perm;
  k := t;                              {k is the initial working node}

  repeat   {is there a better path from k?}
    for i := 1 to n do
      if (a [k,i] <> 0) and (state [i].labl = tent) then      {i is adjacent & tent.}
        if state [k].length + a [k,i] < state [i].length then
          begin
            state [i].predecessor := k;
            state [i].length := state [k].length + a [k,i]
          end;

    {Find the tentatively labeled node with the smallest label.}
    min := infinity;    k := 0;
    for i := 1 to n do
      if (state [i].labl = tent) and (state [i].length < min) then
        begin
          min := state [i].length;
          k := i                       {unless superseded, k will be next working node}
        end;
    state [k].labl := perm

  until k = s;                         {repeat until we reach the source}

  {Copy the path into the output array.}
  k := s;   i := 0;
  repeat
    i := i + 1;
    path [i] := k;
    k := state [k].predecessor;
  until k = 0
end;  {ShortestPath}
```

Fig. 5-11. A procedure to compute the shortest path through a graph.

choice is made among the various alternatives for that packet, independent of the choices made for other packets to that same destination in the past. For virtual circuit subnets, whenever a virtual circuit is set up, a route is chosen, but different virtual circuits (on behalf of different users) are routed independently.

Multipath routing can be implemented as follows. Each IMP maintains a table with one row for each possible destination IMP. A row gives the best, second best, third best, etc. outgoing line for that destination, together with a relative weight. Before forwarding a packet, an IMP generates a random number and then chooses among the alternatives, using the weights as probabilities. The tables are worked out manually by the network operators, loaded into the IMPs before the network is brought up, and not changed thereafter.

As an example, consider the subnet of Fig. 5-12(a). IMP J's routing table is given in Fig. 5-12(b). If J receives a packet whose destination is A, it uses the row labeled A. Here three choices are presented. The line to A is the first choice, followed by the lines to I and H respectively. To decide, J generates a random number between 0.00 and 0.99. If the number is below 0.63, line A is used; if the number is between 0.63 and 0.83, I is used; otherwise, H is used. The three weights are therefore the respective probabilities that A, I, or H will be used.

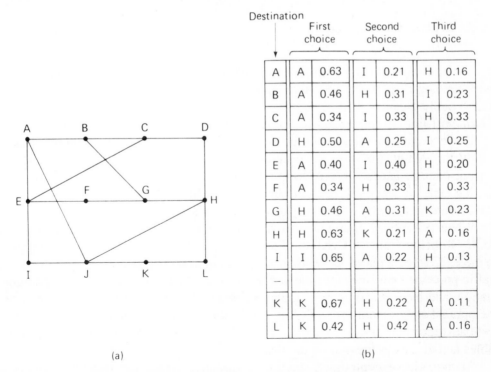

Destination	First choice		Second choice		Third choice	
A	A	0.63	I	0.21	H	0.16
B	A	0.46	H	0.31	I	0.23
C	A	0.34	I	0.33	H	0.33
D	H	0.50	A	0.25	I	0.25
E	A	0.40	I	0.40	H	0.20
F	A	0.34	H	0.33	I	0.33
G	H	0.46	A	0.31	K	0.23
H	H	0.63	K	0.21	A	0.16
I	I	0.65	A	0.22	H	0.13
–						
K	K	0.67	H	0.22	A	0.11
L	K	0.42	H	0.42	A	0.16

(a)   (b)

Fig. 5-12. (a) An example subnet. (b) Routing table for node J.

An advantage of multipath routing over shortest path routing is the possibility of sending different classes of traffic over different paths. For example, a connection between a terminal and a remote computer that consists of short packets that must be delivered quickly could be routed via terrestrial lines, whereas a long file transfer requiring high bandwidth could go via a satellite link. Not only does this method give the file transfer the high bandwidth it needs, but it also prevents short terminal packets from being delayed behind a queue of long file transfer packets.

Although multipath routing is widely used to improve performance, it can also be used to improve the reliability of the subnet. In particular, if the routing tables contain n disjoint routes between each pair of IMPs, then the subnet can withstand the loss of $n - 1$ lines without being broken into two parts.

One simple way to make sure all the alternative routes are disjoint is to first compute the shortest path between the source and destination. Then remove from the graph all the nodes and arcs used on the shortest path and compute the shortest path through the new graph. This algorithm insures that IMP or line failures on the first path will not also bring the second one down. By removing the second path from the graph as well, we can compute a third path that is completely independent of the first two. Even (1975) has devised a more sophisticated algorithm for finding disjoint paths in a graph.

5.2.3. Centralized Routing

The routing algorithms discussed above all require information about the network topology and traffic to make good decisions. If the topology is static and the traffic rarely changes, it is straightforward to build the routing tables once and for all time off-line and download them into the IMPs.

However, if IMPs and lines go down and come back up, or the traffic varies wildly throughout the day, some mechanism is needed to adapt the tables to the current circumstances. In this section we will discuss techniques for building the routing tables in a central location. In the succeeding ones we will see how this job can be done in a totally or partially decentralized fashion.

When centralized routing is used, somewhere within the network there is an **RCC (Routing Control Center)**. Periodically, each IMP sends status information to the RCC (e.g., a list of its neighbors that are up, current queue lengths, amount of traffic processed per line since the last report, etc.). The RCC collects all this information, and then, based upon its global knowledge of the entire network, computes the optimal routes from every IMP to every other IMP, for example using the shortest path algorithm discussed above. From this information it can build new routing tables and distribute them to all the IMPs.

At first glance centralized routing is attractive: since the RCC has complete information, it can make perfect decisions. Another advantage is that it relieves the IMPs of the burden of the routing computation.

Unfortunately, centralized routing also has some serious, if not fatal, drawbacks. For one thing, if the subnet is to adapt to changing traffic, the routing calculation will have to be performed fairly often. For a large network, the calculation will take many seconds, even on a substantial CPU. If the purpose of running the algorithm is to adapt to changes in the topology rather than changes in the traffic, however, running it every minute or so may be adequate, depending on how stable the topology is.

A more serious problem is the vulnerability of the RCC. If it goes down or becomes isolated by line failures, the subnet is suddenly in trouble. One solution is to have a second machine available as a backup, but this amounts to wasting a large computer. An arbitration method is also needed to make sure that the primary and backup RCCs do not get into a fight over who is the boss.

Yet another problem with centralized routing concerns distributing the routing tables to the IMPs. The IMPs that are close to the RCC will get their new tables first and will switch over to the new routes before the distant IMPs have received their tables. Inconsistencies may arise here, so packets may be delayed. Among the packets delayed will be the new routing tables for the distant IMPs, so the problem feeds upon itself.

If the RCC computes the optimal route for each pair of IMPs and no alternates, the loss of even a single line or IMP will probably cut some IMPs off from the RCC, with disastrous consequences. If the RCC does use alternate routing, the argument in favor of having an RCC in the first place, namely that it can find the optimal routes, is weakened.

A final problem with centralized routing is the heavy concentration of routing traffic on the lines leading into the RCC. Figure 5-13 illustrates this problem. The figure was drawn by tracing the shortest path from each machine to the RCC, and placing an arrow on each line. A line with n arrows means that n IMPs are reporting to the RCC via it. The heavy load and consequent vulnerability of lines near the RCC is apparent.

As an example of how centralized routing works in practice, consider TYM-NET, a commercial packet-switching network with over 1000 nodes that has been running since 1971. TYMNET is primarily used to allow terminals to log into remote computers, so the subnet offers connection-oriented service and uses virtual circuits to implement this service. The TYMNET IMPs periodically send the RCC information about their status: lines that are up or down, queue lengths, and other statistics. The RCC maintains tables keeping track of all this incoming information.

When a new user logs in and specifies which host he wants to connect to, a packet is sent to the RCC informing it of the login. The RCC then computes the best route, using all the information at its disposal. It then sends a **needle packet** back to the IMP to which the user is connected. The needle packet contains the route chosen by the RCC. This packet then threads its way through the subnet, making entries in the IMPs tables as it goes, and thus setting up the virtual circuit. When the user logs out, a similar process is used to release the virtual circuit.

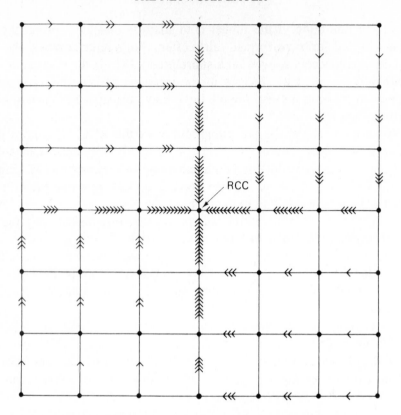

Fig. 5-13. Paths followed from the outgoing IMPs to the RCC.

5.2.4. Isolated Routing

All the problems with centralized routing algorithms suggest that decentralized algorithms might have something to offer. In the simplest decentralized routing algorithms, the IMPs make routing decisions based only upon information they themselves have gleaned; they do not exchange routing information per se with other IMPs. Nevertheless, they try to adapt to changes in topology and traffic. These are usually called **isolated adaptive** routing algorithms.

One simple isolated adaptive algorithm is Baran's (1964) **hot potato** algorithm. When a packet comes in, the IMP tries to get rid of it as fast as it can, by putting it on the shortest output queue. In other words, when a packet arrives, the IMP counts the number of packets queued up for transmission on each of the output lines. It then attaches the new packet to the end of the shortest output queue, without regard to where that line leads. In Fig. 5-14, the inside of IMP J from Fig. 5-12 is shown at a certain instant of time. There are four output queues, corresponding to the four output lines. Packets are queued up on each line waiting for transmission. In this example, queue I is the shortest, with only one packet queued up. The hot potato algorithm would therefore put the newly arrived packet on this queue.

A variation of this idea is to combine static routing with the hot potato algorithm. When a packet arrives, the routing algorithm takes into account both the static weights of the lines and the queue lengths. One possibility is to use the best static choice, unless its queue exceeds a certain threshold. Another possibility is to use the shortest queue, unless its static weight is too low. Yet another way is to rank the lines in terms of their static weights, and again in terms of their queue lengths, taking the line for which the sum of the two ranks is lowest. Whatever algorithm is chosen should have the property that under light load the line with the highest static weight is usually chosen, but as the queue for this line builds up, some of the traffic is diverted to less busy lines.

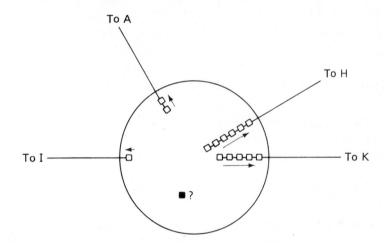

Fig. 5-14. Queueing within the IMP.

Another isolated routing algorithm, also due to Baran, is **backward learning**. In the 1950s and 1960s, when newspaper reporters from Western countries were rarely allowed to visit China, it was common to see news stories beginning with "According to travelers recently arriving in Hong Kong from China ...." The idea was that instead of the reporter going to place X, she could talk to people who just came from X and ask them what was going on there. The backward learning algorithm does the same thing.

One way to implement backward learning is to include the identity of the source IMP in each packet, together with a counter that is incremented on each hop. If an IMP sees a packet arriving on line k from IMP H with hop count 4, it knows that H cannot be more than four hops away via line k. If its current best route to H is estimated at more than four hops, it marks line k as the choice for traffic to H and records the estimated distance as four hops. After a while, every IMP will discover the shortest path to every other IMP.

Alas, there is a fly in the ointment. Since IMPs only record changes for the better, if a line goes down or becomes overloaded, there is no mechanism for recording the fact. Consequently, IMPs must periodically forget everything they have learned and start all over again. During the new learning period, the routing will be far from optimal. If the tables are purged frequently, the IMPs route a substantial number of packets using routes of unknown quality; if the tables are purged rarely, the adaptation process is slow.

Rudin (1976) has described an interesting hybrid between centralized routing and isolated routing, which he calls **delta routing**. In this algorithm, each IMP measures the "cost" of each line (i.e., some function of the delay, queue length, utilization, bandwidth, etc.) and periodically sends a packet to the RCC giving it these values.

Using the information sent to it by the IMPs, the RCC computes the k best paths from IMP i to IMP j, for all i and all j, where only paths that differ in their initial line are considered. Let C_{ij}^1 be the total cost of the best i-j path, C_{ij}^2 be the total cost of the next best path, etc. If $C_{ij}^n - C_{ij}^1 < \delta$, path n is declared to be equivalent to path 1, since their costs differ by so little. When the routing computation is finished, the RCC sends each IMP a list of all the equivalent paths for each of its possible destinations. (Actually, only the initial lines are needed, not the full paths.)

To do actual routing, the IMP is permitted to choose any of the equivalent paths. It may decide among them at random or use the current measured value of the line costs, that is, choose the path from the allowed set whose current initial line is cheapest. By adjusting k and δ, the network operators can transfer authority between the RCC and the IMPs. As $\delta \to 0$, all other paths are deemed inferior to the best path, and the RCC makes all the decisions. However, as $\delta \to \infty$, all the paths considered will be deemed equivalent, and the routing decisions are made in the IMPs based on local information only. Rudin's simulations have shown that δ can be chosen to provide better performance than either pure centralized routing or pure isolated routing.

5.2.5. Flooding

An extreme form of isolated routing is **flooding**, in which every incoming packet is sent out on every outgoing line except the one it arrived on. Flooding obviously generates vast numbers of duplicate packets, in fact, an infinite number unless some measures are taken to damp the process. One such measure is to have a hop counter contained in the header of each packet, which is decremented at each hop, with the packet being discarded when the counter reaches zero. Ideally, the hop counter should be initialized to the length of the path from source to destination. If the sender does not know how long the path is, it can initialize the counter to the worst-case, namely, the full diameter of the subnet.

An alternative technique for damming the flood is to have the source IMP put a sequence number in each packet it receives from its hosts. Each IMP then needs a list per source IMP telling which sequence numbers originating at that source have already been seen. To prevent the list from growing without bound, each list should be augmented by a counter, k, meaning that all sequence numbers through k have been seen. When a packet comes in, it is easy to check if the packet is a duplicate; if so, it is discarded.

Flooding is not practical in most applications, but it does have some uses. For example, in military applications, where large numbers of IMPs may be blown to bits at any instant, the tremendous robustness of flooding is highly desirable. In distributed data base applications, it is sometimes necessary to update all the data bases concurrently, in which case flooding can be useful. A third possible use of flooding is as a metric against which other routing algorithms can be compared. Flooding always chooses the shortest path, because it chooses every possible path in parallel. Consequently, no other algorithm can produce a shorter delay (if we ignore the overhead generated by the flooding process itself).

A variation of flooding that is slightly more practical is **selective flooding**. In this algorithm the IMPs do not send every incoming packet out on every line, only on those lines that are going approximately in the right direction. There is usually little point in sending a westbound packet on an eastbound line unless the topology is extremely peculiar.

Yet another nonadaptive algorithm is **random walk**. The IMP simply picks a line at random and forwards the packet on it. Here, also, the IMP can make some attempt to get the packet heading in roughly the right direction. If the subnet is richly interconnected, this algorithm has the property of making excellent use of alternative routes. It is also highly robust.

5.2.6. Distributed Routing

In this class of routing algorithms, originally used in the ARPANET, each IMP periodically exchanges explicit routing information with each of its neighbors. Typically, each IMP maintains a routing table indexed by, and containing one entry for, each other IMP in the subnet. This entry contains two parts: the preferred outgoing line to use for that destination, and some estimate of the time or distance to that destination. The metric used might be number of hops, estimated time delay in milliseconds, estimated total number of packets queued along the path, excess bandwidth, or something similar.

The IMP is assumed to know the "distance" to each of its neighbors. If the metric is hops, the distance is just one hop. If the metric is queue length, the IMP simply examines each queue. If the metric is delay, the IMP can measure it directly with special "echo" packets that the receiver just timestamps and sends back as fast as it can.

As an example, assume that delay is used as a metric and that the IMP knows the delay to each of its neighbors. Once every T msec each IMP sends to each neighbor a list of its estimated delays to each destination. It also receives a similar list from each neighbor. Imagine that one of these tables has just come in from neighbor X, with X_i being X's estimate of how long it takes to get to IMP i. If the IMP knows that the delay to X is m msec, it also knows that it can reach IMP i via X in $X_i + m$ msec via X. By performing this calculation for each neighbor, an IMP can find out which estimate seems the best, and use that estimate and the corresponding line in its new routing table. Note that the old routing table is not used in the calculation.

This updating process is illustrated in Fig. 5-15. Part (a) shows a subnet. The first four columns of part (b) show the delay vectors received from the neighbors of IMP J. A claims to have a 12-msec delay to B, a 25-msec delay to C, a 40-msec delay to D, etc. Suppose that J has measured or estimated its delay to its neighbors, A, I, H, and K as 8, 10, 12, and 6 msec, respectively.

Consider how J computes its new route to IMP G. It knows that it can get to A in 8 msec, and A claims to be able to get to G in 18 msec, so J knows it can count on a delay of 26 msec to G if it forwards packets bound for G to A. Similarly, it computes the delay to G via I, H, and K as 41 $(31 + 10)$, 18 $(6 + 12)$, and 37 $(31 + 6)$ msec respectively. The best of these values is 18, so it makes an entry in its routing table that the delay to G is 18 msec, and that the route to use is via H. The same calculation is performed for all the other destinations, with the new routing table shown in the last column of the figure.

5.2.7. Optimal Routing

Even without knowing the details of the subnet topology and traffic it is possible to make some general statements about optimal routes. One such statement is known as the **optimality principle**. It states that if IMP J is on the optimal path from IMP I to IMP K, then the optimal path from J to K also falls along the same route. To see this, call the part of the route from I to J r_1 and the rest of the route r_2. If a route better than r_2 existed from J to K, it could be concatenated with r_1 to improve the route from I to K, contradicting our statement that $r_1 r_2$ is optimal.

As a direct consequence of the optimality principle, we can see that the set of optimal routes from all sources to a given destination form a tree rooted at the destination. Such a tree is called a **sink tree** and is illustrated in Fig. 5-16. Since the sink tree is indeed a tree, it does not contain any loops, so each packet will be delivered within a finite and bounded number of hops.

In general, if traffic from IMP X passes through IMP Y as it flows along the sink tree to the destination, X is said to be **upstream** from Y and Y is said to be **downstream** from X. To illustrate these notions, consider the subnet of Fig. 5-17(a), with the sink tree for destination H shown in Fig. 5-17(b). (Throughout this example we will use shortest path routing, with ties broken alphabetically; for example, B routes to H via $BCEH$ rather than $BDGH$ because $BCEH < BDGH$.)

With the sink tree in mind, consider what happens when a line goes down, blocking the path to a certain destination. An IMP cannot simply divert its traffic to

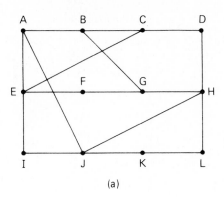

(a)

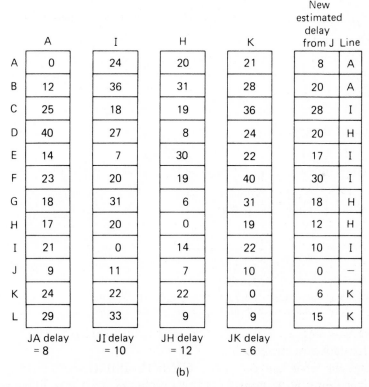

	A	I	H	K	New estimated delay from J	Line
A	0	24	20	21	8	A
B	12	36	31	28	20	A
C	25	18	19	36	28	I
D	40	27	8	24	20	H
E	14	7	30	22	17	I
F	23	20	19	40	30	I
G	18	31	6	31	18	H
H	17	20	0	19	12	H
I	21	0	14	22	10	I
J	9	11	7	10	0	–
K	24	22	22	0	6	K
L	29	33	9	9	15	K
	JA delay = 8	JI delay = 10	JH delay = 12	JK delay = 6		

(b)

Fig. 5-15. (a) A subnet. (b) Input from A, I, H, K, and the new routing table J.

another IMP that is upstream from it with respect to that destination. It must seek out a neighbor that is attached to another (independent) branch of the sink tree. In Chu's (1978) algorithm, each IMP maintains a routing table with one row per destination, as in Fig. 5-17(c). Each column gives the number of hops to the destination via a specific output line. For IMP G, the output lines are D, F, and H. The best route is indicated by a circle. Entries that refer to upstream IMPs are left blank.

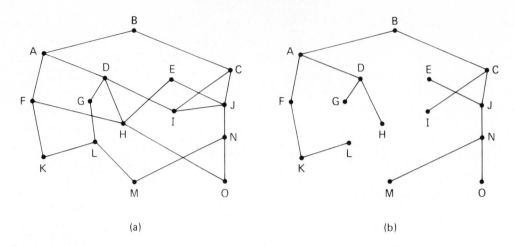

Fig. 5-16. (a) A subnet. (b) The sink tree for IMP *B*, using number of hops as metric.

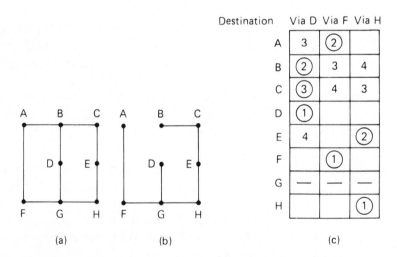

Fig. 5-17. (a) A subnet. (b) Sink tree for *H*. (c) Routing table used by *G*.

Note that the sink tree used to determine who is upstream and who is downstream is different for each row of the table.

Now let us see what happens if line *GH* fails. IMP *G* starts out by marking all the entries in column *H* as unusable. It then checks each row for which the best route has been wiped out to see if an alternative route is available. For destination *E*, for example, an alternative route is available via *D*. (Remember that in this example *D* routes to *E* via *B* because *DBCE* < *DGHE*.)

For destination *H* the situation is worse because both neighbors are upstream from *G*. Consequently, *G* sends each of them a control packet saying "I cannot reach *H* any more. Please help me." Upon receiving the packet each neighbor checks to see if it has an alternative (previously suboptimal) route. *D* has such an alternative, and sends a reply back announcing it. F, however, has no alternative, because its only other neighbor, A, is upstream from it, so it acts in much the same way that it would have if line FG had gone down, namely, by asking A for help. Control packets continue propagating upstream until someone finds an alternate route. When G finally receives replies from all its upstream neighbors, it can make new entries in its routing table and choose the best. The only condition under which the algorithm fails is when none of the IMPs upstream from the failed link can make contact with any IMP on another branch of the sink tree. This condition occurs only when the subnet has been broken into two separate components.

5.2.8. Flow-Based Routing

To some extent, all the algorithms discussed so far are largely empirical, rather than being derived from some fundamental theory. However, under certain limited conditions it is possible to find routing algorithms that are provably optimal. In this section we will give a brief introduction to this subject. Bertsekas and Gallager (1987) give a more comprehensive treatment.

In some networks, the mean data flow between each pair of nodes is relatively stable and predictable. For example, in a corporate network for a retail store chain, each store might send orders, sales reports, inventory updates, and other well-defined types of messages to known sites in a pre-defined pattern, so that the total volume of traffic varied little from day to day. Under conditions in which the average traffic from i to j is known in advance and, to a reasonable approximation, constant in time, it is possible to analyze the flows mathematically to optimize the routing.

The basic idea behind the analysis is that for a given line, if the capacity and average flow are known, it is possible to compute the mean packet delay on that line from queueing theory. From the mean delays on all the lines, it is straightforward to calculate a flow-weighted average to get the mean packet delay for the whole network. The routing problem then reduces to finding the routing algorithm that produces the minimum average delay for the network.

To use this technique, certain information must be known in advance. First the network topology must be known. Second, the traffic matrix, F_{ij}, must be given. Third, the line capacity matrix, C_{ij}, specifying the capacity of each line in bps must be available. Finally, a (possibly tentative) routing algorithm must be chosen.

As an example of this method, consider the full-duplex network of Fig. 5-18(a). The weights on the arcs give the capacities, C_{ij}, in each direction in kbps. The matrix of Fig. 5-18(b) has an entry for each source-destination pair. The entry for source i to destination j shows the route to be used for i - j traffic, and also the number of packets/sec to be sent from i to j. For example, 3 packets/sec go from B to D, and they use route BFD. Notice that some routing algorithm has already been applied to derive the routes shown in the matrix.

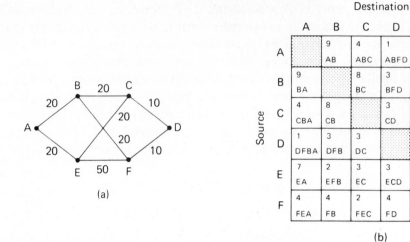

Fig. 5-18. (a) A network with line capacities shown in kbps. (b) The traffic in packets/sec and the routing matrix.

Given this information, it is straightforward to calculate the total in line i λ_i. For example, the B-D traffic contributes 3 packets/sec to the BF line and also 3 packets/sec to the FD line. Similarly, the A-D traffic contributes 1 packet/sec to each of three lines. The total traffic in each eastbound line is shown in the λ_i column of Fig. 5-19. In this example, all the traffic is symmetric, that is the XY traffic is identical to the YX traffic, for all X and Y. The figure also shows the mean number of packets/sec on each line, μC_{ij} assuming a mean packet size of $\mu = 800$ bits.

i	Line	λ_i (pkts/sec)	C_i (kbps)	μC_i (pkts/sec)	T_i (ms)
1	AB	14	20	25	91
2	BC	12	20	25	77
3	CD	6	10	12.5	154
4	AE	11	20	25	71
5	EF	13	50	62.5	20
6	FD	8	10	12.5	222
7	BF	10	20	25	67
8	EC	8	20	25	59

Fig. 5-19. Analysis of the network of Fig. 5-18 using a mean packet size of 800 bits. The reverse traffic (BA, CB, etc.) is the same as the forward traffic.

The last column of Fig. 5-19 gives the mean delay for each line derived from the queueing theory formula

$$T = \frac{1}{\mu C - \lambda}$$

where μ is the mean packet size in bits, C is the capacity in bps, and λ is the mean flow in packets/sec. For example, with a capacity $\mu C = 25$ packets/sec and an actual flow $\lambda = 14$ packets/sec, the mean delay is 91 msec. Note that with $\lambda = 0$, the mean delay is still 40 msec, corresponding to the fact that the capacity is 25 packets/sec. In other words, the "delay" includes both queueing time and service time.

To compute the mean delay time for the entire network, we take the weighted sum of each of the eight links, with the weight being the fraction of the total traffic using that link. In this example, the mean turns out to be 114 msec.

To evaluate a different routing algorithm, we can repeat the entire process, only with different flows to get a new average delay. If we restrict ourselves to only single-path routing algorithms, there are only a finite number of ways to route packets from each source to each destination. It is simple enough to write a program to simply try them all and find out which one has the smallest mean delay. This one is then the best routing algorithm.

If we allow multipath routing, the situation is more complicated because there are then an infinite number of ways to route traffic from A to D, for example, a fraction α of the traffic via $ABCD$ and the rest via $AEFD$, where α can take on any real value between 0 and 1. However, in this case we can write down the flow in each line as a function of the load-splitting parameter α (and similar parameters for other flows). This approach yields an expression for the mean delay as a function of all the parameters. Various techniques exist for minimizing this expression to find the optimum value for α and the other parameters, which effectively determines the routing algorithm.

5.2.9. Hierarchical Routing

As networks grow in size, the IMP routing tables grow proportionally. Not only is IMP memory consumed by ever increasing tables, but more CPU time is needed to scan them and more bandwidth is needed to send status reports about them. At a certain point the network may grow to the point where it is no longer feasible for every IMP to have an entry for every other IMP, so the routing will have to be done hierarchically, as it is in the telephone network.

When hierarchical routing is used, the IMPs are divided into **regions**, with each IMP knowing all the details about how to route packets to destinations within its own region, but knowing nothing about the internal structure of other regions. When different networks are connected together, it is natural to regard each one as a separate region in order to free the IMPs in one network from having to know the topological structure of the other ones.

For huge networks, a two-level hierarchy may be insufficient; it may be necessary to group the regions into clusters, the clusters into zones, the zones into groups, and so on, until we run out of names for aggregations. As an example of a multilevel hierarchy, consider how a packet might be routed from Berkeley, California to Malindi, Kenya. The Berkeley IMP would know the detailed topology within California, but would send all out-of-state traffic to the Los Angeles IMP. The Los Angeles IMP would be able to route traffic to other domestic IMPs, but would send foreign traffic to New York. The New York IMP would be programmed to direct all traffic to the IMP in the destination country responsible for handling foreign traffic, say in Nairobi. Finally, the packet would work its way down the tree in Kenya until it got to Malindi.

Figure 5-20 gives a quantitative example of routing in a two-level hierarchy with five regions. The full routing table for IMP $1A$ has 17 entries, as shown in Fig. 5-20(b). When routing is done hierarchically, as in Fig. 5-20(c), there are entries for all the local IMPs as before, but all other regions have been condensed into a single IMP, so all traffic for region 2 goes via the $1B-2A$ line, but the rest of the remote traffic goes via the $1C-3B$ line. Hierarchical routing has reduced the table from 17 to 7 entries. As the ratio of the number of regions to the number of IMPs within a region grows, the savings in table space grow proportionally.

Unfortunately, these gains in space are not free. There is a penalty to be paid, and this penalty is in the form of increased path length. For example, the best route from $1A$ to $5C$ is via region 2, but with hierarchical routing all traffic to region 5 goes via region 3, because that is a better choice for most destinations in region 5.

When a single network becomes very large, an interesting question is how many levels should the hierarchy have? For example, consider a subnet with 720 IMPs. If there is no hierarchy, each IMP needs 720 routing table entries. If the subnet is partitioned into 24 regions of 30 IMPs each, each IMP needs 30 local entries plus 23 remote entries for a total of 53 entries. If a three-level hierarchy is chosen, with eight clusters, each containing 9 regions of 10 IMPs, each IMP needs 10 entries for local IMPs, 8 entries for routing to other regions within its own cluster, and seven entries for distant clusters, for a total of 25 entries. Kamoun and Kleinrock (1979) have discovered that the optimal number of levels for an N IMP subnet is $\ln N$, requiring a total of $e \ln N$ entries per IMP. They have also discovered that the increase in effective mean path length caused by hierarchical routing is sufficiently small that it is not objectionable.

5.2.10. Broadcast Routing

For some applications, hosts need to send messages to all other hosts. Typical examples might be for scheduling: a host wants to find out which other hosts are willing and able to perform a certain task for it, or distributed data base updates. In

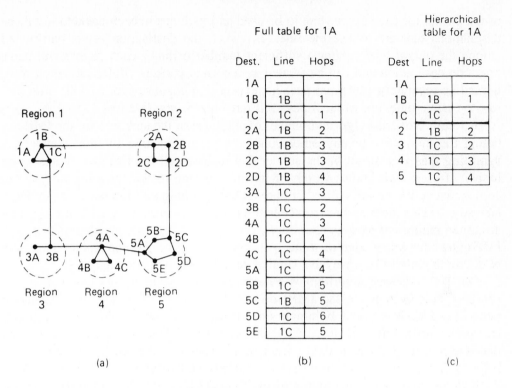

	Full table for 1A			Hierarchical table for 1A	
Dest.	Line	Hops	Dest	Line	Hops
1A	—	—	1A	—	—
1B	1B	1	1B	1B	1
1C	1C	1	1C	1C	1
2A	1B	2	2	1B	2
2B	1B	3	3	1C	2
2C	1B	3	4	1C	3
2D	1B	4	5	1C	4
3A	1C	3			
3B	1C	2			
4A	1C	3			
4B	1C	4			
4C	1C	4			
5A	1C	4			
5B	1C	5			
5C	1B	5			
5D	1C	6			
5E	1C	5			

(a)   (b)   (c)

Fig. 5-20. Hierarchical routing.

some networks the IMPs may also need such a facility, for example to distribute routing table updates. Sending a packet to all destinations simultaneously is called **broadcasting**, and various methods have been proposed for implementing it. Our treatment is based on the work of Dalal and Metcalfe (1978).

One broadcasting method that requires no special features from the subnet is for the source to simply send a distinct packet to each destination. Not only is the method wasteful of bandwidth but it also requires the source to have a complete list of all destinations. In practice this may be the only possibility, but it is the least desirable of the methods.

Flooding is another obvious candidate. Although flooding is ill-suited for ordinary point-to-point communication, for broadcasting it might rate serious consideration, especially if none of the methods described below are applicable. The problem with flooding as a broadcast technique is the same problem it has as a point-to-point routing algorithm: it generates too many packets and consumes too much bandwidth.

A third algorithm is **multidestination routing**. If this method is used, each packet contains either a list of destinations or a bit map indicating the desired destinations. When a packet arrives at an IMP, the IMP checks all the destinations to determine the set of output lines that will be needed. (An output line is needed if it is the best route to at least one of the destinations.) The IMP generates a new copy of the packet for each output line to be used and includes in each packet only those destinations that are to use the line. In effect, the destination set is partitioned among the output lines. After a sufficient number of hops, each packet will carry only one destination and can be treated as a normal packet. Multidestination routing is like separately addressed packets, except that when several packets must follow the same route, one of them pays full fare and the rest ride free.

A fourth broadcast algorithm makes explicit use of the sink tree for the IMP initiating the broadcast, or any other convenient spanning tree for that matter. (A **spanning tree** is a subset of the subnet that includes all the IMPs but contains no loops.) If each IMP knows which of its lines belong to the spanning tree, it can copy an incoming broadcast packet onto all the spanning tree lines except the one it arrived on. This method makes excellent use of bandwidth, generating the absolute minimum number of packets necessary to do the job. The only problem is that each IMP must have knowledge of some spanning tree for it to be applicable, and many of the routing algorithms we have studied do not have such knowledge.

Our last broadcast algorithm is an attempt to approximate the behavior of the previous one, even when the IMPs do not know anything at all about spanning trees. The idea is remarkably simple once it has been pointed out. When a broadcast packet arrives at an IMP, the IMP checks to see if the packet arrived on the line that is normally used for sending packets *to* the source of the broadcast. If so, there is an excellent chance that the broadcast packet itself followed the best route from the IMP and is therefore the first copy to arrive at the IMP. This being the case, the IMP forwards copies of it onto all lines except the one it arrived on. If, however, the broadcast packet arrived on a line other than the preferred one for reaching the source, the packet is discarded as a likely duplicate.

An example of the algorithm, called **reverse path forwarding**, is shown in Fig. 5-21. Part (a) shows a subnet, part (b) shows a sink tree for IMP I of that subnet, and part (c) shows how the reverse path algorithm works. On the first hop, I sends packets to F, H, J, and N, as indicated by the second row of the tree. Each of these packets arrives on the preferred path to I (assuming that the preferred path falls along the sink tree) and is so indicated by a circle around the letter. On the second hop, eight packets are generated, two by each of the IMPs that received a packet on the first hop. As it turns out, all eight of these arrive at previously unvisited IMPs, and all but one arrive along the preferred line. Of the nine packets generated on the third hop, only two arrive on the preferred path (at C and L), and so only these generate further packets. After five hops and 24 packets, the broadcasting terminates, compared with four hops and 14 packets had the sink tree been followed exactly.

The principal advantage of reverse path forwarding is that it is both reasonably efficient and easy to implement. It does not require IMPs to know about spanning trees, nor does it have the overhead of a destination list or bit map in each broadcast packet as does multidestination addressing. Nor does it require any special mechanism to stop the process, as flooding does (either a hop counter in each

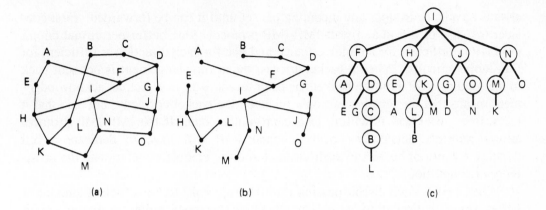

Fig. 5-21. Reverse path forwarding.

packet and a priori knowledge of the subnet diameter, or a list of packets already seen per source).

5.3. CONGESTION CONTROL ALGORITHMS

In this section we will examine five strategies for controlling congestion. These strategies involve allocating resources in advance, allowing packets to be discarded when they cannot be processed, restricting the number of packets in the subnet, using flow control to avoid congestion, and choking off input when the subnet is overloaded.

5.3.1. Preallocation of Buffers

If virtual circuits are used inside the subnet, it is possible to solve the congestion problem altogether, as follows. When a virtual circuit is set up, the call request packet wends its way through the subnet, making table entries as it goes. When it has arrived at the destination, the route to be followed by all subsequent data traffic has been determined and entries made in the routing tables of all the intermediate IMPs.

Normally, the call request packet does not reserve any buffer space in the intermediate IMPs, just table slots. However, a simple modification to the setup algorithm could have each call request packet reserve one or more data buffers as well. If a call request packet arrives at an IMP and all the buffers are already reserved, either another route must be found or a "busy signal" must be returned to the caller. Even if buffers are not reserved, some aspiring virtual circuits may have to be rerouted or rejected for lack of table space, so reserving buffers does not add any new problems that were not already there.

By permanently allocating buffers to each virtual circuit in each IMP, there will always be a place to store any incoming packet until it can be forwarded. First consider the case of a stop-and-wait IMP-IMP protocol. One buffer per virtual circuit per IMP is sufficient for simplex circuits, and one for each direction is sufficient for full-duplex circuits. When a packet arrives, the acknowledgement is not sent back to the sending IMP until the packet has been forwarded. In effect, an acknowledgement means that the receiver not only received the packet correctly, but also that it has a free buffer and is willing to accept another one. If the IMP-IMP protocol allows multiple outstanding packets, each IMP will have to dedicate a full window's worth of buffers to each virtual circuit to completely eliminate the possibility of congestion.

When each virtual circuit passing through each IMP has a sufficient amount of buffer space dedicated to it, packet switching becomes quite similar to circuit switching. In both cases an involved setup procedure is required. In both cases substantial resources are permanently allocated to specific connections, whether or not there is any traffic. In both cases congestion is impossible because all the resources needed to process the traffic have already been reserved. And in both cases there is a potentially inefficient use of resources, because resources not being used by the connection to which they are allocated are nevertheless unavailable to anyone else.

Because dedicating a complete set of buffers to an idle virtual circuit is expensive, some subnets may use it only where low delay and high bandwidth are essential, for example on virtual circuits carrying digitized speech. For virtual circuits where low delay is not absolutely essential all the time, a reasonable strategy is to associate a timer with each buffer. If the buffer lays idle for too long, it is released, to be reacquired when the next packet arrives. Of course, acquiring a buffer might take a while, so packets will have to be forwarded without dedicated buffers until the chain of buffers can be set up again.

5.3.2. Packet Discarding

Our second congestion control mechanism is just the opposite of the first one. Instead of reserving all the buffers in advance, nothing is reserved in advance. If a packet arrives and there is no place to put it, the IMP simply discards it. If the subnet offers datagram service to the hosts, that is all there is to it: congestion is resolved by discarding packets at will. If the subnet offers virtual circuit service, a copy of the packet must be kept somewhere so that it can be retransmitted later. One possibility is for the IMP sending the discarded packet to keep timing out and retransmitting the packet until it is received. Another possibility is for the sending IMP to give up after a certain number of tries, and require the source IMP to time out and start all over again.

Discarding packets at will can be carried too far. It is clearly stupid in the extreme to ignore an incoming packet containing an acknowledgement from a neighboring IMP. That acknowledgement would allow the IMP to abandon a by-now-received packet and thus free up a buffer. However, if the IMP has no spare buffers, it cannot acquire any more incoming packets to see if they contain acknowledgements. The solution is to permanently reserve one buffer per input line to allow all incoming packets to be inspected. It is quite legitimate for an IMP to examine a newly arrived packet, make use of any piggybacked acknowledgement, and then discard the packet anyway. Alternatively, the bearer of good tidings could be rewarded by keeping it, using the just freed buffer as the new input buffer.

If congestion is to be avoided by discarding packets, a rule is needed to tell when to keep a packet and when to discard it. Irland (1978) studied this problem and came up with a simple, yet effective heuristic for discarding packets. In the absence of any explicit rule to the contrary, a single output line might hog all the available buffers in an IMP, since they are simply assigned first come, first served. Figure 5-22(a) shows an IMP with a total of 10 buffers. Three of these are permanently assigned to the input lines. The remaining seven are holding packets queued for transmission on one of the output lines.

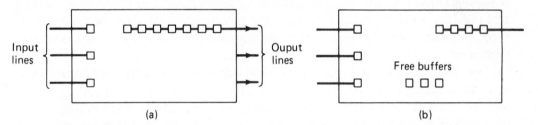

Fig. 5-22. Congestion can be reduced by putting an upper bound on the number of buffers queued on an output line.

Even though two output lines are idle, any incoming packets destined for these lines must be discarded because there are no spare buffers. This is obviously wasteful. Irland's idea is to limit the number of buffers that may be attached to any one output queue. For example, if the limit were set at four, the situation of Fig. 5-22(b) would prevail: three unassigned buffers. A newly arrived packet wanting to go out on the first output line would be discarded rather than allowing it to increase the queue length to five.

This strategy is not really as drastic as it may appear. After all, that output line is already running at maximum capacity. Having seven packets queued instead of four will not pump the bits out any faster, but it will allow traffic for the other lines to be forwarded immediately, possibly doubling or tripling the output rate of the IMP. In any case, the discarded packet will be retransmitted shortly. If the system is well tuned, it will even be retransmitted before the queue empties, so its initial rejection will not even be noticed.

Irland studied several different algorithms for determining maximum queue length, m, for an IMP with k buffers (buffers permanently dedicated for input do not count). The uncontrolled case is $m = k$. If there are s output lines, the case $m = k/s$ effectively means that each buffer is dedicated to a given output line. No line may borrow even one buffer from an idle line, ever. Intuitively this is not efficient, and the study bears this out.

It turns out that the optimal value of m is a complicated function of the mean traffic. Although the IMP could attempt to measure its traffic and continually adjust m, if the traffic were bursty, this probably would not work well. Irland did, however, discover a simple rule of thumb that usually gives good, but not optimal, performance: $m = k/\sqrt{s}$. For example, for seven pool buffers and three lines, $m = 7/\sqrt{3}$, so 4 buffers would be allocated.

A related idea, due to Kamoun (1976), directly prevents any line or lines from starving: a minimum number of buffers is dedicated to each line. If there is no traffic, the empty buffers are reserved. Irland's method can be combined with Kamoun's by having a minimum and a maximum number of buffers for each line. The ARPANET uses this method.

Although discarding packets is easy, it has some disadvantages. Chief among these is the extra bandwidth needed for the duplicates. If the probability of a packet being discarded is p, the expected number of transmissions before it is accepted is $1/(1 - p)$. A related issue is how long the timeout interval should be. If it is too short, duplicates will be generated when they are not needed, making the congestion worse. If it is too long, the delay will suffer.

One way to minimize the amount of bandwidth wasted on the retransmission of discarded packets is to systematically discard packets that have not yet traveled far and hence do not represent a large investment in resources. The limiting case of this strategy is to discard newly arrived packets from hosts in preference to discarding transit traffic. For example, IMPs could refuse or discard new packets from attached hosts whenever the number of buffers tied up by new packets (or total packets) exceeds some threshold.

5.3.3. Isarithmic Congestion Control

Congestion occurs when there are too many packets in the subnet. A direct approach to controlling it is to limit the number of packets in the subnet. Davies (1972) proposed a method that enforces precisely such a limit.

In this method, called **isarithmic** because it keeps the number of packets constant, there exist **permits**, which circulate about within the subnet. Whenever an IMP wants to send a packet just given to it by its host, it must first capture a permit and destroy it. When the destination IMP finally removes the packet from the subnet, it regenerates the permit. These simple rules ensure that the number of packets in the subnet will never exceed the number of permits initially present.

However, this method has some problems. First, although it does guarantee that the subnet as a whole will never become congested, it does not guarantee that a given IMP will not suddenly be swamped with packets.

Second, how to distribute the permits is far from obvious. To prevent a newly generated packet from suffering a long delay while the local IMP tries to scout up a permit, the permits must be uniformly distributed, so that every IMP has some. On the other hand, to permit high-bandwidth file transfer, it is undesirable for the sending IMP to have to go hunting all over the place to find enough permits. It would be nicer if they were all centralized, so that requests for substantial numbers could be honored quickly. Some compromise must be found, such as having a maximum number of permits that may be present at any IMP, with excess permits required to hunt for an IMP with space. Note that the random walk of the excess permits itself puts a load on the subnet.

Third, and by no means least, if permits ever get destroyed for any reason, (e.g., transmission errors, malfunctioning IMPs, being discarded by a congested IMP), the carrying capacity of the network will be forever reduced. There is no easy way to find out how many permits still exist while the network is running.

5.3.4. Flow Control

Some networks (notably the ARPANET) have attempted to use flow control mechanisms to eliminate congestion. Although flow control schemes can be used by the transport layer to keep one host from saturating another, and flow control schemes can be used to prevent one IMP from saturating its neighbors, it is difficult to control the total amount of traffic in the network using end-to-end flow control rules. Still, if the hosts are forced to stop transmitting due to strict flow control rules, the subnet will not be as heavily loaded.

Flow control cannot really solve congestion problems for a good reason: computer traffic is bursty. Most of the time an interactive user sits at his terminal scratching his head, but once in a while he may want to scan a large file. The potential peak traffic is vastly higher than the mean rate. Any flow control scheme which is adjusted so as to restrict each user to the mean rate will provide bad service when the user wants a burst of traffic. On the other hand, if the flow control limit is set high enough to permit the peak traffic to get through, it has little value as congestion control when several users demand the peak at once. (If half the people in the world suddenly picked up their telephones to call the other half, there would be a lot of busy signals; the telephone system is also designed for average traffic, not worst case.)

When flow control is used in an attempt to quench congestion, it can apply to the traffic between pairs of:

1. User processes (e.g., one outstanding message per virtual circuit).

2. Hosts, irrespective of the number of virtual circuits open.

3. Source and destination IMPs, without regard to hosts.

In addition, the number of virtual circuits open can be restricted.

5.3.5. Choke Packets

Although limiting the volume of traffic between each pair of IMPs or hosts may indirectly alleviate congestion it does so at the price of potentially reducing throughput even when there is no threat of congestion. What is really needed is a mechanism that is triggered only when the system is congested.

One way is to have each IMP monitor the percent utilization of each of its output lines. Associated with each line is a real variable, u, whose value, between 0.0 and 1.0, reflects the recent utilization of that line. To maintain a good estimate of u, a sample of the instantaneous line utilization, f (either 0 or 1), can be made periodically and u updated according to

$$u_{new} = au_{old} + (1-a)f$$

where the constant a determines how fast the IMP forgets recent history.

Whenever u moves above the threshold, the output line enters a "warning" state. Each newly arriving packet is checked to see if its output line is in warning state. If so, the IMP sends a **choke packet** back to the source host, giving it the destination found in the packet. The packet itself is tagged (a header bit is turned on) so that it will not generate any more choke packets later, and is forwarded in the usual way.

When the source host gets the choke packet, it is required to reduce the traffic sent to the specified destination by X percent. Since other packets aimed at the same destination are probably already under way and will generate yet more choke packets, the host should ignore choke packets referring to that destination for a fixed time interval. After that period has expired, the host listens for more choke packets for another interval. If one arrives, the line is still congested, so the host reduces the flow still more and begins ignoring choke packets again. If no choke packets arrive during the listening period, the host may increase the flow again. The feedback implicit in this protocol should prevent congestion, yet not throttle any flow unless trouble occurs.

Several variations on this congestion control algorithm have been proposed. For one, the IMPs could maintain two critical levels. Above the first level, choke packets are sent back. Above the second, incoming traffic is just discarded, the theory being that the host has probably been warned already. Without extensive tables it is difficult for the IMP to know which hosts have been warned recently about which destinations, and which hosts have not.

Another variation is to use queue lengths instead of line utilization as the trigger signal. The same exponential weighting can be used with this metric as with u, of course. Yet another possibility is to have the IMPs propagate congestion information along with routing information, so that the trigger is not based on only one IMPs observations, but on the fact that somewhere along the path there is a bottleneck. By propagating congestion information around the subnet, choke packets can be sent earlier, before too many more packets are under way, thus preventing congestion from building up.

5.3.6. Deadlocks

The ultimate congestion is a **deadlock**, also called a **lockup**. The first IMP cannot proceed until the second IMP does something, and the second IMP cannot proceed because it is waiting for the first IMP to do something. Both IMPs have ground to a complete halt and will stay that way forever. Deadlocks are not considered a desirable property to have in your network.

The simplest lockup can happen with two IMPs. Suppose that IMP A has five buffers, all of which are queued for output to IMP B. Similarly, IMP B has five buffers, all of which are occupied by packets needing to go to IMP A [see Fig. 5-23(a)]. Neither IMP can accept any incoming packets from the other. They are both stuck. This situation is called **direct store-and-forward lockup**. The same thing can happen on a larger scale, as shown in Fig. 5-23(b). Each IMP is trying to send to a neighbor, but nobody has any buffers available to receive incoming packets. This situation is called **indirect store-and-forward lockup**. Note that when an IMP is locked up, all its lines are effectively blocked, including those not involved in the lockup.

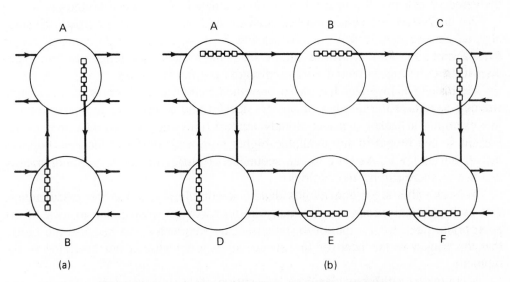

Fig. 5-23. Store-and-forward lockup. (a) Direct. (b) Indirect.

Merlin and Schweitzer (1980) have presented a solution to the problem of store-and-forward lockup. In their scheme, a directed graph is constructed, with the buffers being the nodes of the graph. Arcs connect pairs of buffers in the same IMP or adjacent IMPs. The graph is constructed in such a way that if all packets move from buffer to buffer along the arcs of the graph, then no deadlocks can occur.

As a simple example of their method, consider a subnet with N IMPs in which the longest route from any source to any destination is of length M hops. Each IMP needs $M + 1$ buffers, numbered from 0 to M. The buffer graph is now constructed by drawing an arc from buffer i in each node to buffer $i + 1$ in each of the adjacent nodes. The legal routes from buffer i at IMP A are those to a buffer labeled $i + 1$ at IMPs adjacent to A, and then to a buffer labeled $i + 2$ at IMPs two hops from A, etc.

A packet from a host can only be admitted to the subnet if buffer 0 at the source IMP is empty. Once admitted, this packet can only move to a buffer labeled 1 in an adjacent IMP, and so on, until either it reaches its destination and is removed from the subnet, or it reaches a buffer labeled M, in which case it is discarded. (If M is chosen longer than the longest route, then only looping packets will be discarded.) A packet in buffer i in some IMP may only be moved if buffer $i + 1$ in the IMP chosen by the routing algorithm is free. Note that numbering the buffers does not restrict the choice of routing algorithm, which can be static or dynamic.

To see that this algorithm is deadlock free, consider the state of all buffers labeled M at some instant. Each buffer is in one of three states: empty, holding a packet destined for a local host, or holding a packet for a distant host. In the second case the packet can be delivered, in the third case the packet is looping and must be dropped. In all three cases the buffer can be made free. Consequently, all the packets in buffers labeled $M - 1$ can now be moved forward, one at a time, to be delivered or discarded. Once all the buffers labeled $M - 1$ are free, the packets in buffers labeled $M - 2$ can be moved forward and delivered or discarded. Eventually, all packets can be delivered or discarded. If the routing algorithm guarantees that packets cannot loop, then M can be set to the longest path length, and all packets will be correctly delivered with no discards and no deadlocks.

Merlin and Schweitzer have also presented many improvements to this simple strategy to reduce the number of buffers needed and to improve the performance. For example, a packet that has already made i hops (i.e., is currently in a buffer labeled i), can be put in any available higher numbered buffer at the next hop, not just in buffer $i + 1$. As long as the sequence of buffer numbers is monotonically increasing, there can be no deadlocks.

Although this algorithm avoids deadlock completely, it has the disadvantage that under normal circumstances many buffers will be wasted due to lack of the appropriate packets. Furthermore, lines will be frequently idle because the buffer that the packet at the head of the queue happens to need is not available at the moment.

A completely different deadlock prevention algorithm that does not have these properties has been published by Blazewicz et al. (1987a). In their algorithm, each packet bears a globally unique timestamp. This stamp contains the time the packet was created in the high-order bits and the machine number in the low-order bits. It is not essential that all the clocks be synchronized, although the algorithm tends to give fairer service if the clocks are not too far apart.

The algorithm requires each IMP to reserve one buffer per input line as a special receive buffer. All the other buffers can be used for holding packets in transit. These packets are queued in timestamp order in a separate queue for each output line, as illustrated in Fig. 5-24. In the absence of any deadlock prevention algorithm, the three IMPs in Fig. 5-24 would be deadlocked because although each one can receive a packet from its neighbors, it has nowhere to store it while the packet waits its turn for the next hop.

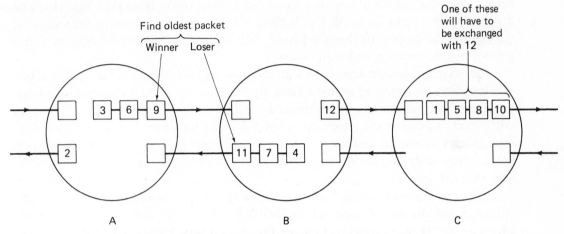

Fig. 5-24. Three potentially deadlocked IMPs.

The essence of the algorithm is that it makes a distinction between three conditions. In all three cases we assume that A has an important packet that it wants to send to B. The conditions are:

1. B has a free buffer.

2. B does not have a free buffer, but it does have a packet for A.

3. B has neither a free buffer nor a packet for A.

In case 1, A just sends its packet. In case 2, A and B exchange packets, so that the newly arrived packet can be put in the buffer just freed by the packet going the other way. In case 3, B is forced to choose a packet not destined for A (preferably, one that is at least going in the same general direction as A) and this packet is exchanged with A as in case 2.

Now we can explain the algorithm and prove that it is deadlock free. Whenever a line goes idle, the two IMPs at the ends of it exchange control packets giving the timestamp of its oldest packet that wants to use the line. The one with the lowest number (oldest packet) wins and that packet is sent, even if case 3 applies and the losing IMP is forced to send another packet in the wrong direction to free up buffer space for the winner. At any instant, one packet in the subnet has the honor of being the oldest. This packet will always come on top in any IMP-IMP discussion about age, so this packet will make nonstop progress to its destination. As soon as it has been delivered, some other packet becomes the oldest, and it can then proceed unobstructed to its destination. As time marches on, every packet eventually becomes the oldest and is delivered.

Two criticisms can be leveled at this algorithm. First, a young packet may be sent far out of its way before it acquires enough seniority to start consistently winning the IMP-IMP timestamp comparisons. However, in practice, case 3 only occurs when the subnet is heavily loaded (all buffers full). If an IMP has, say, 3 or 4 outgoing lines and 20 to 50 full buffers, chances are that none of the outgoing queues will be empty, so that the losing IMP will nearly always be able to find a good packet to exchange with the winner.

The second criticism has to do with clock synchronization. If one IMP's clock is a few seconds ahead of all the others, its packets will be at a competitive disadvantage when timestamps are compared. Still, within a few seconds, its packets will get delivered, so the condition is annoying but not fatal. If each pair of adjacent IMPs periodically exchanges clock values, each IMP can then set its time to the average of its neighbor's times. In this way, no clock can get very far out of step with the rest.

Store-and-forward lockups are not the only kind of deadlocks that plague the subnet. Consider the situation of an IMP with 20 buffers and lines to four other IMPs, as shown in Fig. 5-25. Four of the buffers are dedicated to the four input lines, to help alleviate congestion. Assume that a sliding window protocol is being used, with window size seven. Further, assume that packets are accepted out of order by the IMP, but must be delivered to the host in order. At the time of the snapshot, four virtual circuits, 0, 1, 2, and 3, are open between the host and other hosts.

Rather than dedicate a full window load of buffers to each open virtual circuit, buffers are simply assigned on a first come, first served basis. As soon as the next sequence number expected by the host becomes available, that packet is passed to the host (with each virtual circuit independent of all the others). However higher number packets within the window are buffered in the usual way.

In Fig. 5-25 *v* and *s* indicate the virtual circuit and sequence number of each packet, respectively. The host is waiting for sequence number 0 on all four virtual circuits, but none of them have arrived undamaged yet. Nevertheless, all the buffers are occupied.

If packet 0 should arrive, it would have to be discarded due to lack of buffer space. As a result, no more packets can be passed to the host and no buffers freed. This deadlock occurred in the ARPANET in a slightly different form, and was called **reassembly lockup**.

In the ARPANET there are multipacket messages (i.e., messages too large to fit into a single packet). By allowing hosts to pass relatively large chunks of information to the IMPs in a single transfer, the number of host interrupts could be reduced. The sending IMP splits multipacket messages into individual packets and sends

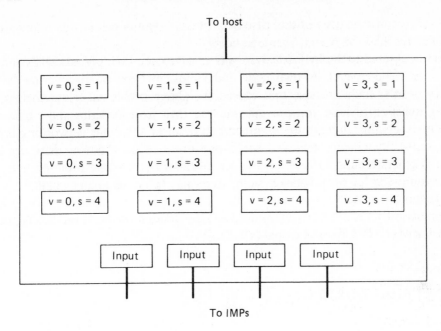

Fig. 5-25. Reassembly lockup.

each one separately. The destination IMP must put all the pieces together before passing the reassembled message to the host. If pieces of several multipacket messages have managed to commandeer all the available buffer space in the destination IMP, the missing pieces will have to be rejected and the IMP (and host) will be deadlocked.

The ARPANET solution is to have the source IMP ask the destination IMP permission to send a multipacket message. The destination IMP then dedicates enough buffers to reassemble the full message before telling the source to go ahead. The sliding window version of the deadlock can only be prevented by dedicating a full window's worth of buffers to each open virtual circuit. The reason this strategy is more attractive in the ARPANET case is that there most (96%) messages are single packet, not multipacket, whereas in the sliding window case, in effect, all messages are multipacket.

Two other problems discovered in the ARPANET are worth mentioning here. Both were caused by malfunctioning IMPs. All of a sudden, one IMP announced that it had zero delay to all other IMPs in the entire subnet. The adaptive routing algorithm spread the good news far and wide. The other IMPs were ecstatic. Within a few seconds, practically all of the traffic in the entire subnet was headed toward the only IMP that was not working properly. Although not a deadlock, this certainly brought the whole network to a grinding halt.

The other problem was also caused by a failing memory. One fine day the Aberdeen IMP (on the East Coast) decided that it was the UCLA IMP (on the West

Coast). The consequences of this case of mistaken identity can be easily imagined, especially for the UCLA and Aberdeen hosts.

The fix applied to the IMP software was to have each IMP periodically compute a software checksum of its own code and tables, in hope of discovering failing memory words, such as those that caused the above problems. Nevertheless the nagging question of how you prevent one bad IMP from bringing the whole network down remains. One of the arguments in favor of computer networking is that higher reliability can be achieved so: if one machine goes down, there are still plenty of others around. However, if a single failure at one site often pollutes the entire nationwide (or worldwide) system, there may be no advantage at all.

An exhaustive catalog of other network deadlocks and possible solutions to them is given by Lai (1982). Other deadlock prevention methods are discussed by Blazewicz et al. (1987b), and Gopal (1985).

5.4. INTERNETWORKING

Up until now, we have implicitly assumed that there is a single homogeneous network, with each machine using the same protocol in each layer. Unfortunately, this assumption is wildly optimistic. Many different networks exist. More than 20,000 SNA networks, more than 2000 DECNET networks, and uncountably many LANs of every kind imaginable are in daily operation all over the world (Green, 1986). Very few of these use the OSI model. In this section we will take a careful look at the issues that arise when it becomes necessary to interconnect two or more networks together to form an **internet**. Additional detail can be found in (Burg et al. 1984; Hinden et al. 1983; Israel and Weissberger, 1987; Postel 1980; Schneidewind 1983; Stallings 1987; and Weissberger and Israel, 1987).

Enormous controversy exists about the question of whether today's abundance of network types is a temporary condition that will go away as soon as everyone realizes how wonderful OSI is, or whether it is an inevitable, but permanent feature of the world that is here to stay. We believe that a variety of different networks will always be around, for the following reasons. First of all, the installed base of non OSI systems is already very large and growing rapidly. IBM is still selling new SNA systems. Most UNIX shops run TCP/IP. LANs are rarely OSI. This trend will continue for years because not all vendors perceive it in their interest for their customers to be able to easily migrate to another vendor's system.

Second, as computers and networks get cheaper, the place where decisions get made moves downward. Many companies have a policy to the effect that purchases costing over a million dollars have to be approved by top management, purchases costing over 100,000 dollars have to be approved by middle management, but purchases under 100,000 dollars can be made by department heads without any higher approval. This can easily lead to the accounting department installing an

Ethernet, the engineering department installing a token bus, and the personnel department installing a token ring.

Third, different networks (e.g., LAN and satellite) have radically different technology, so it should not be surprising that as new hardware developments occur, new software will be needed that does not fit the OSI model.

Let us assume that multiple, incompatible networks are going to be a fact of life for a while, and take a look at some circumstances where it is desirable to connect them together. At most universities, the computer science and electrical engineering departments have their own LANs, often different. These LANs have numerous personal computers, workstations, and minicomputers on them. People interested in number crunching (physicists) or letter crunching (poets) frequently use the computer center's mainframe, in the former case due to the computing power available, and in the latter due to a lack of interest in maintaining hardware. Both the departmental LANs and the mainframes are often connected to national or international WANs, as well as to each other.

The following scenarios are easy to imagine:

1. LAN-LAN: A computer scientist downloading a file to engineering.

2. LAN-WAN: A computer scientist sending mail to a distant physicist.

3. WAN-WAN: Two poets exchanging sonnets.

4. LAN-WAN-LAN: Engineers at different universities communicating.

Figure 5-26 illustrates these four types of connections as dotted lines. In each case, it is necessary to insert a "black box" at the junction between two networks, to handle the necessary conversions as packets move from one network to the other. The generic term for these devices is **relay**. We will discuss the various types (bridges and gateways) later in this chapter. Relays can be **bilateral**, connecting just two networks, or **multilateral**, connecting several networks.

5.4.1. OSI and Internetworking

In the OSI model, internetworking is done in the network layer. In all honesty, this is not one of the areas in which ISO has devised a model that has met with universal acclaim (network security is another one). From looking at the documents, one gets the feeling that internetworking was hastily grafted onto the main structure at the last minute. In particular, the objections from the ARPA Internet community did not carry as much weight as they perhaps should have, inasmuch as DARPA had 10 years experience running an internet with hundreds of interconnected networks, and had a good idea of what worked in practice and what did not.

ISO is not alone in this failing, however. When CCITT drew up its international network numbering plan, for example, it decided that four decimal digits

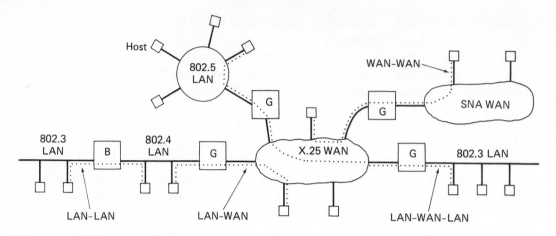

Fig. 5-26. Network interconnection. The boxes marked B are bridges. Those marked G are gateways.

(i.e., 10,000 networks) would be enough for the entire world for years to come. With 20,000 SNA networks and probably even more LANs already around, four decimal digits is grossly inadequate.

The problem is not one of poor estimation; it is a question of mentality. In CCITT's view, each country *ought* to have just one or two public networks, run by the national PTT (or carriers such as TELENET and TYMNET in the U.S.). All the private networks do not count for very much in CCITT's vision. However, not all the users share this viewpoint. Even if all 20,000 SNA networks could somehow miraculously be converted overnight to OSI, it is very unlikely that their owners would be willing to give up administrative control and merge them all into one big, homogeneous public network.

All this said, let us see how internetworking is handled in the OSI model. Where needed, the network layer can be divided into three sublayers: the **subnet access sublayer**, the **subnet enhancement sublayer**, and the **internet sublayer**, as shown in Fig. 5-27. The purpose of the subnet access layer is to handle the network layer protocol for the specific subnet being used. It generates and receives data and control packets and performs the ordinary network layer functions. The software is designed to interface to the real subnet available. There is no guarantee that it will also work with other subnets.

The subnet enhancement sublayer is designed to harmonize subnets that offer different services. In the relay of Fig. 5-27, the upper boundary of 3a is different from 3a′. However, the upper boundary of 3b and 3b′ are the same, so that 3c can work with either subnet.

Subnets can differ in many ways. As one example, consider addressing. The internet sublayer uses NSAPs for addressing. Remember that an NSAP address refers not only to a specific machine, but also to a specific access point within that machine to which a transport process can attach itself. Thus NSAP addresses are

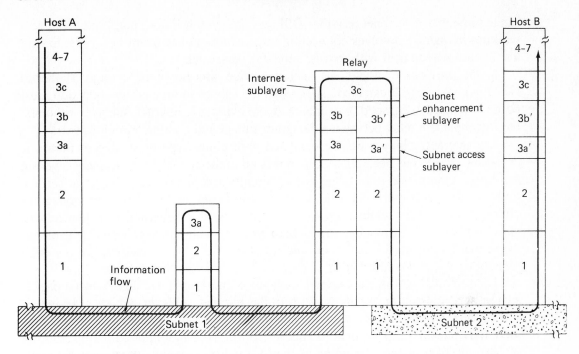

Fig. 5-27. The internal structure of the network layer. The solid line shows how information flows from host *A* to host *B*. The relay is connected to both subnets.

ultimately used to refer to transport layer processes, not to machines. The *N-CONNECT* primitives all use NSAP addresses as parameters (see Fig. 5-4).

Let us first see how a network connection is established in a subnet that conforms to the OSI model. When the connection request comes in from above, the internet sublayer passes it down to the subnet access sublayer (the enhancement sublayer is null for OSI subnets since they need not be enhanced—they are fine as is). The subnet access sublayer constructs a *CALL REQUEST* packet containing the caller and callee's NSAP addresses and gives it to the data link layer for transmission. Later it receives a reply and the connection is established.

Now let us consider what happens if the subnet does not conform to the OSI model, but, for example, uses the 1980 version of the X.25 protocol. This protocol has a *CALL REQUEST* packet, but the addresses used in it are machine addresses, not NSAP addresses. There is no convenient place to put the NSAP addresses. What happens is that the subnet enhancement sublayer first sets up a network layer connection to the proper machine. Then it sends a special data packet containing the NSAP addresses. The result of this extra exchange is that the subnet enhancement sublayer can offer a service (connection to a specific NSAP) that the subnet access sublayer cannot. As packets move along this connection, the subnet enhancement sublayer intercepts each one, routing it to the proper NSAP.

In this manner the actual subnet service is brought up to the level demanded by the internet sublayer. The effect of this enhancement is that the internet sublayer can assume that the subnet provides OSI service, even if it does not. Since internetworking frequently involves connecting one or more nonstandard networks, having a structural way to deal with strange subnets is essential.

In the previous example, the subnet service was not good enough (it lacked NSAP addressing). It can also happen that the subnet service is too good, and must be de-enhanced (degraded?) to match up to what the internet sublayer requires. One example is a relay between a datagram subnet and a virtual circuit subnet.

The internet sublayer can be designed with either type of service in mind. If datagram service has been chosen, then it is up to the subnet enchancement layer on the virtual circuit side to hide the virtual circuits and just provide datagram service to the internet sublayer. If it cannot devise any better strategy, for every datagram offered to it, it can establish a virtual circuit, send the datagram, and then release the virtual circuit. In practice, the subnet enhancement sublayer would not release the virtual circuit until it had been idle for several minutes because there is a high probability it could be used again.

The principal task of the internet sublayer is end-to-end routing. When a packet arrives at a relay, it works its way up to the internet sublayer, which examines it and decides whether to forward it, and if so, using which subnet (a multilateral relay may have several subnets to choose from). To a first approximation, routing across multiple subnets is similar to routing within a single subnet, and the techniques we have studied earlier are relevant. For a large internet, hierarchical routing is an obvious candidate, since it frees the relays from having to know about the internal structure of distant subnets.

The relay of Fig. 5-27 extends up as far as layer 3 and moves packets between networks in that layer. In the general (non OSI) case, relaying can be done in any layer. Four common types of relays are as follows:

Layer 1: **Repeaters** copy individual bits between cable segments.

Layer 2: **Bridges** store and forward frames between LANs.

Layer 3: **Gateways** store and forward packets between dissimilar networks.

Layer 4: **Protocol converters** provide interfacing in higher layers.

Repeaters are low-level devices that amplify just electrical signals. They are needed to provide current to drive long cables. In 802.3, for example, the timing properties of the MAC protocol (the value of τ chosen) allow cables up to 2.5 km, but the transceiver chips can only provide enough power to drive 500 meters. The solution is to use repeaters to extend the cable length where that is desired.

Unlike repeaters, which copy the bits as they arrive, bridges are store-and-forward devices. A bridge accepts an entire frame and passes it up to the data link layer where the checksum is verified. Then the frame is sent down to the physical layer for forwarding on a different subnet. Bridges can make minor changes to the frame before forwarding it, such as adding or deleting some fields from the frame header. Since they are data link layer devices, they do not deal with headers at layer 3 and above, and cannot make changes or decisions that depend on them.

Gateways are conceptually similar to bridges, except that they are found in the network layer. The relay of Fig. 5-27 is a gateway. Some people use the term gateway in a generic sense, applicable to any layer, and the term **router** for a network layer gateway. In this chapter "gateway" will refer to the network layer.

As a general rule, the networks connected by a gateway can differ much more than those connected by a bridge. In Fig. 5-26, the LANs are connected by a bridge; the LAN-WAN and WAN-WAN relays are gateways. A major advantage of gateways over bridges is that they can connect networks with incompatible addressing formats, for example, an 802 LAN using 48-bit binary addresses and an X.25 network using 14 decimal digit X.121 addresses.

At the transport layer and above, the relays are usually called protocol converters, although the term "gateway" is used by some people, as mentioned above. The job of a protocol converter is much more complex than that of a gateway. The protocol converter must convert from one protocol to another without losing too much meaning in the process. An example of a protocol converter is a relay that translates the OSI transport protocol to the protocol used in the ARPA Internet (TCP). Another example of protocol conversion is converting OSI mail messages (MOTIS) to ARPA Internet format (RFC 822).

Regardless of which layer the relaying is done in, the complexity of the job depends mostly on how similar the two networks are in terms of frames, packets, messages, and protocols. Some of the ways networks can differ are frame, packet, and message size, checksum algorithms, maximum packet lifetimes, connection-oriented vs. connectionless protocols, and timer values. Sometimes the conversion is not even possible, for example, when trying to forward expedited data (someone hit the DEL key) through a network not having any concept of expedited data.

5.4.2. Bridges

In this section we will look at bridge design. In the following ones we will study gateways. In a sense, the material about bridges might logically have been covered in Chapter 3 or Chapter 4, but as a convenience to the reader, we have decided to put all the material on internetworking in one place. Most bridges connect 802 LANs, so we will concentrate primarily on 802 bridges.

Before getting into the technology of bridges, it is worthwhile taking a look at some common situations in which bridges are used. We will mention six reasons why a single organization may end up with multiple LANs. First, many university and corporate departments have their own LANs, primarily to connect their own personal computers, workstations, and minicomputers. Since the goals of the various departments differ, different departments choose different LANs, without regard to what other departments are doing. Sooner or later, there is a need for interaction, so a bridge is needed. In this example, multiple LANs came into existence due to the autonomy of their owners.

Second, the organization may be geographically spread over several buildings separated by considerable distances. It may be cheaper to have separate LANs in each building and connect them with bridges and infrared links than to run a single coaxial cable over the entire campus.

Third, it may be necessary to split what is logically a single LAN into separate LANs to accommodate the load. At Carnegie-Mellon University, for example, thousands of workstations are available for student and faculty computing (Morris, 1988; Morris et al., 1986). Files are normally kept on file server machines, and are downloaded to users' machines upon request. The enormous scale of this system precludes putting all the workstations on a single LAN—the total bandwidth needed is far too high. Instead multiple LANs connected by bridges are used, as shown in Fig. 5-28. Each LAN contains a cluster of workstations with its own file server, so that most traffic is restricted to a single LAN.

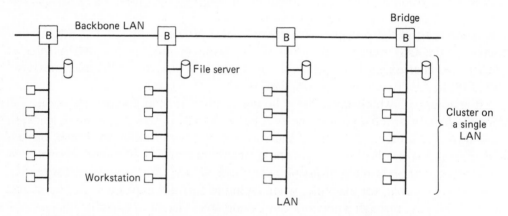

Fig. 5-28. Multiple LANs connected by a backbone to handle a total load higher than the capacity of a single LAN.

Fourth, in some situations, a single LAN would be adequate in terms of the load, but the physical distance between the most distant machines is too great (e.g., more than 2.5 km for 802.3). Even if laying the cable is easy to do, the network would not work due to the excessively long round-trip delay. The only solution is to partition the LAN and install bridges between the segments.

Fifth, there is the matter of reliability. On a single LAN, a defective node that keeps outputting a continuous stream of garbage will cripple the LAN. Bridges can be inserted at critical places, like fire doors in a building, to prevent a single node gone berserk from bringing down the entire system. Unlike a repeater, which just copies whatever it sees, a bridge can be programmed to exercise some discretion about what it forwards and what it does not forward.

Sixth, and last, bridges can contribute to the organization's security. Most LAN interfaces have a **promiscuous mode**, in which *all* packets are given to the computer, not just those addressed to it. Spies and busybodies love this feature. By inserting bridges at various places and being careful not to forward sensitive traffic, it is possible to isolate parts of the network so that its traffic cannot escape.

Having seen why bridges are needed, let us now turn to the question of how they work. Figure 5-29 illustrates the operation of a simple bilateral bridge. Host *A* has a packet to send. The packet descends into the LLC sublayer and acquires an LLC header. Then it passes into the MAC sublayer and an 802.3 header is prepended to it (also a trailer, not shown in the figure). This unit goes out onto the cable and eventually is passed up to the MAC sublayer in the bridge, where the 802.3 header is stripped off. The bare packet (with LLC header) is then handed off to the LLC sublayer in the bridge. In this example, the packet is destined for an 802.4 subnet connected to the bridge, so it works its way down the 802.4 side of the bridge and off it goes. Note that a bridge connecting *k* different LANs will have *k* different MAC sublayers and *k* different physical layers, one for each type.

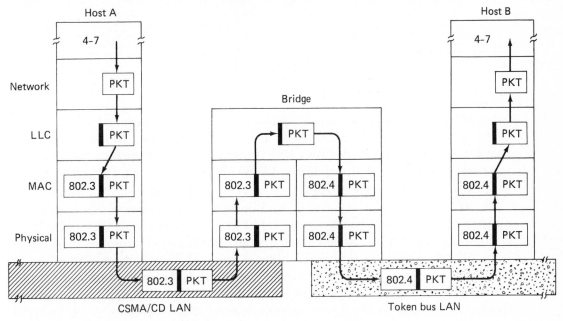

Fig. 5-29. Operation of a LAN bridge from 802.3 to 802.4.

Bridges from 802.x to 802.y

You might naively think that a bridge from one 802 LAN to another one would be completely trivial. Such is not the case. In the remainder of this section we will point out some of the difficulties that will be encountered when trying to build a bridge between the various 802 LANs. More details can be found in Berntsen et al. (1985) and Hawe et al. (1984).

Each of the nine combinations of 802.x to 802.y has its own unique set of problems. However, before dealing with these one at a time, let us look at some general problems common to all the bridges. To start with, each of the LANs uses a different frame format (see Fig. 5-30). There is no valid technical reason for this incompatibility. It is just that none of the corporations supporting the three standards (Xerox, GM, and IBM) wanted to change *theirs*. As a result, any copying between different LANs requires reformatting, which takes CPU time, requires a new checksum calculation, and introduces the possibility of undetected errors due to bad bits in the bridge's memory. None of this would have been necessary if the three committees had been able to agree on a single format.

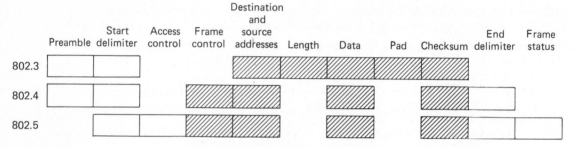

Fig. 5-30. The IEEE 802 frame formats.

A second, and far more serious problem, is that interconnected LANs do not necessarily run at the same data rate. Each of the standards allows a variety of speeds. The 802.3 standard allows 1 to 20 Mbps; the 802.4 standard permits various speeds from 1 to 10 Mbps; finally, the 802.5 standard calls for 1 or 4 Mbps. In practice, 802.3 is 10 Mbps, 802.4 is frequently 10 Mbps, and 802.5 is 4 Mbps.

When forwarding a long run of back-to-back frames from 802.3 or 802.4 to 802.5, a bridge will not be able to get rid of the frames as fast as they come in. It will have to buffer them, hoping not to run out of memory. The problem also exists from 802.4 to 802.3 to some extent because some of 802.3's bandwidth is lost to collisions. It does not really have 10 Mbps, whereas 802.4 really does.

A subtle, but important problem related to the bridge-as-bottleneck problem is the value of timers in the higher layers. Suppose the network layer on an 802.4 LAN is trying to send a very long message as a sequence of frames. After sending the last one it starts a timer to wait for an acknowledgement. If the message has to transit a bridge to an 802.5 LAN, there is a danger that the timer will go off before the last frame has been forwarded onto the slower LAN. The network layer will assume the problem is due to a lost frame, and just retransmit the entire sequence again. After *n* failed attempts it may give up and tell the transport layer that the destination is dead. Precisely this problem with mismatched speeds at a gateway was reported by Nagle (1984) in a slightly different context.

A third, and potentially most serious problem of all, is that all three 802 LANs have a different maximum frame length. For 802.3 it depends on the parameters of the configuration, but for the standard 10-Mbps system it is 1518 bytes. For 802.4 it is fixed at 8191 bytes. For 802.5 there is no upper limit, except that a station may not transmit longer than the token holding time. With the default value of 10 msec, the maximum frame length is 5000 bytes.

The obvious problem is what happens when a long frame must be forwarded onto a LAN that cannot accept it? Splitting the frame into pieces is out of the question in this layer. All the protocols assume that frames either arrive or they do not. There is no provision for reassembling frames out of smaller units. This is not to say that such protocols could not be devised. They could be and have been. It is just that 802 does not provide this feature. Basically, there is no solution. Frames that are too large to be forwarded must be discarded. So much for transparency.

Now let us briefly consider each of the nine cases of 802.x to 802.y bridges to see what other problems are lurking in the shadows. From 802.3 to 802.3 is easy. The only thing that can go wrong is that the destination LAN is so heavily loaded that frames keep pouring into the bridge, but the bridge cannot get rid of them. If this situation persists long enough, the bridge might run out of buffer space and begin dropping frames. Since this problem is always potentially present when forwarding onto an 802.3 LAN, we will not mention it further. With the other two LANs, each station, including the bridge is guaranteed to acquire the token periodically, and cannot be shut out for long intervals.

From 802.4 to 802.3 two problems exist. First, 802.4 frames carry priority bits that 802.3 frames do not have. As a result, if two 802.4 LANs communicate via an 802.3 LAN, the priority will be lost the intermediate LAN.

The second problem is caused by a specific feature in 802.4: temporary token handoff. It is possible for an 802.4 frame to have a header bit set to 1 to temporarily pass the token to the destination, to let it send an acknowledgement frame. However, if such a frame is forwarded by a bridge, what should the bridge do? If it sends an acknowledgement frame itself, it is lying because the frame really has not been delivered yet. In fact, the destination may be dead.

On the other hand, if it does not generate the acknowledgement, the sender will almost assuredly conclude that the destination is dead and report back failure to its superiors. There does not seem to be any way to solve with this problem.

From 802.5 to 802.3 we have a similar problem. The 802.5 frame format has A and C bits in the frame status byte. These bits are set by the destination to tell the sender whether the station addressed saw the frame, and whether it copied it. Again here, the bridge can lie and say the frame has been copied, but if it later turns out that the destination is down, serious problems may arise. In essence, the insertion of a bridge into the network has changed the semantics of the bits.

From 802.3 to 802.4 we have the problem of what to put in the priority bits. A good case can be made for having the bridge retransmit all frames at the highest priority, because they have probably suffered enough delay already.

From 802.4 to 802.4 the only problem is what to do with the temporary token handoff. At least here we have the possibility of the bridge managing to forward the frame fast enough to get the response before the timer runs out. Still it is a gamble. By forwarding the frame at the highest priority, the bridge is telling a little white lie, but it thereby increases the probability of getting the response in time.

From 802.5 to 802.4 we have the same problem with the *A* and *C* bits as before. Also, the definition of the priority bits is different for the two LANs, but beggars can't be choosers. At least the two LANs have the same number of priority bits. All the bridge can do is copy the priority bits across and hope for the best.

From 802.3 to 802.5 the bridge must generate priority bits, but there are no other special problems. From 802.4 to 802.5 there is a potential problem with frames that are too long and the token handoff problem is present again. Finally, from 802.5 to 802.5 the problem is what to do with the *A* and *C* bits again. Figure 5-31 summarizes the various problems we have been discussing.

		Destination LAN		
		802.3(CSMA/CD)	802.4 (Token bus)	802.5 (Token ring)
Source LAN	802.3		1, 4	1, 2, 4, 8
	802.4	1, 5, 9, 8, 10	9	1, 2, 3, 8, 9, 10
	802.5	1, 2, 5, 6, 7, 10	1, 2, 3, 6, 7	6, 7

Actions:
1. Reformat the frame and compute new checksum.
2. Reverse the bit order.
3. Copy the priority, meaningful or not.
4. Generate a ficticious priority.
5. Discard priority.
6. Drain the ring (somehow).
7. Set A and C bits (by lying).
8. Worry about congestion (fast LAN to slow LAN).
9. Worry about token handoff ACK being delayed or impossible.
10. Panic if frame is too long for destination LAN.

Parameters assumed:

802.3:	1518-byte frames,	10 Mbps (minus collisions)
802.4:	8191-byte frames	10 Mbps
802.5:	5000-byte frames	4 Mbps

Fig. 5-31. Problems encountered in building bridges from 802.x to 802.y.

When the IEEE 802 committee set out to come up with a LAN standard, it was unable to agree on a single standard, so it produced *three* incompatible standards, as we have just seen in some detail. For this failure, it has been roundly criticized. When it was later assigned the job of designing a standard for bridges to interconnect its three incompatible LANs, it resolved to do better. It did. It came up with *two* incompatible bridge designs. So far nobody has asked it to design a gateway standard to connect its two incompatible bridges, but at least the trend is in the right direction.

This section has dealt with the problems encountered in connected two LANs via a single bridge. The next two sections deal with the problems of connecting large internetworks containing many LANs and many bridges and the two IEEE approaches to designing these bridges.

Transparent Bridges

The first 802 bridge is a **transparent bridge** or **spanning tree bridge** (Backes, 1988). The overriding concern of the people who supported this design was complete transparency. In their view, a site with multiple LANs should be able to go out and buy bridges designed to the IEEE standard, plug the connectors into the bridges, and everything should work perfectly, instantly. There should be no hardware changes required, no software changes required, no setting of address switches, no downloading of routing tables or parameters, nothing. Just plug in the cables and walk away. The existing LANs should not be affected by the bridges at all. Surprisingly enough, they actually succeeded.

The transparent bridge operates in promiscuous mode, accepting every frame transmitted on all the LANs to which it is attached. As an example, consider the configuration of Fig. 5-32. Bridge 1 is connected to LANs 1 and 2, and bridge 2 is connected to LANs 2, 3, and 4. A frame arriving at bridge 1 on LAN 1 destined for *A* can be discarded immediately, because it is already on the right LAN, but a frame arriving on LAN 1 for *B*, *C*, or *D* must be forwarded.

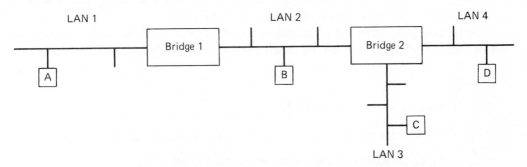

Fig. 5-32. A configuration with four LANs and two bridges.

When a frame arrives, a bridge must decide whether to discard or forward it, and if the latter, on which LAN to put the frame. This decision is made by looking up the destination address in a big (hash) table inside the bridge. The table can list each possible destination, and tell which output line (LAN) it belongs on. For example, bridge 2's table would list *A* as belonging to LAN 2, since all bridge 2 has to know is which LAN to put frames for *A* on. That, in fact, more forwarding happens later is not of interest to it.

When the bridges are first plugged in, all the hash tables are empty. None of the bridges know where any of the destinations are, so they use the flooding algorithm: every incoming frame for an unknown destination is output on all the LANs to which the bridge is connected except the one it arrived on. As time goes on, the bridges learn where destinations are, as described below. Once a destination is known, frames destined for it are put on only the proper LAN, and are not flooded.

The algorithm used by the transparent bridges is Baran's backward learning. As mentioned above, the bridges operate in promiscuous mode, so they see every frame sent on any of their LANs. By looking at the source address, they can tell which machine is accessible on which LAN. For example, if bridge 1 in Fig. 5-32 sees a frame on LAN 2 coming from C it knows that C must be reachable via LAN 2, so it makes an entry in its hash table noting that frames going to C should use LAN 2. Any subsequent frame addressed to C coming in on LAN 1 will be forwarded, but a frame for C coming in on LAN 2 will be discarded.

The topology of the internetwork can change as machines and bridges are powered up and down and moved around. To handle dynamic topologies, whenever a hash table entry is made, the arrival time of the frame is noted in the entry. Whenever a frame that is already in the table arrives, its entry is updated with the current time. Thus the time associated with every entry tells the last time a frame from that machine was seen.

Periodically, a process in the bridge scans the hash table and purges all entries more than a few minutes old. In this way, if a computer is unplugged from its LAN, moved around the building, and replugged in somewhere else, within a few minutes it will be back in normal operation, without any manual intervention. This algorithm also means that if a machine is quiet for a few minutes, any traffic sent to it will have to be flooded, until it next sends a frame itself.

The routing procedure for an incoming frame depends on the LAN it arrives on (the source LAN) and the LAN its destination is on (the destination LAN), as follows:

1. If destination and source LANs are the same, discard the frame.

2. If the destination and source LANs are different, forward the frame.

3. If the destination LAN is unknown, use flooding.

As each frame arrives, this algorithm must be applied. Special purpose VLSI chips exist to do the lookup and update the table entry, all in a few microseconds.

To increase reliability, some sites use two or more bridges in parallel between pairs of LANs, as shown in Fig. 5-33. This arrangement, however, also introduces some additional problems because it creates loops in the topology.

A simple example of these problems can be seen by observing how a frame, F, with unknown destination is handled in Fig. 5-33. Each bridge, following the normal rules for handling unknown destinations, uses flooding, which in this example, just means copying it to LAN 2. Shortly thereafter, bridge 1 sees F_2, a frame with an unknown destination, which it copies to LAN 1, generating F_3. Similarly, bridge

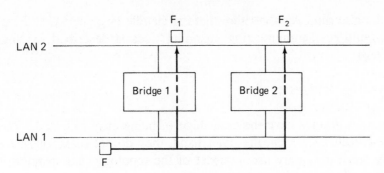

Fig. 5-33. Two parallel transparent bridges.

2 copies F_1 to LAN 1 generating F_4. Bridge 1 now forwards F_4 and bridge 2 copies F_3. This cycle goes on forever.

The solution to this difficulty is for the bridges to communicate with each other and overlay the actual topology with a spanning tree that reaches every LAN. Fig. 5-16(b) shows one of the many spanning trees that can be overlayed on the network of Fig. 5-16(a). Once the bridges have agreed on the spanning tree, all forwarding between LANs follows the spanning tree. Since there is a unique path from each source to each destination, loops are impossible.

To build the spanning tree, every few seconds each bridge broadcasts its identity (e.g., a serial number installed by the manufacturer and guaranteed to be unique) and the list of all other bridges it knows about on its LANs. A distributed algorithm is then used to select one bridge as the root of the tree, for example, the bridge with the lowest serial number. Once the root is selected, the tree is constructed by having each bridge choose the shortest path to the root. In case of ties, the lowest serial number wins.

The result of this algorithm is that a unique path is established from every LAN to the root, and thus to every other LAN. Although the tree spans alls the LAN, not all the bridge are necessarily present in the tree (to prevent loops). Even after the spanning tree has been established, the algorithm continues to run in order to automatically detect topology changes and update the tree.

Bridges can also be used to connect LANs that are widely separated. In this model, each site consists of a collection of LANs and bridges, one of which has a connection to a WAN. Frames for remote LANs travel over the WAN. The basic spanning tree algorithm can be used, preferably with certain optimizations to select a tree that minimizes the amount of WAN traffic. Hart (1988) discusses bridging over WANs in more detail.

When the internetwork becomes very large, problems of scale appear. For example, when each of the 150 million telephones in the United States is eventually replaced by an intelligent telephone, the basic spanning tree algorithm will take much too long to run. An algorithm that can handle large networks by partitioning them into multiple communicating spanning trees is described by Sincoskie and Cotton (1988).

Source Routing Bridges

Transparent bridges have the advantage of being easy to install. You just plug them in and walk away. On the other hand, they do not make optimal use of the bandwidth, since they only use a subset of the topology (the spanning tree). The relative importance of these two (and other) factors led to a split within the 802 committees (Pitt, 1988). The CSMA/CD and token bus people chose the transparent bridge. The ring people (with encouragement from IBM) preferred a scheme called **source routing**, which we will now describe. For addition details, see (Dixon and Pitt, 1988; Hamner and Samsen, 1988; and Pitt and Winkler, 1987).

Reduced to its barest essentials, source routing assumes that the sender of each frame knows whether or not the destination is on its own LAN. When sending a frame to a different LAN, the source machine sets the high-order bit of the destination address to 1, to mark it. Furthermore, it includes in the frame header the exact path that the frame is to follow.

This path is constructed as follows. Each LAN has a unique 12-bit number, and each bridge has a 4-bit number that uniquely identifies it in the context of its LANs. Thus, two bridges far apart may both have number 3, but two bridges on the same LAN must have different bridge numbers. A route is then a sequence of bridge, LAN, bridge, LAN, ... numbers. Referring to Fig. 5-32, the route from A to C would be (B1, L2, B2, L3), where we have added the codes B and L for convenience, to show which items are bridges and which are LANs.

A source routing bridge is only interested in those frames with the high-order bit of the destination set to 1. For each such frame that it sees, it scans the route looking for the number of the LAN on which the frame arrived. If this LAN number is followed by its own bridge number, the bridge forwards the frame onto the LAN whose number follows its bridge number in the route. If the incoming LAN number is followed by the number of some other bridge, it does not forward the frame.

This algorithm lends itself to three possible implementations:

1. Software: the bridge runs in promiscuous mode, copying all frames to its memory to see if they have the high-order destination bit set to 1. If so, the frame is inspected further, otherwise it is not.

2. Hybrid: the bridge's LAN interface inspects the high-order destination bit and only gives it frames with the bit set. This interface is easy to build into hardware and greatly reduces the number of frames the bridge must inspect.

3. Hardware: the bridge's LAN interface not only checks the high-order destination bit, but it also scans the route to see if this bridge must do forwarding. Only frames that must actually be forwarded are given to the bridge. This implementation require the most complex hardware, but wastes no bridge CPU cycles because all irrelevant frames are screened out.

These three implementations vary in their cost and performance. The first one has no additional hardware cost for the interface, but may require a very fast CPU to handle all the frames. The last one requires a special VLSI chip, but offloads much of the processing from the bridge to the chip, so that a slower CPU can be used, or alternatively, the bridge can handle more LANs.

Implicit in the design of source routing is that every machine in the internetwork knows the exact path to every other machine. How these routes are discovered is an important part of the source routing algorithm. The basic idea is that if a destination is unknown, the source issues a broadcast frame asking where it is. This **discovery frame** is copied by every bridge so that it reaches every LAN on the internetwork. When the reply comes back, the bridges record their identity in it, so that the original sender can see the exact route taken and ultimately choose the best route.

While this algorithm clearly finds the best route (it finds *all* routes), it suffers from a frame explosion. Consider the configuration of Fig. 5-34, with N LANs linearly connected by triple bridges. Each discovery frame sent by machine A is copied by each of the three bridges on LAN 1, yielding three discovery frames on LAN 2. Each of these is copied by each of the bridges on LAN 2, resulting in nine frame on LAN 3. By the time we reach LAN N, $3^N - 1$ frames are circulating. If a dozen sets of bridges are traversed, more than half a million discovery frames will have to be injected into the last ring, causing severe congestion.

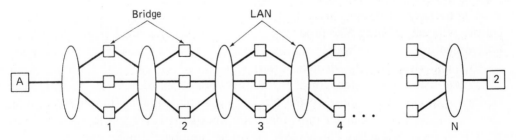

Fig. 5-34. A series of LANs connected by triple bridges.

A somewhat analogous process happens with the transparent bridge, only not nearly so severe. When an unknown frame arrives, it is flooded, but only along the spanning tree, so the total volume of frames sent is linear with the size of the network, not exponential.

Once a host has discovered a route to a certain destination, it stores the route in a cache, so that the discovery process will not have to be run next time. While this approach greatly limits the impact of the frame explosion, it does put some administrative burden on all the hosts, and the whole algorithm is definitely not transparent.

Comparison of 802 Bridges

The transparent and source routing bridges each have advantages and disadvantages. In this section we will discuss some of the major ones. They are summarized in Fig. 5-35 and covered in more detail in (Soha and Perlman, 1988; and Zhang, 1988). Be warned, however, that every one of the points is highly contested.

Issue	Transparent bridge	Source routing bridge
Orientation	Connectionless	Connection-oriented
Transparency	Fully transparent	Not transparent
Configuration	Automatic	Manual
Routing	Suboptimal	Optimal
Locating	Backward learning	Discovery frames
Failures	Handled by the bridges	Handled by the hosts
Complexity	In the bridges	In the hosts

Fig. 5-35. Comparison of transparent and source routing bridges.

At the heart of the difference between the two bridge types is the distinction between connectionless and connection-oriented networking. The transparent bridges have no concept of a virtual circuit at all, and route each frame independently from all the others. The source routing bridges, in contrast, determine a route using discovery frames and then use that route thereafter.

The transparent bridges are completely invisible to the hosts and are fully compatible with all existing 802 products. The source bridges are neither transparent nor compatible. To use source routing, hosts must be fully aware of the bridging scheme, and must actively participate in it.

When using transparent bridges, no network management is needed. The bridges configure themselves to the topology automatically. With source routing bridges, the network manager must manually install the LAN and bridge numbers. Mistakes, such as duplicating a LAN or bridge number, can be very difficult to detect, as they may cause some frames to loop, but not others on different routes. Furthermore, when connecting two previously disjoint internetworks, with transparent bridges there is nothing to do except connect them, whereas with source routing, it may be necessary to manually change many LAN numbers to make them unique in the combined internetwork.

One of the few advantages of source routing is that, in theory, it can use optimal routing, whereas transparent bridging is restricted to the spanning tree. Furthermore, source routing can also make good use of parallel bridges between two LANs to split the load. Whether actual bridges will be clever enough to make use of these theoretical advantages is questionable.

Locating destinations is done using backward learning in the transparent bridge and using discovery frames in source routing bridges. The disadvantage of backward learning is that the bridges have to wait until a frame from a particular machine happens to come along in order to learn where that machine is. The disadvantage of discovery frames is the exponential explosion in moderate to large internetworks with parallel bridges.

Failures handling is quite different in the two schemes. Transparent bridges learn about bridge and LAN failures and other topology changes quickly and automatically, just from listening to each other's control frames. Hosts do not notice these changes at all.

With source routing, the situation is quite different. When a bridge fails, machines that are routing over it initially notice that their frames are no longer being acknowledged, so they time out and try over and over. Finally, they conclude that something is wrong, but they still do not know if the problem is with the destination itself, or with the current route. Only by sending another discovery frame can they see if the destination is available. Unfortunately, when a major bridge fails, a large number of hosts will have to experience timeouts and send new discovery frames before the problem is resolved, even if an alternative route is available. This greater vulnerability to failures is one of the major weaknesses of all connection-oriented systems.

Finally, we come to complexity and cost, a very controversial topic. If source routing bridges have a VLSI chip that reads in only those frames that must be forwarded, these bridges will experience a lighter frame processing load and deliver a better performance for a given investment in hardware. Without this chip they will do worse because the amount of processing per frame (searching the route in the frame header) is substantially more.

In addition, source routing puts extra complexity in the hosts: they must store routes, send discovery frames, and copy route information into each frame. All of these things require memory and CPU cycles. Since there are typically one to two orders of magnitude more hosts than bridges, it may be better to put the extra cost and complexity into a few bridges, rather than in all the hosts.

5.4.3. Gateways

In contrast to bridges, gateways operate at the network level. This gives them more flexibility, for example, in translating addresses between very dissimilar networks, but it also makes them slower. As a consequence, gateways are commonly used in WANs, where no one expects them to handle more than 10,000 packets/sec, a common requirement for LAN bridges.

Two styles of gateways are common, one for connection-oriented networks and one for connectionless networks. We will study both of these in turn below.

Connection-Oriented Gateways

The OSI model permits two styles of internetworking: a connection-oriented concatenation of virtual circuit subnets, and a datagram internet style. In this section we will look at the virtual circuit approach; in the next one we will examine the datagram method.

The virtual circuit method differs from interconnection using bridges in that it happens in the network layer (see Fig. 5-27) rather than the data link layer, but it also differs in other ways. One of these differences stems from the nature of a bridge. It is a small minicomputer or microcomputer. When the bridge and all the LANs are owned by the same organization, ownership and operation of the bridge do not generate any special problems. However, when a gateway is between two WANs run by different organizations, possibly in different countries, the joint operation of a small minicomputer can lead to a lot of finger pointing.

To eliminate these problems, a slightly different approach is taken. The relay of Fig. 5-27 is effectively ripped apart in the middle and the two parts of 3c are connected with a wire, as shown in Fig. 5-36. Each of the halves is called a **half-gateway** and each one is owned and operated by one of the network operators. The whole problem of gatewaying then reduces to agreeing to a common protocol to use on the wire. As long as both parties use the common protocol on the wire, they can arrange their sublayers 3a, 3b, and 3c any way that is convenient for them.

The protocol that the half-gateways speak over the wire is CCITT's **X.75** protocol, which is almost identical to X.25 (discussed later in this chapter). The X.75 model is based on the idea of building up an internetwork connection by concatenating a series of intranetwork and half-gateway to half-gateway virtual circuits. The model is shown in Fig. 5-37(a) The connection between the source host, in one network, and the destination host, in another network, is composed of five adjacent virtual circuits, marked VC 1-5. VC 1 goes from the source host to a half-gateway (called a **signaling terminal** or **STE** by CCITT), in its own network. VC 2 goes from the half-gateway in the source network to a half-gateway in an intermediate network, assuming that there is no direct connection between the source and destination networks. VCs 3 and 5 are also intranet, like VC 1, and VC 4 is internet, like VC 2.

In this model a connection to a host in a distant network is set up the same way normal connections are established. The subnet sees that the destination is remote, chooses an appropriate (half-) gateway and builds a virtual circuit to the gateway. The first gateway records the existence of the virtual circuit in its tables and

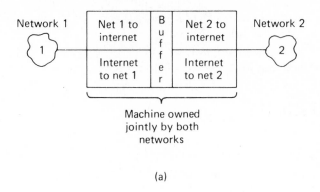

Machine owned
jointly by both
networks

(a)

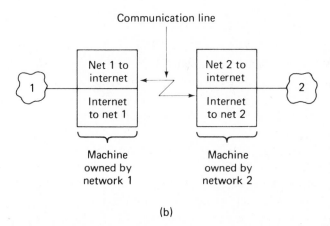

(b)

Fig. 5-36. (a) A full gateway. (b) Two half-gateways.

proceeds to build another virtual circuit to the next gateway. This process continues until the destination host has been reached.

Once data packets begin flowing along the path, each gateway relays incoming packets, converting between packet formats and virtual circuit numbers as needed. Clearly all data packets must traverse the same sequence of gateways, although VCs 1, 3, and 5 in Fig. 5-37(a) might be implemented internally using datagrams, so that not all packets need follow precisely the same route from source to destination. In practice, networks that use virtual circuits *between* networks also use them internally.

The essential feature of this approach is that a sequence of virtual circuits is set up from the source through one or more gateways to the destination. Each gateway maintains tables telling which virtual circuits pass through it, where they are to be routed, and what the new virtual circuit number is. The whole arrangement is similar to the fixed routing of Fig. 5-6, except that only the sequence of gateways is fixed, not (necessarily) the full sequence of IMPs.

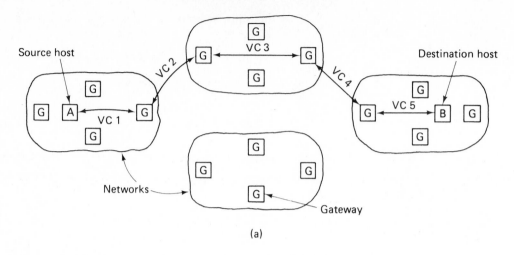

(a)

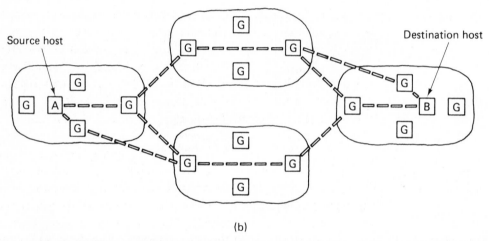

(b)

Fig. 5-37. (a) Internetworking using concatenated virtual circuits. (b) Internetworking using datagrams.

Figure 5-38 shows the protocols used on the various lines when two X.25 networks are connected. The source host talks to the subnet using X.25. The internal IMP-IMP protocol is not specified by CCITT and probably will be different in every network. The protocol used between the gateways and the rest of the subnet is also left open, but here there are clearly two distinct choices: the internal IMP-IMP protocol, or X.25. If this protocol is the IMP-IMP protocol, the network regards the gateway as an IMP. If it is X.25, the subnet regards the gateway as a host.

Although the X.75 protocol itself only applies to the gateway-to-gateway lines, it effectively dictates the concatenated virtual circuit architecture by requiring all packets on a connection to pass over the same gateway-to-gateway virtual circuit in sequence. It is hard to see how different packets could use different gateways and

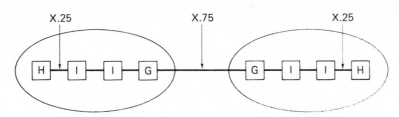

Fig. 5-38. Protocols in the CCITT internetwork model.

still meet this requirement. The X.75 protocol only differs in minor ways from X.25, such as the range of facilities available.

Connectionless Gateways

The alternative internetwork model to CCITT's is the datagram model, shown in Fig. 5-37(b). In this model, the only service the network layer offers to the transport layer is the ability to inject datagrams into the subnet, and hope for the best. There is no notion of a virtual circuit at all in the network layer, let alone a concatenation of them. This model does not require all packets belonging to one connection to traverse the same sequence of gateways. In Fig. 5-37(b) datagrams from A to B are shown taking a wide variety of different routes through the internetwork. On the other hand, no one guarantees that the packets arrive at the destination in order, assuming that they arrive at all.

To see how the internet datagram model works, let us follow the path of the transport message of Fig. 5-39 from host A to host B. Datagrams have a fixed maximum size, so if the message is longer than the limit, the transport layer chops it up into as many datagrams as necessary. It is these datagrams that move from network to network on their way from source to destination. Only at the end of their journey does the transport layer at the destination machine reassemble the datagrams back into the original message.

In order for a datagram to go from gateway to gateway in the internet, the datagram must be encapsulated in the data link format for each network it passes through. In Fig. 5-39, the datagram is given a header and a trailer to form frame 1, which is then passed transparently through network 1. When the datagram reaches gateway 1, the data link header and trailer are stripped off, and the naked datagram emerges again, like a butterfly coming out of its cocoon. While traveling through network 2, the wrapping is different, but the same datagram emerges again at the next gateway. This process of wrapping and unwrapping the datagram occurs repeatedly until the datagram reaches the destination host.

Each network imposes some maximum size on its packets. These limits have various causes, among them:

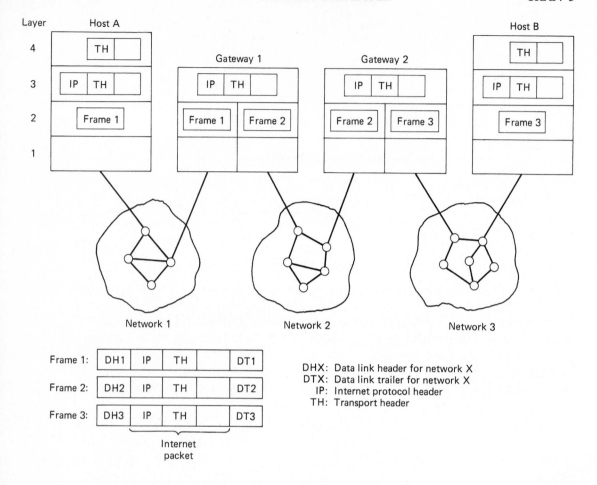

Fig. 5-39. A datagram moving from network to network.

1. Hardware (e.g., the width of a TDM transmission slot).

2. Operating system (e.g., all buffers are 512 bytes).

3. Protocols (e.g., the number of bits in the packet length field).

4. Compliance with some (inter)national standard.

5. Desire to reduce error induced retransmissions to some level.

6. Desire to prevent one packet from occupying the channel too long.

The result of all these factors is that the network designers are not free to choose any maximum packet size they wish. Some typical examples of maximum packet lengths in actual networks are:

1. HDLC: in principle infinite.

2. 802.4: 65,528 bits.

3. X.25: 32768 bits.

4. ARPA Packet Radio Network: 2032 bits.

5. ARPANET: 1008 bits.

6. University of Hawaii ALOHANET: 640 bits.

An obvious problem appears when a large packet wants to travel through a network whose maximum packet size is too small. This problem has received a great deal of attention in the literature and some proposals for solving it have been made.

One solution is to make sure the problem does not occur in the first place. In other words, the internet should use a routing algorithm that avoids sending packets through networks that cannot handle them. However, this solution is no solution at all. What happens if the original source packet is too large to be handled by the destination network? The routing algorithm can hardly bypass the destination. Nevertheless, intelligent routing can minimize the extent of the problem.

Basically, the only solution to the problem is to allow gateways to break packets up into **fragments**, sending each fragment as a separate internet packet. However, as every parent of a small child knows, converting a large object into small fragments is considerably easier than the reverse process. (Physicists have even given this effect a name: the second law of thermodynamics.) Packet-switching networks, too, have trouble putting the fragments back together again.

Two opposing strategies exist for recombining the fragments back into the original packet. The first strategy is to make fragmentation caused by a "small-packet" network transparent to any subsequent networks through which the packet must pass on its way to the ultimate destination. This option is shown in Fig. 5-40(a). When an oversized packet arrives at a gateway, the gateway breaks it up into fragments. Each fragment is addressed to the same exit gateway, where the pieces are recombined. In this way passage through the small-packet network has been made transparent. Subsequent networks are not even aware that fragmentation has occurred.

Transparent fragmentation is simple but has some problems. For one thing, the exit gateway must know when it has received all the pieces, so that either a count field or an "end of packet" bit must be included in each packet. For another thing, all packets must exit via the same gateway. By not allowing some fragments to follow one route to the ultimate destination, and other fragments a disjoint route, some performance may be lost. A third problem is possible reassembly lockup at the exit gateway. A last problem is the overhead required to repeatedly reassemble and then refragment a large packet passing through a series of small-packet networks.

The other fragmentation strategy is to refrain from recombining fragments at

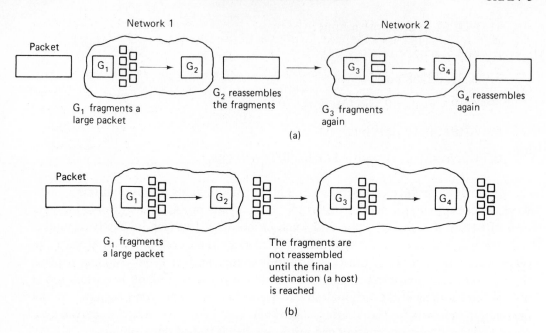

Fig. 5-40. (a) Transparent fragmentation. (b) Nontransparent fragmentation.

any intermediate gateways. Once a packet has been fragmented, each fragment is treated as though it were an original packet. All fragments are passed through the exit gateway (or gateways), as shown in Fig. 5-40(b). Recombination occurs only at the destination host.

Nontransparent fragmentation also has some problems. For example, it requires *every* host to be able to do reassembly. Yet another problem is that when a large packet is fragmented the total overhead increases, because each fragment must have a header. Whereas in the first method this overhead disappears as soon as the small packet network is exited, in this method the overhead remains for the rest of the journey. An advantage of this method, however, is that multiple exit gateways can now be used. Of course, if the concatenated virtual circuit model is being used, this advantage is of no use.

Shoch (1979) has proposed having each packet carry a bit specifying whether or not the ultimate destination is prepared to reassemble fragments. If it is not, any gateway fragmenting a packet must arrange for some other gateway to reassemble the pieces. If the ultimate destination is prepared to do reassembly itself, fragmentation may or may not be transparent, at each gateway's discretion.

When a packet is fragmented, the fragments must be numbered in such a way that the original data stream can be reconstructed. One way of numbering the fragments is to use a tree. If packet 0 must be split up, the pieces are called 0.0, 0.1, 0.2, etc. If these fragments must themselves be fragmented at a subsequent gateway, the pieces are numbered 0.0.0, 0.0.1, 0.0.2, ..., 0.1.0, 0.1.1, 0.1.2, etc. If enough fields have been reserved in the header for the worst case and if there are no duplicates generated anywhere, this scheme is sufficient to ensure that all the pieces can be correctly reassembled at the destination, no matter what order they arrive in.

However, if even one network loses or discards packets, there is a need for end-to-end retransmissions, with unfortunate effects for the numbering system. Suppose that a 1024-bit packet is initially fragmented into four equal-sized fragments, 0.0, 0.1, 0.2, and 0.3. Fragment 0.1 is lost, but the other parts arrive at the destination. Eventually, the source times out and retransmits the original packet again. Only this time the route taken passes through a network with a 512-bit limit, so two fragments are generated. When the new fragment 0.1 arrives at the destination, the receiver will think that all four pieces are now accounted for and reconstruct the packet incorrectly.

A completely different (and better) numbering system is for the internetwork protocol to define an elementary fragment size small enough that the elementary fragment can pass through every network. When a packet is fragmented, all the pieces are equal to the elementary fragment size except the last one, which may be shorter. An internet packet may contain several fragments, for efficiency reasons. The internet header must provide the original packet number, and the number of the (first) elementary fragment contained in the frame. As usual, there must also be a bit indicating that the last elementary fragment contained within the internet packet is the last one of the original packet.

This approach requires two sequence fields in the internet header: the original packet number, and the fragment number. There is clearly a trade-off between the size of the elementary fragment and the number of bits in the fragment number. Because the elementary fragment size is presumed to be acceptable to every network, subsequent fragmentation of an internet packet containing several fragments causes no problem. The ultimate limit here is to have the elementary fragment be a single bit or byte, with the fragment number then being the bit or byte offset within the original packet, as shown in Fig. 5-41.

Some internet protocols take this method even further, and consider the entire transmission on a virtual circuit to be one giant packet, so that each fragment contains the absolute byte number of the first byte within the fragment. Some other issues relating to fragmentation are discussed in (Kent and Mogul, 1987).

5.4.4. Comparison of Connection-Oriented and Connectionless Gateways

The concatenated virtual circuit and datagram approaches have different strengths and weaknesses. The concatenated virtual circuit model has essentially the same advantages as using virtual circuits within a single subnet: buffers can be reserved in advance (in the gateways) to ease congestion, sequencing can be guaranteed, short headers can be used, and the troubles caused by delayed duplicate packets can be avoided.

It also has the same disadvantages: table space required in the gateways for each open connection, whether or not there is any traffic, no alternate routing to

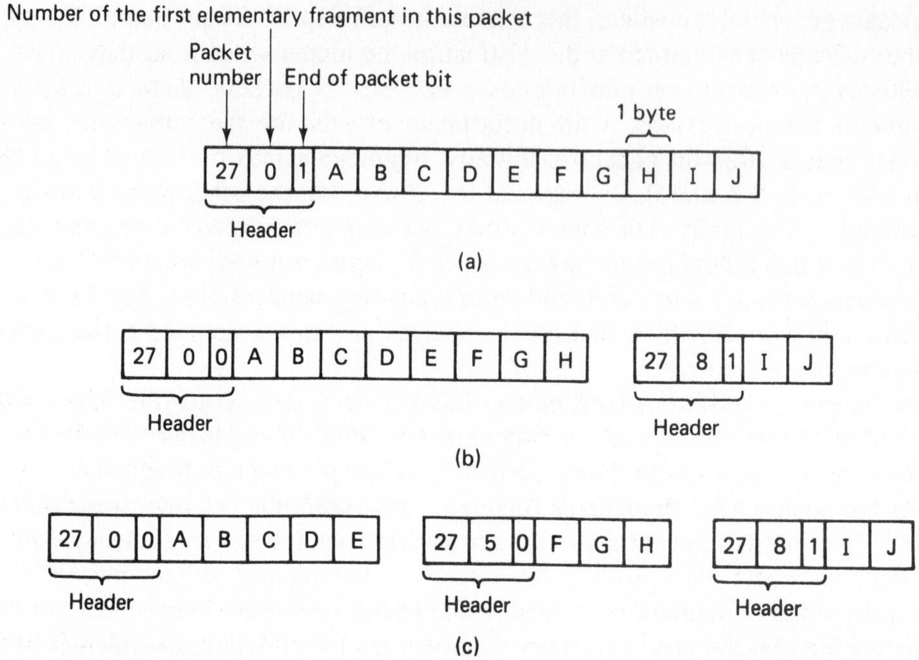

Number of the first elementary fragment in this packet

Packet
number | End of packet bit

1 byte

| 27 | 0 | 1 | A | B | C | D | E | F | G | H | I | J |

Header

(a)

| 27 | 0 | 0 | A | B | C | D | E | F | G | H | | 27 | 8 | 1 | I | J |

Header   Header

(b)

| 27 | 0 | 0 | A | B | C | D | E | | 27 | 5 | 0 | F | G | H | | 27 | 8 | 1 | I | J |

Header   Header   Header

(c)

Fig. 5-41. Fragmentation when the elementary data size is 1 byte. (a) Original packet, containing 10 data bytes. (b) Fragments after passing through a network with maximum packet size of 8 bytes. (c) Fragments after passing through a size 5 gateway.

avoid congested areas, and vulnerability to gateway failures anywhere along the path. It also has the disadvantage of being difficult, if not impossible, to implement if one of the networks involved is an unreliable datagram network.

The properties of the datagram approach to internetworking are the same as those of datagram subnets: more potential for congestion, but also more potential for adapting to it, robustness in the face of gateway failures, and longer headers needed. Various adaptive routing algorithms are possible in the internet, just as they are within a single datagram network.

A major advantage of the datagram approach to internetworking is that it can be used over subnets that do not use virtual circuits inside. Many LANs, mobile networks (e.g., aircraft and naval fleets), and even some WANs fall into this category. When an internet includes one of these, serious problems occur if the internetworking strategy is based on virtual circuits.

5.4.5. Bridge and Gateway Software

The software used in a bridge or gateway is quite different from ordinary host software, and as such it is worth looking at a little bit. The reason for this difference is not hard to find. The performance requirements here are critical. Bridges and gateways are expected to accept and forward traffic from one network to another in real time without slowing down the operation of either network.

Consider the worst case requirements for a LAN bridge. Imagine that a continuous stream of 64-byte packets must be forwarded from one 10-Mbps LAN to another. The 64-byte packets arrive at a rate of one frame per 51 μsec (almost 20,000 frames/sec). Thus the bridge must get an interrupt, process a packet and retransmit it, all in a time of 51 μsec. If packets can arrive from both sides simultaneously, the required throughput is doubled. Even with intelligent front-end processors that collect the bits of the incoming packets and assemble them in memory before causing an interrupt, 51 μsec is not much time. Bridges are nearly always CPU bound.

As a consequence of the heavy workload, the software must be carefully structured for maximum efficiency. At one extreme, the entire bridge or gateway could be interrupt driven. In this model, each arriving packet causes an interrupt, which disables further interrupts and processes the packet to completion right in the interrupt routine. While this approach is very fast, it leads to poorly structured software and should be avoided.

At the other extreme, the software is divided into processes, with each process having a well-defined task. Figure 5-42 shows a simple example of a trilateral gateway (or bridge). Each of the nine processes runs in its own address space. When a packet arrives from network 1, 2, or 3, process 2, 3, or 5, respectively, is made runnable. That process verifies the checksum, converts the packet to an internal network-independent format if needed, and deposits it in the work queue for process 7, the routing process. These input processes must have the highest priority to avoid losing input packets.

When none of the high priority processes, 2, 3, or 5, or medium priority processes, 1, 4, or 6 are able to run and process 7 has work in its queue, it takes the first queued packet, determines how to route it, and puts the packet in the work queue for one of the output processes (1, 4, or 6), which converts it to the appropriate output format and starts the transmitter (if it was idle). As soon as packet transmission has started, the output process terminates to let another process run. When the interrupt comes in at the end of the transmission, the output process is enabled for running, at which time it dequeues the packet just transmitted and starts the next one.

Packet filtering is also done by the routing process. If the packet under examination is a control packet or a packet whose destination is in the same network as its source, it is not queued for output, but just ignored.

The background processes 8 and 9 run periodically at the lowest priority. This process-oriented approach is well structured but slow due to the process switching overhead (each process switch requires setting up a new memory map).

A reasonable compromise is to keep the process model, but have all the processes run within a single address space in kernel mode. For a general-purpose operating system this approach would not work, but since all the gateway processes

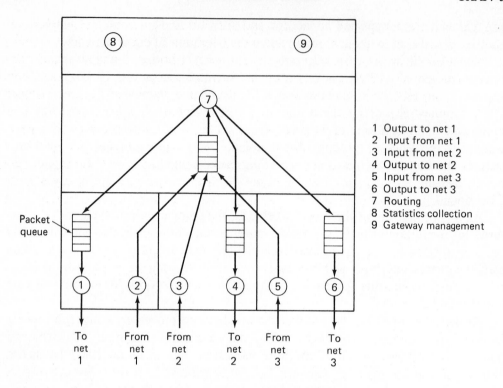

Packet
queue

1 Output to net 1
2 Input from net 1
3 Input from net 2
4 Output to net 2
5 Input from net 3
6 Output to net 3
7 Routing
8 Statistics collection
9 Gateway management

To net 1   From net 1   From net 2   To net 2   From net 3   To net 3

Fig. 5-42. A process-structured trilateral gateway.

can be assumed to be well-behaved, the gain in speed is worth the loss of security.

The gateway scheduling algorithm is also critical. Rather than using round-robin scheduling or some other form of time-slicing, it is probably better to let each process run to completion. Not only does run-to-completion reduce the number of process switches, but when a process finishes with the current packet it has no state information to remember so its registers and stack need not be saved. In fact, it can simply schedule its own successor by finding the highest priority runnable process and jumping to it. That process thus inherits the registers and empty stack of its predecessor. Only one stack is needed, no matter how many processes there are.

On some machines, interrupt processing overhead is substantial. One way to avoid it is to run the gateway with interrupts disabled. When a process finishes, it examines (polls) each network interface to see if a transmission has finished. If so, the corresponding process is marked as runnable, and the highest priority runnable process is executed.

The interprocess communication between the processes is critical. Actually passing messages between processes by copying them would be unbearably slow. It is better to pass buffer pointers. However, if one process allocates a packet buffer and puts a pointer to it in another process' work queue, how does the first process know when to deallocate the buffer? In general, it does not, so the receiving process must either reuse the buffer itself, or explicitly free it.

Buffer management is complicated by the fact that packets may change size as they move around the gateway, with headers being attached and stripped in various places. This effect is most pronounced if multiple protocol layers must be traversed within the gateway. One way to solve the problem is to set up the packet receive hardware to read packets into buffers not at the start of the buffer, but at a distance from the start equal to the size of the largest header. For example, if networks 1, 2, and 3 of Fig. 5-42 have headers of 8, 16, and 24 bytes, respectively, then all packets read in from network 1 should begin at byte 16, as shown in Fig. 5-43(a). That way, if the packet must eventually be transmitted onto network 3, with a 24-byte header, there is room in the buffer for the new header, as shown in Fig. 5-43(b). If packet fragmentation is potentially required, the situation becomes much more complex and a more sophisticated buffer management strategy is needed.

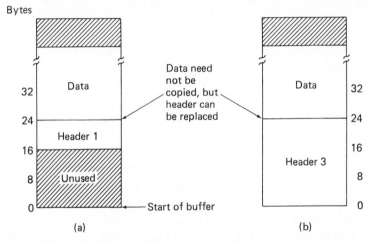

Fig. 5-43. Packets should be read in at an offset from the start of the buffer to allow enough room for the worst case header to be prepended to the data.

Timer management is another important issue. Depending on the layer and nature of the gateway, it may be necessary to wait until a packet has been acknowledged before releasing its buffer. Because most packets are not lost, most timers do not expire. Therefore, what is important is that setting a timer does not take much time. The amount of time required to handle a timer that has gone off is less critical.

Some gateways must reverse the order of the bits in a byte (e.g., for transmission between 802.3 and 802.5). The fastest way to invert the bits is to hardwire bit 0 on the input side to bit 7 on the output side, bit 1 on the input side to bit 6 on the output side, and so forth, so that the reversal is done during transmission between the interface chip and memory. If this special hardware is not available, the next best thing to do is have a 256-entry table indexed by byte value. The i-th entry in this table is the inverted bit pattern for byte i. For inversion in both directions, two 256-byte tables are needed. However, bit reversal is very expensive, even with table lookup, because it means that every byte must be examined; it is even worse than copying, since that can usually be done with a single BLOCK MOVE instruction.

It is worth noting the design of our example gateway is not all that different from the design of an ordinary IMP. There too, packets come in on various input lines, are routed, and are retransmitted. The main difference is that no format conversions or header changes are needed in the IMPs.

More details about gateways, their software, and their problems are given in (Benhamou and Estrin, 1983; Bosack and Hedrick, 1988; and Seifert, 1988). LAN-WAN gateways are described in (Folts, 1984; and Spiegelhalter, 1984).

5.5. EXAMPLES OF THE NETWORK LAYER

The above material should give you a good feeling for the choices and options available to subnet designers. In the remainder of this chapter we will examine our usual example networks to see what choices their designers actually made in practice.

5.5.1. The Network Layer in Public Networks

To prevent networks in different countries from developing mutually incompatible interfaces, in 1974 CCITT proposed international standard network access protocols for layers 1, 2, and 3. These protocols were revised in 1976, 1980, 1984, and so on, *ad infinitum*. These standards are collectively known as **X.25** The layer 3 protocol is often called the **X.25 PLP (Packet Layer Protocol)** to distinguish it from the lower two layers. The significance of X.25 PLP is that it is widely used as the connection-oriented network layer protocol in the OSI model.

X.25 defines the interface between the host, called a **DTE (Data Terminal Equipment)** by CCITT, and the carrier's equipment, called a **DCE (Data Circuit-terminating Equipment)** by CCITT. An IMP is known as a **DSE (Data Switching Exchange)**. In this section we will adhere to the CCITT terminology because it is in widespread use in public network circles. X.25 defines the format and meaning of the information exchanged across the DTE - DCE interface for the layer 1, 2, and 3 protocols (see Fig. 5-44). Since this interface separates the carrier's equipment (the DCE) from the user's equipment (the DTE), it is important that the interface be very carefully defined. Notice that CCITT's use of the word "interface" differs from the OSI usage, as we have already pointed out in Fig. 2-30.

X.25 layer 1 deals with the electrical, mechanical, procedural, and functional interface between the DTE and DCE. Actually, X.25 does not define these things, but rather references two other standards, X.21 and X.21 *bis*, which define the digital and analog interfaces, respectively. We discussed X.21 in Chapter 2. X.21 *bis*

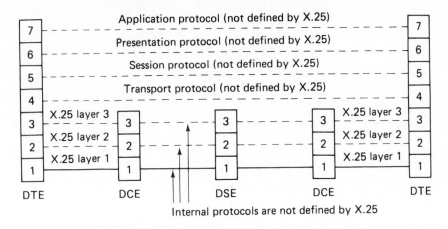

Fig. 5-44. The place of X.25 in the protocol hierarchy.

is an interim standard to be used on analog networks until digital networks become widely available. It is essentially RS-232-C.

The job of layer 2 is to ensure reliable communication between the DTE and the DCE, even though they may be connected by a noisy telephone line. The protocols used are LAP and LAPB, as discussed in Chapter 4.

Layer 3 manages connections between a pair of DTEs. Two forms of connection are provided, **virtual calls** and **permanent virtual circuits**. A virtual call is like an ordinary telephone call: a connection is established, data are transferred, and then the connection is released. In contrast, a permanent virtual circuit is like a leased line. It is always present, and the DTE at either end can just send data whenever it wants to, without any setup. Permanent virtual circuits are normally used in situations with a high volume of data. Since data transfer on a permanent virtual circuit is the same as on a virtual call, we will not discuss permanent virtual circuits any further.

Connections (virtual calls in CCITT terminology) are made as follows. When a DTE wants to communicate with another DTE, it must first set up a connection. To do this, the DTE builds a *CALL REQUEST* packet and passes it to its DCE. The subnet then delivers the packet to the destination DCE, which then gives it to the destination DTE. If the destination DTE wishes to accept the call, it sends a *CALL ACCEPTED* packet back. When the originating DTE receives the *CALL ACCEPTED* packet, the virtual circuit is established. (Actually, when a packet comes into the originating DTE it is called a *CALL CONNECTED* packet, but it is in fact identical to the *CALL ACCEPTED* packet sent by the remote DTE.)

At this point both DTEs may use the full-duplex connection to exchange data packets. When either side has had enough, it sends a *CLEAR REQUEST* packet to the other side, which then sends a *CLEAR CONFIRMATION* packet back as an acknowledgement. The three phases of an X.25 connection are shown in Fig. 5-45.

The originating DTE may choose any idle virtual circuit number to identify the

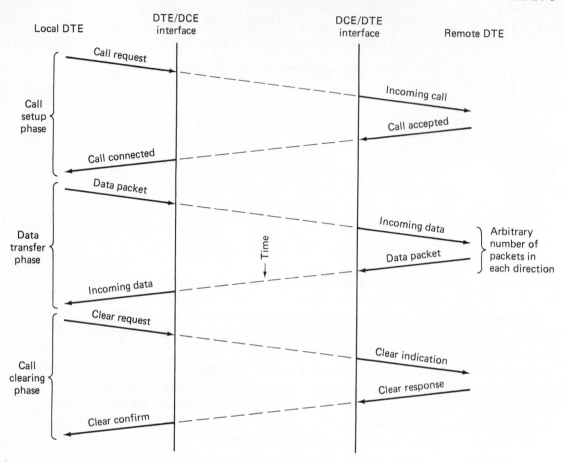

Fig. 5-45. The three phases of an X.25 connection.

connection. If this virtual circuit number is in use at the destination DTE, the destination DCE must replace it by an idle one before delivering the packet. Thus the choice of circuit number on outgoing calls is determined by the DTE, and on incoming calls by the DCE. It might happen that both simultaneously choose the same one, leading to a **call collision**. X.25 specifies that in the event of a call collision, the outgoing call is put through and the incoming one is canceled. Many networks will attempt to put the incoming call through shortly thereafter using a different virtual circuit. To minimize the chance of getting a call collision, the DTE normally chooses the highest available identifier for outgoing calls and the DCE chooses the lowest one for incoming calls.

The format of the *CALL REQUEST* packet is shown in Fig. 5-46(a). This packet, as well as all other X.25 packets, begins with a 3-byte header. (CCITT calls bytes **octets**.)

The *Group* and *Channel* fields together form a 12-bit virtual circuit number.

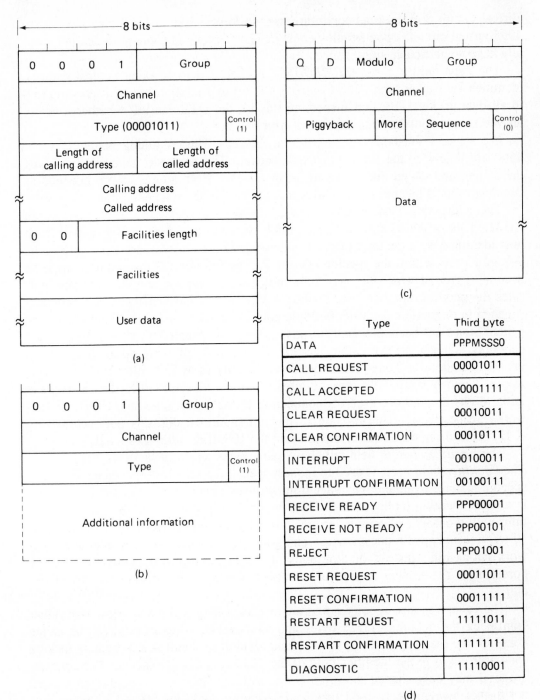

Fig. 5-46. X.25 packet formats. (a) Call request format. (b) Control packet format. (c) Data packet format. (d) Type field (P = Piggyback, S = Sequence, M = More).

Virtual circuit 0 is reserved for future use, so in principle, a DTE may have up to 4095 virtual circuits open simultaneously. The *Group* and *Channel* fields individually have no particular significance.

The *Type* field in the *CALL REQUEST* packet, and in all other control packets, identifies the packet type. The *Control* bit is set to 1 in all control packets and to 0 in all data packets. By first inspecting this bit the DTE can tell whether a newly arrived packet contains data or control information.

We are now finished with the (3-byte) header. The remaining fields of Fig. 5-46(a) are unique to the *CALL REQUEST* packet. The next two fields tell how long the calling and called addresses are, respectively. Both addresses are encoded as decimal digits, 4 bits per digit. Old habits die hard in the telephone industry.

The addressing system used in X.25 is defined in CCITT recommendation **X.121**. This system is similar to the public switched telephone network, with each host identified by a decimal number consisting of a country code, a network code, and an address within the specified network. The full address may contain up to 14 decimal digits, of which the first three indicate the country, and the next one indicates the network number. For countries expected to have many public networks engaged in international traffic, multiple country codes have been allocated e.g., the United States has been allocated country codes 310 through 329, allowing up to 200 networks, Canada has been allocated 302 through 307, allowing up to 60 networks, but the Kingdom of Tonga has been allocated only code 539, allowing for 10 networks. Country codes with initial digits of 0 and 1 are reserved for future use, and initial digits 8 and 9 are used for connecting to the public telex and telephone networks, respectively. The division of the remaining 10 digits is not specified by X.121, permitting each network to allocate the 10 billion addresses itself.

The *Facilities length* field tells how many bytes worth of facilities field follow. The *Facilities* field itself is used to request special features for this connection. The specific features available may vary from network to network. One possible feature is reverse charging (collect calls). This facility is especially important to organizations with thousands of remote terminals that initiate calls to a central computer. If all terminals always request reverse charging, the organization only gets one "network phone bill" instead of thousands of them. High-priority delivery is also a possibility. Yet another feature is a simplex, instead of a full-duplex, virtual circuit.

The caller can also specify a maximum packet length and a window size rather than using the defaults of 128 bytes and two packets, respectively. If the callee does not like the proposed maximum packet length or window size he may make a counterproposal in the facilities field of the *CALL ACCEPTED* packet. The counterproposal may only change the original one to bring it closer to the default values, not further away. Figure 5-47 lists some common facilities offered by many networks.

Some facilities may be selected when the customer becomes a network subscriber rather than on a call-by-call basis. These include closed user groups (no

Use extended (7–bit) sequence numbers
Set nonstandard window size
Set nonstandard packet size
Set throughput class (75 bps to 48 kbps)
Request reverse charging
Accept reverse charging
Select carrier (e.g., TELENET or TYMNET)
Outgoing data only (no incoming data)
Incoming data only (no outgoing data)
Select go-back-n vs. selective repeat
Use fast select

Fig. 5-47. Examples of X.25 facilities.

user can call outside the group, for security reasons), maximum window sizes smaller than seven (for terminals with limited buffer space), line speed (e.g., 2400 bps, 4800 bps, 9600 bps), and prohibition of outgoing calls or incoming calls (terminals place calls but do not accept them).

The *User data* field allows the DTE to send up to 16 bytes of data together with the *CALL REQUEST* packet. The DTEs can decide for themselves what to do with this information. They might decide, for example, to use it for indicating which process in the DTE the caller wants to be connected with. Alternatively, it might contain a login password.

The format of the other control packets is shown in Fig. 5-46(b). Some have only a header; others have an additional byte or two. The fourth byte of the *CLEAR REQUEST* packet, for example, tells why the connection is being cleared. *CLEAR REQUEST* packets are automatically generated by the subnet when a *CALL REQUEST* cannot be put through. When this happens, the cause is recorded here. Typical causes are: callee refuses to accept reverse charging, the number is busy, the destination is down, or the network is congested.

Because X.25 makes a distinction between *CLEAR REQUEST* and *CLEAR CONFIRMATION,* there is the possibility of a **clear collision** (i.e., both sides decide to terminate the connection simultaneously). However, it is always obvious what is happening, so there is no ambiguity, and the connection can be simply cleared.

The data packet format is shown in Fig. 5-46(c). The *Q* bit indicates Qualified data. The standard is silent as to what distinguishes qualified from unqualified data, but the intention is to allow protocols in the transport and higher layers to set this bit to 1 to separate their control packets from their data packets. The *Control* field is always 0 for data packets. The *Sequence* and *Piggyback* fields are used for flow control, using a sliding window. The sequence numbers are modulo 8 if *Modulo* is 01, and modulo 128 if *Modulo* is 10. (00 and 11 are illegal.) If modulo 128 sequence numbers are used, the header is extended with an extra byte to accommodate the longer *Sequence* and *Piggyback* fields. The meaning of the *Piggyback* field is determined by the setting of the *D* bit. If *D* = 0, a subsequent acknowledgement means only that the local DCE has received the packet, not that the remote DTE has received it. If *D* = 1, the acknowledgement is a true end-to-end acknowledgement, and means that the packet has been successfully delivered to the remote DTE.

Even if delivery is not guaranteed (i.e., *D* = 0), the *Piggyback* field can be useful. Consider, for example, a carrier that offers a high delay service for bargain hunters. Incoming packets are written onto a magnetic tape, which is then mailed to the destination the next day. In this case the *Piggyback* field is used strictly for flow control. It tells the DTE that the DCE is prepared to accept the next packet, and nothing more.

One point worth noting about acknowledgements in X.25 is that instead of returning the number of the last packet correctly received (as in our examples of Chapter 4), the DTEs are required to return the number of the next packet expected (i.e., one higher). This choice is an arbitrary one, but to be X.25-compatible, DTEs must play the game according to CCITT's rules.

The *More* field allows a DTE to indicate that a group of packets belong together. In a long message, each packet except the last one would have the *More* bit on. Only a full packet may have this bit set. The subnet is free to repackage data in different length packets if it needs to, but it will never combine data from different messages (as indicated by the *More* bit) into one packet.

The standard says that all carriers are required to support a maximum packet length of 128 data bytes. However, it also allows carriers to provide optional maximum lengths of 16, 32, 64, 256, 512, 1024, 2048, and 4096 bytes. In addition, maximum packet length can be negotiated when a connection is set up. The point of maximum packet lengths longer than 128 is for efficiency. The point of maximum packet lengths shorter than 128 is to allow terminals with little buffer space to be protected against long incoming packets.

The other kinds of control packets are listed in Fig. 5-46(d). *INTERRUPT* packets allow a short (32-byte) signal to be sent out of sequence. Since control packets do not bear sequence numbers, they can be delivered as soon as they arrive, without regard to how many sequenced data packets are queued up ahead of them. A typical use for this packet is to convey the fact that a terminal user has hit the quit or break key. An *INTERRUPT* packet is acknowledged by an *INTERRUPT CONFIRMATION* packet.

The *RECEIVE READY (RR)* packet is used to send separate acknowledgements when there is no reverse traffic to piggyback onto. The *PPP* field tells which packet is expected next. When sequence numbers are modulo 128, an extra byte is needed for this packet.

The *RECEIVE NOT READY (RNR)* packet allows a DTE to tell the other side to stop sending packets to it for a while. *RECEIVE READY* can then be used to tell the DCE to proceed.

The *REJECT* packet allows a DTE to request retransmission of a series of packets. The *PPP* field gives the first sequence number desired.

The *RESET* and *RESTART* packets are used to recover from varying degrees of trouble. A *RESET REQUEST* applies to a specific connection and has the effect of reinitializing the window parameters to 0. A common use of *RESET REQUEST* is for the DCE to inform the DTE that the subnet has crashed. After receiving a *RESET REQUEST*, the DTE has no way of knowing if packets that were outstanding at the time have been delivered. Recovery must be done by the transport layer. Up to two extra bytes in the *RESET REQUEST* packet allow the requester to try to explain what the cause of the reset is. The DTE can also initiate a *RESET REQUEST*, of course.

A *RESTART REQUEST* is much more serious. It is used when a DTE or DCE has crashed and is forced to abandon all of its connections. A single *RESTART REQUEST* is equivalent to sending a *RESET REQUEST* separately for each virtual circuit.

A *DIAGNOSTIC* packet is also provided, to allow the network to inform the user of problems, including errors in the packets sent by the user (e.g., an illegal *Type* field).

The X.25 standard contains several state diagrams to describe event sequences such as call setup and call clearing. The diagram of Fig. 5-48 shows the subphases of call setup. Initially, the interface is in state *P1*. A *CALL REQUEST* or *INCOMING CALL* (i.e., the arrival of a *CALL REQUEST* packet) changes the state to *P2* or *P3*, respectively. From these states the data transfer state, *P4*, can be reached, either directly, or via *P5*. Similar diagrams are provided for call clearing, resetting, and restarting.

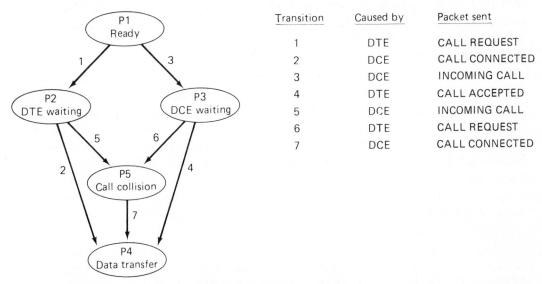

Transition	Caused by	Packet sent
1	DTE	CALL REQUEST
2	DCE	CALL CONNECTED
3	DCE	INCOMING CALL
4	DTE	CALL ACCEPTED
5	DCE	INCOMING CALL
6	DTE	CALL REQUEST
7	DCE	CALL CONNECTED

Fig. 5-48. Call setup in X.25.

The original (1976) X.25 standard was more-or-less as we have described it so far (minus the *D* bit, DIAGNOSTIC packet, the packet length and window size negotiation, and a few other minor items). However, there was considerable demand for a datagram facility, in addition to the virtual circuits. Both the United States and Japan made (conflicting) proposals for the architecture of the datagram service. In the great tradition of international bureaucracies, CCITT accepted *both* of them in 1980, making the protocol even more complicated than it already was.

However, the PTTs, with 100 years of telephone-mentality behind them, did not implement datagrams. Several years later it was noticed that no one was using datagrams, so they were dropped in the 1984 standard.

Nevertheless, the demand for a connectionless service remained. Applications such as point-of-sale terminals, credit card verification, and electronic funds transfer all have the property that the calling party initiates a call with a request, and the called party provides a response. No connection is needed thereafter. To satisfy this demand, CCITT agreed to add a **fast select** feature in 1984.

When fast select is used, the *CALL REQUEST* packet is also expanded to include 128 bytes of user data. Fast select is requested as a facility. As far as the network is concerned, the packet really is an attempt to establish a virtual circuit. When fast select is used, the called DTE may reject the attempted call with a *CLEAR REQUEST* packet, which has also been expanded to include 128 bytes of reply data. However, it may also accept the call, in which case the virtual circuit is set up normally.

Using X.25 for the Network Layer Connection-Oriented Service

When the X.25 protocol is used to provide the OSI connection-oriented network service, the OSI service primitives must be mapped onto the various features of X.25. ISO standard 8878 describes how this mapping is to be done. We will describe it briefly below.

In general, when the transport layer issues a request, a packet is sent. The arrival of this packet at the destination causes an indication primitive to happen. Responses are analogous to requests. Figure 5-49 shows the mapping between primitives and X.25 actions. It is more-or-less straightforward, except that the *N-DATA-ACKNOWLEDGEMENT* primitives do not have any exact correspondence in X.25. They can be handled using the sequence numbers in the RR and RNR packets.

5.5.2. The Network Layer in the ARPANET (IP)

The network layer in the ARPANET has gone through several iterations as problems appeared and were solved. The current network layer protocol, **IP (Internet Protocol)**, was introduced in the early 1980s and has been running ever since. Many other networks have since adopted it, usually in conjunction with the ARPANET transport protocol, TCP, which we will study in the chapter on the transport layer.

Network Service Primitive	X.25 Action
N-CONNECT.request	Send CALL REQUEST
N-CONNECT.indication	CALL REQUEST arrives
N-CONNECT.response	Send CALL ACCEPTED
N-CONNECT.confirm	CALL ACCEPTED arrives
N-DISCONNECT.request	Send CLEAR REQUEST
N-DISCONNECT.indication	CLEAR REQUEST arrives
N-DATA.request	Send Data packet
N-DATA.indication	Data packet arrives
N-DATA-ACKNOWLEDGE.request	No packet
N-DATA-ACKNOWLEDGE.indication	No packet
N-EXPEDITED-DATA.request	Send INTERRUPT
N-EXPEDITED-DATA.indication	INTERRUPT arrives
N-RESET.request	Send RESET REQUEST
N-RESET.indication	RESET REQUEST arrives
N-RESET.response	none
N-RESET.confirm	none

Fig. 5-49. Mapping of network layer connection-oriented services onto X.25

Unlike the X.25 protocol, which is connection-oriented, the ARPANET network layer protocol is connectionless. It is based on the idea of internet datagrams that are transparently, but not necessarily reliably, transported from the source host to the destination host, possibly traversing several networks while doing so, as shown in Fig. 5-39.

The decision to have the network layer provide an unreliable connectionless service evolved gradually from an earlier reliable connection-oriented service as the ARPANET itself evolved into the ARPA Internet, which contains many networks, not all of them reliable. By putting all the reliability mechanisms into the transport layer, it was possible to have reliable end-to-end connections even when some of the underlying networks were not very dependable.

The IP protocol works as follows. The transport layer takes messages and breaks them up into datagrams of up to 64K bytes each. Each datagram is transmitted through the Internet, possibly being fragmented into smaller units as it goes. When all the pieces finally get to the destination machine, they are reassembled by the transport layer to reform the original message.

An IP datagram consists of a header part and a text part. The header has a 20-byte fixed part and a variable length optional part. The header format is given in Fig. 5-50. The *Version* field keeps track of which version of the protocol the datagram belongs to. By including the version in each datagram, the possibility of changing protocols while the network is operating is not excluded.

Since the header length is not constant, a field in the header, *IHL*, is provided to tell how long the header is, in 32-bit words. The minimum value is 5.

The *Type of service* field allows the host to tell the subnet what kind of service

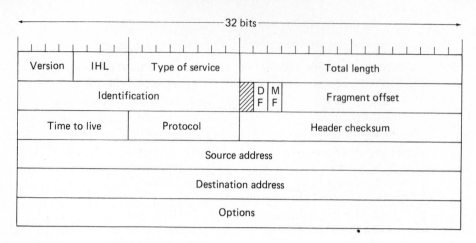

Fig. 5-50. The IP (Internet Protocol) header.

it wants. Various combinations of reliability and speed are possible. For digitized voice, fast delivery is far more important than correcting transmission errors. For file transfer, accurate transmission is far more important than speedy delivery. Various other combinations are also possible from routine traffic to flash override.

The *Total length* includes everything in the datagram—both header and data. The maximum length is 65,536 bytes.

The *Identification* field is needed to allow the destination host to determine which datagram a newly arrived fragment belongs to. All the fragments of a datagram contain the same *identification* value.

Next comes an unused bit and then two 1-bit fields. *DF* stands for Don't Fragment. It is an order to the gateways not to fragment the datagram because the destination is incapable of putting the pieces back together again. For example, a datagram being downloaded to a small micro for execution might be marked with *DF* because the micro's ROM expects the whole program in one datagram. If the datagram cannot be passed through a network, it must either be routed around the network or discarded.

MF stands for More Fragments. All fragments except the last one must have this bit set. It is used as a double check against the *Total length* field, to make sure that no fragments are missing and that the whole datagram is reassembled.

The *Fragment offset* tells where in the current datagram this fragment belongs. All fragments except the last one in a datagram must be a multiple of 8 bytes, the elementary fragment unit. Since 13 bits are provided, there is a maximum of 8192 fragments per datagram, giving a maximum datagram length of 65,536 bytes, in agreement with the *Total length* field.

The *Time to live* field is a counter used to limit packet lifetimes. When it becomes zero, the packet is destroyed. The unit of time is the second, allowing a maximum lifetime of 255 sec.

When the network layer has assembled a complete datagram, it needs to know what to do with it. The *Protocol* field tells which of the various transport processes the datagram belongs to. TCP is certainly one possibility, but there may be others.

The *Header checksum* verifies the header only. Such a checksum is useful because the header may change at a gateway (e.g., fragmentation may occur).

The *Source address* and *Destination address* indicate the network number and host number. Four different formats are used, as illustrated in Fig. 5-51. The four schemes allow for up to 128 networks with 16 million hosts each, 16,384 networks with up to 64K hosts, 2 million networks, presumably LANs, with up to 256 hosts each, and multicast, in which a datagram is directed at a group of hosts. Nearly 1000 networks are currently part of the ARPA Internet, at research, DOD, other governmental, and commercial sites. Addresses beginning with 1111 are reserved for future use.

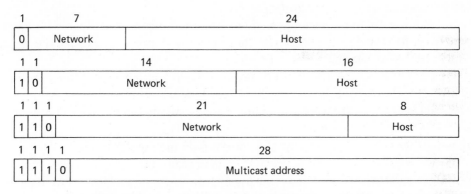

Fig. 5-51. Source and destination address formats in IP.

The *Options* field is used for security, source routing, error reporting, debugging, time stamping, and other information. Basically it provides an escape to allow subsequent versions of the protocol to include information not present in the original design, to allow experimenters to try out new ideas, and to avoid allocating header bits to information that is rarely needed.

The operation of the ARPANET is monitored closely by the IMPs and gateways. When something suspicious occurs, the event is reported by the **ICMP (Internet Control Message Protocol)**, which is also used to test the Internet. About a dozen types of ICMP messages are defined. Each message type is encapsulated in an IP packet.

The *DESTINATION UNREACHABLE* message is used when the subnet or a gateway cannot locate the destination, or a packet with the *DF* bit cannot be delivered because a "small-packet" network stands in the way.

The *TIME EXCEEDED* message is sent when a packet is dropped due to its counter reaching zero. This event is a symptom that packets are looping, that there is enormous congestion, or that the timer values are being set too low.

The *PARAMETER PROBLEM* message indicates that an illegal value has been detected in a header field. This problem indicates a bug in the sending host's IP software, or possibly in the software of a gateway transited.

The *SOURCE QUENCH* message is used to throttle hosts that are sending too many packets. When a host receives this message, it is expected to slow down.

The *REDIRECT* message is used when a gateway notices that a packet seems to be routed wrong. For example, if a gateway in Los Angeles sees a packet that came from New York and is headed for Boston, this message would be used to report the event and help get the routing straightened out.

The *ECHO REQUEST* and *ECHO REPLY* messages are used to see if a given destination is reachable and alive. Upon receiving the *ECHO* message, the destination is expected to send an *ECHO REPLY* message back. The *TIMESTAMP REQUEST* and *TIMESTAMP REPLY* messages are similar, except that the arrival time of the message and the departure time of the reply are recorded in the reply. This facility is used to measure network performance.

In addition to these messages, there are four others that deal with internet addressing, to allow hosts to discover their network numbers and to handle the case of multiple LANs sharing a single IP address.

Originally, the ARPANET used the distributed routing algorithm described in Sec. 5.2.6. After about 10 years, that algorithm was replaced because it caused some packets to loop for a long time and did not use alternate routes. Furthermore, the ARPANET had grown to such a size that the traffic generated by routing table exchanges was getting so large as to interfere with the regular traffic.

In the successor algorithm, each IMP maintains internally a representation of the entire ARPANET, including the delays on each line. Using this data base, every IMP computes the shortest path from itself to every other IMP, using delay as the metric. Since every IMP runs the shortest path algorithm on (almost) the same data base, the paths are consistent and there is little looping.

To provide adaptation to traffic and topology changes, each IMP measures the delay on each of its lines averaged over a 10-sec period. The results of these measurements, along with an update sequence number, are then broadcast to all other IMPs using a flooding algorithm.

5.5.3. The Network Layer in MAP and TOP

The network layer in both MAP and TOP provides the OSI connectionless service to the transport layer. The network protocol used is ISO 8473, which is the ISO connectionless network layer protocol based on the ARPANET's IP protocol. Thus the transport layer in MAP and TOP builds and sends internet datagrams.

The choice of IP by MAP and TOP is both surprising and not surprising. It is surprising because most large organizations tend to accept X.25 at the network layer as a fact of life, whether they like it or not. It is not surprising because both MAP and TOP are very concerned about internetworking, especially between 802 LANs and various WANs. Running all the 802 LANs as X.25 networks and then connecting them with the virtual circuit oriented X.75 is unattractive. Furthermore, both GM and Boeing clearly wanted a system that would actually work, and the fact that the ARPANET had a decade of experience running IP over a very heterogeneous collection of networks clearly made an impression on them.

However, a problem arises when trying to run IP over public networks that offer only connection-oriented X.25 service. The solution is to set up a connection between two X.25 end points, and then just use the public network as a big, dumb wire to transmit the IP packets. In this mode of operation, the subnet enhancement sublayer of Fig. 5-27 effectively de-enhances X.25 to get rid of its connection orientation and just provide a raw connectionless service to the transport layer. When running IP over an 802 LAN, the subnet enhancement layer is null.

The OSI internet packet format described in ISO 8473 contains almost exactly the same fields as the ARPA Internet IP packet (Fig. 5-50), although the order is slightly different. Two differences, however, are the format of the address fields and an extra flag bit. The ARPA Internet uses 32-bit source and destination addresses, which are certainly not adequate for a worldwide network. The corresponding OSI fields are variable length, with count fields telling how long they are, just as in X.25. The extra flag bit can be set to request that if the packet is discarded along the way (e.g., due to congestion), a report is sent back to the source.

The MAP and TOP standards specify the form of the addresses to be used and how they relate to routing. Basically, these addresses have three subparts, the company, the LAN, and the machine number. This numbering plan leads to a hierarchical routing, with packets first being routed to the proper company, then to the proper LAN, and finally to the destination.

5.5.4. The Network Layer in USENET

USENET does not have a network layer in the sense of something that offers a service to the transport layer. However, with something like 10,000 hosts on the network, most of them only connecting to a handful of other hosts, routing is a major issue. The routing algorithm has gone through several iterations, which we will describe below.

The initial routing algorithm was pure source routing. Each mail message contained a line of the form:

To: ucbvax!decvax!mcvax!marvin

In this example, the originating machine would call up, or wait to be called up by *ucbvax* (a VAX computer at Berkeley) to transfer the message to it. The next time *ucbvax* and *decvax* were in contact, the message would be forwarded to *decvax*, which in turn would eventually forward it to *mcvax* where it would be put in Marvin's mailbox.

This algorithm had the advantage of not requiring any routing on the part of the network. Users had to figure out how to route their own messages, with the aid of large maps of the network topology. On the other hand, as the network grew to thousands of hosts, the map got very large, and paths with dozens of hops became increasingly common. Users often made typing mistakes, which resulted in problems when their messages got to the point in the path where the typing error occurred. If the host holding the message did not recognize the name of the host it was supposed to forward the message to, all it could do was discard it or return it to the sender.

To further complicate matters, the network topology changed daily, and the maps were always out of date. (Actually, this was not so much of a problem because they were unreadable anyway.) Finally, sending mail between USENET, BITNET, CSNET, and ARPANET was difficult because each network had its own naming and routing conventions.

To bring some order to this chaos, it was decided to introduce a uniform naming scheme to all four networks. The idea was to group all the hosts into **domains**, which in turn could be divided into subdomains, which also could be subdivided. In effect, all the hosts would be organized into a naming tree.

At the top level in the U.S. the following domains exist:

1. COM- Companies, including nonprofit corporations

2. EDU- Educational institutions such as universities and high schools

3. GOV- Nonmilitary city, state, and federal government agencies

4. MIL - Military organizations

5. ORG- Everything else

In addition, each foreign country is also a top-level domain, for example, NL for The Netherlands, UK for the United Kingdom, and so on. It is sometimes possible to generate multiple names for the same site. The IBM research laboratory in Switzerland, for example, has chosen to be in the COM domain, rather than in the Swiss domain.

Each domain is divided into subdomains. For example, EDU has subdomains BERKELEY.EDU, MIT.EDU, and many others for other universities. These second level domains are typically divided into third level domains for departments or major projects. Thus CS.HARVARD.EDU could be the computer science department at Harvard University. In the domain system, mail is addressed not by giving an explicit route to follow, but rather by giving a name and a domain, as in MARVIN@CS.HARVARD.EDU.

While domain naming makes it much easier for people to type addresses correctly, it completely ruins the USENET routing algorithm. Instead, a new method was devised. This method consists of a program that can run on any host, read the network topology map stored online there, and produce a file giving the shortest path to each known destination. When it is time to forward a piece of mail, the mailing system can look in this file to find out what the first hop along the path is, and forward the message there.

Although this routing algorithm sounds simple, there are a few points worth making. To start with, the idea of precomputing all the shortest paths in advance rather than doing it per message is really essential. With over 10,000 hosts and 30,000 links in the map, computing the shortest path to any given host requires a substantial amount of computation.

A more serious issue is how to assign costs to links. The connections differ in terms of bandwidth (1200 bps, 2400 bps, etc.), telephone cost per minute, and frequency of connection. Suppose mail to host X can go via a 9600 bps telephone line that is activated once a day, seven days a week and costs 20 cents/minute or via a 300 bps X.25 connection that is activated twice a day on weekdays only and costs 0.1 cent per byte and 2 cents/minute for connect time. Which route is shorter? To make a long story short, the weights on the arcs of the graph have been assigned empirically to make the results reasonable, but not optimal. The routing procedure is described in more detail by Partridge (1986).

5.6. SUMMARY

The network layer provides services to the transport layer. These services can be either connection-oriented or connectionless. The connection-oriented services have primitives for establishing, using and releasing connections, whereas the connectionless ones just have primitives for sending and receiving data. The OSI model supports both styles.

Functionally, the main task of the network layer is routing packets from source to destination. Some networks do routing at the time a connection is set up, and use that route for all packets on the connection. Others route each packet individually. Each approach has its own advantages and disadvantages.

Many routing algorithms are known. Shortest path routing is conceptually simple and widely used. Multipath routing spreads the traffic over several routes, both to gain improved performance and higher reliability. In centralized routing, a single routing machine computes all the routes and downloads them to the IMPs. In isolated routing, each IMP makes its own decisions based on local traffic conditions. In between is distributed routing, in which each IMP makes local routing decisions, but exchanges information with its neighbors. Hierarchical routing is important in large networks.

If too many packets are present in the subnet, it may become congested and the throughput will drop off. Congestion can be dealt with by preallocating buffers, discarding packets, or limiting the number of packets in the subnet by various means such as the isarithmic scheme or having IMPs send choke packets to slow down the input rate when they get overloaded. Various kinds of deadlocks can occur, but algorithms for avoiding them are known.

Internetworking involves connecting two networks together. The interconnection can occur in the data link layer (bridges) or network layer (gateways). IEEE has standardized two types of 802 bridges, a spanning tree bridge and a source routing bridge. In the former, the bridges are fully transparent and acquire routing information via backward learning. In the latter, the hosts are involved, and they learn about the topology using discovery frames.

In the network layer, two types of interconnections have evolved: concatenated virtual circuits (X.75) and internet datagrams (IP). As with virtual circuits and datagrams within a single subnet, the virtual circuit approach is simple and avoids congestion, but is inflexible and wastes resources. Similarly, the datagram approach is flexible and robust, but can suffer from congestion.

Two network layer protocols are in widespread use around the world. The X.25 protocol, which is connection-oriented, is used in public data networks. The IP protocol, which is connectionless, is used in the ARPA Internet, at universities, and at most UNIX installations.

PROBLEMS

1. Give two example applications for which connection-oriented service is appropriate. Now give two examples for which connectionless service is best.

2. Are there any circumstances when a virtual circuit service will (or should) deliver packets out of order? Explain.

3. Give three examples of protocol parameters that might be negotiated when a connection is set up.

4. Referring to Fig. 5-6, what new table entries would be needed to add a path *AEFD*?

5. Consider the following design problem concerning implementation of virtual circuit service. If virtual circuits are used internal to the subnet, each data packet must have a 3-byte header, and each IMP must tie up 8 bytes of storage for circuit identification. If datagrams are used internally, 15-byte headers are needed but no IMP table space is required. Transmission capacity costs 1 cent per 10^6 bytes, per hop. IMP memory can be purchased for 1 cent per byte and is depreciated over 2 years (business hours only). The statistically average session runs for 1000 sec, in which time 200 packets are transmitted. The mean packet requires four hops. Which implementation is cheaper, and by how much?

6. Assuming that all IMPs and hosts are working properly and that all software in both is free of all errors, is there any chance, however small, that a packet will be delivered to the wrong destination?

7. What is the difference, if any, between static routing using two equally weighted alternatives, and selective flooding using only the two best paths?

8. Give a simple algorithm for finding two paths through a network from a given source to a given destination that can survive the loss of any communication line. The IMPs are considered reliable enough, so it is not necessary to worry about the possibility of IMP crashes.

9. A certain network uses hot potato routing, that is, incoming packets are put on the shortest queue. One of the IMPs has only two outgoing lines, hence two queues. If the queues are equally long, packets are put on a queue at random. Write down the equation expressing the conservation of flow into and out of the state in which the length of queue 1 is i and the length of queue 2 is j, with $i > j + 1$ and $j > 1$.

10. Propose a good routing algorithm for a network in which each IMP knows the path length in hops to each destination for each output line, and also the queue lengths for each line. For simplicity assume that time is discrete and that a packet can move one hop per time interval.

11. An IMP uses a combination of hot potato and static routing. When a packet comes in, it goes onto the first choice queue if and only if that queue is empty and the line is idle, otherwise it uses the second-choice queue. There is no third choice. If the arrival rate at the IMP for a certain destination is λ packets/sec and the service rate is μ packets/sec, what fraction of the packets get routed via the first choice queue? Assume Poisson arrivals and service times.

12. If delays are recorded as 8-bit numbers in a 50 IMP network, and delay vectors are exchanged twice a second, how much bandwidth per (full-duplex) line is chewed up by the distributed routing algorithm? Assume that each IMP has 3 lines to other IMPS.

13. For hierarchical routing with 4800 IMPs, what region and cluster sizes should be chosen to minimize the size of the routing table for a three layer hierarchy?

14. Looking at the subnet of Fig. 5-16, how many packets are generated by a broadcast from B, using
    (a) reverse path forwarding?
    (b) the sink tree?

15. Irland's method for controlling congestion requires discarding packets if the required queue exceeds a certain length. Use an M/M/1 finite buffer queueing model to derive an expression telling what fraction of the packets will be discarded.

16. As a possible congestion control mechanism in a subnet using virtual circuits internally, an IMP could refrain from acknowledging a received packet until (1) it knows its last transmission along the virtual circuit was received successfully and (2) it has a free buffer. For simplicity, assume that the IMPs use a stop-and-wait protocol and that each virtual circuit has a one buffer dedicated to it for each direction of traffic. If it takes T sec to transmit a packet (data or acknowledgement), and there are n IMPs on the path, what is the rate at which packets are delivered to the destination host? Assume that transmission errors are rare, and that the host-IMP connection is infinitely fast.

17. A datagram subnet allows IMPs to drop packets whenever they need to. The probability of an IMP discarding a packet is p. Consider the case of a source host connected to the source IMP, which is connected to the destination IMP, and then to the destination host. If either of the IMPs discards a packet, the source host eventually times out and tries again. If both host-IMP and IMP-IMP lines are counted as hops, what is the mean number of
    (a) hops a packet makes per transmission?
    (b) transmissions a packet makes?
    (c) hops required per received packet?

18. Does the Merlin-Schweitzer buffering algorithm guarantee that every packet will be delivered within a finite time? If so, prove it, if not, what is needed to fix it?

19. The Blazewicz et al. algorithm uses timestamps as unique numbers so that some packet will have the lowest value and this move unimpeded to its destination. Would checksums do just as well as timestamps?

20. Consider the operation of a bridge between two LANs using LAPB as the data link protocol. Which of the problems cited in Fig. 5-32 would occur in this bridge and which would not?

21. Imagine two LAN bridges, both connecting a pair of 802.4 networks. The first bridge is faced with 1000 512-byte packets per second that must be forwarded. The second is faced with 200 4096-byte packets per second. Which bridge do you think will need the faster CPU? Discuss.

22. Suppose that the two bridges of the previous problem each connected an 802.4 LAN to an 802.5 LAN. Would that change have any influence on the previous answer?

23. Why do you think CCITT provided flow control in X.25 in both LAPB and PLP instead of just in one layer?

24. When an X.25 DTE and DCE both decide to put a call through at the same time, a call collision occurs and the incoming call is canceled. When both sides try to clear simultaneously, the clear collision is resolved without canceling either request. Do you think that simultaneous resets are handled like call collisions or clear collisions? Defend your answer.

25. An IP datagram of 1024 bytes is fragmented into pieces. Each piece is sent as a separate fragment over an X.25 network whose packet size allows 128 bytes of data per packet. How many fragments are needed, and what is the efficiency of the transmission, counting both the X.25 and IP packet overhead, but ignoring that of lower layers?

26. Describe a way to do reassembly of IP fragments at the destination.

27. Write a program to simulate routing using flooding. Each packet should contain a counter that is decremented on each hop. When the counter gets to zero, the packet is discarded. Time is discrete, with each line handling one packet per time interval. Make three versions of the program: all lines are flooded, all lines except the input line

are flooded, and only the (statically chosen) best k lines are flooded. Compare flooding with deterministic routing ($k = 1$) in terms of delay and bandwidth used.

28. Simulate routing using a combination of hot potato and static routing. Time is discrete as above. Use the statically best route unless the queue length is k or more, in which case use the next best route, etc. Investigate the effect of k on mean delay.

29. Write a program that simulates a computer network using discrete time. The first packet on each IMP queue makes one hop per time interval. Each IMP has only a finite number of buffers. If a packet arrives and there is no room for it, it is discarded and not retransmitted. Instead, there is an end-to-end protocol, complete with timeouts and acknowledgement packets, that eventually regenerates the packet from the source IMP. Plot the throughput of the network as a function of the end-to-end timeout interval, parametrized by error rate.

6

THE TRANSPORT LAYER

The transport layer is not just another layer. It is really the heart of the whole protocol hierarchy. Its task is to provide reliable, cost-effective data transport from the source machine to the destination machine, independent of the physical network or networks currently in use. Without the transport layer, the whole concept of layered protocols would make little sense. In this chapter we will study the transport layer in detail, including its design, services, and protocols.

Many networking applications need only a method to reliably transmit a stream of bits from one machine to another. For example, pipes between machines in a distributed UNIX system just need bit transport. They do not need or want any session or presentation services to get in the way. In fact, there are a surprisingly large number of applications that do not need any services from the session layer or above, but it is considered in poor taste to point this out publicly. The ARPANET does not even have session or presentation layers, and few complaints have been voiced about their absence.

This chapter will rely on the OSI model and its terminology more than any of the previous ones. This change in emphasis is due to the fact that many networks were already in operation before the OSI model was designed. These networks generally were well thought out up through the network layer, but began to get excessively fuzzy around the transport layer. As a result, a substantial body of terminology, literature, and operational experience for layers 1 through 3 was well established before the OSI model came along, and is likely to continue developing for years to come. Most of the previous chapters have drawn heavily on this experience (e.g., the term "packet" had been long established before the OSI term "NPDU" came along). This chapter will also emphasize connection-oriented transport, since that is by far the most common type.

Starting with the transport layer, however, the pre-OSI influence has been much weaker. Only one pre-OSI transport protocol (the ARPANET's TCP) is well-established, and even that one may eventually be replaced by its OSI equivalent. Relatively little pre-OSI terminology relating to the transport layer (and almost none relating to the session and presentation layers) is in common use. Considering all these factors, this chapter will have much more of an OSI flavor than its predecessors, a harbinger of things to come. However, we will still treat the general principles first and the details of the various example protocols in a separate section at the end of the chapter, as before.

6.1. TRANSPORT LAYER DESIGN ISSUES

In this section we will provide an introduction to some of the issues that the designers of the transport layer must grapple with. They include the kind of service provided to the session layer, the quality of this service, and the transport layer primitives provided to invoke the service. Finally, we will conclude the section with an initial discussion of the protocols needed to realize the transport service.

6.1.1. Services Provided to the Session Layer

The ultimate goal of the transport layer is to provide efficient, reliable, and cost-effective service to its users, normally entities (e.g., processes) in the session layer. To achieve this goal, the transport layer makes use of the services provided by the network layer. The hardware and/or software within the transport layer that does the work is called the **transport entity**. The relationship of the network, transport, and session layers is illustrated in Fig. 6-1.

Just as there are two types of network service, there are also two types of transport service: connection-oriented and connectionless. The connection-oriented transport service is similar to the connection-oriented network service in many ways. In both cases, connections have three phases: establishment, data transfer, and release. Addressing and flow control are also similar in both layers. Furthermore, the connectionless transport service is also very similar to the connectionless network service.

The obvious question is then: "If the transport layer service is so similar to the network layer service, why are there two distinct layers? Why is one layer not adequate?" The answer is subtle, but crucial, and goes back to Fig. 1-7. In this figure we can see that the network layer is part of the communication subnet and is run by the carrier (at least for WANs). What happens if the network layer offers

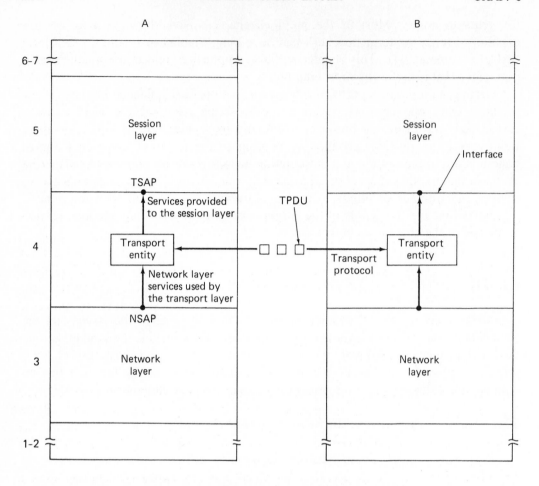

Fig. 6-1. The network, transport, and session layers.

connection-oriented service, but is unreliable? Suppose it frequently loses packets? What happens if it crashes or issues *N-RESET*s all the time?

Since the users have no control over the subnet, they cannot solve the problem of poor service by using better IMPs or putting more error handling in the data link layer. The only possibility is to put another layer on top of the network layer that improves the quality of the service. If a transport entity is informed halfway through a long transmission that its network connection has been abruptly terminated, with no indication of what has happened to the data currently in transit, it can set up a new network connection to the remote transport entity. Using this new network connection, it can send a query to its peer asking which data arrived and which did not, and then pick up from where it left off.

In essence, the existence of the transport layer makes it possible for the transport service to be more reliable than the underlying network service. Lost packets, mangled data, and even network *N-RESET*s can be detected and compensated for by the transport layer. Furthermore, the transport service primitives can be designed to be independent of the network service primitives, which may vary considerably from network to network (e.g., connectionless LAN service may be quite different than connection-oriented WAN service).

Thanks to the transport layer, it is possible for application programs to be written using a standard set of primitives, and to have these programs work on a wide variety of networks, without having to worry about dealing with different subnet interfaces and unreliable transmission. If all real networks were flawless and all had the same service primitives, the transport layer would probably not be needed. However, in the real world it fulfills the key function of isolating the upper layers from the technology, design, and imperfections of the subnet.

For this reason, many people have made a distinction between layers 1 through 4 on the one hand, and layers 5 through 7 on the other. The bottom four layers can be seen as the **transport service provider**, whereas the upper three layers are the **transport service user**. This distinction of provider vs. user has a considerable impact on the design of the layers, and puts the transport layer in a key position, since it forms the major boundary between the provider and user of the reliable data transmission service.

6.1.2. Quality of Service

Another way of looking at the transport layer is to regard its primary function as enhancing the **QOS (Quality Of Service)** provided by the network layer. If the network service is impeccable, the transport layer has an easy job. If, however, the network service is poor, the transport layer has to bridge the gap between what the transport users want and what the network layer provides.

While at first glance, quality of service might seem like a vague concept (getting everyone to agree what constitutes "good" service is a nontrivial exercise), QOS can be characterized by a number of specific parameters. The OSI transport service allows the user to specify preferred, acceptable, and unacceptable values for these parameters at the time a connection is set up. Some of the parameters also apply to connectionless transport. It is up to the transport layer to examine these parameters, and depending on the kind of network service or services available to it, determine whether it can provide the required service. In the remainder of this section we will discuss the QOS parameters. They are summarized in Fig. 6-2.

The **connection establishment delay** is the amount of time elapsing between a transport connection being requested and the confirm being received by the user of the transport service. It includes the processing delay in the remote transport entity. As with all parameters measuring a delay, the shorter the delay, the better the service.

The **connection establishment failure probability** is the chance of a connection not being established within the maximum establishment delay time, for example, due to network congestion, lack of table space, or other internal problems.

Connection establishment delay
Connection establishment failure probability
Throughput
Transit delay
Residual error rate
Transfer failure probability
Connection release delay
Connection release failure probability
Protection
Priority
Resilience

Fig. 6-2. Transport layer quality of service parameters.

The **throughput** parameter measures the number of bytes of user data transferred per second, measured over some recent time interval. The throughput is measured separately for each direction. Actually, there are two kinds of throughput: the actual measured throughput and the throughput that the network is capable of providing. The actual throughput may be lower than the network's capacity because the user has not been sending data as fast as the network is willing to accept it.

The **transit delay** measures the time between a message being sent by the transport user on the source machine and its being received by the transport user on the destination machine. As with throughput, each direction is handled separately.

The **residual error rate** measures the number of lost or garbled messages as a fraction of the total sent in the sampling period. In theory, the residual error rate should be zero, since it is the job of the transport layer to hide all network layer errors. In practice it may have some (small) finite value.

The **transfer failure probability** measures how well the transport service is living up to its promises. When a transport connection is established, a given level of throughput, transit delay, and residual error rate are agreed upon. The transfer failure probability gives the fraction of times that these agreed upon goals were not met during some observation period.

The **connection release delay** is the amount of time elapsing between a transport user initiating a release of a connection, and the actual release happening at the other end.

The **connection release failure probability** is the fraction of connection release attempts that did not complete within the agreed upon connection release delay interval.

The **protection** parameter provides a way for the transport user to specify interest in having the transport layer provide protection against unauthorized third parties (wiretappers) reading or modifying the transmitted data.

The **priority** parameter provides a way for a transport user to indicate that some of its connections are more important than other ones, and in the event of congestion, to make sure that the high-priority connections get serviced before the low-priority ones.

Finally, the **resilience** parameter gives the probability of the transport layer itself spontaneously terminating a connection due to internal problems or congestion.

The QOS parameters are specified by the transport user when a connection is requested. Both the desired and minimum acceptable values can be given. In some cases, upon seeing the QOS parameters, the transport layer may immediately realize that some of them are unachievable, in which case it tells the caller that the connection attempt failed, without even bothering to contact the destination. The failure report specifies the reason for the failure.

In other cases, the transport layer knows it cannot achieve the desired goal (e.g., 1200 bytes/sec throughput), but it can achieve a lower, but still acceptable rate (e.g., 600 bytes/sec). It then sends the lower rate and the minimum acceptable rate to the remote machine, asking to establish a connection. If the remote machine cannot handle the proposed value, but it can handle a value above the minimum, it may lower the parameter to its value. If it cannot handle any value above the minimum, it rejects the connection attempt. Finally, the originating transport user is informed of whether the connection was established or rejected, and if it was established, the values of the parameters agreed upon.

This process is called **option negotiation**. Once the options have been negotiated, they remain that way throughout the life of the connection. The OSI Transport Service Definition (ISO 8072) does not give the encoding or allowed values for the QOS parameters. These are normally agreed upon between the carrier and the customer at the time the customer subscribes to the network service. To keep customers from being too greedy, most carriers have the tendency to charge more money for better quality service.

6.1.3. The OSI Transport Service Primitives

The OSI transport service primitives provide for both connection-oriented and connectionless service. The transport primitives are listed in Fig. 6-3. A comparison of Fig. 6-3 with Fig. 5-4 will show that the transport and network services are (intentionally) similar.

Despite the similarities with the network service, there are also some important differences. The main difference is that the network service is intended to model the service offered by real networks (e.g., X.25 networks), warts and all. These networks can lose packets and can spontaneously issue *N-RESET*s due to internal network problems. Thus the network service provides a way for its users to deal with acknowledgements and *N-RESET*s.

The transport service, in contrast, does not mention either acknowledgements or

```
T-CONNECT.request(callee, caller, exp_wanted, qos, user_data)
T-CONNECT.indication(callee, caller, exp_wanted, qos, user_data)
T-CONNECT.response(qos, responder, exp_wanted, user_data)
T-CONNECT.confirm(qos, responder, exp_wanted, user_data)
```

```
T-DISCONNECT.request(user_data)
T-DISCONNECT.indication(reason, user_data)
```

```
T-DATA.request(user_data)
T-DATA.indication(user-data)
T-EXPEDITED-DATA.request(user_data)
T-EXPEDITED-DATA.indication(user_data)
```

(a)

```
T-UNITDATA.request(callee, caller, qos, user_data)
T-UNITDATA.indication(callee, caller, qos, user_data)
```

(b)

Notes on terminology:
  Callee: Transport address (TSAP) to be called
  Caller: Transport address (NSAP) used by calling transport entity
  Exp_wanted: Boolean flag specifying whether expedited data will be sent
  Qos: Quality of service desired
  User_data: 0 or more bytes of data transmitted but not examined
  Reason: Why did it happen
  Responder: Transport address connected to at the destination

Fig. 6-3. (a) OSI connection-oriented transport service primitives. (b) OSI connectionless transport service primitives.

*N-RESET*s. From the transport user's point of view, the service is error-free. Of course real networks are not error-free, but that is precisely the purpose of the transport layer—to provide a reliable service on top of an unreliable network. The acknowledgements and *N-RESET*s that come from the network service are intercepted by the transport entities and the errors are recovered from by the transport protocol. If a network connection is reset, the transport layer can just establish a new one, and continue from where it left off with the old one.

Another important difference between the network service and transport service is who the services are intended for. The network service is used by the transport entities, which normally are part of the operating system or located on a special hardware board or chip. Few users write their own transport entities, and thus few users or programs ever see the bare network service.

In contrast, many users have no use for the session and presentation layers, and do see the transport primitives. As we mentioned earlier, the ARPANET does not even have session or presentation layers, so all programs that use the network interact with the transport primitives (which are different from the OSI transport primitives, but are roughly comparable). To illustrate this point, consider processes connected by pipes in UNIX. They assume the connection between them is perfect.

They do not want to know about acknowledgements or *N-RESET*s or network congestion or anything like that. What they want is a perfect connection. Process *A* puts data into one end of the pipe, and process *B* takes it out of the other. This is what the connection-oriented transport service is all about—hiding the imperfections of the network service so that user processes can just assume the existence of an error-free bit stream.

Just for the record, the situation is not quite so black-and-white as we have just sketched it. The quality of service parameter provides a large number of gray values between perfect service and perfectly awful service. Still, the basic point we have made remains: the transport service is designed to relieve programs that use it from having to worry about dealing with network errors.

Figure 6-4 shows the relationship among the OSI primitives. In each of the eight parts of the figure, one transport user is shown to the left of the double lines, the other transport user is shown to the right of the double lines, and the transport service provider (i.e., the transport layer itself) is shown between the double lines. Furthermore, time runs downward, so that events at the top occur before events at the bottom.

The normal connection setup is illustrated in Fig. 6-4(a). Four primitives are used. One of the transport entities executes a *T-CONNECT.request* primitive to signal its desire to establish a connection with the transport user attached to the **transport service access point** (**TSAP**) address named in the *CONNECT.request* primitive. This primitive results in a *T-CONNECT.indication* occurring at the destination. The transport user attached to the TSAP addressed gets the indication and can either accept it with a *T-CONNECT.response*, as shown in Fig. 6-4(a), or reject it with a *T-DISCONNECT.request*, as shown in Fig. 6-4(b). The result of an acceptance comes back to the initiator as a *T-CONNECT.confirm*. The result of a rejection comes back as a *T-DISCONNECT.indication*.

One other scenario is also possible for an attempt to establish a connection. This scenario is illustrated in Fig. 6-4(c), and occurs when the transport service provider itself rejects the connection. Such a rejection may be the transport user's fault (e.g., a bad parameter in the *T-CONNECT.request* primitive) or the transport provider's fault (e.g., the transport provider has run out of internal table space). In this scenario, nothing is transmitted across the network, so the remote site does not even hear about the failed attempt.

In Fig. 6-4(d)-(f) we see three ways a connection can be released. The normal way is that one of the parties issues a *T-DISCONNECT.request*, which is signaled to the other party as a *T-DISCONNECT.indication*. Either the calling or called party may initiate the release of the connection. If both parties simultaneously issue a *T-DISCONNECT.request* primitive, the connection is released without either side getting an indication.

Finally, the transport provider itself can terminate a connection by issuing *T-DISCONNECT.indication* primitives on both ends, as shown in Fig. 6-4(f). In a way, the last scenario is a little like the network layer issuing an *N-RESET.indication*.

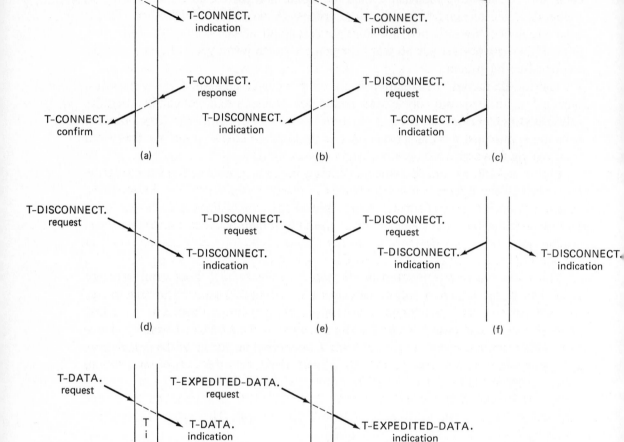

Fig. 6-4. Some valid sequences of OSI transport primitives. (a) Connection setup. (b) Connection rejected by called user. (c) Connection rejected by transport layer. (d) Normal connection release. (e) Simultaneous release by both sides. (f) Transport layer initiated release. (g) Normal data transfer. (h) Expedited data transfer.

The connection is terminated. Clearly, a well-designed transport service provider should not issue spontaneous *T-DISCONNECT.indication* primitives too lightly, but there are circumstances in which no other course of action is possible. For example, if the underlying network crashes and refuses to react to repeated attempts to communicate with it, there is little else the transport service provider can do than break all the connections. Unless the session layer has taken special precautions against this problem, the failure will have to be reported back to the highest level, and may require human intervention to retry the failed command.

The final two diagrams in Fig. 6-4 show normal and expedited data transport. In neither case is an explicit acknowledgement or other indication provided back to the sender. The transport layer uses the same queue model (Fig. 5-3) as the network layer, with data normally delivered in sequence.

However, the *T-EXPEDITED-DATA* primitive can be used to send data that skips ahead of other data already in the queue. This primitive is normally only used to transmit the BREAK, DEL, or interrupt key that people can type from their terminals to interrupt the current program. If there were no expedited data, consider what would happen if a user started a program from a remote terminal connected to the host by a transport connection, and then typed a line ahead while waiting for the program just started to terminate. If that program got into an infinite loop and the user typed a BREAK character, the BREAK would be carefully added to the tail of the queue, and would not be delivered to the host until the running program terminated and read the line queued ahead of the BREAK. The use of *T-EXPEDITED-DATA.request* causes the BREAK to be delivered immediately, no matter what is in the queue.

Strict rules govern the order in which the transport primitives may be used. For example, it is not permitted to issue a *T-DISCONNECT.request* when no connection is established (or at least in the process of being established). The diagram of Fig. 6-5 shows the four legal states that a connection endpoint may have at a TSAP and the relations among the states. The two endpoints are not necessarily in the same state. During the establishment phase, for example, the initiating party goes from the IDLE state to the OUTGOING CONNECTION PENDING state before anything happens at the other endpoint.

The four states are:

1. IDLE—No connection is established or trying to be established. Both incoming and outgoing connections are possible.

2. OUTGOING CONNECTION PENDING—A *T-CONNECT.request* has been done. The reply from the remote peer has not yet been received.

3. INCOMING CONNECTION PENDING—A *T-CONNECT.indication* has come in. It has not yet been accepted or rejected.

4. CONNECTION ESTABLISHED—A valid connection has been established. The establishment phase is completed and data transfer can begin.

Two ways exist to get from the IDLE state to the CONNECTION ESTABLISHED state. The left-hand route (1-2-4) is used when an outgoing call is being placed. The intermediate state (2) is entered after the *T-CONNECT.request* has been issued, and holds until the *T-CONNECT.confirm* comes in. The remote side rejects the

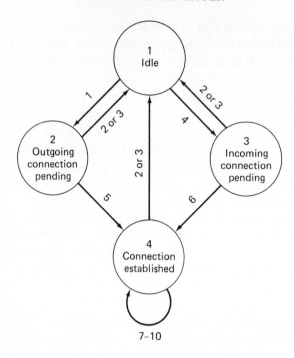

Transitions:
1. T–CONNECT.request received from transport user
2. T–DISCONNECT.indication received from transport service provider
3. T–DISCONNECT.request received from transport user
4. T–CONNECT.indication received from transport service provider
5. T–CONNECT.confirm received from transport service provider
6. T–CONNECT.response received from transport user
7. T–DATA.request received from transport user
8. T–DATA.indication received from transport service provider
9. T–EXPEDITED–DATA.request received from transport user
10. T–EXPEDITED–DATA.indication received from transport service provider

Fig. 6-5. Transport connection endpoint states and transport primitives.

connection or the caller changes its mind and issues a *T-DISCONNECT.request*, the IDLE state is entered again.

The right-hand route (1-3-4) is used when an incoming call is received. The intermediate state is entered after the *T-CONNECT.indication* comes in. If the connection is intentionally rejected or a *T-DISCONNECT.indication* comes in (either from a fickle caller or from the transport layer itself), we return to the IDLE state. However, if the connection is accepted, state 4 is reached.

From state 4 there are two ways back to the IDLE state. These correspond to the local transport user releasing the connection and the transport layer releasing the connection. The latter event may happen either upon request of the remote transport user or of necessity by the transport service provider.

The set of states and transitions governing connection endpoints shown in Fig. 6-5 is a finite state machine. This one is called the **transport protocol**

machine. Similar protocol machines exist for the other layers. This one is particularly simple. For some of the upper layer protocols, the protocol machine has dozens of states and dozens of transitions, typically one transition for each primitive that can be invoked and each PDU that can arrive from the outside.

6.1.4. Transport Protocols

The transport service is implemented by a **transport protocol** used between the two transport entities. In some ways, transport protocols resemble the data link protocols we studied in detail in Chapter 4. Both have to deal with error control, sequencing, and flow control, among other issues.

However, significant differences between the two also exist. These differences are due to major dissimilarities between the environments in which the two protocols operate, as shown in Fig. 6-6. At the data link layer, two IMPs communicate directly via a physical channel, whereas at the transport layer, this physical channel is replaced by the entire subnet. This difference has many important implications for the protocols.

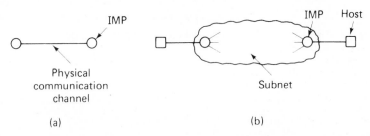

Fig. 6-6. (a) Environment of the data link layer. (b) Environment of the transport layer.

For one thing, in the data link layer, it is not necessary for an IMP to specify which IMP it wants to talk to—each outgoing line uniquely specifies a particular IMP. In the transport layer, explicit addressing of destinations is required.

For another thing, the process of establishing a connection over the wire of Fig. 6-6(a) is simple: the other end is always there (unless it has crashed, in which case it is not there). Either way, there is not much to do. In the transport layer, initial connection establishment is more complicated, as we will see.

Another exceedingly annoying, difference between the data link layer and the transport layer is the potential existence of storage capacity in the subnet. When an IMP sends a frame, it may arrive or be lost, but it cannot bounce around for a while, go into hiding in a far corner of the world, and then suddenly emerge at an inopportune moment 30 sec later. If the subnet uses datagrams and adaptive routing inside, there is a nonnegligible probability that a packet may be stored for a number of seconds and then delivered later. The consequences of this ability of the subnet to store packets can be disastrous, and require the use of special protocols.

A final difference between the data link and transport layers is one of amount rather than of kind. Buffering and flow control are needed in both layers, but the presence of a large and dynamically varying number of connections in the transport layer may require a different approach than we used in the data link layer. In Chapter 4, some of the protocols allocate a fixed number of buffers to each line, so that when a frame arrives there is always a buffer available. In the transport layer, the larger number of connections that must be managed make the idea of dedicating many buffers to each one less attractive.

From the transport protocol designer's point of view, the actual properties of the subnet (Fig. 6-6) are less important than the *service* offered by the network layer, although the latter is, of course, strongly influenced by the former. To some extent, however, the network layer service may mask the least desirable aspects of the subnet and provide a better interface.

For the purposes of studying transport protocols, we will group the various kinds of network services into three categories as shown in Fig. 6-7. The first category, type A, consists of service that is essentially perfect. The fraction of packets lost, duplicated, or garbled is negligible. *N-RESET*s are so rare that they can be ignored. In effect, the environment in which the transport layer operates is that of Fig. 6-6(a). Public WANs offering type A service are scarcer than hen's teeth, but some LANs come fairly close. The transport protocols needed to operate over a type A network are straightforward.

Network type	Description
A	Flawless, error-free service with no N-RESETS
B	Perfect packet delivery, but with N-RESETS
C	Unreliable service with lost and duplicated packets and possibly N-RESETS

Fig. 6-7. Types of service that can be offered by the network layer.

A more common situation for WANs is type B service. Individual packets are rarely, if ever, lost (because the network and data link layer protocols recover from these losses transparently) but from time to time the network layer issues *N-RESET*s, either due to internal congestion, hardware problems, or software bugs. It is then up to the transport protocol to pick up the pieces, establish a new network connection, resynchronize, and continue, so that the *N-RESET* is completely hidden from the transport user. Most public X.25 networks are type B. Transport protocols for type B networks are more complex than those for type A.

The third type is the network service that is not reliable enough to be trusted at all. WANs offering pure connectionless (datagram) service, packet radio networks, and many internetworks fall into this category. Transport protocols that must live with type C service are the most complex of all, and must solve all the problems that we saw in the data link layer, and many more as well.

Thus different transport protocols will be needed for different situations. The worse the network service, the more complex the transport protocol. OSI has recognized this problem, and devised a transport protocol with five variants, as listed in Fig. 6-8.

Protocol class	Network type	Name
0	A	Simple class
1	B	Basic error recovery class
2	A	Multiplexing class
3	B	Error recovery and multiplexing class
4	C	Error detection and recovery class

Fig. 6-8. Transport protocol classes.

Class 0 is the simplest class. It sets up a network connection for each transport connection requested and assumes the network connection does not make errors. The transport protocol does no sequencing or flow control, relying on the underlying network layer to get everything right. It does however, provide mechanisms for establishing and releasing transport connections.

Class 1 is like class 0 except that it has been designed to recover from *N-RESET*s. If the network connection being used for a given transport connection is ever subject to an *N-RESET*, the two transport entities resynchronize and continue from where they left off. To achieve resynchronization, they must use and keep track of sequence numbers, something not required with class 0. Other than the ability to recover from *N-RESET*s, class 1 does not provide any error control or flow control on top of what the network layer itself provides.

Class 2, like class 0 is designed to be used with reliable networks (type A). It differs from class 0 in that two or more transport connections may be sent (multiplexed) over the same network connection. This feature is useful when there are many transport connections open, each with relatively little traffic, and the carrier has a high charge for connect time for each open network connection. For example, in an office full of airline reservation terminals, each terminal might have a separate transport connection to a remote computer, with all the transport connections going over one (or a few) network connections, to reduce networking costs. We will look at multiplexing in more detail later in this chapter.

Class 3 combines the features of classes 1 and 2. It allows multiplexing and can also recover from *N-RESET*s. It also uses explicit flow control.

Class 4 is designed for type C network service. It is completely paranoid and takes Murphy's Law (If something can go wrong, it will) as a given. It must therefore be able to handle lost, duplicate, and garbled packets, *N-RESET*s, and everything else the network can throw at it. Needless to say, class 4 protocols are much more complex than the other ones. We will study some of the problems that class 4 protocols must deal with later in this chapter.

It should be pointed out that having a simple-minded connectionless network service and putting all the complexity in the transport protocol is not necessarily a bad idea. Doing a lot of work to make the service almost reliable in the data link and network layers, and then discovering that it is not quite good enough to satisfy the transport layer, so that class 4 must be used there anyway, may be inefficient.

The choice of which protocol class will be used on any given connection is determined by the transport entities at the time the connection is established. The initiator can propose a preferred class, and zero or more alternative classes. The responder then chooses the protocol class to use from the list supplied. If none of the choices offered are acceptable, the connection is rejected.

This negotiation is required because different users may have different concepts of what "reliable" means. To a casual user behind a terminal who wants to access a remote computer to see if any electronic mail has arrived, a network that loses an average of one packet per week may well be considered a type A (perfect) network, and the class 0 protocol may be sufficient. A bank doing multimillion dollar funds transfers all day long may view the same network as definitely type C, and may insist upon the heavy-duty class 4 protocol. Empirical studies of the transport protocols have been made by Meister (1987) and Cole and Lloyd (1986).

6.1.5. Elements of Transport Protocols

The exact features provided by a transport protocol depend on the environment in which it operates (e.g., the type of network service available) and the type of service it must provide. Nevertheless, it is possible to give a list of basic elements which are common to many transport protocols. Figure 6-9 gives such a list, and furthermore shows which features are applicable to each of the five OSI protocol classes. This list should not be taken too literally because the details of the features sometimes differ among the various protocol classes, and not all the alternatives and variants are mentioned in the list.

In the following paragraphs we will briefly discuss each of the protocol elements listed in Fig. 6-9. All connection-oriented protocols must provide a mechanism for establishing connections. Furthermore all of them provide a way for the called party to accept or refuse a requested connection. Establishing and releasing connections will be discussed in detail in the next section.

To actually move bits across the network, the transport entities normally establish a network connection, and keep track of the mapping between transport

Protocol element	Class				
	0	1	2	3	4
Connection establishment	x	x	x	x	x
Connection refusal	x	x	x	x	x
Assignment to network connection	x	x	x	x	x
Splitting long messages into TPDUs	x	x	x	x	x
Association of TPDUs with connection	x	x	x	x	x
TPDU transfer	x	x	x	x	x
Normal release	x	x	x	x	x
Treatment of protocol errors	x	x	x	x	x
Concatenation of TPDUs to the user		x	x	x	x
Error release	x		x		
TPDU numbering		x	o	x	x
Expedited data transfer		o	o	x	x
Transport layer flow control			o	x	x
Resynchronization after a RESET		x		x	x
Retention of TPDUs until ack		x		x	x
Reassignment after network disconnect		x		x	x
Frozen references		x		x	x
Multiplexing			x	x	x
Use of multiple network connections					x
Retransmission upon timeout					x
Resequencing of TPDUs					x
Inactivity timer					x
Transport layer checksum					o

x = present   o = optional   (blank) = absent

Fig. 6-9. Elements of transport protocols and their relationships to the five OSI connection-oriented transport protocol classes.

connections and network connections. However, it is also possible for the transport entities to use a connectionless network protocol for data transport, provided that the transport protocol is class 4 (or a non-OSI protocol with the same functionality).

Before going on to the next item, let us first say a few words about terminology. When discussing the data link layer we called the units exchanged "frames." In the network layer we called them "packets." Both of these terms are widely used (e.g., in the CCITT X.25 recommendation). For the "transport packet" there is no comparable word, so we will use the OSI term **TPDU** (**Transport Protocol Data Unit**). We will call the item of information passed by the transport user to the transport provider a **message** since the OSI term, **TSDU** (**Transport Service Data Unit**), is rarely used. In some cases, the distinction between a message and a TPDU is not important, in which case we will use whichever term seems most appropriate in the context.

The messages to be transmitted may be of any length, so it is up to the transport layer to split them into TPDUs for transport. If a TPDU does not fit in a single packet, each TPDU may have to be split as well. One of the tasks of all five OSI protocol classes is to split long messages into the TPDU size used by the protocol, and then reassemble the pieces transparently at the other end.

If multiple connections are open on a machine, the transport entities will have to give each connection a number, and put the connection number in each TPDU, so that when a TPDU arrives at the other end, the receiving transport entity will know which connection to associate it with. Needless to say, transport of TPDUs is also a feature of all transport protocols.

Normal release of a connection is also found in all protocols, although it works slightly differently in class 0. In this class, there is always a one-to-one mapping between transport connections and network connections. The transport connection is released implicitly by just releasing the underlying network connection. With the other classes, releasing is explicit, by exchange of control TPDUs.

All protocols must deal with protocol errors. If an invalid TPDU arrives, there must be rules governing what to do. In some cases the action may be to ignore it; in others it may be to release some connection (or all connections). Protocol errors are not supposed to happen, of course, but allowing a transport entity just to crash if one occurs is not a good idea.

The remaining items on the list do not apply to all five OSI protocol classes. For example, concatenation of TPDUs applies to classes 1 through 4, but not 0. This feature allows the transport entity to collect several TPDUs and send them together as a single packet, thus reducing the number of calls to the network layer.

Error release refers to the fact that for protocol classes 0 and 2, an *N-RESET* or *N-DISCONNECT* terminates the transport connection(s) using that network connection. No attempt is made to recover.

TPDU numbering is used to keep track of the TPDUs. By assigning successive TPDUs on a connection successively higher sequence numbers, explicit acknowledgements and flow control are possible, and there is a way to figure out after an *N-RESET* which TPDU was the last one received. Class 0 (and optionally class 2) do not use sequence numbers.

Expedited data transfer is a possibility in the four upper protocol classes, but is not available in class 0.

Transport layer flow control consists of having an explicit part of the transport protocol dealing with how many TPDUs may be sent at any instant. A sliding window scheme can be used, but there are also other possibilities. If no explicit flow control scheme is used at the transport layer, the underlying flow control of the network connection is used.

Resynchronization after an *N-RESET* is done in classes 1, 3, and 4 to allow each side to discover which of the TPDUs it sent have arrived. Closely related to resynchronization is the necessity for transport entities to retain copies of TPDUs sent until they have been acknowledged, so that they can be retransmitted in the event of an *N-RESET*. Since classes 0 and 2 give an error release after an *N-RESET*, rather than attempting to resynchronize, they do not have to handle retention of TPDUs until they are acknowledged.

Reassignment after a network disconnect is related to the above problems. If the network breaks the connection altogether, rather than just resetting it, then it is up to the transport layer to establish a new connection on which to work.

Frozen references are important in networks that can store packets for a non-negligible time. The idea here is to refrain from giving a TPDU an identification that is identical to that of an older TPDU that is still in existence, just in case the old one pops up in an unexpected moment. We will discuss this subtle matter in detail later.

Next come multiplexing and use of multiple network connections. Both of these have to do with having several transport connections on one network connection or vice versa. We will also study these later.

Retransmission upon timeout is only needed in class 4, because this is the only class in which lost packets are common enough to require error control in the transport layer. We saw how the timer mechanism worked in the data link layer. It is essentially the same in the transport layer, although choosing good timeout values is more difficult (Karn and Partridge, 1987).

If TPDUs may be lost (class 4 again), the destination may have received TPDUs in the wrong order, and has to put them together again. This mechanism was also present in protocol 6 in Chapter 4.

The inactivity timer is different from the timer used to detect lost TPDUs. It is used to detect a dead network connection. If there is no sign of life from the network layer for the period of time governed by this timer, despite repeated attempts to communicate with it, the transport layer must assume something is radically wrong. The normal recovery procedure is to try to establish a new network connection.

Finally, the last item is the use of software checksums. TPDUs can be checksummed in software, to guard against networks whose own lower layer checksumming is inadequate. The checksum algorithm (Fletcher, 1982) has been designed to be easy to compute in software (basically, adding up the bytes modulo 256).

6.2. CONNECTION MANAGEMENT

As we mentioned before, in many ways transport protocols resemble data link protocols. Sliding window protocols, for example, can be used in both layers. One significant difference, however, is how connections are managed. In the data link layer, there is little connection management. The lines between the IMPs are always there and always ready for use. In the transport layer, the establishment, release, and general management of connections is much more complex. In this section we will look at some of the issues surrounding connection management in detail. We will see that special protocols are sometimes needed.

6.2.1. Addressing

When a (transport) user wishes to set up a connection to another user, he must specify which remote user to connect to. (Connectionless transport has the same problem: to whom should each message be sent?) The method normally used is to define transport service access points (TSAPs) to which processes can attach themselves and wait for connection requests to arrive. TSAPs are completely analogous to the NSAPs we saw in the previous chapter, only they exist at the top of the transport layer, rather than at the top of the network layer.

Figure 6-10 illustrates the relationship between the NSAP, TSAP, network connection, and transport connection. A possible connection scenario is as follows.

1. A time-of-day server process on machine B attaches itself to TSAP 122 to wait for a *T-CONNECT.indication*. How a process attaches itself to a TSAP is outside the OSI model and depends entirely on the local operating system.

2. A process on machine A wants to find out the time-of-day, so it issues a *T-CONNECT.request* specifying TSAP 6 as the source and TSAP 122 as the destination.

3. The transport entity on A selects an NSAP on its machine and on the destination machine, and sets up a network connection (e.g., an X.25 virtual circuit) between them. Using this network connection, it can talk to the transport entity on B.

4. The first thing the transport entity on A says to its peer on B is: "Good morning. I would like to establish a transport connection between my TSAP 6 and your TSAP 122. What do you say?"

5. The transport entity on B then issues the *T-CONNECT.indication*, and if the time-of-day server at TSAP 122 is agreeable, the transport connection is established.

Note that the transport connection goes from TSAP to TSAP, whereas the network connection only goes part way, from NSAP to NSAP (e.g., from X.121 address to X.121 address).

The picture painted above is fine, except we have swept one little problem under the rug: How does the user process on A know that the time-of-day server is attached to TSAP 122? One possibility is that the time-of-day server has been attaching itself to TSAP 122 for years, and gradually all the network users have learned this. In this model, services have stable TSAP addresses which can be printed on paper and given to new users when they join the network.

While stable TSAP addresses might work for a small number of key services

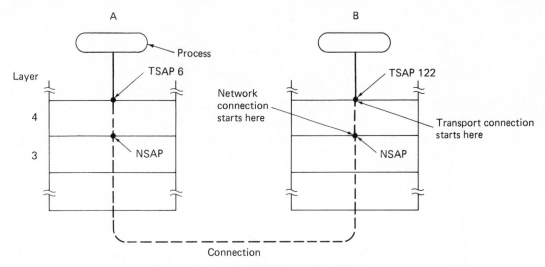

Fig. 6-10. TSAPs, NSAPs, and connections.

that never change, in general, user processes often want to talk to other user processes that only exist for a short time and do not have a TSAP address that is known in advance. Furthermore, if there are potentially many server processes, most of which are rarely used, it is wasteful to have each of them active and listening to a stable TSAP address all day long. In short, a better scheme is needed.

One such scheme, pioneered in the ARPANET, is shown in Fig. 6-11 in a simplified form. It is known as the ARPANET **initial connection protocol**. Instead of every conceivable server listening at a well-known TSAP, each machine that wishes to offer service to remote users has a special **process server** (or **logger**) through which all services must be requested. Whenever the process server is idle, it listens to a well-known TSAP. Potential users of any service must begin by doing a *T-CONNECT.request*, specifying the TSAP address of the process server.

Once the connection has been established, the user sends the process server a message telling which program it wants to run (e.g., the time-of-day program). The process server then chooses an idle TSAP and spawns a new process, telling the new process to listen to the chosen TSAP. Finally, the process server sends the remote user the address of the chosen TSAP, terminates the connection, and goes back to listening on its well-known TSAP.

At this point the new process is listening on a TSAP that the user now knows, so it is possible for the user to release the connection to the process server and connect to the new process. Once this connection has been set up, the new process executes the desired program, the name of which was passed to it by the process server, together with address of the TSAP to listen to. When the server has performed its job, it releases the connection and terminates itself.

While the ARPANET initial connection protocol works fine for those servers that can be created as they are needed, there are many situations in which services do exist independently of the process server. A file server, for example, needs to

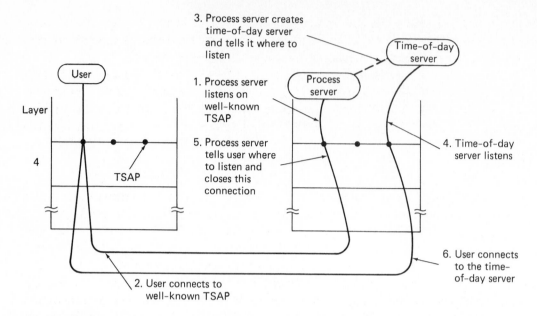

Fig. 6-11. How a user process in host *A* establishes a connection with a time-of-day server in host *B*.

run on special hardware (a machine with a disk) and cannot just be created on-the-fly when someone wants to talk to it.

To handle this situation, an alternative scheme is often used. In this model, there exists a special process called a **name server** or sometimes a **directory server**. To find the TSAP address corresponding to a given service name, such as "time-of-day," a user sets up a connection to the name server (which listens to a well-known TSAP). The user then sends a message specifying the service name, and the name server sends back the TSAP address. Then the user releases the connection with the name server and establishes a new one with the desired service.

In this model, when a new service is created, it must register itself with the name server, giving both its service name (typically an ASCII string) and the address of its TSAP. The name server records this information in its internal data base, so that when queries come in later, it will know the answers.

The function of the name server is analogous to the directory assistance operator in the telephone system—it provides a mapping of names onto numbers. Just as in the telephone system, it is essential that the address of the well-known TSAP used by the name server (or the process server in the initial connection protocol) is indeed well-known. If you do not know the number of the information operator, you cannot call the information operator to find it out. If you think the number you dial for information is obvious, try it in a foreign country some time.

Now let us suppose that the user has successfully located the address of the TSAP to be connected to. Another interesting question is how does the local transport entity know on which machine that TSAP is located? More specifically, how does the transport entity know which NSAP to use to set up a network connection to the remote transport entity that manages the TSAP requested?

The answer depends on the structure of TSAP addresses. One possible structure is that TSAP addresses are **hierarchical addresses**. With hierarchical addresses, the address consists of a sequence of fields used to disjointly partition the address space. For example, a truly universal TSAP address might have the following structure:

address = <galaxy> <star> <planet> <country> <network> <host> <port>

With this scheme, it is straightforward to locate a TSAP anywhere in the known universe. Equivalently, if a TSAP address is a concatenation of an NSAP address and a port (a local identifier specifying one of the local TSAPs), then when a transport entity is given a TSAP address to connect to, it uses the NSAP address contained in the TSAP address to reach the proper remote transport entity.

As a simple example of a hierarchical address, consider the telephone number 19076543210. This number can be parsed as 1-907-654-3210, where 1 is a country code (U.S. + Canada), 907 is an area code (Alaska), 654 is an end office in Alaska, and 3210 is one of the "ports" (subscriber lines) in that end office.

The alternative to a hierarchical address space is a **flat address space**. If the TSAP addresses are not hierarchical, a second level of mapping is needed to locate the proper machine. There would have to be a name server that took TSAP addresses as input and returned NSAP addresses as output. Alternatively, in some situations, it might be possible to broadcast a query asking the destination machine to please identify itself.

6.2.2. Establishing a Connection

Establishing a connection sounds easy, but it is actually surprisingly tricky, especially in a type C network. At first glance, it would seem sufficient for one transport entity to just send a *CR (CONNECTION REQUEST)* TPDU to the destination and wait for a *CC (CONNECTION CONFIRM)* reply. The problem occurs when the network can lose, store, and duplicate packets.

Imagine a subnet that is so congested that acknowledgements never get back in time, and each packet times out and is retransmitted two or three times. Suppose the subnet uses datagrams inside, and every packet follows a different route. Some of the packets might get stuck in traffic jams and take a long time to arrive, that is, they are stored in the subnet and pop out much later.

The worst possible nightmare is as follows. A user establishes a connection with a bank, sends messages telling the bank to transfer a large amount of money to the account of a not entirely trustworthy person, and then releases the connection. Unfortunately, each packet in the scenario is duplicated and stored in the subnet. After the connection has been released, all the packets pop out of the subnet and arrive at the destination in order, asking the bank to establish a new connection, transfer money (again), and release the connection. The bank has no way of telling that these are duplicates, assumes this is a second, independent transaction, and transfers the money again. For the remainder of this section we will study the problem of delayed duplicates, with special emphasis on algorithms for establishing connections in a reliable way, so that nightmares like the one above cannot happen.

The crux of the problem is the existence of delayed duplicates. It can be attacked in various ways, none of them very satisfactory. One way is to use throwaway TSAP addresses. In this approach, each time a TSAP address is needed, a new, unique address is generated, typically based on the current time. When a connection is released, the addresses are discarded forever. This strategy makes the process server model of Fig. 6-11 impossible.

Another possibility is to give each connection a connection identifier (i.e., a sequence number incremented for each connection established), chosen by the initiating party, and put in each TPDU, including the one requesting the connection. After each connection is released, each transport entity could update a table listing obsolete connections as (peer transport entity, connection identifier) pairs. Whenever a connection request came in, it could be checked against the table, to see if it belonged to a previously released connection.

Unfortunately, this scheme has a basic flaw: it requires each transport entity to maintain a certain amount of history information indefinitely. If a machine crashes and loses its memory, it will no longer know which connection identifiers have already been used.

Instead, we need to take a different tack. Rather than allowing packets to live forever within the subnet, we must devise a mechanism to kill off very old packets that are still wandering about. If we can ensure that no packet lives longer than some known time, the problem becomes somewhat more manageable.

Packet lifetime can be restricted to a known maximum using one of the following techniques:

1. Restricted subnet design.

2. Putting a hop counter in each packet.

3. Time stamping each packet.

The first method includes any method that prevents packets from looping, combined with some way of bounding congestion delay over the (now known) longest possible path. The second method consists of having the hop count incremented each time the packet is forwarded. The data link protocol simply discards any packet whose hop counter has exceeded a certain value. The third method requires each packet to bear the time it was created, with the IMPs agreeing to discard any packet older than some agreed upon time. This latter method requires the IMP clocks to be synchronized, which itself is a nontrivial task unless synchronization is achieved external to the network, for example by listening to WWV or some other radio station that broadcasts the exact time periodically.

In practice, we will need to guarantee not only that a packet is dead, but also that all acknowledgements to it are also dead, so we will now introduce T, which is some small multiple of the true maximum packet lifetime. The multiple is protocol-dependent and simply has the effect of making T longer. If we wait a time T after a packet has been sent, we can be sure that all traces of it are now gone and that neither it nor its acknowledgements will suddenly appear out of the blue to complicate matters.

With packet lifetimes bounded, it is possible to devise a foolproof way to establish connections safely. The method described below is due to Tomlinson (1975). It solves the problem, but introduces some peculiarities of its own. The method was further refined by Sunshine and Dalal (1978).

To get around the problem of a machine losing all memory of where it was after a crash, Tomlinson proposed equipping each host with a time of day clock. The clocks at different hosts need not be synchronized. Each clock is assumed to take the form of a binary counter that increments itself at uniform intervals. Furthermore, the number of bits in the counter must equal or exceed the number of bits in the sequence numbers. Last, and most important, the clock is assumed to continue running even if the host goes down.

The basic idea is to ensure that two identically numbered TPDUs are never outstanding at the same time. When a connection is set up, the low-order k bits of the clock are used as the initial sequence number (also k bits). Thus, unlike our protocols of Chapter 4, each connection starts numbering its TPDUs with a different sequence number. The sequence space should be so large (e.g., 32 bits) that by the time sequence numbers wrap around, old TPDUs with the same sequence number are long gone. This linear relation between time and initial sequence numbers is shown in Fig. 6-12.

Once both transport entities have agreed on the initial sequence number, any sliding window protocol can be used for data flow control. In reality, the initial sequence number curve (shown by the heavy line) is not really linear, but a staircase, since the clock advances in discrete steps. For simplicity we will ignore this detail.

A problem occurs when a host crashes. When it comes up again, its transport entity does not know where it was in the sequence space. One solution is to require transport entities to be idle for T sec after a recovery to let all old TPDUs die off. However, in a complex internetwork T may be large, so this strategy is unattractive.

To avoid requiring T sec of dead time after a crash, it is necessary to introduce a new restriction on the use of sequence numbers. We can best see the need for this restriction by means of an example. Let T, the maximum packet lifetime, be 60 sec, and let the clock tick once per second. As shown in Fig. 6-12, the initial sequence number for a connection opened at time x will be x. Imagine that at $t = 30$ sec, an

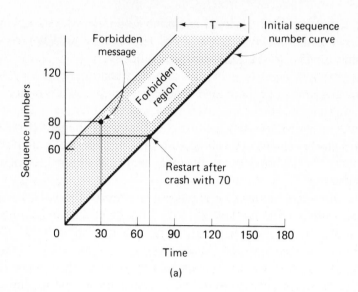

(a)

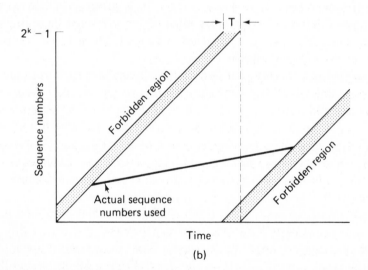

(b)

Fig. 6-12. (a) TPDUs may not enter the forbidden region. (b) The resynchronization problem.

ordinary data TPDU being sent on (a previously opened) connection 5 is given sequence number 80. Call this TPDU *X*. Immediately after sending TPDU *X*, the host crashes and then quickly restarts. At $t = 60$, it begins reopening connections 0 through 4. At $t = 70$, it reopens connection 5, using initial sequence number 70 as required. Within the next 15 sec it sends data TPDUs 70 through 80. Thus at $t = 85$ a new TPDU with sequence number 80 and connection 5 has been injected into the subnet. Unfortunately, TPDU *X* still exists. If it should arrive at the receiver before the new TPDU 80, it will be accepted and the correct TPDU rejected.

To prevent such problems, we must prevent sequence numbers from being used (i.e., assigned to new TPDUs) for a time T before their potential use as initial sequence numbers. The illegal combinations of time and sequence number are shown as the **forbidden region** in Fig. 6-12(a). Before sending any TPDU on any connection, the transport entity must read the clock and check to see that it is not in the forbidden region.

The protocol can get itself into trouble in two different ways. If a host sends too much data too fast on a newly opened connection, the actual sequence number versus time curve may rise more steeply than the initial sequence number versus time curve. This means that the maximum data rate on any connection is one TPDU per clock tick. It also means that the transport entity must wait until the clock ticks before opening a new connection after a crash restart, lest the same number be used twice. Both of these points argue for a short clock tick (a few milliseconds).

Unfortunately, entering the forbidden region from underneath by sending too fast is not the only way to get into trouble. From Fig. 6-12(b), it should be clear that at any data rate less than the clock rate, the curve of actual sequence numbers used versus time will eventually run into the forbidden region from the left. The greater the slope of the actual sequence number curve, the longer this event will be delayed. As we stated above, just before sending every TPDU, the transport entity must check to see if it is about to enter the forbidden region, and if so, either delay the TPDU for T sec or resynchronize the sequence numbers.

The clock based method solves the delayed duplicate problem for data TPDUs, but for this method to be useful, a connection must first be established. Since control TPDUs may also be delayed, there is a potential problem in getting both sides to agree on the initial sequence number. Suppose, for example, that connections are established by having one machine A, send a CR TPDU containing the proposed initial sequence number and destination port number to a remote peer, B. The receiver, B, then acknowledges this request by sending a CC TPDU back. If the CR TPDU is lost but a delayed duplicate CR suddenly shows up at B, the connection will be established incorrectly.

To solve this problem, Tomlinson (1975) has introduced the **three-way handshake**. This establishment protocol does not require both sides to begin sending with the same sequence number, so it can be used with synchronization methods other than the global clock method. The setup procedure when A initiates is shown in Fig. 6-13. In this figure, A is the transport entity (not transport user) to the left of the vertical lines, and B is the transport entity to the right. The arrows denote TPDUs sent and received, not transport user primitives, as was the case when we were discussing the service rather than the protocol. A chooses a sequence number somehow, say x, and sends it to B. B replies with a CC TPDU acknowledging x and announcing its own initial sequence number, y (which may be equal to x, of course). Finally, A acknowledges B's choice of an initial sequence number in its first data TPDU.

Now let us see how the three-way handshake works in the presence of delayed

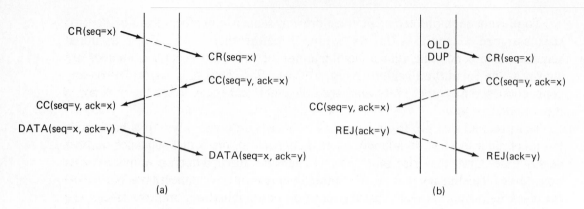

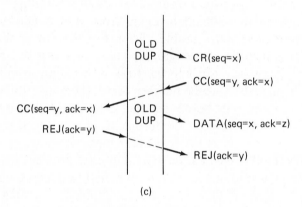

Fig. 6-13. Three protocol scenarios for establishing a connection using a three-way handshake. (a) Normal operation. (b) Old duplicate *CR* appearing out of nowhere. (c) Duplicate *CR* and duplicate ACK.

duplicate control TPDUs. In Fig. 6-13(b), the first TPDU is a delayed duplicate *CR* from a connection since released. This TPDU arrives at *B* without *A*'s knowledge. *B* reacts to this TPDU by sending *A* a *CC* TPDU, in effect asking for verification that *A* was indeed trying to set up a new connection. When *A* rejects *B*'s attempt to establish, *B* realizes that it was tricked by a delayed duplicate and abandons the connection.

The worst case is when both a delayed *CR* and an acknowledgement to a *CC* are floating around in the subnet. This case is shown in Fig. 6-13(c). As in the previous example, *B* gets a delayed *CR* and replies to it. At this point it is crucial to realize that *B* has proposed using *y* as the initial sequence number for *B* to *A* traffic, knowing full well that no TPDUs containing sequence number *y* or acknowledgements to *y* are still in existence. When the second delayed TPDU arrives at *B*, the fact that *z* has been acknowledged rather than *y* tells *B* that this, too, is an old duplicate.

6.2.3. Releasing a Connection

Releasing a connection is much easier than establishing one. Nevertheless, there are more pitfalls than one might expect. In Fig. 6-4(d)-(f) we see three ways that a connection can be released. The first one is the most common, with one of the users issuing a *T-DISCONNECT.request* primitive. The transport layer then generates a *T-DISCONNECT.indication* on the other end, and the connection is released.

The second way that release can happen is when both users issue a *T-DISCONNECT.request* simultaneously. The third way is when the transport layer throws in the towel and issues *T-DISCONNECT.indications* on both ends of the connection. Theoretically, there is also a fourth way, in which one user issues a *T-DISCONNECT.request* and before the *T-DISCONNECT.indication* can happen at the other end, the transport layer itself disconnects the other end.

All of these forms of disconnect have one feature in common: they are abrupt and may result in data loss. Consider the scenario of Fig. 6-14. After the connection is established, *A* sends a TPDU that arrives properly at *B*. Then *A* sends another TPDU and disconnects. Unfortunately, *B* issues a *T-DISCONNECT.request* before the second TPDU arrives. The result is that the connection is released and data are lost.

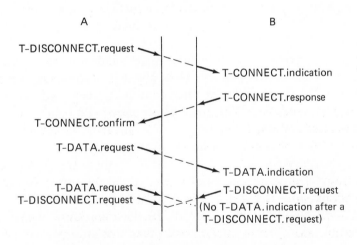

Fig. 6-14. Abrupt disconnection with loss of data.

Clearly a more sophisticated release protocol is required to avoid data loss. An obvious way to handle release is not to have either side issue a *T-DISCONNECT.request* until it is sure that the other side has received all data that has been sent, and has no more data to send itself. In other words, the protocol could be something like *A* saying: "I am done. Are you done too?" If *B* responds: "I am done too. Goodbye." the connection can be safely released.

Unfortunately, this protocol does not always work. There is a famous problem that deals with this issue. It is called the **two-army problem**. Imagine that a white army is encamped in a valley, as shown in Fig. 6-15. On both of the surrounding hillsides are blue armies. The white army is larger than either of the blue armies alone, but together they are larger than the white army. If either blue army attacks by itself, it will be defeated, but if the two blue armies attack simultaneously, they will be victorious.

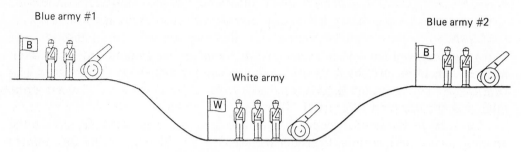

Fig. 6-15. The two-army problem.

The blue armies obviously want to synchronize their attacks. However, their only communication medium is to send messengers on foot down into the valley, where they might be captured and the message lost (i.e., they have to use an unreliable communication channel). The question is, does a protocol exist that allows the blue armies to win?

Suppose that the commander of blue army #1 sends a message reading: "I propose we attack at dawn on March 29. How about it?" Now suppose that the message arrives, and the commander of blue army #2 agrees, and that his reply gets safely back to blue army #1. Will the attack happen? Probably not, because commander #2 does not know if his reply got through. If it did not, blue army #1 will not attack, so it would be foolish for him to charge into battle.

Now let us improve the protocol by making it a three-way handshake. The initiator of the original proposal must acknowledge the response. Assuming no messages are lost, blue army #2 will get the acknowledgement, but the commander of blue army #1 will now hesitate. After all, he does not know if his acknowledgement got through, and if it did not, he knows that blue army #2 will not attack. We could now make a four-way handshake protocol, but that does not help either.

In fact, it can easily be proven that no protocol exists that works. Suppose that some protocol did exist. Either the last message of the protocol is essential or it is not. If it is not, remove it (and any other unessential messages) until we are left with a protocol in which every message is essential. What happens if the final message does not get through? We just said that it was essential, so if it is lost, the attack does not take place. Since the sender of the final message can never be sure of its arrival, he will not risk attacking. Worse yet, the other blue army knows this, so it will not attack either.

To see the relevance of the two-army problem to releasing connections, just substitute "disconnect" for "attack." If neither side is prepared to disconnect until it is convinced that the other side is prepared to disconnect too, the disconnection will never happen.

In practice, one is usually prepared to take more risks when releasing connections than when attacking white armies, so the situation is not entirely hopeless. Figure 6-16 illustrates four scenarios of releasing using a three-way handshake. While this protocol is not infallible, it is usually adequate. Note that it shows the TPDUs sent and received by the transport entities, not the primitives seen by the transport users.

In Fig. 6-16(a), we see the normal case in which one of the users sends a *DR* (*DISCONNECT REQUEST*) TPDU in order to initiate the connection release. When it arrives, the recipient sends back a *DC* (*DISCONNECT CONFIRM*) TPDU and starts a timer, just in case the *DC* is lost. When the *DC* arrives, the original sender sends back an *ACK* TPDU and deletes the connection. Finally, when the ACK arrives, the receiver also deletes the connection. Note that "delete connection" in this context means that the transport entity removes the information about the connection from its table of open connections, and signals the connection's owner (the transport user) somehow. This action is completely different from a transport user issuing a *T-DISCONNECT.request* primitive.

If the final ACK is lost, as shown in Fig. 6-16(b), the situation is saved by the timer. When the timer expires, the connection is deleted anyway.

Now consider the case of the *DC* (or *DR)* being lost. The user initiating the disconnect will not receive the *DC,* will time out, and will start all over again. In Fig. 6-16(c) we see how this works, assuming that the second time no TPDUs are lost.

Our last scenario, Fig. 6-16(d), is the same as Fig. 6-16(c) except that now we assume all the repeated attempts to retransmit the *DR* also fail due to lost TPDUs. After *n* retries, the sender just gives up and deletes the connection. Meanwhile, the receiver times out and also exits.

While this protocol usually suffices, in theory it can fail if the initial DR and *n* retransmissions are all lost. The sender will give up and delete the connection, while the other side knows nothing at all about the attempts to disconnect and is still fully active. This situation results in a half-open connection.

We could have avoided this problem by not allowing the sender to give up after *n* retries, but forcing it to go on forever until it gets a response. However, if the other side is allowed to time out, then the sender will indeed go on forever, because no response will ever be forthcoming. If we do not allow the receiving side to time out, then the protocol hangs in Fig. 6-16(b).

One way to kill off half-open connections is to have a rule saying that if no TPDUs have arrived for a certain number of seconds, the connection is automatically disconnected. That way, if one side ever disconnects, the other side will detect the lack of activity and also disconnect. Of course, if this rule is introduced, it is necessary for each transport entity to have a timer that is stopped and then re-

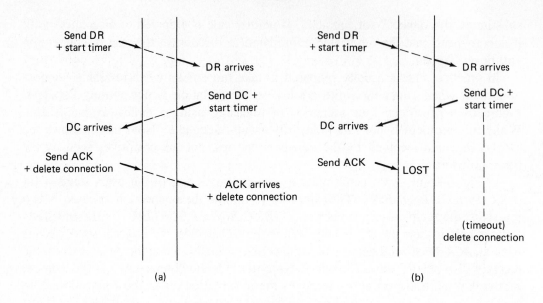

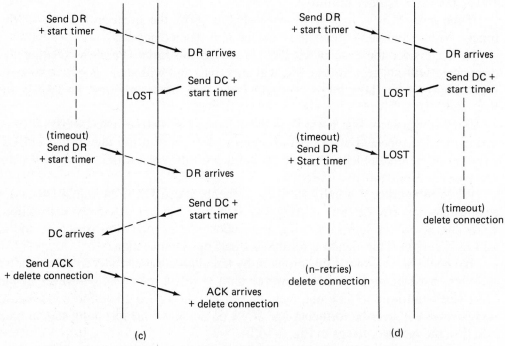

Fig. 6-16. Four protocol scenarios for releasing a connection. (a) Normal case of three-way handshake. (b) Final *ACK* lost. (c) *DC* lost. (d) *DC* lost and subsequent *DRs* lost.

started whenever a TPDU is sent. If this timer expires, a dummy TPDU is transmitted, just to keep the other side from disconnecting. On the other hand, if the automatic disconnect rule is used and too many dummy TPDUs in a row are lost on an otherwise idle connection, first one side, then the other side will automatically disconnect.

We will not belabor this point any more, but by now it should be clear that releasing a connection is not nearly as simple as it at first appears.

6.2.4. Timer-Based Connection Management

Let us take a step back. The original problem we posed was how to avoid the nightmare of old, duplicate packets containing *CR, DATA,* and *DR* TPDUs suddenly appearing from nowhere and being accepted as legitimate. One way is for each transport entity to assign a unique connection identifier to each connection so it can recognize TPDUs from previous connections. A second way is to use three-way handshakes for establishing connections. Fletcher and Watson (1978) and Watson (1981) have proposed a third way based on timers. We will describe their method in this section.

The basic idea is closely related to the proposal earlier to have a connection simply time out if there is no activity. What Fletcher and Watson have done, is arrange for the transport entity to refrain from deleting information about a connection until all the TPDUs relating to it have died off. Thus in their scheme, a transport entity's table entry about a connection is not deleted when the connection is released, but when a carefully chosen time interval has expired.

The heart of their scheme is this: when a sender wishes to send a stream of consecutive TPDUs to a receiver, it creates a **connection record** internally. This connection record keeps track of which TPDUs have been sent, which acknowledgements have been received, and so on. Whenever a connection record is created a timer is started. Whenever a TPDU is sent using a previously created connection record, the timer is started all over again. If the timer expires (meaning nothing has been sent for a certain interval), the connection record is deleted. The time intervals for sender and receiver are different and carefully chosen so that the receiver will always time out and delete its connection record well before the sender.

The first TPDU in the stream contains a 1-bit flag called *DRF* (Data Run Flag), which identifies it as the first in a run of TPDUs. When any TPDU is sent, a timer is started. If the TPDU is acknowledged, the timer is stopped. If the timer goes off, the TPDU is retransmitted. If, after *n* retransmissions, there is still no acknowledgement, the sender gives up. This give-up time plays an important role in the protocol.

When a TPDU with the *DRF* flag set arrives at the receiver, the receiver notes its sequence number and creates a connection record. Subsequent TPDUs will only be accepted if they are in sequence. If the first TPDU to arrive at the receiver does not have the *DRF* flag set, it is discarded. Eventually the first TPDU (original or retransmission) will arrive and the connection record can be created. In other words, a connection record is only created when a TPDU with *DRF* set arrives.

Whenever a TPDU arrives in sequence, it can be passed to the transport user and an acknowledgement returned to the sender. If a TPDU arrives out of sequence when a connection record exists, it may be buffered (like protocol 6 in Chapter 4). It may also be acknowledged. However, an acknowledgement does not imply that all the previous TPDUs have been received as well, unless a flag, *ARF* (Acknowledgment Run Flag), is set.

Let us first consider a simple case of how this protocol works. A sequence of TPDUs is sent and all are received in order and acknowledged. When the sender gets the acknowledgement of the final TDPU sent and sees the *ARF* flag, it stops all the retransmission timers. If no more data are forthcoming from the transport user, eventually the receiver's connection record times out and then later the sender's does too. No explicit establishment or release TPDUs are needed (although the *DRF* flag is somewhat analogous to a *CR* TPDU).

Now consider what happens if the TPDU bearing the *DRF* flag is lost. The receiver will not create a connection record. Eventually the sender will time out and retransmit the TPDU, repeatedly if necessary, until it is acknowledged. Once a connection record has been created by the receiver, a gap in the TPDU stream is easily detected and repaired by sender timeouts and retransmissions.

Suppose a stream of TPDUs is sent and correctly received, but some of the acknowledgements are lost. Subsequent retransmissions are also lost, so the receiver's connection record times out and is deleted. What is to prevent an old duplicate of the TPDU with the *DRF* flag from now appearing at the receiver and triggering a new connection record? The trick is to make the receiver's connection record timer much longer than the sender's give-up timer plus the maximum TPDU lifetime. Thus once the initial TPDU is accepted, the connection record will be kept in existence until the receiver is certain that the sender has stopped sending the TPDU with the *DRF* flag (either because it got an acknowledgement or it gave up). In this way, once the initial TPDU has been accepted, there is no danger that it will appear after the connection record has been deleted—all copies of it are definitely gone. The other TPDUs in the run are harmless because the receiver will not accept them (only TPDUs with the *DRF* flag are acceptable when the receiver has no connection record).

Furthermore, if some TPDUs remain unacknowledged, the sender will keep retransmitting them, thus keeping its connection record alive. As long as the connection record shows unacknowledged TPDUs outstanding, no new TPDU with *DRF* set will be sent.

Now let us see what happens if the transport user sends messages in bursts. Suppose a burst of TPDUs is sent and all are acknowledged. When the transport user finally gets around to sending a new message, one of three situations must hold:

1. Both sender and receiver still have their connection records.

2. The sender has its connection record but the receiver does not.

3. Both connection records have been deleted.

It cannot happen that the sender's record has been deleted while the receiver's is still around because the timer for the sender's record is intentionally longer to prevent just this case. In case 1, the next TPDU will carry a *DRF* flag and will start a new run; it will be numbered one higher than the previous TPDU because the connection record still exists. The receiver will accept it without problems. In case 2, the receiver will create a new connection record and regard it as the start of a new run, since it has already forgotten the previous run. In case 3, the sender will create a new connection record, which means that the TPDU will not be numbered in sequence with the previous ones. However, the receiver no longer knows what the previous ones were, so it does not matter. It should be clear now that the fourth case (receiver knowing which TPDU to expect but sender not knowing which one to send) has been carefully forbidden for good reason.

In summary, this protocol has an interesting mixture of connectionless and connection-oriented properties. The minimum exchange is two TPDUs, which makes it as efficient as a connectionless protocol for query-response applications. Unlike a connectionless protocol, however, if it turns out that a sequence of TPDUs must be sent, they are guaranteed to be delivered in order. Finally, connections are released automatically by the clever use of timers.

6.2.5. Flow Control and Buffering

Having examined connection establishment and release in some detail, let us now look at how connections are managed while they are in use. One of the key issues has come up before: flow control. In some ways the flow control problem in the transport layer is the same as in the data link layer, but in other ways it is different. The basic similarity is that in both layers a sliding window or other scheme is needed on each connection to keep a fast transmitter from overrunning a slow receiver. The main difference is that the IMP usually has relatively few lines whereas the host may have numerous connections. This difference makes it impractical to implement the data link buffering strategy in the transport layer.

In the data link protocols of Chapter 4, frames were buffered at both the sending IMP and at the receiving IMP. In protocol 6, for example, both sender and receiver are required to dedicate $MaxSeq + 1$ buffers to each line, half for input and half for output. For a host with a maximum of, say, 64 connections, and a 4-bit sequence number, this protocol would require 1024 buffers.

In the data link layer, the sending side must buffer outgoing frames because they might have to be retransmitted. If the subnet provides datagram service, the sending transport entity must also buffer, and for the same reason. If the receiver knows that the sender buffers all TPDUs until they are acknowledged, the receiver may or may not dedicate specific buffers to specific connections, as it sees fit. The receiver may, for example, maintain a single buffer pool shared by all connections. When a TPDU comes in, an attempt is made to dynamically acquire a new buffer. If one is available, the TPDU is accepted, otherwise it is discarded. Since the sender is prepared to retransmit TPDUs lost by the subnet, no harm is done by having the receiver drop TPDUs. The sender just keeps trying until it gets an acknowledgement.

In summary, if the network service is unreliable (i.e., type B or C), the sender must buffer all TPDUs sent, just as in the data link layer. However, with reliable (type A) network service, other trade-offs become possible. In particular, if the sender knows that the receiver always has buffer space, it need not retain copies of the TPDUs it sends. However, if the receiver cannot guarantee that every incoming TPDU will be accepted, the sender will have to buffer anyway. In the latter case, the sender cannot trust the network layer's acknowledgement, because the acknowledgement means only that the TPDU arrived, not that it was accepted. We will come back to this important point later.

Even if the receiver has agreed to do the buffering, there still remains the question of the buffer size. If most TPDUs are nearly the same size, it is natural to organize the buffers as a pool of identical size buffers, with one TPDU per buffer, as in Fig. 6-17(a). However, if there is wide variation in TPDU size, from a few characters typed at a terminal to thousands of characters from file transfers, a pool of fixed-sized buffers presents problems. If the buffer size is chosen equal to the largest possible TPDU, space will be wasted whenever a short TPDU arrives. If the buffer size is chosen less than the maximum TPDU size, multiple buffers will be needed for long TPDUs, with the attendant complexity.

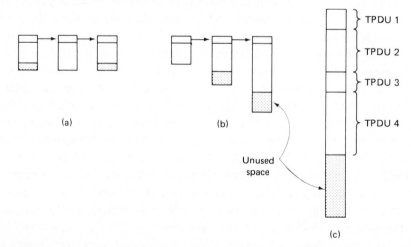

(a)　　　　(b)

Unused space

(c)

Fig. 6-17. (a) Chained fixed-size buffers. (b) Chained variable-size buffers. (c) One large circular buffer per connection.

Another approach to the buffer size problem is to use variable-size buffers, as in Fig. 6-17(b). The advantage here is better memory utilization, at the price of far more complicated buffer management. A third possibility is to dedicate a single large circular buffer per connection, as in Fig. 6-17(c). This system also makes good use of memory, provided that all connections are heavily loaded, but is poor if some connections are lightly loaded.

The optimum trade-off between source buffering and destination buffering depends on the type of traffic carried by the connection. For low-bandwidth bursty traffic, such as that produced by an interactive terminal, it is better not to dedicate any buffers, but rather to acquire them dynamically at both ends. Since the sender cannot be sure the receiver will be able to acquire a buffer, the sender must retain a copy of the TPDU until it is acknowledged. On the other hand, for file transfer and other high-bandwidth traffic, it is better if the receiver does dedicate a full window of buffers, to allow the data to flow at maximum speed. Thus for low-bandwidth bursty traffic, it is better to buffer at the sender, and for high-bandwidth, smooth traffic it is better to buffer at the receiver.

As connections are opened and closed, and as the traffic pattern changes, the sender and receiver need to dynamically adjust their buffer allocations. Consequently, the transport protocol should allow a sending host to request buffer space at the other end. Buffers could be allocated per connection, or collectively, for all the connections running between the two hosts. Alternatively, the receiver, knowing its buffer situation (but not knowing the offered traffic), could tell the sender "I have reserved X buffers for you." If the number of open connections should increase, it may be necessary for an allocation to be reduced, so the protocol should provide for this possibility.

A reasonably general way to manage dynamic buffer allocation is to decouple the buffering from the acknowledgements, in contrast to the sliding window protocols of Chapter 4. Dynamic buffer management means, in effect, a variable-sized window. Initially, the sender requests a certain number of buffers, based on its perceived needs. The receiver then grants as many of these as it can afford. Every time the sender transmits a TPDU, it must decrement its allocation, stopping altogether when the allocation reaches zero. The receiver then separately piggybacks both acknowledgements and buffer allocations onto the reverse traffic.

Figure 6-18 shows an example of how dynamic window management might work in a datagram subnet with 4-bit sequence numbers. Assume that buffer allocation information travels in separate TPDUs, as shown, and is not piggybacked onto reverse traffic. Initially, A wants eight buffers, but is only granted four of these. It then sends three TPDUs, of which the third is lost. TPDU 6 acknowledges receipt of all TPDUs up to and including sequence number 1, thus allowing A to release those buffers, and furthermore informs A that it has permission to send three more TPDUs starting beyond 1 (i.e., TPDUs 2, 3, and 4). A knows that it has already sent number 2, so it thinks that it may send TPDUs 3 and 4, which it proceeds to do. At this point it is blocked, and must wait for more buffer allocation. Timeout induced retransmissions (line 9), however, may occur while blocked, since they use buffers that have already been allocated. In line 10, *B* acknowledges receipt of all TPDUs up to and including 4, but refuses to let *A* continue. Such a situation is impossible with the fixed window protocols of Chapter 4. The next TPDU from *B* to *A* allocates another buffer and allows *A* to continue.

	A	Message	B	Comments
1	→	< request 8 buffers >	→	A wants 8 buffers
2	←	< ack = 15, buf = 4 >	←	B grants messages 0–3 only
3	→	< seq = 0, data = m0 >	→	A has 3 buffers left now
4	→	< seq = 1, data = m1 >	→	A has 2 buffers left now
5	→	< seq = 2, data = m2 >	. . .	Message lost but A thinks it has 1 left
6	←	< ack = 1, buf = 3 >	←	B acknowledges 0 and 1, permits 2–4
7	→	< seq = 3, data = m3 >	→	A has 1 buffer left
8	→	< seq = 4, data = m4 >	→	A has 0 buffers left, and must stop
9	→	< seq = 2, data = m2 >	→	A times out and retransmits
10	←	< ack = 4, buf = 0 >	←	Everything acknowledged, but A still blocked
11	←	< ack = 4, buf = 1 >	←	A may now send 5
12	←	< ack = 4, buf = 2 >	←	B found a new buffer somewhere
13	→	< seq = 5, data m5>	→	A has 1 buffer left
14	→	< seq = 6, data = m6 >	→	A is now blocked again
15	←	< ack = 6, buf = 0 >	←	A is still blocked
16	. . .	< ack = 6, buf = 4 >	←	Potential deadlock

Fig. 6-18. Dynamic buffer allocation. The arrows show the direction of transmission. An ellipsis (...) indicates a lost TPDU.

Potential problems with buffer allocation schemes of this kind can arise in datagram networks if control TPDUs can get lost. Look at line 16. *B* has now allocated more buffers to *A*, but the allocation TPDU was lost. Since control TPDUs are not sequenced or timed out, *A* is now deadlocked. To prevent this situation, each host should periodically send control TPDUs giving the acknowledgement and buffer status on each connection. That way, the deadlock will be broken, sooner or later.

Up until now we have tacitly assumed that the only limit imposed on the sender's data rate is the amount of buffer space available in the receiver. As memory prices continue to fall dramatically, it may become feasible to equip hosts with so much memory that lack of buffers is rarely, if ever, a problem.

When buffer space no longer limits the maximum flow, another bottleneck will appear: the carrying capacity of the subnet. If adjacent IMPs can exchange at most *x* frames/sec and there are *k* disjoint paths between a pair of hosts, there is no way that those hosts can exchange more than *kx* TPDUs/sec, no matter how much buffer space is available at each end. If the sender pushes too hard (i.e., sends more than *kx* TPDUs/sec), the subnet will become congested, because it will be unable to deliver TPDUs as fast as they are coming in.

What is needed is a mechanism based on the subnet's carrying capacity rather than on the receiver's buffering capacity. Clearly, the flow control mechanism must be applied at the sender, to prevent it from having too many unacknowledged TPDUs outstanding at once. Belsnes (1975) has proposed using a sliding window flow control scheme in which the sender dynamically adjusts the window size to match the network's carrying capacity. If the network can handle c TPDUs/sec and the cycle time (including transmission, propagation, queueing, processing at the receiver, and return of the acknowledgement) is r, then the sender's window should be cr. With a window of this size the sender normally operates with the pipeline full. Any small decrease in network performance will cause it to block.

In order to adjust the window size periodically, the sender could monitor both parameters and then compute the desired window size. The carrying capacity can be determined by simply counting the number of TPDUs acknowledged during some time period and then dividing by the time period. During the measurement, the sender should send as fast as it can, to make sure that the network's carrying capacity, and not the low input rate, is the factor limiting the acknowledgement rate. The time required for a transmitted TPDU to be acknowledged can be measured exactly and a running mean maintained. Since the capacity of the network depends on the amount of traffic in it, the window size should be adjusted frequently, to track changes in the carrying capacity.

6.2.6. Multiplexing

Multiplexing several conversations onto connections, virtual circuits, and physical links plays a role in several layers of the network architecture. In the transport layer the need for multiplexing can arise in a number of ways. For example, in networks that use virtual circuits within the subnet, each open connection consumes some table space in the IMPs for the entire duration of the connection. If buffers are dedicated to the virtual circuit in each IMP as well, a user who left his terminal logged into a remote machine during a coffee break is nevertheless consuming expensive resources. Although this implementation of packet switching defeats one of the main reasons for having packet switching in the first place—to bill the user based on the amount of data sent, not the connect time—a number of PTTs have chosen this approach, presumably because it so closely resembles the circuit switching model to which they have grown accustomed over the decades.

The consequence of a price structure that heavily penalizes installations for having many virtual circuits open for long periods of time is to make multiplexing of different transport connections onto the same network connection attractive. This form of multiplexing, called **upward multiplexing**, is shown in Fig. 6-19(a). In this figure, four distinct transport connections all use the same network connection (e.g., X.25 virtual circuit) to the remote host. When connect time forms the major component of the carrier's bill, it is up to the transport layer to group transport connections according to their destination and map each group onto the minimum number of network connections. If too many transport connections are mapped onto one network connection, the performance will be poor, because the window will usually be full, and users will have to wait their turn to send one message. If too few transport connections are mapped onto one network connection, the service will be expensive. When upward multiplexing is used with X.25, we have the ironic (tragic?) situation of having to identify the connection using a field in the transport header, even though X.25 provides more than 4000 virtual circuit numbers expressly for that purpose.

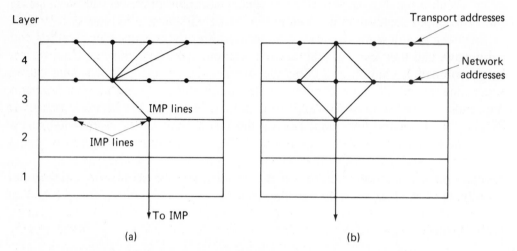

Fig. 6-19. (a) Upward multiplexing. (b) Downward multiplexing.

Multiplexing can also be useful in the transport layer for another reason, related to carrier technical decisions rather than carrier pricing decisions. Suppose, for example, that a certain important user needs a high-bandwidth connection from time to time. If the subnet enforces a sliding window flow control with a 3-bit sequence number, the user must stop sending as soon as seven packets are outstanding, and must wait for the packets to propagate to the remote host and be acknowledged. If the physical connection is via a satellite, the user is effectively limited to seven packets every 540 msec. With 128-byte packets, the usable bandwidth is about 13 kbps, even though the physical channel bandwidth is more than 1000 times higher.

One possible solution is to have the transport layer open multiple network connections, and distribute the traffic among them on a round-robin basis, as indicated in Fig. 6-19(b). This modus operandi is called **downward multiplexing**. With k network connections open, the effective bandwidth is increased by a factor of k. With 4095 X.25 virtual circuits, 128-byte packets, and a 3-bit sequence number, it is theoretically possible to achieve data rates in excess of 50 Mbps. Of course, this performance can be achieved only if the host-IMP line can support 50 Mbps, because all 4095 virtual circuits are still being sent out over one physical line, at least in Fig. 6-19(b). If multiple host-IMP lines are available, downward multiplexing can also be used to increase the performance even more.

6.2.7. Crash Recovery

If hosts and IMPs are subject to crashes, recovery from these crashes becomes an issue. If the network layer issues an *N-RESET*, for example, the transport entities must exchange information after the crash to determine which TPDUs were received and which were not. In effect, after a crash host *A* can ask host *B*: "I have four unacknowledged TPDUs outstanding, 2, 3, 4, and 5; have you received any of them?" Based on the answer, *A* can retransmit the appropriate TPDUs, provided that it has kept copies of them. If the host simply assumes that the subnet is reliable and does not keep copies, it will not be able to recover in this manner.

A more troublesome problem is how to recover from host crashes. To illustrate the difficulty, let us assume that one host, the sender, is sending a long file to another host, the receiver, using a simple stop-and-wait protocol. The transport layer on the receiving host simply passes the incoming TPDUs to the transport user, one by one. Part way through the transmission the receiver crashes. When it comes back up, its tables are reinitialized, so it no longer knows precisely where it was.

In an attempt to recover its previous status, the receiver might send a broadcast TPDU to all other hosts, announcing that it had just crashed and requesting the other hosts to inform it of the status of all open connections. The sender can be in one of two states: one TPDU outstanding, *S1*, or no TPDUs outstanding, *S0*. Based on only this state information, the sender must decide whether or not to retransmit the most recent TPDU.

At first glance it would seem obvious that the sender should retransmit only if it has an unacknowledged TPDU outstanding (i.e., is in state *S1*) when it learns of the crash. However, a closer inspection reveals difficulties with this naive approach. Consider, for example, the situation when the receiving host first sends an acknowledgement, and then, when the acknowledgement has been sent, performs the write. Writing a TPDU onto the output stream and sending an acknowledgement are considered as two distinct indivisible events that cannot be done simultaneously. If a crash occurs after the acknowledgement has been sent, but before the write has been done, the other host will receive the acknowledgement and thus be in state *S0* when the crash recovery announcement arrives. The sender will therefore not retransmit, thinking the TPDU has arrived correctly, leading to a missing TPDU.

At this point you may be thinking: "That problem can be solved easily. All you have to do is reprogram the transport entity to first do the write, and then send the acknowledgement." Try again. Imagine that the write has been done but the crash occurs before the acknowledgement can be sent. The sender will be in state *S1* and thus retransmit, leading to an undetected duplicate TPDU in the output stream.

No matter how the sender and receiver are programmed, there are always situations where the protocol fails to recover properly. The receiver can be programmed in one of two ways: acknowledge first or write first. The sender can be programmed in one of four ways: always retransmit the last TPDU, never retransmit the last TPDU, retransmit only in state *S0*, or retransmit only in state *S1*. This gives eight combinations, but as we shall see, for each combination there is some set of events that makes the protocol fail.

Three events are possible at the receiver: sending an acknowledgement (*A*), writing to the output process (*W*), and crashing (*C*). The three events can occur in six different orderings: *AC(W)*, *AWC*, *C(AW)*, *C(WA)*, *WAC*, and *WC(A)*, where the parentheses are used to indicate that neither *A* nor *W* may follow *C* (i.e., once it has crashed, it has crashed). Figure 6-20 shows all eight combinations of sender and receiver strategy and the valid event sequences for each one. Notice that for each strategy there is some sequence of events that causes the protocol to behave incorrectly. For example, if the sender always retransmits, the *AWC* event will generate an undetected duplicate, even though the other two events work properly.

Strategy used by receiving host

Strategy used by sending host	First ACK, then write			First write, then ACK		
	AC(W)	AWC	C(AW)	C(WA)	W AC	WC(A)
Always retransmit	OK	DUP	OK	OK	DUP	DUP
Never retransmit	LOST	OK	LOST	LOST	OK	OK
Retransmit in S0	OK	DUP	LOST	LOST	DUP	OK
Retransmit in S1	LOST	OK	OK	OK	OK	DUP

OK = Protocol functions correctly
DUP = Protocol generates a duplicate message
LOST = Protocol loses a message

Fig. 6-20. Different combinations of sender and receiver strategy.

Making the protocol more elaborate does not help. Even if the sender and receiver exchange several TPDUs before the receiver attempts to write, so that the sender knows exactly what is about to happen, the sender has no way of knowing whether a crash occurred just before or just after the write. The conclusion is inescapable: under our ground rules of no simultaneous events, host crash/recovery cannot be made transparent to higher layers.

Put in more general terms, this result can be restated as recovery from a layer *N* crash can only be done by layer *N* + 1, and then only if the higher layer retains enough status information. As mentioned above, the transport layer can recover from failures in the network layer, provided that each end of a connection keeps track of where it is.

This problem gets us into the issue of what a so-called end-to-end acknowledgement really means. In principle, the transport protocol is end-to-end and not chained like the lower layers. Now consider the case of a user entering requests for transactions against a remote data base. Suppose that the remote transport entity is programmed to first pass TPDUs to the next layer up, and then acknowledge. Even in this case, the receipt of an acknowledgement back at the user's machine does not necessarily mean that the remote host stayed up long enough to actually update the data base. A truly end-to-end acknowledgement, whose receipt means that the work has actually been done, and lack thereof means that it has not, is probably impossible to achieve. This point is discussed in more detail by Saltzer et al. (1984).

6.3. A SIMPLE TRANSPORT PROTOCOL ON TOP OF X.25

To make the ideas discussed so far more concrete, in this section we will study an example transport layer in detail. The example has been carefully chosen to be reasonably realistic, yet still simple enough to be easy to understand. The abstract service primitives are the OSI connection-oriented primitives, with the exception of the expedited data feature, which just adds complexity without providing any new insight into how the transport layer works.

6.3.1. The Example Service Primitives

Our first problem is how to express the OSI transport primitives in Pascal. *CONNECT.request* is easy: we will just have a library procedure *connect*, that can be called with the appropriate parameters necessary to establish a connection. However, *CONNECT.indication* is much harder. How do we signal the called transport user that there is an incoming call? In essence, an incoming call is an interrupt, a difficult concept to deal with in a high-level language and poor programming practice as well. The *CONNECT.indication* primitive is an excellent way of modeling how telephones work (telephones really do generate interrupts, by ringing), but is a not a good way of modeling how computers work.

To provide a reasonable interface to our transport layer, we will have to do what all real networks do, and invent a different, and much more computer-oriented, model for connection establishment. In our model, there are two procedures available, *listen* and *connect*. When a process (i.e., a transport user) wants to be able to accept incoming calls, it calls *listen*, specifying a particular TSAP to listen to. The process then blocks (i.e., goes to sleep) until some remote process attempts to establish a connection to its TSAP.

The other procedure, *connect*, can be used when a process wants to initiate the establishment of a connection. The caller specifies the local and remote TSAPs, and is blocked while the transport layer tries to set up the connection. If the connection succeeds, both parties are unblocked, and can start exchanging data.

Note that this model is highly asymmetric. One side is passive, executing a *listen* and waiting until something happens. The other side is active and initiates the connection. An interesting question arises of what to do if the active side begins first. One strategy is to have the connection attempt fail if there is no listener at the remote TSAP. Another strategy is to have the initiator block (possibly forever) until a listener appears.

A compromise, used in our example, is to hold the connection request at the receiving end for a certain time interval. If a process on that host calls *listen* before the timer goes off, the connection is established; otherwise, it is rejected and the caller is unblocked.

To release a connection, we will use a procedure *disconnect*. When both sides have disconnected, the connection is released.

Data transmission has precisely the same problem as connection establishment: although *T-DATA.request* can be implemented directly with a call to a library procedure, *T-DATA.indication* cannot be. We will use the same solution for data transmission as for connection establishment, an active call *send* that transmits data, and a passive call *receive* that blocks until a message has arrived.

Our concrete service definition thus consists of five primitives: *CONNECT*, *LISTEN*, *DISCONNECT*, *SEND*, and *RECEIVE*. Each primitive corresponds exactly with a library procedure that executes the primitive (unlike the OSI model, in which there is barely any correspondence at all between the primitives and the library procedures). The parameters for the service primitives and library procedures are as follows:

```
connum = CONNECT(local, remote)
connum = LISTEN(local)
status = DISCONNECT(connum)
status = SEND(connum, buffer, bytes)
status = RECEIVE(connum, buffer, bytes)
```

The *CONNECT* primitive takes two parameters, a local TSAP (i.e., transport address), *local*, and a remote TSAP, *remote*, and tries to establish a transport connection between the two. If it succeeds, it returns in *connum* a nonnegative number used to identify the connection on subsequent calls. If it fails, the reason for failure is put in *connum* as a negative number. In our simple model, each TSAP may participate in only one transport connection, so a possible reason for failure is that one of the transport addresses is currently in use. Some other reasons are: remote host down, illegal local address, and illegal remote address.

The *LISTEN* primitive announces the caller's willingness to accept connection requests directed at the indicated TSAP. The user of the primitive is blocked until an attempt is made to connect to it. There is no timeout.

The *DISCONNECT* primitive terminates a transport connection. The parameter *connum* tells which one. Possible errors are: *connum* belongs to another process, or *connum* is not a valid connection identifier. The error code, or 0 for success, is returned in *status*.

The *SEND* primitive transmits the contents of the buffer as a message on the indicated transport connection, possibly in several units if it is too big. Possible errors, returned in *status*, are: no connection, illegal buffer address, or negative count.

The *RECEIVE* primitive indicates the caller's desire to accept data. The size of the incoming message is placed in *bytes*. If the remote process has released the connection or the buffer address is illegal (e.g., outside the user's program), *status* is set accordingly to an error code.

6.3.2. The Example Transport Entity

Before looking at the code of the example transport entity, please be sure you realize that this example is analogous to the early examples presented in Chapter 4: it is more for pedagogical purposes than a serious proposal. Many of the technical details (such as extensive error checking) that would be needed in a production system have been omitted for the sake of simplicity. Nevertheless, most of the basic ideas found in the transport entity for the class 0 OSI protocol are present in our example.

The transport layer makes use of the network service primitives to send and receive TPDUs. Just as the OSI transport service primitives cannot be mapped directly onto library procedures, neither can the network service procedures. In this example we get around this problem by using X.25 as the network layer interface. Each TPDU will be carried in one packet and each packet will correspond to one TPDU. We will call these units "packets" below. In this example we will assume that X.25 is completely reliable (type A), neither losing packets nor resetting the circuit. Figure 6-21 gives an example program for implementing our transport service. Such a program (effectively the code of the transport entity) may be part of the host's operating system or it may be a package of library routines running within the user's address space. It may also be contained on a co-processor chip or network board plugged into the host's backplane. For simplicity, the example of Fig. 6-21 has been programmed as though it were a library package, but the changes needed to make it part of the operating system are minimal (primarily how user buffers are accessed).

It is worth noting, however, that in this example, the "transport entity" is not really a separate entity at all, but part of the user process. In particular, when the user executes a primitive that blocks, such as *LISTEN*, the entire transport entity blocks as well. While this design is fine for a host with only a single user process, on a host with multiple users, it would be more natural to have the transport entity be a separate process, distinct from all the user processes.

The interface to the network layer (X.25) is via the procedures *ToNet* and *FromNet* (not shown). Each has six parameters: the connection identifier, which maps one-to-one onto network virtual circuits; the X.25 *Q* and *M* bits, which indicate control message and more data from this message follows in the next packet, respectively; the packet type, chosen from the set *CALL REQUEST, CALL*

```
const MaxConn = ... ;  MaxMsg = ... ;  MaxPkt = ... ;
      TimeOut = ... ; cred = ... ;
      q0 = 0; q1 = 1; m0 = 0; m1 = 1; ok = 0;
      ErrFull = −1;  ErrReject = −2;  ErrClosed = −3;  LowErr = −3;

type bit = 0..1;
      TransportAddress = integer;
      ConnId = 0 .. MaxConn;              {connection identifier}
      PktType = (CallReq, CallAcc, ClearReq, ClearConf, DataPkt, credit);
      cstate = (idle, waiting, queued, established, sending, receiving, disconnecting);
      message = array [0 .. MaxMsg] of 0 .. 255;
      msgptr = ↑message;      {pointer to a message}
      ErrorCode = LowErr .. 0;
      ConnIdOrErr = LowErr .. MaxConn;
      PktLength = 0 .. MaxPkt;
      packet = array[PktLength] of 0 .. 255;

var ListenAddress: TransportAddress; {local address being listened to}
      ListenConn: ConnId;                    {connection identifier for listen}
      data: packet;                          {scratch area for packet data}
      conn: array[ConnId] of record
        LocalAddress, RemoteAddress: TransportAddress;
        state: cstate;               {state of this connection}
        UserBufferAddress: msgptr;   {pointer to receive buffer}
        ByteCount: 0 .. MaxMsg;      {send/receive count}
        ClrReqReceived: boolean;     {set when CLEAR REQUEST packet received}
        timer: integer;              {used to time out CALL REQUEST packets}
        credits: integer            {number of messages that may be sent}
      end;

function listen(t: TransportAddress): ConnIdOrErr;
{User wants to listen for a connection.  See if CALLREQ has already arrived.}
var i: integer; found: boolean;
begin
  i := 1;
  found := false;

  while (i <= MaxConn) and not found do
    if (conn[i].state = queued) and (conn[i].LocalAddress = t)
      then found := true
      else i := i + 1;

  if not found then
    begin    {no CALLREQ is waiting.  Go to sleep until arrival or timeout.}
      ListenAddress := t; sleep; i := ListenConn
    end;
  conn[i].state := established;    {connection is established}
  conn[i].timer := 0;             {timer is not used}
  listen := i;                    {return connection identifier}
  ListenConn := 0;                {0 is assumed to be an invalid address}
  ToNet(i, q0, m0, CallAcc, data, 0)    {tell net to accept connection}
end; {listen}
```

Fig. 6-21. A sample transport entity.

```
function connect (l , r : TransportAddress ): ConnIdOrErr ;
{User wants to connect to a remote process.  Send CALLREQ packet.}
var i : integer ;
begin i := MaxConn ;              {search table backwards}
   data [0] := r ;  data [l ] := l ;        {CALL REQUEST packet needs these}
   while (conn [i ].state <> idle ) and (i > 1) do i := i − 1;
   if conn [i ].state = idle then
      with conn [i ] do
         begin                    {make a table entry that CALLREQ has been sent}
            LocalAddress := l ;  RemoteAddress := r ;   state := waiting ;
            ClrReqReceived := false ;   credits := 0;  timer := 0;
            ToNet (i , q0, m0, CallReq , data , 2);
            sleep ;               {wait for CALLACC or CLEARREQ}
            if state = established then connect := i ;
            if ClrReqReceived then
               begin              {other side refused call}
                  connect := ErrReject ;
                  state := idle ;     {back to idle state}
                  ToNet (i , q0, m0, ClearConf , data , 0)
               end
         end
      else connect := ErrFull      {reject CONNECT: no table space}
end; {connect}

function send (cid : ConnId ; bufptr : msgptr ; bytes : integer ): ErrorCode ;
{User wants to send a message.}
var i , count : integer ;   m : bit ;
begin
   with conn [cid ] do
      begin                          {enter sending state}
         state := sending ;
         ByteCount := 0;
         if (not ClrReqReceived ) and (credits = 0) then sleep ;
         if not ClrReqReceived then
            begin {credit available; split message into packets}
               repeat
                  if bytes − ByteCount > MaxPkt
                     then begin count := MaxPkt ;  m := 1 end
                     else begin count := bytes − ByteCount ;  m := 0 end;
                  for i := 0 to count − 1 do data [i ] := bufptr↑[ByteCount + i ];
                  ToNet (cid , q0, m , DataPkt , data , count );
                  ByteCount := ByteCount + count ;
               until ByteCount = bytes ;   {loop until whole message sent}
               credits := credits − 1;    {one credit used up}
               send := ok
            end
         else send := ErrClosed ;          {SEND failed: peer wants to disconnect}
         state := established
      end
end; {send}
```

```
function receive (cid : ConnId ; bufptr : msgptr ; var bytes : integer ): ErrorCode ;
{User is prepared to receive a message.}
begin
  with conn [cid ] do
    begin
      if not ClrReqReceived then
        begin                    {connection still established; try to receive}
          state := receiving ;
          UserBufferAddress := bufptr ;   ByteCount := 0;
          data [0] := cred ;  data [1] := 1;
          ToNet (cid , q1, m0, credit , data , 2);        {send credit}
          sleep ;            {block awaiting data}
          bytes := ByteCount
        end;
      if ClrReqReceived then receive := ErrClosed else receive := ok ;
      state := established
    end
end; {receive}

function disconnect (cid : ConnId ): ErrorCode ;
{User wants to release a connection.}
begin
  with conn [cid ] do
    if ClrReqReceived
      then begin state := idle ; ToNet (cid , q0, m0, ClearConf, data , 0) end
      else begin state := disconnecting ;  ToNet (cid , q0, m0, ClearReq, data , 0) end;
  disconnect := ok
end; {disconnect}

procedure PacketArrival ;
{A packet has arrived, get and process it.}
var cid : ConnId ;                {connection on which packet arrived}
    q , m : bit ;
    ptype : PktType ;             {CallReq, CallAcc, ClearReq, ClearConf, DataPkt, credit}
    data : packet ;               {data portion of the incoming packet}
    count : PktLength ;           {number of data bytes in packet}
    i : integer ;                 {scratch variable}

begin
  FromNet (cid , q , m , ptype , data , count );   {go get it}
  with conn [cid ] do
  case ptype of
  CallReq :                       {remote user wants to establish connection}
    begin
      LocalAddress := data [0];  RemoteAddress := data [1];
      if LocalAddress = ListenAddress
        then begin ListenConn := cid ; state := established ; wakeup end
        else begin state := queued ; timer := TimeOut end;
      ClrReqReceived := false ;   credits := 0
    end;
```

CallAcc :   {remote user has accepted our CALL REQUEST}
  begin
    state := *established* ;
    wakeup
  end;

ClearReq :   {remote user wants to disconnect or reject call}
  begin
    ClrReqReceived := *true* ;
    if *state* = *disconnecting* **then** *state* := *idle* ;   {clear collision}
    if *state* **in** [*waiting* , *receiving* , *sending*] **then** *wakeup*
  end;

ClearConf :   {remote user agrees to disconnect}
  state := *idle* ;

credit :   {remote user is waiting for data}
  begin
    credits := *credits* + *data* [1];
    if *state* = *sending* **then** *wakeup*
  end;

Datapkt :   {remote user has sent data}
  begin
    for *i* := 0 **to** *count* − 1 **do** *UserBufferAddress*↑[*ByteCount* + *i*] := *data* [*i*];
    ByteCount := *ByteCount* + *count* ;
    if *m* = 0 **then** *wakeup*
  end
  end;
end; {PacketArrival}

procedure *clock* ;
{The clock has ticked, check for timeouts of queued connect requests.}
var *i* : *ConnId* ;
begin
  for *i* := 1 **to** *MaxConn* **do**
    with *conn* [*i*] **do**
      if *timer* > 0 **then**
        begin {timer was running}
          timer := *timer* − 1;
          if *timer* = 0 **then**
            begin   {timer has expired}
              state := *idle* ;
              ToNet (*i* , *q0*, *m0*, *ClearReq* , *data* , 0)
            end
        end
end; {*clock*}

ACCEPTED, CLEAR REQUEST, CLEAR CONFIRMATION, DATA, and *CREDIT;* a pointer to the data itself; and the number of bytes of data.

On calls to *ToNet,* the transport entity (i.e., some procedure in Fig. 6-21) fills in all the parameters for the network layer to read; on calls to *FromNet,* the network layer dismembers an incoming packet for the transport entity. By passing information as procedure parameters rather than passing the actual outgoing or incoming packet itself, the transport layer is shielded from the details of the network layer protocol. If the transport entity should attempt to send a packet when the underlying virtual circuit's sliding window is full, it is suspended within *ToNet* until there is room in the window. This mechanism is transparent to the transport entity and is controlled by the network layer using commands like *EnableTransportLayer* and *DisableTransportLayer* analogous to those described in the protocols of Chapter 4. The management of the X.25 packet layer window is also done by the network layer.

In addition to this transparent suspension mechanism, there are also explicit *sleep* and *wakeup* procedures (not shown) called by the transport entity. The procedure *sleep* is called when the transport entity is logically blocked waiting for an external event to happen, generally the arrival of a packet. After *sleep* has been called, the transport entity (and user process, of course) stop executing.

Each connection maintained by the transport entity of Fig. 6-21 is always in one of seven states, as follows:

1. Idle—Connection not established yet.

2. Waiting—*CONNECT* has been executed and *CALL REQUEST* sent.

3. Queued—A *CALL REQUEST* has arrived; *LISTEN* has not been done.

4. Established—The connection has been established.

5. Sending—The user is waiting for permission to transmit a packet.

6. Receiving—A *RECEIVE* has been done.

7. Disconnecting—A *DISCONNECT* has been done locally.

Transitions between states can occur when primitives are executed, when packets arrive, or when the timer expires.

The collection of procedures shown in Fig. 6-21 are of two types. Most are directly callable by user programs. *PacketArrival* and *clock* are different, however. They are spontaneously triggered by external events: the arrival of a packet and the clock ticking, respectively. In effect, they are interrupt routines. We will assume that they are never invoked while a transport entity procedure is running. Only when the user process is sleeping or executing outside the transport entity may they be called. This property is crucial to the correct functioning of the transport entity.

The existence of the *Q* (Qualifier) bit in the X.25 header allows us to avoid the overhead of a transport protocol header. Ordinary data messages are sent as X.25 data packets with $Q = 0$. Transport protocol control messages, of which there is only one (*CREDIT*) in our example, are sent as X.25 data packets with $Q = 1$. These control messages are detected and processed by the receiving transport entity, of course.

The main data structure used by the transport entity is the array *conn*, which has one record for each potential connection. The record maintains the state of the connection, including the transport addresses at either end, the number of messages sent and received on the connection, the current state, the user buffer pointer, the number of bytes of the current messages sent or received so far, a bit indicating that the remote user has issued a *DISCONNECT*, a timer, and a permission counter used to enable sending of messages. Not all of these fields are used in our simple example, but a complete transport entity would need all of them, and perhaps more. Each *conn* entry is assumed initialized to the *idle* state.

When the user calls *CONNECT*, the network layer is instructed to send a *CALL REQUEST* packet to the remote machine, and the user is put to sleep. When the *CALL REQUEST* packet arrives at the other side, the transport entity is interrupted to run *PacketArrival* to check if the local user is listening on the specified address. If so, a *CALL ACCEPTED* packet is sent back and the remote user is awakened; if not, the *CALL REQUEST* is queued for *TimeOut* clock ticks. If a *LISTEN* is done within this period, the connection is established; otherwise, it times out and is rejected with a *CLEAR REQUEST* packet. This mechanism is needed to prevent the initiator from blocking forever in the event that the remote process does not want to connect to it.

Although we have eliminated the transport protocol header, we still need a way to keep track of which packet belongs to which transport connection, since multiple connections may exist simultaneously. The simplest approach is to use the X.25 virtual circuit number as the transport connection number as well. Furthermore, the virtual circuit number can also be used as the index into the *conn* array. When a packet comes in on X.25 virtual circuit k, it belongs to transport connection k, whose state is in the record *conn*[k]. For connections initiated at a host, the connection number is chosen by the originating transport entity. For incoming calls, the X.25 network makes the choice, choosing any unused virtual circuit number.

To avoid having to provide and manage buffers within the transport entity, a flow control mechanism different from the traditional sliding window is used here. Instead, when a user calls *RECEIVE*, a special **credit message** is sent to the transport entity on the sending machine and is recorded in the *conn* array. When *SEND* is called, the transport entity checks to see if a credit has arrived on the specified connection. If so, the message is sent (in multiple packets if need be) and the credit decremented; if not, the transport entity puts itself to sleep until a credit arrives. This mechanism guarantees that no message is ever sent unless the other side has already done a *RECEIVE*. As a result, whenever a message arrives there is guaranteed to be a buffer available into which it can be put. The scheme can easily be generalized to allow receivers to provide multiple buffers and request multiple messages.

You should keep the simplicity of Fig. 6-21 in mind. A realistic transport entity would normally check all user supplied parameters for validity, handle recovery from network resets, deal with call collisions, and support a more general transport service including such facilities as interrupts, datagrams, and nonblocking versions of the *SEND* and *RECEIVE* primitives.

6.3.3. The Example as a Finite State Machine

Writing a transport entity is difficult and exacting work, especially for the higher transport protocol classes. To reduce the chance of making an error, it is often useful to represent the state of the protocol as a finite state machine.

We have already seen that our example protocol has seven states per connection. It is also possible to isolate 12 events that can happen to move a connection from one state to another. Five of these events are the five service primitives. Another six are the arrivals of the six legal packet types. The last one is the expiration of the timer. Figure 6-22 shows the main protocol actions in matrix form. The columns are the states and the rows are the 12 events.

Each entry in the matrix (i.e., the finite state machine) of Fig. 6-22 has up to three fields: a predicate, an action, and a new state. The predicate indicates under what conditions the action is taken. For example, in the upper left-hand entry, if a *LISTEN* is executed and there is no more table space (predicate *P1*), the *LISTEN* fails and the state does not change. On the other hand, if a *CALL REQUEST* packet has already arrived for the transport address being listened to (predicate *P2*), the connection is established immediately. Another possibility is that *P2* is false, that is, no *CALL REQUEST* has come in, in which case the connection remains in the *Idle* state, awaiting a *CALL REQUEST* packet.

It is worth pointing out that the choice of states to use in the matrix is not entirely fixed by the protocol itself. In this example, there is no state *listening*, which might have been a reasonable thing to have following a *LISTEN*. There is no *listening* state because a state is associated with a connection record entry, and no connection record is created by *LISTEN*. Why not? Because we have decided to use the X.25 virtual circuit numbers as the connection identifiers, and for a *LISTEN*, the virtual circuit number is ultimately chosen by the X.25 network when the *CALL REQUEST* packet arrives.

The actions *A1* through *A12* are the major actions, such as sending packets and starting timers. Not all the minor actions, such as initializing the fields of a connection record are listed. If an action involves waking up a sleeping process, the actions following the wakeup also count. For example, if a *CALL REQUEST* packet comes in and a process was asleep waiting for it, the transmission of the *CALL ACCEPT* packet following the wakeup counts as part of the action for *CALL*

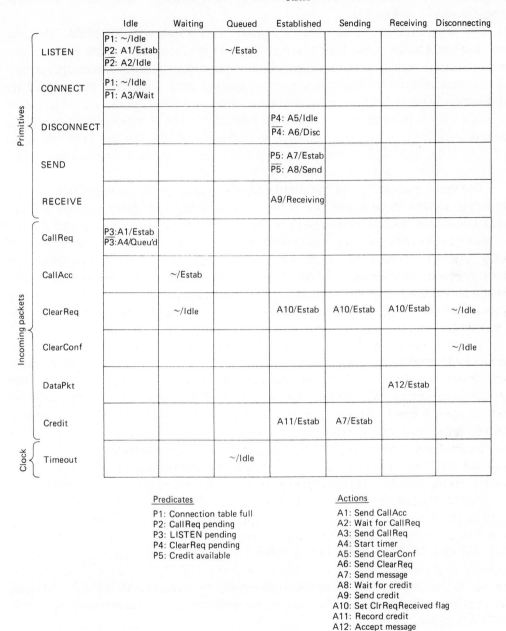

Status

		Idle	Waiting	Queued	Established	Sending	Receiving	Disconnecting
Primitives	LISTEN	P1: ~/Idle P2: A1/Estab $\overline{P2}$: A2/Idle		~/Estab				
	CONNECT	P1: ~/Idle $\overline{P1}$: A3/Wait						
	DISCONNECT				P4: A5/Idle $\overline{P4}$: A6/Disc			
	SEND				P5: A7/Estab $\overline{P5}$: A8/Send			
	RECEIVE				A9/Receiving			
Incoming packets	CallReq	$\overline{P3}$:A1/Estab P3:A4/Queu'd						
	CallAcc		~/Estab					
	ClearReq		~/Idle		A10/Estab	A10/Estab	A10/Estab	~/Idle
	ClearConf							~/Idle
	DataPkt						A12/Estab	
	Credit				A11/Estab	A7/Estab		
Clock	Timeout			~/Idle				

Predicates

P1: Connection table full
P2: CallReq pending
P3: LISTEN pending
P4: ClearReq pending
P5: Credit available

Actions

A1: Send CallAcc
A2: Wait for CallReq
A3: Send CallReq
A4: Start timer
A5: Send ClearConf
A6: Send ClearReq
A7: Send message
A8: Wait for credit
A9: Send credit
A10: Set ClrReqReceived flag
A11: Record credit
A12: Accept message

Fig. 6-22. The example protocol as a finite state machine. Each entry has an optional predicate, and optional action, and the new state. The tilde indicates that no major action is taken. An overbar above a predicate indicates the negation of the predicate. Blank entries correspond to impossible or invalid events.

REQUEST. After each action is performed, the connection may move to a new state, as shown in Fig. 6-22.

The advantage of representing the protocol as a matrix is threefold. First, in this form it is much easier for the programmer to systematically check each combination of state and event to see if an action is required. In production implementations, some of the combinations would be used for error handling. In Fig. 6-22 no distinction is made between impossible situations and illegal ones. For example, if a connection is in *waiting* state, the *DISCONNECT* event is impossible because the user is blocked and cannot execute any primitives at all. On the other hand, in *sending* state, data packets are not expected because no credit has been issued. The arrival of a data packet is a protocol error that should be checked for.

The second advantage of the matrix representation of the protocol is in implementing it. One could envision a two-dimensional array in which element $a[i][j]$ was a pointer or index to the procedure that handled the occurrence of event i when in state j. One possible implementation is to write the transport entity as a short loop, waiting for an event at the top of the loop. When an event happens, the relevant connection is located and its state is extracted. With the event and state now known, the transport entity just indexes into the array a and calls the proper procedure. This approach gives a much more regular and systematic design than our transport entity.

The third advantage of the finite state machine approach is for protocol description. In some standards documents, including the OSI connection-oriented transport protocol standard (ISO 8073), the protocols are given as finite state machines of the type of Fig. 6-22. Going from this kind of description to a working transport entity is much easier if the transport entity is also driven by a finite state machine based on the one in the standard.

The primary disadvantage of the finite state machine approach is that it may be more difficult to understand than the straight programming example we used initially. However, this problem may be partially solved by drawing the finite state machine as a graph, as is done in Fig. 6-23.

6.4. EXAMPLES OF THE TRANSPORT LAYER

In this section we will once again examine our running examples to see what their transport layers are like. As usual, we will emphasize the protocol aspects in these examples.

6.4.1. The Transport Layer in Public Networks

Nearly all public networks use the connection-oriented OSI transport service (ISO 8072) and OSI transport protocols (ISO 8073). We have already looked at the OSI transport service; let us now look at the protocols.

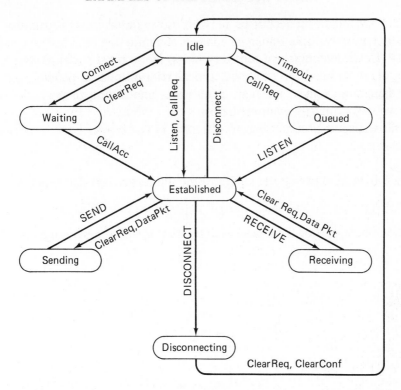

Fig. 6-23. The example protocol in graphical form. Transitions that leave the connection state unchanged have been omitted for simplicity.

As mentioned earlier, the OSI transport protocol has five variations, Classes 0 through 4. Each variation is intended for a specific type of network reliability, ranging to perfect to completely unreliable. We will briefly review the five protocol classes below. Class 0 (Simple class) is intended for use with type A (perfect) networks. It is primarily concerned with connection establishment and release, data transfer, and breaking large messages up into smaller TPDUs, if necessary. It uses the underlying network connection to do all the rest of the work (flow control, error control, and so on).

Class 1 (Basic error recovery class) differs from Class 0 in its ability to recover from *N-RESET*s generated by the network layer. After a network layer connection is broken, the transport entities establish a new network layer connection and continue from where they left off. In order to accomplish this recovery, the transport entities number the TPDUs, a feature not present in Class 0. Class 0 just gives up if the network connection breaks.

Class 2 (Multiplexing class) is the same as Class 0, except that it also supports multiplexing of multiple transport connections onto one network connection. Also, it permits explicit flow control using a credit scheme analogous to the one used in the example of Sec. 6-3. Finally, Class 2 also permits the use of expedited data.

Class 3 (Error recovery and multiplexing class) includes the features of Classes

1 and 2, namely, it can recover from network layer failures and it can also support the multiplexing of multiple transport connections onto one network connection.

Class 4 (Error detection and recovery class) is the most sophisticated and most interesting class. It has been designed to deal with unreliable network service, for example, datagram subnets that can lose, store, and duplicate packets. It is this class that we will primarily examine below.

The OSI transport protocol has 10 different TPDU types. Each TPDU has up to four parts:

1. A 1-byte field giving the length of the fixed plus variable headers.

2. A fixed part of the header (length depends on the TPDU type).

3. A variable part of the header (length depends on the parameters).

4. A user data.

The first byte of each TPDU is the *LI* (*Length Indicator*) field. It gives the total header length (fixed plus variable parts) in bytes, excluding the *LI* field itself, up to a maximum of 254 bytes. Code 255 is reserved for future use.

Next comes the fixed part of the header. These fields are important enough that they are included in each TPDU of the relevant type. The fields are TPDU dependent. In other words, the fixed part of all *CONNECTION REQUEST* TPDUs have the same fields, but these are different from the fields in a *DATA* TPDU.

Following the fixed part of the header is the variable part. This part of the header is used for options that are not always needed. The recipient of a TPDU can tell how many bytes of variable-part header are present by looking at the *LI* field and subtracting off the length of the fixed-part header for the TPDU type. The variable part is divided into fields, each starting with a 1-byte type field, then a 1-byte length field, followed by the data itself. For example, when setting up a transport connection, the initiating transport entity can use the variable part to propose a nonstandard maximum TPDU size.

Following the header come the user data. The *DATA* TPDU obviously contains user data, but some of the other TPDUs also contain a limited amount too. The formats of the 10 TPDU types are shown in Fig. 6-24. Some of these have minor variants that are not shown.

The *CONNECTION REQUEST, CONNECTION CONFIRM, DISCONNECT REQUEST*, and *DISCONNECT CONFIRM* TPDUs are completely analogous to the *CALL REQUEST, CALL ACCEPTED, CLEAR REQUEST*, and *CLEAR CONFIRM* packets used in X.25. To establish a connection, the initiating transport entity sends a *CONNECTION REQUEST* TPDU and the peer replies with *CONNECTION CONFIRM*. Similarly, to release a connection, either one of the transport entities sends a *DISCONNECT REQUEST* and the peer replies with *DISCONNECT CONFIRM*. The *DATA* and *EXPEDITED DATA* TPDUs are used for regular and expedited data,

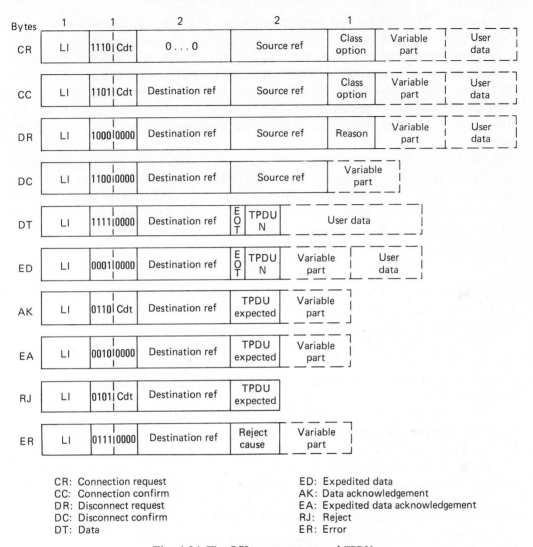

Bytes	1	1	2	2	1		
CR	LI	1110|Cdt	0 . . . 0	Source ref	Class option	Variable part	User data
CC	LI	1101|Cdt	Destination ref	Source ref	Class option	Variable part	User data
DR	LI	1000|0000	Destination ref	Source ref	Reason	Variable part	User data
DC	LI	1100|0000	Destination ref	Source ref	Variable part		
DT	LI	1111|0000	Destination ref	E O T / TPDU N	User data		
ED	LI	0001|0000	Destination ref	E O T / TPDU N	Variable part	User data	
AK	LI	0110|Cdt	Destination ref	TPDU expected	Variable part		
EA	LI	0010|0000	Destination ref	TPDU expected	Variable part		
RJ	LI	0101|Cdt	Destination ref	TPDU expected			
ER	LI	0111|0000	Destination ref	Reject cause	Variable part		

CR: Connection request   ED: Expedited data
CC: Connection confirm   AK: Data acknowledgement
DR: Disconnect request   EA: Expedited data acknowledgement
DC: Disconnect confirm   RJ: Reject
DT: Data   ER: Error

Fig. 6-24. The OSI transport protocol TPDUs.

respectively. These two types are acknowledged by the *DATA ACKNOWLEDGE-MENT* and *EXPEDITED DATA ACKNOWLEDGEMENT* TPDUs, respectively. Finally, the *REJECT* and *ERROR* TPDUs are used for error handling.

Let us now look at the various TPDU types one at a time in more detail. *CONNECTION REQUEST* is used to establish a connection. Like all TPDUs, it contains a 1-byte *LI* field giving the total header length (excluding the *LI* field itself).

Next comes a byte containing a 4-bit TPDU type and the *cdt* (credit) field. The Class 4 protocol uses a credit scheme for flow control, rather than a sliding window scheme, and this field tells the remote transport entity how many TPDU's it may initially send.

The *Destination reference* and *Source reference* fields identify transport connections. They are needed because in Classes 2, 3, and 4 it is possible to multi-plex several transport connections over one network connection. When a packet comes in from the network layer, the transport entities use these fields to determine which transport connection the TPDU in the packet belongs to. The *CONNECTION REQUEST* TPDU provides an identifier in the *Source reference* field that will be used by the initiator. The *CONNECTION CONFIRM* TPDU adds to that identifier the *Destination reference*, which is used by the destination for connection identification.

The *Class option* field is used by the transport entities for negotiating the proto-col class to be used. The initiator makes a proposal, which the responder can either accept or reject. The responder can also make a counterproposal, suggesting a lower, but not a higher, protocol class. The field also contains two bits that are used to enable 4-byte TPDU sequence numbers instead of the standard 1-byte numbers, and enable or disable explicit flow control in Class 2.

The *Variable part* of the *CONNECTION REQUEST* TPDU may contain any of the following options:

1. TSAP to be connected to at the remote host.

2. TSAP being connected to at the local host.

3. Proposed maximum TPDU size (128 to 8192 bytes, in powers of 2).

4. Version number.

5. Protection parameter (e.g., an encryption key).

6. Checksum.

7. Some option bits (e.g., use of expedited data, use of checksum).

8. Alternative protocol classes that are acceptable to the initiator.

9. Maximum delay before acknowledging a TPDU, in milliseconds.

10. Throughput expected (average desired and minimum acceptable).

11. Residual error rate (average desired and maximum acceptable).

12. Priority (0 to 65535, with 0 being the highest priority).

13. Transit delay (average and maximum acceptable, in milliseconds).

14. How long to keep trying to recover after an *N-RESET*.

Some of the parameters, such as the alternative protocol classes, are intended for the remote peer. However, others, such as the quality of service parameters (throughput, residual error rate, etc.), are aimed at the network layer. If the network layer is unable to provide at least the minimum service required, then the network layer itself rejects the connection with a *DISCONNECT REQUEST,* rather than putting it through.

The *User data* field may contain up to 32 bytes of data in Classes 1 through 4. It is not permitted in Class 0. This field may be used for any purpose the users wish (e.g., a password for remote login).

When the *CONNECTION REQUEST* TPDU arrives at the remote host, the transport entity there causes a *CONNECT.indication* primitive to the transport user. If the user decides to accept the incoming call, the remote transport layer replies to the initiator with a *CONNECTION CONFIRM* TPDU. The format and options in the *CONNECTION CONFIRM* TPDU are the same as those in the *CONNECTION REQUEST* TPDU.

In type A and B networks, this establishment procedure is sufficient, but in type C networks it is not, due to the possibility of delayed duplicate packets. To eliminate the possibility of old packets interfering with a connection establishment, a three-way handshake is used, with the *CONNECTION CONFIRM* TPDU itself being acknowledged with an *ACK* TPDU. Furthermore, after a connection is released, the *Source reference* and *Destination reference* are considered **frozen references** and not reused for an interval long enough to guarantee that all old duplicates have died out. Unlike Tomlinson's clock scheme, the OSI transport protocol does not describe how to deal with crashes. The safest way is just to wait for the maximum packet lifetime before rebooting.

To release a connection, a transport entity sends a *DISCONNECT REQUEST* TPDU to its peer. The format of the fixed part of the header is the same as for the *CONNECTION REQUEST* TPDU, except that the *Class option* field is replaced with the *Reason* field telling why the connection is being released. Among other possibilities are: the transport user executed a *DISCONNECT.request* primitive, there was a bad parameter in a TPDU, the TSAP to be connected to does not exist, or the network is congested. The *Variable part* of the header and the *User data* field (up to 64 bytes) can provide additional explanations.

The required response to a *DISCONNECT REQUEST* TPDU is a *DISCONNECT CONFIRM* TPDU. The only field that may be present in the *Variable part* is the checksum, if checksums are being used on the connection.

The formats of the *DATA* TPDU and *EXPEDITED DATA* TPDU shown in Fig. 6-24 are the normal types for Class 4. An additional format with a 4-byte *TPDU Nr* is also permitted to make sure that TPDU sequence numbers will not wrap around for a very long time. The *EOT* flag is set to 1 to indicate End Of Transport message. This flag is needed so the remote transport entity knows when to stop reassembling TPDUs and pass the resulting message to the remote transport user. The only *Variable part* field is the checksum, when it is in use.

The *DATA ACKNOWLEDGEMENT* and *EXPEDITED DATA ACKNOWLEDGEMENT* TPDUs acknowledge the receipt of TPDUs up to, but not including, the one whose sequence number is given in the acknowledgement. Thus that one is the one expected next. The *Variable part* of both contain the checksum, if checksums are being used.

In addition, the *DATA ACKNOWLEDGEMENT* TPDU also contains information about the flow control window. In particular, the receiver can explicitly specify the lower edge and size of the window of sequence numbers that the sender is permitted to send. It is explicitly permitted for the receiver to reduce the window size (i.e., take back credits). For example, suppose the receiver has acknowledged TPDU 3 and given a window size of 8, thus permitting TPDUs 4 through 11. Shortly thereafter, the receiver notices that it is short on buffer space and decides to reduce the window to 3 by sending a new acknowledgement for 3 with a window of 2. This action permits only TPDUs 4 and 5 and forbids 6 through 11, even though these were previously permitted.

With a type C network, a problem arises if the two acknowledgements are delivered in the wrong order. The sender will wrongfully conclude that it may send TPDUs up to 11. To eliminate this problem, the protocol allows a *subsequence* field in the *Variable part*. Normally this field is not used, but when a second acknowledgement is sent for the same TPDU, a *subsequence* field is included with the value 1. A third acknowledgement carries a *subsequence* value of 2, and so on. This method allows the sender to deduce the order in which the acknowledgements were sent, and only accept the last one as valid.

The *REJECT* TPDU is only used in Classes 1 and 3, and is primarily used when resynchronizing after an *N-RESET*. Its function is to signal a problem and invite the peer to retransmit all TPDUs starting at the sequence number indicated. The credit value is also reset.

The final TPDU type is used to report protocol errors. The *Reject cause* field tells what was wrong. Possibilities include: invalid parameter code in the *Variable part*, invalid TPDU type, and invalid TPDU value.

As we mentioned earlier, the OSI transport layer defines a connectionless service and protocol, in addition to the connection-oriented service and protocol we have been describing at length. The purpose of the OSI connectionless transport service is to allow its users to send messages with the *T-UNITDATA* primitive without the overhead of first establishing and later releasing a connection.

The OSI connectionless transport service can work using either connection-oriented network service or connectionless network service. To a large extent, putting connectionless transport service on top of connection-oriented network service defeats the purpose of having connectionless transport service, but in some cases the only network service available is connection-oriented (e.g., a public X.25 network), so that case has been provided for.

When operating the connectionless transport service on top of a connectionless network service, each TPDU goes into a single packet. These TPDUs are not acknowledged and are not guaranteed to be reliably delivered. No promise is given about the order in which TPDUs are delivered.

The OSI connectionless service uses a connectionless protocol. Only one TPDU format is used, as shown in Fig. 6-25. This TPDU is similar to those used in the connection-oriented service. The *Variable part* contains the source and destination TSAP addresses, and optionally a checksum.

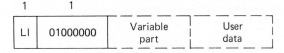

Fig. 6-25. The OSI connectionless TPDU format.

Work on the implementation of OSI and related transport protocols is discussed in (Chong, 1986; and Watson and Mamrak, 1987).

6.4.2. The Transport Layer in the ARPANET (TCP)

In the original ARPANET design, the subnet was assumed to offer virtual circuit service (i.e., be perfectly reliable). The first transport layer protocol, **NCP** (**Network Control Protocol**), was designed with a perfect subnet in mind. It just passed TPDUs (called messages) to the network layer and assumed that they would all be delivered in order to the destination. Experience showed that the ARPANET was indeed reliable enough for this protocol to be completely satisfactory for traffic within the ARPANET itself.

However, as time went on, and the ARPANET grew into the ARPA Internet, which included many LANs, a packet radio subnet, and several satellite channels, the end-to-end reliability of the subnet decreased. This development forced a major change in the transport layer and led to the gradual introduction of a new transport layer protocol, **TCP** (**Transmission Control Protocol**), which was specifically designed to tolerate an unreliable subnet (type C in OSI terms). Associated with TCP was a new network layer protocol, **IP**, which we studied in the previous chapter. Today TCP/IP is not only used in the ARPANET and ARPA Internet, but in many commercial systems as well.

A TCP transport entity accepts arbitrarily long messages from user processes, breaks them up into pieces not exceeding 64K bytes, and sends each piece as a separate datagram. The network layer gives no guarantee that datagrams will be delivered properly, so it is up to TCP to time out and retransmit them as need be. Datagrams that do arrive may well do so in the wrong order; it is also up to TCP to reassemble them into messages in the proper sequence.

Every byte of data transmitted by TCP has its own private sequence number. The sequence number space is 32 bits wide to make sure that old duplicates have long since vanished by the time the sequence numbers have wrapped around. TCP does, however, explicitly deal with the problem of delayed duplicates when attempting to establish a connection, using the three-way handshake for this purpose.

Figure 6-26 shows the header used by TCP. The first thing that strikes one is that the minimum TCP header is 20 bytes. Unlike OSI Class 4, with which it is roughly comparable, TCP has only one TPDU header format. Let us dissect this large header field by field. The *Source port* and *Destination port* fields identify the end points of the connection (the TSAP addresses in OSI terminology). Each host may decide for itself how to allocate its ports.

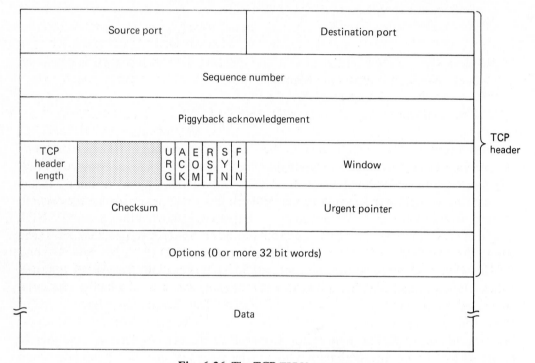

Fig. 6-26. The TCP TPDU structure.

The *Sequence number* and *Piggyback acknowledgement* fields perform their usual functions. They are 32 bits long because every byte of data is numbered in TCP.

The *TCP header length* tells how many 32-bit words are contained in the TCP header. This information is needed because the *Options* field is variable length, so the header is too.

Next come six 1-bit flags. *URG* is set to 1 if the *Urgent pointer* is in use. The *Urgent pointer* is used to indicate a byte offset from the current sequence number at which urgent data are to be found. This facility is in lieu of interrupt messages. The *SYN* bit is used to establish connections. The connection request has *SYN* = 1 and *ACK* = 0 to indicate that the piggyback acknowledgement field is not in use. The connection reply does bear an acknowledgement, so it has *SYN* = 1 and *ACK* = 1. In essence the *SYN* bit is used to denote *CONNECTION REQUEST* and *CONNECTION CONFIRM*, with the *ACK* bit used to distinguish between those two possibilities. The *FIN* bit is used to release a connection. It specifies that the sender has no more data. After closing a connection, a process may continue to receive data indefinitely. The *RST* bit is used to reset a connection that has become confused due to delayed duplicate *SYN*s or host crashes. The *EOM* bit indicates End Of Message.

Flow control in TCP is handled using a variable-size sliding window. A 16-bit field is needed, because *Window* tells how many bytes may be sent beyond the byte acknowledged, not how many TPDUs.

A *Checksum* is also provided for extreme reliability. The checksum algorithm is simply to add up all the data, regarded as 16-bit words, and then to take the 1's complement of the sum.

The *Options* field is used for miscellaneous things, for example to communicate buffer sizes during the setup procedure.

Unlike most of the non-OSI protocols, TCP has a well-defined service interface. Calls are provided to actively and passively initiate connections (effectively, the *CONNECT* and *LISTEN* primitives from our example transport protocol, except that the *LISTEN* has two variants, one to accept connection requests from any caller and one to accept connection requests only from some specified caller). Calls are also provided to send and receive data, gracefully and abruptly terminate connections, and ask for the status of a connection.

Like OSI, the ARPANET also provides a connectionless transport protocol, **UDP (User Datagram Protocol)**. Like its OSI counterpart, it allows users to send messages without connection establishment and without any guarantee of delivery or sequencing. In effect, UDP is simply a user interface to IP. Its format is shown in Fig. 6-27.

Fig. 6-27. The ARPANET UDP format.

Comparison of OSI Class 4 and TCP

The OSI Class 4 transport protocol (often called **TP4**), and TCP have numerous similarities but also some differences. In this section we will examine these similarities and differences (Groenbaek, 1986). Let us start with the points on which the two protocols are the same. Both protocols are designed for providing a reliable, connection-oriented, end-to-end transport service on top of an unreliable network that can lose, garble, store, and duplicate packets. Both must deal with the worst case problems, such as a subnet that can store a valid sequence of packets and then "play them back" later.

The two protocols are also alike in that both have a connection establishment phase, a data transfer phase, and then a connection release phase. The general concepts of establishing, using, and releasing connections are also similar, although some of the details differ. In particular, both TP4 and TCP use three-way handshakes to eliminate potential difficulties caused by old packets suddenly emerging and causing trouble.

However, the two protocols also have some notable differences, which are listed in Fig. 6-28. First, TP4 uses nine different TPDU types, whereas TCP only has one. This difference results in TCP being simpler, but it also needs a larger header, because all fields must be present in all TPDUs. The minimum size of the TCP header is 20 bytes; the minimum size of the TP4 header is 5 bytes. Both protocols allow optional fields that can increase the header size above the minimum.

Feature	OSI TP4	TCP
Number of TPDU types	9	1
Connection collision	2 connections	1 connection
Addressing format	Not defined	32 bits
Quality of service	Open ended	Specific options
User data in CR	Permitted	Not permitted
Stream	Messages	Bytes
Important data	Expedited	Urgent
Piggybacking	No	Yes
Explicit flow control	Sometimes	Always
Subsequence numbers	Permitted	Not permitted
Release	Abrupt	Graceful

Fig. 6-28. Differences between the OSI TP4 protocol and TCP.

A second difference is what happens if two processes simultaneously attempt to set up connections between the same two TSAPs (i.e., a connection collision). With TP4, two independent, full-duplex connections are established. With TCP, a connection is identified by a pair of TSAPs, so only one connection is established.

A third difference is in the addressing format used. TP4 does not specify the exact format of a TSAP address; TCP uses 32-bit numbers as TSAPs.

The issue of quality of service is also handled differently in the two protocols and forms the fourth difference. TP4 has a rather elaborate and open-ended mechanism for a three-way negotiation of the quality of service. This negotiation involves the calling process, the called process, and the transport service itself. Many parameters can be specified, and both target and minimum acceptable values can be given. TCP, in contrast, does not have a quality of service field at all, but the underlying IP service has an 8-bit field that allows a choice to be made out of a limited number of combinations of speed and reliability.

A fifth difference is that TP4 allows user data to be carried in the *CR* TPDU, but TCP does not allow user data in the initial TPDU. The initial data (e.g., a password) might be necessary to decide whether or not a connection should be established. With TCP, making establishment depend on user data is not possible.

The previous four differences relate to the connection establishment phase. The next five concern the data transfer phase. A very basic difference is the model of data transport. The TP4 model is that of an ordered series of messages (TSDUs in OSI terminology). The TCP model is that of a continuous stream of bytes, without any explicit message boundaries. In practice, however, the TCP model is not really a pure byte stream because a library procedure, *push*, can be called to flush out any data buffered but not yet sent. When the remote user does a read, data from before and after the *push* will not be combined, so in a sense *push* can be thought of as defining a sort of message boundary.

The seventh difference concerns how important data that need special processing (such as BREAK characters) are dealt with. TP4 has two independent message streams, regular data and expedited data, multiplexed together. Only one expedited message may be outstanding at any instant. TCP uses the *Urgent* field to indicate that some number of bytes within the current TPDU are special and should be processed out of order.

The eighth difference is the absence of piggybacking in TP4 and its presence in TCP. This difference is not quite as significant as it may first appear since it is possible for a transport entity to put two TPDUs, for example, DT and AK in a single network packet.

The ninth difference is the way flow control is handled. TP4 can use a credit scheme, but it can also rely on the window scheme of the network layer to regulate the flow. TCP always uses an explicit flow control mechanism with the window size specified in each TPDU.

The tenth difference relates to this window scheme. In both protocols the receiver is entitled to reduce the window at will. This possibility potentially gives rise to problems if the grant of a large window and its subsequent retraction arrive in the wrong order. In TCP there is no solution to this problem. In TP4 it is solved by the subsequence number that is included in the retraction, thus allowing the sender to determine that the small window followed, rather then preceded, the large one.

Finally, our eleventh and last difference between the two protocols is in the way connections are released. TP4 uses an abrupt disconnection in which a series of data TPDUs may be followed directly by a *DR* TPDU. If the data TPDUs are lost, they will not be recovered by the protocol and information will be lost. TCP uses a three-way handshake to avoid data loss upon disconnection. The OSI model handles this problem in the session layer. It is worth noting that the U.S. National Bureau of Standards was so displeased with this property of TP4 that it introduced extra TPDUs into the transport protocol to allow disconnection without data loss. As a consequence, the U.S. and international versions of TP4 are not identical.

NETWORKING IN UNIX

A large number of machines on the ARPANET and the ARPA Internet run Berkeley UNIX. For this reason, it is worth taking a short look at how it handles networking. Berkeley UNIX supports TCP/IP, which is accessed through a set of primitives.

In contrast to the OSI primitives, which are highly abstract, the Berkeley primitives are much more specific. They are implemented as a set of system calls that allow users to access the transport service. The major system calls are listed in Fig. 6-29. Several minor calls and some variants of the major calls are not shown, for simplicity.

Socket	Create a TSAP of a given type
Bind	Associate an ASCII name to a previously created socket
Listen	Create a queue to store incoming connection requests
Accept	Remove a connection request from the queue or wait for one
Connect	Initiate a connection with a remote socket
Shutdown	Terminate the connection on a socket
Send	Send a message through a given socket
Recv	Receive a message on a given socket
Select	Check a set of sockets to see if any can be read or written

Fig. 6-29. The principal transport service calls in Berkeley UNIX.

Central to the service interface is the concept of a **socket**, which is similar to an OSI TSAP. Sockets are end points to which connections can be attached from the bottom (the operating system side) and to which processes can be attached from the top (the user side). The *socket* system call creates a socket (a data structure within the operating system). The parameters to the call specify the address format (e.g., an ARPA Internet name), the socket type (e.g., connection-oriented or connectionless), and the protocol (e.g., TCP/IP).

Once a socket has been created, buffer space can be allocated to it for storing incoming connection requests. This space is allocated using the *listen* call. A socket specified in a *listen* call then becomes a passive end point waiting for a connection request to arrive from outside.

In order for a remote user to send a connection request to a socket, the socket has to have a name (TSAP address). Names can be attached to sockets by the *bind* system call. Once bound, a name can be published or distributed in some way, so that remote processes can address the socket.

The way a user process attaches itself to a socket to passively await the arrival of a connection request is the *accept* call (essentially the same as the *listen* call in our example). If a request has already arrived, it will be taken from the socket's queue; otherwise, the process will block until a request comes in (unless the socket has been specified as nonblocking). Either way, when a request is available, a new socket is created and the new socket is used for the connection end point. In this manner, a single well-known port can be used to establish many connections.

To initiate a connection to a remote socket, a process can make the *connect* system call specifying a local socket and a remote name as parameters. This call establishes a connection between the two sockets. Alternatively, if the sockets are of the connectionless type, the operating system records an association between the two, so that *send*s on the local socket result in messages being sent to the remote one, even though no formal connection exists.

To terminate a connection or association the *shutdown* call is used. The two directions of a full duplex connection can be independently shut down.

The calls *send* and *recv* are used to send and receive messages. Several variations of the basic call are present.

Finally, we have the *select* call. This system call is useful for processes that have several connections established. In many cases such a process wants to do a *recv* on any socket that has a message waiting for it. Unfortunately it does not know which sockets have messages pending and which do not. If it picks one socket at random, it may end up blocking for a long time waiting for a message, while messages are waiting on several other sockets. The *select* call allows it to block until reads (or writes) are possible on some set of sockets specified by the parameters. For example, a process can say that it wants to block until a message is available on any one of a given set of sockets. When the call terminates, the caller is told which sockets have messages pending and which do not.

6.4.3. The Transport Layer in MAP and TOP

MAP and TOP use the OSI transport protocol. Since they use a connectionless protocol (ISO 8473) in the network layer, they are forced to use the TP4 variant in the transport layer.

TP4 contains several options that can be negotiated at the time a connection is established. Specific choices have been made for some of them. To start with, the computer initiating the connection is required to specify the use of Class 4 in the *CR* TPDU, and the responder is required to accept it in the *CC* TPDU. If either side is unable or unwilling to do this, the connection cannot be established.

Both the 7-bit and 31-bit sequence number options must be supported. Implementations are encouraged to use the 31-bit option all the time, except in those circumstances in which the underlying network cannot support it.

Expedited data must be supported by all implementations, even though the OSI standard says that it is optional. If during the connection establishment either peer rejects this option, the connection must be rejected because some of the upper layers use this facility.

Finally, all MAP and TOP implementations must be prepared to use the software checksum option, in which transport entities checksum each TPDU before sending it or after receiving it. Doing the checksum in software is very expensive in terms of CPU time, but guards against the possibility of losing data due to memory errors. Use of this option for any given connection is optional, but if it is desired, it must be available.

6.4.4. The Transport Layer in USENET

USENET does not have an official transport protocol. Each pair of communicating machines can negotiate the use of any desired transport protocol (or none at all). Many pairs of machines use TCP/IP, but X.25 and the *uucp* protocol described in Chap. 4 are also widely used.

The upper layers do not require any specific transport protocol, although they do need a way to establish a reliable connection between machines for the purpose of logging in. If this goal can be achieved, each pair of machines can use any mutually agreeable transport protocol, or none at all, if the underlying communication is reliable enough (e.g., over a LAN).

6.5. SUMMARY

The purpose of the transport layer is to bridge the gap between what the network layer offers and what the transport user wants. It also serves to isolate the upper layers from the technology of the network layer by providing a standardized service definition. In this way, changes in the network technology will not require changes to software in the higher layers.

The OSI transport service definition views a connection as having three phases: establishment, use, and release. For each phase, service primitives are available to perform the required actions. Connectionless service is also provided for.

Network layer service can be categorized as A, B, or C, depending on how reliable it is. For type A (reliable) networks, simple protocols can be used. For type B (almost reliable) networks, the transport protocol must be able to recover from *N-RESET*s. For type C networks, the transport protocol must use complex mechanisms to deal with many subtle errors that may occur.

Connection management is a key responsibility of the transport layer. For type C networks, connection establishment needs to be quite elaborate, usually involving a three-way handshake. Connection release can also be a problem, as our example of the two-army problem demonstrated. One possible solution is to use timer-based connections.

After finishing with connection management, we studied a sample transport layer using X.25 as the network service. In this example we saw one possible way of relating the abstract OSI service primitives to executable procedures. We also saw how the protocol can be represented as a finite state machine.

Finally, we examined the transport layer in our usual running examples and looked at the two main transport protocols currently in use, the OSI transport protocol and TCP. The similarities and differences between these two protocols were pointed out.

PROBLEMS

1. The dynamic buffer allocation scheme of Fig. 6-18 tells the sender how many buffers it has beyond the acknowledged message. An alternative way of conveying the same information would be for the buffer field to simply tell how many additional buffers, if any, had been allocated. In this method the sender maintains a counter that is incremented by the contents of the buffer field in arriving messages, and decremented when a message is sent for the first time. Are the two methods equally good?

2. A user process sends a stream of 128-byte messages to another user process over a connection. The receiver's main loop consists of two actions, fetch message and process message. The time required to fetch and process a message has an exponential probability density, with mean 10 msec. The window mechanism allows up to 16 outstanding messages at any instant. All communication lines in the subnet are 230 kbps, but due to delays in the subnet, the arrival pattern at the receiver is approximately Poisson. Measurements show that the time for an acknowledgement to get back to the sender, measured from the first bit of transmission, is 200 msec. Use queueing theory to determine the mean number of bytes of buffer space required at the receiving host.

3. A group of N users located in the same building are all using the same remote computer via an X.25 network. The average user generates L lines of traffic (input + output) per hour, on the average, with the mean line length being P bytes, excluding the X.25 headers. The packet carrier charges C cents per byte of user data transported, plus X cents per hour for each X.25 virtual circuit open. Under what conditions is it cost effective to multiplex all N transport connections onto the same X.25 virtual circuit, if such multiplexing adds 2 bytes of data to each packet? Assume that even one X.25 virtual circuit has enough bandwidth for all the users.

4. Class 0 of the OSI transport protocol does not have any explicit flow control procedure. Does this mean that a fast sender can transmit data can drown a slow receiver in data?

5. Imagine a generalized n-army problem, in which the agreement of any two of the armies is sufficient for victory. Does a protocol exist that allows blue to win?

6. In a network that has a maximum packet size of 128 bytes, a maximum packet lifetime

of 30 sec, and an 8-bit packet sequence number, what is the maximum data rate per connection?

7. Suppose that the clock-driven scheme for generating initial sequence numbers is used with a 15-bit wide clock counter. The clock ticks once every 100 msec, and the maximum packet lifetime is 60 sec. How often need resynchronization take place
   (a) in the worst case?
   (b) when the data consumes 240 sequence numbers/min?

8. Why does the maximum packet lifetime, T, have to be large enough to ensure that not only the packet, but also its acknowledgements have vanished?

9. Imagine that a two-way handshake rather than a three-way handshake were used to set up connections. In other words, the third message was not required. Are deadlocks now possible? Give an example or show that none exist.

10. Consider the problem of recovering from host crashes (i.e., Fig. 6-20). If the interval between writing and sending an acknowledgement, or vice versa, can be made relatively small, what are the two best sender-receiver strategies for minimizing the chance of a protocol failure?

11. Are deadlocks possible with the transport entity described in the text?

12. What happens when the user of the transport entity given in Fig. 6-21 sends a zero length message? Discuss the significance of your answer.

13. Out of curiosity, the implementer of the transport entity of Fig. 6-21 has decided to put counters inside the *sleep* procedure to collect statistics about the *conn* array. Among these are the number of connections in each of the seven possible states, n_i ($i = 1, \ldots, 7$). After writing a massive FORTRAN program to analyze the data, our implementer discovered that the relation $\sum n_i = MaxConn$ appears to always be true. Are there any other invariants involving only these seven variables?

14. For each event that can potentially occur in the transport entity of Fig. 6-21, tell whether it is legal or not when the user is sleeping in *sending* state.

15. The X.25 protocol does not use subsequence numbers like TP4. Is this simply because X.25 was invented years ago, before the idea of subsequence numbers had been thought of, or is there a different reason?

16. Consider the problem of internetworking with type C connectionless subnets. If a TPDU passes through a network whose maximum packet size is smaller than the standard TPDU size, will this cause problems with TP4? How about with TCP?

17. TCP only allows one connection to exist between any pair of TSAPs. Do you think this is also true of TP4? Discuss your answer.

18. Discuss the advantages and disadvantages of credits versus sliding window protocols.

19. TCP uses a single transport protocol header, whereas OSI has many of them. Discuss the advantages and disadvantages of each method.

20. Datagram fragmentation and reassembly is handled by IP, and is invisible to TCP. Does this mean that TCP does not have to worry about data arriving in the wrong order?

21. Modify the program of Fig. 6-21 to do error recovery. Add a new packet type, *reset*, that can arrive after a connection has been opened by both sides but closed by neither. This event, which happens simultaneously on both ends of the connection, means that any packets that were in transit have either been delivered or destroyed, but in either case no longer are in the subnet.

22. Modify the program of Fig. 6-21 to multiplex all transport connections onto a single X.25 virtual circuit. This change will probably require you to create and manage an explicit transport header to keep track of which packet belongs to which connection.

23. Write a program that simulates buffer management in a transport entity using a sliding window for flow control rather than the credit system of Fig. 6-21. Let higher layer processes randomly open connections, send data, and close connections. To keep it simple, have all the data travel from machine A to machine B, and none the other way. Experiment with different buffer allocation strategies at B, such as dedicating buffers to specific connections versus a common buffer pool, and measure the total throughput achieved by each one.

7

THE SESSION LAYER

The session, presentation, and application layers form the **upper layers** in the OSI Reference Model. In contrast to the lower four layers, which are concerned with providing reliable end-to-end communication, the upper layers are concerned with providing user-oriented services. They take the bare-bones, error-free channel provided by the transport layer, and add additional features that are useful to a wide variety of applications, so that the writers of these applications will not each have to re-implement these features over and over as part of each separate program.

The session layer is basically an invention of ISO. Prior to the OSI model, no existing network had a session layer (although some of the OSI session services are present in SNA, albeit scattered over several layers). During the development of OSI, there was considerable debate about the need for a session layer. The British proposal to ISO, for example, had only five layers and did not include a session layer.

Although a majority of the ISO committee eventually decided to include a session layer, it should be clear from the brevity of this chapter that the session layer is a "thin" layer, with relatively few features compared to the lower layers. Furthermore, when a session layer connection is established, options can be selected to disable most of the available features. It is not nearly as important as, say, the transport layer, and many applications do not need even the few features that it does have. Nevertheless, it is now part of the OSI Reference Model, so let us turn to it and see what services it offers and how they work.

7.1. SESSION LAYER DESIGN ISSUES

In this section we will discuss some of the design issues relevant to the session layer. These include dialog management, synchronization, and activity management, among others. They can all be regarded as "value-added" services put on top of the naked transport connection.

7.1.1. Services Provided to the Presentation Layer

The session layer provides services to the presentation layer. Its position in the hierarchy is shown in Fig. 7-1. This figure is analogous to Fig. 6-1, except that the service access points are called **session service access points (SSAPs)** and the protocol data units are called **session protocol data units (SPDUs)**. Analogously with the transport layer, we will use the terms **session service provider** and **session entity** interchangeably.

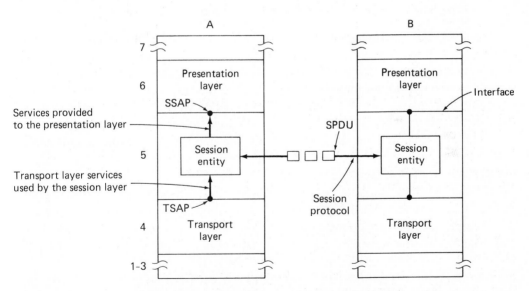

Fig. 7-1. The transport, session, and presentation layers.

The main function of the session layer is to provide a way for the session users (e.g., presentation entities or sometimes just ordinary user processes) to establish connections, called **sessions**, and transfer data over them in an orderly way. A session might be used for a remote login from a terminal to a distant computer, or for a file transfer, or for any of many other purposes. Although connectionless primitives are available in the session layer, a connectionless session cannot make any use of the user-oriented features for which the session layer was designed. For this reason we will initially focus on the connection-oriented model. However, later in this chapter we will discuss an interesting application of connectionless sessions.

A session bears a close resemblance to a transport connection, but the two are not identical. Usually, when a request comes into the session layer to establish a session, a transport connection must be established to carry the connection. When the session is terminated, the transport connection is released. In this example there is a one-to-one mapping between the session and transport connection. This situation is illustrated in Fig. 7-2(a).

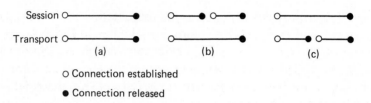

Fig. 7-2. Three ways of mapping sessions onto transport connections. (a) One-to-one mapping. (b) Consecutive sessions use the same transport connection. (c) One session spans multiple transport connections. The horizontal axis is time.

However, other mappings are also possible. Consider the case of an airline with reservation offices in many cities. Each office has agents with terminals connected to a minicomputer in the local office. The minicomputers are connected by a wide-area network to the main computer holding the reservation data base. Whenever an agent answers a call, a session is established to the main computer. When the call has been processed, the session is terminated, but there is no need to go to the trouble of releasing the underlying transport connection, because it will surely be needed again within a few seconds. It is simpler to allow sequential sessions to use the same transport connection, as shown in Fig. 7-2(b).

A third possible mapping between sessions and transport connections is given in Fig. 7-2(c). Here we see a session that spans multiple transport connections. If for example, a transport connection fails (for whatever reason), the session layer can establish a new transport connection, and continue the session over the new one. If the transport entities reside in the hosts, this situation should not occur because the transport entities are expected to recover from network layer (i.e., subnet) failures themselves. However, if the transport entities are external to the hosts, the problem of recovery from external failures is pushed up to the session layer because it then becomes the lowest layer of software that can survive subnet crashes.

As an aside, it is not permitted to multiplex several sessions onto a single transport connection simultaneously the way the transport layer can multiplex several transport connections onto a network connection. At any instant of time, each transport connection carries at most one session. Multiplexing is done to reduce cost or improve performance, which are transport layer functions.

7.1.2. Data Exchange

The most important feature of the session layer is data exchange. A session, like a transport connection, goes through three phases: establishment, use, and release. The primitives provided to the presentation layer for establishing, using, and releasing sessions are very similar to the primitives provided to the session layer for establishing, using and releasing transport connections. In many cases, all the session entity has to do when a primitive is invoked by the session user, is invoke the corresponding transport primitive to get the work done.

For example, when a session user issues an *S-CONNECT.request* primitive to establish a session, the session provider just issues a *T-CONNECT.request* to establish a transport connection (assuming that no transport connection happens to be available). Similarly, session establishment, like transport connection establishment, involves negotiation between the peers (users) to set the values of various parameters. Some of these parameters actually pertain to the transport connection, such as quality of service and the flag telling whether or not expedited data are permitted. These are just passed to the transport connection without modification. Others are specifically related to the session layer. For example, if a session is being established between two computers for the purpose of exchanging electronic mail in both directions, one of the session parameters might specify which side was to go first.

Nevertheless, despite these similarities, important differences do exist between a session and a transport connection. Chief among these is the way sessions and transport connections are released. Transport connections are terminated with the *T-DISCONNECT.request* primitive, which gives an **abrupt release** and may result in data in transit at the time of the release being irretrievably lost. Sessions are ended with the *S-RELEASE.request* primitive, which results in an **orderly release** (also called a **graceful release**) in which no data are ever lost. An abrupt release, like *T-DISCONNECT.request*, is also available in the form of *S-U-ABORT.request*.

The difference between an orderly and an abrupt release can be seen in Fig. 7-3. In the abrupt release, as soon as either user has issued the appropriate primitive to disconnect, no more data can be delivered to it. In Fig. 7-3(a), once *B* has invoked *T-DISCONNECT.request*, its end of the connection is immediately released. It may not receive the message that is currently in transit for it, even if that message arrives before the *DR* TPDU arrives at *A*. Furthermore, *A* may not refuse the request to release the connection. The transport service provider just issues a *T-DISCONNECT.indication* and that is that. It is like a telephone connection: when one party hangs up, the connection is terminated, no matter what the other one wants.

Orderly release works differently. It uses a full handshake, with *request*, *indication*, *response*, and *confirm* primitives. In Fig. 7-3(b), even after *B* has issued an *S-RELEASE.request* primitive, it can still accept messages until *A* has confirmed the release. Just issuing an *S-RELEASE.request* does not terminate the session by itself.

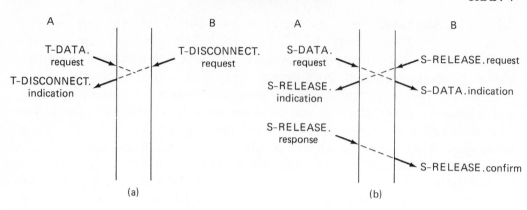

Fig. 7-3. (a) Abrupt release. (b) Orderly release.

The remote user must agree. If the remote user wants to continue the session, it can reject the attempt to release (by setting a parameter in the *S-RELEASE.response* primitive), and the session continues as if nothing had happened. A session is only terminated when both parties have had enough.

If you think it strange that orderly release is present in the session layer but not in the transport layer, rest assured that you are not alone. When drafting the transport layer standard for the U.S. Government, the National Bureau of Standards (NBS) also thought it pretty strange, and decided to add an orderly release option to the transport layer, thus solving the problem and simultaneously making the U.S. standard different from that used by the rest of the world. People in the standards business frequently have to choose between doing it right and doing it the way everybody else does it. This is why there are so many standards.

Addressing is another area in which the session and transport layers differ, although only slightly. To establish a session, one must specify the SSAP address (rather than TSAP address) to connect to. Although the standards do not tell how SSAP addresses are to be constructed, it is likely that in practice an SSAP address will consist of a TSAP address plus some additional identifying information.

One more way in which session data exchange differs from transport data exchange is the number of different kinds of data. The transport layer has two logically independent data streams, regular data and expedited data. The session layer has both of these, and two more (typed data and capability data). The other two streams relate to features of the session layer that we have not yet covered, so we will defer our discussion of them until later in this chapter.

7.1.3. Dialog Management

In principle, all OSI connections are full duplex, that is, PDUs can move in both directions over the same connection simultaneously. Full-duplex communication is shown in Fig. 7-4(a). However, there are many situations in which the upper-layer software is structured to expect the users to take turns (half-duplex communication). This design has nothing to do with the limitations of some ancient terminals still in existence that cannot work in full-duplex mode, but with designing upper-layer software in a convenient way.

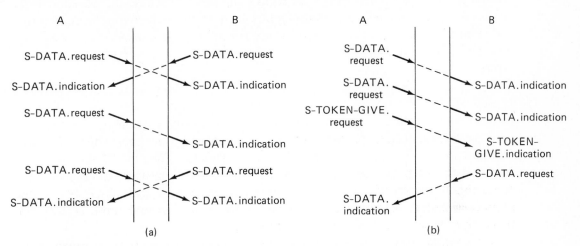

Fig. 7-4. (a) Full-duplex communication.   (b) Half-duplex communication managed with a token.

As an example, consider a database management system that can be accessed from remote terminals (e.g., airline reservation or home banking). The most natural mode of operation is for the user to send a query to the database system and then wait for the reply. Allowing users to send a second and a third query before the first one has been answered needlessly complicates the system. Logically, it is desirable to operate the system in half-duplex mode: either it is the user's turn to transmit or the database system's. Keeping track of whose turn it is to talk (and enforcing it) is called **dialog management**, and is one of the services that can be provided by the session layer when requested.

The way that dialog management is implemented is by the use of a **data token**. When a session is established, half-duplex operation is one of the options that can be selected. If half-duplex operation is chosen, the initial negotiation also determines which side gets the token first. Only the user holding the token may transmit data; the other one must remain silent. When the token holder has finished transmitting, it passes the token to its peer using the *S-TOKEN-GIVE.request* primitive, as shown in Fig. 7-4(b).

What happens if the user not holding the token wants to transmit some data? It can politely ask for the token using the *S-TOKEN-PLEASE.request* primitive. The token holder can agree, and pass the token, or it can refuse, in which case the other user will just have to wait (or send an emergency message using expedited data, which does not require the token). If full-duplex operation is selected when the session is established, no token is used for data transmission.

7.1.4. Synchronization

Another service of the session layer is **synchronization**, which is used to move the session entities back to a known state in the event of an error or disagreement. At first glance, such a service would seem unnecessary because the transport layer has been carefully designed to transparently recover from all communication errors and subnet crashes. However, closer study shows that the transport layer has been designed to mask only *communication* errors. It cannot recover from *upper layer* errors.

As an example of the problems that can occur, consider the **teletex** service that is gradually replacing telex (TWX) for sending hard copy messages from one company to another. Subscribers to this service use a device containing an embedded CPU, keyboard, display, printer, modem, telephone and sometimes a disk. The user first composes a message using the CRT and keyboard. Then the CPU calls up the company to which the message is to be sent, establishes a session, and transfers the message. If the receiving device has no disk storage, a real possibility in the cheaper versions, incoming messages must be printed in real time, as they are received.

As soon as each SPDU is received, it is acknowledged and text is given to the printer to print. Now suppose that a paper or ribbon jam occurs. Even if the human operator notices the problem quickly and hits a button on the device to stop printing, some information may be lost. Since it has already been acknowledged, the sender will no longer have a copy, and the message transmission will fail. There is nothing that the transport layer can do about this problem. After all, it has done its job perfectly: it moved all the bits reliably from sender to receiver. Only after handing the SPDU to the session layer did it send back an acknowledgement. It is not the transport layer's fault that the upper layers dropped the ball.

The solution lies in the session layer. The session users can split the text up into pages and insert a **synchronization point** between each page, as shown in Fig. 7-5. In case of trouble, it is possible to reset the state of the session to a previous synchronization point and continue from there. Of course, in order to make this process, called **resynchronization**, possible, the sending session user (not the session entity) must continue to hold data as long as it might be needed.

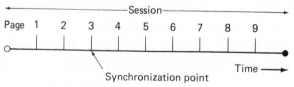

Fig. 7-5. Synchronization points.

It is important to understand what the semantics of synchronization are in the session layer. Session users can insert synchronization points in the message stream. Each synchronization point bears a serial number. When one user issues a primitive to request a synchronization point, the other one gets an indication. Similarly, when one issues a primitive to resynchronize, the other one gets an indication of that, too. The saving of messages and subsequent retransmission later is all handled *above* the session layer. All the session layer provides is a way of conveying numbered synchronization and resynchronization signals across the network.

The mechanism is actually slightly more complex than we have sketched so far. Two different kinds of synchronization points exist, **major** and **minor**, each with its own primitives. The units delimited by major synchronization points are called **dialog units**, and usually represent logically significant pieces of work. When transmitting a book, for example, the chapters might be delimited by major synchronization points and the pages by minor ones. Figure 7-6 shows a session with three major and four minor synchronization points.

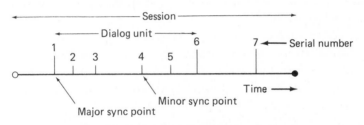

Fig. 7-6. Major and minor synchronization points.

Major and minor synchronization points differ in several ways. For one thing, when resynchronizing, it is only possible to go back as far as the most recent major synchronization point and no further. Thus in the time interval between synchronization points 6 and 7 in Fig. 7-6, it is permitted to resynchronize back to 6, but not to 1, 2, 3, 4, or 5. By erecting a brick wall at each major synchronization point, the sender knows that data that were sent before it can be safely discarded. Minor synchronization points do not have this property. Just before synchronization point 6 in Fig. 7-6 it is permitted to resynchronize to 1, 2, 3, 4, or 5. The choice of which type of synchronization point to use and where to use it is up to the session users, of course.

Major synchronization points are so significant that each one inserted into the data stream is explicitly confirmed (acknowledged). Minor synchronization points are not confirmed. On a satellite channel, where the minimum delay to send a message and get an acknowledgement is 540 msec, this distinction can be significant.

Setting a synchronization point, either major or minor, requires possession of the relevant tokens. Two independent tokens are available (for major and minor synchronization). They are distinct from each other and also distinct from the token used to control data flow in half-duplex connections. When resynchronization occurs, all the tokens are restored to the positions they had at the instant that the synchronization point was set.

7.1.5. Activity Management

Another key feature of the session layer, closely related to synchronization, is **activity management**. The idea behind activity management is to let the user split the message stream up into logical units called **activities.** Each activity is completely independent of any other activities that may have come before it or will come after it.

It is up to the user to determine what an activity is. As a first example, consider a session that has been set up for the purpose of transferring several files between two computers. Some way is needed of marking the place where one file ends and the next one begins. Using the ASCII FS (File Separator) character is not a good idea because if the files contain binary information, this character might appear in the data and accidentally signal end of file when that is not intended. Using some form of character stuffing, as is done in the data link layer, is a possibility, but in the session layer the stuffing will probably have to be done in software rather than hardware, so it will be slow.

What is really needed is some way to insert a marker into the message stream that is itself distinct from a data message (sometimes called **out of band** information). One way of achieving this goal is to define each file transfer as a separate activity, as illustrated in Fig. 7-7. In this figure, before each file transfer is started, the sender issues an *S-ACTIVITY-START .request* primitive. This comes in on the other side as an *S-ACTIVITY-START .indication* to mark the start of the file. Similarly, after each file transfer is completed, the *S-ACTIVITY-END* primitive can be used to denote end-of-file.

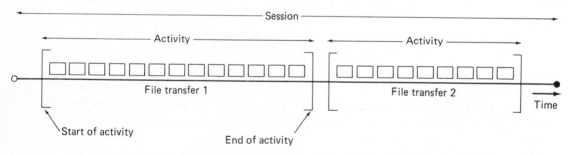

Fig. 7-7. Use of activities to mark file boundaries.

It is important to emphasize here that the choice of what constitutes an activity is made by the users, not the session layer. All the session layer does is ensure that when one of the *S-ACTIVITY* requests is made by one user, the other user gets the corresponding indication. *When* such requests are made and *how* the recipient reacts to the indications are of no interest to the session layer. The session layer is only concerned with the execution of the primitives, not their meaning (semantics) or use. It is worth noting that an activity covers all traffic sent in *both* directions.

As a second example of how activity management can be used, consider a home banking system in which people can pay bills by using their personal computers to transfer money from their accounts to those of the companies issuing the bills. The program running on the personal computer might start out by asking for the number of the account to be debited and send that information to the bank as the first message. Then it could successively ask for the number of the account to be credited and the amount, and send these items in messages two and three.

When the first message arrives at the bank's computer, the disk record containing the account to be debited is located and locked to prevent any concurrent access. When the second message arrives, the record for the account to be credited is also locked. When the third message arrives, the money is transferred and both accounts are unlocked.

Imagine what would happen if an electrical power failure blacked out the user's home just after the first message had been sent, received at the bank, and processed. The transaction would never be completed and the locked account would remain locked forever. To avoid situations like this, the banking transaction might be structured as a session layer activity. After receiving the *S-ACTIVITY-START.indication*, the bank's computer could simply accumulate incoming messages until the *S-ACTIVITY-END.indication* signaled that there were no more. Only then would processing and locking begin. In this way, no external failures could cause the bank's computer to get stuck half way in a transaction.

The technique of collecting messages in an input buffer until all of them have arrived before starting to process any of them is called **quarantining**. In early drafts of the session layer, quarantining was an explicit session service. However, later, the ISO committee realized that quarantining could equally well be accomplished using activity management, so the quarantine service was not included in the published standard.

Our third and last example of activity management makes use of a property that we have not yet mentioned: activities can be interrupted (i.e., suspended) and later restarted without loss of information. Consider the case of someone who has started to download a very long file from his computer at work to his personal computer at home. Half-way through the transfer, he needs to make an urgent telephone call and needs to look up the telephone number in his on-line telephone directory at work, preferably without ruining the file transfer.

The solution to this problem is given in Fig. 7-8. The file transfer is started as an activity. Part way through it is possible to issue an *S-ACTIVITY-INTERRUPT.request* to suspend the file transfer. Then another activity can be started and completed, and finally the original activity can be resumed from the point where it was interrupted.

Activity management is the primary way to structure a session. For this reason, it is essential that both parties agree on what the activity structure is. A problem could arise if both of them tried to start activities simultaneously. To prevent this event from occurring, activity management is controlled by a token (in fact the same token used for major synchronization points). To invoke an activity service, a

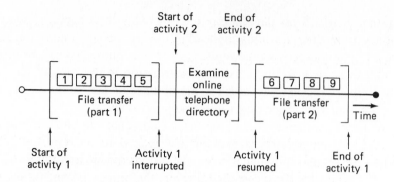

Fig. 7-8. Activities can be interrupted and later resumed.

user must be in possession of the activity token. This token can be passed and requested independently of the data and synchronize-minor tokens.

Actually, the situation is somewhat more complicated than we have just sketched. It started out as we have described it, but later on, ISO realized that problems could occur if one user started an activity while the other was doing a minor synchronization. To prevent this situation, the rules were changed to require a user to hold both the activity and synchronize-minor tokens, as well as the data token (if used) before initiating an activity or a synchronization operation. This strategy eliminated the original problems, but created a new one: what happens if one user holds the activity token and the other one holds the synchronize-minor token, and both users want both tokens. Each sits in a loop issuing *S-TOKEN-PLEASE* primitives, getting nowhere. A deadlock ensues. The only solution is for all applications to try to be very, very careful. In retrospect, a single token might have been better.

Activities are intimately related to synchronization points. When an activity is started, the synchronization serial numbers are reset to 1 and a major synchronization point is made. It is possible to make additional synchronization points, both major and minor, within an activity, as shown in Fig. 7-9.

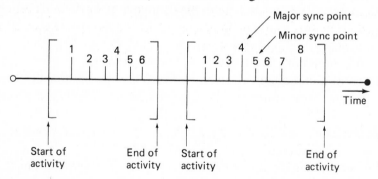

Fig. 7-9. Activities, major synchronization points, and minor synchronization points.

Because the start of each activity also corresponds to a major synchronization

point, once an activity has started, it is not possible to resynchronize to a point earlier than the start of that activity. In particular, it is not possible to resynchronize to
a synchronization point in a previous activity.

7.1.6. Exception Reporting

Another session layer feature is a general-purpose mechanism for reporting
unexpected errors. If the user runs into trouble, for whatever reason, this trouble
can be reported to the peer using a *S-U-EXCEPTION-REPORT.request* primitive.
Some user data may be transferred using this primitive. The user data typically will
explain what happened.

As an example, suppose a programmer designs a complex special-purpose layer
7 protocol for some specific application. During debugging of the protocol (or even
after it is supposedly debugged) protocol errors may occur. These can be reported
to the peer using the session layer exception reporting mechanism.

Exception reporting does not only apply to user-detected errors. The service
provider can generate an *S-P-EXCEPTION-REPORT.indication* to notify the user
about internal problems within the session layer or problems reported to it from the
transport or lower layers. These reports contain a field describing the nature of the
exception. It is up to the user to decide what action to take, if any.

7.1.7. The OSI Session Service Primitives

In this section we will systematically examine all the OSI session primitives
and describe the function of each one. They are listed in Fig. 7-10. Each line in the
table corresponds to between 1 and 4 primitives as noted. Potentially, each primitive type has *request*, *indication*, *response*, and *confirm* versions. However, not all
the combinations are valid. *S-DATA*, for example, only has *request* and *indication*.
Acknowledgements (i.e., *response* and *confirm*) are taken care of by lower layers.

Although there are 58 connection-oriented session service primitives they can
be better understood by dividing them into seven groups:

1. Connection establishment.

2. Connection release.

3. Data transfer.

4. Token management.

5. Synchronization.

6. Activity management.

7. Exception reporting.

OSI session primitive	Request	Indication	Response	Confirm	Meaning
S-CONNECT	X	X	X	X	Establish a session
S-RELEASE	X	X	X	X	Terminate a session gracefully
S-U-ABORT	X	X			User-initiated abrupt release
S-P-ABORT		X			Provider-initiated abrupt release
S-DATA	X	X			Normal data transfer
S-EXPEDITED-DATA	X	X			Expedited data transfer
S-TYPED-DATA	X	X			Out-of-band data transfer
S-CAPABILITY-DATA	X	X	X	X	Control information data transfer
S-TOKEN-GIVE	X	X			Give a token to the peer
S-TOKEN-PLEASE	X	X			Request a token from the peer
S-CONTROL-GIVE	X	X			Give all the tokens to the peer
S-SYNC-MAJOR	X	X	X	X	Insert a major sync point
S-SYNC-MINOR	X	X	X	X	Insert a minor sync point
S-RESYNCHRONIZE	X	X	X	X	Go back to a previous sync point
S-ACTIVITY-START	X	X			Start an activity
S-ACTIVITY-END	X	X	X	X	End an activity
S-ACTIVITY-DISCARD	X	X	X	X	Abandon an activity
S-ACTIVITY-INTERRUPT	X	X	X	X	Suspend an activity
S-ACTIVITY-RESUME	X	X			Restart a suspended activity
S-U-EXCEPTION-REPORT	X	X			Report of a user exception
S-P-EXCEPTION-REPORT		X			Report of a provider exception

(a)

	Request	Indication	Response	Confirm	
S-UNITDATA	X	X			Connectionless data transfer

(b)

Fig. 7-10. (a) OSI connection-oriented session service primitives. (b) OSI connectionless session service primitives.

The first group contains four primitives of the form *S-CONNECT.xxx*. *S-CONNECT.request* specifies a session identifier, the calling and called SSAP addresses, the quality of service, the initial synchronization point number, the initial assignment of the tokens, some user data (optional), and possibly various options.

The options are provided because not all sessions require all the services that are potentially available. Synchronization, activity management, exception reporting, and certain kinds of data transfer to be discussed below may be individually enabled or disabled for each session, depending on the needs of the users.

The second group contains seven primitives concerned with releasing sessions. *S-RELEASE.request* is used to request orderly termination of a session. An alternative to this ordinary release is a negotiated release, which uses a **release token**. When this option has been selected at session establishment time, only the user holding this token may initiate a release. This facility is sometimes useful when the two ends of a session are not equals, but exhibit a master-slave relationship.

Two forms of abrupt release are also provided. One is user initiated and the other is provider initiated. The latter only occurs if some fatal error has been detected by the session entity.

The third group deals with data transfer. As we mentioned briefly earlier, there are four independent data streams. These are:

1. Regular data.

2. Expedited data.

3. Typed data.

4. Capability data.

The first two have already been discussed at length, so let us look at the other two. **Typed data** is like regular data, except that it may always be sent, without regard to the ownership of any tokens. In contrast to arrival of ordinary data, which is signaled by an *S-DATA.indication* primitive, the arrival of typed data is signaled by an *S-TYPED-DATA.indication* primitive so the recipient can tell them apart. Typed data may be used by the session service user for control messages or any other purpose it wishes.

The session layer standards do not specify how typed data are to be used. However, the intention of the ISO committee was to provide an out-of-band data stream for higher layer control information, network maintenance, and system management. For this reason, typed data may be sent at any time, without regard to any tokens. We have seen this concept of a special channel for control information before. In the X.25 protocol, there is a Q bit in the header to indicate qualified data. It would have been nice if typed data could have been sent using the Q bit. Unfortunately the transport layer service has no concept of typed data, so there is no way for the session entity to tell the transport layer that a message contains typed data.

The fourth data stream is called **capability data**. It, too, is intended for control purposes, but for control of the session layer itself. Its real function is to allow session options and parameters to be changed during a session (although, in theory, it can be used for anything the session users mutually agree to). Unlike typed data, capability data are fully acknowledged. Furthermore, to avoid confusion, capability data may only be sent outside (i.e., between) activities, and then only when the data, synchronization, and activity tokens are held.

The fourth group of primitives deals with token management. The session layer has four tokens, as shown in Fig. 7-11. The *S-TOKEN-GIVE.request* primitive can be used to pass one or more tokens to the peer entity. Parameters specify which tokens are to be given. The *S-TOKEN-PLEASE.request* primitive can be used to announce that the user issuing the primitive wants the specified tokens. Finally, the *S-CONTROL-GIVE.request* can be used to surrender all the tokens at once. It can only be used outside activities. Logically, this primitive is not necessary, but it was included at the request of CCITT for compatibility with their teletex protocol, which works in terms of control, rather than in terms of tokens.

Token type	Controls
Data token	Data transfer in half-duplex mode
Release token	Initiation of orderly release
Synchronize-minor token	Insertion of minor sync points
Major/activity token	Activity or major sync operations

Fig. 7-11. The session layer tokens.

The fifth group contains the synchronization primitives. Primitives are provided for both major and minor synchronization, as well as resynchronization. All of the primitives are confirmed. Each primitive specifies the serial number of the synchronization point that it wants to set or go back to. These serial numbers are in the range 0 to 999,999. All synchronization primitives require possession of the relevant tokens.

The sixth group of primitives relates to activity management. Activities can be started, interrupted, resumed, and discarded (abandoned). Like synchronization, activity management is controlled by tokens.

The seventh and last group contains the exception reporting primitives. Note that *S-P-EXCEPTION*, like *S-P-ABORT* cannot be requested. The service provider decides when and if to issue it.

The OSI primitives are implemented by the session entity using the session protocol. We will discuss this protocol later in this chapter.

7.2. REMOTE PROCEDURE CALL

The primary concern of the session layer is managing the dialog and dealing with errors (e.g., system crashes) occurring above the transport layer. In the OSI Reference Model, a connectionless session makes little sense. However, there has been considerable research at universities and in industry on a radically different model for dialog and error control based on the connectionless model. This work, which goes under the name **RPC** (**Remote Procedure Call**), has been widely implemented in networks and (especially) distributed systems.

RPC does not fit into the OSI Reference Model especially well. It has been designed to be fast, and therefore does not contain a multilayer structure. Logically, remote procedure call is concerned with roughly the same issues as the session layer (although from a very different perspective), so we will examine it in this chapter. Please note, however, that RPC can also be implemented in the application layer (although less efficiently), so one sometimes finds discussions of it in that context.

7.2.1. The Client-Server Model

Up until now, we have tacitly assumed that the two processes communicating over a session or transport connection are symmetric. In practice, this assumption is frequently violated. A common example is a network of diskless personal computers or workstations, called **clients**, that are communicating over a network with a **file server** having a disk on which all the files are stored. In this system, clients access their data by sending requests to the server, which carries out the work and sends back the replies. Communication always takes the form of request-reply pairs, always initiated by the clients, never by the server. This model is called the **client-server model**. It is illustrated in Fig. 7-12.

Fig. 7-12. In the client-server model, the client sends a request and the server sends a reply.

While it is obviously possible to establish sessions between clients and servers and then use half-duplex communication over these sessions, the high overhead caused by multiple layers of connections is frequently unattractive for applications, such as file servers, where performance is critical. A fully connectionless form of communication built right on top of the raw datagram facility (especially on LANs) is often a much better choice.

Even if the performance problems can be solved by using connectionless mode, the model still has a major flaw: the conceptual basis of all communication is I/O (input/output). Programs communicate with other programs using commands such as *X-DATA.request* and *X-DATA.indication*, the former of which is I/O and the latter of which is an interrupt. These are hardly the proper tools for building well-structured applications.

The RPC school of thought approaches the client-server model from a completely different perspective. In this view, a client sending a message to a server and getting a reply is like a program calling a procedure and getting a result. In both cases, the caller initiates an action and waits until it is completed and the results are available. Although in the ordinary (local) case, the procedure runs on the same machine as the caller, and with RPC it runs on a different machine, the caller need not be aware of this distinction.

To help hide the difference between local and remote calls even more, it is possible to embed RPC in the programming language. Suppose, for example, that we provide each of the file server's clients with a (library) procedure, *read*, that can be called with three parameters: an identifier telling which file to read, a buffer to read the data into, and a count of the number of bytes to read. A call like

    read(fileid, buffer, count)

is then an ordinary call to a local procedure (i.e., a procedure included in the caller's address space by the linker). This procedure sends a message to the file server and waits for the reply. Only after the reply arrives, does *read* return control to the caller.

The beauty of this scheme is that client-server communication now takes the form of procedure calls instead of I/O commands (or worse yet, interrupts). All the details of how the network works can be hidden from the application program by putting them in the local procedures such as *read*. These procedures are called **stubs**.

In this example, the stub procedure actually transfers data, but a stub procedure can equally well send a message requesting the server to perform an arbitrary operation. For example, a call

    delete(filename)

might cause the stub procedure, *delete*, to send a message to the file server asking it to destroy the specified file. By providing appropriate stub procedures, we can have the client invoke arbitrary actions on the server in a way that is much more natural for the applications programmer to deal with than I/O and interrupts. The ultimate goal is to make a remote procedure call look no different than a local procedure call.

7.2.2. Implementation of Remote Procedure Call

In this section we will take a closer look at how RPC is implemented. More information can be found in the work of Birrell and Nelson (1984). Figure 7-13 shows one way of implementing a remote procedure call system. In this figure, the remote call takes ten steps. Step 1 consists of the client program (or procedure) calling the stub procedure linked within its own address space. Parameters may be passed in the usual way. The client does not notice anything unusual about this call because it is a normal, local call.

The client stub then collects the parameters and packs them into a message. This operation is known as **parameter marshalling**. After the message has been constructed, it is given to the transport layer for transmission (step 2). In a connectionless LAN system, the transport entity will probably just attach a header to the

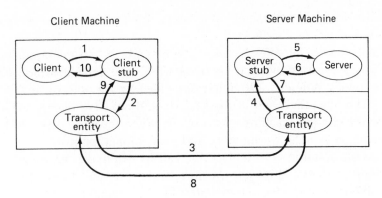

Fig. 7-13. The ten steps required to execute a remote procedure call.

message and put it out on the network without further ado (step 3). In a WAN, the actual transmission may be more complicated. In many systems, step 2 is a trap to the operating system.

When the message arrives at the server, the transport entity there passes it to the server stub (step 4), which unmarshalls the parameters. The server stub then calls the server procedure (step 5), passing the parameters in the standard way. The server procedure has no way of telling that it is being activated remotely because its immediate caller is a local procedure that obeys all the standard rules. Only the stubs know that something peculiar is going on.

After it has completed its work, the server procedure returns (step 6), the same way as any other procedure returns when it is finished. It may also return a result to its caller. The server stub then marshalls the result into a message and hands it off at the transport interface (step 7), possibly by making a system call, just as in step 2. After the reply gets back to the client machine (step 8), it is handed to the client stub (step 9). Finally, the client stub returns to its caller, the client procedure. Any value returned by the server in step 6 is given to the client in step 10.

The purpose of the whole mechanism of Fig. 7-13 is to give the client procedure the illusion that it is making a direct call on the distant server procedure. To the extent that the illusion succeeds and the client cannot tell that the server is remote, the mechanism is said to be **transparent**. However, a closer inspection reveals some difficulties in achieving full transparency.

The principal problem occurs with the parameter passing. Passing integers, floating point numbers, and character strings by value is easy. The client stub just puts them in the message. At worst, a conversion to some network standard format might be needed (such conversions are part of the presentation layer, and will be discussed at length in the next chapter). Passing structures, records, or arrays of these types is equally straightforward.

The trouble comes when the language allows parameters to be passed by *reference*, rather than by *value*. For a local call, a pointer (the address of the parameter) is normally passed to the called procedure. The called procedure knows that it is dealing with a reference parameter, so it can follow the pointer to access the parameter.

This strategy fails completely for a remote call. When the compiler produces code for the server, it knows nothing about RPC, and generates the usual instructions for following pointers. Of course the object being pointed to is not even on the server's machine, and even if it were, it would not have the same address there as it had on the client's machine. As a result, when the server tries to use a reference parameter, it gets the wrong value and the computation fails.

One possible solution is to replace the call-by-reference parameter mechanism by call-by-copy/restore. With copy/restore, the client stub locates the item being pointed to, and passes it to the server stub. The server stub puts it in memory somewhere, and passes a pointer to it to the server procedure. The server is then able to access the item in the usual way. When the server procedure returns control to the stub, the stub sends the (possibly modified) data item back to the client stub, which uses it to overwrite the original reference parameter.

Although the copy/restore mechanism frequently works, it can fail in certain pathological situations. Consider, for example, the program of Fig. 7-14. When this program runs locally, both of the parameters in the call to *doubleincr* are pointers to *a*, which gets incremented twice. The number 2 is printed.

```
program test (output);
var a :integer;


procedure doubleincr(var x ,y :integer);
begin
  x := x+1;
  y := y+1
end;


begin                          {main program}
  a := 0;
  doubleincr(a , a);
  writeln(a)
end.
```

Fig. 7-14. If the procedure *doubleincr* is run remote, the program fails.

Now let us see what happens if *doubleincr* is called as a remote procedure using copy/restore. The client stub processes each parameter separately, so it sends two copies of *a* to the server stub. The server procedure increments each copy once, and both are passed back to the client stub, which then restores them sequentially. First *a* is restored to 1 and then it is restored to 1 again. Thus the final value is 1 instead of the correct answer, 2.

Pointers give problems similar to reference parameters. They are especially troublesome if they point into the middle of complex lists or graphs or data structures involving variant records. Procedure or function parameters also are difficult to handle, although it may be possible for the server stub to replace them by procedures local to the server's machine that invoke the called procedures back on the client's machine using reverse RPC.

Many RPC systems finesse the whole problem by prohibiting the use of reference parameters, pointers, and procedure or function parameters on remote calls. Such a decision makes the implementation easier, but breaks down the transparency because the rules for local and remote calls are then different.

Let us now turn from parameter passing to another implementation issue: How does the client stub know who to call? In traditional connection-oriented networks, sessions are established between SSAPs, each of which has a fixed "telephone number." For RPC a simpler, yet more dynamic, scheme is needed.

Birrell and Nelson (1984) have described a scheme involving not only clients and servers, but also a specialized kind of data base system. In their method, illustrated in Fig. 7-15, when a server is booted, it registers with the data base system by sending a message containing its name (as an ASCII string), its network address (e.g., an NSAP, TSAP, or SSAP), and a unique identifier (e.g., a random 32-bit integer). This registration is done by having the server call a procedure *export*, which is handled by the stub (steps 1 and 2).

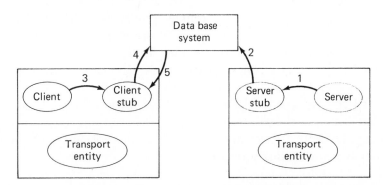

Fig. 7-15. Client-server binding is done via a data base.

Later, when the client makes its first call (step 3) and its stub is faced with the problem of locating the server, the stub sends its name, which is also the server's name, in ASCII, to the data base system (step 4). The data base system then returns the server's network address and the unique identifier (step 5). This process is called **binding**. From this point on, the stub knows how to locate the server, so binding is not required on subsequent calls.

The unique 32-bit identifier is included in each RPC call. It is used by the transport entity on the server's machine to tell which of the potentially many server stubs to give the incoming message to. It also has another role. If the server crashes and reboots, it re-registers with the data base system using a new unique number. Attempts by clients to communicate with it using the old unique identifier will fail, making them aware of the crash and forcing them to rebind.

Another key implementation issue is the protocol used. In the simplest case, the RPC protocol can consist of two messages: a request and a reply. Both the request and the reply contain the unique number identifying the server, a transaction identifier, and the parameters. When sending a request, the client stub (in some systems) may set a timer. If the timer goes off before the reply comes back, the stub can query the server to see if the request arrived. If not, it can retransmit it. The purpose of the transaction identifier is to allow the server to recognize and reject duplicate requests. Recognizing duplicate requests is only possible if the server keeps track of the most recent transaction identifier from each client.

A final implementation issue is **exception handling**. Unlike local procedure calls, where nothing can go wrong, many things can go wrong with RPC, for example, the server could be down. If the programming language allows it, the occurrence of an RPC error should not give control back to the caller, but should raise an exception to be handled by an exception handler. The design of the exception handling mechanism is language dependent, but a method is clearly needed to distinguish unsuccessful calls from successful ones.

7.2.3. Semantics of Remote Procedure Call

Also unlike local procedure calls, remote procedure calls are subject to lost messages, server crashes, and client crashes. These effects influence the semantics of RPC and the goal of making it transparent. In this section we will look at the problems caused by server crashes; in the following one we will examine client crashes.

The normal operation of the RPC protocol is shown in Fig. 7-16(a). However, consider what happens if the server crashes after carrying out the request, but before sending the reply. There are at least three possible ways of programming the client stub to deal with this situation.

1. Just hang forever waiting for the reply that will never come.

2. Time out and raise an exception or report failure to the client.

3. Time out and retransmit the request.

The first approach is similar to what happens when a program calls a local procedure containing an infinite loop. No timers are used locally and the procedure never returns. Manual intervention is required to kill the program. If the goal is to make the semantics of RPC similar to local procedure calls, there is something to be said for this approach.

The second approach to handling server crashes is to have the client stub time out and raise an exception (if the programming language supports exceptions), or report an error otherwise. This method is analogous to what happens if a called procedure gets a memory protection error or tries to divide by zero. If there is an

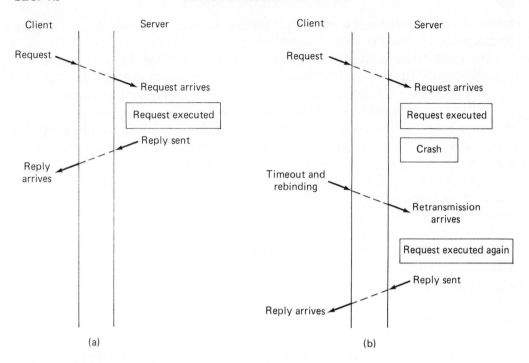

Fig. 7-16. (a) Ordinary two-message RPC. (b) RPC with a server crash and timeout by the client.

appropriate handler enabled, the exception will be caught and processed. If not, the program will be killed.

The third approach is to have the client stub time out and retransmit the request. Since the server will reregister a new unique identifier with the data base system after a crash, the retransmission will be rejected by the transport entity on the server's machine when it sees the old, now-invalid, unique identifier. If the transport entity sends back an error reply, the client stub can either give up (essentially the previous approach), or rebind and try again. If the client stub rebinds and repeats the call, it is conceivable that the operation will be carried out twice, as shown in Fig. 7-16(b). In fact, we can get repeated execution even without crashes if the reply gets lost and we allow the client stub to try again.

Whether or not repeated execution is acceptable depends on the kind of operation being performed. If the operation consists of reading block 4 from a file, there is no harm if it is repeated 1000 times. Each time it yields the same results and there are no side effects. On the other hand, if the operation consists of appending a block to the end of a file, then it matters very much how many times the operation is performed. Operations that can be repeated over and over with no harm are said to be **idempotent**.

If all operations could be cast into an idempotent form, then the third approach would obviously be the best one. Unfortunately, some operations are inherently nonidempotent (e.g., transferring money from one bank account to another). As a result of these problems, the exact semantics of remote procedure call systems can be categorized in various ways (Nelson, 1981).

The most desirable kind of semantics is **exactly once**, where every call is carried out exactly one time, no more and no less. This goal is unachievable because after a server crash it is not always possible to tell whether the operation was performed or not. Imagine, for example, a chocolate factory, in which vats of liquid chocolate are filled by having a computer set a bit in some device register to open a valve. After recovering from a crash, there is no way for the chocolate server to see if the crash happened one microsecond before or after the bit was set.

A weaker form of exactly once semantics is achievable if the programming language supports exception handling. In this variation, if a call returns normally, it means that no crashes have occurred and the operation has been executed exactly once. If the server crashes or any other serious error is detected, the call does not return at all. Instead, an exception is raised and the appropriate handler invoked. With these semantics, client procedures do not have to be programmed to deal with errors, but exception handlers do.

A second kind of semantics is **at most once**. When this form is used, control always returns to the caller. If everything has gone right, the operation will have been performed exactly once. However, if a server crash is detected, the client stub will give up and return an error code. Retransmission is not attempted. In this case, the client knows that the operation has been performed either zero or one times, but no more. Further recovery is up to the client.

A third kind of semantics for RPC is **at least once**. This type corresponds to Fig. 7-16(b). The client stub just keeps trying over and over until it gets a proper reply. When the caller gets control back, it knows that the operation has been performed one or more times. For idempotent operations, this situation is ideal. For nonidempotent operations, we can distinguish several variations. Probably the most useful of these is that the result returned is guaranteed to be the result of the final operation, not one of the earlier ones. If the client stub uses a different transaction identifier in each retransmission, it will be possible for it to tell which reply belongs to which request and thus filter out all but the last one. These semantics are called **last of many**.

In summary, the goal of fully transparent RPC semantics is considerably complicated by the possibility of crashes that affect the server but not the client. In single processor systems this situation does not occur because a crash that wipes out the server also wipes out the client and the whole computation is totally lost.

7.2.4. Orphans

We have just looked at the impact of server crashes; now let us take a look at what happens when a client crashes after starting a remote procedure call. Once a server procedure has been started up, its process continues to run, even if its parent has crashed. A running server with no waiting parent is called an **orphan**.

Orphans can cause trouble in a variety of ways. At the very least, they waste CPU cycles and other resources. In addition, they may lock files and other objects, thus denying other processes their rightful access to them. Finally, if a client is rebooted and starts an RPC all over again, results sent back by orphans may cause confusion.

Nelson (1981) has described four ways to deal with orphans. In the first way, called **extermination**, when a machine recovers after crashing, it checks to see if it had any RPCs in progress at the time of the crash. If so, it asks the server machine(s) to kill any processes running on its behalf. To use the extermination algorithm, it is necessary that client stubs log RPCs before executing them. When RPCs complete, their entries are deleted from the log of pending RPCs. The log must be kept in such a way that it survives processor crashes (e.g., on disk).

Orphans may themselves make remote procedure calls, thus creating **grand-orphans** (and even great grandorphans). Thus the extermination algorithm must be run recursively to kill off the whole chain all the way to the bottom.

The second way to kill orphans is **expiration**. This technique does not require any log. When an RPC is started, the server is given a certain amount of time to complete the call. If the call does not complete within the original interval, the server stub must ask the client stub for a new quantum. If the client machine has crashed or rebooted, this event will be detected, the timer will not be renewed, and the server will be allowed to die. When expiration is used, all a client has to do is make sure that one quantum has elapsed since the last crash before issuing the first RPC.

The third technique for getting rid of orphans is called **reincarnation**. It may happen that extermination fails to eliminate all orphans. For example, if the network is partitioned at the time the extermination algorithm is run, some orphans may be unreachable. In that case a blunderbuss approach can be taken that effectively kills off all remote activity in the network.

In this method, time is divided into sequentially numbered epochs. When a recovering client fails to exterminate its orphans, it broadcasts the start of a new epoch to all machines. They react by killing off all their server processes. Since all requests and replies always contain the number of the epoch in which they were started, any replies that eventually come back from orphans will bear an obsolete epoch number, and thus be detectable.

The fourth approach to eliminating orphans is similar to the third one, but somewhat less Draconian. It also uses epochs, but instead of each machine killing off all remote activity when a new epoch is declared, it tries to locate the client that started the server. Only if that client cannot be found is the server killed. This algorithm is called **gentle reincarnation**.

So far in this discussion we have assumed that as soon as an orphan can be found, it can be killed. In fact, matters are actually more complex. An orphan may be running inside a critical region, or have just locked some files. Under these circumstances, killing the orphan may create inconsistencies in data bases or deadlocks. Furthermore, an orphan may have already scheduled future work. For example, an orphan may have made an entry in a queue for a file to be printed later or some other future action to be taken. Even if the orphan itself is killed, the queued work may eventually be executed. The problem of orphan elimination is discussed in more detail by Shrivastava and Panzieri (1982).

7.2.5. Discussion of RPC

In this section we will briefly look at some of the key issues that confront the designer of any RPC system. They fall into four broad categories:

1. Interface design.

2. Client design.

3. Server design.

4. Protocol design.

Let us start with the first one. The heart of the matter is how far transparency will be pursued. Given the problems with **var** parameters and pointers, and the near impossibility of achieving exactly once semantics in the face of crashes, Hamilton (1984) has argued that transparency should not even be attempted at all. He favors adding a keyword, **remote**, in front of the declaration of any procedure that may be called remotely to warn the compiler and avoid misleading the programmer. On the other hand, although the RPC problems look formidable on paper, in practice crashes are rare, and most of the other problems can be handled by careful stub and compiler design.

An important matter that we have not touched on yet is how the stubs are produced. One possibility is to have them all written by hand. Another is to have the compiler produce them as a byproduct of the compilation process. The latter is much more convenient, but is quite tricky unless the language is very strongly typed.

Another language issue is exception handling. If there is no adequate mechanism to have RPC errors caught by some piece of code other than the client procedure, then each client procedure will have to test for all possible error returns and be prepared to handle them, a highly nontransparent situation.

Last, comes the issue of binding. Precisely how servers export their names, how clients can select a specific instance of a server when there are several identical ones, and how and when rebinding works are all issues that need careful attention.

The main client design questions involve timeouts and orphans. Should client stubs time out after getting no response, or should they just wait forever? If they time out, what action should they take, what semantics should be provided, and how should orphans be handled?

The main issue concerning server design is that of parallelism. At one extreme, whenever a request comes in for execution of a server procedure, a new process is created and the procedure run as part of that process. If other requests come in from other clients before the first one is finished, more processes are created, and all of them run in parallel, independent of one another. At the other extreme, there exists a single process associated with each server procedure. If a second request comes in before the first one is finished, it must wait its turn. The first approach bears the burden of process creation on each RPC, but potentially allows parallel execution of calls. The second is simpler and faster if there is only one call at a time, but does not allow any parallelism if there are multiple calls.

Finally, the main issue with protocol design is achieving high performance. There has been a great deal of controversy on this point. Many researchers believe that the only way to make RPC go fast is to run it on top of the bare packet interface, effectively with null transport and network layers.

On the other hand, some of the more connection-minded people feel that RPC can run adequately in the application layer, even if there are many protocol layers below it. This is the direction that ISO is taking. In this model, there are primitives *BIND*, *UNBIND*, *INVOKE*, and *RESULT*, each with *request*, *indication*, *response*, and *confirm*.

7.3. EXAMPLES OF THE SESSION LAYER

In this section we will look at our running examples to see how they handle the session layer, if at all.

7.3.1. The Session Layer in Public Networks

Public networks and other OSI networks generally implement the full session layer services as described earlier in this chapter. The session protocol (see Fig. 7-1) is complex, due to the large number of service primitives, but follows the service definitions closely. Furthermore, the complexity was made worse by the political decision to require the protocol to be compatible with the much older CCITT teletex protocol.

For each service primitive, there is a corresponding SPDU (Session Protocol Data Unit) that is sent when the protocol is invoked. For those primitives with responses, there is an SPDU that is generated by the response. The list of service primitives and their corresponding SPDUs is given in Fig. 7-17.

Of the 21 primitive types listed in Fig. 7-17 all but two can be invoked by user processes. In each case, issuing an *XXX.request* causes the session entity to transmit an SPDU. To start with, consider the *S-CONNECT.request* primitive.

OSI session primitive	Request	Indication	Response	Confirm	SPDU sent on request	SPDU sent on response
S-CONNECT	X	X	X	X	CONNECT	ACCEPT, REFUSE
S-RELEASE	X	X	X	X	FINISH	DISCONNECT, NOT FINISHED
S-U-ABORT	X	X			ABORT	(ABORT ACCEPT)
S-P-ABORT		X			(ABORT)	
S-DATA	X	X			DATA TRANSFER	
S-EXPEDITED-DATA	X	X			EXPEDITED DATA	
S-TYPED-DATA	X	X			TYPED DATA	
S-CAPABILITY-DATA	X	X	X	X	CAPABILITY DATA	CAPABILITY DATA ACK
S-TOKEN-GIVE	X	X			GIVE TOKENS	
S-TOKEN-PLEASE	X	X			PLEASE TOKENS	
S-CONTROL-GIVE	X	X			GIVE TOKENS CONFIRM	(GIVE TOKENS ACK)
S-SYNC-MAJOR	X	X	X	X	MAJOR SYNC POINT	MAJOR SYNC POINT ACK
S-SYNC-MINOR	X	X	X	X	MINOR SYNC POINT	MINOR SYNC POINT ACK
S-RESYNCHRONIZE	X	X	X	X	RESYNCHRONIZE	RESYNCHRONIZE ACK
S-ACTIVITY-START	X	X			ACTIVITY START	
S-ACTIVITY-END	X	X	X	X	ACTIVITY END	ACTIVITY END ACK
S-ACTIVITY-DISCARD	X	X	X	X	ACTIVITY DISCARD	ACTIVITY DISCARD ACK
S-ACTIVITY-INTERRUPT	X	X	X	X	ACTIVITY INTERRUPT	ACTIVITY INTERRUPT ACK
S-ACTIVITY-RESUME	X	X			ACTIVITY RESUME	
S-U-EXCEPTION-REPORT	X	X			EXCEPTION REPORT	
S-P-EXCEPTION-REPORT		X			(EXCEPTION REPORT)	

Fig. 7-17. Session primitives and the corresponding SPDUs.

When it is invoked, the session entity builds a *CONNECT* SPDU and sends it to the destination. When this SPDU arrives at the remote machine, the session entity there causes an *S-CONNECT.indication* to happen. The user addressed can accept or refuse the session by invoking the *S-CONNECT.response* primitive with the appropriate parameter to show acceptance or refusal. This action results in the remote session entity sending either an *ACCEPT* or a *REFUSE* SPDU back to the originating machine, as shown in Fig. 7-17.

Like *S-CONNECT*, *S-RELEASE* also has two variations. When a user requests the end of a session, a *FINISH* SPDU is transmitted. The remote user can either accept the request to terminate or reject it, in which case the session continues. The choice is indicated by a parameter in the *S-RELEASE.response* primitive. If the user has decided to accept the request and end the session, the reply to *FINISH* is *DISCONNECT*. If, however, the offer is declined, the *NOT FINISHED* SPDU is sent back and the session continues as though nothing had happened.

The pattern of SPDU usage for *S-U-ABORT* differs from the normal pattern. Although there is no response possible for this primitive, the *ABORT* SPDU sent when the primitive is invoked is explicitly acknowledged by *ABORT ACCEPT* (shown in parentheses in Fig. 7-17 because it is not generated by the *response* primitive but by the session entity itself). The reason for having this acknowledgement is that it ensures that the transport connection is fully purged of SPDUs, thus allowing the transport connection to be reused immediately for another session. Provider-generated aborts also use the *ABORT* primitive, but these are not acknowledged.

The pattern for the data transfer primitives follows the normal pattern. Each requesting and each responding primitive causes an SPDU of the corresponding type to be sent. The token management, synchronization, and activity management primitives also work this way, except that for *S-CONTROL-GIVE* acknowledgements are generated by the remote session entity for compatibility with the CCITT teletex protocol. Exception reporting also follows the standard pattern.

Let us now briefly look at the formats of the PDUs used by the session protocol. The general format is shown in Fig. 7-18(a). The *SI* (*Session Identifier*) field consists of one byte that gives the SPDU type. Each of the SPDUs in Fig. 7-17 has a distinct type. The *LI* (*Length Identifier*) field is normally a value between 0 and 254 telling how many bytes of parameters follow. If there are more than 254 bytes of parameters, *LI* takes on the value of 255, and two additional bytes follow it immediately, giving the length (up to a maximum of 65,535 bytes). Following the parameters themselves come the user data, if any.

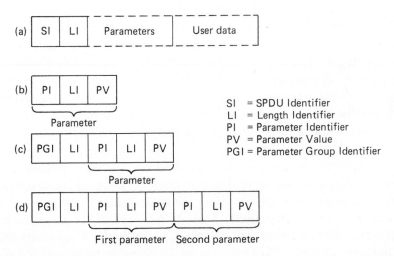

Fig. 7-18. (a) General format of an SPDU. (b) - (d) Examples of the parameters field.

Many session layer service primitives, and hence their SPDUs, carry parameters (e.g., called address or synchronization serial number). Several formats are provided for encoding these parameters. In the simplest form, shown in Fig. 7-18(b), there is a 1-byte *PI* (*Parameter Identifier*) field telling which parameter follows, a 1-byte *LI* (*Length Identifier*) field telling how long the parameter is, and a variable-length *PV* (*Parameter Value*) field containing the numerical value of the parameter.

More general formats are shown in Fig. 7-18(c) and Fig. 7-18(d). In these SPDUs, parameters can be collected into groups. Each group starts with a *PGI* (*Parameter Group Identifier*) followed by an *LI* field giving the length of the group. The individual parameters are described the same way as in Fig. 7-18(b). Although the figure only illustrates one and two parameter groups, larger groups are also allowed. The one-parameter group of Fig. 7-18(c) is no different than the basic form of Fig. 7-18(b). These two forms have been included for compatibility with the CCITT teletex protocol.

When the session entity has constructed an SPDU, it can give it to the transport layer as a message. However, in many cases, the session protocol also allows the session entity to pack several SPDUs together into a single message. This technique reduces the number of transport primitives that must be invoked. It is called **concatenation**. The inverse process (unpacking an incoming message into multiple SPDUs), done by the remote session entity, is called **segmentation**. Note that the transport layer is completely unaware of concatenation and segmentation done by the session entity. Both concatenation and segmentation can be done in other layers as well.

It is not permitted to concatenate an arbitrary SPDU with another arbitrary SPDU. There are bizarre rules for concatenation. The SPDUs are divided into three categories: those that may not be concatenated, those that must be concatenated, and those that may or may not be, at the session entity's discretion. If an SPDU that must be concatenated has to be sent and there is no other SPDU to concatenate it with, the session entity can always generate a *GIVE TOKENS* SPDU and set the parameter to request none of the tokens, effectively creating a null SPDU. Another peculiar aspect of concatenation is an additional set of rules telling the order in which the SPDUs may be glued together, and a third set of rules specifying the order in which the SPDUs must be processed at the other end after they have been segmented. All of these difficulties can be traced to the desire for compatibility with teletex.

Although the OSI session protocol standard (ISO 8327) does not tell how to implement the session protocol in detail, it does describe its basic operation as a large finite state machine called the **SPM (Session Protocol Machine)**. The SPM has 75 events that can trigger actions. Most of these events represent the invocation of a session primitive or the arrival of an SPDU, but timer expirations also play a role. At any instant, the SPM is in one of 29 possible states, so the finite state machine consists of a matrix with 29 columns and 75 rows. Fortunately, most of the 2175 entries are invalid.

Each valid entry may contain one or more of 72 different predicates (e.g., if the data token is currently held, then take one action, otherwise take a different action). There are 72 actions listed. Most of these cause some indication to happen or send some SPDU. After each action, the SPM can move to a new state. All in all, a full implementation of the session protocol is conceptually straightforward, but there is a lot of detail.

7.3.2. The Session Layer in the ARPANET

The ARPANET does not have a session layer or anything resembling it. It is up to individual applications to manage their sessions, if need be. On the other hand, a considerable amount of the work on RPC has gone on within the ARPA Internet community, especially at Xerox PARC and Carnegie-Mellon University.

7.3.3. The Session Layer in MAP and TOP

MAP and TOP use a restricted form of the OSI session layer. Session establishment, data transfer, and session release are fully supported for full-duplex mode. Half-duplex mode is not supported. The synchronization service, activity management, exception reporting, typed data, and capability data services are not required. This subset corresponds roughly to the (now-defunct) basic synchronized subset, with the omission of half-duplex mode and typed data.

The MAP/TOP session protocols are subsets of the full OSI session protocols. Those SPDUs needed to implement the MAP/TOP subset must be implemented. The others are optional.

7.3.4. The Session Layer in USENET

Like the ARPANET, USENET does not have a session layer. Unlike the ARPANET, it is not even possible for higher layers to implement the session services themselves. None of the session services are needed at all.

7.4. SUMMARY

The session layer is the first layer we have seen so far that is not concerned with raw communication. Its job is to add value to the reliable communication facility provided by the transport layer. One service that it offers is dialog management—keeping track of whose turn it is to talk on a half-duplex connection. Another service is synchronization, to allow roll back and recovery from noncommunication errors that have been detected by the upper layers. A third service is activity management, which allows logical units of work to be marked as such for quarantining and other purposes. Several other minor services are also provided.

Remote procedure call can be viewed as a kind of connectionless session. In this model, when a client calls a remote procedure, the call is actually made to a local stub. This stub marshalls the parameters and transmits a request message to the server. When the message arrives, the parameters are unmarshalled and the server procedure is called. The result traces the same path in the reverse direction.

A key design issue in RPC systems is transparency, trying to make remote calls look like local ones. This goal is difficult to achieve. One the one hand, pointer parameters, **var** parameters, and function parameters are hard to implement properly. On the other, server and client crashes make it difficult to achieve a reasonable semantics. Various strategies are available for handling crashes, and they lead to slightly different semantics for RPC in each case. Orphans must also be dealt with.

PROBLEMS

1. List three similarities between a session and a transport connection and also three differences.

2. The session layer has four data streams. Could any of them be removed without any loss of functionality? If so, how? If not, why not?

3. Suppose that half-duplex mode is selected on a session. What should be done about people at terminals who try to type when it is not their turn?

4. Is there any way to achieve the effect of quarantining in MAP?

5. The session protocol does not provide for any piggybacking (e.g., MAJOR SYNC ACK is not a header bit, but a separate SPDU). Do you think this design is a serious inefficiency? Discuss.

6. In a large computer network, there are three identical compile servers, all of which can compile Pascal programs. How can the RPC model be adapted to handle this situation?

7. Parameter passing in RPC is easiest if all the computers are identical. Imagine, however, that RPC is being used among machines whose binary representations for integers, floating point numbers, and characters are all different. Suggest two strategies for handling this problem and discuss their strengths and weaknesses.

8. Suppose RPC runs on top of a LAN that can lose packets, but none of whose clients and servers ever crash. What problems can still arise? (*Hint:* think about nonidempotent operations)

9. An RPC might take a long time to complete. If it takes too long, the client may time out and retransmit the request, leading to a variety of complicated situations. Can you think of anything that can be done to reduce the problem of executing long operations?

10. Implement a simple RPC system for carrying out a limited number of remote procedures. Write the stub routines by hand and test your system.

8

THE PRESENTATION LAYER

The presentation layer has evolved considerably since the start of the OSI work. For a long time, it was a layer in search of a function. At one point in the past it was mainly conceived of as the place where conversions could be done to allow ASCII machines to talk to EBCDIC machines. Somewhat later, it was seen as a way to permit visually-oriented programs, like full-screen editors, to work with a variety of terminals. Finally, it was decided to let the presentation layer handle all the problems relating to the representation of transmitted data, including conversion, encryption, and compression. As a result of this evolution, the term "presentation layer" has become something of a misnomer. "Representation layer" would be better now.

Unlike the lower five layers, which merely deal with the orderly movement of bits from source to destination, the presentation layer is concerned with preserving the *meaning* of the information transported. Each computer may have its own way of representing data internally, so agreements and conversions are needed to ensure that different computers can understand each other. These data often take the form of complex data structures. It is the job of the presentation layer to encode structured data from the internal format used on the sending machine to a bit stream suitable for transmission, and then to decode it to the required representation at the destination. How structured data are described in a machine-independent way, and how they are represented "on the wire" (i.e., in between machines), are the subjects of this chapter.

8.1. PRESENTATION LAYER DESIGN ISSUES

The presentation layer has four primary functions:

1. Giving users a way to execute the session service primitives.

2. Providing a way to specify complex data structures.

3. Managing the set of data structures currently required.

4. Converting data between internal and external form.

The first item is straightforward, and needs little explanation. The other three are closely related and have to do with how data structures are described, used, and encoded for transmission. In this section we will give a brief overview of data representation and encoding (compression and encryption). Later in the chapter we will look at each of these topics in considerable detail.

8.1.1. Data Representation

It is a fact of life that different computers have different internal representations for data. All the large IBM mainframes use EBCDIC as the character code, whereas practically all other computers use ASCII. Most microcomputers use two's complement arithmetic on 16- or 32-bit integers, but the CDC Cybers use 60-bit one's complement. The Intel 80286 and 80386 chips number their bytes from right to left, whereas the Motorola 68020 and 68030 chips number theirs from left to right. Since manufacturers rarely change these conventions (to avoid having their new products be incompatible with their old ones), it is unlikely that any universal standards for internal data representation will ever be adopted.

To see the consequence of these different internal formats, consider a one's complement machine that establishes a session with a two's complement machine and then transmits an array of 16-bit integers over it, bit for bit. Due to the differences in representation, even if all the data are received without error, if both machines print the array, they may well have different values. For example, the bit pattern FFF0 (hexadecimal) will print as −15 on the one's complement machine and −16 on the two's complement machine.

To solve this problem, a conversion will have to be made somewhere. However, between two machines using the same integer representation no conversion will be needed (at least not for integers, although their floating point formats might well differ). With structured data, such as records in Pascal, the situation is even more complicated, since some fields may have to be converted and others not.

It is perhaps ironic to realize that layers 1 through 5 have gone to an enormous amount of trouble to make sure that all messages are accurately transmitted bit for bit from sender to receiver, only to discover in layer 6 that for many applications, transmitting exact copies of the data is completely wrong. What one wants is that the meaning is preserved, not the bit pattern. When the number −15 is sent, the number −15 should arrive, even if the representation at the bit level is different.

Many ways have been proposed to deal with this problem. The sender could do the conversion; the receiver could do the conversion; or both could convert to and from a network standard format. In this chapter we will discuss a very general and elaborate scheme for encoding, decoding, and generally representing complex data structures. All of these issues are central to the operation of the presentation layer.

8.1.2. Data Compression

The organizations that operate computer networks frequently expect to be paid for their efforts. In nearly all cases, the cost of using a network depends on the amount of data sent. The cost is not strictly linear because there are usually fixed monthly subscription charges and fixed charges for setting up each connection, both of which are independent of the traffic volume. Still, it is clear the more bytes sent, the more it costs, so the final bill can often be reduced by compressing the data before sending them.

Data compression is closely related to data representation. One way to transmit a 32-bit integer is to simply encode it as four bytes in some representation and send it on its way. However, if it is known that 95 percent of the integers transmitted are between 0 and 250, it may be better to transmit these integers in a single unsigned byte, and to use the code 255 to signify that a true 32-bit integer follows. While it is true that once in a while five bytes will be needed instead of four, the gain from being able to use one byte most of the time more than offsets this loss.

Data compression has been studied in many contexts for years. It is widely used to save space in memory, on disk, and on magnetic tape. In this chapter we will look at some of the methods that are applicable to data representation in the presentation layer.

8.1.3. Network Security and Privacy

Back in the early days when corporations and universities had a single computer center, achieving security was easy. All the organization had to do was station a guard at the door to the computer room. The guard made sure that no one removed any tapes, disks, or cards from the room unless explicitly authorized to do so.

With the advent of networking, the situation has changed radically. No one can manually police the millions of bits of data that daily move between the computers in a network. Moreover, organizations have no way of being sure that their data are not secretly copied by wiretap or other means on the way to their proper destination. Wiretapping is far more common than most people realize (Kahn, 1980; Selfridge and Schwartz, 1980). Worst of all, when satellite links are being employed on the transmission path, the data are available to anyone who wishes to go to the trouble of erecting an antenna to listen. Clearly, some kind of **encryption** (also called **encipherment**) is needed to make the data unintelligible to all but their intended recipient.

Protecting data from prying eyes is not the only security issue in networking. One can imagine at least four security services:

1. Protecting data from being read by unauthorized persons.

2. Preventing unauthorized persons from inserting or deleting messages.

3. Verifying the sender of each message.

4. Making it possible for users to send signed documents electronically.

Encryption can be used to achieve all these goals.

The location of encryption in the OSI model has been so controversial that all mention of the subject was omitted from the initial standard. In theory, encryption can be done in any layer, but in practice three layers seem most suitable: physical, transport, and presentation (Branstad, 1987; Tardo, 1985; and Voydock and Kent, 1985).

When encryption is done in the physical layer, an encryption unit is inserted between each computer and the physical medium. Every bit leaving a computer is encrypted and every bit entering a computer is decrypted. This scheme is called **link encryption**. It is simple, but relatively inflexible.

The primary advantage of link encryption is that the headers as well as the data are encrypted. In some situations, knowledge of the traffic patterns (deducible from the source and destination addresses) is itself secret. For example, if during wartime, an enemy noticed that the amount of traffic to and from the Pentagon in Washington suddenly decreased dramatically, and the amount of traffic to and from East Podunk increased by the same amount, the enemy need not have an IQ of 200 to figure out that something strange is going on. The study of message length and frequency by an enemy is known as **traffic analysis**. It can be made more difficult by the insertion of a large amount of dummy traffic.

For most commercial applications, traffic analysis is not an issue, so end-to-end encryption done in one of the upper layers is the preferred solution. Putting it in the transport layer causes the entire session to be encrypted. A more sophisticated approach is to put it in the presentation layer, so that only those data structures or fields requiring encryption must suffer the overhead of it.

In this chapter we will cover a number of cryptographic methods, dating from the time of Julius Caesar to the present time. We will look at some other closely related topics, such as authentication and several ways for electonic messages to carry unforgeable signatures, similar, or perhaps even superior, to handwritten signatures.

8.1.4. The OSI Presentation Service Primitives

The relation of the presentation layer to its neighbors is analogous to those of Fig. 6-1 and Fig. 7-1 so that another figure is unnecessary. Furthermore, for the most part, the OSI service primitives in the presentation layer are identical to those in the session layer. Users (i.e., application entities) can establish sessions with *P-CONNECT.request*, which simply causes the presentation entity to issue an *S-CONNECT.request*. In effect, nearly all the presentation service primitives are just passed through to the session layer. These primitives are shown in Fig. 8-1.

The last three lines of Fig. 8-1(a) show primitives that originate in the presentation layer and are not just passed on to the session layer. Their function is to allow users to include whatever complex data structures are needed for the application at hand. The data structures needed by an application can be collected into groups, called **contexts**. During the first half of a session, one group might be needed, but during the second half a different group might be needed. The context management services allow the users to change the context.

It is up to the presentation layer to manage the negotiation process by which the users agree which data structures go in which context. The standard negotiation procedure is that one user process gives a list of the data structure libraries that it wants to use. The other party can accept or reject these. At any time, either side can alter the context by proposing to add or delete libraries from the current context.

The presentation layer can (optionally) maintain multiple contexts, to make it easy to switch context repeatedly in mid session. In particular, if the activity or synchronization features of the session layer have been enabled, it is possible to have the presentation layer reset the presentation context whenever an activity is resumed or a resynchronization is done. For example, if a file transfer activity is suspended to allow an interactive query to be made, the presentation layer can remember the file transfer context and restore it when the file transfer activity is resumed. The primitives listed at the end of Fig. 8-1(a) provide these services.

8.2. ABSTRACT SYNTAX NOTATION 1 (ASN.1)

The key to the whole problem of representing, encoding, transmitting, and decoding data structures is to have a way of describing the data structures that is flexible enough to be useful in a wide variety of applications, yet standard enough that everyone can agree on what it means. As part of the OSI development work, ISO has devised just such a notation. It is called **abstract syntax notation 1** or **ASN.1** for short. The suffix "1" indicates that it is the first one standardized, but that additional standards may appear in the future. The ASN.1 notation is described in International Standard 8824. The rules for encoding ASN.1 data structures to a bit stream for transmission are given in International Standard 8825. The format of the bit stream is called the **transfer syntax**. The following three sections will deal

OSI Presentation primitive	Request	Indication	Response	Confirm	Meaning
P–CONNECT	X	X	X	X	Establish a presentation connection
P–RELEASE	X	X	X	X	Graceful termination
P–U–ABORT	X	X			User initiated abrupt release
P–P–ABORT		X			Provider initiated abrupt release
P–DATA	X	X			Normal data transfer
P–EXPEDITED–DATA	X	X			Expedited data transfer
P–TYPED–DATA	X	X			Out–of–band data transfer
P–CAPABILITY–DATA	X	X	X	X	Control information data transfer
P–TOKEN–GIVE	X	X			Give a token to the peer
P–TOKEN–PLEASE	X	X			Request a token from the peer
P–CONTROL–GIVE	X	X			Give all the tokens to the peer
P–SYNC–MAJOR	X	X	X	X	Insert a major sync point
P–SYNC–MINOR	X	X	X	X	Insert a minor sync point
P–RESYNCHRONIZE	X	X	X	X	Go back to a previous sync point
P–ACTIVITY–START	X	X			Start an activity
P–ACTIVITY–END	X	X	X	X	End an activity
P–ACTIVITY–DISCARD	X	X	X	X	Abandon an activity
P–ACTIVITY–INTERRUPT	X	X	X	X	Suspend an activity
P–ACTIVITY–RESUME	X	X			Restart a suspended activity
P–U–EXCEPTION–REPORT	X	X			Report of a user exception
P–P–EXCEPTION–REPORT		X			Report of a provider exception
P–ALTER–CONTEXT	X	X	X	X	Change the context

(a)

	Request	Indication	Response	Confirm	
P–UNITDATA	X	X			Connectionless data transfer

(b)

Fig. 8-1. (a) The connection-oriented presentation service primitives. (b) The connectionless presentation service primitives.

with the general issues of representing data, the ASN.1 abstract syntax, and the transfer syntax, respectively.

8.2.1. Data Structures

As we have already mentioned, many applications exchange complex data structures. A record or structure used to transfer money in a banking application might contain the names, addresses, and branch numbers of the debiting and crediting banks, the account numbers, the amount of money, the currencies and exchange rates being used, the date and time at which the transaction is to take effect, and various other fields.

For other applications it might be necessary to maintain and exchange a large number of different kinds of data structures. Consider, for example, the computer system used by an airline. There are data structures needed for making, changing, and canceling reservations, others for scheduling aircraft, pilots, and cabin crews, and still others for keeping track of plane inspections, maintenance, and spare parts.

In general, each application has some collection of data structures that are relevant to its operation and which must be transmitted over the network. Some of these data structures are used in a great variety of applications (e.g., data structures for file transfer), while others are only used by a specific company or industry.

We have seen some of these data structures in previous chapters. In many places we have looked at figures representing frames, packets, or other kinds of PDUs. A *CALL REQUEST* packet, for example, can be regarded as a data structure with fields for the packet type, calling and called addresses and other parameters. Up until now we have sketched these PDUs with simple pen-and-ink drawings, but as we move towards the application layer, this graphical representation becomes less satisfactory. The application layer contains many different applications, each with a variety of complex structures that are transmitted as **APDUs** (**Application Protocol Data Units**). The fields of these APDUs often have a type (e.g., Boolean or integer) and in many cases fields can be omitted or have default values. The situation has become more complex, so a more formal method for describing data structures is required. This is where ASN.1 comes in.

The basic idea is to define all the data structure types (i.e., data types) needed by each application in ASN.1 and package them together in a **module** (library). When an application wants to transmit a data structure (i.e., an APDU), it can pass the data structure to the presentation layer, along with the ASN.1 name of the data structure. Using the ASN.1 definition as a guide, the presentation layer then knows what the types and sizes of the fields are, and thus knows how to encode them for transmission.

At the other end of the connection, the receiving presentation layer looks at the ASN.1 identity of the data structure (encoded in the first byte or bytes), and thus knows how many bits belong to the first field, how many to the second, their types, and so on. Armed with this information, the presentation layer can do any necessary conversions from the external format used on the wire to the internal format used by the receiving computer. For example, if the agreed upon format for transferring integers is two's complement and the receiver uses one's complement, the presentation layer can convert all the integers to one's complement before passing the APDU to the user.

It is worth pointing out that although using the ASN.1 approach may seem natural, it is not the only possibility. Another one is to require every machine to be aware of the internal format used by every other machine in the network. When an application builds an APDU, it builds it in the form that the receiver expects it. With n different types of machines in the network, $n \times (n - 1)$ different conversion routines must be written, instead of just $2n$ for going to and from ASN.1.

On the other hand, each APDU has only be to converted once, instead of twice. Furthermore, if a one's complement machine is talking to another one's complement machine, they can speak one's complement. In the ASN.1 scheme, conversions are needed on both ends because the ASN.1 transfer syntax specifies that two's complement must be used. The difference between these two approaches is illustrated in Fig. 8-2.

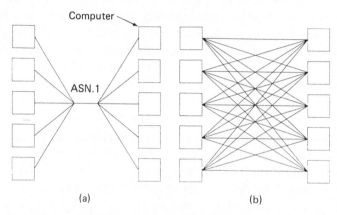

Fig. 8-2. (a) The sender converts to the ASN.1 transfer syntax for transmission and the receiver converts from ASN.1 to its internal format. (b) Each sender converts directly to the receiver's format.

The problems with one's versus two's complement and ASCII versus EBCDIC are not the only ones ASN.1 must solve. A much trickier one has to do with the byte ordering used by different computers. **Little endian** computers, such as the DEC VAX and Intel 8088/286/386, number their bytes with byte 0 being the low-order (i.e., rightmost) byte. **Big endian** computers, such as all the large IBM main-frames and the Motorola 68000/68020/68030, number theirs the other way, with byte 0 being the high-order (i.e., leftmost) byte. This terminology comes from Cohen's (1981) analogy with the politicians in *Gulliver's Travels* who fought wars over whether eggs should be broken at the little end or the big end.

As an example of how the byte ordering wreaks havoc with networking, consider an application in which museums wish to exchange information about their dinosaur collections. A sample data type definition is shown in Pascal in Fig. 8-3. The type contains the name as a string of up to 12 characters, the length of the dinosaur in meters, a Boolean telling whether or not it was carnivorous, the number of bones the museum has, and the year the bones were discovered.

Now let us consider what happens if a value of this type is transmitted from a 32-bit little endian machine (e.g., the Intel 386) to a 32-bit big endian machine (e.g., Motorola 68030). Fig. 8-4 shows the memory representation of our sample

```
type dinosaur = record
        name : array [1..12] of character;
        length : integer;
        carnivorous : boolean;
        bones : integer;
        discovery : integer
end;
```

Fig. 8-3. An example data type definition.

value in the little endian on the left. This record refers to a dinosaur called a stegosaurus, 10 meters long, not carnivorous, with 300 bones, discovered in 1877. The *name* field occupies bytes 0 through 11, with the last one being unused. Each of the three integers requires 2 bytes, at addresses 12, 20, and 24 respectively. For example, byte 20 is a 44 (decimal), byte 21 is a 1, and the 2 high-order bytes of the 32-bit word at address 20 are both 0. This is the correct representation for 300 as a 32-bit integer ($1 \times 256 + 44$).

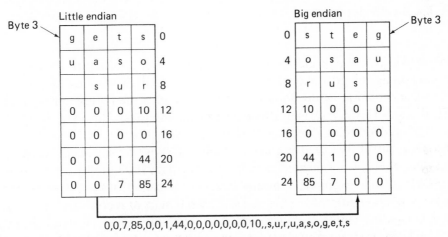

0,0,7,85,0,0,1,44,0,0,0,0,0,0,0,10,,s,u,r,u,a,s,o,g,e,t,s

Fig. 8-4. Transmission of a record from a little endian to a big endian.

If the bytes are transmitted in order, from byte 0 to byte 27, and then deposited in the big endian's memory byte for byte, in the order of arrival, we get the image shown in the right-hand part of Fig. 8-4. When the program tries to address the string at address 0, everything works fine because the computer expects the first character at address 0, the next one at address 1, and so on. However, when the program tries to address the *length* field at address 12, instead of finding the 10 in the low-order byte, it finds it in the high-order byte. Thus the *length* is not 10 meters, but 10×2^{24} or 167,772,160 meters. Even for a stegosaurus, that is pretty impressive. Although the Boolean field is unharmed by the byte reversal, the other two integers are also way above 100 million.

At first glance, it might appear possible to solve this problem by just inverting the order of each group of four incoming bytes. The presentation layer could even make this reversal automatically. The trouble is, we then end up with the memory image of Fig. 8-5. Here the integers and the Boolean are correct, but if the string is printed, it will appear as "getsuaso sur" instead of "stegosaurus" because the computer is expected to store strings in order, starting at the first byte.

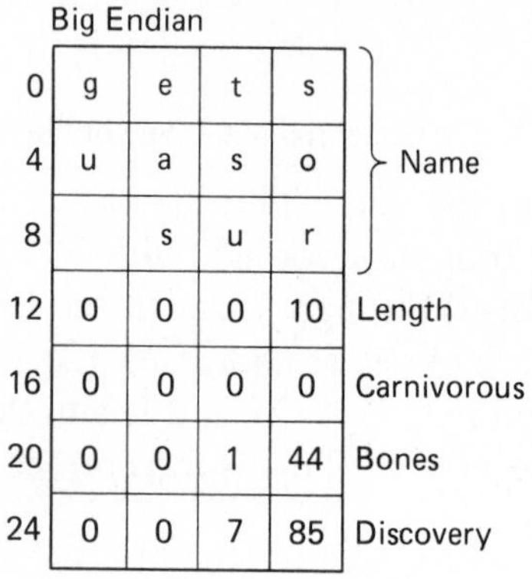

Big Endian

0	g	e	t	s
4	u	a	s	o
8		s	u	r
12	0	0	0	10
16	0	0	0	0
20	0	0	1	44
24	0	0	7	85

Name (rows 0–8), Length (12), Carnivorous (16), Bones (20), Discovery (24)

Fig. 8-5. The big endian of the previous figure with the bytes in each word reversed.

The reason that this brute force byte-swapping tactic failed, of course, is that words containing integers should be reversed but words containing strings should not be. The situation with Booleans has been deliberately left ambiguous. If FALSE is 0 and TRUE is 1, then Booleans are like integers. However, if FALSE is 0 and TRUE is everything else, then byte reversal is optional.

One way out of this bind is to have each data type be self-identifying on the wire. In Fig. 8-6(a) we represent each field in the data structure by a type, a length and a value. In this example, 1 means integer, 2 means Boolean, 3 is unused but might mean floating point, 4 means string, 5 means start of record, and so on. After the type comes the length in bytes, and then the value, using the convention that high-order bytes are transmitted before low-order bytes. Using this encoding, it is a simple matter for the receiver to know which words are to be reversed and which ones are not to be. Furthermore, even if the sender and receiver have different word lengths, it is possible for the presentation layer to figure out what the data mean and store them in memory properly. Figure 8-6(b) shows an optimized variant of Fig. 8-6(a), in which leading zeros and trailing spaces are omitted since they do not contain any information.

Although this example is simple, it illustrates the basic principle of ASN.1. Data types are defined in a language vaguely similar to Pascal. When an application wants to transmit a data structure (i.e., an APDU), it might pass pointers to two items to the presentation layer. The first one points to the formal definition of the data type in ASN.1, and the second one points to the APDU itself. Using this information, an encoding routine outputs an optimized, self-identifying byte stream, as

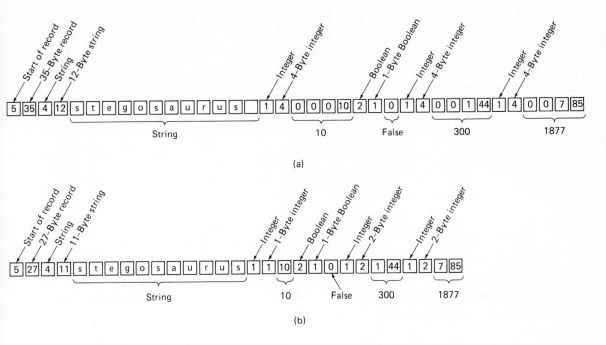

Fig. 8-6. (a) The dinosaur data structure using type, length, value encoding. (b) An optimized form of (a).

in Fig. 8-6(b). At the receiving end, a semantically equivalent data structure is constructed and passed to the application layer.

8.2.2. Abstract Syntax

In this section we will look more closely at the ASN.1 notation used for defining data types. It is worth pointing out that ISO originally conceived of these definitions as being intended exclusively for human readers. In several places, key information (e.g., array bounds) cannot be specified in the notation itself. The standard simply tells the ASN.1 programmer to provide the extra information in a comment.

Now that compilers have been written to translate ASN.1 definitions into C, Pascal, and other languages, ISO is busy modifying the standards to make them more precise and suitable for machine processing. In any event, our discussion will just give an overview of the official, published standard and will ignore all the bug fixes (more formally called **addenda**). We make no pretense of covering every nook and cranny; just the main features of ASN.1 will be discussed here.

As we mentioned earlier, the ASN.1 description of a data type is called its abstract syntax (because no specific representation is implied). The definition of *dinosaur* in Fig. 8-3 is like an abstract syntax, only it is given in Pascal instead of

ASN.1. To give a preview of ASN.1, Fig. 8-7 gives the abstract syntax for the same data type in ASN.1. Very briefly, an ASN.1 SEQUENCE is like a Pascal record. An **OCTET** is OSI jargon for what everyone else in the computer business calls a byte. An OCTET STRING is a list of octets (i.e., a byte array). The size of the array is given in the comment, following the two hyphens.

```
Dinosaur :: = SEQUENCE      {
        name          OCTET STRING, --12 characters
        length        INTEGER,
        carnivorous   BOOLEAN,
        bones         INTEGER
        discovery     INTEGER

}
```

Fig. 8-7. The ASN.1 equivalent of Fig. 8-3.

The ASN.1 primitive types are listed in Fig. 8-8. These types are built into the language and form the building blocks for more complex types. The names of these types are reserved words, and, like all ASN.1 reserved words, are always written in upper case letters.

Primitive type	Meaning
INTEGER	Arbitrary length integer
BOOLEAN	TRUE or FALSE
BIT STRING	List of 0 or more bits
OCTET STRING	List of 0 or more bytes
ANY	Union of all types
NULL	No type at all
OBJECT IDENTIFIER	Object name (e.g., a library)

Fig. 8-8. The ASN.1 primitive types.

Integers are cardinal numbers used for counting. They do not have any specific maximum size; arbitrarily large numbers are valid. There is only one value for zero (i.e., there is no -0 as in one's complement). As a side effect of defining an INTEGER type, it is possible to define names to correspond to specific values, for example, sunday = 1, monday = 2, and so on. This feature is similar to enumerated types in Pascal.

Booleans are used to tell if certain conditions hold. A Boolean can take on one of two values: TRUE or FALSE.

Bit strings are ordered lists of bits. Each bit string has 0 or more bits, with no maximum. The length of a bit string need not be a multiple of eight or any other number. A value of type BIT STRING is written between single quotes, followed by the letter B (binary) or H (hexadecimal), for example, '01001101'B or '4D'H. To avoid ambiguity, the hexadecimal notation should only be used for bit strings that are multiples of 8 bits.

Octet strings are ordered lists of bytes. They can be used to represent characters or any other byte-oriented data for which no other type seems appropriate. Like bit strings, octet strings have no inherent maximum lengths. The binary or hexadecimal notation given above is also used to express values of these strings.

The type ANY is special. If a field of a record is declared of type ANY, it can later be filled in by any valid type. ANY is essentially the union of all types.

NULL is the complement of ANY, no type at all. This type only has one value, also called NULL. When a field of a record is assigned the value NULL, it has no value. If that record is subsequently transmitted, the null fields do not have to be sent. How NULL is represented internally is implementation dependent. On a 16-bit two's complement computer, for example, it is conceivable that the value -32768 could be used to represent NULL, since it is somewhat peculiar, having no positive counterpart.

The final type in our list is the OBJECT IDENTIFIER. When a session is established, the presentation layer manages a negotiation to make sure that both sides agree on which abstract syntaxes, encoding rules, and protocols are to be used by the applications. All of these things are objects (essentially libraries), and are named by object identifiers. Object identifiers generally consist of multiple words enclosed by braces, as in {iso standard 8571 part 4 ftam-pci(1)}, which identifies an object defined in part 4 of ISO 8571.

The primitive types can be combined to build more complex types. Fig. 8-9 shows the five principal constructors used in ASN.1 for this purpose. The first of these is the SEQUENCE, which, as we saw in Fig. 8-7, is used to combine a collection of other types to form a type analogous to a record in Pascal. The fields of a SEQUENCE may be any types, including constructed types.

Constructor	Meaning
SEQUENCE	Ordered list of various types
SEQUENCE OF	Ordered list of a single type, like an array
SET	Unordered collection of various types
SET OF	Unordered collection of a single type
CHOICE	Any one type taken from a given list

Fig. 8-9. The principal ASN.1 constructors.

The SEQUENCE OF constructor is for building arrays of a single type. It is possible to have SEQUENCE OF INTEGER or of any other type, including constructed types (e.g., to make an array of records). The SEQUENCE OF types do not have bounds. While knowing the size of an array in advance is not important for data transmission (it can always be terminated by some special marker), it is obviously very important for storage allocation within a computer. While this particular bug is fixed by an addendum, it would have been nicer if the committee had gotten it right the first time.

The SET type is similar to the SEQUENCE type, except that the order of the components is not guaranteed to be the same when deposited in the receiver's memory as it was in the sender's. Since most people programming in high-level languages do not care about the actual memory layout of their data structures, this advantage may seem marginal, at best. However, declaring a data type as a SET gives the presentation layer some additional flexibility. Consider for example, an ASN.1 type containing a large chunk of user data followed by a field telling how much of the data field is currently in use. If the type is declared as a SEQUENCE, the data must be sent first, even though the receiver does not know how much buffer space to allocate. With a SET, the presentation layer has the option of sending the size first.

The SET OF type is a collection of elements of a single type, like a SEQUENCE OF type. In a SET OF type, like a SET type, the elements have no inherent ordering.

The CHOICE type is used when a data structure can hold any one of several different types. Figure 8-10 shows an example of some data types that might be used in a simple remote job entry application. To use this protocol, the user might create an instance of type *Job*, fill in the fields, and then send it. As can be seen from the definition, a *Job* consists of an *Account-PDU*, followed by any number of *Local-commands* and *Remote-commands* followed by a single *Termination-PDU*. The complete abstract syntax definition is not provided here. The last four lines define four types by extracting them from an (imaginary) module called *Joblib*.

```
Job ::= SEQUENCE   {

     header     Account—PDU,
     body       SEQUENCE OF Command—PDU,
     trailer    Termination—PDU

}

Command—PDU ::= CHOICE   {

     Local—command,
     Remote—command

}

Account—PDU   ::= Joblib. account
Local—command ::= Joblib. local
Remote—command ::= Joblib. remote
Termination—PDU ::= Joblib. termination
```

Fig. 8-10. Use of the CHOICE constructor.

In addition to the primitive types and the constructed types, the ASN.1 standard also discusses some predefined types that are useful in many applications. Eight different string types are defined. Each one is a different subset of OCTET STRING. The *NumericString* only includes the ten digits 0 through 9 and the space. The *PrintableString* includes the upper and lower case letters, the ten digits, space, and the 11 characters given here in quotes: "()'+-.,/:=?". Other string types are provided for the teletex character set, the videotex character set, various international versions of ASCII, and some graphics character sets. Other character sets, such as Kanji (Japanese characters), will be added in the future.

Another useful type is *GeneralizedTime*, based on ISO 3307. Using this format avoids endless discussion about whether 5/12 is the 5th of December or the 12th of May. An example value of *GeneralizedTime* is 17760704210538.8, which represents 5 minutes, 38.8 seconds after 9 P.M. on the Fourth of July, 1776.

In practice, it is common for international standards to define complex data types many of whose fields are optional. For example, *CONNECT REQUEST* PDUs frequently have a large number of optional parameters. If these parameters are not used for a particular connection establishment, they need not be transmitted. To handle this situation, ASN.1 allows fields to be declared OPTIONAL. Alternatively, they can be declared DEFAULT, followed by the value to be used by the receiver if the field is not transmitted.

The existence of OPTIONAL and DEFAULT types potentially causes problems with identifying the data when they are received. Suppose that a SEQUENCE has ten fields, all of them of type INTEGER and all OPTIONAL. Now suppose that only three of them are transmitted. How does the receiver know which three they are?

This problem is solved by the concept of **tagging**. ASN.1 allows any data type or field to have a tag that identifies it. Four types of tags are allowed: UNIVERSAL, APPLICATION, PRIVATE, and context specific. Each tag consists of an integer, preceded by one of the reserved words UNIVERSAL, APPLICATION, PRIVATE, or no reserved word, in which case the tag is context specific. Tags are written in square brackets, like this: [APPLICATION 4].

The purpose of tagging is closely related to the encoding rules and the transfer syntax. Whenever an item is transmitted, its type, length, and value are normally sent, as we saw in Fig. 8-6. When a type or field is tagged, the tag is sent as well, to identify it. Most tags are encoded in a single byte, with the 2 high-order bits giving the tag type, and the 5 low-order bits giving the tag number. (The other bit is used to distinguish primitive from constructed types.)

To consider our previous example again, if a data type contains ten integers, all tagged with different values, and only three are transmitted, the receiver can tell which ones they are by looking at the tags. Furthermore, if the receiver can tell which item it is getting by looking at the tag, there is no need to send the type. ASN.1 provides a way to have the type information suppressed when tagged types or fields are sent. To suppress this information, the person writing the abstract syntax can add the reserved word IMPLICIT after the tag, as in [PRIVATE 7] IMPLICIT. If IMPLICIT is not included after a tag, both the tag and the type are sent, as a kind of run-time type checking.

Figure 8-11 shows our by now familiar example fully tagged and with an option and a default. Compared to Fig. 8-6, the encoding would be structurally the same, in terms of each item having a type, length, and value, but all six types would now be tags, the top level one being PRIVATE, and the rest being context specific.

```
Dinosaur ::= [PRIVATE 6] IMPLICIT SEQUENCE {
    name [0] IMPLICIT OCTET STRING, -- 12 characters
    length [1] IMPLICIT INTEGER,
    carnivorous [2] IMPLICIT BOOLEAN DEFAULT TRUE,
    bones [3] IMPLICIT INTEGER,
    discovery [4] IMPLICIT INTEGER OPTIONAL
}
```

Fig. 8-11. An example ASN.1 type using IMPLICIT, OPTIONAL, and DE-FAULT.

Four kinds of tags are possible, as mentioned above. The UNIVERSAL tag is reserved for the primitive types defined in the ASN.1 standard, as well as certain quasi-primitive types, such as the various string types discussed above.

The APPLICATION tag is used by many of the OSI application layer protocols to denote types used in those protocols, but it is not forbidden for users to employ it where there is no ambiguity. However, users are encouraged to use PRIVATE for their own types.

Finally, context specific tags are used where identification is needed to tell fields apart but where the scope of the tag is limited to the inside of some data type. In other words, it is permitted to have a tag of [0] in many data types, but only one type per module may be tagged [PRIVATE 0] or [APPLICATION 0].

ASN.1 not only provides a way to define types, but also a way to define values for these types. An example value for *Dinosaur* is given in Fig. 8-12.

```
{ "stegosaurus", 10, FALSE, 300, 1877 }
```

Fig. 8-12. An example value for the type *Dinosaur*.

The exact structure of an ASN.1 type can be determined by a context-free grammar. A grammar that generates most of the legal types is given in Fig. 8-13. This grammar is not complete, but it includes all the features discussed in this chapter for generating types (but not values).

In the grammar of Fig. 8-13, the terminal symbols are enclosed by quotation marks. Symbols not enclosed by quotation marks are nonterminals, each of which has a production rule that ultimately can be reduced to a (possibly infinite) set of sequences of terminal symbols. All production rules have the form

name ::= rule.

Alternatives within a rule are denoted by the | symbol. The distinguished symbol (starting symbol) of the grammar is *ModuleDefinition*. The grammar does not include the quasi-primitive types such as the teletex and videotex strings, since they are not really part of the basic language.

For people who do not like the syntax generated by Fig. 8-13, ISO has provided a macro mechanism to allow users to define their own notation. Since the macro

```
ModuleDefinition ::= Name "DEFINITIONS ::= BEGIN" ModuleBody "END"
ModuleBody ::= AssignmentList | Empty
AssignmentList ::= Assignment | Assignmentlist Assignment
Assignment ::= Name "::=" Type
Type ::= ExternalType | BuiltinType
ExternalType ::= Name "." Name
BuiltinType ::= PrimitiveType | ConstructedType | TaggedType
PrimitiveType ::= Integer | Boolean | BitStr | OctetStr | Any | Null | ObjId
ConstructedType ::= Sequence | SequenceOf | Set | SetOf | Choice
TaggedType ::= Tag Type | Tag "IMPLICIT" Type
Integer ::= "INTEGER" | "INTEGER" "{" NamedNumberList "}"
Boolean ::= "BOOLEAN"
BitStr ::= "BIT STRING" | "BIT STRING" "{" "NamedBitList" "}"
OctetStr ::= "OCTET STRING"
Any ::= "ANY"
Null ::= "NULL"
ObjId ::= OBJECT IDENTIFIER
Sequence ::= "SEQUENCE" "{" ElementListType "}" | "SEQUENCE {}"
SequenceOf ::= "SEQUENCE OF" Type | "SEQUENCE"
Set ::= "SET" "{" ElementListType "}" | "SET {}"
SetOf ::= "SET OF" Type | "SET"
Choice ::= "CHOICE" "{" AlternativeTypeList "}"
Tag ::= "[" Class UnsignedNumber "]"
Class ::= "UNIVERSAL" | "APPLICATION" | "PRIVATE" | Empty
NamedNumberList ::= NamedNumber | NamedNumberList "," NamedNumber
NamedNumber ::= Name "(" UnsignedNumber ")" | Name "(" "−"UnsignedNumber")"
NamedBitList ::= NamedBit | NamedBitList "," NamedBit
NamedBit ::= Name "(" UnsignedNumber ")"
ElementListType ::= ElementType | ElementTypeList "," ElementType
ElementType ::= NamedType | NamedType "OPTIONAL" | NamedType "DEFAULT" Value
NamedType ::= Name Type | Type
AlternativeTypeList ::= NamedType | AlternativeTypeList "," NamedType
UnsignedNumber ::= Digit | UnsignedNumber Digit
Digit ::= "0" | "1" | "2" | "3" | "4" | "5" | "6" | "7" | "8" | "9"
Empty ::=
```

Fig. 8-13. A grammar for generating most ASN.1 types. The nonterminals *Name* and *Value* are not defined above. A *Name* is an identifier made up of letters, digits, and hyphens and a *Value* is an ASN.1 value of the appropriate type.

mechanism is only syntactic sugar, that is, it does not add to the set of types that can ultimately be produced, we will not discuss it.

8.2.3. Transfer Syntax

The driving force behind ASN.1 is the need to be able to represent data structures in an unambiguous way on the wire. There are numerous strange rules associated with the abstract syntax (which we have spared the reader until now) related to this problem. For example, although IMPLICIT may generally be used to tag a type, it is forbidden to tag ANY or CHOICE types. Why? The reason is straightforward: without the explicit type information, the receiver cannot figure out what kind of value is being sent. Normally the type is uniquely determined by the tag, but not for ANY or CHOICE, so IMPLICIT had to be forbidden for them.

The guiding principle behind the ASN.1 transfer syntax is that each value transmitted, both primitive and constructed ones, potentially consists of four fields:

1. The identifier (type or tag).

2. The length of the data field, in bytes.

3. The data field.

4. The end-of-contents flag, if the data length is unknown.

The first three fields are always present. The last one is optional.

The first field identifies the item that follows. It, itself, has three subfields, as shown in Fig. 8-14. The high-order 2 bits identify the tag type and the next bit tells whether it is primitive (0) or not (1). The tag bits are 00, 01, 10, and 11, for UNIVERSAL, APPLICATION, context-specific, and PRIVATE, respectively. The remaining 5 bits can be used to encode the value of the tag if it is in the range 0 through 30. If the tag is 31 or more, the low-order 5 bits contain 11111, with the true value in the next byte or bytes.

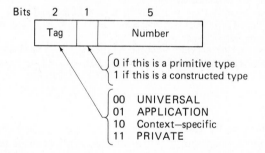

Fig. 8-14. The first byte of each data item sent in the ASN.1 transfer syntax.

The rule used to encode tags greater than 30 has been designed to handle arbitrarily large numbers. Each identifier byte following the first one contains 7 data bits. The high-order bit is set to 0 in all but the last one. Thus tag values up to 2^7-1 can be handled in 2 bytes, and up to $2^{14}-1$ can be handled in three bytes.

The encoding of the UNIVERSAL types is done according to the table of Fig. 8-15. We have seen most of these UNIVERSAL types before. Here is a brief summary of the ones not yet mentioned. The OBJECT DESCRIPTOR is a human readable string identifying an object (in contrast to an OBJECT IDENTIFIER, which is intended for consumption by machines). The EXTERNAL type allows one abstract syntax to refer to something from a different one, without having to textually include the other one. The various strings relate to different CCITT recommendations, no two of which use the same character set. And finally, two different ways to write the time are provided, for historical reasons.

Tag	Meaning
1	BOOLEAN
2	INTEGER
3	BIT STRING
4	OCTET STRING
5	NULL
6	OBJECT IDENTIFIER
7	OBJECT DESCRIPTOR
8	EXTERNAL
16	SEQUENCE and SEQUENCE OF
17	SET and SET OF
18	NumericString
19	PrintableString
20	TeletexString
21	VideotexString
22	IA5String
23	GeneralizedTime
24	UTCTime
25	GraphicString
27	GeneralString

Fig. 8-15. The tags used to encode UNIVERSAL types.

It is worth noting that SEQUENCE and SEQUENCE OF use the same UNIVERSAL type. Similarly, SET and SET OF also use the same type. In effect, some information is lost in the transfer syntax. This decision on the part of ISO does not appear to have any valid technical reason.

Following the identifier field comes one telling how many bytes the data occupy. The same scheme is used here as with tags longer than 30. In other words, lengths shorter than 128 bytes are directly encoded in one byte. Those that are longer use multiple bytes, with 7 data bits per byte and the high-order bit set to 1. For a multibyte number, the most significant 7 bits are transmitted first, then the next most significant 7 bits, and so on. Deep in its heart, ISO is big endian.

In some cases, data may be passed from the application layer to the presentation layer in small units. If the presentation entity has limited buffer space, it may be forced to start transmitting before it finds out how much data there are. To handle this situation, a length code of 128 is used to indicate that the data field is variable length. The data field is then terminated by a special end-of-contents flag.

The encoding of the data field depends on the type of data present. Integers are encoded in two's complement. A positive integer below 128 requires 1 byte, a positive integer below 32768 requires two bytes, and so forth. The most significant byte is transmitted first.

Booleans are encoded with FALSE as 0 and TRUE as any other value. The encoding of a Boolean is always 1 byte.

Bit strings are encoded as themselves. The only problem is how to indicate the length. The length field tells how many *bytes* the value has, not how many *bits*. The solution chosen is to transmit 1 byte before the actual bit string telling how many bits (0 through 7) of the final byte are unused. Thus the encoding of the 9-bit string '010011111' would be 07, 4F, 80 (hexadecimal).

Octet strings are easy. The bytes of the string are just transmitted in standard big endian style, left to right.

The null value is indicated by having a null contents field (zero bytes long). The fact that the length field is 0 indicates that a null value is being sent. No numerical value is actually transmitted.

The four sequence and set types are transmitted by first sending the type or tag for the sequence or set itself, then the total length of the encoding for all the fields, followed by the fields themselves. The fields of a sequence must be sent in order, but the fields of a set may be sent in any order. If any two or more fields of a set have the same type, they must be tagged so that the receiver can tell which is which.

The encoding of a CHOICE value is the same as the encoding of the actual data structure being transferred. If a particular CHOICE is between an INTEGER and a BOOLEAN, and the data structure at hand is an INTEGER, then the rules for INTEGER apply.

All the character strings are encoded with 1 character per byte, the same as OCTET STRINGs.

8.3. DATA COMPRESSION TECHNIQUES

The data sent over a channel can be viewed as a sequence of symbols, $S_1, S_2, \ldots, S_N$. These symbols are assumed to be drawn from some (possibly infinite) set of symbols. A few examples of such sets and some of their members are:

1. Set of bits: 0, 1.

2. Set of decimal digits: 0, 1, 2, 3, 4, 5, 6, 7, 8, 9.

3. Set of letters: A, B, C, . . . , X, Y, Z.

4. Set of English words: anserine, blebby, coypu, dibble, ennead, ...

5. Set of countries: Argentina, Belgium, China, Dahomey, Egypt, ...

Data compression can be approached in three general ways. Respectively, these three approaches are based on:

1. The finiteness of the set of symbols.

2. The relative frequencies with which the symbols are used.

3. The context in which a symbol appears.

Let us now consider each of these in turn.

8.3.1. Encoding a Finite Set of Equally Likely Symbols

In many applications the messages are drawn from a finite set and expressed in ASCII. In a library automation project, for example, the titles in the library's collection might be usefully regarded as a (finite) set of symbols. Suppose that each day a complete list of books requested were sent to each branch library, so each would know which books were most in demand and where. The daily transmission might consist of the branch number, followed by the list of all titles requested at that branch that day.

A typical book has about 20 characters in its title. Expressed in ASCII, such a book title requires 140 bits. Yet no library in the world has anywhere near 2^{140} titles. (The Library of Congress has about 2^{26} titles.) By simply giving each book a sequence number, it is possible to reduce the number of bits needed per title from 140 to 26 or fewer. However, the receiver must have the numbered book list, although this need only be sent once and can be transmitted by mailing a magnetic tape.

In cases where an occasional reference is made to an item not in the numbered list, the name can be spelled out in full, using an escape convention. Using the above example again, book number 0 could mean that an ASCII title follows, de%limited by an ASCII ETX character.

8.3.2. Frequency Dependent Coding

In virtually all text, some symbols occur more often than others. In English text the letter "E" occurs 100 times more often than the letter "Q," and the word "THE" occurs 10 times more often than the word "BE." This observation suggests an encoding scheme in which common symbols are assigned short codes and rare symbols are assigned long codes.

As an example, consider the plight of a brilliant but poor young biologist who has just cracked the genetic code of the wild Bactrian camel. She wants to send a telegram to her mother (as a birthday present) giving the sequence of bases (adenine, cytosine, guanine, and thymine) in the camel's DNA, but cannot afford to send 2 bits per base. Fortunately, she notices that the occurrence probabilities of the bases are 0.50, 0.30, 0.15, and 0.05 respectively. By encoding them as 0, 10, 110, and 111 (instead of 00, 01, 10, and 11), the average symbol now only requires 1.7 bits (instead of 2.0).

In light of the above example, it is interesting to ask what the minimum number of bits per symbol is. According to information theory, if symbol S_i occurs with a probability of P_i, then the information content of each symbol is

$$-\sum_{i=1}^{N} P_i \log_2 P_i$$

where N is the number of symbols. This quantity is often known as the **entropy per symbol**. For the (hypothetical) camel DNA example, the theoretical limit is 1.65 bits/symbol, so the proposed encoding is within 3%. As another example consider a uniform distribution: $P_i = 1/N$. Here the entropy per symbol is $\log_2 N$, as expected.

Unfortunately, there is no way to achieve the theoretical minimum encoding with independently coded symbols, because many of them require a fractional number of bits. However, an algorithm due to Huffman (1952) can be used to produce a reasonable approximation to the theoretical limit. The algorithm, now called **Huffman coding**, is as follows.

1. Write down all the symbols, together with the associated probability of each. As the algorithm proceeds, a binary tree will be built up, with these symbols as the terminal nodes. Initially, all nodes are unmarked.

2. Find the two smallest nodes and mark them. Add a new node, with arcs to each of the nodes just marked. Set the probability of the new node to the sum of the probabilities of the two nodes it is connected to.

3. Repeat step 2 until all nodes have been marked except one. The probability of the unmarked node will always be 1.0.

4. The encoding for each symbol can now be found by tracing the path from the unmarked symbol to that symbol, recording the sequence of left and right branches taken. The code is just the path, with left = 0 and right = 1 (or vice versa).

Huffman coding can also be done in radices other than 2. For example, by choosing the 256 smallest unmarked nodes at each step, and having 256 arcs radiate from each intermediate node, we get a code in which each symbol is an integral number of bytes.

We mentioned above that the theoretical minimum is impossible to achieve with independently coded symbols due to the need to represent each symbol in an integral number of bits. However, if we drop the requirement that each symbol be individually coded, we can improve on Huffman coding and come very close to the actual entropy per symbol. To restate the underlying idea of Huffman coding, what the algorithm does is determine a coding for each symbol, and then transmit the coded symbols independently, one after another. The code that we are now about to examine, called **arithmetic coding**, does not code the symbols independently, so it does not suffer from the problem of having to use 3 bits to represent 2.5 bits worth of information.

Arithmetic coding represents each symbol as a portion of the real number line between 0 and 1. Encoding a sequence of symbols ultimately results in selecting out a (typically very small) portion of the reals and transmitting a number in that portion. The operation of the algorithm can most easily be seen by repeating our camel example in which we want to encode four symbols, A, C, G, and T, whose probabilities are 0.50, 0.30, 0.15 and 0.05 respectively.

With this probability distribution, we use the interval 0.00 to 0.50 for A, the interval 0.50 to 0.80 for C, the interval 0.80 to 0.95 for G, and the interval 0.95 to 1.00 for T, as shown in Fig. 8-16(a). Let us encode the three symbol string CAT. The first symbol is C, so we narrow our range to the interval 0.50 to 0.80. As the algorithm progresses, we will steadily narrow this interval more and more, requiring more and more bits to give the necessary accuracy.

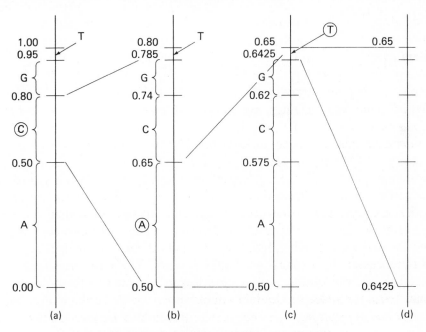

Fig. 8-16. Coding CAT using arithmetic encoding.

The next symbol to encode is A, so we take the next interval as the A portion of Fig. 8-16(b) and get the interval 0.50 to 0.65. If we expand this to unit length as in Fig. 8-16(c) and select the T part from it, we get the interval 0.6425 to 0.6500. If there were more symbols, they would further subdivide the interval again, as shown in Fig. 8-16(d). The encoded result that we transmit is any value in the final range, for example, 0.645.

When the receiver gets this value, it immediately sees that it lies between 0.50 and 0.80, so it knows that the first symbol must be a C. Then it constructs the interval 0.50 to 0.80, just as the sender did, and sees that 0.645 lies between 0.50 and 0.65, meaning that the second symbol must be an A. In this manner, the receiver decodes the message symbol by symbol.

In our example, we did the arithmetic in decimal instead of binary, and ignored the problem of detecting the end of the message, and similar issues, but these can all be handled in a straightforward way. Witten et al. (1987) show how these details can be managed, and give programs to actually do the encoding and decoding. Related work on compression is described in (Bentley et al., 1986).

8.3.3. Context Dependent Encoding

The method above implicitly assumes that the probability of a symbol occurring is independent of its immediate predecessor. To put it more bluntly, it assumes that the probability of a "T" directly following a "Q" is almost four times higher than the probability of a "U" following the "Q." A more sophisticated scheme would determine the conditional probability of each symbol for each possible predecessor. For letters as symbols, this comes down to having 26 tables, one for the frequency distribution following an "A," one for the frequency distribution following a "B," and so on. If there are strong correlations between symbols and their successors, this method yields large savings, even if the symbols themselves have a flat distribution.

The disadvantage of this conditional probability method is the large number of tables required. If there are k symbols, the tables will have k^2 entries. Instead, a variation on the old 5-bit Baudot telegraph code can be used. In our variation there are four cases: uppercase, lowercase, numeric + special, and control. In each case, four codes are allocated to the case shifts, and 28 are allocated to the symbols, allowing for $4 \times 28 = 112$ symbols. (Probably space and newline should be included in each case, leaving 104 distinct symbols, plus space and newline.) To shift between cases, an explicit symbol is needed. The basic assumption behind this model is that the symbol following a lowercase letter is likely to be another lowercase letter (or space or newline), and that the symbol following a number is likely to be another number. The advantage of Baudot code over Huffman code is that all symbols are the same length, making encoding and decoding by table lookup easy to do. Baudot code is also more resilient in the presence of transmission errors.

A related method, **run length encoding**, can be used to encode long binary bit strings containing mostly zeros. Each k-bit symbol tells how many 0 bits occurred between consecutive 1 bits. To handle long zero runs, the symbol consisting of all

1 bits means that the true distance is $2^k - 1$ plus the value of the following symbol (or symbols). For example, the bit string

0001000001000000100000000000000010000001000100000001101 0100000101

consists of runs of length 3, 5, 6, 14, 6, 3, 7, 0, 1, 5, and 1. It would be encoded using 3-bit symbols as

011 101 110 111 111 000 110 011 111 000 000 001 101 001

for a saving of 34%.

Another context dependent compression method is to squash runs of repeated symbols into a count plus the symbol. Runs of blanks, linefeeds, and leading zeros are the most likely candidates here.

A variation of run length encoding can also be used to encode symbols other than 0s and 1s. For example, consider the digital transmission of color television. This signal can be thought of as a sequence of frames (25 or 30 per second), each containing a rectangular array of picture elements or **pixels**. One simple scheme might be to have an image of 1000 by 600 pixels with each pixel being a 16-bit number. Fifteen of these bits would encode the red, green and blue intensities, with 32 levels per color, and the last bit would distinguish data from control signals, such as horizontal and vertical retrace.

A straight encoding of this information would require 600,000 pixels per frame resulting in a data rate of 240 or 288 megabits/sec. With binary encoding, the Nyquist theorem tells us that a bandwidth of 480 MHz or 576 MHz is required. Since current analog televison only uses 6 MHz per channel, this digital scheme is not likely to find widespread acceptance in a world where the spectrum is already oversubscribed.

However, most frames are almost identical to their predecessors. This suggests that if each television could be equipped with a buffer holding one frame (1.2 Mbytes), it would only be necessary to transmit the differences between the current frame and the previous one. We could do the encoding of the 16-bit pixels as follows. Any pixel beginning with 0 would contain 15 data bits. Any pixel beginning with 10 would be a control signal, with the details specified in the remaining 14 bits. Finally, any pixel beginning with 11 would contain a number between 0 and 16383 telling how long a run of pixels to skip because they are identical to the pixels already in the frame buffer.

As the image came in, the television would maintain a pointer to the current pixel. Pixels beginning with 0 would just overwrite the current pixel and advance the pointer by one. Pixels beginning with 10 would set the pointer to a specific pixel such as the next scan line or the top of the screen. Finally, pixels beginning with 11 would advance the pointer by the indicated number of pixels. In practice, this scheme is somewhat naive, but the basic idea of having a frame buffer and skipping runs of unchanged pixels is solid.

8.4. CRYPTOGRAPHY

Cryptography has a long and colorful history. In this section we will just sketch some of the highlights, as background information for what follows. For a complete history, Kahn's (1967) book is still recommended reading. For a theoretical treatment, see Kranakis' (1986) book.

8.4.1. Traditional Cryptography

Historically, four groups of people have used and contributed to the art of cryptography: the military, the diplomatic corps, diarists, and lovers. Of these, the military has had the most important role and has shaped the field. Within military organizations, the messages to be encrypted have traditionally been given to poorly paid code clerks for encryption and transmission. The sheer volume of messages to be sent has prevented this work from being done by a few elite specialists.

Until the advent of computers, one of the main constraints on cryptography had been the ability of the code clerk to perform the necessary transformations, often on a battlefield with little equipment. An additional constraint has been the difficulty in switching over quickly from one cryptographic method to another one, since this entails retraining a large number of people. However, the danger of a code clerk being captured by the enemy has made it essential to be able to change the cryptographic method instantly, if need be. These conflicting requirements have given rise to the model of Fig. 8-17.

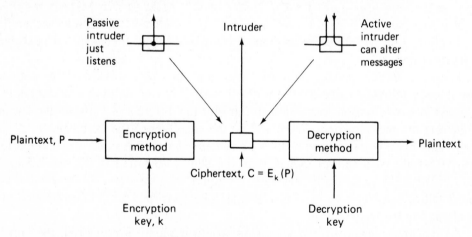

Fig. 8-17. The encryption model.

The messages to be encrypted, known as the **plaintext**, are transformed by a function that is parametrized by a **key**. The output of the encryption process, known as the **ciphertext** or **cryptogram**, is then transmitted, often by messenger or radio. We assume that the enemy, or **intruder**, hears and accurately copies down the complete ciphertext. However, unlike the intended recipient, he does not know what the key is and so cannot decrypt the ciphertext easily. Sometimes the intruder can not only listen to the communication channel (passive intruder), but can also record messages and play them back later, inject his own messages, or modify legitimate messages before they get to the receiver (active intruder). The art of breaking ciphers is called **cryptanalysis**. The art of devising ciphers (cryptography) and breaking them (cryptanalysis) is collectively known as **cryptology**.

A fundamental rule of cryptography is that one must assume that the cryptanalyst knows the general method of encryption used. In other words, the cryptanalyst knows how the encryption method of Fig. 8-17 works. The amount of effort necessary to invent, test, and install a new method every time the old method is compromised or thought to be compromised has always made it impractical to keep this secret, and thinking it is secret when it is not does more harm than good.

This is where the role of the key enters. The key consists of a (usually) short string of characters that selects one of many potential encryptions. In contrast to the general method, which may only be changed every few years, the key can be changed as often as required. Thus our basic model is a stable and publicly known general method parametrized by a secret and easily changed key.

From the cryptanalyst's point of view, the cryptanalysis problem has three variations. When he has a quantity of ciphertext and no plaintext, he is confronted with the **ciphertext only** problem. The cryptograms that appear in the puzzle section of newspapers pose this kind of problem. When he has some matched ciphertext and plaintext, the problem becomes known as the **known plaintext** problem. Finally, when the cryptanalyst has the ability to encrypt pieces of plaintext of his own choosing, we have the **chosen plaintext** problem. Newspaper cryptograms could be broken trivially if the cryptanalyst were allowed to ask such questions as: What is the encryption of ABCDE?

Novices in the cryptography business often assume that if a cipher can withstand a ciphertext only attack, it is secure. This assumption is very naive. In many cases the cryptanalyst can make a good guess at parts of the plaintext. For example, the first thing many time-sharing systems say when you call them up is "PLEASE LOGIN." Equipped with some matched plaintext-ciphertext pairs, the cryptanalyst's job becomes much easier. To achieve security, the cryptographer should be conservative and make sure that the system is unbreakable even if his opponent can encrypt arbitrary amounts of chosen plaintext.

Encryption methods have historically been divided into two categories: substitution ciphers (including codes) and transposition ciphers. We will now deal with each of these in turn, as background information for modern cryptography.

Substitution Ciphers

In a **substitution cipher** each letter or group of letters is replaced by another letter or group of letters to disguise it. The oldest cipher known is the **Caesar cipher**, attributed to Julius Caesar. In this method, *a* becomes *D*, *b* becomes *E*, *c* becomes $F, \ldots$, and z becomes C. For example, *attack* becomes *DWWDFN*. In examples, plaintext will be given in lowercase letters, and ciphertext in uppercase letters. In running text both will be in *italics*.

A slight generalization of the Caesar cipher allows the ciphertext alphabet to be shifted by k letters, instead of always 3. In this case k becomes a key to the general method of circularly shifted alphabets. The Caesar cipher may have fooled the Carthaginians, but it has not fooled anyone since.

The next improvement is to have each of the symbols in the plaintext, say the 26 letters for simplicity, map onto some other letter. For example,

> plaintext: a b c d e f g h i j k l m n o p q r s t u v w x y z
> ciphertext: Q W E R T Y U I O P A S D F G H J K L Z X C V B N M

This general system is called a **monoalphabetic substitution**, with the key being the 26-letter string corresponding to the full alphabet. For the key above, *attack* would be encrypted as *QZZQEA*.

At first glance this might seem a safe system because although the cryptanalyst knows the general system (letter for letter substitution), he does not know which of the $26! = 4 \times 10^{26}$ possible keys is in use. In contrast with the Caesar cipher, trying all of them is not a promising approach. Even at 1 μsec per solution, a computer would take 10^{13} years to try all the keys.

Nevertheless, given a surprisingly small amount of ciphertext, the cipher can be broken easily. The basic attack takes advantage of the statistical properties of natural languages. In English, for example, e is the most common letter, followed by t, o, a, n, i, etc. The most common two letter combinations, or **digrams**, are: *th, in, er, re,* and *an*. The most common three letter combinations, or **trigrams**, are: *the, ing, and,* and *ion*. (See Fig. 8-18 for more statistics of English.)

A cryptanalyst trying to break a monoalphabetic cipher would start out by counting the relative frequencies of all letters in the ciphertext. Then he might tentatively assign the most common one to e and the next most common one to t. He would then look at trigrams to find a common one of the form tXe, which strongly suggests that X is h. Similarly, if the pattern $thYt$ occurs frequently, the Y probably stands for a. With this information, he can look for a frequently occurring trigram of the form aZW, which is most likely *and*. By making guesses at common letters, digrams, and trigrams, the cryptanalyst builds up a tentative plaintext, letter by letter.

Another approach is to guess a probable word or phrase. For example, consider the following ciphertext from an accounting firm (blocked into groups of five characters):

CTBMN BYCTC BTJDS QXBNS GSTJC BTSWX CTQTZ CQVUJ
QJSGS TJQZZ MNQJS VLNSX VSZJU JDSTS JQUUS JUBXJ
DSKSU JSNTK BGAQJ ZBGYQ TLCTZ BNYBN QJSW

Letters		Digrams		Trigrams		Words	
E	13.05	TH	3.16	THE	4.72	THE	6.42
T	9.02	IN	1.54	ING	1.42	OF	4.02
O	8.21	ER	1.33	AND	1.13	AND	3.15
A	7.81	RE	1.30	ION	1.00	TO	2.36
N	7.28	AN	1.08	ENT	0.98	A	2.09
I	6.77	HE	1.08	FOR	0.76	IN	1.77
R	6.64	AR	1.02	TIO	0.75	THAT	1.25
S	6.46	EN	1.02	ERE	0.69	IS	1.03
H	5.85	TI	1.02	HER	0.68	I	0.94
D	4.11	TE	0.98	ATE	0.66	IT	0.93
L	3.60	AT	0.88	VER	0.63	FOR	0.77
C	2.93	ON	0.84	TER	0.62	AS	0.76
F	2.88	HA	0.84	THA	0.62	WITH	0.76
U	2.77	OU	0.72	ATI	0.59	WAS	0.72
M	2.62	IT	0.71	HAT	0.55	HIS	0.71
P	2.15	ES	0.69	ERS	0.54	HE	0.71
Y	1.51	ST	0.68	HIS	0.52	BE	0.63
W	1.49	OR	0.68	RES	0.50	NOT	0.61
G	1.39	NT	0.67	ILL	0.47	BY	0.57
B	1.28	HI	0.66	ARE	0.46	BUT	0.56
V	1.00	EA	0.64	CON	0.45	HAVE	0.55
K	0.42	VE	0.64	NCE	0.45	YOU	0.55
X	0.30	CO	0.59	ALL	0.44	WHICH	0.53
J	0.23	DE	0.55	EVE	0.44	ARE	0.50
Q	0.14	RA	0.55	ITH	0.44	ON	0.47
Z	0.09	RO	0.55	TED	0.44	OR	0.45

Fig. 8-18. Percent occurrences of English letters, digrams, trigrams, and words.

A likely word in a message from an accounting firm is *financial*. Using our knowledge that *financial* has a repeated letter (*i*), with four other letters between their occurrences, we look for repeated letters in the ciphertext at this spacing. We find 12 hits, at positions 6, 15, 27, 31, 42, 48, 56, 66, 70, 71, 76, and 82. However, only two of these, 31 and 42, have the next letter (corresponding to *n* in the plaintext) repeated in the proper place. Of these two, only 31 also has the *a* correctly positioned, so we know that *financial* begins at position 30. From this point on, deducing the key is easy by using the frequency statistics for English text.

To make the cryptanalyst's job more difficult, it is necessary to smooth out the frequencies of the ciphertext, so the letters representing *e*, *t*, etc. do not stand out so clearly. One way of achieving this goal is to introduce multiple cipher alphabets, to be used in rotation, giving what is known as a **polyalphabetic cipher**. As an example, consider the **Vigenère cipher**. It consists of a square matrix containing 26 Caesar alphabets. The first row, called row A, is ABCDEFGH...XYZ. The next row, called row B, is BCDEFGHI...YZA. The last row, called row Z, is ZABCDEFG...WXY.

Like the monoalphabetic cipher, this cipher also has a key, but instead of being a string of 26 distinct characters, the key is usually a short, easy-to-remember word or phrase, such as COOKIEMONSTER. To encrypt a message, the key is written repeatedly above the plaintext, for example:

COOK I EMONS T ERCOOK I EMONS T ERCOOK I EMONS T ERCOOK I EMO
f o u r s c o r e a n d s e v e n y e a r s a g o o u r m o t h e r s b r o u g h t f o r t h

The key letter above each plaintext letter tells which row to use for encryption. The *f* is encrypted using the Caesar alphabet of row C, the *o* and *u* are encrypted using the Caesar alphabet of row O, and so on. It should be clear that a plaintext letter will be represented by different letters in the ciphertext, depending on the position in the plaintext. Similarly, trigrams such as *the* will map onto different trigrams in the ciphertext, depending on their position.

A more powerful polyalphabetic cipher can be constructed by using arbitrary monoalphabetic ciphers for the rows instead of restricting them to Caesar ciphers. The only problem with this scheme is that the 26×26 square table then becomes part of the key and must also be memorized or written down.

Although unquestionably much better than the monoalphabetic cipher, polyalphabetic ciphers can also be broken easily by a ciphertext only attack, provided that the cryptanalyst has a sufficient amount of ciphertext. The trick is to guess the key length. First the cryptanalyst tentatively assumes a key of length k. He then arranges the cipher text in rows, k letters per row. If his guess is correct, all the ciphertext letters in each column will have been encrypted by the same monoalphabetic cipher, in which case they should exhibit the same frequency distribution as normal English text: the most common letter 13%, the next most common letter 9%, etc. If this is obviously not the case, the tentative value for k is wrong, and another should be tried. Once a good fit has been obtained, each column can be attacked as a separate monoalphabetic cipher.

The next step up in complexity for the cryptographer is to use a key longer than the plaintext, making the above attack useless. In fact, constructing an unbreakable cipher is easy. First choose a random bit string as the key. Then convert the plaintext into a bit string, for example by using its ASCII representation. Finally, compute the EXCLUSIVE OR of these two strings, bit by bit. The resulting ciphertext cannot be broken, because every possible plaintext is an equally probable candidate. The ciphertext gives the cryptanalyst no information at all. In a sufficiently large sample of ciphertext, each letter will occur equally often, as will every digram and every trigram.

This method, known as the **one time key**, has a number of practical disadvantages, unfortunately. To start with, the key cannot be memorized, so both sender and receiver must carry a written copy with them. If either one is subject to capture, written keys are clearly undesirable. Additionally, the total amount of data that can be transmitted is limited by the amount of key available. If the spy strikes it rich and discovers a wealth of data, he may find himself unable to transmit it back to headquarters because the key has been used up. Another problem is the sensitivity of the method to lost messages, or messages that arrive in the wrong order. If the sender and receiver get out of synchronization as to where in the key they are, they are in trouble.

All of these problems can be overcome by simply having sender and receiver agree to start each message anew at the start of the key and to break up long messages into multiple messages. Now the key is no longer a one-time key and can be broken, albeit with difficulty. To break the system, the cryptanalyst must acquire a number of encrypted messages and lay them out on top of one another, as a series of rows. The first character of each row can be viewed as a column encrypted by a monoalphabetic cipher and can be attacked in the usual way. In fact, the one-time key is now conceptually the same as a polyalphabetic cipher, only with a longer key, and can be broken the same way.

One note is in order about generating one-time keys. They must be random to be secure. The worst possible way of generating a key is to use a pseudo random number generator based on a Markov chain. When these random numbers are used, not only is the rest of the key not independent of what has come before, it is uniquely determined by what has come before. Thus, if the cryptanalyst ever manages to acquire matched plaintext-ciphertext pairs, he will be able to deduce the key used for those pairs. From this key he may well be able to deduce the algorithm that produced it, and from the algorithm he will be able to generate the rest of the key. To generate a truly random key, the quantum noise in an electrical resistor should be amplified and digitized. The laws of quantum mechanics guarantee that the results will not be reproducible.

Substitution ciphers need not always work one letter (or bit) at a time. For example, **Porta's cipher** uses a 26×26 table, like the Vigenère cipher. The plaintext is encoded two characters at a time. The first character indicates a row, the second, a column. The number or letter pair found at the intersection is the encrypted value. If 26 different tables are prepared, trigrams can be encrypted as units by using the first letter of each trigram to select a table.

Codes

As the units encrypted become longer and longer, the cipher begins to resemble a **code**. The main difference between a cipher and a code is that the former encrypts a fixed-size unit of plaintext with each operation, whereas the latter encrypts a single variable-length linguistic unit, typically a single word or phrase. Prior to computers, codes came in two distinct flavors: one-part codes and two-part codes. In a one-part code, both the plaintext word and the code symbol are arranged in the same order. For example, the code symbols for *amnesia, amoeba,* *amok, among, amorous, amorphous, amortize* and *ampere* might be 16142, 16144, 16149, 16155, 16160, 16189, 16201, and 16209. In a two-part code these same words might be encoded as 15202, 16902, 40420, 30012, 80032, 76290, 39321, and 10344. With a one-part code, both encoding and decoding can use the same code book, whereas a two-part code requires differently arranged books for encoding and decoding. A one-part code is much easier to break than a two-part code, since the code symbol itself contains approximate information about where the plaintext symbol is in the book. However, a two-part code requires both sender and receiver to carry around twice as much baggage.

Breaking a code is like breaking a giant monoalphabetic cipher. The most common symbol in a code is usually the symbol for *stop*, used to end a sentence. Next come the symbols for *the, of, and, to, a, in,* and *that*. Knowledge of English sentence structure is also helpful for example, most sentences begin with a subject, and subjects are usually of the form ARTICLE ADJECTIVES NOUN.

Codes have the disadvantage of requiring large books, which cannot be replaced as easily as the key to a cipher. However, they have the advantage of generally being harder to break than ciphers. Codes and ciphers can be combined to make the cryptanalyst's life even less pleasant. For example, encoding a message might yield a list of five-digit numbers. These numbers could be concatenated to form a digit sequence, that could then be encrypted using a polyalphabetic cipher. Enciphering a coded message is called **superencipherment**.

Although superenciphered codes may seem impenetrable at first glance, Kahn points out that during World War II, U.S. Intelligence broke a top secret superenciphered code in which the plaintext was Japanese transliterated into Latin letters. When the fact that the code was broken leaked out and was published in a Chicago newspaper, the Japanese government refused to believe that anyone could break their code, and continued to use it for the rest of the war.

Transposition Ciphers

Substitution ciphers and codes preserve the order of the plaintext symbols but disguise them. **Transposition ciphers**, in contrast, reorder the letters but do not disguise them. Figure 8-19 depicts a common transposition cipher, the columnar transposition. The cipher is keyed by a word or phrase not containing any repeated letters. In this example, MEGABUCK is the key. The purpose of the key is to number the columns, column 1 being under the key letter closest to the start of the alphabet, and so on. The plaintext is written horizontally, in rows. The ciphertext is read out by columns, starting with the column whose key letter is the lowest.

To break a transposition cipher, the cryptanalyst must first be aware that he is dealing with a transposition cipher. By looking at the frequency of *E, T, A, O, I, N,* etc., it is easy to see if they fit the normal pattern for plaintext. If so, the cipher is clearly a transposition cipher, because in such a cipher every letter represents itself.

The next step is to make a guess at the number of columns. In many cases a

```
M E G A B U C K          Plaintext:
- - - - - - - -
7 4 5 1 2 8 3 6              pleasetransferonemilliondollarsto
- - - - - - - -              myswissbankaccountsixtwotwo
p l e a s e t r
a n s f e r o n          Ciphertext:
e m i l l i o n
d o l l a r s t              AFLLSKSOSELAWAIATOOSSCTCLNMOMANT
o m y s w i s s              ESILYNTWRNNTSOWDPAEDOBUOERIRICXB
b a n k a c c o
u n t s i x t w
o t w o a b c d
```

Fig. 8-19. A transposition cipher.

probable word or phrase may be guessed at from the context of the message. For example, suppose that our cryptanalyst suspected the plaintext phrase *milliondollars* to occur somewhere in the message. Observe that digrams *MO, IL, LL, LA, IR* and *OS* occur in the ciphertext as a result of this phrase wrapping around. The ciphertext letter *O* follows the ciphertext letter *M* (i.e., they are vertically adjacent in column 4) because they are separated in the probable phrase by a distance equal to the key length. If a key of length seven had been used, the digrams *MD, IO, LL, LL, IA, OR,* and *NS* would have occurred instead. In fact, for each key length, a different set of digrams is produced in the ciphertext. By hunting for the various possibilities, the cryptanalyst can often easily determine the key length.

The remaining step is to order the columns. When the number of columns, k, is small, each of the $k(k-1)$ column pairs can be examined to see if its digram frequencies match that for English plaintext. The pair with the best match is assumed to be correctly positioned. Now each remaining column is tentatively tried as the successor to this pair. The column whose digram and trigram frequencies give the best match is tentatively assumed to be correct. The predecessor column is found in the same way. The entire process is continued until a potential ordering is found. Chances are that the plaintext will be recognizable at this point (e.g., if *milloin* occurs, it is clear what the error is).

Some transposition ciphers accept a fixed-length block of input and produce a fixed-length block of output. These ciphers can be completely described by just giving a list telling the order in which the characters are to be output. For example, the cipher of Fig. 8-19 can be seen as a 64 character block cipher. Its output is 4, 12, 20, 28, 36, 44, 52, 60, 5, 13 , . . . , 62. In other words, the fourth input character, a, is the first to be output, followed by the twelfth, f, and so on.

8.4.2. The Data Encryption Standard

While describing the various classical cryptographic schemes, we have tried to make it clear how computers can be used as powerful tools by the cryptanalyst, both for collecting frequency statistics and for trying out large numbers of tentative solutions. Now we will remove our cryptanalyst hat and put on our cryptographer hat: we will think about making the encrypting process so complicated that not even a computer can break it.

Although modern cryptography uses the same basic ideas as traditional cryptography, transposition and substitution, its emphasis is different. Traditionally, cryptographers have used simple algorithms and relied on long keys for their security. Nowadays the reverse is true: the object is to make the encryption algorithm so complex and involuted that even if the cryptanalyst acquires vast mounds of enciphered text of his own choosing, he will not be able to make any sense of it at all.

Transpositions and substitutions can be implemented with simple circuits. Figure 8-20(a) shows a device, known as a **P-box** (P stands for permutation), used to effect a transposition on an 8-bit input. If the 8 bits are designated from top to bottom as 01234567, the output of this particular P-box is 36071245. By appropriate internal wiring, a P-box can be made to perform any transposition.

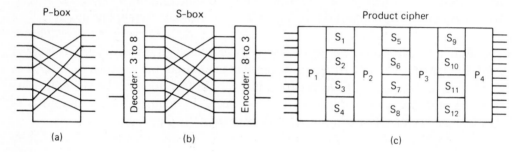

Fig. 8-20. Basic elements of product ciphers.

Substitutions are performed by **S-boxes**, as shown in Fig. 8-20(b). In this example a 3-bit plaintext is entered and a 3-bit ciphertext is output. The 3-bit input selects one of the eight lines exiting from the first stage and sets it to 1; all the other lines are 0. The second stage is a P-box. The third stage encodes the selected input line in binary again. With the wiring shown, if the eight octal numbers 01234567 were input one after another, the output sequence would be 24506713. In other words, 0 has been replaced by 2, 1 has been replaced by 4, etc. Again, by appropriate wiring of the P-box, any substitution can be accomplished.

The real power of these basic elements only becomes apparent when we cascade a whole series of ciphers, as shown in Fig. 8-20(c). In this example, 12 input lines are transposed by the first stage. Theoretically, it would be possible to have the second stage be an S-box that mapped a 12-bit number onto another 12-bit number. However, such a device would need $2^{12} = 4096$ crossed wires in its middle stage. Instead, the input is broken up into four groups of 3 bits, each of which is substituted independently of the others. Although this method is less general, it is still powerful. By including a sufficiently large number of stages in the product cipher, the output can be made to be a nonlinear function of the input.

In January 1977, the U.S. government adopted a product cipher developed by

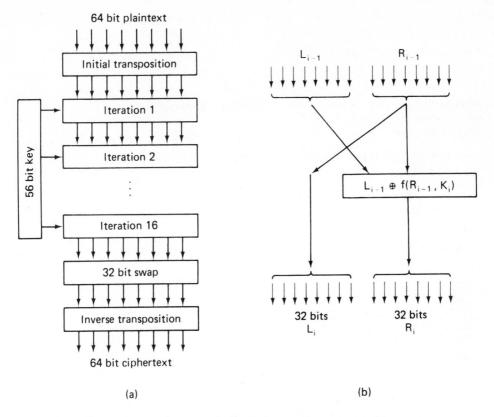

Fig. 8-21. The data encryption standard. (a) General outline. (b) Detail of one iteration.

IBM as its official standard for unclassified information. This adoption, in turn, has stimulated a number of manufacturers to implement the encryption algorithm, known as the **Data Encryption Standard** (National Bureau of Standards, 1977) in hardware, thus making it fast. The availability of fast and cheap hardware (Abbruscato, 1984), in turn, has stimulated many other users to adopt DES.

We will now explain the DES algorithm. An outline of it is shown in Fig. 8-21. Plaintext is encrypted in blocks of 64 bits, yielding 64 bits of ciphertext. The algorithm, which is parametrized by a 56-bit key, has 19 distinct stages. The first stage is a key independent transposition on the 64-bit plaintext. The last stage is the exact inverse of this transposition. The stage prior to the last one exchanges the leftmost 32 bits with the rightmost 32 bits. The remaining 16 stages are functionally identical but are parametrized by different functions of the key. The algorithm has been designed to allow decryption to be done with the same key as encryption. The steps are just run in the reverse order.

The operation of one of these intermediate stages is illustrated in Fig. 8-21(b). Each stage takes two 32-bit inputs and produces two 32-bit outputs. The left output is simply a copy of the right input. The right output is the bitwise EXCLUSIVE

```
type block = array[1 .. 64] of 0 .. 1;        {64 bit vector}
     ordering = array[1 .. 64] of 1 .. 64;    {defines a transposition}

var InitialTr, FinalTr, swap, KeyTr1, KeyTr2, etr, ptr: ordering;
    s: array[1 .. 8, 1 .. 64] of 0 .. 15;
    rots: array[1 .. 16] of 1 .. 2;

procedure transpose(var data: block; t: ordering; n: integer);
var x: block; i: 1 .. 64;
begin x := data;   for i := 1 to n do data[i] := x[t[i]] end;  {transpose}

procedure rotate(var key: block);   {1 bit left rotate on two 28 bit units}
var i: 1 .. 55;  x: block;
begin x := key;
   for i := 1 to 55 do x[i] := x[i + 1];
      x[28] := key[1];   x[56] := key[29];   key := x
end;  {rotate}

procedure f(i: integer;   var key,a,x: block);
var e,ikey,y: block;   r: 0 .. 64;  k: 1 .. 8;   j: 1 .. 48;
begin   e := a;
   transpose(e, etr, 48);                      {expand e to 48 bits}
   for j := 1 to rots[i] do rotate(key);
   ikey := key;   transpose(ikey, KeyTr2,48);
   for j := 1 to 48 do if e[j] + ikey[j] = 1 then y[j] := 1 else y[j] := 0;
   for k := 1 to 8 do                          {substitute part}
      begin   r := 32*y[6*k − 5] + 16*y[6*k] +
            8*y[6*k − 4] + 4*y[6*k − 3] + 2*y[6*k − 2] + y[6*k − 1] + 1;
      if odd(s[k,r] div 8) then x[4*k − 3] := 1 else x[4*k − 3] := 0;
      if odd(s[k,r] div 4) then x[4*k − 2] := 1 else x[4*k − 2] := 0;
      if odd(s[k,r] div 2) then x[4*k − 1] := 1 else x[4*k − 1] := 0;
      if odd(s[k,r]) then x[4*k] := 1 else x[4*k] := 0
      end;
   transpose(x, ptr, 32)
end;  {f}

procedure des(plaintext, key: block; var ciphertext: block);
var i: 1 .. 16;   j: 1 .. 32;   a,b,x: block;
begin   a := plaintext;                   {copy plaintext to a}
   transpose(a, InitialTr, 64);           {initial transposition}
   transpose(key, KeyTr1, 56);            {mix up key and reduce to 56 bits}
   for i := 1 to 16 do                    {here come the 16 iterations}
      begin   b := a;                      {a contains current ciphertext}
      for j := 1 to 32 do a[j] := b[j + 32];{current left taken from old right}
      f(i, key, a, x);                     {compute x = f(r[i − 1], k[i])}
      for j := 1 to 32 do if b[j]+x[j]=1 then a[j + 32] := 1 else a[j + 32] :=0;
      end;
   transpose(a, swap, 64);                {swap left and right halves}
   transpose(a, FinalTr, 64);             {final transposition}
   ciphertext := a
end;  {des}
```

Fig. 8-22. DES. (a) General outline. (b) Detail of one iteration.

InitialTr
```
58 50 42 34 26 18 10 02 60 52 44 36 28 20 12 04 62 54 46 38 30 22 14 06 64 56 48 40 32 24 16 08
57 49 41 33 25 17 09 01 59 51 43 35 27 19 11 03 61 53 45 37 29 21 13 05 63 55 47 39 31 23 15 07
```

FinalTr
```
40 08 48 16 56 24 64 32 39 07 47 15 55 23 63 31 38 06 46 14 54 22 62 30 37 05 45 13 53 21 61 29
36 04 44 12 52 20 60 28 35 03 43 11 51 19 59 27 34 02 42 10 50 18 58 26 33 01 41 09 49 17 57 25
```

swap
```
33 34 35 36 37 38 39 40 41 42 43 44 45 46 47 48 49 50 51 52 53 54 55 56 57 58 59 60 61 62 63 64
01 02 03 04 05 06 07 08 09 10 11 12 13 14 15 16 17 18 19 20 21 22 23 24 25 26 27 28 29 30 31 32
```

KeyTr1
```
57 49 41 33 25 17 09 01 58 50 42 34 26 18 10 02 59 51 43 35 27 19 11 03 60 52 44 36
63 55 47 39 31 23 15 07 62 54 46 38 30 22 14 06 61 53 45 37 29 21 13 05 28 20 12 04
```

KeyTr2
```
14 17 11 24 01 05 03 28 15 06 21 10 23 19 12 04 26 08 16 07 27 20 13 02
41 52 31 37 47 55 30 40 51 45 33 48 44 49 39 56 34 53 46 42 50 36 29 32
```

etr
```
32 01 02 03 04 05 04 05 06 07 08 09 08 09 10 11 12 13 12 13 14 15 16 17
16 17 18 19 20 21 20 21 22 23 24 25 24 25 26 27 28 29 28 29 30 31 32 01
```

ptr
```
16 07 20 21 29 12 28 17 01 15 23 26 05 18 31 10
02 08 24 14 32 27 03 09 19 13 30 06 22 11 04 25
```

S−boxes: $s[1:1..64]$, $s[2:1..64]$, ... , $s[8,1..64]$
```
14 04 13 01 02 15 11 08 03 10 06 12 05 09 00 07 00 15 07 04 14 02 13 01 10 06 12 11 09 05 03 08
04 01 14 08 13 06 02 11 15 12 09 07 03 10 05 00 15 12 08 02 04 09 01 07 05 11 03 14 10 00 06 13

15 01 08 14 06 11 03 04 09 07 02 13 12 00 05 10 03 13 04 07 15 02 08 14 12 00 01 10 06 09 11 05
00 14 07 11 10 04 13 01 05 08 12 06 09 03 02 15 13 08 10 01 03 15 04 02 11 06 07 12 00 05 14 09

10 00 09 14 06 03 15 05 01 13 12 07 11 04 02 08 13 07 00 09 03 04 06 10 02 08 05 14 12 11 15 01
13 06 04 09 08 15 03 00 11 01 02 12 05 10 14 07 01 10 13 00 06 09 08 07 04 15 14 03 11 05 02 12

07 13 14 03 00 06 09 10 01 02 08 05 11 12 04 15 13 08 11 05 06 15 00 03 04 07 02 12 01 10 14 09
10 06 09 00 12 11 07 13 15 01 03 14 05 02 08 04 03 15 00 06 10 01 13 08 09 04 05 11 12 07 02 14

02 12 04 01 07 10 11 06 08 05 03 15 13 00 14 09 14 11 02 12 04 07 13 01 05 00 15 10 03 09 08 06
04 02 01 11 10 13 07 08 15 09 12 05 06 03 00 14 11 08 12 07 01 14 02 13 06 15 00 09 10 04 05 03

12 01 10 15 09 02 06 08 00 13 03 04 14 07 05 11 10 15 04 02 07 12 09 05 06 01 13 14 00 11 03 08
09 14 15 05 02 08 12 03 07 00 04 10 01 13 11 06 04 03 02 12 09 05 15 10 11 14 01 07 06 00 08 13

04 11 02 14 15 00 08 13 03 12 09 07 05 10 06 01 13 00 11 07 04 09 01 10 14 03 05 12 02 15 08 06
01 04 11 13 12 03 07 14 10 15 06 08 00 05 09 02 06 11 13 08 01 04 10 07 09 05 00 15 14 02 03 12

13 02 08 04 06 15 11 01 10 09 03 14 05 00 12 07 01 15 13 08 10 03 07 04 12 05 06 11 00 14 09 02
07 11 04 01 09 12 14 02 00 06 10 13 15 03 05 08 02 01 14 07 04 10 08 13 15 12 09 00 03 05 06 11
```

rots
```
1 1 2 2 2 2 2 2 1 2 2 2 2 2 2 1
```

OR of the left input and a function of the right input and the key for this stage, K_i. All the complexity lies in this function.

The function consists of four steps, carried out in sequence. First, a 48-bit number, E, is constructed by expanding the 32 bit R_{i-1} according to a fixed transposition and duplication rule. Second, E and K_i are EXCLUSIVE-ORed together. This output is then partitioned into eight groups of 6 bits each, each of which is fed into a different S-box. The S-boxes produce 4, instead of 6 output bits. Each of the 64 possible inputs to an S-box is mapped onto a 4-bit output. Obviously different inputs can produce the same output. The result is a list of eight 4-bit numbers. Finally, these 32 bits are passed through a P-box.

In each of the 16 iterations, a different key is used. Before the algorithm starts, a 56-bit transposition is applied to the key. Just before each iteration, the key is partitioned into two 28-bit units, each of which is rotated left by a number of bits dependent on the iteration number. K_i is derived from this rotated key by applying yet another 56-bit transposition to it. Despite all this complexity, DES is basically a monoalphabetic substitution cipher using a 64-bit character.

A procedure to perform the DES algorithm is given in Fig. 8-22(a). The values to which the tables are to be initialized are given in Fig. 8-22(b). In case anyone cares, the ciphertext corresponding to the plaintext of 64 zeros and a key of 56 zeros is 8CA64DE9C1B123A7 (hexadecimal).

One way to strengthen DES (or any cipher, for that matter) is to insert random characters into the plaintext according to a well defined rule (e.g., every nth character is real, the rest are just noise). In addition, dummy messages can be inserted between the real ones according to yet another rule. This principle is called a **null cipher**. Null ciphers are obviously wasteful of bandwidth, but they are difficult to break, because the position of the real characters and messages is a carefully guarded secret and is changed whenever the key is changed. On leased private lines, there is something to be said for transmitting garbage whenever the line would otherwise be idle.

Stream Encryption

Another way to make cryptanalysis of DES much harder is to operate it as a **stream cipher**, as shown in Fig. 8-23, rather than as a **block cipher**, as we have described up until now. When being used as a stream cipher, both sender and receiver operate their DES chips in encryption (as opposed to decryption) mode. Each DES chip has a 64-bit input register, which operates as a shift register, and a 64-bit output register, which does not. When a plaintext character arrives, it is EXCLUSIVE-ORed with 8 bits of the output register, O_1. (O_2 through O_8 are never used.) The character thus created is both transmitted to the receiver and shifted into the input register, pushing I_8 off the end. Then the chip is activated and the output computed for the new input.

At the receiving end, the incoming character is first EXCLUSIVE-ORed with

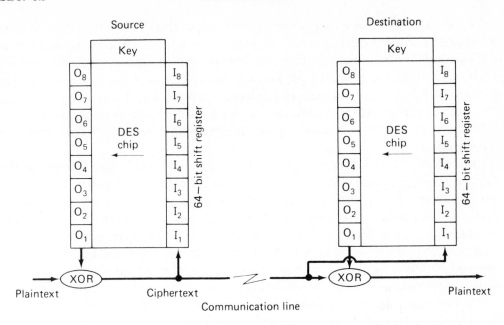

Fig. 8-23. Stream encryption.

O_1 (yielding the plaintext), and then shifted into I_1. If the sender and receiver start out with identical input registers, they remain identical forever, which means that O_1 at the transmitter will always be the same as O_1 at the receiver. Since the incoming plaintext character at the transmitter is being EXCLUSIVE-ORed with the same character as the incoming ciphertext character at the receiver, the output at the receiver is the original plaintext. The property of stream ciphers that makes them valuable is that O_1 depends on the entire history of the plaintext, so that a repeated pattern in the plaintext will not generate a repeated pattern in the cipher-text. Stream ciphers are also convenient for use with terminals, because they do not have to collect eight characters before emitting ciphertext. Each keystroke generates output immediately, as it is typed.

The DES Controversy

Before leaving the subject of DES, it is worthwhile pointing out that this cipher has been surrounded by controversy since its inception (Diffie and Hellman, 1977; Kolata, 1977). A number of computer scientists have made the claim that 56 bits is too small a key size, making it too easy to attack by brute force. The key size in IBM's original design was 128 bits, which unquestionably eliminates any chance of an exhaustive search of the key space. At the request of the U.S. National Security Agency, the key size was reduced to 56 bits. The reason the cipher was weakened has not been made public.

What has also bothered a number of scientists is IBM's refusal to make public the reasons the specific S-boxes in the cipher were chosen. All IBM has said is that the National Security Agency requested that it keep the design principles secret. Without knowing the design principles, it is difficult to exclude the possibility that a trick exists by which the cipher can be easily broken. There was also an incident that some observers interpreted as an attempt by a government employee to stifle publication of academic research aimed at developing stronger ciphers (Shapley and Kolata, 1977).

The net effect of a short key, secret design principles, and other factors has led some critics (e.g., Kahn, 1980; Smith, 1980) to believe that the government might not be unhappy with a standard cipher just strong enough to keep everyone except itself from breaking it. To understand the significance of these developments, you should realize that in the future, telephones may contain microcomputers capable of digitizing and encrypting speech, and mail may be sent electronically, from home terminal to home terminal. If unbreakable encryption algorithms were used in these applications, it would be impossible for governments to tap phones and surreptitiously read mail. As Kahn (1980) and Selfridge and Schwartz (1980) point out, electronic eavesdropping is currently practiced on a large scale, so technical advances making it impossible in the future may not be viewed with great joy in all quarters. Although the federal government decided to decertify DES effective in 1988 (Hellman, 1987), its widespread use in the commercial sector will no doubt continue for years to come.

8.4.3. The Key Distribution Problem

Another problem with DES is that it requires the receiver of a message to use the same key for decrypting it that the sender used for encrypting it. As a consequence, the question of how to distribute keys securely arises. Traditionally, identical key pairs were invented at a central key generating facility and transmitted to their destinations by personal courier. For a bank, or other organization with hundreds or thousands of offices, such a key distribution method is highly unsatisfactory, especially if security requirements dictate changing keys daily. It would be much more convenient if keys could be distributed via the network itself. Of course, key exchange must itself be encrypted, and encrypted with a key that has not already been compromised.

One solution to this problem is use a key hierarchy (Balenson, 1985). Each organization chooses a master key at random and distributes it by personal courier to each of its offices. The offices are grouped into regions, with the head office of each region choosing a regional key. The regional keys are encrypted using the master key and distributed via the network. Whenever any two offices within a region wish to communicate, one of them chooses a session key and sends it to the other, encrypted by the regional key. Alternatively, a key manager process chooses the session key and sends it to both parties, encrypted by the regional key.

The philosophy behind this design is that master keys and regional keys are so rarely used that no intruder will ever be able to collect enough ciphertext to break them. Furthermore, the plaintext of these messages consists of 56-bit random numbers, making it virtually impossible to cryptanalyze them. In practice, the messages must start out with a header saying in essence "I AM A NEW KEY," but to prevent the cryptanalyst from acquiring a matched plaintext-ciphertext pair, this header should be sent unencrypted.

Nevertheless, it remains clear that physical transport of master keys by a means external to the network is required to make the system work. Whenever the master key is thought to be compromised or whenever an employee who knew it or who might have known it (e.g., one of the couriers) leaves the organization, a new master key must be generated and physically transported to all the offices.

Worst of all, there is no easy way for two total strangers who belong to different organizations to communicate in a secure way, except by physically getting together and agreeing upon a key right then and there. It is as though you were not allowed to call someone on the telephone until the person had physically handed you his business card. Obviously, a better method is needed.

Puzzles

Fortunately, several ingenious methods for solving the key distribution problem are known. Merkle's method (Merkle, 1978) explicitly uses the model of Fig. 8-17. He assumes that two parties, A and B, have never previously communicated, but now wish to communicate in a secure way. They must use the channel between them for establishing the key, even though the intruder can copy down everything they send on this channel.

The method is based on what Merkle calls **puzzles**. A puzzle is a cryptogram that is intended to be broken. Suppose that A initiates the conversation. His first message to B (in plaintext) might be something like this.

Dear B,
I am now going to send you 20,000 puzzles. Each puzzle is a cryptogram whose plaintext starts out with 128 zero bits, followed by a 16-bit puzzle number, and then a 56-bit key. The cryptograms have been encrypted using the DES standard with a key whose final 22 bits are zeros. Please pick one cryptogram at random and break it by brute force, trying all 2^{34} keys ending in 22 zeros. You know you have broken it when you find a key that yields a plaintext starting with 128 zeros. After breaking the cryptogram, extract the 56-bit random number and use it as your key. As your first message, send me back the puzzle number in plaintext, so that I know which key you are going to use.

Your secretive correspondent, A

This plaintext message is followed by 20,000 puzzles, as promised. The intruder hears everything, including all the puzzles. From the intruder's point of view, the difficulty is in choosing the correct puzzle to begin working on. In effect, he must begin attacking puzzles in a random order, hoping to find the one B chose. On the average he will have to try 10,000 puzzles before striking pay dirt.

Assume that an encryption takes 1 μsec. Breaking a puzzle will require, on the average, 2^{33} encryptions, which takes a little under 3 hours. This means that, statistically, the intruder will need more than 3 years to find the key. By adjusting the difficulty and number of puzzles, we can adjust the time to set up a conversation and the chance of the intruder's finding the key in a short time interval.

Key Protection

Although hiding the key from potential intruders is important, it is often equally important to hide the key from oneself. To be more precise, a corporation may not wish to delegate unlimited authority (in the form of a key) to any one employee. Banks, for example, normally do not give the complete vault combination to any one employee, but give half to one employee and half to another. Shamir (1979) has devised a clever technique for sharing cryptographic keys among multiple employees in a flexible way.

Let us illustrate Shamir's idea with an example. Suppose that a nervous company wants certain important messages to be sent only by the company president, or any two of the three dozen vice presidents, or any four of the thousands of other managers, or one VP plus two managers. Giving each person a few bits of the key does not work, because picking two VPs or four managers at random does not ensure having a full key.

To use Shamir's system, the company mathematician picks a polynomial of degree 3:

$$p(x) = a_3 x^3 + a_2 x^2 + a_1 x + a_0$$

where a_3, a_2, and a_1 are chosen at random, and a_0 is the key, expressed as an integer. (With k managers instead of four, the polynomial is of degree $k - 1$.) Each manager is given one point on the curve: $(x, p(x))$; each VP is given two such points. The president is given four points. All the x values must be unique. Any time a collection of executives can assemble an arbitrary four points (in general, k points), they can find the polynomial and hence its coefficients, including a_0, the key, because four points uniquely determine a polynomial of degree 3. For the benefit of executives who have forgotten whatever linear algebra they once knew, each one could be given a machine-readable plastic card for insertion into the cryptographic terminal.

To prevent fewer than the critical number of executives from gaining any information at all about the key, all arithmetic should be done modulo a prime number. Figure 8-24 gives an example of the method.

Company with 1 VP and 10 managers

Key = 11, prime = 41   polynomial: $p(x) = (x^3 + 4x^2 + 3x + 11) \bmod 41$

$p(1) = 19$	$p(4) = 28$	$p(7) = 38$	$p(10) = 6$
$p(2) = 0$	$p(5) = 5$	$p(8) = 24$	$p(11) = 14$
$p(3) = 1$	$p(6) = 20$	$p(9) = 25$	$p(12) = 14$

The VP is given the (x, y) points $(1, 19)$ and $(2, 0)$

Each manager is given a different (x, y) point from the list

$(3, 1), (4, 28), (5, 5), (6, 20), (7, 38), (8, 24), (9, 25), (10, 6), (11, 14), (12, 14)$

If the VP and managers 1 and 4 get together they have four points:

$(1, 19), (2, 0), (3, 1)$ and $(6, 20)$

To solve the equation

$$a_3 x^3 + a_2 x^2 + a_1 x + a_0 = y$$

This leads to the four simultaneous linear equations in four unknowns:

$$a_3 + a_2 + a_1 + a_0 = 19 \bmod 41$$
$$8a_3 + 4a_2 + 2a_1 + a_0 = 0 \bmod 41$$
$$27a_3 + 9a_2 + 3a_1 + a_0 = 1 \bmod 41$$
$$216a_3 + 36a_2 + 6a_1 + a_0 = 20 \bmod 41$$

These can be solved by any standard technique, doing all arithmetic modulo 41. The solution is $a_3 = 1$, $a_2 = 4$, $a_1 = 3$, $a_0 = 11$.

Fig. 8-24. Key sharing using Shamir's method.

8.4.4. Public Key Cryptography

Now let us return to the problem of setting up secure communication between people who have never previously communicated. Although Merkle's puzzle method allows strangers to establish secure communication, it has the clear drawbacks of requiring both a large amount of computing time and a large amount of transmission bandwidth to agree upon the key. This brings us to another method, due to Diffie and Hellman (1976), which has neither of these drawbacks and which has caused a basic revolution in the way people think about cryptographic systems.

Until Diffie and Hellman's article, all cryptographers simply took for granted that both the encryption and decryption keys had to be kept secret. If one thinks in terms of ciphers such as monoalphabetic substitution, it is obvious that the encryption key, for example *abc* becomes *XYZ*, and the corresponding decryption key, *XYZ* becomes *abc*, can each be trivially derived from the other one. What Diffie and Hellman proposed was to use an encryption algorithm, *E*, and a decryption algorithm, D, with E and D chosen so that deriving D even given a complete description of E would be effectively impossible.

Since these requirements differ so strikingly from those of conventional cryptographic systems, it is worth repeating them. There are three requirements:

1. $D(E(P)) = P$.

2. It is exceedingly difficult to deduce D from E.

3. E cannot be broken by a chosen plaintext attack.

The first requirement says that if we apply D to an encrypted message, $E(P)$, we get the original plaintext message, P, back. The second requirement speaks for itself. The third requirement is needed because, as we shall see in a moment, intruders may experiment with the algorithm to their heart's content.

Under these conditions, there is no reason that E cannot be made public. The method works like this. Any person or organization wanting to receive secret messages first devises two algorithms, E and D, meeting the above requirements. The encryption algorithm or key is then made public, hence the name **public key cryptography**. This might be done by putting it in a file that anyone who wanted to could read.

Now let us see if we can solve the problem of establishing a secure channel between two parties, A and B, who have never had any previous contact. Both A's encryption key, E_A, and B's encryption key, E_B, are assumed to be in a publicly readable file. (Basically, all users of the network are expected to publish their encryption keys as soon as they become network users.) Now A takes his first message, P, computes $E_B(P)$, and sends it to B. B then decrypts it by applying his secret key D_B [i.e., he computes $D_B(E_B(P)) = P$]. No one else can read the encrypted message, $E_B(P)$, because the encryption system is assumed strong and because it is too difficult to derive D_B from the publicly known E_B. The problem has been solved, and without requiring 3 hours of computing time to establish communication.

The MIT Algorithm

The only catch is that we need to find algorithms that indeed satisfy all three requirements. Due to the potential advantages of public key cryptography, many researchers are hard at work, and some algorithms have already been published. One good method was discovered by a group at MIT (Rivest et al., 1978). Their method is based on some principles from number theory. We will now summarize how to use the method below; for details, consult the paper.

1. Choose two large primes, p and q, each greater than 10^{100}.

2. Compute $n = p \times q$ and $z = (p - 1) \times (q - 1)$.

3. Choose a number relatively prime to z and call it d.

4. Find e such that $e \times d = 1 \bmod z$.

With these parameters computed in advance, we are ready to begin encryption. Divide the plaintext (regarded as a bit string) into blocks, so that each plaintext message, P falls in the interval $0 \le P < n$. This can be done by grouping the plaintext into blocks of k bits, where k is the largest integer for which $2^k < n$ is true.

To encrypt a message, P, compute $C = P^e \pmod n$. To decrypt C, compute $P = C^d \pmod n$. It can be proven that for all P in the specified range, the encryption and decryption functions are inverses. To perform the encryption, you need e and n. To perform the decryption, you need d and n. Therefore, the public key consists of the pair (e, n) and the secret key consists of (d, n), or just d, actually.

The security of the method is based on the difficulty of factoring large numbers. If the cryptanalyst could factor the (publicly known) n, he could then find p and q, and from these z. Equipped with knowledge of z and e, d can be found using Euclid's algorithm. Fortunately, mathematicians have been trying to factor large numbers for at least 300 years, without much success. All the known evidence suggests that it is an exceedingly difficult problem.

According to Rivest et al., factoring a 200-digit number requires 4 billion years of computer time; factoring a 500-digit number requires 10^{25} years. In both cases, they assume the best known algorithm and a computer with a 1 μsec instruction time. Even if computers continue to get faster by an order of magnitude per decade, it will be centuries before factoring a 500-digit number becomes feasible, at which time our descendants can simply choose p and q still larger. However, it should be pointed out that no one has proven the absence of a trick that would allow the cipher to be broken without factoring n. Neither has anyone demonstrated the presence of any such trick.

A trivial pedagogical example of the MIT algorithm is given in Fig. 8-25. For this example we have chosen $p = 3$ and $q = 11$, giving $n = 33$ and $z = 20$. A suitable value for d is $d = 7$, since 7 and 20 have no common factors. With these choices, e can be found by solving the equation $7e = 1 \pmod{20}$, which yields $e = 3$. The ciphertext, C, for a plaintext message, P, is given by $C = P^3 \pmod{33}$. The ciphertext is decrypted by the receiver according to the rule $P = C^7 \pmod{33}$. The figure shows the encryption of the plaintext "SUZANNE" as an example.

Because the primes chosen for this example are so small, P must be less than 33, so each plaintext block can contain only a single character. The result is a monoalphabetic substitution cipher, not very impressive. If instead we had chosen p and $q \approx 10^{100}$, we would have $n \approx 10^{200}$, so each block could be up to 664 bits $(2^{664} \approx 10^{200})$ or 83 8-bit characters, versus eight characters for DES.

Plaintext (P)			Ciphertext (C)		After decryption		
Symbolic	Numeric	P^3	P^3 (mod 33)	C^7	C^7 (mod 33)	Symbolic
S	19	6859	28	13492928512	19	S
U	21	9261	21	1801088541	21	U
Z	26	17576	20	1280000000	26	Z
A	01	1	1	1	1	A
N	14	2744	5	78125	14	N
N	14	2744	5	78125	14	N
E	05	125	26	8031810176	5	E

Sender's computation

Receiver's computation

Fig. 8-25. An example of the MIT algorithm.

8.4.5. Authentication and Digital Signatures

In the real world, people make a big distinction between originals and copies. For example, if you go to your friendly local bank with a check, they will be happy to cash it, provided that you can adequately identify yourself. On the other hand, if you go to the same bank with a photocopy of the check, or better yet, with a large pile of photocopies of the check, they will suddenly become a lot less friendly. Banks take the difference between originals and copies quite seriously.

A related issue is that of handwritten signatures. The authenticity of many legal, financial, and other documents is ultimately determined by the presence or absence of an authorized handwritten signature. And photocopies do not count. For computerized message systems to replace the physical transport of paper and ink documents, a solution must be found to these problems.

The problem of devising a replacement for handwritten signatures is a difficult one. Basically, what is needed is a system by which one party can send a "signed" message to another party in such a way that

1. The receiver can verify the claimed identity of the sender.

2. The sender cannot later repudiate the message.

The first requirement is needed, for example, in financial systems. When a customer's computer orders a bank's computer to buy a ton of gold, the bank's computer needs to be able to make sure that the computer giving the order really belongs to the company whose account is to be debited. The second requirement is needed to protect the bank against fraud. Suppose that the bank buys the ton of gold, and immediately thereafter the price of gold drops sharply. A dishonest customer might sue the bank, claiming that he never issued any order to buy gold. When the bank produces the message in court, the customer denies having sent it.

Authentication

In connection-oriented systems, authentication can be done when a session is established. The traditional approach is to have a user prove his identity by typing in a password. Not only does this method expose the user to passive wiretapping, but it may require the authenticating computer (e.g., the bank) to maintain a list of passwords internally, which is itself a potential security problem. Using public key cryptography, it is possible to perform the authentication in a secure way, without storing any passwords (Anderson et al., 1987; Sidhu, 1986).

To continue with our banking example, when opening an account, a customer chooses a public key and a private key. He gives the public key to the bank and keeps the private key himself. When the customer calls the bank to establish a session, the bank chooses a random number, encrypts it with the alleged customer's public key, and challenges the caller to send it back unencrypted. Only the person knowing the decryption key is able to perform the decryption, so impostors will fail the test. Furthermore, an intruder recording all the traffic will have no benefit because next time the bank will choose a different random number.

Even after the initial authentication, for additional security, it might be desirable to provide at least some authentication in each message (Jueneman et al., 1985). The bank above might require its customers to include in each message a secret password, a sequence number, the time and date of transmission, and a checksum of the entire plaintext, including the time, date, and sequence number. The sequence numbers make it pointless for an intruder to record and subsequently play back messages, because the bank can see that they are just duplicates of earlier messages. The time and date make it useless for the intruder to save a recorded message until the sequence numbers have cycled around. The checksum makes it highly improbable that an intruder could forge or modify a (ciphertext) message and still have the (plaintext) checksum be correct.

Digital Signatures with Public Key Cryptography

In any event, there is still the problem of preventing dishonest users from repudiating their previous messages. Under certain conditions, public key cryptography can make an important contribution to solving this problem. To use public key cryptography for sending signed messages, it is necessary that the encryption and decryption algorithms have the property that $E(D(P)) = P$ in addition to the usual property that $D(E(P)) = P$. Assuming that this is the case, A can send a signed plaintext message P to B by transmitting $E_B(D_A(P))$. Note carefully that A knows his own (secret) decryption key, D_A, as well as the public key of B, E_B.

When B receives the message, he transforms it using his private key, as usual, yielding $D_A(P)$, as shown in Fig. 8-26(b). He stores this text in a safe place and then decrypts it using E_A to get the original plaintext.

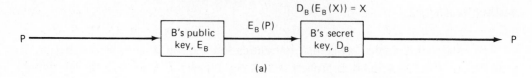

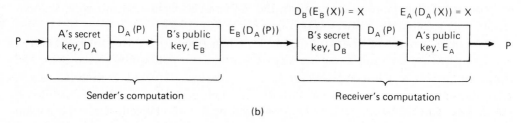

Fig. 8-26. Secure message transmission using public key cryptography. (a) Without signature. (b) With signature.

To see how the signature property works, suppose that A subsequently denies having sent the message P to B. When the case comes up in court, B can produce both P and $D_A(P)$. The judge can easily verify that B indeed has a valid message encrypted by D_A by simply applying E_A to it. Since B does not know what A's secret key is, the only way B could have acquired a message encrypted by it is if A did indeed send it. While in jail, A will have plenty of time to devise interesting new public key algorithms.

One criticism of this signature method is that it couples two distinct functions: authentication and secrecy. In many applications, authentication is essential but secrecy is not. Since public key cryptography is slow, it is frequently desirable to be able to send signed plaintext documents. Below we will describe an authentication scheme that does not require encrypting the entire message (de Jonge and Chaum, 1987).

This authentication mechanism is based on the idea of a **one-way checksum** function, CK. Given a plaintext message, P, it must be relatively easy to calculate $CK(P)$, but given $CK(P)$ it must be nearly impossible to find a P that yields this checksum. The checksum, $CK(P)$, should be much smaller than the message, for example, 256 bits. Many mathematical functions with this one-way property exist.

To sign a plaintext message, P, the sender, A, first computes $CK(P)$ and then applies his private key to it, to yield $D_A(CK(P))$. He then transmits the pair $[P, D_A(CK(P))]$ to B. The message itself can be sent in plaintext (or encrypted with public key or conventional cryptography) followed by the encrypted checksum.

When everything arrives, B applies E_A to the signature part to yield $CK(P)$. At this point B holds three items: P, $CK(P)$, and $D_A(CK(P))$. B now applies CK to P

to see if the checksum so computed agrees with the checksum received along with the message. If it does, he knows that the message has not been tampered with. If the checksum disagrees, the message has been forged.

If a dispute arises later, B can show all three items to a judge to prove that A indeed sent the message. After all, the judge knows that even if B fabricated P and $CK(P)$, there is no way B could have computed $D_A(CK(P))$ without access to A's private key. The beauty of this scheme is that only the short checksum has to undergo the expensive public key encryption, no matter how long the message is.

Note the importance of the one-way property of CK. If it were possible to find a plaintext message P that corresponded to $CK(P)$, then B could cheat by generating a new message, P' with the same checksum as P and show P', $CK(P)$, and $D_A(CK(P))$ to the judge.

Although both of these signature methods are elegant, they have some problems that are related to the environment in which they operate rather than with the algorithms themselves. For one thing, B can prove that a message was sent by A only as long as D_A remains secret. If A discloses his secret key, the argument no longer holds, because anyone could have sent the message, including B. The problem might arise, for example, when A and B are corporations. At a certain point the management of A may realize that sending the message was a mistake. For example, they may have discovered a cheaper supplier for some important part they need. To repudiate the message to the original supplier they make their secret key public and then run to the police claiming that their office had been broken into and the key stolen. Depending on the local laws, the corporation may or may not be legally liable for the misuse of property stolen from it.

Another problem with the signature scheme is what happens if A decides to change his key. Doing so is clearly legal and may even be standard operating procedure within many companies. If a court case later arises, as described above, the judge will apply the current E_A to $D_A(P)$ or $D_A(CK(P))$ and discover that it does not produce P or $CK(P)$, respectively. B will look pretty stupid at this point. Consequently, it appears that some central authority is needed to record all key changes and their dates.

Digital Signatures with Conventional Cryptography

However, once we are resigned to having a central authority that knows everything, say Big Brother (BB), both secrecy and digital signatures can be obtained using conventional cryptography (Needham and Schroeder, 1978). One way to achieve secrecy is to require each user to choose a secret key and hand carry it to BB's office. Thus only A and BB know A's secret key, K_A. When A wants to talk to B, A asks BB to choose a session key, K_S, and send him two copies of it, one encrypted with K_A, and one encrypted with K_B. A then sends the latter to B with instructions to decrypt it using K_B and then use the plaintext as the session key. *BB* can also provide a signature service. To do so, he needs a special key, *X*, kept secret from everyone. To use the signature service, *B*, a bank for example, could insist that the following procedure be followed for every signed, encrypted plaintext message, *P*, sent to it:

1. The customer, *A*, sends $K_A(P)$ to *BB*.

2. *BB* decrypts $K_A(P)$ to get *P*, then builds a new message consisting of *A*'s name and address concatenated with the date, *D*, and the original message. This new message, $A + D + P$, is then encrypted with *X*, yielding $X(A + D + P)$ and sent back to *A*. Note that *BB* can verify that the request indeed came from *A*, because only *A* and *BB* know K_A. An impostor would not be able to send *BB* a message that made sense when decrypted by K_A. The ability of *BB* to authenticate *A* is the heart of the signature mechanism.

3. The customer, *A*, sends $X(A + D + P)$ to the bank, *B*.

4. The bank sends $X(A + D + P)$ to *BB*, requesting $K_B(A + D + P)$ as a result.

5. The bank then decrypts $K_B(A + D + P)$ to recover the plaintext information *A*, *D*, and *P*.

If a customer denies sending *P* to the bank, the bank can show $X(A + D + P)$ to a judge. The judge then orders *BB* to decrypt it. When the judge sees *A*, *D*, and *P*, he knows the customer is lying, because the bank does not know *X*, and therefore could not have fabricated $X(A + D + P)$. Of course, the problem of the customer claiming that his K_A was stolen still exists, just as in public key cryptography.

Figure 8-27 illustrates secure message transmission between total strangers using conventional cryptography. When signatures are not needed, as in Fig. 8-27(a), after the session key has been established by steps 1, 2a, 2b, and 3, *BB* is no longer needed. In contrast, for the signed messages of Fig. 8-27(b), *BB* must be invoked twice for each message. The public key system of Fig. 8-26 is also more complicated for signed than for unsigned messages, but does not require sending any extra messages, except perhaps to look up the public keys initially.

8.5. EXAMPLES OF THE PRESENTATION LAYER

In this section we will look at our usual examples to see how they deal with the presentation layer issues. As usual, for the public networks, we will emphasize the protocol, since we have already discussed the service.

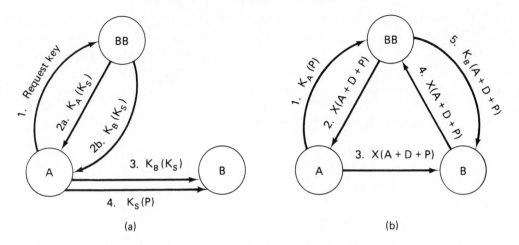

Fig. 8-27. Secure message transmission between strangers using conventional cryptography. (a) Without signature. (b) With signature.

8.5.1. The Presentation Layer in Public Networks

Public networks that implement the session layer also implement the presentation layer. After all, most of what the presentation layer does is just make the session services available to application layer users. The only real service originating in the presentation layer itself is the negotiation and management of presentation contexts.

Of course, another feature of the presentation layer (although it is not formally a service) is the use of ASN.1. This facility is normally supported in full, if for no other reason than that many of the standard applications expect it. The OSI file transfer, virtual terminal, and other protocols are based entirely on the use of ASN.1 for representing and transmitting data structures and APDUs.

The presentation protocol is surprisingly simple because most of the presentation service primitives simply cause the corresponding session primitive to be invoked. The sending of PDUs is done by the session layer. For example, when a presentation layer user invokes the *P-TOKEN-PLEASE.request*, all that the presentation entity has to do is invoke the *S-TOKEN-PLEASE.request*. It is up to the session layer to send the PDU that actually asks for the token. No presentation PDUs are sent. This situation is an example of the more general phenomenon of a service that is offered by one layer being propagated up through higher layers without change. When the service is invoked in the highest layer, the request simply propagates downward until it reaches the layer where the work is done.

Figure 8-28 shows the 14 PDUs used by the presentation protocol. They fall into four groups: connection establishment, abnormal release, data transfer, and context management.

When an application entity invokes the *P-CONNECT.request* primitive, the presentation layer first establishes a session, and then sends a *CP* **PPDU**

PDDU	Name	Request	Indication	Response	Confirm
CP	Connect Presentation	X	X		
CPA	Connect Presentation Accept			X	X
CPR	Connect Presentation Reject			X	X
ARU	Abnormal Release, User initiated	X	X		
ARP	Abnormal Release, Provider initiated		X		
TD	Transfer Data	X	X		
TE	Transfer Expedited	X	X		
TTD	Transfer Typed Data	X	X		
TC	Transfer Capability	X	X		
TCC	Transfer Capability Confirm			X	X
AC	Alter Context	X	X		
ACA	Alter Context Acknowledge			X	X
RS	Resynchronize	X	X		
RSA	Resynchronize Acknowledge			X	X

Fig. 8-28. The presentation PDUs and their associated primitives.

(**Presentation PDU**) over the new session. The columns *request* and *indication* are marked in Fig. 8-28 because this PDU is sent when a *request* is done and arrives at the other side as an *indication*.

The *CP* PPDU contains among its parameters a proposed list of presentation contexts. Each item in this list contains three parts: an integer identifying the context, the name of the abstract syntax (an object identifier), and a list of transfer syntaxes that the initiating party is willing to use for the abstract syntax. Normally there is only one transfer syntax for each abstract syntax, but in theory there could be more.

After the peer receives the PDU, it can accept or reject the connection with *CPA* or *CPR* respectively. If the connection is accepted, the receiver gives a list of those contexts that it is willing to use, and for each one, selects which transfer syntax it prefers. If none of the transfer syntaxes are acceptable, the call must be rejected.

Interestingly enough, there is no PDU for disconnecting. Instead, the presentation connection is implicitly terminated when the session is released. The *ARU* and *ARP* PDUs are used for the *ABORT* primitives.

Five PDUs are present for data transfer, one for each of the four kinds supported by the session layer, and one for acknowledging the fourth kind, capability data, since that is a confirmed service.

Two PDUs are provided for altering the context, one to request a new context and one to confirm (or reject) the request. This PDU contains two parameter lists, one for adding new contexts and one for deleting existing ones. The format of the list of additions is the same as in the initial negotiation. For deletions, it is sufficient just to give the context numbers.

Finally, the last two PDUs are for the session resynchronization service and carry the synchronization point numbers.

The presentation layer protocol standard (ISO 8823) uses ASN.1 for defining the format of all the PPDUs. This is a step up from the previous layers, where the entire descriptions are verbal. However, only the syntax is formally defined; the semantics of the various fields are given as comments.

Like the session layer, the actions of the protocol machine to the various events are described by a finite state machine. There are 60 incoming events, mmostly *request* and *response* primitives from the presentation layer, but also some *indication* primitives from the session layer and some PPDU arrivals. Only seven states exist in this protocol machine, so the matrix has only 420 entries, most of them invalid. The valid entries specify which of 69 actions are to be performed, most of them *request*s to the session layer or *indication*s to the presentation layer.

Although the implementation of the presentation layer is not discussed at all in the standards documents (rightly so), it is perhaps worth saying a few words about the relationship between the presentation layer and reality. To the extent that the standards convey the impression that the presentation entity is a distinct process to which application processes can send messages or pass pointers to get services, this impression may be slightly misleading. One could implement it that way, but that is not required.

An alternative implementation is to put the presentation primitives into a library, so they can be called by application programs. In this way, the problems of converting data from the internal format to the proper transfer syntax can be done without having an interpreter in the way. For example, to convert an EBCDIC string to IA5 (CCITT's international ASCII), a library routine *OutputString* could map each EBCDIC character to IA5 by table look up and put it directly into the outgoing buffer. Eliminating the interpreter from the presentation layer by merging the encoding function into the application layer may result in better performance.

An implementation that actually did what the standard suggests would pass both the string and abstract syntax type to the presentation process, which would then have to examine the abstract syntax to figure out what to do. Thus in practice, the presentation layer will not actually exist at run time as a distinct entity, but be contained in library procedures bound in with the applications.

8.5.2. The Presentation Layer in the ARPANET

The ARPANET does not have a presentation layer. There is no general purpose way to pass arbitrary data structures between incompatible machines. Of course the ARPANET has a large variety of machines, so the problem certainly exists. The solution used is to have each application define its own standards. Thus the file transfer protocol specifies that the length field shall be a 32-bit two's complement integer, and all implementations must use that format on the wire, regardless of what they use internally.

While the ARPANET approach is less general than the OSI approach, it is a lot what the protocol uses externally, so it just makes the conversions directly. The price that is paid for this efficiency is that each implementation of each protocol is somewhat machine dependent, although these low-level dependencies can usually be well isolated from the rest of the code.

8.5.3. The Presentation Layer in MAP and TOP

MAP and TOP support the basic OSI presentation layer functions of establishing connections and managing multiple contexts. The primitives associated with context switches at activity boundaries are not supported because the whole concept of activities is not supported in the session layer.

The use of ASN.1 is mandatory. The MAP and TOP documents contain references to various abstract syntaxes for file transfer, message transfer, network management, and directory services that must be supported by all MAP and TOP implementations. The transfer syntaxes for these abstract syntaxes are also specified.

8.5.4. The Presentation Layer in USENET

Like the ARPANET, USENET has no general solution to the problem of incompatible machines. Each application has to solve the problem for itself. However, since there are only two applications, mail and news, and these two are closely related, the solution is not difficult. As in the ARPANET case, each application has a built-in knowledge of the external formats required, and just makes all the conversions internally before offering any messages for transmission.

8.6. SUMMARY

The presentation layer is concerned with the manipulation of data structures, their abstract types, and their external representations on the wire (transfer syntaxes). When a session is established, the peers negotiate one or more contexts, each consisting of some data types and their transfer syntaxes. These contexts can be changed as the session progresses. Once these have been agreed upon, each machine is free to represent the data structures internally in the most convenient form, with the knowledge that they can be transmitted and understood by the remote peer, even if a different internal representation is used there.

The ASN.1 notation can be used to describe data types and values. ASN.1 supports the primitive types of Booleans, integers, bit strings, and octet strings, and also provides constructors for combining these into more complex data types, similar to arrays and records in Pascal. Associated with ASN.1 is a transfer syntax that allows data types expressed in ASN.1 to be coded unambiguously for transmission.

Data compression is closely related to transfer syntax. ASN.1 provides a little bit of data compression, for example, by representing small integers in a single byte. Other compression techniques include Huffman coding, arithmetic coding, and run length coding.

Many of the issues relating to network privacy and security can be implemented in the presentation layer. The output of the presentation layer, expressed in one or more transfer syntaxes, can be encrypted before being given to the session layer, for example. Encryption can be done using conventional or public key cryptography. Encryption also plays a major role for authentication and providing digital signatures.

PROBLEMS

1. Write a type definition in ASN.1 for an ordered, untagged structure called *computer* with a 10-byte string *name*, two integers *wordlength* and *mips*, and a Boolean *bigendian*. Also write a value of this type for the Intel 386, which has a 32-bit word, runs at 4 MIPS, and is big endian.

2. Suppose that the text "to be or not to be that is the question" is transmitted from a 16-bit little endian computer to a 16-bit big endian computer. The bytes of each word are swapped before they are deposited into memory. When the string is printed, what does it say?

3. Show how the tagging of Fig. 8-12 affects the transfer syntax of Fig. 8-6(b). How is the length changed by tagging?

4. Is the following type allowed according to the ASN.1 grammar given in the text?

    s ::= SEQUENCE OF { [APPLICATION 49] IMPLICIT INTEGER }

5. Why is it permitted to have several data types in an ASN.1 module with [0] as the tag of some field, but it is not permitted to have several data types tagged at the top level with [PRIVATE 0]?

6. Why isn't the length code of 128 ambiguous in the ASN.1 transfer syntax?

7. How many bits per symbol are required to conditionally Huffman encode the four DNA bases A, C, G, and T, given the following conditional probabilities. Note that all four bases occur equally often, so straightforward Huffman coding yields 2.00 bits/symbol. (XY means the probability of Y following X.)

AA	AC	AG	AT	CA	CC	CG	CT	GA	GC	GG	GT	TA	TC	TG	TT
.45	.35	.15	.05	.30	.50	.18	.02	.15	.04	.60	.21	.10	.11	.07	.72

8. Four symbols are to be encoded using a Huffman code. Their respective probabilities are P_1, P_2, P_3 and P_4, with $P_i > P_{i+1}$ ($i = 1, 2, 3$). What is the mean number of bits per symbol? (Consider all possible cases.)

9. Compute the compression factor (input bits/output bits) for run length encoding, assuming each input bit is generated randomly with a probability α of it being a 0. Do the calculation for output symbols of width 3, 4, 5, and 6 bits. For $\alpha = 0.9$, which output symbol length is most efficient?

10. In a number of countries, the Post Office offers a facsimile transmission system for intercontinental mail. The original document is optically scanned, converted to a bit matrix, and transmitted digitally for reconstruction at a foreign post office. The copy is then put in an envelope and injected into the domestic mail system. Suppose that a document has 20×15 cm of text, with 5 char/cm and 2.4 lines/cm. If digitization uses a 40×40 dot matrix per cm^2, with 1 bit per dot, compare the bandwidth needed for facsimile transmission to the bandwidth needed for transmission as ASCII characters. List some advantages of facsimile over ASCII transmission.

11. The coding scheme proposed in the text for digital television uses a special code for control information in order to issue horizontal and vertical retrace commands. Why are these necessary? After all, the receiver knows how many pixels the screen has, so it knows when to retrace.

12. What is the biggest problem with the digital television scheme described in the text?

13. Break the following monoalphabetic cipher. The plaintext, consisting of letters only, is a well-known excerpt from a poem by Lewis Carroll.

    kfd ktbd fzm eubd kfd pzyiom mztx ku kzyg ur bzha kfthcm
    ur mfudm zhx mftnm zhx mdzythc pzq ur ezsszcdm zhx gthcm
    zhx pfa kfd mdz tm sutythc fuk zhx pfdkfdi ntcm fzld pthcm
    sok pztk z stk kfd uamkdim eitdx sdruid pd fzld uoi efzk
    rui mubd ur om zid uok ur sidzkf zhx zyy ur om zid rzk
    hu foiia mztx kfd ezindhkdi kfda kfzhgdx ftb boef rui kfzk

14. Break the following columnar transposition cipher. The plaintext is taken from a popular computer textbook, so "computer" is a probable word. The plaintext consists entirely of letters (no spaces). The ciphertext is broken up into blocks of five characters for readability.

    aauan cvlre rurnn dltme aeepb ytust iceat npmey iicgo gorch srsoc
    nntii imiha oofpa gsivt tpsit lbolr otoex

15. What is the output of iteration 1 of the DES algorithm when the plaintext and key are both 0?

16. In Fig. 8-20(c), the P-boxes and S-boxes alternate. Although this arrangement is esthetically pleasing, is it any more secure than first having all the P-boxes and then all the S-boxes?

17. How many 2400 foot magnetic tapes are required to store the DES encrypted values of a known plaintext for all keys composed of six uppercase letters? The tape density is 6250 bytes/inch. What are the implications of this result for network security?

18. Design an attack on DES based on the knowledge that the plaintext consists

exclusively of uppercase ASCII letters, plus space, comma, period, semicolon, carriage return, and line feed. Nothing is known about the plaintext parity bits.

19. If stream encryption is being used on a virtual circuit and an undetected transmission error occurs, what happens to the subsequent plaintext at the receiver? Remember that with stream encryption the entire previous plaintext affects the encryption of each character.

20. A very ecology-conscious company has decided to replace all its nonbiodegradable plastic cryptographic keys, which use Shamir's key sharing algorithm for $k = 3$, with a (biodegradable) computer scientist, namely you. One day, three managers come to you and whisper their newly memorized $(x, p(x))$ pairs in your ear: (2,29), (3,12), and (4,28). The prime modulus is 31. What is the key?

21. Using the MIT public key cryptosystem, with $a = 1, b = 2$, etc.
   (a) If $p = 7$ and $q = 11$, list five legal values for d.
   (b) If $p = 13, q = 31$ and $d = 7$, find e.
   (c) Using $p = 5, q = 11$, and $d = 27$, find e and encrypt "abcdefghij"

22. Write a parser for the ASN.1 grammar in the text. The parser should accept alleged ASN.1 modules and tell whether they are legal or not.

23. Write a program to break monoalphabetic substitution ciphers consisting of English prose (uppercase letters only). The program should compute single letter, digram, and trigram frequencies of the ciphertext, make guesses about which letter is which, and see if they lead to reasonable plaintext digrams and trigrams. The program should output the plaintext.

9

THE APPLICATION LAYER

The application layer holds the user (also known as application) programs that do the actual work for which the computers were purchased. These programs make use of the services offered by the presentation layer for their communication needs. However, certain applications, such as file transfer, are so common that standards have been developed for them to eliminate the need for each company to develop its own, and to make sure that everyone uses the same protocols. In this chapter we will examine several of these common applications in detail, both to see the general principles involved and to see how they fit in to the OSI Reference Model. We will also briefly look at some building blocks that the application layer provides for all applications to use.

9.1. APPLICATION LAYER DESIGN ISSUES

In this section we will provide a short introduction and overview of the applications to be studied in this chapter, just to get an idea of what kinds of issues must be dealt with in the application layer. These include file transfer, electronic mail, and virtual terminals, among others. Later in the chapter we will return to each topic to examine it in detail.

Furthermore, we will also briefly examine two building blocks that are often used by these and other applications. One of these deals with connection management and the other is concerned with concurrency.

9.1.1. File Transfer, Access, and Management

File transfer and remote file access are two of the most common applications in any computer network. People who are working together on a project commonly need to share files. One approach is to have a machine where the original of each file is held, and have copies transferred to other machines as needed. Another approach is to have each file "live" on the machine where it was created (or where it is maintained), and have users on other machines ask for copies when they need them.

Another situation in which file transfer is used is at a university that has many diskless workstations spread around campus along with one or more machines with large disks. Students can log into any workstation and access their files over the network. In an alternative design, the workstations can be equipped with small disks, allowing students to download their files to their workstations at the start of each terminal session and upload them back to the main machine when they are done. This arrangement means that a student can log into any workstation on campus (or perhaps even at the dorm), not just the one specific workstation where his files are.

Remote file access (as in the case of diskless workstations) is similar to file transfer, except that only pieces of files are read or written, rather than entire files. The techniques used for file transfer and remote file access are similar, so we will not make much of a distinction between them until we come to the subject of file replication. Furthermore, access to a file located on a remote computer that has its own users is hardly different from accessing a file on a dedicated **file server** machine that has no local users, so we will not make much of a distinction between these two cases either. For simplicity, we will assume that files are located on file server machines, with users on **client** machines wanting to transfer these files in whole or in part for reading and writing.

In contrast to the session and presentation layers, on which there has been very little work done outside of OSI, there has been a great deal of research about file transfer done at universities and in industry. Many file servers have been built and experimented with (Svobodova, 1984). As a result, our discussion of file transfer will reflect both OSI and nonOSI work.

The key idea behind most modern file servers is that of a **virtual filestore**, an abstract file server, either freestanding or running as a process on a timeshared computer. The virtual filestore presents a standardized interface to its clients, and provides a set of standardized operations that the clients can execute. Transfers to and from the virtual filestore use standardized protocols. If the real file server has a different internal structure than that of the virtual filestore, it will need some application layer software to hide the truth from the clients and make only the virtual filestore interface visible. By standardizing on a particular virtual filestore interface, as OSI has done, it is possible for application programs to access and transfer remote files without knowing all the details of numerous incompatible file servers.

In this chapter we will look at some of the characteristics of the OSI virtual filestore, as well as other ones, and also discuss some of the issues involved in designing and implementing file servers and file transfer protocols.

9.1.2. Electronic Mail

When the ARPANET first went into operation, its designers expected that process-to-process traffic would dominate. They were wrong. From its very inception, the volume of electronic mail between people has overshadowed the volume of communication between processes. While neither snow, nor rain, nor heat, nor gloom of night may stay the post office's couriers from the swift completion of their appointed rounds, the ARPANET's ability to deliver a message from coast to coast in a few seconds started a revolution in the way people communicate.

The attraction of electronic mail, of course, is that it is very fast. However, there are other advantages that are not as well known. The telephone also provides instantaneous access, but studies have shown that about 75% of all business calls fail to reach the intended party ("I am very sorry, but Mr. Smith is in a meeting/out of town/away from his desk."). Electronic mail has the speed of the telephone without requiring that both parties be available at the same instant. It also leaves a written copy of the message that can be filed away or forwarded. Furthermore, a message can be sent to many people at once.

Although electronic mail can be viewed as just a special case of file transfer, it has a number of specific characteristics not common to all file transfers. For one thing, the ultimate senders and receivers are nearly always people, not machines. This fact has resulted in electronic mail systems being constructed as two distinct, but closely related parts: one providing for the human interface (e.g., composition, editing, and reading mail), and one for transporting mail (e.g., managing mailing lists and providing notification of delivery).

Another difference between electronic mail and general purpose file transfer is that mail messages are highly structured documents. In many systems, each message has a large number of fields in addition to its content. These include the sender's name and address, the recipient's name and address, the date and time of posting, a list of people to receive carbon copies, the expiry date, importance level, security clearance, and many more.

Many telephone companies and PTT's are interested in offering electronic mail as a standard service to companies and individual subscribers. To prevent world-wide chaos, in 1984 CCITT defined a series of protocols for what it calls **MHS** (**Message Handling Systems**) in its **X.400** series of recommendations. ISO tried to incorporate them into the OSI application layer under the name **MOTIS** (**Message-Oriented Text Interchange Systems**), although such incorporation is not entirely straightforward given the lack of structure in X.400. In 1988, CCITT modified X.400 in an attempt to converge with MOTIS. We will discuss MOTIS later in this chapter. Additional material on electronic mail can be found in (Huffman, 1987; Hutchison and Desmond, 1987; and Solman, 1987; Taylor, 1988).

9.1.3. Virtual Terminals

For some reason or other, terminal standardization has been a complete failure. Nearly all terminals accept certain character sequences, called **escape sequences**, for cursor motion, entering and leaving reverse video mode, inserting and deleting characters and lines, and so on. There are ANSI and other standards for these escape sequences, but nobody uses them. Each manufacturer has it own escape sequences, incompatible with those of every other manufacturer. Furthermore, the input (keyboard) problem is even worse than the output (screen) problem.

As a result, it is difficult for anyone to write a screen editor that works with an arbitrary keyboard and display. Even if a given terminal has a key labeled "insert character," it is very unlikely that an existing editor will be able to use that key for the function for which it was intended.

Similarly, if an airline reservations program displays a list of available flights, it would be nice if the user could just move the cursor to the desired flight using the arrow keys on the keyboard or the mouse and then hit the carriage return key or click a mouse button to select the flight. The airlines solve this problem by buying the main computer, all the terminals, and the software from a single manufacturer, so everything works together. However, as more and more people gain access to reservation systems from their terminals and personal computers over networks, the incompatibility problem can no longer be swept under the rug.

The OSI approach to solving it is to define a **virtual terminal**, which is really an abstract data structure that represents the abstract state of the real terminal. This data structure can be manipulated by both the keyboard and the computer, with the current state of the data structure being reflected on the display. The computer can query the abstract data structure to find out about keyboard input and can change the abstract data structure to cause output to appear on the screen. In the section on virtual terminals we will describe in some detail how this idea works.

9.1.4. Other Applications

Numerous other applications have been or are being standardized. Many of these pertain to some specific industry, such as banking. Still, there are a few others that are general enough to warrant saying at least a few words about in this book. Among these are directory services, remote job entry, graphics, and telematics.

Directory services are the electronic equivalent of the telephone book. They provide a way to find the network address of people and services available on the network. Even leaving aside the question of whether that address should be the

NSAP, TSAP, SSAP, PSAP, or something else, there are a variety of interesting design issues for directory service. We will discuss these in this chapter.

Remote job entry allows a user working on one computer to submit a job for execution on another computer. Typically it is the user of a personal computer submitting a batch job for execution on a large mainframe somewhere else. In many cases, the program, data files, and job control statements must all be collected, possibly from diverse machines, bundled together and submitted as a unit. Finally, the output must be directed to the appropriate destinations.

Not all applications are text oriented. Some primarily use drawings. Thus there is a need to send, for example, engineering drawings over networks for remote display and plotting. Considerable work has been done in this area and we will discuss some of the ideas behind it later.

Telematics is the collective name for public information services for home and office use. **Teletex** is a simple system in which a small amount of information can be sent to a large number of people using conventional television broadcasting. **Videotex** (formerly called **viewdata**) is an interactive service in which users can access large public data bases and perform simple transactions like making reservations.

9.1.5. OSI Service Elements—ACSE and CCR

After ISO had been working on the above and other applications for a while, it became apparent that many applications had a certain amount in common. Almost all of them needed to manage connections and many had to coordinate activities among three or more parties. To avoid forcing each new application to solve these programs all over again, ISO decided to standardize some of these building blocks. Below we will describe two of the most important ones.

Association Control Service Element

ACSE (**Association Control Service Element**) is designed to manage connections, which in the application layer are called **associations**. Figure 9-1 shows the ACSE primitives.

Each ACSE primitive maps one to one with the corresponding presentation layer service primitive. Consequently, one could legitimately ask what use they are. Surely applications could just as well use the presentation primitives directly. Two reasons are offered for their existence. The first one is symmetry. All the other layers have their own primitives for connection establishment, so it would be strange if the application layer did not. The second reason is that future changes to ACSE may give *A-ASSOCIATE* more work to do, for example, user authentication. Such a function is clearly inappropriate for the presentation layer.

OSI ACSE Primitive	Description
A-ASSOCIATE	Establish an association
A-RELEASE	Release an association
A-ABORT	User-initiated abort
A-P-ABORT	Provider initiated abort

Fig. 9-1. The ACSE primitives.

Commitment, Concurrency, and Recovery

CCR (Commitment, Concurrency, and Recovery) is a service element that coordinates multiparty interactions in a foolproof way, even in the face of repeated system crashes. Nearly all applications that need to operate reliably use CCR.

To see the kind of problem that CCR has been designed to solve, consider a simple banking transaction. Marvin has instructed his bank to transfer 1 million dollars from his account in Amsterdam to the account of Simon at a different bank in distant Amstelveen. The instruction is passed to the electronic clearinghouse that handles all interbank transfers.

The straightforward protocol is for the clearinghouse to simultaneously send messages to both banks instructing them to debit or credit the appropriate account and then acknowledge that they have done so. The trouble comes in when one of the banks does it and the other is unable to for some reason such as a network failure. What we need is a protocol that either completely succeeds or does nothing at all, rather than one that does part of the work and leaves the banking system in an inconsistent state.

CCR solves this problem by providing atomic actions. An **atomic action** is a collection of messages and operations that either completely succeeds or can be rolled back to the original state, as if no actions at all had occurred.

Atomic actions are implemented using **two-phase commit**, a technique first used in distributed data bases, but which is applicable to almost any multiparty operation. It is illustrated in Fig. 9-2.

In the first phase, the master (the clearinghouse in our example) tells each slave (other bank) what it wants done. Each slave checks to see if it can carry out its request. If it can, it records the request on **stable storage** (some medium, such as a replicated disk, that is known to survive crashes), locks the data so that no other requests from other masters can interfere, and reports back success. It also records the initial state of the data (e.g., the balance in the account) on stable storage. On the other hand, if a slave cannot execute the request, it just reports back failure immediately and does nothing else.

When all the replies have come back, the master sees if all the slaves can perform their assigned tasks. If so, it sends each one a **commit** message, instructing it to go ahead and do the work. Since message loss is handled by lower layers, the

```
Master                                Slave

Begin atomic action;
Send Request 1;
   ⋮
Send Request n;
Send "Prepare to commit" message;
                                      if action can be performed
                                        then
                                          begin
                                            Lock data;
                                            Store initial state on disk;
                                            Store requests on disk;
                                            Send "OK" message
                                          end
                                        else
                                            Send "Failure"
if all slaves said "OK"
   then send "Commit" message
   else send "Rollback" message;
Wait for acknowledgements
                                      if master said commit
                                        then begin
                                            Do work;
                                            Unlock data;
                                        end;
                                      Send "Acknowledgement" message
```

Fig. 9-2. Two phase commit.

only thing that can go wrong is that a slave can crash before carrying out its work. However, it can recover when it comes back up by looking at stable storage to see what the initial state was and what it was supposed to do.

If any of the slaves report failure back in the first phase, the master aborts the action and tells all the slaves to unlock their data and restore the initial state. The net result is that no work is done and no data are changed.

CCR provides primitives for each of the essential actions in the two-phase commit. They are shown in Fig. 9-3.

OSI CCR primitive	From	Description
C-BEGIN	Master	Begin an atomic action
C-PREPARE	Master	End of phase 1; prepare to commit
C-READY	Slave	Slave is able to do its work
C-REFUSE	Slave	Slave is not able to do its work
C-COMMIT	Master	Commit the action
C-ROLLBACK	Master	Abort the action
C-RESTART	Either	Announce that a crash occurred.

Fig. 9-3. The CCR primitives.

The first six have already been discussed. The last one is used when either the master or a slave has rebooted after a crash. Its purpose is to reset the state of the action back to its initial state so it can be repeated.

9.2. FILE TRANSFER, ACCESS, AND MANAGEMENT

File handling is one of the principal services in any network or distributed system. In this section we will look at file server design, concurrency control, file replication, and some key implementation issues. We will take examples from various sources (including the OSI virtual filestore), but we will look specifically at OSI later in this chapter. Considerable literature on file servers exists. A few papers are: (Brown et al., 1985; Hagmann, 1987; Howard, 1988; Rodriguez et al., 1986; Sidebotham, 1986; Svobodova, 1984; Vandome, 1986; Zwaenepoel, 1985).

9.2.1. File Servers

A file server (or a virtual filestore) can be characterized by three properties:

1. File structure.

2. File attributes.

3. File operations.

We will now describe each of these in turn.

Every file server has some conceptual model of what a file is. Different file servers have different models. Three models, however, are widely used. In the first model, a file is an unstructured lump of data without any substructure known to the file server. Since the file server does not know anything about the internal structure of its files, it cannot perform any operations on parts of files. Typically the only operations possible in this model are reading or writing entire files. Fig. 9-4(a) illustrates an unstructured file.

The next step up is the **flat file**, which consists of an ordered sequence of records. The records of a file need not all be of the same size and type. Furthermore, some or all of the records may have labels (keys) associated with them. These labels are not part of the data of the file, just as the file name is not either. With these files, it is possible for clients to address specific records, either by their labels or their positions, so the file server may support operations on individual records such as extending, replacing, or deleting them. A flat file is shown in Fig. 9-4(b). A UNIX file, for example, can be regarded as being a sequence of 1-byte records that are individually addressable by position.

The most general model of a file is the **hierarchical file**, which takes the shape of a tree. Each node of the tree may have a label, a data record, both, or neither.

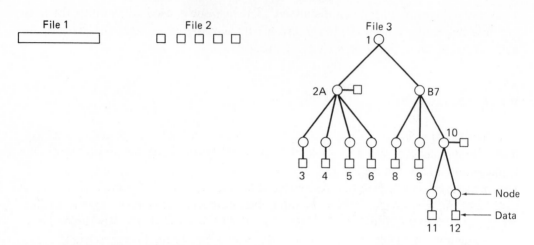

Fig. 9-4. Files. (a) Unstructured. (b) Sequence of records. (c) Hierarchical.

Fig. 9-4(c) depicts a hierarchical file with 12 nodes, two of which have labels (A, and B), and 10 of which have data records (all but nodes 1 and 7).

It is frequently useful to have a standard ordering for all the nodes, not only to allow unlabeled nodes to be addressed by node position for delete and replace operations, but also for transferring entire files. In this example, the nodes are numbered by depth-first search, in which the tree is walked by always visiting the leftmost unvisited node next. Alternatively, if all the nodes are labeled, a specific node can be addressed by giving its path from the root (provided that all sister nodes have unique labels). It is also worth pointing out that node indices or labels also serve for addressing entire subtrees. Thus an operation to delete a subtree applied to node 10 would also remove nodes 11 and 12.

All files have **attributes** that describe them. As a bare minimum, each file must have a name or other identifier, and a size telling how much storage it currently occupies. In practice, most file servers maintain various other attributes as well. Figure 9-5 shows the OSI virtual filestore attributes as an example. Each attribute has a name, a type, and a value (possibly a set or list).

Some attributes are created when the file is created, and are forever frozen thereafter. Others can be explicitly changed by user operations. Still others (e.g., time of last modification) are automatically maintained by the file server. Which attributes are user changeable varies from file server to file server.

Although most of the attributes are straightforward, a few of them require some comment. The *Allowed operations* attribute allows the creator of a file to specify, for example, that some operations are not valid on this file. Insertion of records in the middle of UNIX files could be prohibited in this way.

Access control determines who may access the file, and how. We will discuss this important issue in detail later.

The *File available* attribute can be used to indicate that there may be a slight delay when opening the file (e.g., to fetch it from a bank vault on the other side of

Attribute	Type	Set when file is created	User changeable	Maintained by server
File Name	String	X	X	
Allowed operations	Bit map	X		
Access control	List		X	
Account number	Integer	X	X	
Date and time of file creation	Time	X		
Date and time of last file modification	Time	X		X
Date and time of last file read	Time	X		X
Date and time of last attribute modification	Time	X		X
Owner	User id	X		
Identity of last modifier	User id	X		X
Identity of last reader	User id	X		X
Identity of last attribute modifier	User id	X		X
File availability	Boolean	X	X	
Contents type	Object id	X	X	
Encryption key	String	X		
Size	Integer	X		X
Maximum future size	Integer	X	X	
Legal qualifications	String	X	X	
Private use	String	X	X	

Fig. 9-5. The OSI virtual filestore attributes.

town). The *Contents type* attribute could tell something about the record structure, for example, by giving an object identifier corresponding to the ASN.1 definition of its records.

The *Legal qualifications* attribute is a string that might contain information relating to various national privacy laws, for example: "This file contains personal information about Swedish citizens and may not be transferred outside of Sweden." Finally, *Private use* is a catchall for any information not provided for by other attributes (e.g., whether or not the information in the file is trustworthy enough to be worth believing).

File operations can apply to a file as a whole or to its contents, that is, to the individual records. Figure 9-6 gives a list of possible operations (also taken from the OSI virtual filestore). The column labeled *Bitmap* shows which operations are included in the *Allowed operations* attribute of Fig. 9-5. For example, a file can be created with permission to read it, but not permission to insert, replace, extend, or erase any of its records. Thus the file cannot be changed after it has been created.

In addition to the operations listed in Fig. 9-6, some file servers also support directory operations. Clients can create and delete directories, and move files about from one directory to another.

Operation	Applies to whole file	Applies to contents	Bitmap	Description
Create file	X			Create a new file
Delete file	X		X	Destroy an existing file
Select file	X			Pick a file for attribute management
Deselect file	X			Terminate the current selection
Open file	X			Open a file for reading or modification
Close file	X			Close an open file
Read attribute	X		X	Read a file attribute
Change attribute	X		X	Modify a file attribute
Locate		X		Locate a record
Read		X	X	Read data from the file
Insert		X	X	Insert new data in the file
Replace		X	X	Overwrite existing data
Extend		X	X	Append data to some record
Erase		X	X	Delete a record

Fig. 9-6. The OSI virtual filestore operations.

All file servers must deal with access control and protection in some way. The simplest and least reliable way is to assume that all the client machines are trustworthy and just carry out all requests that come in. If all the client machines are large mainframe computers with elaborate protection schemes of their own that prevent users from even making unauthorized server requests, this approach may be justified. In a wide-area X.25 public network, the caller's address provided by the carrier during connection setup may be sufficient to authenticate the caller as a trusted mainframe. On the other hand, trusting personal computers on a LAN is foolhardy, so a better method is needed for that case.

One such method is to verify the sender of each request, either by having the sender include a password in each request, or by using one of the digital signature methods discussed in Chapter 8. If wiretappers are potentially a problem, a cryptographically-based digital signature is much better than just sending a plaintext password, unless, of course, the entire session is encrypted. Once the server knows the identity of the client, it can use any of the traditional schemes used by time-sharing systems for protection. For example, the owner could designate the access rights for himself, other members of his group, and everyone else, as in UNIX, or for each file he could give a list of who can access it.

A more elaborate method is to have one or more passwords per file (e.g., one for reading and another for writing). In this system, anyone presenting a valid password is allowed to perform the corresponding operations, without regard to the sender's true identity. Sparse capability-based protection, with a bit map to indicated permitted operations (Tanenbaum et al., 1986), is a variant of this idea.

9.2.2. Concurrency Control

Network file servers have multiple clients to take care of. If two or more clients should accidentally happen to decide to access the same file at more or less the same time, problems can occur. Consider the following scenario. Two clients open the same file for writing. Then each of them simultaneously issues a request to replace the first record of the file. Whichever request happens to get serviced last wins, and overwrites the other one. It is difficult to build reliable applications under these conditions.

One widely implemented solution is to permit clients to lock files before using them. Two kinds of locks are used, **shared locks** and **exclusive locks**. When a client requests a shared lock on a file, typically at the time the file is opened, the lock will be granted only if the file is unlocked or has other shared locks on it. If there is an exclusive lock on it, the open request cannot be granted. Exclusive locks are only granted on unlocked files.

Shared locks are typically used for reading; exclusive locks are normally used for writing. When reading a file, a client generally does not mind the existence of other readers, but wants the shared lock simply to prevent the file from being changed while it is busy. However, when writing a file, the client needs to make sure no other readers or writers are active.

When a file is in heavy use by multiple clients, mostly for reading but occasionally for writing, a problem can occur if ungrantable requests are just rejected. As time goes on, some readers finish, but new readers enter, so that there are always readers active and no writers can ever get started. As an alternative to rejecting requests for exclusive locks out of hand, the server could queue them, and also queue any new requests for shared locks. When the current readers finally finish, the first queued writer is then given a chance. After the writer finishes, the server would have to make a policy decision about whether writers or readers should be allowed to go next.

The granularity of the locking is an important design issue. Obviously it is possible to lock entire files, but it is also possible to lock specific records or subtrees. The finer the grain of the locking, the more concurrency is possible. If two clients need to update the same file, there is no reason to stop them from doing it simultaneously if they are working on disjoint subtrees that can be independently locked.

Locking introduces several annoying problems. First, if a client needs to access several files, as is commonly the case when transferring money in banking applications, there is a potential for deadlock. If client 1 has a lock on file A and client 2 has a lock on file B and each one is trying to get the other file, neither will ever succeed. Ad hoc solutions are sometimes possible, such as having all clients lock files in alphabetical order, thus preventing cycles, but in general deadlock avoidance is up to the clients, not the file server.

Another problem with locking is what happens if a client holding some locks crashes? Unless something is done, the locked files will remain locked forever. If the server is not informed about client crashes, the only thing it can do is adopt a policy of automatically breaking locks on files that are not accessed for some specified time interval. However, if a client is too slow, it may discover that some of its locks have timed out part way through a complex multifile update, leading to chaos.

As an alternative to having clients set individual locks, some file servers support atomic actions, often called **transactions** in the context of file servers. When this facility is available, a client can tell the server to begin a transaction, followed by any number of opens and file operations, and finished by a command to end the transaction. It is up to the server to carry out all the requests in an atomic (i.e., indivisible) way, without interference from other client requests. If the client decides to abort the transaction, or if it times out or something else goes wrong, all files are restored to the state they had before the transaction started.

Transactions can be implemented by having the server make a copy of each file that is opened for writing. Changes that are made by subsequent writes are made on the copy, not the original. If the transaction completes successfully, the copies replace the originals. If multiple servers are involved, the CCR techniques described earlier in this chapter can be used.

If two clients use the same file in simultaneous transactions, the first one to finish wins and makes all its changes, and the second one is aborted. Although this strategy means that the second client has wasted some CPU time, he is effectively rolled back to the start of his transaction, so no damage has been done to any of his files. It is as though he never even started. The beauty of the transaction model is that there are no user-visible locks and the server can prevent deadlock.

The entire discussion of concurrency control so far has been centered around the problem of what to do when multiple users want to update the same file. A completely different approach is to prevent all updates. In this view, files are **immutable**. Once a file has been created, it can never be changed.

To permit new information to be incorporated into a file, a client can create a new **version** of a file, which replaces (but does not modify) the original. Thus a file becomes a sequence of immutable versions. When a client opens a file, the most recent version is opened. Subsequent reads use that version for consistency, even if a new version has been created by another client in the meanwhile. Since creating a new version is an atomic operation, there are no problems with files containing updates from multiple clients. Mullender and Tanenbaum (1985) describe the FUSS system, a multiversion file server, in some detail.

9.2.3. Replicated Files

Having tackled file systems with a single server and multiple clients, let us now look at systems with multiple servers and multiple clients. Networks often have multiple file servers for several reasons:

1. To split the workload over multiple servers.

2. To allow file access to occur even if one file server is down.

3. To increase reliability by having independent backups of each file.

One strategy for file replication is to let each user open accounts with as many file servers as he wants, and manage all the replication himself. This puts a considerable administrative burden on the user, and human nature being what it is, not much replication is to be expected. Nevertheless, when a server crash destroys a users' files, statements from the computer center management to the effect, "It's your own fault," are not likely to be well received.

Thus we would prefer the replication to be done automatically by the file servers themselves. As long as files are never modified, maintaining multiple copies is easy. The trouble comes when one copy is updated: the others must be updated too. The simplest solution, and one which is widely used in practice, is **primary copy replication**. In this scheme, one copy is designated as the master, and all the others are slaves. Updates are always made to the master, which then propagates them to the slaves. Although this method is simple and unambiguous, it has the serious disadvantage of making updates impossible when the master is currently unavailable, either due to a crash of its server or a partition of the network (e.g., due to a broken gateway).

A more robust method, especially with multiple clients active, is **voting** (Gifford, 1979). Call the number of servers with copies of a file N. To read a file, it is required to obtain a **read quorum**, N_r. To modify a file, one needs a **write quorum**, N_w, subject to the constraint $N_r + N_w > N$. Only after the appropriate number of servers have been asked if they are willing to participate and agree, can the operation be performed.

The point of requiring quora can be seen by an example. In Fig. 9-7(a) we have $N = 9$, $N_r = 2$, and $N_w = 8$. Suppose one client has acquired two servers, A and B for reading. In order for another client to perform an update, a write quorum of eight servers must be acquired, but this is impossible since there are only nine of them and two are already busy. Would-be writers must wait until the reader has finished. (As an aside, the reader need not read one copy from each server; a single copy is enough.)

Similarly, in Fig. 9-7(b) we have a client who has acquired five servers for writing, precluding any reads, which also need five. In general, making N_r low means that reads are easy, but writes are hard, and vice versa. The optimal choice depends on whether reads or writes are more common.

Since writes do not update every copy of the file, a read quorum will usually contain some obsolete copies as well as the latest one. In order to allow readers to tell which is the most recent one, each copy maintains a version number. Each write creates a new version with a number higher than any previous version, so that

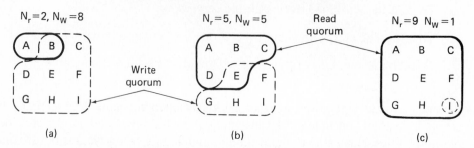

Fig. 9-7. Three examples of a read quorum and a write quorum.

when a reader gets a quorum it can tell which copy or copies are up-to-date (there is always at least one).

An interesting variation on voting is **voting with ghosts** (Van Renesse and Tanenbaum, 1988). In most applications, reads are much more common than writes, so N_r is typically a small number and N_w is nearly N. This choice means that if a few servers are down, it may be impossible to obtain a write quorum at all.

Voting with ghosts solves this problem by creating a dummy server, with no storage, for each real server that is down. A ghost is not permitted in a read quorum (it does not have any files, after all), but it may join a write quorum, in which case it just throws away the file written to it. A write only succeeds if at least one server is real.

When a failed server is rebooted, it must obtain a read quorum to locate the most recent version, which it then copies to itself before starting normal operation. The algorithm works because it has the same basic property as the basic voting scheme, namely, N_r and N_w are chosen so that acquiring a read quorum and a write quorum at the same time is impossible. The only difference here is that dead machines are allowed in a write quorum, subject to the condition that when they come back up they immediately obtain the current version before going into service.

Other replication algorithms are described in (Bernstein and Goodman, 1984; Brereton, 1986; Pu et al., 1986; and Purdin et al., 1987).

9.2.4. Implementation Issues

File servers are so important and widespread that it is worth saying a little bit about how they are implemented. The simplest way is to organize the server as a single process, with the main loop as shown in Fig. 9-8. Requests for work come in, are processed, and the results are sent back. The server handles one request at a time. While it is busy with the current request, all new requests are simply queued until the server is ready.

The approach of Fig. 9-8 is certainly usable, but it has the disadvantage that if the processing of a request requires several disk accesses (for directories and

begin   {Main loop of file server}
   GetMessage (*buffer*);
   DoWork (*buffer*, *result*);
   SendReply (*result*)
end

Fig. 9-8. Overview of a simple file server.

various internal tables) the server will be idle while waiting for the disk accesses to complete. A more sophisticated design that has higher performance is illustrated in Fig. 9-9. In this design the file server is split up into several **tasks** that share a common address space. Each task is a separate thread of control, with its own program counter and its own stack. However, the tasks share global data, such as file system tables and buffers.

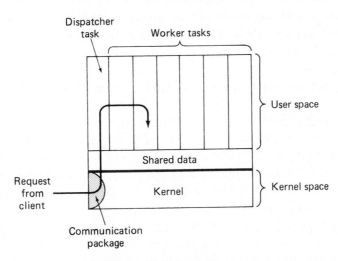

Fig. 9-9. A multithreaded server.

When a request message from a client comes in, the kernel accepts it and passes it to the **dispatcher task**, which is normally waiting. The dispatcher then inspects it and hands it off to an idle **worker task**. Since the dispatcher and worker tasks are in the same address space, only a pointer has to be passed, not the message.

Each task handles a single request to completion. However, if a task blocks while waiting for the disk, another task can run. In this way, the CPU is never idle when there is work to do. When a worker finishes its assigned job, it updates its entry in the master status table in global memory, so the dispatcher will know that it is available to handle another request.

Most file servers are block oriented, that is, they divide the disk up into blocks (e.g., 1K bytes) and represent files as sequences of blocks. A bit map or free list keeps track of blocks unassigned to any file. When a file grows, a free block is allocated and assigned to the file. Some file servers attempt to keep all the blocks of a file within a few cylinders to reduce arm motion, but in general the blocks are not consecutive on the disk.

A widely used technique to improve performance is to have the server maintain a **buffer cache** in memory (e.g., as part of the shared data in Fig. 9-9). The buffer cache consists of the n most recently used disk blocks. When a disk block is read in, it is put in the cache, and the least recently used block is purged (after being rewritten to the disk if it has been modified). If the cache is large enough, the hit rate can be 90 percent or more, thus eliminating a large fraction of the disk accesses.

A completely different approach is taken in the Amoeba system. The Amoeba file server is not block oriented. Instead, it stores each file contiguously on the disk. The cache is also organized this way, with entire files cached, each file occupying some number of consecutive bytes in the server's memory. Files can be transferred between disk and memory in a single disk operation. When a client requests a file that is in the cache, the entire file can be sent as a sequence of back-to-back packets. Measurements on Amoeba have shown that the file server can operate at close to the full bandwidth of the underlying LAN, something that block-oriented servers cannot even approach.

Although caching on the server machine improves performance, an even bigger gain can be had by caching on the client machines, either instead of or in addition to server caching (Howard et al., 1988; Kazar, 1988; Nelson et al., 1988; Ousterhout et al, 1988; and Schroeder et al., 1985). The client caches can be either on disk or in memory. Furthermore, either blocks or whole files can be cached.

When files can be shared among multiple users working on different machines, client caching introduces a serious problem. Suppose several client machines all have cached copies of a particular file. If a user on one of these machines modifies the local copy, the changes will not be visible to the other users. Thus the semantics of file sharing are drastically altered by allowing local caches.

One approach to this problem is simply to accept it, and tell users to be careful. Some commercial systems actually work this way, but it is not an esthetically pleasing solution.

A second attempt is to have the file server keep track of which client has which blocks and files in its cache. Whenever a client modifies a block or file, it tells the file server, so the latter can send an **unsolicited message** to every client holding the modified block or file, instructing it to remove the now-invalid block or file from its cache.

A third possibility is to cache entire files only, and to have the server keep track of which files are cached where and whether they are opened for reading or for writing. If a file has one writer and no readers, everything works fine. If a second user opens that file, the file server sends an unsolicited message to the client machine asking it to upload the modified file back to the server and to cease caching it. The second open is suspended until the upload has completed.

In effect, the file server maintains a central data base of file usage and simply tells clients to disable caching of all shared files that are being modified. Caching is only permitted for read-only files or files with a single writer and no readers. This scheme is only marginally more elegant than the other ones, but at least it is reasonably efficient because in practice files that are heavily shared are rarely updated.

We have saved the best part for last. In the networking world, there is a tremendous controversy about the issue of connectionless vs. connection-oriented file servers. In the connectionless model, one has a **stateless file server**. To read or write (part of) a file, a client sends a request specifying the file, the record position or label, and the amount of data to be transferred. Files do not have to be opened before use or closed after use. Each request is fully self contained. The SUN NFS system is a widely-used stateless server.

In contrast, a connection-oriented server maintains internal state. When a file is opened, the server makes a table entry for the newly-opened file. Usually the index of this entry is returned to the client for use in subsequent requests.

In practice, files are normally read sequentially, so somebody has to keep track of the current file position. In the stateless model, it is the client who maintains the file position and sends it along on each request. In the other model (sometimes called **stateful** although the word seems fairly contrived), it is the server that keeps track of the file position, so the client can just give the table index, to identify the file, and the byte count.

Each model has advantages and disadvantages. The stateless server's main attraction is that it is highly robust. If it crashes and then reboots, there is no state information to lose, so the only thing a client might notice is a longer response time while the server is coming back up. In contrast, a crash of a stateful server effectively closes all open connections and puts full responsibility for recovery on the clients.

The counterargument against the stateless server is that it is difficult to implement normal file system semantics in a stateless way. For one thing, file locking is inherently stateful. If a server crashes and forgets which files are locked, that can hardly be made transparent to the clients.

For a second thing, suppose a client opens a file and then removes it while the file is open (something UNIX programs frequently do with scratch files). With a stateful server, the file can still be used by referring to the table index, but other programs cannot get at the file, which of course, was the purpose of the whole maneuver.

As a third example, suppose a client opens a file and then changes the protection mode of the file so that it is no longer permitted to access the file. Again, as in the second example, with a stateful server there is no problem in continuing to access the already open file, but with a stateful server it is difficult, if not impossible, to achieve the original semantics.

The adherents of the stateless model would argue that these traditional semantics are actually rather bizarre, but due to the way they were implemented on centralized systems, they seemed natural and no one ever complained. Now that their limitations have become painfully obvious, the solution is to change the semantics of file access to something more reasonable.

The stateless versus stateful debate will no doubt go on for years. Taking sides will be left as an exercise for the reader. It is worth making one final point however. Be sure you realize that there is a subtle difference between the concepts of "connectionless" and "stateless." Connectionless refers to communication, whereas stateless refers to file system design. Theoretically one could imagine a stateless, connection-oriented server that accepted fully-specified requests over its connection, but did not maintain any state between requests. Such a design makes little sense, but it is possible, for example, to access an NFS server over an X.25 network. The reverse situation, sending unreliable datagrams to a stateful server, boggles the mind.

9.3. ELECTRONIC MAIL

Electronic mail, or **e-mail**, as it is known to its many fans, has been around for over two decades. The first e-mail systems simply consisted of file transfer protocols, with the convention that the first line of each message (i.e., file) contained the recipient's address. As time went on, the limitations of this approach became more obvious. Some of the complaints were:

1. Sending a message to a group of people was inconvenient.

2. Messages had no internal structure, making computer processing difficult. For example, if a forwarded message was included in the body of another message, extracting the forwarded part was difficult.

3. The originator (sender) never knew if a message arrived or not.

4. If someone was planning to be away on business for several weeks, and wanted all incoming mail to be handled by his secretary, this was not easy to arrange.

5. The user interface was poorly integrated with the transmission system requiring users first to edit a file, then leave the editor and invoke the file transfer program.

6. It was not possible to create and send messages containing a mixture of text, drawings, facsimile, and voice.

As experience was gained, new proposals were made for more ambitious e-mail systems (Bauerfeld et al., 1984; Horak, 1984; Rose et al., 1985). In 1984, CCITT drafted its X.400 recommendation, which was later taken over as the basis for OSI's MOTIS. In 1988, CCITT modified X.400 to align it with MOTIS. Unlike, say, FTAM, which is widely perceived as being unwieldy and which will probably never replace "native" file systems, MOTIS/X.400 is rapidly becoming the dominant form for all electronic mail systems. For that reason, we will concentrate our discussion of electronic mail on it.

9.3.1. Architecture and Services of MOTIS and X.400

In this section we will provide an overview of what e-mail systems, especially MOTIS and X.400, can do and how they are organized. For the sake of brevity, we will refer to them by their OSI name, MOTIS (ISO 10021), but everything in this section also holds for X.400 as well. MOTIS is concerned with all aspects of the electronic mail system, starting at the time the originator decides to write a message, and ending with the time the recipient (receiver) finally throws it in the garbage can. Let us now briefly describe six of the basic aspects of any electronic mail system.

Composition refers to the process of creating messages and answers. Although any text editor can be used for the body of the message, the system itself can provide assistance with addressing and the numerous header fields attached to each message. For example, when answering a message, the mail system can extract the originator's address from the incoming mail and automatically insert it into the proper place in the reply.

Transfer refers to moving messages from the originator to the recipient. In large part, this requires interfacing with ACSE or the presentation layer to establish the necessary connection, output the message, and release the connection. The mail system should do this completely automatically, without bothering the user.

Reporting has to do with telling the originator what happened to the message. Was it delivered? Was it rejected? Was it lost? Numerous applications exist in which confirmation of delivery is important and may even have legal significance, ("Well, Your Honor, my mail system is not very reliable, so I guess the electronic subpoena just got lost somewhere").

Conversion may be necessary to make the message suitable for display on the recipient's terminal or printer. This feature is especially important because the world is full of existing, incompatible sending and receiving devices. For example, sending a message from a computer terminal to a facsimile terminal might require projecting the message onto a screen, then scanning the screen pixel by pixel to build up a facsimile image for the recipient's terminal.

Formatting pertains to the form of the displayed message on the recipient's terminal. This book was typeset using *troff*. If the input file were to be transmitted by e-mail, it would have to be reformatted at the receiving end to give it the desired appearance. Although the message could be saved to a file, *troffed*, and then examined with a special previewer program, it is a lot simpler, especially for unsophisticated users, if the mail system can just display the formatted message directly (very possibly by calling the formatting program itself).

Disposition is the final step and concerns what the recipient does with the message after receiving it. Possibilities include throwing it away immediately, reading it first then throwing it away, reading it then saving it, and so on. There should also be a way to retrieve saved messages to reread them, forward them, or process them in other ways.

In addition to these basic services, most mail systems provide a large variety of advanced features. Let us just briefly mention a few of these. When people move, or when they are away for some period of time, they may want their mail forwarded, so the system should be able to do this automatically.

On the other hand, if someone has decided to take a vacation in Tahiti to "get away from it all" for a few weeks, he may *not* want his mail forwarded. Instead, he may want the mail system to send a canned reply to the originator of each incoming message saying that he is away and telling when he will return. However, the mail system should keep track of who has been sent a reply and not send a second reply even if a second message comes in from the same originator.

Most mail systems allow users to create **mailboxes** to store incoming mail. Commands are needed to create and destroy mailboxes, inspect the contents of mailboxes, insert and delete messages from mailboxes, and so on.

Corporate managers often need to send a message to each of their subordinates, customers, or suppliers. This gives rise to the idea of a **distribution list**, which is a list of electronic mail addresses. When a message is sent to the distribution list, identical copies are delivered to everyone on the list.

Registered mail is another important idea, to allow the originator to know that his message has arrived. Alternatively, automatic notification of undeliverable mail may be desired. In any case, the originator should have some control over the reporting of what happened.

Other advanced features are carbon copies, high-priority mail, secret (encrypted) mail, alternative recipients if the primary one is not available, and the ability for secretaries to handle their bosses' mail.

A key idea in all modern e-mail systems is the distinction between the **envelope** and its contents. The envelope encapsulates the message, just as a TPDU encapsulates an SPDU. The envelope contains parameters needed for transporting and interpreting the message, such as the destination address, priority, security level, and terminal type required, all of which are distinct from the message itself. Envelopes and messages are illustrated in Fig. 9-10.

Mail systems generally distinguish three types of messages: user messages, replies, and probes. **User messages** contain information sent from one user to another. These are the most important messages carried by the mail system, and are its reason for existence. They can be arbitrarily long and can contain anything the originator chooses to include.

Replies are system-generated messages sent back to an originator to report on

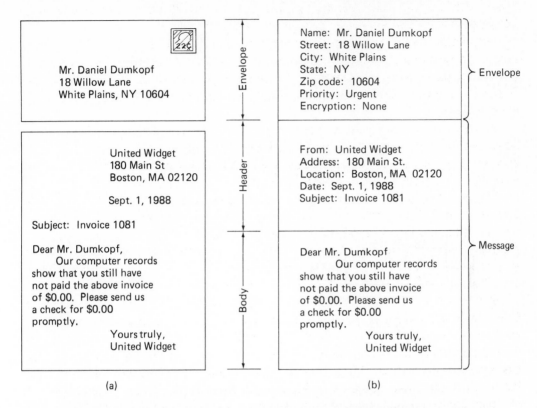

Fig. 9-10. Envelopes and messages. (a) Postal mail. (b) Electronic mail.

whether his message was delivered or not. In MOTIS, users can request that a message generate a reply only if it is delivered, only if it is not delivered, in all cases, or in no cases.

Probes are special test messages consisting of empty envelopes. The purpose of sending a probe is to find out if the destination is reachable. Furthermore, from the time and location stamps attached by all the intermediate machines along the way, the sender can also determine what route the message followed and how long each hop took.

Figure 9-11 shows the model used by MOTIS and most other electronic mail systems. The **user agent** is a program that provides the interface to the mail system. It allows users to compose, send, and receive mail, and manipulate mailboxes.

The **message transfer agent** accepts mail from user agents and sees to it that the mail is started on its way. The message transfer agent is the electronic post office. Just as with the postal system (known in e-mail circles as **snail mail**) a message may visit several (electronic) post offices before being delivered.

While it is possible for the user agent and the message transfer agent to reside on the same host computer, in the future this will be the exception rather than the rule. Typically, the user agent will run on a personal computer at home or work,

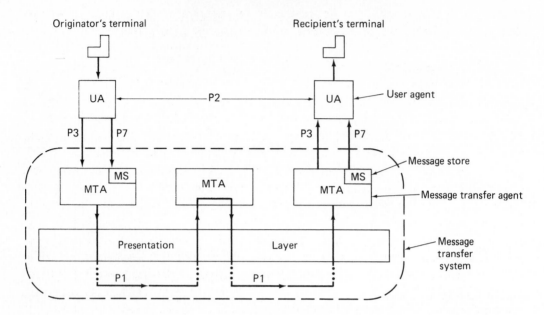

Fig. 9-11. The general model of an electronic mail system.

and the message agent will run on a mainframe operated by the post office, telephone company, PTT, or some other common carrier. In telephone terms, the user agent is the telephone and the message transfer agent is the carrier's end office.

Personal computers have a limited storage capacity and are furthermore only connected to the message transfer agent a short fraction of the day. This gives rise to the question of what to do with very large messages or messages that come in when the user agent is not logged in. The solution is to have the message transfer agent maintain electronic mailboxes for each user in an area called the **message store**. Incoming messages can be placed in these mailboxes until the user logs in to read them, delete them, move them to other mailboxes, selectively upload them, and so on.

If the user agent and message transfer agent run on separate machines, the interaction between them, *P3*, becomes a subject for standardization. OSI has defined service and protocol standards for it. Similarly, the interaction with the message store, *P7*, has also been standardized, as has *P1*, the protocol between the message transfer agents.

The collection of all message transfer agents is called the **message transfer system**. It is divided up into **administrative domains**. Different domains are operated by different authorities. Some domains are public, operated by a common carrier or PTT, whereas others are private, entirely local to a single company.

The (virtual) protocol between the user agents, *P2*, has also been standardized. In effect, *P2* is defined by the header and body of Fig. 9-10 whereas *P1* deals with the envelope. *P2* is known as **IPM (interpersonal messaging)**, and is intended for human to human messages. As time goes on, no doubt other protocols will be defined for ordering products, sending invoices, and other activities.

9.3.2. The User Agent

Electronic mail systems have two basic parts, as we have seen: the user agents and the message transfer agents. In this section we will look at the user agents; in the next one we will study the message transfer agents. The user agent has three different kinds of interactions, as shown in Fig. 9-11. It manages the dialog with the user at the terminal, it talks to the message transfer system about accepting and delivering messages, and it deals with the message store.

Let us consider the user interface first. The user agent is typically invoked by calling a program that accepts a variety of commands that relate to composing, sending, and receiving messages and manipulating mailboxes. Some mail programs have fancy menu or icon driven front ends that are used with a mouse, while others have a list of 1 character keyboard commands to provide the various functions. Typically the mail program will go look at the user's mailbox for incoming mail before displaying anything on the screen. Then it will announce the number of messages in the mailbox and wait for a command.

As an example of how a user agent works, let us take a look at a typical mail scenario. After starting up the mail program, the user asks to see the messages in the mailbox used for incoming mail. A display like that of Fig. 9-12 then appears on the screen. Each line refers to one message. In this example, the mailbox contains eight messages.

#	Flags	Bytes	Sender	Subject
1	K	1030	Johan	Bug in MINIX file system
2	K F	2146	Ann L. Jones	Request for information
3	K A	7136	RVR	Comments about performance paper
4		3124	Erik	Improvement to the basic model
5		610	Henri	Meeting postponed until Tuesday
6		724	janlo	I think the solution is 0-0
7		3240	Peter Smith	Invitation to come see kangaroos
8		425	Edith	Don't forget to prepare your exam

Fig. 9-12. An example display of the contents of a mailbox.

Each display line contains several fields extracted from the envelope or header of the corresponding message. In a simple mail system, the choice of fields displayed is built into the program. In a more sophisticated system, the user can specify which fields are to be displayed by providing a **user profile**, a file describing the display format. In this example, the first field is the message number. The second field, *Flags*, can contain a *K*, meaning that the message is not new, but was read previously and kept in the mailbox; an *A*, meaning that the message has already been answered; and/or an *F*, meaning that the message has been forwarded to someone else. Other flags are also possible.

The third field tells how long the message is and the fourth one tells who sent the message. Since this field is simply extracted from the message, this field may contain first names, full names, initials, login names, or whatever else the sender chooses to put in that field. Finally, the *Subject* field gives a brief summary of what the message is about. People who fail to include a *Subject* field often discover that answering their mail tends not to get the highest priority.

After the headers have been displayed, the user can perform any of the commands listed in Fig. 9-13. Some of the commands require a parameter. The # sign means that the number of a message (or perhaps several messages) is expected. Alternatively, the letter *a* can be used to mean all messages. The display of Fig. 9-12 was produced by the *h a* command.

Command	Parameter	Description
h	#	Display header(s) on screen
c		Display current header on screen
t	#	Type message(s) on screen
s	address	Send a message
f	#	Forward message(s)
a	#	Answer message(s)
d	#	Delete message(s)
u	#	Undelete previously deleted message(s)
m	#	Move message(s) to another mailbox
k	#	Keep message(s) after exiting
r	mailbox	Read a new mailbox
n		Go to next message and display it
b		Back up to previous message and display it
g	#	Go to a specific message but do not display it
e		Exit mail system and update mailbox

Fig. 9-13. Typical mail handling commands to the user agent.

Our example mail program (patterned after the *mmdf* program used on UNIX) keeps track of the current message. The *c* command prints the current message's header. The *t* command types (i.e., displays on the screen) the requested message or messages. Possible commands are *t 3*, to type message 3, *t 4–6*, to type messages 4 through 6, and *t a* to type them all.

The next group of three commands deals with sending messages rather than receiving them. The *s* command sends a message by calling an appropriate editor (e.g., specified in the user's profile) to allow the user to compose the message. Spelling, grammar, and diction checkers can see if the message is syntactically correct. Unfortunately, the current generation of mail programs do not have checkers to see if the sender knows what he is talking about. When the message is finished, it is prepared for transmission to the message transfer agent.

The *f* command forwards a message from the mailbox, prompting for an address to send it to. The *a* command extracts the source address from the message to be answered and calls the editor to allow the user to compose the reply.

The next group of commands is for manipulating mailboxes. Users typically have one mailbox for each person with whom they correspond, in addition to the mailbox for incoming mail that we have already seen. The *d* command deletes a message from the mailbox, but the *u* command undoes the delete. (The message is not actually deleted until the mail program is exited.) The *m* command moves a message to another mailbox. This is the usual way to save important mail after reading it. The *k* command keeps the indicated message in the mailbox even after it is read. If a message is read but not explicitly kept, some default action is taken when the mail program is exited, such as moving it to a special default mailbox. Finally, the *r* command is used to finish up with the current mailbox and go read another one.

The *n*, *b*, and *g* commands are for moving about in the current mailbox. It is common for a user to read message 1, answer, move, or delete it, and then type *n* to get the next one. The value of this command is that the user does not have to keep track of where he is. It is possible to go backwards using *b* or to a given message with *g*.

Finally, the *e* command exits the mail program and makes whatever changes are required, such as deleting some messages and marking others as kept. This command overwrites the mailbox, replacing its contents.

It should be clear from this example that electronic mail has come a long way from the days when it was just file transfer. Sophisticated user agents make it possible to manage a large volume of correspondence easily. For people (such as the author) who receive and send thousands of messages a year, such tools are indispensable.

Let us now turn from the user interface to the protocol used between user agents (*P2* in Fig. 9-11). This protocol is, to a large extent, defined by the header fields included in each message. Some of the common header fields are shown in Fig. 9-14.

The *Originator* field contains the name of the person who actually sent the message. The *Authorizing users* field tells who gave authority to send it. In most cases these two will be identical, but they might differ when a secretary sends a message on behalf of the boss.

The next three fields determine who gets copies of the message. The *Primary recipients* are the people it is really intended for. Carbon copies are sent to the *Copy recipients*, often for administrative purposes. The *Blind copy recipients* also get copies, but their names are not included in the copies sent to the others. Thus the primary recipients get to know who received carbon copies, but not who received blind carbon copies. This feature is widely used in many companies.

Field	Description
Originator	Who actually sent the message
Authorizing users	On whose behalf was it sent
Primary recipients	To whom is the message addressed
Copy recipients	Who gets carbon copies
Blind copy recipients	Who gets carbon copies secretly
Reply recipients	To whom should the reply be sent
Reply time	By when the reply desired
Message id	Message identifier
In reply to	Message to which this is a reply
Obsoleted messages	Messages invalidated by this one
Related messages	Other messages relevant to this one
Subject	What is the message about
Importance	Message priority
Sensitivity	Public, company confidential, etc.
Expiry time	Time when message ceases to be valid

Fig. 9-14. Some header fields for interpersonal messages.

The next group of fields relate to the reply. The reply does not necessarily have to go to the person who sent the message, and there may be a deadline by which it is required.

Then comes a group containing message identifiers: of this message, of the message it is replying to, of previous messages superseded by this one, and of other relevant messages.

The *Subject* field summarizes the message. We saw how this field is used in Fig. 9-12. The *Importance* field can specify the message to be urgent or of some other priority. *Sensitivity* has to do with how secret the contents are and whether the sender wishes them disclosed to third parties.

Finally, the *Expiry date* field tells how long the message is valid. For example, someone might offer to buy or sell some goods for a certain price, but the offer is only valid until a certain date.

Although the body of the message is not as tightly structured as the header, it does have some structure. The body consists of a main part and optionally one or more attachments (appendices). In the future, many people will be receiving electronic mail at home via videotex, using their television sets as the display device. Generally, televisions only have enough resolution to display 40 characters of text per line. If the originator assumed that a line contains 80 characters, a problem arises.

One solution is to encode the body as a standard **simple formatted document**. In such a document, the text is composed of paragraphs, with blank lines between the paragraphs. The user agent on the recipient's end displays as many words per line as fit, preserving only the paragraph boundaries, not the line boundaries.

A more sophisticated solution is to have all messages contain standardized typesetting commands of the sort used in *troff*, *scribe*, T_EX, and other **markup languages**. The user agent can then display sophisticated text, including mathematical and chemical formulas, tables, line drawings, and footnotes in a form suitable for the recipient's terminal or printer. Work is progressing in this area.

9.3.3. The Message Transfer Agent

The message transfer system is concerned with relaying the message from the originator to the recipient. This process is fundamentally different than setting up an application-layer association, as is done in FTAM. With FTAM, you cannot read a remote file if the file server is currently down. With mail, you *can* send a message to someone, even if that person is currently on vacation, or if his user agent is not currently logged in. Electronic mail is thus modeled on a store-and-forward system that works hop-by-hop, not end-to-end.

When a message comes in to a message transfer agent, the processing goes something like this. If the message is from a user agent, the syntax is checked for validity, and if found invalid, it is sent back with an explanation. If it is valid, a message identifier and time stamp are affixed, and it is then treated the same way as a message arriving from another message transfer agent.

The next step is to see if the recipient's user agent or mailbox is local. If so, the message can be delivered, queued for delivery, or stored in the mailbox. If necessary, a reply message confirming delivery is generated and sent back. If the recipient is not local, the message is forwarded to another message transfer agent. International mail may have to transit a gateway at each national boundary.

In most systems, a log of message agents that have handled the message is appended to the envelope. Not only does this make it easier to track down problems, but it also makes it possible to check for loops. If a message transfer agent receives a message containing itself in the log, it knows the message is looping, and has to take special measures to break the loop.

Delivery to a local user agent is not always trivial, because the originator and recipient may have different types of equipment. Possible message types include:

1. ASCII text.
2. Analog facsimile.
3. Digital facsimile.
4. Digitized voice.
5. Videotex.
6. Telex.
7. External (some other system).

If the recipient cannot directly accept the message type, the message transfer agent can attempt to convert it before delivery. Not all conversions are feasible. For example, converting digitized voice to ASCII or facsimile is a nontrivial project. If the conversion cannot be done, the message cannot be delivered.

It will be many years before everyone has the necessary equipment to receive e-mail. In the meanwhile, conversions to other systems will be of great value. For example, when sending a message to someone not having any kind of terminal, the message could be sent electronically to the post office closest to the destination address. There it could be printed on a mechanical printer, laser printer, or facsimile device. Digitized voice could be spoken by a speech synthesizer and then recorded on an audio cassette. The final output could be hand delivered by the postal system.

Alternatively, if the recipient has a personal computer without e-mail capability, the message could be written to floppy disk and the disk physically delivered by the letter carrier. When this mixed-system scheme is not as elegant as an end-to-end electronic one, sending the message to the final post office electronically and then having the printout, audio cassette, or floppy disk sent special delivery, means that it should be possible to have a message entered from a terminal be delivered almost anywhere to the final destination in a few hours at most.

Although ISO has not standardized all the details of the store-and-forward operation between message transfer agents, it has adopted CCITT's general framework for what is called the **remote operation service**. This is none other than our friend the remote procedure call, only now buried inside the mail system, of all places. Four operations have been standardized:

1. Invoke remote operation on another computer.

2. Return result of a remotely invoked operation to the caller.

3. Return error message to the invoker.

4. Reject remote operation call as invalid (e.g., bad parameters).

The remote operation service could be used, for example, by one message transfer agent to execute the operation of entering a message in a processing queue on another one. Why CCITT suddenly embraced the connectionless model after fighting it tooth and nail for seven layers is not obvious. On the other hand, better late than never.

One of the key design issues for the message transfer agents is addressing. We have already seen one possible scheme in Chapter 5, namely, the NAME@DOMAIN system. This is the addressing system used in the ARPANET, ARPA Internet, USENET, and various other networks. Domains can have subdomains, so THOMPSON@CS.YALE.EDU refers to the Thompson in computer science at Yale, whereas THOMPSON@CHEM.YALE.EDU refers to the Thompson in chemistry.

This domain based naming system works fine with a user base of a million people at universities, computer companies, and government installations. CCITT does not believe it would work nearly as well when e-mail reaches the entire population of the industrialized world. Consequently they have devised a radically different addressing scheme. However, we will defer the description of it until later in this chapter after we have covered the directory service, to which it is closely related.

The last aspect of the message transfer system that we will look at here is the envelope (see Fig. 9-10). Some of the fields are listed in Fig. 9-15. They are collected into four rough groups: addressing, delivery, conversion, and security. Although this list is not complete, it gives a reasonable feel for the envelope.

Field	Description
Originator's address	Mail address of the sender
Recipient's address	Mail address of the recipient
Alternate recipient allowed	Is redirection to someone else allowed
Alternate recipient	Second choice recipient
Message id	Message identification
Priority	Slow (cheap), normal, fast (expensive)
Originator report request	What reporting does originator want
MTA report request	What reporting does MTA want
Deferred delivery	Do not deliver before this time
Latest delivery	Do not deliver after this time
Content return	Should content be returned on nondelivery
Information type	Text, facsimile, digitized voice, etc.
Conversion prohibited	No conversion allowed
Lossy conversion prohibited	Only perfect conversion allowed
Explicit conversion	Conversion is known to be required
Encryption identification	Index into encryption key table
Content integrity check	Check sum on contents
Originator's signature	Digital signature
Message security label	Classified, secret, top secret, etc.
Proof of delivery	Recipient's signature

Fig. 9-15. Some of the envelope fields.

The need for the *Originator's address* and the *Recipient's address* are obvious. Less obvious are the next two fields. They deal with the possibility that the message can be delivered to the destination machine but not to the recipient, for example, because the name is spelled wrong or the recipient has moved. Some installations have a default rule that all undeliverable mail is delivered to the "postmaster," who looks at it and tries to figure out what to do with it. If the message is confidential, the originator can set the *Alternate recipient allowed* field to FALSE, so it will not be forwarded to the postmaster. It is also possible to specify a second choice recipient.

The second group concerns delivery. The first two items are self explanatory.

The *Originator's report request* allows the originator to specify that a reply message should be sent back if the message is delivered, if it is not delivered, always, or never. The reply specifies to whom it was actually delivered (the recipient, alternative, postmaster, or other), and when that happened. The *MTA report request* allows the message transfer agent to ask for its own reporting, distinct from the user reporting. This reporting can be more detailed, for example, requiring each message transfer agent along the route to sign and time stamp the envelope.

It is sometimes important that a message not be delivered too early or too late. For example, a company may wish to announce an important new product worldwide at the same moment. It may not want any of its announcement messages to be delivered too early, to avoid information leaking out. The *Deferred delivery time* field gives the earliest allowed delivery time. If the message actually arrives earlier, it must be held.

The reverse situation is when delivery after a certain time is not worth the trouble. This time is indicated by *Latest delivery time*.

Finally, *Content return request* can be set to insure that if the message cannot be delivered, that the entire message, not just the envelope and header, is returned. This feature is especially useful for people who send a lot of mail and do not keep copies of it, so if something comes back as undeliverable, they will know what it was.

The third group deals with conversion between ASCII text, teletex, facsimile, digitized voice, and other information types. If the recipient happens to have the wrong kind of device, sometimes a conversion can be made. However, conversions can result in lost information. For example, teletex terminals do not have the full ASCII character set. The more exotic symbols may have to be replaced by question marks or even dropped altogether. This group of fields gives the originator some control over the conversion process and lets him state whether a lossy conversion is better than no delivery at all.

The final group deals with security. It provides for message encryption, checksums on the contents (to allow message tampering to be detected), the originator's digital signature (to prevent originators from repudiating their messages), security codes, and the recipients digital signature (to prevent recipient's from denying delivery). We have discussed cryptographic algorithms to achieve these goals in the previous chapter. The exact choice of algorithm is up to the users. These fields merely provide a standardized place to put the information.

9.4. VIRTUAL TERMINALS

Terminals fall in three broad classes: scroll mode, page mode, and form mode. Scroll mode terminals are the simplest; form mode terminals are the most sophisticated. For each category, different problems are present and different approaches are needed. We discuss each of the three classes in some detail below. Some additional information on this subject can be found in (Gilmore, 1987).

9.4.1. Scroll Mode Terminals

Scroll mode terminals do not have built-in microprocessors or any local editing capability. When a key is hit, the corresponding character is sent over the line (and possibly also displayed). When a character comes in over the line, it is just displayed. As new lines are displayed, the old ones just scroll upward. Most hardcopy terminals, as well as some CRT terminals are, of this type.

Despite their relative simplicity, scroll mode terminals can differ in many ways, for example, character set, line length, presence or absence of automatic echoing, and overprinting, not to mention the way carriage return, line feed, horizontal tab, vertical tab, backspace, form feed, and break are handled. Some terminals also have potential timing problems, such as the number of filler characters needed following tab and carriage return.

Because scroll mode terminals do not have any processing power, they cannot communicate with the network using any of the network's standard protocols. (A terminal with a built-in CPU can run protocol software internally.) To solve this problem, people normally buy a "black box" that is inserted between the terminal and the network. The black box speaks RS-232 to the terminal, and some standard protocol to the network. It is generally called a **PAD** (**Packet Assembler/Disassembler**) and it can also do various conversions.

The Packet Assembler/Disassembler

CCITT has defined standard PAD interfaces in its X.3, X.28, and X.29 recommendations (triple X). X.3 defines the PAD parameters, X.28 defines the terminal-PAD interface, and X.29 defines the PAD-computer (DTE) interface. The PAD is not exactly a virtual terminal, but it does not really fit into the OSI hierarchy very well anywhere else, either.

When a terminal initially establishes contact with a PAD, the human operator or the computer sets up certain parameters describing the conversation between the terminal and the PAD. The parameters are numbered and so are their option values. A typical command to the PAD might be: SET 1:0, meaning set parameter 1 to value 0. Other commands are available to establish and break connections, read out the values of the parameters, reset the line, and force an interrupt. The complete list is given in Fig. 9-16.

Parameter 1 has to do with whether or not the terminal operator can change PAD parameters in the middle of a session. Parameter 2 must be set according to the terminal type.

Parameters 3 and 4 are needed because some carriers charge per packet, not per character. If a user wishes to be frugal, he will only send full packets, since they

Parameter	Description	Allowed values
1	Can the terminal operator escape from data transfer mode to inspect or change the PAD parameters?	0 = No (escape prohibited) 1 = Yes (escape allowed)
2	Should the PAD echo characters back to the terminal?	0 = No 1 = Yes
3	Which characters should trigger the PAD into sending a partially full packet?	0 = Only send full packets 1 = Carriage return 126 = All control chars + DEL
4	How fast should the PAD time out and send a partially full packet?	0 = No time out 1 — 255 = Time in 50 ms ticks
5	Can the PAD (temporarily) prohibit the terminal from sending characters?	0 = No (Raw mode) 1 = Yes (Flow control)
6	Is the PAD allowed to send service signals to the terminal?	0 = No (suppress signals) 1 = Yes (deliver signals)
7	What should the PAD do upon receiving a break signal from the terminal?	0 = Nothing 1 = Interrupt 2 = Reset 4 = Send a host a control packet 8 = Escape to command mode 16 = Discard output
8	Should the PAD discard computer output intended for the terminal?	0 = No (Deliver) 1 = Yes (Discard)
9	How many fill characters should the PAD insert after outputting a carriage return to the terminal?	0 = None 1 — 7 = Number of fillers
10	Should the PAD automatically fold output to prevent line overflow?	0 = No 1 — 255 (yes) line length
11	Terminal speed (bps)	0 = 110 8 = 200 1 = 134.5 9 = 100 2 = 300 10 = 50
12	Can the terminal (temporarily) prohibit the PAD from sending it output?	0 = No 1 = Yes
13	Should the PAD insert line feed after carriage return?	0 = No 1 — 7 various conditions
14	Should PAD add filler after line feeds?	0 = No 1 — 7 = Yes (How many)
15	Does PAD allow editing	0 = No 1 = Yes
16	Select keystroke for character delete	0 — 127 = character
17	Select keystroke for line delete	0 — 127 = character
18	Select keystroke for line display	0 — 127 = character

Fig. 9-16. The PAD parameters (from CCITT standard X.3).

cost the same as partial packets. The trouble is, that to make intelligent use of an interactive terminal, the host must be notified every time a carriage return is typed. If the typed in characters just pile up in the PAD waiting for the packet to fill, the host will not react to them. Therefore options are provided to override the "send-only-full-packet" rule. Parameter 3 can be set to force a packet to be sent whenever a control character is typed. Parameter 4 can be set to force a packet to be sent whenever no input is received for a specified time interval. Depending on how the host has been programmed, it might be possible for the PAD to collect characters from several terminals and put them in the same packet to reduce costs.

Parameter 5 is used when the terminal also contains a paper tape reader or other relatively high-speed input device. When this parameter is set to 1, the PAD may start and stop the device to regulate the flow. The ASCII control characters DC1 and DC3 are used for on and off, respectively. Parameter 6 can be used to suppress certain status reporting from the PAD. This option is useful when nontechnical personnel (e.g., bank tellers) are using the terminal. Parameter 7 tells the PAD what to do when the user types a break character. The options may be combined. Parameter 8 can be set to cause the PAD to discard computer output (e.g., after receiving a break). Parameter 9 is needed because most hardcopy terminals require filler characters after a carriage return. Even some CRT terminals require filler characters above 4800 bps.

Parameter 10 tells the PAD the terminal line length, so that extra long output lines can be correctly folded. Parameter 11 gives the speed. Other speeds will probably be added in the future. Parameter 12 allows the user to temporarily shut the PAD up using DC1 and DC3, for example, to read the contents of the screen before it scrolls out of view.

Parameters 13 and 14 have to do with the fact that some terminals require a line feed after a carriage return or some filler characters after a line feed. These parameters allow the user to instruct the PAD to insert the necessary line feeds or filler characters.

Parameters 15 through 18 allow the user to edit text that has been typed in but not yet transmitted. If editing is enabled (parameter 15), the user can specify which characters will be used for deleting lines and characters and displaying the current line. CCITT may add new parameters to the PAD in the future, as the need arises.

9.4.2. Page Mode Terminals

Page mode terminals are typically CRT terminals that can display 25 lines of 80 characters each. The computer can move the cursor around the screen to modify selected portions of the display. These terminals have all the same problems as scroll mode terminals, plus a few more such as page length, cursor addressing, and the presence or absence of blinking, reverse video, color, and multiple intensities.

No two terminals have the same escape sequences for using all these fancy features. This makes writing screen editors (and other display-oriented software) difficult. One widely-used solution, pioneered in Berkeley UNIX, is to define a virtual terminal consisting of the commands that most page mode terminals have.

When an editor starts up, it inquires about the terminal type, and then reads in the entry for the terminal from a data base called **termcap** (terminal capabilities). This entry gives the escape sequence required for each virtual command. As long as the software restricts itself to issuing virtual terminal commands, it will run on any terminal having a termcap entry.

Figure 9-17 shows a few of the more common termcap codes. The first group consists of Booleans that are present in the termcap entry if the associated statement is true, and absent if it is false.

The second group provides numerical values, such as the size of the screen. Armed with these numbers, the software knows how many lines of how many characters it can display.

The third group consists of escape sequences for clearing parts of the screen, moving the cursor, entering various special modes, and so on. If a particular code is not present in the termcap data base, the terminal does not have that capability, and the software must avoid it. In many cases missing capabilities can be handled with alternative commands.

For example, if a terminal does not have the *cl* code, but does have *cm* and *cd*, the screen can be cleared by first moving the cursor to the upper left-hand corner, and then clearing the screen from the cursor to the end. Similarly, an editor that wants to have error messages stand out, might prefer reverse video, but settle for bold if reverse video is not available, and use blinking as a last resort.

The fourth group in Fig. 9-17 is an attempt to deal with keyboard input. It is possible to define the escape sequences generated by the arrows and some other keys that move the cursor. In this way, users can move the cursor around the screen with the arrows in a terminal independent manner. The ability of termcap to deal with input is limited, however.

9.4.3. Form Mode Terminals

The most sophisticated terminals are those with built-in microprocessors. In applications such as banking and airline reservations, the computer can download a form to the terminal, with some of the fields being read-only and containing information, with the other fields to be filled in by keyboard input. The microprocessor can allow local editing, macros, and other facilities. These terminals are often called **form mode terminals**.

When the form has been filled in, the microprocessor can run a quick syntax check on it (e.g., bank accounts should be eight decimal digits, with the sum of the digits modulo 9 being 0). If the form is syntactically correct, the modified portion can be uploaded across the network back to the computer. It should be obvious that the termcap model is not adequate for these applications. A radically different virtual terminal model is needed.

Code	Type	Description
bs	Boolean	Terminal can backspace with CTRL-H
hc	Boolean	Terminal prints hard copy
nc	Boolean	Terminal is a CRT but is not able to scroll
os	Boolean	Terminal can overstrike (multiple characters at same position)
ul	Boolean	Terminal can underline text
pt	Boolean	Terminal has hardware tabs

Code	Type	Description
co	Integer	Number of columns in a line
li	Integer	Number of lines on the screen or on a page
dB	Integer	Number of millisec of delay needed for backspace
dC	Integer	Number of millisec of delay needed for carriage return
dN	Integer	Number of millisec of delay needed for line feed
dT	Integer	Number of millisec of delay needed for tab

Code	Type	Description
cd	String	Clear screen from cursor to end of display
ce	String	Clear screen from cursor to end of line
cl	String	Clear entire screen
cm	String	Cursor motion
ct	String	Clear all tab stops
dc	String	Delete character under cursor
dl	String	Delete line containing cursor
ff	String	Go to top of next page (hardcopy terminals)
ic	String	Insert one character at cursor
is	String	String used to initialize terminal (and perhaps set tabs)
mb	String	Enter blinking mode
md	String	Enter bold (extra-bright) mode
us	String	Enter underscore mode
mh	String	Enter dim (half-bright) mode
so	String	Enter reverse video mode
me	String	Enter normal mode (no blinking, bold, dim, reverse video, etc.)
pc	String	Character to use for padding after tab, line feed, etc.
sf	String	Scroll screen forwards
sr	String	Scroll screen backwards

Code	Type	Description
kl	String	Escape sequence sent by left arrow key
kr	String	Escape sequence sent by right arrow key
ku	String	Escape sequence sent by up arrow key
kd	String	Escape sequence sent by down arrow key
kh	String	Escape sequence sent by home key
kb	String	Escape sequence sent by backspace key

Fig. 9-17. A few of the more common entries in the termcap data base.

An alternative model that is well suited for sophisticated display-oriented applications is based on the use of shared data structures. In this model, the virtual terminal software maintains an abstract representation of the display image internally. This representation can be read and updated by both the terminal user and the application program running somewhere on the network. The virtual terminal software has the responsibility for making sure that the screen image is updated whenever its abstract representation is modified.

Actually, this model has two major variants. In the first one, shown in Fig. 9-18(a), there is a single abstract data structure representing the screen image. Two identical copies of it are maintained, one by the virtual terminal software running on (or near) the terminal's microprocessor and the other by the virtual terminal software running near the application program on a distant host computer.

The person at the terminal can modify the microprocessor's copy of the abstract data structure by typing on the keyboard (the arc labeled 1 in Fig. 9-18). These changes are visible on the screen because the screen display is driven by the local data structure. The microprocessor then sends virtual terminal commands to the distant host over the network using the virtual terminal protocol (labeled 2 in Fig. 9-18). These PDUs cause the remote copy of the data structure to be brought up to date with the local one. The modified data structure can be read by the application program using appropriate commands (labeled 3 in Fig. 9-18).

Similarly, the application program can modify its copy of the data structure, which causes PDUs to be sent to the microprocessor to update the terminal's data structure and hence its display. These steps are shown in Fig. 9-18 as 4, 5, and 6.

To prevent both sides from trying to modify the data structure simultaneously, a token is used to control update access. Either the computer or the terminal may hold the token, and only the token holder may update the data structure. The token may be requested and passed back and forth, analogously to the tokens in the session layer, although the virtual terminal token is unrelated to those tokens.

A consequence of the use of the token to control access to the data structure is that the terminal user may only type when the microprocessor holds the token. One could imagine equipping each terminal with two lights, along with a small sign saying:

Dear terminal user:
You may type when the green light is on, but please refrain from typing when the red light is on. The penalty for disobedience is that your typed input will be discarded. Thank you for your cooperation.

The terminal manager

(Actually, the terminal could buffer input without acting on it until the token arrived; nevertheless, the characters could not be echoed to the screen immediately.)

When this **synchronous** model was first proposed, not all users were equally enthusiastic about it. It did not take long for an alternative model to be proposed,

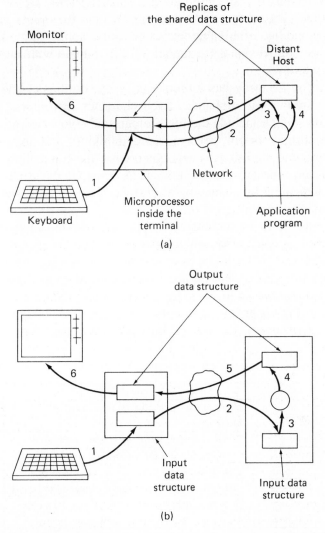

Fig. 9-18. Virtual terminal software using a shared data structure. (a) Synchronous model. (b) Asynchronous model.

namely, the **asynchronous** model of Fig. 9-18(b). The asynchronous model consists of two independent monologs, rather than a single dialog. Each end of the connection has a data structure for input and a second one for output. Changing your own output data structure affects your partner's input data structure, but it does not affect your input data structure or his output data structure.

In the asynchronous model, each copy of the data structure has a single reader and a single writer, so simultaneous write conflicts cannot occur. The price paid is additional storage and more complexity, although this is partly offset by not needing a token. All of what follows applies equally well to both models.

The heart of the abstract data structure is a character array representing the contents of the screen. The array can be one dimensional (to model intelligent typewriters with only one line of editable text), two dimensional (to model simple CRT terminals), or three dimensional (to model CRT terminals with multiple pages of text or multiple windows).

Each element of the array has a unique (x, y, z) coordinate, and can contain a single character from some alphabet. Each character can appear in any one of several **renditions**, which include the font, foreground color, background color, and emphasis (dim, normal, bright, reverse video, blinking, and so on). The set of available alphabets and renditions is negotiated when the connection is established.

At every instant, one (x, y, z) coordinate is designated the **current position**. Most terminals indicate it by displaying a solid, flashing, or underline **cursor** at that position on the screen.

Some basic operations on the character array are shown in Fig. 9-19. They are of four types: moving the cursor, entering text into the array, manipulating attributes, and erasing text. The addressing operations cause a new character to be designated as the current one, but do not cause the contents of the array to change. Both absolute and relative addressing are generally provided, as well as an operation that moves to the upper left-hand corner of page 1. Although in theory absolute addressing is sufficient, the other forms are often used for convenience and efficiency.

Type	Description
Addressing	Move cursor to absolute position (x,y,z)
Addressing	Move cursor by relative amount (Δx,Δy,Δz)
Addressing	Move cursor to home position (1,1,1)
Text	Enter characters starting at current position
Attribute	Change attributes for the entire array
Attribute	Change attributes from cursor forward to (x,y,z)
Attribute	Change attributes from cursor backward to (x,y,z)
Attribute	Change attributes from (x1,y1,z1) to (x2,y2,z2)
Attribute	Change attribute mode on subsequent writes
Erase x	Erase this line from start to cursor
Erase x	Erase this line from cursor to end
Erase x	Erase this line from start to end
Erase y	Erase this page from start to cursor
Erase y	Erase this page from cursor to end
Erase y	Erase this page from start to end
Erase z	Erase from start of first page to cursor
Erase z	Erase from cursor to end of last page
Erase z	Erase from start of first page to end of last page

Fig. 9-19. Basic operations on the virtual terminal character array.

One text operation is generally sufficient. It enters new characters into the array starting at the current position and advances the cursor to the first position beyond the newly entered text. Several attribute operations are commonly provided. Some change the attributes of characters already in the array, but one is needed to change the current attribute, which is used on new characters. Once the current attribute has been set, it remains in effect until changed.

Various commands are available for erasing characters from the current line, page, or multiple pages. Erasing a character causes it to appear on the screen as a blank space. The characters to the right of an erased character do *not* get shifted to the left.

Given only the basic commands, scrolling the screen is difficult: it would require copying an entire subarray almost the full size of the screen. One solution to this problem is to make the *y*-dimension of the array infinite and to introduce the concept of a fixed-size **update window**. Typically, the update window has the width of the screen (e.g., 80 characters) and a height equal to the number of lines on the screen (e.g., 25 lines).

As an example, several hours into a long session, the current *y* position might be 5760, and the update window might extend from 5736 to 5760. As soon as a character was written to an array element on line 5761, the update window would be move automatically to the range 5737 to 5761. Only those characters within the update window are visible on the screen, and only those characters within the update window may be modified.

More advanced virtual terminal systems also provide direct support for forms. Form definitions can be downloaded into the terminal. A typical form consists of multiple fields, each field either containing read-only text, or blank space to be filled in by the terminal user according to some grammar associated with that field. Commands similar to the basic ones are provided: the cursor can be moved absolutely or relatively to a given field, text can be entered into a field, the attributes for certain fields can be changed, and fields can be erased. An example form is shown in Fig. 9-20. This form has nine fields, five of which are read-only (including the title), and four of which are to be filled in from the terminal.

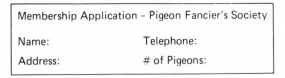

Fig. 9-20. A typical form.

In general, virtual terminal definitions do not specify *when* updates have to be transmitted to the other side. It would be very inefficient to transmit each character typed on the terminal as a separate PDU, although there are some applications that demand this. In many cases it is better to collect an entire line or field, and transmit a single PDU at the end.

In particular, consider what happens when a user enters a line or field, and then part way through notices a typing error, erases the last few characters typed, and then retypes them. Should the virtual terminal software transmit all the characters typed, including the wrong ones, the backspaces, and the corrections? Probably not. Under normal circumstances it is sufficient to transmit the net effect of all the typing, namely the corrected line or field.

Similarly, it might happen that a terminal user decides to fill in the fields of a form in an order different from the top to bottom order. It may be possible to transmit a command sequence involving cursor motion and text that is shorter than what was actually typed, but has the same net effect. Many virtual terminal protocols allow each side to send any legal sequence of commands that achieves the same net effect as the commands that were actually typed in. This optimization is called **net-effecting**.

In general, the issue of how long the microprocessor should collect keystrokes before transmitting them or their net effect is called **delivery control**. The more it collects, the larger the chance that some optimization can be done. However, if it decides to collect several lines, and each line is a command to the computer to do something, then the terminal user will be surprised that nothing happens after the first line has been entered (because nothing has been sent yet).

Virtual terminal models can support various kinds of delivery control. In the simplest model, the virtual terminal software itself decides how much to buffer and when to send. One step up is to have a rule that all the net effect of all accumulated input is transmitted when certain characters (e.g., carriage return, line feed, or form feed) are input. Another rule is that no more than some number of characters will be buffered. Yet another possibility is not to allow input to accumulate for more than some specified time interval.

A more sophisticated form of delivery control is to have a primitive command *FLUSH* that sends the accumulated input. Data are never sent except when this primitive is executed. This scheme gives the user complete control over delivery. It is typically used on the computer side rather than on the terminal side.

One last issue that virtual terminals must address is **attention handling**. All systems have some key that the terminal user can hit to interrupt the current command or program. Sometimes it is the break hit; sometimes it is DEL or rubout. In any event, the virtual terminal software must deal with this event in a special way to allow this signal to overtake any data already in the pipe. One way is to use expedited data.

Suppose a user has asked the computer to list a file, and then after seeing the first few lines, has decided to kill the listing by hitting DEL. It would probably be a good idea for the terminal to start discarding output instantly, to give the user the feeling that the DEL has worked. However, the terminal is then faced with the decision of when to stop discarding output.

In particular, if the computer reacts to the DEL by outputting some kind of response or prompt, these characters must not be discarded. For this reason, the

DEL must be acknowledged in such a way that the terminal can tell which characters were output before the DEL (and must be discarded) and which were output after it (and must be displayed). If the computer acknowledges the DEL with a special character or character sequence in-band (thus not using expedited data), the terminal will be able to tell when to stop discarding (unless the special character happens to occur within the output to be discarded, in which case character stuffing is needed). The protocol has to be robust enough to work with impatient users who hit DEL three or four times in rapid succession, before even the first one has arrived at the computer.

9.5. OTHER APPLICATIONS

Numerous other applications are being developed and standardized. Some of them are for specific industries, such as banking, but others are general purpose. In this section we will take a quick look at a few general-purpose applications.

9.5.1. Directory Service

Services, SAPs, telephones, telex machines and other addressable entities found in telecommunication networks always have long numeric identifiers to make sure they are unambiguous. Since people tend to forget them, telephone books and directory services are provided to map names onto numbers. In the long run, these telephone books and information operators will be replaced by online directory services for looking up telephone numbers, network addresses, and so on. In France, most telephone subscribers already have a PTT terminal for this purpose. To prevent chaos, ISO and CCITT are developing standards for these directory services. In this section, we will provide an outline of this work.

At first glance, it might seem adequate to simply have an alphabetical list of service and subscriber names and their numbers, but different countries have different ways of doing things, so a fairly general scheme is needed. As an example, telephone books everywhere are sorted using the last name, although precisely what constitutes a last name varies from country to country (just ask John von Neumann, Anwar el-Sadat, or Willem de Kooning). In the U.S., all the people with with the same last name are sorted using their first names as the secondary key, whereas in Holland the street address is the secondary key. In some Scandinavian countries, a user-supplied string, such as an occupation or even an academic degree is the secondary sort key.

The basic idea of the OSI directory service is to allow users to look up names based on **attributes**. For example, one could ask the number of a person named Hudson working in IBM's sales office in Los Angeles. To accommodate the conventions of different countries as well as private directory services (company phonebooks), the directory service consists of a hierarchy as shown in Fig. 9-21. Here, the top level directory contains entries of the form "C = country," although other hierarchies are also possible.

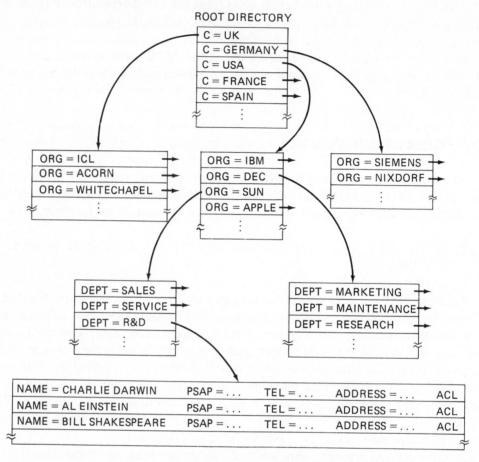

Fig. 9-21. An example directory hierarchy.

One level down, we have organization identifiers, denoted by "ORG = organization name." Below that we have departments, and finally at the bottom, entries for people (or services, machines, printers, etc). Higher level attributes can be inherited, so all entries below "ORG = NIXDORF" would act as though they also had the attribute "C = GERMANY."

To look up an entry, a user provides a set of attributes, such as

C = USA, ORG = SUN, DEPT = R&D, NAME = AL EINSTEIN

and a specification of which attributes of the entry are desired, such as the presentation address, telephone number, or street address. If the specification is unambiguous, the desired value is returned. If there is potential ambiguity and the user knows some piece of information that can resolve it, that information can be used. For example, if there are two Al Einsteins in R&D and the user wants the PSAP address of the one whose telephone extension is 6144, the query could be formulated as

C = USA, ORG = SUN, DEPT = R&D, NAME = AL EINSTEIN, EXT = 6144

An entry consists of a set of attributes and an access control list. The access control list determines who may read the entry and who may modify it. In some situations, users may modify their own entries, and in others, only the organization may do so.

Each attribute has four properties: a type, an interpretation, a qualifier, and a value. The attribute type can be a string or integer, or other data type. The interpretation tells something about how to interpret the value, for example, whether upper and lower case letters are to be considered the same when looking for matches. The qualifier tells whether or not the attribute is inherited by all its subordinates in the tree, whether the attribute is mandatory, optional, or prohibited in queries, and other things. One attribute (or a sequence of attributes) in each directory is mandatory and is called the **key.** The value is the string or numeric value of the attribute.

The directory system also provides for many other features in addition to the basic ones discussed above. For example, an entry can map onto a list of values, rather than just one. Such a feature is useful for building mailing lists. Another feature is the ability to provide aliases, which means that an entry may have two or more immediate superiors. Aliases make it possible to locate entries by organization, geographically, and other ways.

9.5.2. Job Transfer and Management

In many large organizations, individuals have personal computers or workstations on their desks, departments have minicomputers, and the organization as a whole has a computer center with mainframes, supercomputers, and other expensive equipment. It frequently occurs that an individual prepares some work on his personal computer that must be run on a mainframe using files located on his department's minicomputer with the results to be sent back to the personal computer. The application that manages this kind of remote job entry is called **JTM (Job Transfer and Management).**

A typical scenario occurs when a person submits a **work specification** telling what is to be done, where it is to be done, where the input files come from, and where the output files go to. The JTM software must arrange that the program and all its input files end up on the machine where the job will be executed. Work specifications may consist of multiple jobs, so this entire process may have to be repeated several times.

One way is to send a request to each machine holding a file, and direct that machine to send the file to the initiator's machine (e.g., using the standard file transfer protocol). When all the files and programs have been collected in this way, they are shipped to the execution machine.

A second way is for the initiating machine to direct the other machines to send the files directly to the execution machine, for example, to put them in a directory just created for that purpose.

A third way is to have the work specification move to one of the machine's holding input files, pick up the needed files, and then move on to the next machine. This migration continues until all the files have been collected, at which time the whole party moves on to the execution machine.

It is important to realize that JTM knows nothing about the contents of files, job control languages, or the nature of the processing. Its function is to see to it that input files are collected, programs are submitted for execution, and result files are deposited where they should be. It knows as little about the nature of the processing as FTAM does about the files it transfers.

As a concrete example of how execution could be requested without JTM knowing anything about how it works, imagine a computer with a directory called *InputQueue* in which processes can create subdirectories. Each subdirectory contains data files and a special file called *run* consisting of a shell script or job control language program. Whenever it is idle, the computer hunts around in *InputQueue* looking for a subdirectory not yet processed, and executes its *run* file.

As a job executes, it may create subjobs that are also submitted to JTM for remote execution. These subjobs may themselves require files either from the local machine or remote ones. In this manner, a single initial request may ultimately generate a tree of subjobs.

To design a JTM service, several problems must be solved. For one thing, every system involved in a job must have a unique name, so that there is no ambiguity. Telling JTM to run a job on the VAX is not very helpful if there are 50 VAXes around. If jobs may move over public networks, each system needs a worldwide unique name.

A second issue is authentication. When JTM requests an input file on behalf of a user, how does the file system holding the file know if the user has permission to access the requested file? How does the machine that eventually runs the job know who to charge for the CPU time? These are very interesting issues that can only be solved in a definitive way using cryptographic techniques such as digital signatures. In practice, the authentication methods used, such as passwords or trusting everyone are weak.

Finally, in addition to managing file and job movement, JTM is responsible for monitoring progress and reporting it. When complex jobs have been submitted, users are frequently interested in knowing how far along they are (e.g., has the initial job and all its files even reached the execution machine yet)? JTM can provide progress reports by sending report files back to the initiator after designated steps have been completed.

9.5.3. Picture Storage and Transfer

As high resolution displays become more common, there will be a corresponding increase in the number of people and applications interested in transmitting pictures as if they were text files. For this reason, a considerable amount of work has been done on standardizing picture representations so that pictures can be transferred between different locations, different applications, and different vendor's equipment. In this section we will briefly discuss this work.

Before getting started, we should make it clear that we are discussing the storage and transmission of line drawings, not photographs. Typical applications are electrical schematics, VLSI circuits, and architectural blueprints. All the figures in this book are line drawings.

Figure 9-22 shows the basic elements of a picture file. A **polyline** is a sequence of one or more line segments specified by a sequence of (x, y) pairs.

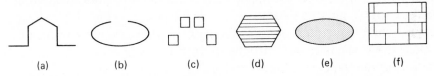

Fig. 9-22. (a) A polyline. (b) An elliptical arc. (c) A polymarker. (d) A filled polygon. (e) A filled ellipse. (f) A cell array.

An **elliptical arc** is a portion of an ellipse. It can be described by giving the coordinates of its foci, the length of the major axis, and the starting and ending angles of the arc. A circle is a special case of an ellipse, with both foci at the same position.

A **polymarker** is a sequence of points, like a polyline, except that they are not connected. The items drawn at each coordinate can be points, squares, circles, or other geometric figures.

A **filled polygon** is a closed figure formed by specifying a polyline that returns to its starting point. The polygon can be filled with a solid color, hatching, lines, dots, or a variety of other textures.

A **filled ellipse** is like a filled polygon, except that it is an ellipse that is filled, rather than a polygon. It is also possible to fill a portion of an ellipse, either as in pie diagrams or by drawing a chord and removing one part.

A **cell array** is a collection of rectangles filled with some pattern. Cells can be combined to give complex pictures.

In addition to these geometric elements, pictures may contain text in one or more alphabets at various positions and orientations.

Each of the picture elements has a variety of attributes that allow a wider variety of pictures to be drawn. For all the line segments, one can specify the type of line (solid, dashed, dotted), the color, and the thickness. Similarly, for polymarkers, the type, color, size, thickness, and orientation of the markers can be specified. For filled figures and cells, the shape and texture must be given. Finally, for text, the fonts, sizes, and colors of the characters must be specified.

With these basics in mind, it should be clear how pictures can be represented as files. A picture file is a sequence of records, each record describing one picture element. Each element starts with a type field, followed by a list of its coordinates and other parameters. In this way, any line drawing can be reduced to a sequence of integers and characters for specifying its types, coordinates, angles, attributes and text. In effect, the picture description is like an assembly language program for an abstract drawing engine.

9.5.4. Teletext and Videotex

Teletext and Videotex are two new information-age services that will soon be widespread among home and business users. **Teletext** (not to be confused with teletex) is a one-way service in which pages of information from a central data base are broadcast on a regular television signal, as illustrated in Fig. 9-23. A small portion of the signal bandwidth is normally wasted while the electron beams in the television sets are engaged in horizontal or vertical retrace. This time can be used for transmitting numbered pages of text.

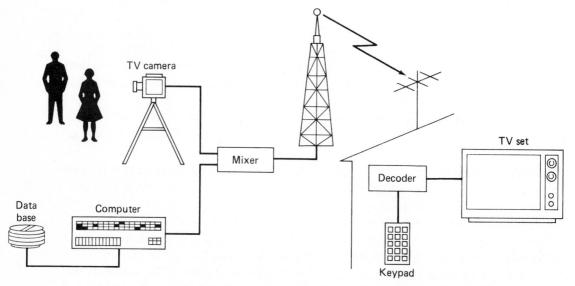

Fig. 9-23. Teletext is a one-way television-based information service.

If, for example, the bandwidth available for teletext is 8 kbytes/sec, and pages consist of 20 lines of 40 characters, the service can transmit 10 different pages in one second. A typical system might transmit 100 different pages in a 10-sec interval, and then repeat the pattern over and over every 10 sec. The contents of a given page may be different on successive passes as the data base is updated.

To use the system, the user types a page number on a keypad attached to the teletext decoder. The next time that page is transmitted (and every subsequent time, as well), it is plucked out of the air and displayed on the screen. With a 10-sec cycle time, there will be an average delay of 5 sec before the page appears. Thus there is a trade-off between the information capacity of the system (number of pages in the cycle) and the response time.

Teletext is most suitable for simple information in which many people are potentially interested. Uses include: weather forecasts, stock market reports, news, recipes, product information, and advertising. A simple file transfer protocol is all that is needed in the application layer.

Videotex is a more sophisticated two-way service using telephone lines. In effect, the home user logs into a large time-sharing system operated by the provider of the videotex service, as shown in Fig. 9-24. In many cases, the "terminal" is a keyboard that generates a video signal, so a standard color television set can be used as the display. Videotex is an interactive service in which users can request specific information. Unlike the teletext data base, which is restricted by the number of pages that can be broadcast in a few seconds, the videotex data base can be arbitrarily large because information is only transmitted when someone wants it. Furthermore, since each user has a dedicated channel into the videotex computer, the total bandwidth is much higher than for teletext.

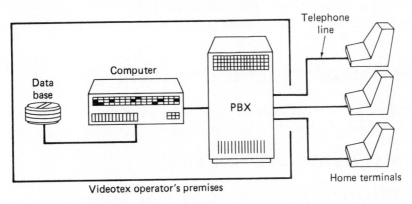

Fig. 9-24. Videotex is a two-way information dialup service.

Two incompatible schemes have developed for videotex. In the **alphamosaic** system, the screen image consists of 24 lines of 40 characters. Each character can be an ASCII character, a graphics symbol, or a mosaic. Mosaics are little 3×2 matrices. Using mosaics transforms the television into a 72×80 bit map display. This is not exactly high resolution, but is good enough for simple graphics.

In the **alphageometric** system, graphics are generated by sending picture drawing commands of the type described in the previous section (polyline, ellipse, and so on). This system gives good results even with low-speed modems, but it requires more hardware and is thus more expensive.

Videotex has two potential audiences: home users and business users. Home users may be interested in information services, such as airline, train and bus schedules, movie listings, restaurant menus, yellow pages, library card catalogs, news, sports, weather, and stock prices. They may also want to use the system in an interactive way, for home banking, catalog shopping, buying stocks, accessing electronic bulletin boards, and making airline, hotel, restaurant, or theater reservations. Sending and receiving electronic mail is also a possibility.

Corporations may use some of these services too (e.g., airline and hotel reservations). Furthermore, they may also want to use videotex to make certain information easily available to all employees nationwide. Some videotex operators offer closed user groups to cater to this audience. With closed user groups, certain information is restricted to members of the group. However, if the expected use is heavy, it may be cheaper to set up a private system and couple it to the public one, so both can be accessed from all terminals (Maurer and Sebestyen, 1983).

Such a coupled public-private system is really a two-level hierarchy. As the size of the system grows, one can imagine a deeper hierarchy developing, with the lowest level holding corporate information, the second level containing local or regional information, the third level supplying national information, with the top level dealing in international information. In this way, information providers could get the coverage they want. Local restaurants would probably want to have their menus available only in region, but major hotel chains could make their reservation systems available world wide by using the top level.

9.6. EXAMPLES OF THE APPLICATION LAYER

In this section we will examine our running examples for the last time to see how they deal with file transfer, electronic mail, virtual terminals, and so on.

9.6.1. The Application Layer in Public Networks

The OSI (and CCITT) work has produced models and standards for file transfer, electronic mail (MOTIS/MHS), virtual terminals, and other applications. We will examine the first three below. The OSI directory service and job transfer and manipulation sections in the text have already described the OSI work.

File Transfer, Access, and Management

The OSI **FTAM** (File Transfer, Access, and Management) model is based on the idea of a virtual filestore that is mapped to a real filestore by software. The OSI virtual filestore definition is highly complex, with many bells and whistles, so our discussion will only give the general flavor, not all the details. For those, please consult the standard itself, ISO 8571.

FTAM has one basic file type, the hierarchical file, but it is possible to specify constraints that give other types as special cases. One special case is the unstructured file, which is manipulated as a unit, with no filestore operations defined on subsections of the file. Another important case is the sequential file, in which the records can be accessed by their labels or positions. Files have the attributes listed in Fig. 9-5.

The virtual filestore is highly connection oriented, with a series of nested **regimes**. Each regime has a series of operations that are permitted during it. When a connection is established, using the *F-INITIALIZE* primitive, FTAM enters what is called the **FTAM association regime**, as shown in Fig. 9-25. During this regime, the FTAM user is permitted to perform operations that manage the virtual filestore.

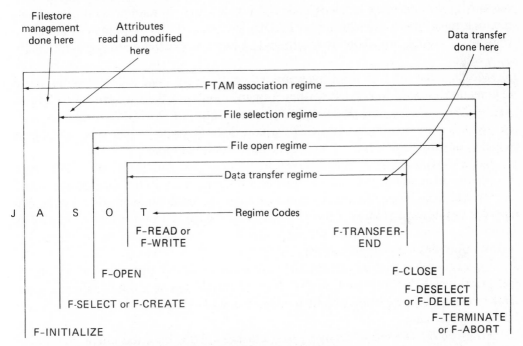

Fig. 9-25. The FTAM regimes.

To access a specific file, the user then executes an *F-SELECT* primitive to select an existing file, or an *F-CREATE* primitive to create a new one. In both cases, the user now enters the **file selection regime**, in which the file attributes can be read or modified. The next step is initiated with *F-OPEN*, which enters the **file open regime**, in which data can be transferred. Normally, the regimes are exited in the reverse order they are entered, although in emergencies it is possible to bail out and abort everything.

While the existence of *F-SELECT* and *F-OPEN* may seem redundant, with some effort it is possible to construct situations where having the two regimes is useful. Since the OSI philosophy is to include every feature that anybody might ever conceivably need, no matter how remote the chance, they were both included. Both primitives have parameters that specify the lock needed, if any. In particular, it is possible to select a file with a shared lock (for reading), then open a file with an exclusive lock (for writing). After exiting the selection regime, the exclusive lock is released, but the shared lock is still in place, so the file can be reopened for reading without any danger of losing the shared lock. In this way, an application can go back and forth between reading and writing phases without any danger of strangers sneaking in and locking the file for writing between an *F-CLOSE* and the following *F-OPEN*.

The list of FTAM primitives is given in Fig. 9-26. Some of these relate to regime management, and others to the specific operations on files, which are listed in Fig. 9-6. A few of the primitives operate on **FADUs** (**File Access Data Units**), essentially the (possibly labeled) nodes of Fig. 9-4(c). To read or write, for example, one must first locate the initial FADU and then specify how many FADUs to transfer. A FADU may contain multiple data records, but these are not individually accessible.

Most of the FTAM primitives are straightforward, but a few require more explanation. *F-INITIALIZE* establishes a connection with the filestore by calling *A-ASSOCIATE*, which calls *P-CONNECT*, which calls *S-CONNECT*, which calls *T-CONNECT*, which calls *N-CONNECT*, which does the work. (Are you starting to understand why some people prefer the connectionless model?)

The *F-BEGIN-GROUP*, *F-END-GROUP*, *F-RECOVER*, *F-CHECK*, and *F-RESTART* primitives all relate to making file transfers reliable, even in the face of client and server crashes. When the open regime is entered, the parameters of *F-OPEN* can specify ordinary or reliable service. If a crash happens when ordinary service is selected, it is up to the user to recover. However, if reliable service is chosen, the system provides considerable assistance.

To start with, the *F-BEGIN-GROUP* and *F-END-GROUP* primitives allow multiple primitives to be bracketed, so that they are carried out as a single atomic action. If they cannot all be carried out, then none of them are carried out and the file is left in its original state.

F-RECOVER is used to recover from crashes. After both the client and server machines are back in operation, the FTAM user can invoke this primitive to return to the regime that was in effect at the time of the crash, with the same parameters and same locks.

F-RESTART is used to resynchronize from minor disturbances that do not break the association, but do cause the user to lose track of the current state of the transfer.

F-CHECK is used to establish checkpoints. It uses the session service's minor sync points. After a checkpoint has been confirmed, any subsequent *F-RECOVER* or *F-RESTART* will fall back to the most recent checkpoint. By making occasional checkpoints during a long file transfer, crashes do not require starting the entire transfer all over from the beginning.

FTAM Service primitive	Confirmed	Regime	Description
F–INITIALIZE	X	I	Establish a connection with the filestore
F–TERMINATE	X	A	Release a connection with the filestore
F–U–ABORT		all	User–initiated abort
F–P–ABORT		all	Provider–initiated abort
F–SELECT	X	A	Select a file for manipulation or transfer
F–DESELECT	X	S	Terminate a selection
F–CREATE	X	A	Create a file
F–DELETE	X	S	Destroy a file
F–READ–ATTRIB	X	S	Read file attributes
F–CHANGE–ATTRIB	X	S	Modify file attributes
F–OPEN	X	S	Open a file for reading or writing
F–CLOSE	X	O	Close an open file
F–BEGIN–GROUP	X	A	Mark start of an atomic action
F–END–GROUP	X	A	Mark end of an atomic action
F–RECOVER	X	A	Recreate open regime after a failure
F–LOCATE	X	O	Move file pointer to a specific FADU
F–ERASE	X	O	Destroy a FADU
F–READ		T	Read one or more FADUs
F–WRITE		T	Write one or more FADUs
F–DATA		T	Data arrival (F–DATA. indication only)
F–DATA–END		T	End of FADU (F–DATA–END. indication only)
F–TRANSFER–END	X	T	End of data transfer regime
F–CANCEL	X	T	Abruptly terminate data transfer regime
F–CHECK	X	T	Set a checkpoint
F–RESTART	X	T	Go back to a previous checkpoint

Fig. 9-26. The FTAM primitives.

FTAM uses a protection scheme so general that no real file server can hope to implement all of it, but most will be able to implement at least some of it. Associated with each file is an access control attribute. This attribute is a set of arbitrarily many five-element lists. Each list contains a bit map, a concurrency key, a user identifier, a list of passwords, and a user location, as shown in Fig. 9-27.

When a user selects a file, the *F-SELECT* contains parameters telling the operations that are needed, the concurrency needed, and optionally some passwords. The user and location identifiers are already known from the *F-INITIALIZE*. Each list in the control attribute is checked in turn to see if it grants permission. Permission can be granted on the basis of user identifier, password, or location (one of these in one list is enough).

In the example of Fig. 9-27, two lists are associated with the file. The first list grants permission to read the attributes, read the data, or extend the file (see the column *bitmap* in Fig. 9-6 for the list of operations that can be specified). The

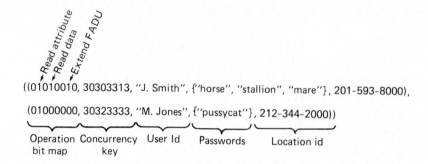

Fig. 9-27. An example access control attribute.

second list only allows reading of the attributes but not reading or writing the data or anything else.

If any of the operations requested by the *F-SELECT* are turned off in the bit map, that list fails. If all the operations are valid, the concurrency key for the list entry is checked against the type of locking the user wants for each operation. There are four possibilities per operation:

0: I want a shared lock (for reading).

1: I want an exclusive lock (for writing).

2: I will not do the operations, but others may.

3: No one may do the operation.

In Fig. 9-27, for example, J. Smith will not be granted access if he wants an exclusive lock for reading attributes because the second digit of the concurrency key is a 0 (shared lock). If the concurrency is all right, then either the user identifier, the passwords, or the location identifier must agree. It is only necessary to pass one test, so an installation could decide just to check who was making the request or where it was coming from. Alternatively, it could allow anyone quoting the proper passwords to perform the operations, without regard to who they were or where they were.

FTAM is so complex that it is unlikely that anyone will implement the whole thing. To prevent the appearance of many incompatible subsets, the FTAM standard has split the features up into 9 subsets, one of which is required and eight of which are optional. This organization reduces the number of possible combinations to 2^8. At *F-INITIALIZE* time, a check is made to see what the user and the filestore have in common. Requests falling outside the common subset cannot be used.

The FTAM protocol is very complicated, but it could hardly have been otherwise given all the features that have to be supported. Each primitive has one or more PDUs associated with it, each of which is defined in ASN.1. The standard also defines a finite state machine telling which actions are to be done for each possible event, such execution of a primitive or arrival of a PDU.

Electronic Mail

The OSI electronic mail system, MOTIS, is based on CCITT's X.400 series of recommendations. The general description given in the text, including all the figures, apply to MOTIS. There are only a few points that need to be added.

One of these is addressing. MOTIS does not use NAME@DOMAIN addressing. Instead, it uses the same type of names used by the directory service. In the context of MOTIS, they are called **O/R** (**Originator/Recipient**) names. Thus a name is any string of attributes that allows the name to be unambiguously looked up by the directory service. The value of this system should be immediately obvious: the directory service can be consulted for PSAP addresses, routes, and any other technical information people are likely to forget.

In practice, certain additional requirements will be added to this basic scheme. For example, for international traffic, the country name must be specified even if the attributes given are unambiguous. Thus an O/R name of:

ORG = KANGAROO EXPORTS LTD, DEPT = SUPPLY, NAME = BRUCE BOOMER

would be allowed in Australia but not elsewhere, even if no other organization in the world was called Kangaroo Exports Ltd. The reason is obvious: without a country specification, the originator's message transfer agent would have to search the top-level directory of every country in the world to find the right organization. Even if by luck the search was successful quickly, the rest of the world would still have to be searched to see if there were multiple matches (and thus an ambiguous O/R name).

The detailed mechanism for sending mail works like this. The user constructs the message using a user agent (mail program) of the type described in the text (and Fig. 9-13). The user agent then passes the message to the message transfer agent using a *SUBMIT.request* primitive. The parameters of this primitive consist of the fields in the envelope, plus the message itself (header plus body).

After the message transfer agent has accepted the envelope and message, it looks up the address of the next message transfer agent along the route and hands it the whole thing using **RTS** (**Reliable Transfer Service**), which uses the *P1* protocol of Fig. 9-11.

The reliable transfer service is designed to avoid losing mail, even in the face of repeated crashes. This service has seven primitives, as shown in Fig. 9-28. The service is implemented by establishing an association between the message transfer agents, and using a stop-and-wait protocol on it. After each message is sent, it is confirmed before another one may be sent.

Reliability is achieved by using session activities. Each message is sent as a separate APDU bracketed by its own activity. If the association is broken due to a

RTS Service primitive	Confirmed	Description
RT-OPEN	X	Establish an association
RT-CLOSE	X	Release an association
RT-U-ABORT		User-initiated abort
RT-P-ABORT		Provider-initiated abort
RT-TRANSFER	X	Transfer one message
RT-TURN-PLEASE		Please give me the "token"
RT-TURN-GIVE		Here is the "token"

Fig. 9-28. The reliable transfer service primitives.

crash of either partner, the session layer recovery mechanism is used to redo the activity in an unambiguous way. For long messages, minor sync points can be used to reduce the amount of retransmission needed for recovery.

It may seem strange that MOTIS does not use FTAM for transporting messages, even though FTAM also provides for reliable transfer using session activities. The reason is that MOTIS is rooted in the 1984 X.400, which predates FTAM.

Virtual Terminals

The OSI VTS (**Virtual Terminal Service**) is very similar to the form mode virtual terminal described in the text. Both the synchronous and asynchronous modes are supported. The central idea behind the model is that of a **conceptual communication area**, which is the shared data structure. This area contains five different kinds of objects, which we will now discuss in turn.

The **conceptual data store** is a three-dimensional array of characters chosen from some agreed upon alphabet. One consequence of this standard having been written by an international committee was the demand for support of diacritical marks, something not needed in English, but required in many other languages. Symbols such as é and è are used in French, and umlauts are used in German, for example. The solution chosen by OSI was to have a special character set of nonspacing diacritical marks that may overlay regular characters. Other than superimposing one of these on a regular character, overstriking is not permitted.

Associated with each character position are attributes for the font, emphasis, foreground color, and background color. The choice of character sets and the allowed values for the attributes are determined when the virtual terminal association (connection) is established.

The second kind of object in the conceptual communication area is the **control object**. Control objects can be used for handling terminal functions that are not related to displaying text, such as ringing bells, turning lights on and off, and modeling function keys and mouse buttons.

The standard does not specify the semantics of control objects in general, although it does provide one example—echo control. If an asynchronous mode virtual terminal were set up to collect entire lines before forwarding them, no characters would appear on the screen until after the entire line had been typed and transmitted and a response received. To get around this problem, there is a control object that can be set to enable local echoing, so that characters appear on the screen as they are typed. However, the computer can disable echoing when passwords have to be typed, by setting the echo control object to FALSE.

The third kind of object in the conceptual communication area is the **device object**. There is one device object for each real device attached to the terminal (e.g., keyboard, display, printer). It handles the interface with the real device, making whatever conversions are necessary.

The fourth kind of object in the conceptual communication area deals with token ownership when the virtual terminal is being operated in synchronous mode. It keeps track of who has the token, and is concerned with token passing.

The fifth kind of object holds the parameters and ASN.1 definitions used by the virtual terminal service and protocol. When a virtual terminal association is established, the two parties have to agree on a large number of parameters and options. One side can propose a value and then the other side can accept or reject it. This negotiation process continues until all the values have been settled. Alternatively, the two sides can agree to use a standard profile, providing a complete parametrized description of the virtual terminal properties. Some of the OSI virtual terminal parameters are listed in Fig. 9-29.

Mode: synchronous or asynchronous
Number of dimensions: 1, 2, or 3
Is the terminal capable of erasing (CRTs) or not (hardcopy)
Character sets allowed
Fonts allowed
Emphasis types allowed
Foreground colors allowed
Background colors allowed
Maximum x coordinate (or infinite)
Maximum y coordinate (or infinite)
Maximum z coordinate (or infinite)
Addressing constraints

Fig. 9-29. Some of the OSI virtual terminal parameters.

The mode, number of dimensions, erasure capability and attributes are straightforward. The maximum bounds on the (up to) three dimensions are also what you would expect. Infinite bounds are allowed, in which case the scrolling mechanism with the update window scheme described earlier in the chapter is used. In addition, several parameters are present to allow addressing constraints to be described.

Some terminals may not be able to backspace, for example, and simple hard copy terminals may not permit any random access at all.

The virtual terminal can perform all the operations listed in Fig. 9-19, as well as several others related to cursor motion within the update window.

It also supports three kinds of delivery control: none, simple, and quarantine. When no delivery control is used, the virtual terminal software determines when to send PDUs. With simple delivery control, the same rule applies, except that a primitive *VT-DELIVER* is provided to flush the buffer. Finally, with quarantine deliver, PDUs are only sent when *VT-DELIVER* is invoked.

The basic VTS primitives are listed in Fig. 9-30. The first four primitives are the same as in FTAM and many other applications. The next one allows the peers to negotiate the use of a standard profile, instead of negotiating the individual parameters one by one. If no standard profile is available, the six primitives with *NEG* in their names can be used to negotiate the parameters one by one.

VTS Service primitive	Confirmed	Description
VT–ASSOCIATE	X	Establish a connection
VT–RELEASE	X	Release a connection
VT–U–ABORT		User-initiated abort
VT–P–ABORT		Provider-initiated abort
VT–SWITCH–PROFILE	X	Negotiate the use of a standard profile
VT–START–NEG	X	Start the parameter negotiation phase
VT–END–NEG	X	End the parameter negotiation phase
VT–NEG–INVITE		Invite the peer to propose a parameter value
VT–NEG–OFFER		Propose a parameter value
VT–NEG–ACCEPT		Accept a proposed parameter value
VT–NEG–REJECT		Reject a proposed parameter value
VT–DATA		Data operation
VT–DELIVER		Flush out all buffered data
VT–ACK–RECEIPT		Acknowledge VT–DELIVER
VT–GIVE–TOKEN		Pass the token in synchronous mode
VT–REQUEST–TOKEN		Request the token in synchronous mode

Fig. 9-30. The basic VTS primitives.

The *VT-DATA* primitive is used for all the operations listed in Fig. 9-19. A parameter is used to specify the operation. There does not appear to be any overriding reason to lump all the data operations in one primitive. The committee could equally well have decided to have a single primitive *NEGOTIATE* with a parameter telling which of the six possibilities was desired and have had each of the operations of Fig. 9-19 be a separate primitive.

In fact, that would have made more sense, since the most common PDU is the one corresponding to *VT-DATA*, and this PDU will need a field giving its type, and then a second field giving the operation. If each operation were a separate primitive, corresponding to a separate PDU, these important PDUs would be shorter.

The last primitives deal with delivery control and token management. We have already seen *VT-DELIVER*. *VT-ACK-RECEIPT* is used to acknowledge it.

VTS also has facilities for handling forms. A form is constructed as a sequence of fields, each field built up from one or more rectangles. The composite field need not be rectangular. Each field is addressed by its field number, independent of its position in the character array.

Field addressing is useful for making application programs independent of the screen geometry. Consider, for example, an application that uses many fields. When run on a 66×80 terminal the position of the fields on the screen will be different than on a 25×132 terminal. By allowing the program to address fields by number instead of by position, the program does not have to be aware of the layout of the fields on the screen. At the time the association is established, the terminal downloads the form layout from the library for its terminal type, and thereafter screen coordinates need not be used.

Commands are available to create fields, delete fields, display text in fields, and erase text from fields. Furthermore, restrictions can be imposed on fields, such as requiring that the input entered into a field consist of exactly four decimal digits. Fields can also be made read only to prevent operator input.

Directory Service

The directory service model described in the text is the one ISO has chosen. The details of this service are being carefully worked out with CCITT, since it is the telephone companies and PTTs that have traditionally provided telephone books and operator-supplied information.

To prevent different names from being used for the same attribute in different countries and organizations, work is in progress to standardize a certain number of common attribute names and the forms of their values. It is also likely that all queries will be required to include certain attributes, such as the country and administrative domain, although certain defaults will be provided if they are not listed.

Job Transfer and Management

OSI JTM also closely follows the model described earlier in the chapter. Rather than talking about files, OSI uses the term **document** as a kind of generalized information carrier. A document may contain several files. The JTM service deals with the manipulation of documents.

The JTM software performs its work by interacting with four kinds of agencies:

1. **Initiation agency**: the process (or person) that submits the work.

2. **Source agencies**: file systems that provide needed files.

3. **Sink agencies**: file systems that accept files for storage.

4. **Execution agencies**: machines that run jobs.

JTM's main function is to issue primitives to these agencies giving them work to do and to accept primitives from them containing information and work for JTM itself. The OSI JTM primitives are listed in Fig. 9-31. They fall cleanly into four groups.

The first group consists of *J-INITIATE* (which has several variants), and is used to pass work specifications to JTM for processing. Each work specification tells in detail what is to be done.

Issued by

JTM Service primitive	Initiator	JTM provider	Execution agency	Sink agency	Source agency	Description
J-INITIATE	X					Create and initiate a work specification
J-GIVE		X				Ask source agency to give JTM a document
J-DISPOSE		X				Pass a document to execution or sink agency
J-ENQUIRE		X				Ask source or execution agency for document names
J-SPAWN			X			Create a subjob
J-MESSAGE			X			Report on work in progress
J-END-SIGNAL			X	X		Report completion of JTM work
J-STATUS		X				Ask about status of work
J-HOLD		X				Temporarily suspend work
J-RELEASE		X				Continue suspended work
J-KILL		X				Abort work abruptly
J-STOP		X				End work gracefully

Fig. 9-31. The JTM primitives.

The second group contains three primitives issued by the JTM provider to ask for documents, deposit documents, and inquire about document availability. All of them are confirmed, with the agency addressed accepting or rejecting the work request, or providing (or not providing) the requested information.

The third group consists of three primitives used by execution and sink agencies to create subjobs, give status reports, and announce completion of work.

The fourth and last group of primitives is used by the JTM provider to control the behavior of previously issued work requests. JTM can ask about the status of the work, suspend and resume it, and kill it. Two ways are provided for terminating work, one abrupt, which just kills it immediately without regard to the consequences, and one that makes an attempt to kill it gracefully, preferably with a report on how far things were and so on. On *J-KILL*, execution agencies are expected to roll back any permanent effects of actions already taken, to the extent possible (using CCR primitives), but on *J-STOP* permanent actions are committed (using CCR primitives).

9.6.2. The Application Layer in the ARPANET

The ARPANET has standard protocols for file transfer, electronic mail, virtual terminals, and many other applications. They differ from their OSI counterparts in a fundamental way: they were all designed bottom up. In the beginning, the protocols were simple, with few features. As it became obvious that new features were needed, they were added. The result of this process is a set of protocols that actually handle the situations that people need.

In contrast, the OSI designers often had little practical experience to guide them and tended to include every feature that anyone thought might conceivably be of some use. On the other hand, for every OSI service, there is a semiformal service specification telling what the service does. The ARPANET lacks these service specifications.

File Transfer

The ARPANET file transfer model is not based on the idea of a virtual filestore. Instead, it is based on the idea of transferring a file from one real machine to another, taking into account differences between the machines. These differences may require some conversions to be performed during the transfer, something the protocol can handle. For example, transferring a file for subsequent retrieval, bit-for-bit, is different than transferring a file to a printer that requires certain carriage control conventions.

Many of the original ARPANET hosts were 36-bit machines, including DEC-10s and DEC-20s, as well as MULTICS machines. Other machines, such as IBM mainframes, had 32-bit words. Consequently the problem of transferring data between machines with different word sizes was taken seriously. OSI essentially ignores the problem.

As a simple example of the problems that can occur, consider transferring a file from a 32-bit machine to a 36-bit machine (the easy case—the other way is harder). At least four reasonable models exist, as shown in Fig. 9-32. In Fig. 9-32(a) three 32-bit words are shown. Each contains four characters. In Fig. 9-32(b) and (c), each 32-bit word is placed in a 36-bit word, left and right adjusted, respectively, with 4 zero bits. In Fig. 9-32(d) each 8-bit character is placed in a 9-bit character, with the high-order bit zero. In Fig. 9-32(e) the bits are packed tight, with no wasted space. Nine characters are packed into two words.

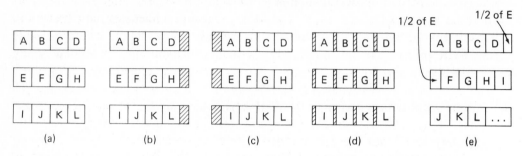

Fig. 9-32. (a) 32-bit words. (b) - (e) Different ways of storing the bits in 36-bit words.

The file transfer protocol, **FTP**, distinguishes four file types: image, ASCII, EBCDIC, and logical byte files. Image files are transferred bit for bit, without change. ASCII files are the standard for text exchange, except between IBM mainframes, in which case EBCDIC is used. Logical byte files are binary files with a byte size different from 8 bits.

FTP recognizes certain types of structure, roughly analogous to the OSI unstructured, sequential, and hierarchical files. There are unstructured files, files that are sequences of records, and random access files that are collections of pages. An unstructured file can be of image, ASCII, EBCDIC, or logical byte type.

A record-oriented file consists of a sequence of fixed size records. Many mainframes expect all input to be 80-character card images and all output to be 132-character print files. Many of these files contain a large number of space characters.

Paged files consist of blocks of data, each with a header giving its size, position and type. One place where these files are useful is for files with holes in them. In UNIX, a process can create a file and write 1 byte into it, then seek to byte 1 billion and write a second byte. On the disk, only two blocks are used, but most file transfer protocols would send the file as 1,000,000,001 bytes. With paged files this can be avoided. Paged files are also used to indicate that some pages may contain bad data due to magnetic tape read errors or measuring instrument problems.

File transfer can occur in three different modes. Stream mode is used for ordinary files. Compressed mode is used to squeeze out runs of consecutive characters, typically spaces, in record-oriented files. Block mode is used for paged files, in which each page has its own header. Checkpointing and error recovery is provided for compressed and block mode files.

A wide variety of commands are supported by FTP. Some of them have to do with sending and receiving files, others manipulate directories, and others relate to setting parameters and modes for transfers. All in all, the model is quite different from the OSI virtual filestore model.

In addition to FTP, a second file transfer protocol, **NETBLT (NETwork BLock Transfer)** is used for very fast file transfers (Clark et al., 1987). It runs directly on top of IP, bypassing the transport layer (TCP) and all higher layers. The idea behind NETBLT is to transfer files in large chunks without explicit flow control, and have the receiver report back to the sender which chunks it received and which were lost.

A NETBLT scenario goes like this. A sender opens a connection to a receiver and negotiates the values of certain parameter settings, such as buffer sizes, packet sizes, and the rate at which the receiver expects that it can accept data. The sender then passes a buffer of data to the NETBLT program, which breaks it up into packets and sends them at the rate (in packets/sec) previously negotiated.

In the simplest version, after sending one buffer, NETBLT waits for a report about which packets arrived safely and which were lost or damaged. The packets that did not make it are then sent again. At this point the sender is informed that the buffer has been sent, and allowed to offer a new one. This algorithm is repeated until the entire file has been transmitted.

An improvement to the basic algorithm is not to use stop-and-wait per buffer, but to allow the sender to supply several buffers at once. In this manner, NETBLT can start sending the second buffer, even before the first one has been acknowledged.

Unlike nearly all other protocols we have studied, which use a flow control algorithm permitting a sender to send a certain number of packets before stopping, the NETBLT protocol uses a rate-based flow control. A sender can transmit packets whenever it wants to, but it must not send more than a certain number of packets per second. If the rate negotiated initially proves unsatisfactory, it may be renegotiated up or down during the transfer. Experience has shown that this protocol can achieve extremely high data rates on networks ranging from LANs to satellite channels due to its low overhead.

Electronic Mail

Electronic mail was essentially pioneered by the ARPANET and is still its primary use. The mail format is defined in a document called **RFC 822**, the only name it has. It has evolved over the years from earlier mail standards. The protocol is called **SMTP (Simple Mail Transfer Protocol)**.

RFC 822 has been designed for sending messages containing lines of ASCII text. No other character sets are supported. Neither are mechanisms for sending facsimile, digitized voice, pictures, or other forms of communication, although other ARPANET standards do deal with some of these.

RFC 822 does not make any distinction between the envelope and the message. Instead, each piece of mail is simply a file containing certain header fields at the top. Each header field is an ASCII keyword, followed by a colon, followed by the value. For example, consider a typical line identifying the sender:

From: TOM@PHYSICS.HARVARD.EDU (Tom Jones)

Any string in parentheses is treated as a comment and is ignored. There are some specific rules about how long lines are treated, the significance of white space (spaces and tabs), and other layout issues, but we will not go into them here.

One contrast between RFC 822 and MOTIS is worth mentioning. In RFC 822, the headers are all in ASCII and are part of the message (in-band signaling), making it easy for people to change them with their editors. While this feature is often convenient, it also provides unwary users with enough rope to hang themselves. MOTIS decided to avoid this problem by clearly separating the headers and the content, and furthermore encoding all the headers in binary (by defining an ASN.1 type for the envelope) to make it much harder for users to casually tamper with them.

The ARPANET (and ARPA Internet) use NAME@DOMAIN addressing. Among the top-level domains are EDU (educational institutions), COM (companies), GOV (government), MIL (military sites), ORG (nonprofit organizations), and the two- and three-character abbreviations for countries other than the U.S. Domains can have subdomains, as we have pointed out before. All addresses in header fields have this format.

The RFC 822 headers shown in Fig. 9-33 are divided into four rough groupings: envelope functions, address headers, message contents, and miscellaneous. The *Sender* and *To* fields are the originator's and recipient's network addresses.

As messages move around the network, *Receive* header lines are added at each hop. These lines list the immediate neighbor that passed the message, the identity of the receiving machine, the physical medium on which the message arrived (e.g., the ARPANET or some LAN), and the protocol that was used for delivery. They also give the date and time. As a result, when a message reaches its destination, it contains enough information that its exact path can be reconstructed to monitor network operation.

The remaining fields are straightforward. With the exception of *Keywords*, all of them have a reasonable counterpart in MOTIS. In addition to the ones we have shown, about a half-dozen other fields exist. These mostly relate to forwarded mail (who forwarded it, from where, to whom, when, and so on).

One field that is worth mentioning is *Encryption*. Because RFC 822 does not make any distinction between envelopes and messages, all the header fields are in plaintext. Only the body is encrypted. An intruder is free to read the *Subject*, *Keywords*, and other header lines, which may provide valuable information. In MOTIS, encryption is handled by the envelope, so the entire message, including the headers, is encrypted. Only the envelope parameters are in plaintext, and none of these relate to the content of the message.

With RFC 822 so widely used and MOTIS so up-and-coming, there is a serious

Field	Description
Sender	Address of the person who sent the message
To	Recipient's address
Received from	Where did message come from
Received by	Who received the message
Received via	On which physical medium did it arrive
Received with	Which protocol did it use
From	Name of the person who sent the message
Reply-To	Address to reply to
Cc	Addresses to which copies are to be sent
Bcc	Addresses of blind copies
In-Reply-To	Message-ID being replied to
References	Other messages cited
Subject	What the message is about
Keywords	Content descriptors
Date	When was the message sent
Message-ID	Message identification
Comments	User defined
Encrypted	Index into encryption key table

Fig. 9-33. RFC 822 header fields. The fields concerned with forwarded mail are not listed.

compatibility problem. One solution is **mail gateways**, which accept messages in one format and forward them in the other. Conversion from RFC 822 to MOTIS is relatively straightforward. The *Keywords* field is just dropped and the rest can be mapped onto some MOTIS field.

The hardest part of the mapping is the addressing since the RFC 822 NAME@DOMAIN addresses are radically different from the attribute-based O/R addressing used by MOTIS. If the *domain* field is structured hierarchically, as in Tom Jones' address above, an implicit mapping is

C = USA, ORG = HARVARD, DEPT = PHYSICS, NAME = TOM

The problem mapping between RFC 822 and X.400 (MOTIS) addresses is studied in more detail by Henken (1987).

Going from MOTIS to RFC 822 is much harder, since many of the MOTIS fields do not exist in RFC 822. Those fields that are irrelevant (e.g., everything about conversions) can just be dropped. For those fields that might be important, such as digital signatures, RFC 822 provides an escape hatch. Header fields starting with *X-* are accepted by the mail software as syntactically valid headers, but are not examined or acted upon. Thus the mail gateway could create special fields such as *X-Sender-Signature* to encode these MOTIS fields. As time goes on, some of these will probably become "legal" and drop the *X-* prefix. As an aside, frivolous headers (e.g., X-Fruit-Of-The-Day: Kumquat) are not totally unknown on the net.

Most mail is transported using the SMTP protocol. To use it, a host initiates a TCP connection to another host, which may either be the ultimate destination or an intermediate stop along the way. Once the connection has been set up, the initiator sends a *MAIL* command, identifying the sender, primarily so the destination knows where to send error messages, should they be required. If the receiver is prepared to accept the mail, it sends a positive acknowledgement.

Next, the initiator sends a *RCPT* command identifying the recipient of the mail. Again, the receiver can accept or reject it. If the recipient is known and acceptable, the sender issues a *DATA* command, followed by the message as a series of ASCII lines and terminated by a line containing only a period. Character stuffing is used to allow such lines to appear within messages. Other commands are available for verifying addresses, expanding mailing lists, switching roles, and terminating connections.

Virtual Terminals

The ARPANET virtual terminal protocol, known as **TELNET**, was designed with scroll mode rather than page or form mode, terminals in mind, although some page mode terminal properties can be negotiated. The default network virtual terminal has a single line of unlimited length.

The protocol is concerned with setting up and manipulating two simplex data streams, one in each direction. It has no concept of a data structure that must be kept identical at both ends by the protocol. As keys are hit on the terminal, a stream of 8-bit bytes is transmitted over the line. The terminal process must convert whatever character code the terminal outputs to the network standard, ASCII. In addition to the 95 ASCII graphics, the CR, LF, BEL, BS, HT, VT, and FF control characters are also legal.

Furthermore, there also exists a group of 15 commands, which may be freely interspersed with the ordinary data. The list of commands is shown in Fig. 9-34. Commands are preceded by the IAC character (Interpret As Command, code 255), which says that the next character is a command. If the command is longer than one character (i.e., if it has parameters), codes 250 and 240 are used like **begin** and **end** in Pascal, to delimit the command.

Code 244 is used to interrupt a process. *Break* (243) is used to mean whatever the remote machine normally uses it for, not necessarily kill process. *Mark* is used to indicate to the terminal process where it should resume output, as above. *Abort output* is only meaningful if the remote machine has a way to terminate the output from the running process without killing it. Similarly, *Are you there* is provided by some operating systems to allow the user to confirm that although the machine may be slow, it is still there.

Codes 247 and 248 are important because they allow the user to use the local host's erase conventions on the remote machine. The clear implication of these

Code

240	End of command	248	Erase line
241	No operation	249	Go ahead
242	Mark	250	Start of command
243	Break	251	Will
244	Interrupt process	252	Won't
245	Abort output	253	Do
246	Are you there?	254	Don't
247	Erase character	255	Interpret as command

Fig. 9-34. The ARPANET TELNET protocol commands.

codes is that when the user wants to erase a character or a line, the terminal process merely converts the local erase key into this network standard and transmits it.

The *Go ahead* command is used with synchronous terminals, to authorize the other side to send. In OSI terms, it passes the token.

Like our first example, TELNET provides for option negotiation to change the defaults and set parameters on the virtual terminal. Option negotiation may be initiated at any time, by either side, using *WILL*, *WON'T*, *DO*, and *DON'T*.

As an example of how these commands are used, a computer capable of handling full-duplex (free running) terminals, might want to find out if the terminal could also work in full-duplex mode. To do so it would send a *WILL* command, specifying its willingness to use full-duplex. The terminal would then reply with either *DO* or *DON'T*. Negotiation can also take the form of one side sending a *DO* or *DON'T* to the other one, requesting some option, with the answer being either *WILL* or *WON'T*. About two dozen options have been defined, including binary transmission, remote echoing, line and page length, and the meaning of tabs.

9.6.3. The Application Layer in MAP and TOP

MAP and TOP implement a subset of the OSI layer 7 applications. ACSE, FTAM, and directory service are fully supported. CCR and JTM are not supported. VTS is fully supported in TOP and partially supported in MAP (because virtual terminals are more important in office applications than on the factory floor). TOP also differs from MAP in another way: TOP supports X.400 whereas MAP supports a completely different kind of messaging system called **MMS (Manufacturing Message Standard)**. MMS is intended for machine-to-machine communication, such as computer-to-robot, whereas X.400 is intended for human-to-human messages.

Nevertheless, MAP and TOP have different goals than OSI, and this leads to another difference between MAP and TOP on the one hand and OSI on the other that shows up for the first time in the application layer. The idea behind OSI is to make it possible for computers from different manufacturers to communicate with one another. This leads to an emphasis on protocols. Service definitions are also provided, but all of them are in the form of abstract primitives as shown in Fig. 9-35.

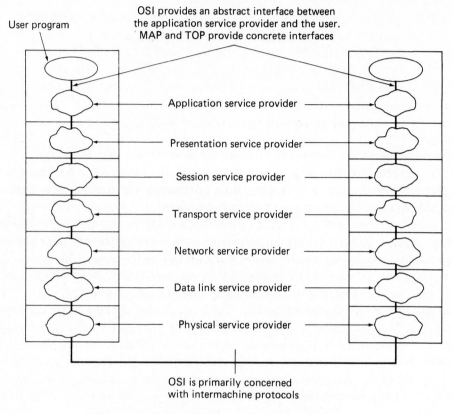

Fig. 9-35. Abstract versus concrete user interfaces.

For the intermediate layers, these abstract service definitions do not cause problems unless a user foolishly decides to acquire each layer from a different manufacturer. For a system produced by a single company, the user does not really care what the interfaces among the lower six layers are. All that matters is how programs talk to the application layer. However, the OSI standards do not specify this top-level interface in much detail, and the specifications that are given (e.g., *indication*) are not even implementable.

As a consequence of this incomplete specification, each manufacturer has necessarily defined its own interface between user programs and the application service provider. A program written using *A*'s interface will not run on *B*'s machine.

In the mainframe world, this situation does not cause problems because computer centers are like newly hatched ducklings: whatever they see first, they follow around for the rest of their lives. In ducklings it is called imprinting; in computer centers it is called compatibility. If a computer center standardizes on brand X computers, the users write their programs using brand X's application service interface and are not bothered by the fact that their programs will not run on brand Y's computers. They do not have any of these, after all.

The MAP and TOP committees found this situation unacceptable. In factories and offices, small computers predominate. The committees envisioned many companies producing plug-in boards containing a full MAP or TOP implementation. In order for the user to be in a position to choose among competing boards on the basis of performance and price, it is essential that the boards all have exactly the same interface between the user program and the board. In other words, there is a need for a standard application service interface so that a changing from one board to another does not require changing user programs. MAP and TOP define this interface.

The MAP and TOP documents thus provide additional specification above and beyond OSI by providing a few more details. In MAP, this runs to about 2300 single-spaced pages (excluding the OSI standards themselves, which are many thousands of additional pages). TOP is not far behind. In the remaining paragraphs of this section, we will briefly compare one aspect of the abstract OSI connection establishment service with that provided by a real implementation, as an example.

Figure 9-36 shows the basic model for connection establishment. Each process wanting to use the network must start out by making an *ACTIVATION* call. This call authenticates the process and registers it as a legal network user. The call returns a 32-bit integer to the caller by which the process identifies itself in subsequent calls.

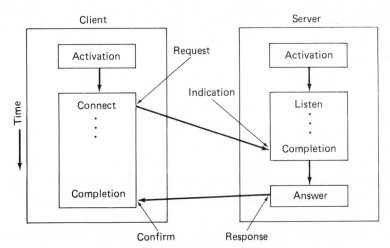

Fig. 9-36. Connection establishment in MAP and TOP.

Next, the server does a *LISTEN*. Both blocking and nonblocking versions are available. If the blocking option is chosen, the server is suspended until some client attempts a connection. If the nonblocking option is chosen, the server can compute for a while and then block later using the *WAIT* call.

When some client does a *CONNECT* call (effectively *A-ASSOCIATE.request*) the server is awakened and given the parameters contained in the incoming PDU. The awakening of the server is the *A-ASSOCIATE.indication*.

After inspecting the parameters, the server accepts or rejects the association by making an *ANSWER* call. This action is the *A-ASSOCIATE.response*. Finally, the PDU sent by *ANSWER* arrives at the client, completing the *CONNECT* (the *A-ASSOCIATE.confirm*) and establishing or denying the connection.

The similarity of this model with our detailed example of the transport layer is not entirely a coincidence. There is really no other sane way to do it. *Request* and *response* can easily be implemented by calls to library routines, but *indication* and *confirm* are fundamentally different, and cannot be implemented the same way.

MAP and TOP not only provide a model that is conceptually implementable, but they also define library procedures that can be called by user programs. By requiring MAP and TOP products to support these calls, users can ensure that their software will work without modification. The details of how the library procedures transmit their parameters to the boards (i.e., which bits go in which device registers) is not standardized because it does not affect program portability.

The parameters of the calls shown in Fig. 9-36 are given in Fig. 9-37. Some of the parameters contain explicit values passed by the caller to the application provider. Other parameters are pointers to records containing even more parameters. Result parameters are also divided this way.

The idea behind this split is that unlike ISO, which hopes to have stable standards some day, the MAP and TOP people have abandoned all hope and are constantly revising the documents in response to experience from users and implementers. The parameters explicitly included in the parameter lists are said to be **exposed**, and are thought to have a higher probability of surviving new versions intact. The parameters hidden away in the records pointed to can be changed more easily (and new ones added) with minimal impact on existing programs.

```
XX-aeactivation (who, how, inpointer, Permit, Result)
XX-listen (permit, how, Outpointer, Connid)
XX-connect (permit, how, callee, inpointer, Outpointer, Connid)
XX-answer (connid, how, inpointer, Result)
```

Fig. 9-37. Details of the calls shown in Fig. 9-36. Parameters beginning with a lower case letter are filled in by the caller. The other ones are result parameters filled in by the application provider.

Let us briefly examine the calls one by one. Just for the record, the parameters listed in Fig. 9-37 are not the official MAP/TOP names, which are somewhat obscure. The *xx_aeactivation* procedure activates an application entity (process). The *xx_* is a dummy prefix that is different for each application. For example, for FTAM, the activation call is *ft_aeactivation*.

The *who* parameter identifies the caller to the application provider (e.g., a plug-in board). The *how* parameter specifies if the call is blocking or nonblocking, not only in this call, but in all the rest as well. The *inpointer* parameter points to a record containing the authentication information.

The remaining two parameters are filled in by the application service provider upon completion of the call. *Permit* is a random 32-bit integer used to identify the caller in subsequent calls, and *Result* is a status code that tells if the call succeeded or not. It could fail, for example, if the board can only handle a limited number of processes and it is already at the limit.

The *xx_listen* procedure contains the 32-bit identifier returned by *xx_aeactivation*, and the blocking/nonblocking flag as input parameters. The output parameters are a pointer to a record and the connection identifier. The record contains information taken from the incoming PDU, including the caller's presentation address, the proposed application context name, and a status code indicating success or failure.

The *xx_connect* procedure is used to establish an association. The remote entity can be specified either by giving its full presentation address or its entity name, in which case the the presentation address must be looked up in a directory. If the call is to a specific application entity name (e.g., "Fileserver3"), the *callee* field is used to specify it. The *inpointer* and *Outpointer* parameters point to records with parameters and results, respectively. If the connection is established, *Connid* is filled in with a 32-bit identifier for that connection.

The parameter record pointed to by *inpointer* contains the presentation address (which is null if the *callee* field is nonnull). It also contains two parameters telling how often to retry the connection if the first time fails due to a transient cause such as network congestion, and how long to wait between retries.

The record also contains a timer that gives the maximum time to wait for local resources, such as a table slot on the board. If, for example, the board can only handle *n* connections at once, and all are in use, the process calling *xx_connect* could specify that it was prepared to wait up to one minute for a connection slot.

The next parameter in the record is the application context (library of ASN.1 definitions) that the caller is proposing to use. This name is made available to the server by a field in the record returned to *xx_listen*, as we mentioned above.

Finally, there is a special application-dependent field, a pointer to yet another record. This pointer is a hook for parameters that apply only to, say, FTAM, but not to VTS.

When the server is awakened from *LISTEN*, it accepts or rejects the connection by calling the procedure *xx_answer*. The *connid* parameter must be the same one returned by *xx_listen*, to identify which call is being answered. *Result* gives the status of the call. Again here, the call could fail due to lack of table space, a parameter error, or other causes.

The record pointed to by *inpointer* provides the server's name (something the caller may not know if the connection was made to a presentation address), and the server's proposed application context. The use of a context in *xx_connect* and one in *xx_answer* constitutes a primitive option negotiation using only a tiny fraction of the possibilities provided by OSI. If the two contexts agree, then that context is established and is used for the duration of the connection.

If they do not agree, it is anyone's guess what happens next. Presumably if the client likes the server's proposal, the connection can go on using it. Otherwise, the client will have to release the connection. This example shows how the enormous wealth of unbearably complicated options provided by OSI are often reduced to the simplest possible case in practice.

9.6.4. The Application Layer in USENET

USENET offers two services, mail and news. USENET mail has been designed to be compatible with the ARPANET mail system described above, so let us concentrate on news. News is effectively a worldwide electronic bulletin board, with hundreds of newsgroups on a great variety of subjects, both technical and other. The total traffic is many megabytes a day. Subscribers to any newsgroup can read all the messages **posted** to (i.e., deposited in) that group, and can post messages of their own. Every message posted to a newsgroup is delivered to all of its subscribers, frequently all over the earth.

The newsgroups are divided into eight broad categories based on their subject:

1. Comp: computers and their software.

2. Misc: Miscellaneous topics not otherwise classifiable.

3. News: The news system itself and its operation.

4. Rec: Recreational activities and hobbies.

5. Soc: Social issues and socializing.

6. Sci: Physics, chemistry, biology, and the other sciences.

7. Talk: Debate-oriented subjects that generate much heat and no light.

8. Alt: Alternative groups that do not fit into any other category.

Figure 9-38 lists a few of the groups, just to give the flavor of what exists. In many cases, the reader can infer the existence of other groups. For example, *comp.binaries.mac* is used for distributing Macintosh binary programs. Analogous groups exist for other popular computers. Similarly, *comp.sys.ibm.pc* is for general discussions of the IBM PC and its clones, but groups also exist for general discussions of virtually every other computer, large and small. Groups also exist for most popular computer languages.

Groups also exist for most areas of computer science, almost all programming languages, as well as for many sciences and hobbies, and political topics. Newsgroups also exist for discussing the operation of the network itself and for

comp.ai	Artificial intelligence discussions
comp.binaries.mac	Encoded Macintosh programs in binary
comp.databases	Database and data management issues and theory
comp.dcom.lans	Local area network hardware and software
comp.edu	Computer science education
comp.graphics	Computer graphics, art, animation, image processing
comp.lang.pascal	Discussion about Pascal
comp.newprod	Announcements of new products of interest
comp.os.minix	Discussion of Tanenbaum's MINIX system
comp.os.research	Operating systems and related areas
comp.protocols.iso	The ISO protocol stack
comp.sources.unix	Postings of complete, UNIX–oriented sources
comp.sys.ibm.pc	Discussion about IBM personal computers
misc.consumers.house	Discussion about owning and maintaining a house
misc.handicap	Items of interest for/about the handicapped
misc.forsale	Short, tasteful postings about items for sale
misc.jobs.offered	Announcements of positions available
misc.kids	Children, their behavior and activities
news.groups	Discussions and lists of newsgroups
rec.arts.poems	For the posting of poems
rec.bicycles	Bicycles, related products and laws
rec.food.cooking	Food, cooking, cookbooks, and recipes
rec.games.chess	Chess & computer chess
rec.humor.funny	Jokes that are funny
rec.photo	Hobbyists interested in photography
sci.astro	Astronomy discussions and information
sci.bio	Biology and related sciences
sci.space	Space, space programs, space related research, etc.
soc.college	College, college activities, campus life, etc.
soc.singles	Newsgroup for single people, their activities, etc.
talk.politics.misc	Political discussions and ravings of all kinds
talk.rumors	For the posting of rumors

Fig. 9-38. A few of the USENET newsgroups.

distributing new news software. There is even a group *rec.nude* for nudists, although it is not obvious to outsiders if a medium supporting only ASCII text is the appropriate vehicle in this case. Since each site pays its own communication costs, not every site accepts every group. In particular, many companies take only the technical groups and refuse most of *misc*, *rec*, *soc*, *talk*, and *alt*.

New groups come and go all the time. When someone proposes creating a new group, the proposal is first discussed in *news.groups* and then a vote is held. If enough people approve, the group is created. It is sometimes hard to tell whether USENET is a glimpse into the 21st century, or a New England town meeting gone international.

In principle, anyone can post a message to any group. However, experience has shown that some people abuse this privilege. When too large a percentage of the traffic is perceived by the readers as a waste of their time, the group can become a **moderated newsgroup**. In such a group, one person is designated as moderator, and is the only one able to post to the group. All attempts by other people to post to the group are automatically converted by the news software into ordinary e-mail messages to the moderator. The moderator then sifts the wheat from the chaff and posts those messages thought to be worthwhile. Moderation raises the quality of the group, but it does tend to reduce the spontaneity of the moderated groups. Some topics have both a moderated and an unmoderated group.

The news system consists of user agents and message transfer agents, just like mail systems. Let us look at each of these in turn.

The news user agent is a program that is invoked to read and send news. When it starts up, it looks in the user's news profile to see which groups the user subscribes to. It then hunts around in the analog of the message store to see if there is any unread news in these groups. If so, it displays a message announcing the first group with news and telling how many messages are present.

At that point, the user has a variety of commands available for reading the news, similar to the mail commands. It is possible to ask for a display of the subject lines, similar to Fig. 9-12. After seeing all the subjects, the user can choose to read a specific message, or just start reading them all, in order. He can also decide that none are very interesting, and ask to move on to the next group. The unread messages can either be left in their original state so that they will also be available next time, or they can be marked as "read" so they will not be mentioned next time.

If a message looks interesting, it can be read, and possibly saved to a file or printed, as well. Having read a particular message, the user now has several options. He can proceed automatically to the next message on the same topic or continue with the next message in the group, regardless of its subject.

However, he also has the possibility of reacting to the message by either sending a reply to the originator of the message (using e-mail), or by posting the reply to the newsgroup. In the former case, the reply only goes to the person who posted the message; in the latter case, it goes to all the subscribers. A message or reply may also be **crossposted** to more than one group. The news software takes care that a user only sees a given message once, even if he subscribes to several groups to which a message has been crossposted.

Since many replies refer to the original message, the user agent has an option of building a properly formatted reply that includes the original message, and then calling the editor to allow the user to edit this reply. Typically, this editing consists of removing the irrelevant portions and adding some text to the relevant parts. When the editing has been completed, the user agent delivers the message to the message transfer agent for delivery as mail or posting as news.

When a message or reply is posted, the poster is asked about the geographic coverage desired. Messages can be posted to all members of the group, wherever they may be anywhere in the world, or they can be restricted to group members in the U.S., North America, Europe, or a smaller area such as a state or in some cases even a city. If someone in Berkeley wants to announce next Tuesday's colloquium speaker, it is unlikely that there will be many potential attendees in, say, Finland or Japan. On the other hand, someone distributing software might well be interested in reaching readers everywhere.

Discussions on USENET can go on for an extended period of time. For the benefit of newcomers, some newsgroups maintain an archive of old messages, to allow people to see what was said before they joined. Partridge et al. (1987) describe how such archive servers work in CSNET, but the same principles apply to USENET as well.

The message transfer agent for news is in many ways similar to the message transfer agent for RFC 822 mail (see Collyer and Spencer, 1987 for a discussion of the news software). This is not entirely surprising, since the formats of news messages and RFC 822 mail messages are structurally the same to permit news messages to be carried the same way as mail messages. Only the exact list of legal header fields differ. The news headers are described in RFC 1036 and listed in Fig. 9-39. News addressing uses the ARPANET NAME@DOMAIN format.

Field	Description
Newsgroups	List of newsgroups to which this message belongs
Subject	What is the message about
From	Who wrote the message
Date	When was the message posted
Path	Route the message has followed so far
Message-ID	Message identifier
Followup-To	Which newsgroups should this reply go to
References	Messages to which this is a followup
Summary	Subject of a followup message
Keywords	Descriptive terms
Distribution	Geographic distribution: NY, USA, Europe, world, etc.
Reply-To	Address to be used for e-mail replies
Sender	Who actually posted the message
Organization	Sender's employer
Lines	Number of lines in the message
Expires	When should the message be considered obsolete
Approved	Moderator's name (for moderated groups)
Control	Used for administering the news system itself

Fig. 9-39. The USENET news header fields. The first six are required. The rest are optional.

The *Newsgroups* field provides a list of groups to which the message has been posted. A reader subscribing to any one of these groups will see the message (once). The *Subject, From,* and *Date* fields have the same function as in RFC 822.

News is propagated hop-by-hop over a complex and ever-changing topology of about 10,000 sites in several dozen countries. At each hop, the current receiver adds its name to the *Path* field. By looking at it, one can see how the message propagated from the source to the current site. Before forwarding a message, the news software checks to see if the destination is already in the *Path* field, in which case the message is not forwarded there. In addition, this information is used by the system administrators to see what paths are being used and to tune the routing algorithms.

The remaining 12 fields are optional. The *Followup-To, References,* and *Summary* fields are used for messages that are followups to an earlier posting. The *Followup-To* field is used when a message is initially posted to multiple groups, but the sender wants subsequent discussions to occur in one specific group. When anyone responds to a message, his user agent checks to see if the original message contained a *Followup-To* field, and if so, uses that as the *Newsgroups* field of the response.

When a message is a followup to an earlier message, the *References* field is included to hold the *Message-ID* of the message (or messages) being responded to. In this case, the *Subject* consists of the prefix *Re:* followed by the original subject. The *Summary* field allows the responder to provide additional information about the response.

The *Keywords* field allows a few keywords to be mentioned. Some sites archive (store) old messages for certain groups. New users can go to the archive and ask for a list of all messages containing specific keywords.

The remaining fields are straightforward and need little explanation, with the exception of *Control*. This field contains the protocol used between the message transfer agents for operating the news system. News messages are distributed over a wide variety of media, including telephone lines, leased lines, X.25 networks, the ARPANET, and other means. Conceptually, USENET is a directed graph, with the nodes being the machines, and the arcs being the transmission lines. Most arcs are bidirectional, but unidirectional arcs also exist. The graph for news is similar, but not identical, to the graph for mail.

Each arc is labeled by the newsgroups that are exchanged over it. For each link, there is a bilateral agreement about which side will call the other, how often that will occur, and which transport protocol will be used. Most of the links are short, but there are also long-haul paths between major organizations that form the **backbone**.

After two machines have established contact, one of them typically begins by sending the other all the news messages that are carried by that link, except for those that list the destination in the *Path* field. Then the flow reverses and messages travel the other way.

This algorithm is essentially flooding, but in practice, most sites receive all their news from a single site, so it works reasonably well. The only time it breaks down is when the primary news feed is down and a site calls an alternative site. Unlike the primary, the alternative has no idea which messages have already been sent. Sending all the messages on its disk is not an attractive proposition. To solve this problem, the called machine can send a message whose *Control* field contains the value *Ihave*. The body contains the message identifiers of its message collection.

After the caller has had time to digest this message and check which ones it has and which ones it does not have, it sends a reply with *Control* set to *Sendme*, with the body containing the message identifiers of the messages it wants.

The exact mechanism by which a message posted on a small machine in some far corner of the earth is propagated to more than 10,000 machines worldwide can now be explained. When the message is posted, it is stored locally in one of the news system's internal directories. When contact is established with another machine, the message is propagated to that machine, which, in the course of time, sends it to all its neighbors. In this way, messages diffuse around the network the same way a drop of red dye diffuses into a glass of water (or the way an epidemic spreads in a population). On the average, most news is delivered within one or two days.

Ihave and *Sendme* are not the only control messages. Two others are *Newgroup* and *Rmgroup*. These are used to create and delete newsgroups, respectively. Only certain authorized people may send these messages. Several other control messages exist for administration and statistics gathering.

Although the flooding algorithm is used on most lines, within the backbone, a protocol called **NNTP (Network News Transfer Protocol)** is commonly used. It is described in RFC 977. The reason for the distinction is that most sites only have a single news feed, so there is little danger of receiving a message twice from independent sites. Backbone sites connect to multiple sites, so a more sophisticated protocol is needed to avoid wasting bandwidth.

NNTP provides about half a dozen commands that allow messages to be selectively downloaded. The *NEWSGROUPS* command allows one machine to ask another if it knows about any newsgroups created after a given date and time (specified as a parameter). In this way, the existence of new groups can be propagated.

Similarly, the *NEWNEWS* command allows one machine to ask for a list of news messages received after a a given date and time, usually the date and time of the last contact. Once the receiver has this list, it can request the messages it is missing with the *ARTICLE* command. The *LIST* and *GROUP* commands can be used to ask for numbers of the first and last messages held for all newsgroups or one specific newsgroup, respectively. New messages can be posted to the network with the *POST* command.

No discussion of news would be complete without some mention of the security problems it raises. Allowing foreign machines to call up and login to send or receive mail and news is a potential security threat. The protocols have to be defined carefully to limit what remote users may do. If all that a remote user can do is deposit files in, or read files from, a specific directory, there is relatively little danger. However, if remote users can execute arbitrary programs, they can potentially do more damage.

We are now finished with our study of computer networks. However, there is still more to learn. New subjects are developing all the time, for example, network management (Klerer, 1988), and old ones are evolving. The reader who wishes to keep up-to-date on this fascinating subject will certainly have plenty to do. See Chap. 10 for some suggested readings to get started.

9.7. SUMMARY

In this chapter we have examined some of the key aspects of the application layer. We started with ACSE and CCR, which manage associations and two-phase commit, respectively. Many applications use these service elements to do their jobs.

Next we looked at file servers. All file servers have an implicit model of what a file is and what operations can be performed on it. The OSI virtual filestore regards a file as a tree of independently addressable elements. It also associates a large number of attributes with a file, and provides operations to read and modify them.

If two or more users try to access the same file at the same time, problems, including deadlocks can arise. For this reason, file servers use concurrency control algorithms to manage simultaneous access. To provide more reliable service, some file servers replicate their files. This practice makes reads easier but updates harder. Various algorithms have been devised to handle multicopy updates, including primary copy and voting.

Another major application is electronic mail. Electronic mail systems have two major components, the user agent and the message transfer agent. Mail sent electronically consists of the content (header plus body) and the envelope. The user agent is concerned with the content whereas the message transfer agent deals with the envelope.

Most mail systems have a facility to manage mailboxes for their users. Commands are typically provided to read, answer, move, and delete messages, as well as send new mail.

Virtual terminals are used to allow screen-oriented software to be written in a terminal independent way. Three types of terminals exist, each with their own properties: scroll mode, page mode, and form mode. Scroll mode terminals can be handled with a stream-oriented character protocol. Page mode terminals can be dealt with using a scheme such as termcap, in which programs execute abstract terminal commands that are mapped onto device dependent escape sequences.

Form mode terminals are typically modeled using a two- or three-dimensional character array. Characters can be entered into the array either from the keyboard or by the computer. The problem of simultaneous access is solved in the asynchronous model by having two arrays and in the synchronous model by controlling access with a token.

Finding the name of a network user or service in a large network requires a directory service. For a small network, having a file mapping user or service names onto network addresses is sufficient. For a large network, a hierarchical directory system in which objects can be located by various attributes is more satisfactory.

Remote job entry is another application layer function. The OSI JTM service provides a way for a user to collect programs and input files from various source agencies and have them shipped to an execution agency for processing. The results can then be stored with sink agencies and reports returned to the person who submitted the job.

Other applications are picture storage and transfer, videotex and teletext. Pictures are built up from basic elements, such as polylines and ellipses. By combing the basic elements, complex pictures can be represented in a small number of bits. Videotex and teletext are telematic services for home and office use. Videotex allows remote access to large public data bases, and teletext allows for broadcasting of mass market information.

PROBLEMS

1. If CCR and two-phase commit are used on computers that may crash, serious problems may develop. Give an example of such a scenario and propose a solution to the problem.

2. A UNIX file is a linear sequence of bytes, numbered from 0 up to some maximum. An operation, *LSEEK*, is provided to move the file pointer to an arbitrary byte position, after which data can be read or written. Discuss how an OSI virtual filestore could be implemented on a UNIX system to provide remote access to the UNIX files using the OSI primitives.

3. Earlier versions of FTAM only allowed a single FADU to be read or written in one operation. How would such a restriction affect the solution to the previous problem?

4. Some of the OSI virtual filestore attributes can be changed by the owner of a file and others cannot be. For example, the owner can change the *Account number* attribute, but not the *Owner* attribute. Give a plausible reason for this restriction.

5. A replicated file has 5 servers. List all the possible ways of choosing the read quorum and the write quorum for the voting algorithm.

6. Consider the previous problem again. Suppose that reads are very common and writes are very infrequent. Which choice is most efficient?

7. Devise a method by which users of a stateless file server can gain exclusive access to files for update purposes without using locks.

8. The FTAM *F-SELECT* and *F-OPEN* primitives both allow concurrency control to be specified. However, if *F-SELECT* has already asked for and been granted exclusive access, it is not permitted for *F-OPEN* to change to shared access upon entering the open regime, even though this cannot fail. Why was such a rule introduced?

9. In Fig. 9-11 the message storage area (mailbox) is part of the message transfer agent rather than the user agent. Inasmuch as manipulating the mailbox is something that users do from terminals, it would seem to be in the wrong place. Why was it placed in the message transfer agent?

10. Electronic mail systems use people's names in some of the header fields. Discuss the possibility of breaking up names into standard components with an eye to finding a standard representation. Consider all the components that are in common use and would cause problems if they could not be handled.

11. The originator is mentioned in both the envelope and header in the electronic mail example given in the text. Why?

12. In Fig. 9-19 we listed 18 commands for manipulating the character array of a virtual terminal. Leaving the question of efficiency aside, devise the smallest set of primitives that can perform all the functions of the commands in the figure.

13. The OSI virtual terminal committee has been discussing adding a "ripple delete" feature to the virtual terminal service. This feature would allow a block of text to be deleted, and have the text following it move leftward and upward to take the place of the deleted text. What could such a feature be used for?

14. Explain in your own words what net-effecting is good for.

15. Look at the list of termcap escape sequences (not the Booleans or integers) given in Fig. 9-17. Are there any things termcap can do that cannot be handled directly or simulated easily with the OSI VTS?

16. The OSI directory service requires each directory to have a key attribute. Why? (Hint: think about implementing telephone directories with millions of entries.)

17. Which attributes are inherited by DEC's marketing department in Fig. 9-21?

18. How many picture drawing commands of the type discussed in this chapter are needed to draw a regular hexagon?

19. Imagine that 5 percent of a 6 MHz television channel is available for teletext, and that teletext pages are 20 lines of 40 characters, with the characters set in ASCII using binary encoding. How many pages can the system handle and still have an average response time under 1 second?

20. Consider an alphageometric videotex system operating on a 256 × 256 bit map display. Design a byte-oriented protocol for transmitting polylines and circles.

21. Can you see any advantage to adding the type rectangle to the protocol of the previous problem? After all, a rectangle can be drawn as a polyline.

22. Write a program that simulates that subset of the OSI virtual filestore described in this chapter. The simulator should take the form of a program running on your computer that accepts filestore commands and carries them out. Invent a simple protocol for requests and replies.

23. Write a simple user agent that expects to find mail in a certain directory. Each file is one message. The user agent should provide a way to get an overview of the currently available mail. It should also allow users to read and delete specific messages. Furthermore, it should allow users to compose messages, by calling an editor. When the editor exits, the user agent should get control again and send the mail by putting it in a system spooling directory.

24. Write a program that provides that subset of the OSI directory service described in this chapter. There should be commands to make entries, delete entries and look up entries, plus whatever other commands you need (e.g., managing directories). To make it simpler, an entry should only contain a name, in the form of a 32-character ASCII string, and network address, in the form of a 16-digit decimal number.

10

READING LIST AND BIBLIOGRAPHY

We have now finished our study of computer networks, but this is only the beginning. Many interesting topics have not been treated in as much detail as they deserve, and others have been omitted altogether for lack of space. In this chapter we provide some suggestions for further reading and a bibliography, for the benefit of readers who wish to continue their study of computer networks.

10.1. SUGGESTIONS FOR FURTHER READING

There is an extensive literature on all aspects of computer networks and distributed systems. Four journals that frequently publish papers in this area are *IEEE Transactions on Communications*, *IEEE Journal on Selected Areas in Communications*, *Computer Networks*, and *Computer Communication Review*. Many other journals also publish occasional papers on the subject.

IEEE also publishes two magazines, *IEEE Network Magazine* and *IEEE Communications Magazine* that contain surveys, tutorials, and case studies on networking. The former emphasizes architecture, standards, and software, and the latter tends toward communications technology (fiber optics, satellites, and so on).

In addition, there are several annual or biannual conferences that tend to attract many papers on networks and distributed systems, in particular, *International Conference on Distributed Computer Systems*, *Symposium on Operating System*

Principles, N-th Data Communications Symposium, International Conf. on Computer Communication (ICCC), *International Conf. on Communications* (ICC), and *National Telecommunications Conf.* (NTC). Furthermore, IEEE has published several volumes of network paper reprints in convenient paperback form.

Below we list some suggestions for supplementary reading, keyed to the chapters of this book.

10.1.1. Introduction and General Works

Bertsekas and Gallager, *Data Networks*
A discussion of layers 1 through 3, with an emphasis on the formal, mathematical aspects. Queueing theory and its applications, the MAC sublayer, routing, and flow control are all analyzed mathematically.

Day and Zimmermann, "The OSI Reference Model"
A short introduction to the OSI Reference Model, starting with its history, architecture, and terminology. Next comes an overview of each layer. The paper concludes with a discussion of issues that are still unresolved.

Henshall and Shaw, *OSI Explained. End to End Computer Communication Standards*
If you are looking for more detailed information about the OSI upper layers in a comprehensible form, this is the book for you. It covers the transport, session, and presentation layers in their entirety, and parts of the application layer, notably FTAM and MOTIS. The style is highly readable and numerous explantory figures are provided.

Linington, "Fundamentals of the Layer Service Definitions and Protocol Specifications"
A clear introduction the the OSI concepts of services, layers, protocols, and interfaces. Important OSI conventions and terms are also introduced.

Schwartz, *Telecommunication Networks: Protocols, Modeling and Analysis*
Another highly mathematical treatment of networks from the viewpoint of queueing theory. The book is similar to Bertsekas and Gallager, except that it also treats the transport layer, LANs, and circuit-switched networks, again, all from a highly formal perspective.

Sloman and Kramer, *Distributed Systems and Computer Networks*
Both distributed systems and networks are covered in this easy-to-read introductory text. In addition to a chapter on each OSI layer, there are chapters relating to distributed systems, communication primitives and software.

Stallings, *Data and Computer Communications, 2nd ed.*

A look at networking from the engineering perspective. The first half of this book looks at traditional data communications and transmission technology (the physical layer). The second half covers topics from layers 2 through 7.

10.1.2. The Physical Layer

Cooper, *Broadband Network Technology*

For the hardware-oriented reader interested in the technology of broadband systems, this book contains a wealth of engineering information.

IEEE Communications Magazine, Dec. 1987

This special issue contains 16 short, slightly technical articles on ISDN. Among other topics, it covers business issues, user perceptions, implementations, and future applications.

IEEE Journal on Selected Areas in Communications, May 1986

A complete issue focusing on ISDN. Unlike most of the literature about ISDN, which more wishful thinking than anything else, the papers in this issue are all highly technical, discussing the various ISDN layers and protocols in detail.

McClelland, "Services and Protocols of the Physical Layer"

An introduction to the physical layer, its services and its protocols. Examples are drawn from ISDN, X.21, and RS-232-C. The paper also discusses how testing can be done in the physical layer.

Luetchford, "CCITT Recommendations—Network Aspects of the ISDN"

A discussion of ISDN from an implementation standpoint. The topics covered include ISDN architecture, addressing, internetworking, routing, and maintenance.

10.1.3. The Medium Access Control Sublayer

Currie, *LANs Explained*

An up-to-date introduction to LANs covering technology, architecture, and protocols. The IEEE 802 standards are discussed extensively, with chapters on 802.3, 802.4, and 802.5. In addition, various other related topics are examined, including the OSI lower layers, internetworking, IBM's NETBIOS and network management.

Kummerle et al., *Advances in Local Area Networks*

A collection of 34 key papers on LANs and related topics taken from the scientific literature. The papers are organized in seven sections, covering introduction, evolution of LANs, fiber optics, performance, integrated traffic, gateways, and software.

Li, "Multiple Access Communications Networks,"
An introduction to the idea of multiple access, starting with ALOHA, and continuing with splitting algorithms, CSMA, TDM, and reservation schemes. Satellites, LANs, and packet radio are all discussed.

Stallings, *Local Networks, an Introduction, 2nd ed.*
A discussion of LANs, covering technology, topology, protocols, PBXes, Internetworking and Design issues. There is a considerable amount of material here, although the division of material into chapters is somewhat haphazard.

Tagney and O'Mahony, *Local Area Networks and Their Applications*
An easy-to-read introduction to LANs, including transmission tecnhology, topology, implementation, protocols, protocols, servers, distributed systems and office and factory automation. Not as technical as Stallings, but with more emphasis on software and case studies of existing LANs.

10.1.4. The Data Link Layer

Budkowski and Dembinski, "An Introduction to Estelle"
Along with LOTOS, Estelle is one of the official OSI formal techniques for describing protocols. This paper provides an introduction to the syntax and semantics of Estelle, and gives some examples of it use.

Conard, "Services and Protocols of the Data Link Layer"
Data link layer protocols have been around for over two decades, so a great deal is known about them. This paper summarizes their functions, services, and design issues

Rudin, "An Informal Overview of Formal Protocol Specification"
In this paper, Rudin tries to make the formal techniques used by professional protocol provers accessible to mere mortals, and with considerable success.

Schwartz, *Telecommunication Networks: Protocols, Modeling and Analysis*
Chapter 4 describes both the stop-and-wait and go back *n* protocols in detail, and then proceeds to give a detailed performance analysis for both of them. HDLC and its performance is also treated.

10.1.5. The Network Layer

Bell and Jabbour, "Review of Point-to-Point Network Routing Algorithms"
An overview and taxonomy of routing, including both adaptive and nonadaptive algorithms. The routing algorithms used in the ARPANET, Tymnet, SNA, Decnet, and Telenet are described and compared.

Bertsekas and Gallager, *Data Networks*

Chapter 5 contains over 100 pages of material on routing algorithms and their mathematical analyses. About half of the chapter is devoted to optimal routing in networks where the traffic is continuous and known in advance.

Chapin, "Connections and Connectionless Data Transmission"

Although the controversy between connection-oriented and connectionless communication occurs in every layer, it is most heated in the network layer (e.g., X.25 versus IP). In this paper, Chapin discusses the key differences between these two approaches in some detail within the context of OSI networks.

Deasington, *X.25 Explained: Protocols for Packet Switched Networks*

A detailed exposition of X.25. All the packet formats are covered, as well as the various options and error messages. In addition, triple X and some transport protocols are also discussed.

Dhas and Konangi, "X25: An Interface to Public Packet Networks"

An overview of the CCITT X.25 recommendation. Among the topics explained are virtual call setup, data transfer, error recovery, and user facilities. The evolution of X.25 is also discussed.

Green, "Protocol Conversion"

One of the most difficult aspects of internetworking is converting protocols between dissimilar networks. This paper discusses the conversion process and points out places where mismatches can cause problems.

IEEE Network Magazine, Jan. 1988

This issue contains 15 articles and one polemic about LAN bridges, routers, and gateways. The editors admit that six of the articles were rejected by the referees, but they published them anyway because they feel that this subject is so controversial that not even the experts can agree on what is true and what is false.

Tucker, "Naming and Addressing Issues—OSI Network Addresses"

One of the most important network layer issues is addressing. The OSI model for addressing is quite complicated, as it tries to encompass all existing schemes. The various issues involved are described in this short paper.

10.1.6. The Transport Layer

Chong, "Software Development and Implementation of NBS Class-4 Transport Protocol"

An overview of the implementation of the OSI Class 4 protocol is described. The transport entity maintains four event queues, sorted by priority. Whenever it becomes active, it takes work from the highest nonempty queue and processes the work. The techniques used to test and debug the code are also discussed.

Comer, *Internetworking with TCP/IP: Principles, Protocols, and Architecture*
An entire book about TCP/IP and its use in the ARPA internet. In addition to a detailed description of the protocols, addressing, domains, control messages, gateways, and interfaces are all carefully described.

Groenbaek, "Conversion between the TCP and ISO Transport Protocols as a Method of Achieving Interoperability Between Data Communications Systems"
Although TCP and the OSI class 4 protocol have many similarities, they also have some subtle differences that causes problems when building a gateway between them. Groenbaek points out that there is a large common subset, and suggests that applications restrict themselves to using only features from the subset to make interworking easier.

Henshall and Shaw, *OSI Explained. End to End Computer Communication Standards*
Chapter 7 describes the OSI transport layer. The main topics treated are the transport service, the realization of the transport service, expedited data, and the quality of service.

Rose and Cass, "OSI Transport Services on Top of the TCP"
The ARPA Internet community is not going to give up TCP/IP without a fight. One solution to the problem of interfacing OSI to TCP/IP is to implement the OSI transport protocol on top of TCP. This paper tells how.

Schwartz, *Telecommunication Networks: Protocols, Modeling and Analysis*
In contrast to the rest of this book, the chapter on the transport layer contains almost no mathematics. It does, however, cover the OSI class 4 transport protocol qualitatively and in great detail.

Watson and Mamrak, "Gaining Efficiency in Transport Services by Appropriate Design and Implementation Choices"
The efficiency of a protocol is frequently determined more by the implementation than by the PDU formats. Mechanisms and techniques for efficient protocol implementation are described at length here.

10.1.7. The Session Layer

Birrell and Nelson, "Implementing Remote Procedure Calls"
The classic paper on RPC. It describes both the concepts behind remote procedure call and the implementation at Xerox PARC.

Emmons and Chandler, "OSI Session Layer: Services and Protocols"

An overview of the OSI session layer, including both the services provided and the protocol used.

Henshall and Shaw, *OSI Explained. End to End Computer Communication Standards*

Chapter 6 describes the OSI session layer. Both the service and the protocol are covered. All the functional units and phases are described.

10.1.8. The Presentation Layer

Caneschi and Merelli, "Standardizing the Presentation Layer: Why and What"

An overview of the presentation layer is given covering the functions, components and protocol machine of this layer. It also makes the remarkable statement: "...Presentation is quite a new standard, therefore we cannot expect that everything in it be clearly understandable ..." Perhaps we should just stick to old standards.

Davies and Price, "Digital Signatures—An Update"

A concise summary of the state-of-the art in digital signatures. Both DES-based and public key schemes are examined. Some applications to banking are also mentioned.

Henshall and Shaw, *OSI Explained. End to End Computer Communication Standards*

Chapter 5 looks at the OSI presentation layer, in particular connection establishment and release and the management of presentation contexts. Unfortunately, ASN.1 is not covered here.

IEEE Network Magazine, April 1987

This issue contains five papers about security in networks. Commerical schemes, public key cryptography, and authentication mechanisms are discussed.

Tardo, "Standardizing Cryptographic Services at OSI Higher Layers"

This paper describes security services in relation to the OSI Reference Model. In particular, the thorny issue of which services to place in which layer is addressed. Considering the various factors, transport and presentation seem to be the best candidates.

Witten et al., "Arithmetic Coding for Data Compression"

Despite a widespread belief that Huffman coding is the best way to compress text, there are other algorithms that yield better results. One of these is arithmetic coding, described in detail in this article.

10.1.9. The Application Layer

Henshall and Shaw, *OSI Explained. End to End Computer Communication Standards*

Two applications are covered in detail in this book: FTAM and MOTIS. The chapter on FTAM looks at the virtual filestore, the FTAM services and the FTAM protocol. The chapter on MOTIS discusses the functional model and the various services.

Huffman, "E-mail—the Glue to Office Automation"

A case study of one electronic mail system, covering both the user agent and the message transfer agent. The issue of private vs. public systems, and network design are also treated. The article concludes with some tips for e-mail users (e.g., do not become so dependent on e-mail that you forget how to communicate verbally).

Hutchison and Desmond, "Electronic Data Exchange"

As electronic mail comes into widespread use, the first application will be interpersonal messages. The next phase is specialized protocols for applications (ordering, billing, etc) and specific industries (banking, transportation, etc.). This article discusses some issues concerned with these more specialized uses of electronic mail.

Linington, "The Virtual Filestore Concept"

The concept of a virtual filstore is described, along with the notions of interfaces, services, and protocols. The OSI filestore is then discussed.

McLeod-Reisig and Huber, "ISO Virtual Terminal Protocol and its Relationship to Mil-Std Telnet"

After an initial description of the OSI virtual terminal model, and its operations, parameters, and PDUs, the authors compare it to the ARPANET standard, TEL-NET.

10.2. ALPHABETICAL BIBLIOGRAPHY

Conerence abbreviations and publishers:

Compcon (IEEE Computer Society Internat. Conf.), IEEE, Long Beach, CA
N-th Data Communications Symp., ACM, N.Y.; and IEEE, Long Beach, CA
ICC (International Conf. on Communications), IEEE, Long Beach, CA
ICCC (Int. Comp. Commun. Conf.), Int. Council for Comp. Comm., Wash. DC
NCC (National Computer Conf.), AFIPS Press, Montvale, NJ

NTC (National Telecommunications Conf.), IEEE, Long Beach, CA
SJCC (Spring Joint Computer Conf.), AFIPS Press, Montvale, NJ

ABBRUSCATO, C.R.: "Data Encryption Equipment," *IEEE Commun. Magazine*, vol. 22, pp. 15-21, Sept. 1984.

ABRAMSON, N.: "Develoment of the ALOHANET," *IEEE Trans. on Inform. Theory*, vol. IT-31, pp. 119-123, March 1985.

ANDERSON, D.P., FERRARI, D., RANGAN, P.V., and SARTIRANA, B.: "A Protocol for Secure Communication and Its Performance," *Proc. Seventh Int'l Conf. on Distr. Computer Sys.*, IEEE, pp. 473-480, 1987.

APPENZELLER, H.R.: "Signaling System No. 7 ISDN User Part," *IEEE Journal on Selected Areas in Commun.*, vol. SAC-4, pp. 366-371, May 1986.

BACKES, F.: "Transparent Bridges for Interconnection of IEEE 802 LANs," *IEEE Network Magazine*, vol. 2, pp. 5-9, Jan. 1988.

BALENSON, D.M.: "Automated Distribution of Cryptographic Keys Using the Financial Insitution Key Management Standard," *IEEE Commun. Magazine*, vol. 23, pp. 41-46, Sept. 1985.

BARAN, P.: "On Distributed Communication Networks," *IEEE Trans. on Commun. Systems*, vol. CS-12, pp. 1-9, March 1964.

BAUERFELD, W.L., KAUFMANN, P., TSCHICHHOLZ, M., and WEIKART, C.: "DIN-A-MIT: An Adaptable, Distributed Computer-Based Message System," *Computer Networks*, vol. 8, pp. 93-105, 1984.

BELL, P.R., and JABBOUR, K.: "Review of Point-to-Point Routing Algorithms," *IEEE Commun. Magazine*, vol. 24, pp. 34-38, Jan. 1986.

BELSNES, D.: "Flow Control in the Packet Switching Networks," *Communications Networks*. Uxbridge, England: Online, pp. 349-361, 1975.

BENHAMOU, E., and ESTRIN, J.: "Multilevel Internetworking Gateways: Architecture and Applications," *IEEE Computer Magazine*, vol. 16, pp. 27-34, Sept. 1983.

BENTLEY, J.L., SLEATOR, D.D., TARJAN, R.E., and WEI, V.K.: "A Locally Adaptive Data Compression Scheme," *Commun. ACM*, vol. 29, pp. 320-330, April 1986.

BERNSTEIN, P.A., and GOODMAN, N.: "An Algorithm for Concurrency Control and Recovery in Replicated Distributed Databases," *ACM Trans. on Database Systems*, vol. 9, pp. 596-615, Dec. 1984.

BERNTSEN, J.A., DAVIN, J.R., PITT, D.A., and SULLIVAN, N.G.: "MAC Layer Interconnection of IEEE 802 Local Area Networks," *Computer Networks and ISDN Systems*, vol. 10, pp. 259-273, Dec. 1985.

BERTSEKAS, D., and GALLAGER, R.: *Data Networks*, Englewood Cliffs, NJ: Prentice-Hall, 1987.

BINDER, R.: "A Dynamic Packet Switching System for Satellite Broadcast Channels," *Proc. ICC*, pp. 41-1 to 41-5a, 1975.

BIRRELL, A.D., and NELSON, B.J.: "Implementing Remote Procedure Calls," *ACM Trans. on Computer Systems*, vol. 2, pp. 39-59, Feb 1984.

BLAZEWICZ, J., BRZEZINSKI, J., and GAMBOSI, G.: "Time-Stamp Approach to Store-and-Forward Deadlock Prevention," *IEEE Trans. on Commun.*, vol. COM-35, pp. 490-495, May 1987a.

BLAZEWICZ, J., BRZEZINSKI, J., and GAMBOSI, G.: "Time-Stamp Approach to Prevention of Different Deadlock Types in Store-and-Forward Networks," *IEEE Trans. on Commun.*, vol. COM-35, pp. 564-566, May 1987b.

BOSACK, L., and HEDRICK, C.: "Problems in Large LANS," *IEEE Network Magazine*, vol. 2, pp. 49-56, Jan. 1988.

BRANSTAD, D.: "Considerations for Security in the OSI Architecture," *IEEE Network Magazine*, vol. 1, pp. 34-39, April 1987.

BRERETON, O.P.: "Management of Replicated Files in a UNIX Environment" , *Software - Practice & Experience*, vol. 16, pp. 771-780, Aug. 1986.

BRINKSMA, H., and KARJOTH, H.: "A Specification of the OSI Transport Service in LOTOS," in *Proc. Fourth Int'l Workshop on Protocol Specification, Testing, and Verification*, Y.Yemini (Ed.), Amsterdam: North-Holland, pp. 227-251, 1984.

BRINKSMA, H., SCOLLO, G, and STEENBERGEN, C.: "LOTOS Specifications, Their Implementations and Their Tests" in *Proc. Sixth Int'l Workshop on Protocol Specification, Testing and Verification*, B. Sarikaya (Ed.), Amsterdam: North Holland, pp. 349-360, 1986.

BROWN, M.R., KOLLING, K.N., and TAFT, E.A.: "The Alpine File System," *ACM Trans. on Computer Systems*, vol. 3, pp. 261-293, Nov. 1985.

BUCCIARELLI, P., and CANESCHI, F.: "Connectionless Services in the OSI Reference Model," *Proc. ICCC*, pp. 564-569, 1984.

BUDKOWSKI, S., and DEMBINSKI, P.: "An Introduction to Estelle,Q *Computer Networks and ISDN Systems*, vol. 14, pp. 3-23, Jan. 1988.

BURG, F.M., CHEN, C.T., and FOLTS, H.C.: "Of Local Networks, Protocols, and the OSI Reference Model," *Data Communication*, pp. 129-150, Nov. 1984.

BURR, W.E.: "The FDDI Optical Data Link," *IEEE Commun. Magazine*, vol. 25, pp. 18-23, May 1986.

BUX, W.: "Local-Area Subnetworks, a Performance Comparison," in *Advances in Local Area Networks*, Kummerle, K., Tobagi, F., and Limb, J.O. (Eds.), New York: IEEE Press, 1987.

CANESCHI, F., and MERELLI, "Standardizing the Presentation Layer: Why and What," *Proc. Seventh Int'l Conf. on Distr. Computer Sys.*, IEEE, pp. 35-39, 1987.

CAPETANAKIS, J.I.: "Tree Algorithms for Packet Broadcast Channels," *IEEE Trans. on Inform. Theory*, vol. IT-25, pp. 505-515, Sept. 1979.

CHANG, J.-F. "A Packet Satellite System with Multiuplinks and Priority Discipline," *IEEE Trans. on Commun.*, vol. COM-30, pp. 1143-1152, May 1982.

CHANG, J.-F. "A Multibeam Packet Satellite Using Random Access Techniques," *IEEE Trans. on Commun.*, vol. COM-31, pp. 1143-1153, Oct. 1983.

CHAPIN, A.L.: "Connections and Connectionless Data Transmission," *Proc. of the IEEE*, vol. 71, pp. 1365-1371, Dec. 1983.

CHLAMTAC, I.: "Radio Packet Broadcasted Computer Network—The Broadcast Recognition Access Method," M.S. thesis, Dept. of Mathematical Sciences, Tel Aviv University, 1976.

CHLAMTAC, I., and GANZ, A.: "Design and Analysis of very High Speed Network Architectures," *IEEE Trans. on Commun.*, vol. COM-36, pp. 252-262, March 1988.

CHLAMTAC, I., and GANZ, O.: "An Optimal Hybrid Demand Access Protocol for Unrestricted Topology Broadcast Networks," *Infocom 86*, 1986a.

CHLAMTAC, I., and GANZ, O.: "Performance of Multibeam Packet Satellite Systems with Conflict Free Scheduling," *IEEE Trans. on Commun.*, vol. COM-34, pp. 1016-1023, Oct. 1986b.

CHLAMTAC, I., and KUTTEN, S.: "On Broadcasting in Packet Radio—Problem Analysis and Protocol Design," *IEEE Trans. on Commun.*, vol. COM-35, pp. 1240-1246, Dec. 1985.

CHOI, T.Y.: "Formal Techniques for the Specification, Verification, and Construction of Communication Protocols," *IEEE Commun. Magazine*, vol. 23, pp. 46-52, 1985.

CHONG, H.Y.: "Software Development and Implementation of NBS Class-4 Transport Protocol," *Computer Networks and ISDN Systems*, vol. 11, pp. 353-365, May 1986.

CHOUDHURY, G.L. and RAPPAPORT, S.S. "Diversity ALOHA—A Random Access Scheme for Satellite Communication," *IEEE Trans. on Commun.*, vol. COM-31, pp. 450-457, March 1983.

CHU, K.: "A Distributed Protocol for Updating Network Topology Information," Report RC 7235, IBM T.J. Watson Research Center, 1978.

CIDON, I., KODESH, H., and SIDI, M.: "Erasure, Capture, and Random Power Level Selection in Multiple-Access Systems," *IEEE Trans. on Commun.*, vol. COM-36, pp. 263-271, March 1988.

CLARK, D., LAMBERT, M., and ZHANG, L.: "NETBLT: A High Throughput Transport Protocol," *Proc. ACM SIGCOMM '87 Workshop*, ACM, pp. 353-359, 1987.

COHEN, D.: "On Holy Wars and a Plea for Peace," *IEEE Computer Magazine*, vol. 14, pp. 48-54, Oct. 1981.

COLE, R., and LLOYD, P.: "OSI Transport Protocol—User Experience," *Open Systems 86*, Online Publications, pp. 33-43, 1986.

COLLYER, G., and SPENCER, H.: "News Need Not be Slow," *Proc. Winter USENIX Conf.*, pp. 181-190, 1987.

COMER, D.:: *Internetworking with TCP/IP: Principles, Protocols, and Architecture*, Englewood Cliffs, NJ: Prentice-Hall, 1988.

COMER, D.: "The Computer Science Research Network CSNET: A History and Status Report," *Commun. ACM*, vol. 26, pp. 747-753, Oct. 1983.

COMER, D., and NARTEN, T.: "UNIX Systems as Cypress Implets," *Proc. Winter USENIX Conf.*, pp. 55-62, 1988.

CONARD, J.W.: "Services and Protocols of the Data Link Layer," *Proc. of the IEEE*, vol. 71, pp. 1378-1383, Dec. 1983.

COOPER, E. *Broadband Network Technology*, Englewood Cliffs, NJ: Prentice-Hall, 1986.

COURTIAT, J.P., PEDROZA, A., and AYACHE, J.M.: "A Simulation Environment for Protocol Specifications in Estelle," in *Proc. Fifth Int'l Workshop on Protocol Specification, Testing and Verification*, M. Diaz (Ed.), Amsterdam: North Holland, 1986.

CRICHLOW, J.M.: *Distributed and Parallel Computing* Englewood Cliffs, NJ: Prentice-Hall Int'l, 1988.

CROWTHER, W., RETTBERG, R., WALDEN, D., ORNSTEIN, S., and HEART, F.: "A System for Broadcast Communication: Reservation-Aloha," *Proc. Sixth Hawaii Int. Conf. System Sci.*, pp. 371-374, 1973.

CURRIE, W.S.: *LANs Explained*, Chichester, England: Ellis Horwood, 1988.

DALAL, Y., and METCALFE, R.: "Reverse Path Forwarding of Broadcast Packets," *Commun. ACM*, vol. 21, pp. 1040-1048, 1978.

DANTHINE, A.A.S.: "Protocol Representation with Finite-State Models," *IEEE Trans. on Commun.*, vol. COM-28, pp. 632-643, April 1980.

DAVIES, D.W.: "The Control of Congestion in Packet Switching Networks," *IEEE Trans. on Commun.*, vol. COM-20, pp. 546-550, June 1972.

DAVIES, D.W., and PRICE, W.L.: "Digital Signatures—An Update" *Proc. ICCC*, pp. 843-847, 1984.

DAY, J.D., and ZIMMERMANN, H.: "The OSI Reference Model," *Proc. of the IEEE*, vol. 71, pp. 1334-1340, Dec. 1983.

DE JONGE, W., and CHAUM, D.: "Some Variations on RSA Signatures and Their Security," in *Advances in Cryptology—CRYPTO '86*, Odlyzko, A.M. (Ed.), Berlin: Spring Verlag, 1987.

DEASINGTON, R.J.: *X.25 Explained: Protocols for Packet Switched Networks. 2nd ed.*, Chichester, England: Ellis Horwood, 1988.

DECINA, M.: "CCITT Recommendations on the ISDN: A Review," *IEEE Journal on Selected Areas in Commun.*, vol. SAC-4, pp. 320-325, May 1986.

DHAS, C.R., and KONANGI,V.K.: "X25: An Interface to Public Packet Networks," *IEEE Commun. Magazine*, vol. 24, pp. 118-125, Sept. 1986.

DIFFIE, W., and HELLMAN, M.E.: "Exhaustive Cryptanalysis of the NBS Data Encryption Standard," *IEEE Computer Magazine*, vol. 10, pp. 74-84, June 1977.

DIFFIE, W., and HELLMAN, M.E.: "New Directions in Cryptography," *IEEE Trans. on Inform. Theory*, vol. IT-22, pp. 644-654, Nov. 1976.

DIJKSTRA, E.W.: "A Note on Two Problems in Connexion with Graphs," *Numer. Math.*, vol. 1, pp. 269-271, Oct. 1959.

DIRVIN, R.A., and MILLER, A.R.: "The MC68824 Token Bus Controller: VLSI for the Factory LAN," *IEEE Micro Magazine*, vol. 6, pp. 15-25, June 1986.

DIXON, R.C.: "Lore of the Token Ring," *IEEE Network Magazine*, vol. 1, pp. 11-18, Jan. 1987.

DIXON, R.C., and Pitt, D.A.: "Addressing, Bridging, and Source Routing," *IEEE Network Magazine*, vol. 2, pp. 25-32, Jan. 1988.

DORFMAN, R.: "Detection of Defective Members of a Large Population," *Annals Math. Statistics*, vol. 14, pp. 436-440, 1943.

EMMONS, W.F., and CHANDLER, A.S.: "OSI Session Layer: Services and Protocols," *Proc. of the IEEE*, vol. 71, pp. 1397-1400, Dec. 1983.

EVEN, S.: *Graph Algorithms.* Potomac, Md.: Computer Science Press, 1979.

EVEN, S.: "An Algorithm for Determining Whether the Connectivity of a Graph Is at Least *k*," *SIAM Journal on Comput.*, vol. 4, pp. 393-396, Sept. 1975.

FERGUSON, M.J.: "Computation of the Variance of the Waiting Time for Token Rings," *IEEE Journal on Selected Areas in Commun.*, vol. SAC-4, pp. 775-782, Sept. 1986.

FIELD, J.A.: "Efficient Computer-Computer Communication," *Proc. IEE*, vol. 123, pp. 756-760, Aug. 1976.

FLETCHER, J.G.: "An Arithmetic Checksum for Serial Transmission," *IEEE Trans. on Commun.*, vol. COM-30, pp. 247-252, Jan. 1982.

FLETCHER, J.G., and WATSON, R.W.: "Mechanisms for a Reliable Timer-Based Protocol," *Computer Networks*, vol. 2, pp. 271-290, Sept. 1978.

FOLTS, H.C.: "802 LAN/X.25 WAN Internetworking—A Prgamatic Approach," *ICCC 84*, pp. 577-583, 1984.

FRASER, A.G.: "Towards a Universal Data Transport System," in *Advances in Local Area Networks*, Kummerle, K., Tobagi, F., and Limb, J.O. (Eds.), New York: IEEE Press, 1987.

FRASER, A.G.: "Delay and Error Control in a Packet Switched Network," *Proc. ICC*, pp. 22.4-121 to 22.4-125, 1977.

FRATTA, P.R.L. and GERLA, M.: "Tokenless Protocols for Fiber Optic Local Area Networks," *IEEE Journal on Selected Areas in Commun.*, vol. SAC-3, pp. 928-940, Nov. 1985.

GALLAGER, R.G. "A Perspective on Multiaccess Channels," *IEEE Trans. on Inform. Theory*, vol. IT-31, pp. 124-142, March 1985.

GIFFORD, D.K.: "Weighted Voting for Replicated Data," *Proc. Seventh Symp. on Operating Systems Prin.* ACM, pp. 150-162, 1979.

GIFFORD, W.S.: "ISDN User—Network Interfaces" *IEEE Journal on Selected Areas in Commun.*, vol. SAC-4, pp. 343-348, May 1986.

GILMORE, B.: "A User View of Virtual Terminal Standardisation," *Computer Networks and ISDN Systems*, vol. 13, pp. 229-233, 1987.

GITMAN, I., VAN SLYKE, R.M., and FRANK, H.: "Routing in Packet-Switching Broadcast Radio Networks," *IEEE Trans. on Commun.*, vol. COM-24, pp. 926-930, Aug. 1976.

GOPAL, I.S.: "Prevention of Store-and-Forward Deadlock in Computer Networks," *IEEE Trans. on Commun.*, vol. COM-33, pp. 1258-1264, Dec. 1985.

GRAY, J.P., PITT, D.A., and POZEFSKY, D.P.: "LAN-PBX Gateway Alternatives," in *Local Communication Systems: LAN and PBX*, Cabanel, J.P., Pujolle, G., and Danthine, A. (Eds.), Amsterdam: North-Holland, 1987.

GREEN, P.E.: "Protocol Conversion," *IEEE Trans. on Commun.*, vol. COM-34, pp/ 257-268, March 1986.

GREENE, E.P., and EPHREMIDES, A.: "Distributed Reservation Control Protocols for Random Access Broadcasting Channels," *IEEE Trans. on Commun.*, vol. COM-29, pp. 726-735, May 1981.

GROENBAEK, I: "Conversion between the TCP and ISO Transport Protocols as a Method of Achieving Interoperability Between Data Communications Systems," *IEEE Journal on Selected Areas in Commun.*, vol. SAC-4, pp. 288-296, March 1986.

HAGMANN, R.: "Reimplementing the Cedar File System Using Logging and Group Commit," *Proc. Eleventh Symp. on Operating Systems Prin.*, ACM, pp. 155-162, 1987.

HAMILTON, K.G.: *A Remote Procedure Call System*, Ph.D. thesis, University of Cambridge, 1984.

HAMMING, R.W.: "Error Detecting and Error Correcting Codes," *Bell System Tech. Journal*, vol. 29, pp. 147-160, April 1950.

HAMMOND, J.L., and O'REILLY, P.J.P.: *Performance Analysis of Local Computer Networks*, Reading, MA: Addison-Wesley, 1986.

HAMNER, M.C., and SAMSEN, G.R.: "Source Routing Bridge Implementation," *IEEE Network Magazine*, vol. 2, pp. 33-36, Jan. 1988.

HART, J.: "Extending the IEEE 802.1 MAC Bridge Standard to Remote Bridges," *IEEE Network Magazine*, vol. 2, pp. 10-15, Jan. 1988.

HAWE, B., KIRBY, A., and STEWART, B.: "Transparent Interconnection of Local Area Networks with Bridges," *Journal of Telecommun. Networks*, vol. 3, pp. 116-130, Summer 1984.

HAYES, J.F.: *Modeling and Analysis of Computer Communication Networks*, New York: Plenum Press, 1984.

HELLMAN, M.E.: "Commercial Encryption," *IEEE Network Magazine*, vol. 1, pp. 6-10, April 1987.

HELLMAN, M.E.: "A Cryptanalytic Time-Memory Tradeoff," *IEEE Trans. on Inform. Theory*, vol. IT-26, pp. 401-406, July 1980.

HENKEN, G.: "Mapping of X.400 and RFC822 Addresses," *Computer Networks and ISDN Systems*, vol. 13, pp. 161-164, 1987.

HENSHALL, J., and SHAW, A.: *OSI Explained. End to End Computer Communication Standards*, Chichester, England: Ellis Horwood, 1988.

HINDEN, R., Haverty, J., and SHELTZER, A.: "The DARPA Internet: Interconnecting Heterogeneous Computer Networks with Gateways," *IEEE Computer Magazine*, vol. 16, pp. 38-48, Sept. 1983.

HOPKINS, G.T., and MEISNER, N.B.: "Choosing Between Broadband and Baseband Local Networks," in *Advances in Local Area Networks*, Kummerle, K., Tobagi, F., and Limb, J.O. (Eds.), New York: IEEE Press, 1987.

HORAK, W.: "Concepts of the Document Interchange Protocol for Telematic Services," *Computer Networks*, vol. 8, pp. 175-185, 1984.

HOWARD, J.: "An Overview of the Andrew File System," *Proc. USENIX Winter Conf.*, pp. 23-26, 1988.

HOWARD, J., KAZAR, M., MENEES, S., NICHOLS, D., SATYANARAYANAN, M., SIDEBOTHAM, R., and WEST. M: "Scale and Performance in a Distributed File System," *ACM Trans. on Computer Systems*, vol. 6, pp. pp. 51-81, Feb. 1988.

HUFFMAN, A.J.: "E-mail— the Glue to Office Automation," *IEEE Network Magazine* vol. 1, pp. 4-10, Oct. 1987.

HUFFMAN, D.: "A Method for the Construction of Minimum Redundancy Codes," *Proc. IRE*, vol. 40, pp. 1098-1101, Sept. 1952.

HUTCHISON, G., and DESMOND, C.L.: "Electronic Data Exchange," *IEEE Network Magazine* vol. 1, pp. pp. 16-20, Oct. 1987.

IEEE: *802.3: Carrier Sense Multiple Access with Collision Detection*, New York: IEEE, 1985a.

IEEE: *802.4: Token-Passing Bus Access Method*, New York: IEEE, 1985b.

IEEE: *802.5: Token Ring Access Method*, New York: IEEE, 1985c.

IEEE: Special Issue on Congestion Control. *IEEE Trans. on Commun.* vol. COM-29, April 1981.

IRLAND, M.I.: "Buffer Management in a Packet Switch," *IEEE Trans. on Commun.*, vol. COM-26, pp. 328-337, March 1978.

ISRAEL, J.E., and WEISSBERGER, A.J.: "Communicating Between Heterogenous Networks," *Data Communication*, Feb. 1987.

JACKSON, R.: "Job Shop-like Queueing Systems," *Management Science*, vol. 10, pp. 131-142, 1963.

JACOBS, I.M., BINDER, R., BRESSLER, R.D., EDMOND, W.B., and KILLIAN, E.A.: "Packet Satellite Network Design Issues," *Proc. NTC*, IEEE, pp. 45.2.1 to 45.2.12, Nov. 1979.

JOSHI, S.P.: "High-Performance Networks—A Focus on the Fiber Distributed Data Interface (FDDI) Standard," *IEEE Micro Magazine*, vol. 6, pp. 8-14, June 1986.

JUBIN, J.: "Current Packet Radio Network Protocols," *Proc. INFOCOM 85*, 1985.

JUENEMAN, J.J., MATYAS, S.M., and MEYER, C.H.: "Message Authentication," *IEEE Commun. Magazine*, vol. 23, pp. 29-40, 1985.

JULIO, U. DE, and PELLEGRINI, G.: "Layer 1 ISDN Recommendations," *IEEE Journal on Selected Areas in Commun.*, vol. SAC-4, pp. 349-354, May 1986.

KAHN, D.: "Cryptology Goes Public," *IEEE Commun. Magazine*, vol. 18, pp. 19-28, March 1980.

KAHN, D.: *The Codebreakers*. New York: MacMillan, 1967.

KAHN, R.E.: "The Introduction of Packet Satellite Communications," *Proc. NTC*, IEEE, pp. 45.1.1 to 45.1.8, Nov. 1979.

KAMOUN, F.: "Design Considerations for Large Computer Communications Networks," Ph.D. thesis, Computer Science Dept., UCLA, 1976.

KAMOUN, F., and KLEINROCK, L.: "Stochastic Performance Evaluation of Hierarchical Routing for Large Networks," *Computer Networks*, vol. 3, pp. 337-353, Nov. 1979.

KANO, S.: "Layers 2 and 3 ISDN Recommendations," *IEEE Journal on Selected Areas in Commun.*, vol. SAC-4, pp. 355-359, May 1986.

KARN, P., Price, H., and Diersing, R.: "Packet Radio in the Amateur Service," *IEEE Journal on Selected Areas in Commun.*, vol. SAC-3, pp. 431-439, May 1985.

KARN, P., and PARTRIDGE, C.: "Improving Round-Trip Time Estimates in Reliable Transport Protocols," *Proc. ACM SIGCOMM '87 Workshop*, ACM, pp. 2-7, 1987.

KAZAR, M.L.: "Synchronization and Caching Issues in the Andrew File System," *Proc. Winter USENIX Conf.*, pp. 27-36, 1988.

KENT, C.A., and MOGUL, J.C.: "Fragmentation Considered Harmful," *Proc. ACM SIGCOMM '87 Workshop*, ACM, pp. 390-401, 1987.

KLEINROCK, L.: *Queueing Systems*, Vol. 2: *Computer Applications*. New York: John Wiley, 1976.

KLEINROCK, L.: *Communication Nets*. New York: Dover, 1964.

KLEINROCK, L., and TOBAGI, F.: "Random Access Techniques for Data Transmission over Packet-Switched Radio Channels," *Proc. NCC*, pp. 187-201, 1975.

KLEINROCK, L., and YEMINI, Y.: "An Optimal Adaptive Scheme for Multiple Access Broadcast Communication," *Proc. ICC*, pp. 7.2.1 to 7.2.5, 1978.

KLERER, S.M.: "The OSI Management Architecture: an Overview," *IEEE Network Magazine*, vol. 2, pp. 20-29, March 1988.

KNOTT, J.D.: "A Fairness Evaluation of the Bit-Map Access Protocol," *Globecom 85*, IEEE, pp. 34.4.1-34.4.3, 1985.

KOLATA, G.B.: "Computer Encryption and the National Security Agency Connection," *Science*, vol. 197, pp. 438-440, July 29, 1977.

KRANAKIS, E.: *Primality and Cryptography*, New York: Wiley-Teubner, 1986.

KUMMERLE, K., TOBAGI, F., and LIMB, J.O. (Eds.): *Advances in Local Area Networks*, New York: IEEE Press, 1987.

LAI, W.S.: "Protocol Traps in Networks—A Catalog," *IEEE Trans. on Commun.*, vol. COM-30, pp. 1434-1449, June 1982.

LANDWEBER, L.H., JENNINGS, D.M., and FUCHS, I.: "Research Computer Networks and Their Interconnection," *IEEE Commun. Magazine*, vol. 24, pp. 5-17, June 1986.

LANGSFORD, A.: "The Open System User's Programming Interfaces," *Computer Networks*, vol. 8, pp. 3-12, 1984.

LEE, H.W., and MARK, J.W.: "Combined Random/Reservation Access for Packet-Switched Transmission over a Satellite," *IEEE Trans. on Commun.*, vol. COM-32, pp. 1093-1104, Oct. 1984.

LI, V.O.K.: "Multiple Access Communications Networks," *IEEE Commun. Magazine*, vol. 25, pp. 41-48, June 1987.

LIMB, J.O.: "Performance of Local Area Networks at High Speed," *IEEE Commun. Magazine*, vol. 22, pp. 41-45, Aug. 1984.

LIMB, J.O., and FLORES, C.: "Description of FASNET: A Unidirectional Local Area Communications Network," in *Advances in Local Area Networks*, Kummerle, K., Tobagi, F., and Limb, J.O. (Eds.), New York: IEEE Press, 1987.

LIN, F., CHU, P., LIU, M.: "Protocol Verification Using Reachability Analysis: The State Space Explosion Problem and Relief Strategies," *Proc. ACM SIGCOMM '87 Workshop*, ACM, pp. 126-135, 1987.

LINN, R., Jr.: "The Features and Facilities of Estelle," *Proc. Fifth Int'l Workshop on Procotcol Specification, Testing, and Verification*, June 1985.

LINNINGTON, P.F.: "The Virtual Filestore Concept," *Computer Networks*, vol. 8, pp. 13-16, 1984.

LINNINGTON, P.F.: "Fundamentals of the Layer Service Definitions and Protocol Specifications," *Proc. of the IEEE*, vol. 71, pp. 1341-1345, Dec. 1983.

LITTLE, D.: "A Proof for the Queueing Formula: $L = \lambda W$," *Oper. Res.*, vol. 9, pp. 383-387, May 1961.

LIU, M.T.: "Distributed Loop Computer Networks," in *Advances in Computers*, M.C. Yovits (Ed.), New York: Academic Press, pp. 163-221,

LUETCHFORD, J.C.: "CCITT Recommendations—Network Aspects of the ISDN," *IEEE Journal on Selected Areas in Commun.*, vol. SAC-4, pp. 334-342, May 1986.

MAEBARA, K., and TAKEUCHI, T. "Network Interconnection between Digital PBX and LAN," in *Local Communication Systems: LAN and PBX*, Cabanel, J.P., Pujolle, G., and Danthine, A. (Eds.), Amsterdam: North-Holland, 1987.

MAURER, H.A., and SEBESTYEN, I.: "Inhouse Versus Public Videotex Systems," *Computer Networks and ISDN Systems*, vol. 7, pp. 329-342, 1983.

MCCLELLAND, F.M.: "Services and Protocols of the Physical Layer," *Proc. of the IEEE*, vol. 71, pp. 1372-1377, Dec. 1983.

MCLEOD-REISIG, S.E., and HUBER, K.: "ISO Virtual Terminal Protocol and its Relationship to Mil-Std TELNET," *Proc. Computer Networking Symp.*, IEEE, pp. 110-119, 1986.

MEHRAVARI, N.: "TDMA in a Random-Access Environment: An Overview," *IEEE Commun. Magazine*, vol. 22, pp. 54-59, Nov. 1984.

MEIJER, A.: *Systems Network Architecture*, London: Pitman, 1987.

MEISTER, B.: "A Performance Study of the ISO Transport Protocol," *Proc. Seventh Int'l Conf. on Distr. Computer Sys.*, IEEE, pp. 398-405, 1987.

MERKLE, R.C.: "Secure Communications Over an Insecure Channel," *Commun. ACM*, vol. 21, pp. 294-299, April 1978.

MERLIN, P.M., and SCHWEITZER, P.J.: "Deadlock Avoidance—Store-and-Forward Deadlock," *IEEE Trans. on Commun.*, vol. COM-28, pp. 345-354, March 1980.

METCALFE, R.M., and BOGGS, D.R.: "Ethernet: Distributed Packet Switching for Local Computer Networks," *Commun. ACM*, vol. 19, pp. 395-404, July 1976.

MILLS, D., and BRAUN, H.: "The NSFNET Backbone Network," *Proc. ACM SIGCOMM '87 Workshop*, ACM, pp. 191-196, 1987.

MOK, A.K., and WARD, S.A.: "Distributed Broadcast Channel Access," *Computer Networks*, vol. 3, pp. 327-335, Nov. 1979.

MORRIS, J.H.: "Make or Take Decisions in Andrew," *Proc. Winter USENIX Conf.*, pp. 1-8, 1988.

MORRIS, J.H., SATYANARAYANAN, CONNER, M.H., HOWARD, J.H., ROSENTHAL, D.S.H., and SMITH, F.D.: "Andew: A Distributed Personal Computing Environment," *Commun. ACM*, vol. 29, pp. 184-201, March 1986.

MULLENDER, S.J. and TANENBAUM, A.S.: "A Distributed File Service Based on Optimistic Concurrency Control," *Proc. Tenth Symp. on Operating System Prin.*, ACM, pp. 51-62, 1985.

NAGLE, J.: "Congestion Control in TCP/IP Internetworks," *Computer Commun. Rev.*, vol. 14, pp. 11-17, Oct. 1984.

NATIONAL BUREAU OF STANDARDS: "Data Encryption Standard," Fed. Inf. Process. Stand. Publ. 46, Jan. 1977.

NEEDHAM, R.M., and SCHROEDER, M.D.: "Using Encryption for Authentication in Large Networks of Computers," *Commun. ACM*, vol. 21, pp. 993-999, Dec 1978.

NELSON, B.J.: *Remote Procedure Call*, Ph.D. thesis, Carnegie-Mellon University, 1981.

NELSON, M., WELCH, B., and OUSTERHOUT, J.: "Caching in the Sprite Network File System," *ACM Trans. on Computer Systems*, vol. 6, pp. 134-154, Feb. 1988.

OUSTERHOUT, J.K., CHERENSON, A.R., DOUGLIS, F., NELSON, M.N., and WELCH, B.B.: "The Sprite Network Operating System," *IEEE Computer Magazine*, vol. 21, pp. 23-36, Feb. 1988.

PARTRIDGE, C.: "Mail Routing using Domain Names: An Informal Tour," *Proc. USENIX Summer Conf.*, 1986.

PARTRIDGE, C., MOOERS, C., and LAUBACH, M.: "The CSNET Information Server: Automatic Document Distribution using Electronic Mail," *Computer Commun. Rev.*, vol. 17, pp. 3-10, Oct. 1987.

PETERSON, W.W., and BROWN, D.T.: "Cyclic Codes for Error Detection," *Proc. IRE*, vol. 49, pp. 228-235, Jan. 1961.

PHINNEY, T.L., and JELATIS, G.D.: "Error Handling in the IEEE 802 Token-Passing Bus LAN," *IEEE Journal on Selected Areas in Commun.*, vol. SAC-1, pp. 784-789, Nov. 1983.

PIERCE, J.: "How Far Can Data Loops Go?" *IEEE Trans. on Commun.*, vol. COM-20, pp. 527-530, June 1972.

PITT, D.A.: "Bridging—The Double Standard," *IEEE Network Magazine*, vol 2., pp. 94-95, Jan. 1988.

PITT, D.A.: "Standards for the Token Ring," *IEEE Network Magazine*, vol. 1, pp. 19-22, Jan. 1987.

PITT, D.A., and WINKLER, J.L.: "Table-Free Bridging," *IEEE Journal on Selected Areas in Commun.*, vol. SAC-5, pp. 1454-1462, Dec. 1987.

POSTEL, J.B.: "Internetwork Protocol Approaches," *IEEE Trans. on Commun.*, vol. COM-28, pp. 604-611, April 1980.

PU, C., NOE, J.D., and PROUDFOOT, A.: "Regeneration of Replicated Objects: A Technique and Its Eden Implementation," *Proc. Int'l Conf. on Data Engineering*, 1986.

PURDIN, T.D.M., SCHLICHTING, R.D., and ANDREWS, G.R.: "A File Replication Facility for Berkeley UNIX," *Software - Practice & Experience*, vol. 17, pp. 923-940, Dec. 1987.

QUARTERMAN, J., and HOSKINS, J: "Notable Computer Networks," *Commun. ACM*, vol. 29, pp. 932-971, Oct. 1986.

RAYCHAUDHURI, D.: "Announced Retransmission Random Access Protocols," *IEEE Trans. on Commun.*, vol. COM-33, pp. 1183-1190, Nov. 1985.

REEDY, J.W., and JONES, J.R.: "Methods of Collision Detection in Fiber Optic CSMA/CD Networks," *IEEE Journal on Selected Areas in Commun.*, vol. SAC-3, pp. 890-896, Nov. 1985.

RIVEST, R.L., SHAMIR, A., and ADLEMAN, L.: "On a Method for Obtaining Digital Signatures and Public Key Cryptosystems," *Commun. ACM*, vol. 21, pp. 120-126, Feb. 1978.

ROBERTS, L.: "Dynamic Allocation of Satellite Capacity through Packet Reservation," *Proc. NCC*, pp. 711-716, 1973.

ROBERTS, L.: "Extensions of Packet Communication Technology to a Hand Held Personal Terminal," *Proc. SJCC*, pp. 295-298, 1972.

RODRIGUEZ, R., KOEHLER, M., and HYDE, R.: "The Generic File System," *Proc. USENIX Summer Conf.*, pp. 260-269, 1986.

ROSE, M.T. and CASS, D.E.: "OSI Transport Services on Top of the TCP," *Computer Networks and ISDN Systems*, vol. 12, pp. 159-173, 1987.

ROSE, M.T., STEFFERUD, E.A., and SWEET, J.N.: "MH: A Multifarious User Agent," *Computer Networks and ISDN Systems*, vol. 10, pp. 65-80, 1985.

ROSS, F.E.: "Rings are 'Round for Good!," *IEEE Network Magazine*, vol. 1, pp. 31-38, Jan. 1987.

ROSS, F.E.: "FDDI—A Tutorial," *IEEE Commun. Magazine*, col 24, pp. 10-15, May 1986.

ROTHAUSER, E.H., and WILD, D.: "MLMA—A Collision-Free Multi-Access Method," *Proc. IFIP Congr. 77*, pp. 431-436, 1977.

RUDIN, H.: "On Routing and Delta Routing: A Taxonomy and Performance Comparison of Techniques for Packet-Switched Networks" *IEEE Trans. on Commun.*, vol. COM-24, pp. 43-59, Jan. 1976.

RUDIN, H.: "Time in Formal Protocol Specifications," in *Kommunikation in Verteilten Systemen I*, Heger, D. et al. (Eds.), Berlin: Springer-Verlag, 1985a.

RUDIN, H.: "An Informal Overview of Formal Protocol Specification," *IEEE Commun. Magazine*, vol. 23, pp. 46-52, March 1985b.

SACHS, S., KAN, K.-L., and SILVESTER, J.A.: "Token-Bus Protocol Performance Analysis and Comparision with Other LAN Protocols," *Globecom 85*, IEEE, pp. 48.1.1-48.1.7, 1985.

SALTZER, J.H., POGRAN, K.T., and CLARK, D.D.: "Why a Ring?" *Computer Networks*, vol. 7, pp. 223-230, Aug. 1983.

SALTZER, J.H., REED, D.P., and CLARK, D.D.: "End-to-End Arguments in System Design," *ACM Trans. on Computer Systems*, vol. 2, pp. 277-288, Nov. 1984.

SCHLANGER, G.G.: "An Overview of Signaling System No. 7," *IEEE Journal on Selected Areas in Commun.*, vol. SAC-4, pp. 360-365, May 1986.

SCHMIDT, R.V., RAWSON, E.G., NORTON, R.E., Jr., JACKSON, S.B., and BAILEY, M.D.: "Fibernet II — A Fiber Optic Ethernet," *IEEE Journal on Selected Areas in Commun.*, vol. SAC-1, pp. 702-710, Nov. 1983.

SCHNEIDEWIND, N.: "Interconnecting Local Networks to Long-Distance Networks," *IEEE Computer Magazine*, vol. 16, pp. 15-24, Sept. 1983.

SCHOLL, M.: "Multiplexing Techniques for Data Transmission over Packet Switched Radio Systems," Ph.D. thesis, Computer Science Dept., UCLA, 1976.

SCHROEDER, M.D., GIFFORD, D.K., and NEEDHAM, R.M.: "A Caching File System for a Programmer's Workstation," *Proc. Tenth Symp. on Operating Systems Principles*, ACM, pp. 25-34, 1985.

SCHWARTZ, A.: "Modelling and Analysis of a Token Ring," in *Local Communication Systems: LAN and PBX*, Cabanel, J.P., Pujolle, G., and Danthine, A. (Eds.), Amsterdam: North-Holland, 1987a.

SCHWARTZ, M.: *Telecommunications Networks: Protocols, Modeling and Analysis*, Reading, MA: Addison-Wesley, 1987b.

SEIFERT, W.M.: "Bridges and Routers," *IEEE Network Magazine*, vol. 2, pp. 57-64, Jan. 1988.

SELFRIDGE, O.G., and SCHWARTZ, R.T.: "Telephone Technology and Privacy," *Technology Review*, vol. 82, pp. 56-65, May 1980.

SHAMIR, A.: "How to Share a Secret," *Commun. ACM*, vol. 22, pp. 612-613, Nov. 1979.

SHANNON, C.: "A Mathematical Theory of Communication," *Bell System Journal*, vol. 27, pp. 379-423, July 1948; and pp. 623-656, Oct. 1948.

SHAPLEY, D., and KOLATA, G.B.: "Cryptology: Scientists Puzzle over Threat to Open Research, Publication," *Science*, vol. 197, pp. 1345-1349, Sept. 30, 1977.

SHOCH, J.F., DALAL, Y,K., REDELL, D.D., and CRANE, R.C.: "Ethernet," in *Advances in Local Area Networks*, Kummerle, K., Tobagi, F., and Limb, J.O. (Eds.), New York: IEEE Press, 1987.

SHRIVASTAVA, S.K., and PANZIERI, F. "The Design of a Reliable Remote Procedure Call Mechanism," *IEEE Trans. on Computers*, vol. C-31, pp. 692-697, July 1982.

SIDEBOTHAM, B.: "VOLUMES—The Andrew File System Data Structuring Primitive," *Proc.*European pp. 473-480, 1986.

SIDHU, D.P.: "Authentication Protocols for Computer Networks: I," *Computer Networks and ISDN Systems*, vol. 11, pp. 297-310, April 1986.

SINCOSKIE, W.D., and COTTON, C.J.: "Extended Bridge Algorithms for Large Networks," *IEEE Network Magazine*, vol. 2, pp. 16-24, Jan. 1988.

SLOMAN, M., and KRAMER, J.: *Distributed Systems and Computer Networks*, Englewood Cliffs, NJ: Prentice-Hall Int'l, 1987.

SMITH, R.E.: "Civilian Cryptography," *Compcon*, p. 215D, Spring 1980.

SOHA, M., and PERLMAN, R.: "Comparison of Two LAN Bridge Approaches," *IEEE Network Magazine*, vol. 2, pp. 37-43, Jan. 1988.

SOLMAN, J.V.: "Design of a Public Electronic Mail System," *IEEE Network Magazine* vol. 1, pp. pp. 11-15, Oct. 1987.

SPIEGELHALTER, B.: "The Implementation of a LAN Gateway to an X.25 Public Network," *ICCC 84*, pp. 710-715, 1984.

STALLINGS, W.: *Data and Computer Communications. Second Edition.* New York: Macmillan, 1988.

STALLINGS, W.: *Local Networks. Second Edition.* New York: Macmillan, 1987.

STROLE, N.C.: "The IBM Token-Ring Network—A Functional Overview," *IEEE Network Magazine*, vol. 1, pp. 23-30, Jan. 1987.

STUCK, B.W.: "Calculating the Maximum Throughput Rate in Local Area Networks," *Computer*, vol. 16, pp. 72-76, May 1983.

SUNSHINE, C.A., and DALAL, Y.K.: "Connection Management in Transport Protocols," *Computer Networks*, vol. 2, pp. 454-473, 1978.

SVOBODOVA, L.: "File Servers for Network-Based Distributed Systems," *Computing Surveys*, vol. 16, pp. 353-398, Dec. 1984.

TANENBAUM, A.S., MULLENDER, S.J., and RENESSE, R. van: "Using Sparse Capabilities in a Distributed Operating System," *Proc. Sixth Int'l Conf. on Distr. Computer Sys.*, IEEE, pp. 558-563, 1986.

TANENBAUM, A.S., and RENESSE, R. van: "Distributed Operating Systems," *Computing Surveys*, vol. 17, pp. 419-470, Dec. 1985.

TARDO, J.J.: "Standardizing Cryptographic Services at OSI Higher Layers," *IEEE Commun. Magazine*, vol. 23, pp. 25-29, July 1985.

TAYLOR, D.: "The Postman Always Rings Twice: Electronic Mail in a Highly Distributed Environment," *Proc. Winter USENIX Conf.*, pp. 145-154, 1988.

TOBAGI, F.A., BINDER, R., and LEINER, B.: "Packet Radio and Satellite Networks," *IEEE Commun. Magazine*, vol. 22, pp. 24-40, Nov. 1984.

TOBAGI, F.A., BORGONOVO, F.:, and FRATTA, L.: "Expressnet: A High-Performance Integrated Services Local Area Network," in *Advances in Local Area Networks*, Kummerle, K., Tobagi, F., and Limb, J.O. (Eds.), New York: IEEE Press, 1987.

TOBAGI, F.A. and FINE, M.: "Performance of Unidirectionsl Broadcast Local Area Networks: Expressnet and Fasnet," *IEEE Journal on Selected Areas in Commun.*, vol. SAC-1, pp. 913-926, Nov. 1983.

TOKORO, M., and TAMARU, K.: "Acknowledging Ethernet," *Compcon*, pp. 320-325, Fall 1977.

TOMAS, J.G., PAVON, J., and PEREDA, O.: "OSI Service Specification: SAP and CEP Modelling," *Computer Commun. Rev.* vol. 17, pp. 48-70, Jan. 1987.

TOMLINSON, R.S.: "Selecting Sequence Numbers," *Proc. ACM SIGCOMM/SIGOPS Interprocess Commun. Workshop*, ACM, pp. 11-23, 1975.

TSYBAKOV, B.S.: "Survey of USSR Contributions to Random Multiple-Access Communications," *IEEE Trans. on Inform. Theory*, vol. IT-31, pp. 143-161, March 1985.

TURNER, J.S.: "Design of an Integrated Services *Packet* Network," *IEEE Journal on Selected Areas in Commun.*, vol. SAC-4, pp. 1373-1380, Dec. 1986.

ULUG, M.E.: "A Fiber Optic Contention Bus with Bounded Delays," *IEEE Journal on Selected Areas in Commun.*, vol. SAC-3, pp. 908-915, Nov. 1985.

VANDOME, G.: "Comparative Study of some UNIX Distributed Filesystems," *Proc. European UNIX Users Group Conf.*, pp. 73-82, 1986.

VAN EIJK, P: *Software Tools for the Specification Language LOTOS*, Ph.D. thesis, Technical University of Twente, The Netherlands, 1988.

VAN RENESSE, R., and TANENBAUM, A.S.: "Voting with Ghosts," *Proc. Eighth Int'l Conf. on Distr. Computer Sys.*, IEEE, 1988.

VISSERS, C.A., TENNEY, R.L., and BOCHMANN, G.V.: "Formal Description Techniques," *Proc. of the IEEE*, vol. 71, pp. 1356-1364, Dec. 1983.

VOYDOCK, V.L., and KENT, S.T.: "Security in High-level Network Protocols," *IEEE Commun. Magazine*, vol. 23, pp.12-24, July 1985.

WARD, S.A., and TERMAN, C.J.: "An Approach to Personal Computing," *Compcon*, pp. 460-465, Spring 1980.

WATSON, R.W.: "Timer-Based Mechanisms in Reliable Transport Protocol Connection Management," *Computer Networks*, vol. 5, pp. 47-56, Feb. 1981.

WATSON, R.W., and FLETCHER, J.G.: "An Architecture for Support of Network Operating System Services," *Computer Networks*, vol. 4, pp. 33-49, Feb. 1980.

WATSON, R.W., and MAMRAK, S.A.: "Gaining Efficiency in Transport Services by Appropriate Design and Implementation Choices," *ACM Trans. on Computer Systems*, vol. 5, pp. 97-120, May 1987.

WEISSBERGER, A.J., and ISRAEL, J.E.: "What the New Internetworking Standards Provide," *Data Communication*, Feb. 1987.

WILLETT, M.: "Token-Ring Local Area Networks—An Introduction," *IEEE Network Magazine*, vol. 1, pp. 8-9, Jan. 1987.

WITTEN, I.H., NEAL, R.M., and CLEARY, J.G.: "Arithmetic Coding for Data Compression," *Commun. ACM*, vol. 30, pp. 520-540, June 1987.

WU, Z.D., and SPRATT, E.B.: "The Performance Analysis of Multiple Cambridge Rings," in *Local Communication Systems: LAN and PBX*, Cabanel, J.P., Pujolle, G., and Danthine, A. (Eds.), Amsterdam: North-Holland, 1987.

ZHANG, L.: "Comparison of Two Bridge Routing Approaches," *IEEE Network Magazine*, vol. 2, pp. 44-48, Jan. 1988.

ZWAENEPOEL, W.: "Protocols for Large Data Transfers over Local Networks," *Proc. Ninth Data Commun. Symp.*, ACM, pp. 22-32, 1985.

A

INTRODUCTION TO QUEUEING THEORY

One of the most powerful mathematical tools for making quantitative analyses of computer networks is queueing theory. This technique was first developed to analyze the statistical behavior of telephone switching systems, but it has since been applied to many networking problems as well. In this appendix we will show the basic elements of the theory and give a few applications to see how it is used. A more complete treatment of queueing theory and its applications to networking can be found in (Kleinrock, 1976).

A.1. Queueing Systems

Queueing systems can be used to model processes in which customers arrive, wait their turn for service, are serviced, and then depart. Supermarket checkout stands, World Series ticket booths, and doctor's waiting rooms are examples of queueing systems. Queueing systems can be characterized by five components:

1. The interarrival-time probability density function.

2. The service-time probability density function.

3. The number of servers.

4. The queueing discipline.

5. The amount of buffer space in the queues.

It is worth explicitly noting that we are considering only systems with an infinite number of customers (i.e., the existence of a long queue does not so deplete the population of customers that the input rate is materially reduced). (In contrast, in a time-sharing system model, there are only a finite number of customers. If half of them are waiting for a response, the input rate will be significantly reduced.)

The interarrival-time probability density describes the interval between consecutive arrivals. One could imagine hiring someone (e.g., a graduate student, since they do not cost much), to watch customers arrive. At each arrival the graduate student would record the elapsed time since the previous arrival. After a sufficiently long sampling time, the list of numbers could be sorted and grouped: so many interarrival times of 0.1 sec, so many of 0.2 sec, etc. This probability density characterizes the arrival process.

Each customer requires a certain amount of the server's time. The amount of service time varies from customer to customer (e.g., one has a full shopping cart of groceries and the next has only a small box of peanut butter cookies). To analyze a queueing system, the service-time probability density function, like the interarrival density function, must be known.

The number of servers speaks for itself. Many banks, for example, have one big queue for all customers. Whenever a teller is free, the customer at the front of the queue goes directly to that teller. Such a system is a multiserver queueing system. In other banks, each teller has his or her own private queue. In this case we have a collection of independent single-server queues, not a multiserver system.

The queueing discipline describes the order in which customers are taken from the queue. Supermarkets use first come, first served. Hospital emergency rooms often use sickest first rather than first come, first served. In friendly office environments, shortest job first prevails at the photocopy machine.

Not all queueing systems have an infinite amount of buffer space. When too many customers are queued up for a finite number of slots, some customers get lost or rejected.

We will concentrate exclusively on infinite-buffer, single-server systems using first come, first served. The notation A/B/m is widely used in the queueing literature for these systems, where A is the interarrival-time probability density, B the service-time probability density, and m the number of servers. The probability densities A and B are chosen from the set

M - exponential probability density (M stands for Markov)
D - all customers have the same value (D is for deterministic)
G - general (i.e., arbitrary probability density)

The state of the art ranges from the M/M/1 system, about which everything is known, to the G/G/m system, for which no exact analytic solution is yet known.

Throughout this book we use queuing theory as one of our basic tools to analyze network performance. In particular, we usually assume the M/M/1 model. The assumption of an exponential interarrival probability is completely reasonably for any system that has a large number of independent customers. Under such conditions, the probability of exactly n customers arriving during an interval of length t is given by the Poisson law:

$$P_n(t) = \frac{(\lambda t)^n}{n!} e^{-\lambda t} \tag{A-1}$$

where λ is the mean arrival rate.

Now we will show that Poisson arrivals generate an exponential interarrival probability density. The probability, $a(t)\Delta t$, that an interarrival interval is between t and $t + \Delta t$ is just the probability of no arrivals for a time t times the probability of one arrival in the infinitesimal interval Δt:

$$a(t)\Delta t = P_0(t)P_1(\Delta t)$$

$P_0(t)$ is $e^{-\lambda t}$, and $P_1(\Delta t)$ is $\lambda \Delta t e^{-\lambda \Delta t}$. In the limit $\Delta t \to 0$, the exponential factor in P_1 approaches unity, so

$$a(t)dt = \lambda e^{-\lambda t} \, dt \tag{A-2}$$

Note that the integral of Eq. (A-2) from 0 to ∞ is 1, as it should be.

Although the assumption of an exponential interarrival probability density is usually reasonable, the assumption of exponential services times is harder to defend on general grounds. Nevertheless, for situations in which increasingly long service times are increasingly less likely, M/M/1 may be an adequate approximation. We leave it to the reader to show that if the probability of service finishing in some small time interval Δt is $\mu \Delta t$, then the service-time probability density function is $\mu e^{-\mu t}$, with a mean service time of $1/\mu$ sec/customer.

A.2. The M/M/1 Queue in Equilibrium

The state of an M/M/1 queueing system (see Fig. A-1) is completely described by telling how many customers are currently in the system, including both queue and server. At first you might think that it would also be necessary to describe how far along the customer currently being served was, but the exponential density function has no memory: the probability of the remaining service time requiring t seconds is independent of how much service the customer has already received! The exponential function is the only one with this remarkable property, which is why queueing theorists love it so much.

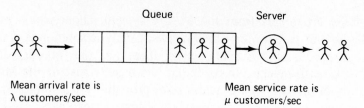

Fig. A-1. A single-server queueing system with four customers, one in service and three in the queue.

Let p_k be the equilibrium probability that there are exactly k customers in the system (queue + server). Once we have derived these probabilities we can find the mean number of customers in the system, the expected waiting time, and other statistical properties of the system. Even when the system is in equilibrium, transitions between states take place. If the system is in state 4 (i.e., four customers in the system) and a new customer arrives, the system moves into state 5. Similarly, when a customer receives his desired service, the system moves down one state. Queueing systems in which the only transitions are to adjacent states are known in the trade as **birth-death systems**.

Figure A-2 shows the states for a single-server queueing system, with the allowed transitions indicated by arrows. To analyze this system, we must know how many of each transition occur per second. If the mean arrival rate is λ customers/sec, the mean number of transitions/sec from state 0 to state 1 is λp_0. Suppose, for example, that 40 customers/sec arrive, there is a 20% chance of finding the system in state 0 (empty), and a 15% chance of finding the system in state 1 (one customer being served, queue empty). There will be eight transitions from 0 to 1 each second on the average, and six transitions from 1 to 2. In general, the transition rate from state k to state $k + 1$ is λp_k.

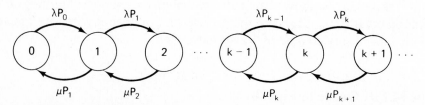

Fig. A-2. State diagram for a single-server queueing system. The transition rates are shown as labels on the arrows.

Similarly, if the server is capable of processing μ customers/sec the transition rate from state $k + 1$ to state k is μp_{k+1}. Note that the transition rate is the completion rate times the probability of the system being in the initial state, not the final state. If you want to know how many transitions per second happen from state 4 to state 3, you need to know what the probability is of finding the system in state 4. You do not need to know what the state 3 probability is.

In equilibrium the probability of finding the system in a given state does not change with time. In particular, the probability of there being more than k customers in the system is constant. The transition from k to $k + 1$ increases this probability, and the transition from $k + 1$ to k decreases it. Therefore, these two transitions must occur at the same rate. If this were not so, the system would not be in equilibrium. If there were many transitions from, say, 4 to 5, but few transitions from 5 to 4, the mean number of customers in states above 4 would increase in time, violating our assumption about the system being in equilibrium. This principle, sometimes referred to as the principle of **detailed balancing**, is the key to solving for the state probabilities.

Looking at Fig. A-2, we see that

$$\lambda p_0 = \mu p_1 \tag{A-3}$$

$$\lambda p_1 = \mu p_2 \tag{A-4}$$

and in general,

$$\lambda p_k = \mu p_{k+1} \tag{A-5}$$

Using Eq. (A-3), we can solve for p_1 in terms of p_0. Using Eq. (A-4), we can solve for p_2 in terms of p_1 and then use the previous result to get p_2 in terms of p_0. The solution for the general case can be found be repeating this process, yielding

$$p_k = \rho^k p_0 \tag{A-6}$$

where we have introduced $\rho = \lambda/\mu$. The variable ρ is known as the **traffic intensity**. It must be less than 1. Queueing systems that receive input faster than the server can process it are inherently unstable, and their queues grow without bound.

To eliminate p_0 from Eq. (A-6), we use the fact that the probabilities must sum to 1:

$$\sum_{k=0}^{\infty} \rho^k p_0 = 1$$

Using the well-known formula for the sum of a geometric series,

$$\sum_{k=0}^{\infty} \rho^k = \frac{1}{1 - \rho} \tag{A-7}$$

we find that $p_0 = 1 - \rho$, and finally

$$p_k = (1 - \rho)\rho^k \tag{A-8}$$

Notice that $\rho = 1 - p_0$ is just the probability that the system is not empty (i.e., the probability that the server is busy).

The mean number of customers in the system, N, can now be found directly from the state probabilities, Eq. (A-8):

$$N = \sum_{k=0}^{\infty} kp_k = (1 - \rho) \sum_{k=0}^{\infty} k\rho^k$$

The value of the summation can be found by differentiating both sides of Eq. (A-7) with respect to ρ and then multiplying through by ρ. Using this result, we find the mean number of customers in the system to be

$$N = \frac{\rho}{1 - \rho} \tag{A-9}$$

As ρ approaches 1, the queue length grows very quickly.

Having found the mean number of customers in the system, we are now ready to determine the total waiting time, T, the mean interval between customer arrival and customer departure, including service time. Imagine that our friend the graduate student stops recording interarrival times once in a while, and in a fit of pique paints one of the customers shocking pink. The pink customers progress along like the other customers and are eventually disgorged from the system. Since the pink customers are in the system for an average time T (the mean time for all customers), the mean number of new arrivals subsequent to the arrival of a pink customer and just prior to his own departure is λT. This result follows directly from the fact that the arrival rate is λ customers/sec. At the instant of the pink customer's departure, all λT of these customers, and no others, are in the system. Since the mean number of customers in the system at any time is N, we have the basic result: $N = \lambda T$. This equation was first proven by D. C. Little (1961) and is known as **Little's result**.

Using Little's result and Eq. (A-9), we can now find the total waiting time, including service time:

$$T = \frac{N}{\lambda} = \frac{\rho/\lambda}{1 - \rho} = \frac{1/\mu}{1 - \rho} = \frac{1}{\mu - \lambda} \tag{A-10}$$

This key result will be the basis of our network delay analysis.

As an example of Eq. (A-10), consider a public birdbath at which birds arrive according to a Poisson distribution. The mean arrival rate is 3 birds/min. The bathing time is exponentially distributed with a mean of 10 sec/bird. How long does a bird have to wait in the queue? The mean arrival rate is $\lambda = 0.05$ customer/sec. The mean service rate is $\mu = 0.10$ customer/sec. From Eq. (A-10) we find that $T = 20$ sec for waiting plus service. Since the mean service-time ($1/\mu$) is 10 sec, the mean queueing time is then $20 - 10 = 10$ sec.

For the sake of generality, we will state, but not derive, the formula for the mean number of customers in the system for an M/G/1 queueing system:

$$N = \rho + \rho^2 \frac{1 + C_b^2}{2(1 - \rho)} \tag{A-11}$$

where C_b is the ratio of the standard deviation to the mean of the service time probability density function. This result, known as the **Pollaczek-Khinchine** equation, is valid for any service-time distribution. It shows that if two service-time distributions have equal means, the one with the larger standard deviation will produce a longer waiting time. For the Poisson distribution, upon which M/M/1 is based, $C_b = 1$.

A.3. Networks of M/M/1 Queues

The results derived above for the M/M/1 queue can be directly applied to the problem of finding the queueing delay for packets in an IMP. But first it is convenient to change the notation slightly to convert the units of service time from customers/sec to bits/sec. Let the probability density function for packet size, x, in bits be $\mu e^{-\mu x}$ with a mean of $1/\mu$ bits/packet. Now introduce the capacity of communication channel i as C_i bits/sec. The product μC_i is then the service rate in packets/sec. The arrival rate for channel i is λ_i packets/sec. Equation (A-10) can now be rewritten for channel i as

$$T_i = \frac{1}{\mu C_i - \lambda_i} \qquad \text{(A-12)}$$

where T_i includes both queueing and transmission time, as can be seen by taking the limit $\lambda_i \to 0$. Notice that the mean packet size does not depend on the channel, as the capacity and input rate do. This application of queueing theory to a communication channel was first due to Kleinrock (1964).

One problem that we face in a network is that the communication channels are not isolated. The output of one channel becomes the input to another. Several lines may converge upon a single IMP dumping packets there. Thus the input to a certain line is no longer a Poisson process outside the network, but the sum of the outputs of several other network lines. Fortunately, if the outputs of several M/M/1 servers feed into the input queue of another server, the resulting input process is also a Poisson process, with mean equal to the sum of the means of the feeding processes. Even better, Jackson (1957) has shown that an open network of M/M/1 queues can be analyzed as though each one were isolated from all the others. All you need to know is the mean input rate.

However, there is still one obstacle in our way. When a packet moves around the network, it maintains its size, of course. This property introduces nonrandom correlations into the system. When a big monster packet comes along, it takes a long time to service, hence causing a noticeable gap in the arrival pattern of the queue being fed into. We can get around this problem by assuming that every time a packet arrives at an IMP, it loses its identity and a new length is chosen for it at random. This assumption, first made by Kleinrock (1964), is known as the **Independence Assumption**. Simulation and actual measurements show that it is quite reasonable to make it. Besides, if we do not make it, we cannot make any progress at all.

A.4. APPLICATIONS OF QUEUEING THEORY

In this section we will look at several examples of how queueing theory can be applied in practice to networking problems.

A.4.1. Terminal Concentrators

As a first example, consider a terminal concentrator with four 4800 bps input lines and one 9600 bps output line. The mean packet size, $1/\mu$, is 1000 bits. Each of four lines delivers Poisson traffic with an average of $\lambda_i = 2$ packets/sec. What is the mean delay experienced by a packet from the moment the last bit arrives at the concentrator until the moment that bit is retransmitted on the output line? Also, what is the mean number of packets in the concentrator, including the one in service?

We can use Eq. (A-12) here with $\lambda_i = 2$ and $\mu C = 9.6$ packets/sec. By adding up all four input lines, we get a total of $\lambda = 8$ so $T = 1/(9.6 - 8)$ or $T = 0.625$ sec. Thus the average delay for a packet arriving at the concentrator is 625 msec. Note that even if $\lambda = 0$, T is not zero because it takes a finite amount of time to transmit the packet over the 9600 bps output line.

The mean number of packets in the concentrator is given by Eq. (A-7) for $\rho = 8/9.6$ which gives $N = 5$. It may seem surprising that a substantial input queue builds up even though the output capacity is adequate to handle the input. Nevertheless, it is true. It is the randomness of the arrivals that causes the queue to build up.

This type of calculation applies not only to terminal concentrators, but to any store-and-forward switch, such as an IMP. It can be used, for example, to calculate the amount of memory required for queue storage.

A.4.2. Dedicated Versus Shared Channels

Two computers are conected by a 64-kbps line. There are eight parallel sessions using the line. Each session generates Poisson traffic with a mean of 2 packets/sec. The packet lengths are exponentially distributed with a mean of 2000 bits. The system designers must choose between giving each session a dedicated 8-kbps piece of bandwidth (via TDM or FDM) or having all packets compete for a single 64-kbps shared channel. Which alternative gives a better response time?

For TDM or FDM, each 8-kbps channel operates as an independent queueing system with $\lambda = 2$ packets/sec and $\mu = 4$ packets/sec. From Eq. (A-12) we find $T = 500$ msec.

Now analyze a single 64-kbps system. Here $\lambda = 16$ and $\mu = 32$, so T is 66.7 msec. This conclusion is very general. Splitting up a single channel into k fixed-size pieces makes the response time k times worse. The reason is that it frequently happens that several of the smaller channels are idle, while other ones are over-loaded. The lost bandwidth can never be regained.

A.4.3. Token Rings

As a second example of how queueing theory is used, let us now briefly analyze the performance of a token ring. More detailed results can be found in (Schwartz, 1987). Assume that frames are generated according to a Poisson process, and that when a station receives permission to send, it empties itself of all queued frames, with the mean queue length being q frames. The total arrival rate of all N stations combined is λ frames/sec. Each station contributes λ/N. The service rate (the number of frames/sec that a station can transmit) is μ. The time it takes for a bit to go all the way around an idle ring, or **walk time**, consisting of both the one bit-per-station delays and the signal propagation delay, plays a key role in the mean delay. Denote the walk time by w. The quantity we intend to compute is the **scan time**, s, the mean interval between token arrivals at a given station.

Each scan time is divided into two parts, the walk time, w, and the time required to service each of the Nq requests queued up to service, each of which requires $1/\mu$ sec. Algebraically,

$$s = w + \frac{Nq}{\mu} \tag{A-13}$$

The mean queue length is easy to derive, since it is just the number of requests that pile up during an interval of length s when the arrival rate is λ/N, namely $q = \lambda s/N$. Substituting into Eq. (A-13) we get

$$s = w + \frac{\lambda s}{\mu}$$

Introducing $\rho = \lambda/\mu$ and solving for s we find

$$s = \frac{w}{1 - \rho} \tag{A-14}$$

The channel-acquisition delay is about half the scan time, so we now have one of the basic performance parameters. Notice that the delay is always proportional to the walk time, both for low load and high. Also note that ρ represents the utilization of the entire ring, not the utilization of a single station, which is ρ/N.

The other key performance parameter is the channel efficiency under heavy load. The only overhead is the walk time between stations. If every station has data to send, this overhead is w/N, compared to the transmission time per station, q/μ. Using these times the channel efficiency can be .S

A.4.4. Connection Establishment Failure Probabilities

In many computer systems, there is a maximum number of connections that can be in existence at any one instant. For example, MAP, TOP, and OSI boards for personal computers normally have some fixed maximum number of allowable connections, determined by table sizes on the board. Companies that subscribe to X.25 networks may only have a certain number of virtual circuits open at once, the number being determined when the company subscribes to the service. PBXes typically have a fixed number of outgoing lines, so here too only a certain number of connections can coexist.

In all these cases, it is interesting to be able to compute the probability that an attempt to establish a new connection fails because the maximum number of connections already exist. We can model this environment by saying that there are m connection servers, each capable of handling one connection. If an attempt is made to establish a connection and no server (i.e., table slot, virtual circuit, or outgoing line) is available, there are two possibilities: the caller is queued or the caller gives up and tries again later. The latter is more realistic, so we will analyze it.

The model for our system is similar to that of Fig. A-2, except that we only have a finite number of states, from 0 to m.. There are no transitions from state m to higher states because new connection attempts simply fail when all the outgoing circuits are full. There are thus $m + 1$ equations, starting with

$$\lambda p_0 = \mu p_1$$

$$\lambda p_1 = 2\mu p_2$$

$$\lambda p_2 = 3\mu p_3$$

and so on until the last one

$$\lambda p_{m-1} = m\mu p_m$$

Note that the probability of dropping from state k to state $k - 1$ increases with k because as more outgoing lines are occupied, the chance that one of them becomes free during a given interval increases as well. The general case can be expressed in terms of p_0 as

$$p_k = p_0 \, \rho^k/k! \quad (k \leq m)$$

By summing all the probabilities and setting the result to 1 we can solve for p_0:

$$p_0 = \frac{1}{\sum_{k=0}^{m} \rho^k / k!}$$

Finally, we can compute the probability of a connection attempt failing. This probability is simply the probability of the system being in state m, which is

$$p_m = \frac{\rho^m / m!}{\sum_{k=0}^{m} \rho^k / k!}$$

INDEX

C